Contents

Introduction

As you stand on the Charles Bridge, like countless visitors before you, the castle looms above. Malá Strana stretches out on the left bank of the Vltava river, arcing through the heart of the city. And on the right are the spires and cobbled lanes of Staré Město, the Old Town. Wander around here as a stranger and you'll soon find yourself lost and disoriented in this medieval Gothic maze, before mercifully re-emerging on to some smartened square. Palaces, pubs and churches from every era, and enough crystal to coat the Empire State Building, serve as constant backdrops.

While taking in the scene from one of the countless pavement tables dotted all over Staré Město, you may begin to wonder whether these stressed-out New Europeans recognise the beauty of their home town. Do they notice the city's squares, colonnades and gables, as inspiring as any in Europe, or the breathtaking ornament and craft on show? Why are they scrambling so hard for status, boxy new apartments and good private schools for the kids? Perhaps a traveller's enthusiasm is difficult to maintain when you pass this magnificence every day and have bills to pay. Lucky you, then, who wisely packed beer goggles and can escape your own bills in Bohemia.

While you're here, perhaps you'll permit yourself to indulge in behaviour you wouldn't countenance at home. We're not alluding to stag party antics, of course. You and Prague can both do better than that. Reading Kafka would qualify, but maybe you'd rather not mix dark literature with precious holiday time. Instead, consider opening your mind to some of the radical and heretical ideas that the city has inspired, through such unlikely bedfellows as 15th-century firebrand preacher Jan Hus and 20th-century playwright-turned-president Václav Havel, astronomer Tycho Brahe and student Jan Palach.

So let the Praguers strive, succeed, study and firm up their market share. Your job is to get away with something crazy and beautiful. Propose to someone. Quit your job and take on an apartment in Malá Strana. Compose jingles or study the stars. You're in the right place. *Will Tizard, Editor*

Prague in Brief

IN CONTEXT

The opening section of *Time Out Prague* details the city's back story, the events and personalities that shaped today's town. Alongside its history, visible on almost every corner, we examine the challenges facing Prague in the 21st century. Elsewhere, we look at the city's most impressive buildings, its literary heritage, and one of Prague's main attractions – beer.
► *For more, see pp15-56.*

SIGHTS

Few first-time visitors leave without seeing Prague Castle, but there's plenty more to the city than the grand old hilltop retreat. Both Malá Strana and Staré Město are rich in historic appeal, lined with churches, palaces and other glorious relics. There are also plenty of great art galleries, both ancient and modern. But perhaps Prague's main attraction is its beguiling, charismatic streetscape.
► *For more, see pp57-121.*

CONSUME

Traditionally, foreign visitors to Prague have approached Czech food with something between apprehension and disdain. However, the restaurants here are better than ever, offering both quality and variety if you know where to look. Also in this section, we spotlight the city's best hotels for all budgets, focus on the improving shopping scene and review the finest cafés, pubs and bars in town.
► *For more, see pp123-210.*

ARTS & ENTERTAINMENT

Praguers have always been a cultured bunch, and the city's artistic heritage is alive today in the shape of an enviable classical music circuit, a rich theatre scene and a vast array of galleries. But night owls have just as much to look forward to as culture vultures, with a welter of rock and jazz venues supplemented by an outlandishly permissive clubbing scene.
► *For more, see pp211-274.*

ESCAPES & EXCURSIONS

Prague has more than enough appeal to detain most visitors for a while, but there's plenty outside the city limits if you're keen on a little exploration. The city is ringed by handsome and historic castles, interspersed with picturesque towns and villages. And beyond here lie more rural escapes, rolling hills and otherworldly forests that could hardly be further in spirit from the city.
► *For more, see pp275-298.*

Prague in Profile

HRADČANY

Hradčany contains both the official and the historic hearts of the Czech Republic in the form of **Prague Castle**. The world's largest such complex of buildings, it's centred around the Gothic spires of **St Vitus's Cathedral**, and is first on many visitors' list of things to see and do in the city. The roots of the old Czech Přemyslid dynasty enfold the oldest parts of the Castle, but the president's office remains here today, flanked by the futuristic early 20th-century architectural accents of Josip Plečnik. Elsewhere, the various courtyards, palaces and chapels show off every significant early period of Prague's architecture, from the Romanesque **Basilica of St George** onwards.

The castle makes a logical starting point for a stroll around the highly walkable city, and not just because everything is downhill from here. For all that, Hradčany can feel like one vast museum, although a handful of characterful pubs, galleries and traditional dining rooms enliven the district as you move toward Loretanské náměstí.

▶ *For more, see pp59-71.*

MALÁ STRANA

Between Hradčany and the Vltava river, the Malá Strana quarter is a tapestry of its former histories: a craftsmen's hovel during the medieval period; prize real estate granted to nobles for supporting the Habsburgs during the late Renaissance; a hotbed of poets bristling against foreign domination in coffeehouse cabals during the 19th century. Today, cottages, fabulous palaces and smoky cafés from each era stand side by side on its narrow streets.

The Baroque architecture in Malá Strana may prove to be the most over-the-top you'll see. It's a style that's epitomised by the immense, eye-catching **Church of St Nicholas**, which dominates the area. The nearby **Church of our Lady Victorious**, which hosts the supposedly miracle-working Bambino di Praga, still draws pilgrims, but the deeply skeptical Czechs never really were won over by all the religious excess.

▶ *For more, see pp72-82.*

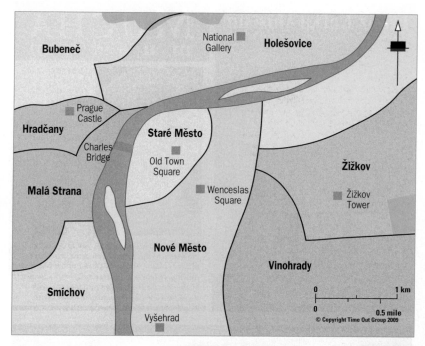

STARÉ MĚSTO

Prague's right bank owes its beguiling layers to the Vltava river, which is responsible for the unique underworld of flat Staré Město (literally, Old Town). These innumerable vaulted, stone-walled spaces once sat at street level, but constant flooding of the Vltava during the 13th century prompted city fathers to raise the streets one storey to the level at which they lie today. Ordinary-looking doorways lead to underground labyrinths; small frontages hide surprisingly expansive buildings.

Prague's layers are such that longtime residents who have lived here for years still stop in amazement when an old passageway between favourite streets is reopened. Many of these walkways, through building courtyards, haven't seen the light of day for over 50 years, but now host designer hotels, one-of-a-kind shops and smart bars. Staré Město ultimately reveals how Prague is rediscovering itself, as it digs itself out from its grey pre-Velvet Revolution days.

► For more, see pp83-99.

NOVÉ MĚSTO

Bordering Staré Město to the south and east is Nové Město, or New Town, so named because it was the first area of the city to be laid out with broad streets when it was planned by Charles IV in 1348. This is where the city's commerce gets done, and is also where the uniquely Czech form of political dissent known as defenestration was perfected.

All of Europe was plunged into the chaos of the 30 Years' War after city mugwumps were tossed from the windows of the New Town Hall, which overlooks **Karlovo náměstí**. The constant traffic gridlock surrounding this square gives no hint of its past as a medieval horse market. **Wenceslas Square**, meanwhile, personifies modern Prague, whether for good or ill. The adjoining street of **Na příkopě** is the place to shop for lifestyle essentials, while the blocks south of the **National Theatre** are still blooming as a fashionable, hedonistic nightlife hub.

▶ *For more, see pp100-110.*

FURTHER AFIELD

A bend of the Vltava river wraps around the once-blighted **Holešovice** district, across the river to the north of Staré Město; Letná park, once home to a massive statue of Stalin, forms the high ground. Holešovice is shaking off its past as the city's slaughterhouse district: international trains stop here first, allowing visitors to hop right off and explore the area's range of hip clubs, award-winning dining rooms, forward-looking art galleries and, less thrillingly but perhaps more lucratively, trade fairs.

To the west, the neighbourhoods of **Dejvice** and **Bubeneč** are lined with sleepy but elegant streets, dotted with embassies and century-old apartment buildings. To the east of Staré Město lie **Vinohrady** and **Žižkov** districts; once home to outlying vineyards and tenements, they now support some of the city's hottest music venues, drinking holes and ethnic restaurants. And south of Malá Strana lies **Smíchov**, newly transformed from an industrial wasteland into a buzzy retail and nightlife hub.

▶ *For more, see pp111-121.*

Prague in 48 Hours

Day 1 Covering the Basics

9AM Start by strolling into the fantastically ornate Art Nouveau café of the **Municipal House** (*see p103 and p242*), and imagine Alfons Mucha rendering Sarah Bernhardt amid the curlicues and foliage as you breakfast on pastries and espresso.

Once replete, rise and follow Celetná west to Staroměstské náměstí and the **Astronomical Clock** at the **Old Town Hall** (it chimes hourly, 8am-8pm daily; *see p87*). Take a close look at the clock face to see if you can work out Babylonian time.

10.05AM From here, it's a short walk to **Josefov**, Prague's Jewish Quarter. Allow two hours to tour the **Jewish Museum** and the **Old Jewish Cemetery** (*see pp94-97*), and take heart in the revival of the district emptied by Hitler.

Backtrack across Staroměstské náměstí toward the Cubist museum at the **House of the Black Madonna** (*see p84*). After checking out the exhibits, grab a coffee and a snack at the museum's café. Or if you're hungrier, there are plenty of restaurants within easy reach.

2PM Just ten minutes away from the House of the Black Madonna is **Wenceslas Square** (*see p100*). Before checking out its eclectic mix of architecture, take in the Gothic **Church of Our Lady of the Snows** (*see p105*) and, nearby, the world's only Cubist streetlamp.

From Wenceslas Square, ramble down Národní třída towards the National Theatre, past historic café **Slavia** (*see p182*) and across the bridge to **Malá Strana** (*see pp72-82*). Walk through lovely **Kampa Park**, maybe stopping at the **Museum Kampa** (*see pp78-79*). Head north to Malostranské náměstí and the Baroque wonders of the **Church of St Nicholas** (*see p74*), then reward yourself with tapas and a pilsner at **Hergetova Cihelna** (*see p155*).

7PM Head back across the Charles Bridge to Staré Město and stroll to Betlémské náměstí, where Jan Hus challenged the Catholic powers. Explore the streets south of Národní to see where the buzz may be tonight, checking the bulletin board at the **Globe Bookstore & Coffeehouse** (*see p185 and p193*). You could start with high culture at the **National Theatre** (*see p105 and p271*) or a jazz jam at **U staré paní** (*see p251*), then continue to **Café Louvre** (*see p183*) – a former fave of Einstein – and on into the night…

NAVIGATING THE CITY

The best way to explore Prague is on foot. The city centre is compact, and most hotels are within an easy walk of the major attractions, worthwhile restaurants, noteworthy shops and interesting cultural venues. However, for outlying areas, there's a decent public transport network here, led by the Metro network. For details, *see pp300-302*.

THE LOCAL CURRENCY

We have listed prices in **koruna česká** (or **Czech crown; Kč**) throughout this guide. The Czech Republic intends to adopt the euro as the national currency in the near future, but the original target date of 2010 has been shelved; it now appears likely that the euro won't be adopted here until 2013 at the earliest. Even so, some hotels do accept payment in euros.

Day 2 Culture & Decadence

9AM Start the day with breakfast of Czech apple strudel and espresso, with a side order of the finest views in town, at **Villa Richter** (*see p151*). A stroll from here to **Prague Castle** (*see p59*), just across the vineyard, will burn off any excess calories you take on board. The royal treasury is rarely displayed, but the 'Story of Prague Castle' exhibition in the **Old Royal Palace** (*see p66*) shows off the finest medieval gold and gem work. The nearby **Schwarzenberg Palace** (*see p71*) adds an incredible collection of late Renaissance and Baroque painting and sculpture to the mix.

1PM Refuel with a sit-down steak at the other great terrace on Hradčany hill: the back patio of **Cowboys** (*see p154*). Take in the red pantiled roofs of the Malá Strana townhouses as you refuel amidst a mix of hip Praguers and foreign visitors.

2PM Head north-east through Letná park and towards Holešovice for a survey of modern art. Start at the **National Gallery Collection of 19th-, 20th- and 21st-Century Art** (*see p114*), a functionalist wonder where Gutfreund and Váchal share space with Picasso. If state-sanctioned art proves too traditional, head for the **DOX Centre for Contemporary Art** (*see p229*), three tram stops east, where edgy work in unusual media is celebrated. Or if that doesn't appeal, cross the river back into Staré Město for a little light shopping.

7PM Hungry yet? If you're near DOX, try a bacon cheeseburger at **Bohemia Bagel**'s Holešovice location (*see p229*). Elsewhere, **Kampa Park** (*see p155*), **Allegro** (*see p158*) and **Maze** (*see p169*) are all great bets if you've got cash to splash.

9.30PM Beer hounds may like to finish the night with a couple of rounds at **Pivovarský dům** (*see p184*), which brews its own. Clubgoers with an artistic bent, though, may prefer to start at the progressive **Cross Club** (*see p254*), before hitting the Žižkov district for louder stuff at the **Akropolis** (*see p190*) and then, if you've still got a litttle energy in reserve, finishing with a late, late nightcap at **Bukowski's** (*see p253*).

PACKAGE DEALS

Available at the Čedok tourism office (at Můstek metro, Nové Město, Prague 1; 224 219 992), the **Prague Card** (790 Kč, or 530 Kč for students) offers three days' entry to the city's major museums and galleries, including Prague Castle but excluding the Old Jewish Cemetery. Public transport is included for an additional 350 Kč .

GUIDED TOURS

The whole city is one great outdoor museum, with free sights aplenty in the centre. We've included a handful of mapped walks in the Sights chapters. But for in-depth guided tours, try **City Walks** (222 244 531), which organises walks that depart from the St Wenceslas equestrian statue in Wenceslas Square at 1.30pm daily (600 Kč, 300 Kč under-12s).

Time Out Prague

Editorial
Editor Will Tizard
Copy Editors Simon Cropper, Will Fulford-Jones, Ros Sales, Elizabeth Winding
Listings Editors Hela Balínová, Kateřina Kadlecová, Helena Vančurová
Proofreader Tamsin Shelton
Indexer Sally Davies

Managing Director Peter Fiennes
Editorial Director Ruth Jarvis
Series Editor Will Fulford-Jones
Business Manager Dan Allen
Editorial Manager Holly Pick
Assistant Management Accountant Ija Krasnikova

Design
Art Director Scott Moore
Art Editor Pinelope Kourmouzoglou
Senior Designer Henry Elphick
Graphic Designers Kei Ishimaru, Nicola Wilson
Advertising Designer Jodi Sher

Picture Desk
Picture Editor Jael Marschner
Deputy Picture Editor Lynn Chambers
Picture Researcher Gemma Walters
Picture Desk Assistant Marzena Zoladz
Picture Librarian Christina Theisen

Advertising
Commercial Director Mark Phillips
International Advertising Manager Kasimir Berger
International Sales Executive Charlie Sokol
Advertising Sales (Prague) Michal Jareš, Prague In Your Pocket; Jarmila Procházková, ARBOMedia

Marketing
Marketing Manager Yvonne Poon
Sales & Marketing Director, North America & Latin America Lisa Levinson
Senior Publishing Brand Manager Luthfa Begum
Marketing Designer Anthony Huggins

Production
Group Production Director Mark Lamond
Production Manager Brendan McKeown
Production Controller Damian Bennett
Production Coordinator Kelly Fenlon

Time Out Group
Chairman Tony Elliott
Chief Executive Officer David King
Group General Manager/Director Nichola Coulthard
Time Out Communications Ltd MD David Pepper
Time Out International Ltd MD Cathy Runciman
Group IT Director Simon Chappell
Marketing & Circulation Director Catherine Demajo

Contributors
Introduction Will Tizard (*Prague in 48 Hours* Steffen Silvis & Will Tizard). **History** Jonathan Cox & Paul Lewis (*It's a Bug's Life* Steffen Silvis; *Spirit of '68* Will Tizard). **Prague Today** Iva Skochová (*Revolt! Radar Love* Dominic Swire). **Architecture** Steffen Silvis. **Writers on the Storm** Dominic Swire. **Cheers!** Dominic Swire. **Sightseeing** Will Tizard (*Revolt! Drinking in the Scenery* Steffen Silvis; *Revolt! Herna Blues* Dominic Swire). **Hotels** Kateřina Kadlecová, Jacy Meyer, Mark Nessmith (*Backpacker Chic, At Home Abroad* Will Tizard). **Restaurants** Will Tizard. **Cafés, Pubs & Bars** Will Tizard. **Shops & Services** Jacy Meyer. **Calendar** Will Tizard (*That's All Folklore!* Steffen Silvis). **Children** Mark Nessmith, Alena Živnůstková. **Film** Will Tizard. **Galleries** Mimi Rogers. **Gay & Lesbian** Wendy Wrangham. **Music** Will Tizard (*Walk: Melody March* Steffen Silvis; *Profile: Gipsy.cz* Dominic Swire). **Nightlife** Will Tizard. **Sport & Fitness** Sam Beckwith (*Profile: Bohemians* Dominic Swire). **Theatre & Dance** Steffen Silvis. **Escapes & Excursions** Pavla Kozáková, Iva Skochová, Will Tizard (*The Sporting Life* Will Tizard). **Directory** Hela Balínová.

Maps john@jsgraphics.co.uk.

Photography Jitka Hynkova except: page 5 (bottom) Czech Tourism; pages 16, 18, 24, 36, 37 Getty Images; 9, 11, 95, 101, 102, 103, 112, 151, 169, 195, 236, 239 Olivia Rutherford; page 20 Bridgeman Art Library; page 22 akg-images; page 28 Associated Press; pages 34, 157, 186 Will Tizard; page 38 Czech News Agency; pages 47, 54, 64, 98, 120, 123, 127, 181, 192, 210, 212, 242, 252, 258, 268 Elan Fleisher; page 48 akg-images/Archiv Klaus Wagenbac; pages 80, 188, 189 Helena Smith; pages 84, 107, 167, 240 Rene Jakl. The following images were provided by the featured establishments/artists: 41, 45, 47, 51, 63, 116, 129, 130, 131, 136, 141, 142, 144, 145, 146, 204, 209, 222, 224, 225, 227, 244, 249, 250, 257, 262, 269, 273.

The Editor would like to thank all contributors to previous editions of *Time Out Prague*, whose work forms the basis for parts of this book.

About the Guide

GETTING AROUND

The back of the book contains street maps of Prague, as well as overview maps of the city and its surroundings. The maps start on page 323; on them are marked the locations of hotels (**❶**), restaurants (**❶**), and cafés, pubs and bars (**❶**). The majority of businesses listed in this guide are located in the areas we've mapped; the grid-square references refer to these maps.

THE ESSENTIALS

For practical information, including visas, disabled access, emergency numbers, useful websites and local transport, please see the Directory. It begins on page 299.

THE LISTINGS

Addresses, phone numbers, websites, transport information, hours and prices are all included in our listings, as are selected other facilities. All were checked and correct at press time. However, business owners can alter their arrangements at any time, and fluctuating economic conditions can cause prices to change rapidly.

The very best venues in the city, the must-sees and must-dos in every category, have been marked with a red star (★). In the Sights chapters, we've also marked venues with free admission with a FREE symbol.

THE LANGUAGE

Most Czechs living in Prague speak a little English; much tourist literature and many menus are available in English. The majority of venues are labelled with their Czech names alone, but we have also included an English name where useful.

PHONE NUMBERS

From within the Czech Republic, dial all phone numbers as listed in this book. From outside the Czech Republic, dial your country's international access code (00 from the UK, 011 from the US), followed by the Czech Republic's country code (420) and the nine-digit number as listed here. For more on phones, *see p311*.

FEEDBACK

We welcome feedback on this guide, both on the venues we've included and on any other locations that you'd like to see featured in future editions. Please email us at guides@timeout.com.

Time Out Guides

Founded in 1968, Time Out has grown from humble beginnings into the leading resource for anyone wanting to know what's happening in the world's greatest cities. Alongside our influential weeklies in London, New York and Chicago, we publish more than 20 magazines in cities as varied as Beijing and Beirut; a range of travel books, with the City Guides now joined by the newer Shortlist series; and an information-packed website. The company remains proudly independent, still owned by Tony Elliott four decades after he launched *Time Out London*.

Written by local experts and illustrated with original photography, our books also retain their independence. No business has been featured because it has advertised, and all restaurants and bars are visited and reviewed anonymously.

ABOUT THE EDITOR

Former California crime reporter **Will Tizard** has lived in the Czech capital for 15 years. A correspondent for *Variety* and *The Guardian*, he also runs AskFilm, a documentary and video production company in the city.

A full list of the book's contributors can be found opposite. We've also included details of our writers in selected chapters through the guide.

In Context

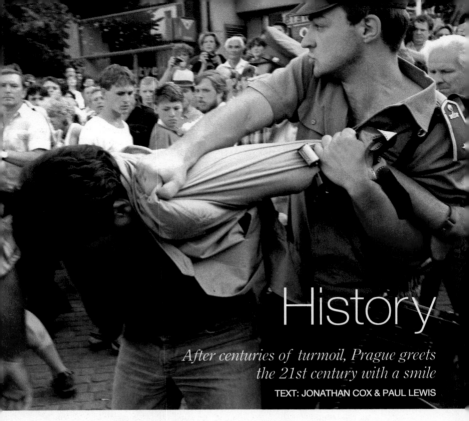

History

After centuries of turmoil, Prague greets the 21st century with a smile

TEXT: JONATHAN COX & PAUL LEWIS

Paul Lewis
writes for the
Economist *and is
the author of* How
the East was Won,
*an exploration of
Eastern Europe's
post-communist
transition.*

Jonathan Cox
*has edited and
written several
guide books for*
Time Out. *He now
works as a primary
school teacher.*

The story of Prague has been one of protest, and of a centuries-long struggle for cultural and national identity. The invasion of Czech lands by the Habsburgs in 1276 was followed by large-scale German immigration and subsequent German dominance of Church and state. Protests in the 15th century against Church corruption and German influence led to martyrdom, further dissent and even religious wars.

Amid such traumas, intellectual firepower has also flourished, ever since Emperor Rudolf II moved his court from Vienna to Prague and the city became a hub of manic creativity. And this intellectual excellence proved crucial in later struggles: the 19th-century culture war to revive the Czech language, for instance, and the Prague Spring of 1968, when freedom of speech flourished before a Soviet crackdown. By the time playwright and future president Václav Havel addressed the masses in Wenceslas Square in 1989, the Czechs were well on the way to the self-determination for which they'd battled during much of their history. But the struggle continues.

EARLY DAYS

The leader of the Celtic tribe known to the Romans as the Boii, a ruddy fellow called Čech, has achieved a posterity beyond all imagining in the Czech lands, which adopted his name after his settlers rose to power around 400 BC. Still known as Čechia to locals, what is now the Czech Republic then witnessed the cunning Boii successfully repelling foreign invaders for the best part of 1,000 years. Although there's little detail in the historical records before the ninth century, it's clear the Boii were eventually driven out by the Germanic Marcomanni and Quadi tribes... who, in turn, were wiped out by Attila the Hun in AD 451. Western Slavonic tribes moved into the area some time during the seventh century; they were ruled over by the Avars, whose harsh regime provoked a successful Slavic rebellion that gave rise to the Great Moravian empire.

MYTHIC ROOTS

Czechs had to wait until the founding of the Přemyslid dynasty in the eighth century for real independence. One of the myths surrounding the origins of the dynasty suggests that in the absence of a male heir, tribe leader Krok was succeeded by his soothsaying daughter Libuše. When the indignant men of the tribe told her to find a husband, she went into a trance and sent her white horse over the hills to find a ploughman with two spotted oxen. His name was Přemysl. However, Prague's own origin myth holds that while standing atop Vyšehrad, Libuše foretold the birth of 'a city whose splendour will reach to the stars'. A craftsman making a door sill (*práh*) was found, for, as Libuše said, 'mighty Lords bend before a low door'. His workshop was promptly declared the site of the Praha and hence Prague was born.

In the ninth century, Charlemagne briefly occupied the region, and the realignment of power caused by his arrival allowed the foundation of a Slavic state in Moravia. Rastislav (who ruled from 846 to 870), the second king of Great Moravia, cemented its cultural and historic importance by asking the Byzantine Emperor Michael III for Slavic-speaking Christian apostles in order to help end the worship of sun gods. The emperor sent brothers Cyril and Methodius, Greek monks who not only converted the people but developed the Cyrillic alphabet still used in many Slavic nations.

Slav leader Svatopluk sided with the Germans and seized power in 871, building an empire that encompassed Moravia, Bohemia and Slovakia. After his death in 894, the Magyars took a piece of Slovakia and held on to it until the early 20th century, disrupting all attempts to unite Slovaks and Czechs. And so, over the next four centuries, Bohemia rode a rollercoaster from chaos to political supremacy in Central Europe.

Many Czech nobles felt that 'Good King' Wenceslas (actually Prince Václav or Wenceslas, who reigned from 921 to 935) sold out to the Germans. They backed Wenceslas's brother, Boleslav the Cruel, who had Wenceslas murdered in 935 in the present-day town of Olomouc and went on to rule until 967. Meanwhile, Prague was made a bishopric in 973, completing the Christianisation of Bohemia that had begun in the previous century.

IN AN EXPANSIVE MOOD

National prestige reached new heights when Přemysl Otakar II (who reigned for 25 years, 1253-78) grabbed Cheb from the Germans, briefly controlling an empire that stretched from Florence to Poland. An invasion by Holy Roman Emperor Rudolf of Habsburg in 1276 soon supplanted the Přemysls when the last one, Václav III, was assassinated in 1306. German emigration to the Czech lands flourished; the new arrivals assumed great influence over the Church and the trades, dividing Prague into three autonomous areas: Malá Strana, Hradčany and Staré Město (Old Town). Malá Strana's Jewish community was forced into a ghetto in Staré Město.

By the 14th century, Czech and German nobles were in conflict, as they would remain from then on. In 1310, John of Luxembourg, the 14-year-old son of the Holy Roman Emperor, was elected king of Bohemia, but his contribution was limited to attempting to recreate the Knights of the Round Table by inviting all the great paladins of Europe to the city. Unfortunately, none turned up, though Prague did gain a town hall, became the dominant centre of Bohemia and scored an archbishopric in 1344.

After John died in a kamikaze charge against Welsh archers at the Battle of Crécy, his son Charles IV was elected Holy Roman Emperor in 1346, making his position as king of Bohemia unassailable. With such prestige to guard him, Charles launched a golden age during his 32-year reign, even managing to help Prague escape the Black Death in 1348. Laying claim to a Přemyslid lineage through his mother, the 'Father of his Country' brought the 23-year-old Swabian architect Peter Parler to Prague to build the Charles Bridge and to work on St Vitus's Cathedral. In 1348, he established Central Europe's first university, then founded the Nové Město (New Town) along modern grid principles, in stark contrast to the warren of workshops that was Staré Město. Charles declared the union of Bohemia, Moravia, Silesia and Upper Lusatia indissoluble and grafted bits of Germany on to Bohemia.

NOT-SO-GOOD KING WENCESLAS

Wenceslas IV, Charles's incorrigible son who was in charge from 1378 to 1419, was a champion of the common man. He would go out shopping dressed in commoners' clothing and execute any swindlers; Prague was soon crime-free. However, he also railed against the Church; he was even alleged to have urinated into the holy water at his christening. He's said to have spent his last years in a drunken stupor and barely escaped imprisonment by the nobles.

Jan Žižka.

'Wenceslas IV railed against the Church; he was even alleged to have urinated into the holy water at his christening.'

In 1403, Jan Hus, the rector of Prague University, took up a campaign against Church corruption. German academics left for Leipzig to found their own university, though, and the Church deemed Hus's arguments heretical. In November 1414, Hus was summoned by Wenceslas's brother, Sigismund, King of Hungary, to appear before the General Council at Constance. He went in good faith but was arrested on arrival and ordered to recant. He refused and, on his 46th birthday, was burned to death.

Hus became a martyr to two vital Czech hopes: reform of the Church and independence from German dominance. His motto of 'truth will prevail' became a rallying cry for his followers, and was even heard during the Velvet Revolution of 1989.

HUSSITES BRISTLE

A mob of several hundred Czech nobles stormed the Nové Město town hall on 30 July 1419 and threw the mayor and his councillors through the window to their deaths. In the process, they minted that quintessentially Czech form of protest: defenestration. When Wenceslas died in an apoplectic fit a few days later, Hussite mobs marked the occasion by rioting and sacking the monasteries. Sigismund elbowed his way on to the Bohemian throne, but radical preachers such as Jan Želivský furiously denounced him and Rome. The Pope called for a holy crusade against Bohemia; in return, radical Hussites burned alive nine monks in Prague.

Rome's call to arms against the heretic nation was taken up all over Europe, and the Czechs were soon surrounded. However, they united behind a powerful moral cause and Jan Žižka, their brilliant one-eyed general. Žižka not only repelled the enemies from Vítkov Hill in what is now Žižkov in Prague, but, by 1432, he and his self-proclaimed Warriors of God had begun to pillage all the way up to the Baltic coast. Women fought and died alongside men.

Most Hussites, known as Praguers, were moderate and middle class; their leaders were based at Prague University. The more extreme group, known as Táborites, were based on a fortified hillside. They banned all class divisions, shared their property and held religious services only in Czech. Unable to win a holy war, the Pope invited the Czechs to discuss a peace settlement. However, it proved unnecessary when, in 1434, the Praguers marched their army down to wipe out 13,000 Táborites at the Battle of Lipany.

During the Hussite wars, the Church's power was devastated and the vacuum was filled by the nobles, who seized Church property and ruled, with considerably less mercy than the monks, over the peasants. George of Poděbrady (Jiří z Poděbrad), the new Czech king, attempted to restore order by choosing successors from the Polish Jagellon dynasty. But after George's death in 1471, Vladislav II, then Ludvík, ruled ineffectually in absentia. After Ludvík's death, the Estates of Bohemia elected the Habsburg Duke Ferdinand I king of Bohemia. The foreign Catholic monarch sent troops into Prague to suppress Protestant dissidents, while inviting the Society of Jesus to Bohemia to spearhead the Counter-Reformation.

MOVING THE CENTRE EAST

In 1583, the Habsburg Rudolf II, who ruled from 1576 to 1611, moved his court from Vienna to Prague. For the first time in 200 years, the city became the centre of an empire. But the Holy Roman Empire badly needed a man of action, vision and direction to deal with Turkish invaders raging to the south, and to the demands of Bohemia's Protestants.

IN CONTEXT

It's a Bug's Life

From ants to fireflies, Prague culture offers plenty of insects appeal.

When two Czech entomologists were recently arrested in India for collecting rare creepy-crawlies without proper permits, the story threw up an interesting fact: there are more entomologists per capita in the Czech Republic than in any other country on earth. How did the Czechs become so fascinated by bugs?

As it turns out, insects have long played a role in Czech popular culture. After the little mole Krtek, perhaps the country's most beloved cartoon character is Ferda Mravenec, or Ferda the Ant. Created for a comic strip by Ondřej Sekora in the 1930s, Ferda was a hardworking black ant who lived in a modern insect society.

Having survived a Nazi concentration camp, Sekora was later happy to set Ferda to work supporting the various five-year plans (*pětiletka*) conjured up by the Czech Communist Party. However, no one holds that against Ferda today: he's still found throughout Prague in bookshops and souvenir shops, in the form of puppets and plush toys, and also appears on a brand of lollies.

One of the best known pieces of bug-inspired Czech work is *The Insect Play* by the Čapek brothers, a piece of expressionist theatre in which various aspects of human nature are depicted by the activities of insects. The Čapeks were less enamoured of ants than Sekora, however: in their universe, ants are used to represent militarism.

Long before Sekora and the Čapeks, there was the popular children's book *Broučci* (*Fireflies*). First published in 1876, Jan Karafiát's collection of moral tales used insects to foster Christian values. Needless to say, his minor classic was banned by the commies, though it was passed from hand to hand like samizdat literature. Copies now fetch good prices at antiquarian stalls. At around the same time, Karafiát's contemporary Svatopluk

Johannes Kepler.

Čech created a set of satirical tales around the title character Pan Brouček (Mr Bug), although this eponymous hero was a narrow-minded and nationalist Czech Everyman.

However, was it Czech literature that produced the current swarm of entomologists? Not everyone thinks so, and there's one alternative theory. In the Rudolfian age, the country's reputation rested upon astronomy: with Tycho Brahe and Johannes Kepler resident in the city, Prague was second only to Galileo's Pisa as a centre of post-Copernican studies. Yet astronomy seems to have withered after the Czechs' defeat at Bílá Hora (White Mountain). In the chaotic decades that followed, did it become easier for the downtrodden Czechs to look down instead of up?

A small, struggling people might very well identify with the smaller lives going on below them. These former masters of their own fate suddenly found themselves under the boot of others: perhaps awakening, like Kafka's Gregor Samsa in that other famous bug tale from Prague, to find that man can easily metamorphose into a cockroach.

'Rudolfine Prague was a dazzling confluence of art, science and mysticism, host to scores of brilliant and sometimes mad creatives.'

What it got was a dour, eccentric monarch engrossed in alchemy, who tended to ignore everyone except Otakar, his pet lion. While Europe headed towards the Thirty Years' War, Prague became a surreal fantasy world.

Even so, Rudolfine Prague was a dazzling confluence of art, science and mysticism, host to scores of brilliant and/or mad creatives. As word of Rudolf's sponsorships spread, the flood began. One recipient of his generosity was Tycho Brahe, the Danish astronomer who first shattered Aristotle's theories, had a metal nose and died of an intestinal implosion after overeating. But as Turkish armies thrust northwards and an attack on Vienna loomed, a coterie of archdukes concluded that Rudolf had to go. His brother Matthias picked up the reins.

TOSS 'EM OUT

Neither Matthias nor his successor, Ferdinand II, both strong Counter-Reformation Catholics, did much to win over Protestants. On 23 May 1618, an assembly of Protestants marched to the Old Royal Palace at Prague Castle. They were met by Slavata and Martinic, the emperor's die-hard Roman Catholic councillors, who were then thrown out the window. However, they landed in a dung heap and survived.

Prague's most famous defenestration turned out to be the first act of the Thirty Years' War. Frederick of the Palatinate, son-in-law of James I of England and Scotland, was elected to the Bohemian throne, but failed spectacularly to rally the Protestant princes of Europe to defend Bohemia. On 8 November 1620, the Protestants were trounced at the Battle of White Mountain (Bílá Hora) on the outskirts of Prague. On the first anniversary of the defenestration, 27 Protestant leaders were beheaded on Old Town Square, their heads then skewered on the towers of Charles Bridge.

Ferdinand maintained that it was 'better to have no population than a population of heretics'. Bohemia soon lost three-quarters of its native nobility, along with its eminent scholars and any remaining vestige of national independence. War further reduced its population from three million to 900,000, and three-quarters of the land in Bohemia was seized to pay war expenses. All Protestants who refused to abandon their faith were driven from the country, and the towns and villages filled with German immigrants. Jesuits swarmed in to 're-educate', and the peasants were forced to stay and work the land.

General Wallenstein (or Valdštejn), a Bohemian-born convert from Protestantism, became leader of the Imperial Catholic armies of Europe. He scored a number of spectacular victories, but the emperor's Jesuit advisors conspired to have him dismissed. So Wallenstein, who had been secretly negotiating with the Swedish enemy, then joined the Protestants. After Wallenstein entered Bohemia in 1634, Czech hopes for a Wallenstein victory were dashed when a band of Irish mercenaries jumped him in Cheb, stabbed him and dragged him down the stairs to his death. The Thirty Years' War eventually petered out on Charles Bridge in 1648, as Swedish Protestants scuffled with newly Catholicised students and Jews.

DEUTSCH UBER ALLES

By the mid-17th century, German had replaced Czech as the official language of government, and the lifeline of Czech heritage now rested entirely with the enslaved and illiterate peasantry. Ironically, this period also saw the construction of Prague's most beautiful baroque palaces and churches.

Tomáš Garrigue Masaryk.

During the 18th century, Empress Maria Theresa centralised Bohemia with a new wave of Germanisation in schools and government. But Maria Theresa's successor, the enlightened despot Joseph II, had little patience with the Church and kicked out the Jesuits, before nationalising the education system, freeing Jews from the ghetto and expanding the Empire's bureaucracy. As the industrial revolution began, this was all good news for the Czechs.

Though the Czech language had gone underground, a revival slowly took root. By the end of the 18th century, suppressed works had been published, notably Balbín's *Defence of the Czech Language*; the Bohemian Diet began to whisper in Czech; the Church, seeing rows of empty pews, started to preach in Czech; and Emperor Leopold II even established a chair in Czech Language at Prague University. The revival continued under Ferdinand V (1835-48) with Josef Dobrovský's *Detailed Textbook of the Czech Language* and František Palacký's *History of the Czech Nation*, while Prague's theatres staged patriotic dramas.

1848 AND ALL THAT

Finally, the Czechs demanded equal rights for their language in government and schools. As the 1848 revolutions swept Europe, Emperor Ferdinand V tossed promises Prague's way. But progress was halted when Prince Windischgrätz, the Habsburg general, fired on

'With 90 per cent of Prague's ancient Jewish community murdered during the war, the culture that had produced Kafka was wiped out.'

a peaceful gathering in Wenceslas Square, provoking a riot in order to give himself an excuse for wholesale suppression. Franz Josef, the new emperor, came to the throne on 2 December 1848 on a tidal wave of terror, then declared all Habsburg territories to be one entity.

A group known as the Young Czechs attacked the more moderate Prague establishment for pursuing a 'policy of crumbs'. Adopting Jan Hus as their hero and supported by Realist Party leader Professor Tomáš Garrigue Masaryk, they swept the 1891 elections to the Diet. At last, Czechs began to forge the political, social and economic infrastructure of a nation. Rapid industrialisation transformed the region, and an efficient rail network soon linked the Czech lands to the European economy. Industrialisation also gave rise to working-class political movements and Czech arts flourished. The era produced composers Smetana, Dvořák and Janáček, and painters such as Mucha. The Czech Academy of Sciences and Arts also achieved renown.

INDEPENDENCE DAY

During World War I, the Czechs assumed that they could win concessions on a federal constitution in return for support for the war effort. The Habsburgs didn't agree, and the Czechs soon realised that their best hopes for autonomy lay in the downfall of the Empire itself. Czechs deserted to the other side; in Prague, an underground society known as the 'Mafia' waged a campaign of agitation against the imperial regime, while Masaryk and Edvard Beneš drummed up Allied support for an independent state.

Europe's elite hardly signed up to such demands. However, the United States took the lead, and granted de jure recognition to a provisional Czechoslovak government under Masaryk. On 28 October 1918, National Committee member Antonín Švehla marched into the Corn Institute and announced that the Committee was going to take over food production. Later that day, the Habsburg government sent a note to US President Woodrow Wilson, acquiescing to Czechoslovak independence.

With a well-developed industrial base, coal and iron, an efficient communications infrastructure, an educated, highly trained workforce and little war damage with which to contend, the new Republic of Czechoslovakia bloomed into a liberal democracy. However, divisions still existed among its population. Unlike the Czechs, the Slovaks were largely an agricultural people; long ruled by Hungarians rather than Habsburgs, they looked upon the Catholic Church as a symbol of freedom. Meanwhile, the Jews, who comprised only 2.5 per cent of the population but formed a significant part of the intelligentsia, spoke German, which created Czech resentment. Indeed, it was the Germans, who formed 23 per cent of the population, who presented the biggest obstacle to a united nation. Still powerful but now resentful of their minority status, they were spread throughout the Czech lands but were concentrated in Prague and the Sudeten area near the German border.

CHAMBERLAIN'S APPEASEMENT

Konrad Henlein, head of the pro-Hitler Sudeten German Fatherland Front, cashed in on these tensions. Having grown into the second largest parliamentary bloc, Henlein's party demanded union with Germany in 1938. British Prime Minister Neville Chamberlain, for whom the Sudeten crisis was a 'quarrel in a faraway country between people of whom we know nothing', went to Munich with the French premier to meet both Mussolini and

IN CONTEXT

Hitler. All the parties involved (except Czechoslovakia, which wasn't invited to attend) were in agreement that Germany should take the Sudetenland in exchange for Hitler's promise of peace.

With Poland and Hungary also eyeing its borders, Czechoslovakia found itself encircled, and abandoned by its allies. Six months later, Hitler took the rest of the country, with Poland snatching Těšín and Hungary grabbing parts of southern Slovakia. On 14 March 1939, one day before Hitler drove into Prague, the Slovaks declared independence and established a Nazi puppet government.

THE REICH MOVES IN

In Czechoslovakia, now the Reich Protectorate of Bohemia & Moravia, everyone except for Jews and Gypsies fared better under occupation than did people in most other European countries. A National Government of Czechs was set up to follow Reich orders; Hitler had often expressed his hatred of 'Hussite Bolshevism', but he needed Czech industrial resources and skilled manpower for his war machine.

Hitler made fierce examples of resisters. Some 1,200 students were sent to concentration camps for demonstrating, and all Czech universities were closed. Reinhard Heydrich, later to chair the infamous Wannsee Conference on the Final Solution, was appointed Reichsprotektor and began rounds of calculated terror, while enticing workers and peasants to collaborate.

Beneš fled to London, where he joined Jan Masaryk (son of Tomáš) to form a provisional Czechoslovak government in exile. They were joined by thousands of Czech soldiers and airmen, who fought alongside the British forces. Czech intelligence agents passed approximately 20,000 messages on to London, including the details of Germany's ambitious plans for the invasion of the Soviet Union.

With the help of the British Special Operations Executive, Beneš hatched a plan for the assassination of Heydrich using British-trained Czech parachutists. Jan Kubiš and Josef Gabčik were dropped into Bohemia and, on 27 May 1942, successfully ambushed Heydrich's open-top Mercedes, fatally injuring the hated Reichsprotektor.

The assassins and their accomplices were hunted down to the crypt of the Orthodox Cathedral of SS Cyril and Methodius, and anyone thought to have any connection to the paratroopers was murdered. The villages of Lidice and Ležáky were mistakenly picked out for aiding the assassins and razed to the ground: the men were murdered, the women were sent to concentration camps or shot, and the children were 're-educated' (placed with German families) or killed. The transportation of Jews to the concentration camps was stepped up.

Of the 300,000-plus Czechoslovaks who perished in the war, the majority of them were Jews, and the country's Jewish population was largely destroyed. Most Jews were rounded up and sent to the supposedly 'model' Theresienstadt (Terezín) ghetto. Many died there, but the remainder were transported to Auschwitz and other concentration camps.

ATTEMPTS AT RESISTANCE

Occasional acts of sabotage continued, but the main resistance took place in the Slovak puppet state, where a four-month uprising began on 30 August 1944. The Czechs' own act of defiance came in the last week of the war: in May 1945, 5,000 died during a four-day uprising in Prague. The US forces that had just liberated Pilsen (Plzeň) to the west were only a few miles from Prague. But Allied leaders at Yalta had promised the Soviets the honour of liberating Prague, so General Eisenhower ordered his troops to pull back. General Patton was willing to ignore the order and sent a delegation to the leaders of the Prague uprising, asking for an official request for the American troops to liberate the capital. The communist leaders refused. Although communist power was not consolidated until 1948, the country already found itself inside the Soviet sphere of influence.

For at least 1,000 years, Prague's Jewish community had been walled into a ghetto in Staré Město, where life was characterised by pogroms, poverty and mysticism. Between

IN CONTEXT

The Nazi occupation.

the late 18th century, when they left the ghetto, and the arrival of the Nazis, Jews had dominated much of Prague's cultural life. But with around 90 per cent of Prague's ancient Jewish community murdered during the war, the rich literary culture that had produced Franz Kafka had been wiped out. Prague's synagogues and communal Jewish buildings were only saved from destruction by the Nazis' morbid intention to use them after the war to house 'exotic exhibits of an extinct race'.

Under the Reich Protectorate, the Czech government actively supported the extermination of its Romany citizens and helped to run dozens of concentration camps for Gypsies all over Bohemia and Moravia. An estimated 90 per cent of the region's Czech Romany died in Nazi concentration camps, mostly in Germany and Poland. Beneš's faith in liberalism had been dented by the way the Western powers had ditched his country. He began to perceive the political future of Czechoslovakia as a bridge between capitalism and communism. But his foreign minister Jan Masaryk was less idealistic, stating that 'cows like to stop on a bridge and shit on it'.

Beneš needed a big-power protector and believed that, if he could win Stalin's trust, he could handle the popular Communist Party of Czechoslovakia while keeping the country independent and democratic. During the war, he signed a friendship and mutual assistance treaty with the Soviet Union, and later established a coalition government comprising principally communists and socialists. For his part, Stalin knew that a straightforward takeover of a formerly democratic state was not politically expedient in 1945, and realised that he needed Beneš as an acceptable front in order to buy himself some time. For all his tightrope diplomacy, Beneš was effectively shuffling his country into Soviet clutches.

THE COUP STOPS TIME

The Soviets and Czech communists were widely regarded as war heroes and won a handsome victory in the 1946 elections, with Klement Gottwald becoming prime minister of a communist-led coalition and Beneš, still hoping that Stalinist communism could co-exist in a pluralistic democracy, remained president. The communists made political hay, setting up workers' militias in the factories, installing communist loyalists in the police force and infiltrating both the army and rival socialist parties.

One of the first acts of the government, approved by the Allies, was to expel more than 2.5 million Germans from Bohemia. It was a popular move and, as Klement Gottwald remarked, 'an extremely sharp weapon with which we can reach to the very roots of the bourgeoisie'. Thousands of Germans were executed or given life sentences and many more were killed in a wave of self-righteous revenge.

In 1947, Czechoslovakia was forced to turn down the American economic aid promised by the Marshall Plan. Stalin knew that such aid came with strings attached, and he was determined to be the only puppetmaster. In February 1948, with elections looming and communist popularity declining, Gottwald sent the workers' militias on to the streets of Prague. The police occupied crucial party headquarters and offices: the country was incapacitated by a general strike, and Beneš's diplomatic skill was no match for the brutal tactics of Moscow-trained revolutionaries. With the Czech army neutralised by communist infiltration and the Soviet army casting a long shadow over Prague, Beneš capitulated and consented to an all-communist government. Gottwald now became Czechoslovakia's first 'working-class president'.

Shortly after the coup, Jan Masaryk fell to his death from his office window. The communists said it was suicide. But when his body was found, the window above was tightly fastened. The defenestration had a distinctly Czech flavour, but the purges that followed had the stamp of Moscow. They were directed against resistance fighters, Spanish Civil War volunteers, Jews (often survivors of concentration camps) and anyone in the party hierarchy who might have posed a threat to Moscow. The most infamous trial was that of Rudolf Slánský, a loyal sidekick of Gottwald who had orchestrated his fair share of purges. After being showered with honours, he was arrested just a few days later.

Spirit of '68

How tanks and troops marked the end of the Prague Spring.

Czechs have a theory about their history, and with good reason. All the major sea changes that have churned or reversed the course of the country seem to come in years ending in '8': Independence in 1918, the Nazi invasion in 1938, the communist coup of 1948, and, of course, the Warsaw Pact invasion of 1968 are the tips of the iceberg. Mercifully, 2008 passed without any major upheaval, at least if you don't count the turmoil in the global markets. But during the year, much thought was given to the events of 40 years earlier and their significance.

Myths still surround that August when heavy Soviet tanks rolled through the streets of Prague, in which the dreams of Prague Spring were so brutally crushed. In movie depictions, such as the one in Philip Kaufman's *The Unbearable Lightness of Being*, the invaders are seen – unsurprisingly – as impassive at best and malevolent at worst. But a series of photographs and eyewitness accounts, solicited for a National Museum exhibition by state-run Czech TV in 2008, led to a more nuanced understanding of events. It seems that Czechs were not the only victims of the plot to 'rescue' the country from dangerous foreign elements.

Many images of the first hours of the invasion show confusion and disbelief on the part of both the invaders and the student demonstrators who turned out to face them. Young Red Army conscripts from Russia, Kazakhstan, Bulgaria and other Eastern bloc nations had no more idea what they were doing in Prague than did the Praguers: many had never been abroad before and barely knew where they were, while others considered the whole outing almost a holiday compared with army life back on home duty.

One account emerged of a Bulgarian soldier who was so taken with Prague that he tried to give his unit the slip and stay on in the city. Czech backpackers travelling through former satellite countries still meet kindly old pensioners who stun them by saying: 'Prague? Oh yes! I was there back in '68. What a lovely place!'

New tales of heroism emerged too. Take Jan Němec, whose footage of the invasion was smuggled out with the help of Italian embassy officials. It inspired a new film this year named after a young woman who aided the effort, known to him then only as Girl Ferrari Dino.

With all the focus in 2008 on the economic problems that affected not just the Czech lands but much of the world, such new perspectives have offered the cynical post-1989 generation food for thought, and no small amount of moving moments as they come to grips with what their parents faced.

IN CONTEXT

In March 1951, Slánský and ten senior communists (mostly Jews) were found guilty of being Trotskyite, Titoist or Zionist traitors in the service of US imperialists. They 'confessed' under torture, and eight were sentenced to death.

PRAGUE SPRING

Gottwald dutifully followed his master, Stalin, to the grave in 1953, but the paranoia that had gripped Prague took a long time to ease. By the 1960s, communist student leaders and approved writers on the fringes of the party hierarchy tentatively began to suggest that Gottwald and Stalin might have taken the wrong route to socialism. Slowly, the drizzle of criticism turned into a shower of anger and increasingly awkward questions. Then, on 5 January 1968, an alliance of disaffected Slovak communists and reformists within the party replaced Antonín Novotný with a reformist Slovak communist named Alexander Dubček.

The Soviet Invasion of 1968.

'For months after the Velvet Revolution, Prague floated in a dream world as playwright-president Havel captured the world's imagination.'

For the next eight months, the world watched the developments in Prague in amazement, as Dubček rehabilitated political prisoners and virtually abandoned press censorship. Understandably, Moscow was deeply alarmed and tried to intimidate Dubček by holding full-scale military manoeuvres in Czechoslovakia, but the reforms continued regardless. On 27 June, 70 leading writers signed the widely published *Two Thousand Word Manifesto* supporting the reformist government. Suppressed literature was published or performed on stage and the whole city was infused with the air of freedom. Dubček called it 'socialism with a human face'.

It didn't last. With Soviet leader Leonid Brezhnev having failed to influence the Czechoslovak leader, nearly half a million Warsaw Pact troops entered the country on the night of 20 August 1968, taking over Prague Castle and abducting Dubček and his closest supporters. The leaders fully expected to be shot, but Brezhnev needed some sort of a front for his policy of repression with a human face, so Dubček was returned to Prague eight days later.

Back on the streets of Prague, crowds of thousands of people confronted the tanks. Free radio stations using army transmitters continued to broadcast; newspapers went underground and encouraged Czechs to refuse any assistance to the occupiers. Street signs and house numbers were removed, and the previously Stalinist workers' militia found a way to defend a clandestine meeting of the national party conference.

The resistance prevented nothing. Dubček stayed in power for eight more months, watching as his collaborators were replaced by pro-Moscow ministers. In April 1969, Dubček too was removed in favour of Gustav Husák, who was eager to push for more of Moscow's 'normalisation'. Husák purged the party and state machinery, the army and the police, the unions, the media, every company and every other organ of the country that might have a voice in the nation's affairs. Anyone who was not for Husák was assumed to be against him.

Within a short time, every aspect of daily Czechoslovak life was dictated by Husák's many mediocre yes-men. Without firing a shot, Husák was able to subdue the nation back into apathy by permitting an influx of consumer goods.

THE ULTIMATE SACRIFICE

On 16 January 1969, a 21-year-old philosophy student called Jan Palach stood at the top of Wenceslas Square, poured a can of petrol over himself and set himself alight. He died four days later. A group of his friends had agreed to burn themselves to death one by one until the restrictions were lifted. On his deathbed, Palach begged his friends not to go through with it, though some did. With malicious irony, Palach's death symbolised the extinguishing of the flame of hope. 'People withdrew into themselves and stopped taking an interest in public affairs,' wrote Václav Havel. 'An era of apathy and widespread demoralisation began, an era of grey, everyday totalitarian consumerism.'

Instead of mass arrests, tortures and show trials, the communists now bound up the nation in an endless tissue of lies and fabrications, and psychologically bludgeoned all critical thought by rewarding people for not asking awkward questions and punishing them for refusing to spy on their neighbours. Punishment could mean spells in prison and severe beatings, but for most it meant losing a good job and being forced into menial work instead. During this time, Prague had an abnormally high percentage of window cleaners with PhDs.

Some, however, refused to be bowed. A diverse alternative culture emerged in which underground (*samizdat*) literature was circulated around a small group of dissidents. In December 1976, a group led by Václav Havel issued a statement demanding that leading Czechoslovak authorities should observe human rights obligations; Charter 77 became a small voice of conscience inside the country, spawning a number of smaller groups trying to defend civil liberties. Despite it, there seemed little hope for real change unless events from outside took a new turn. But then, in the mid 1980s, Mikhail Gorbachev came to power in the Soviet Union and initiated his policies of *perestroika* and *glasnost*.

THE VELVET REVOLUTION

Gorbachev came to Prague in 1988. When his spokesman was asked what he thought the difference was between the Prague Spring and *glasnost*, he replied '20 years'. In the autumn of 1989, the Berlin Wall came down and the communist regimes of Eastern Europe began to falter. The Czechoslovak government, one of the most hardline regimes in Eastern Europe, seemed firmly entrenched until 17 November, when police violently broke up a demonstration on Národní třída commemorating the 50th anniversary of the closure of Czech universities by the Nazis. A rumour, picked up by the Reuters news agency, said that a demonstrator had been killed. Another demonstration was called to protest against police brutality.

On 20 November, 200,000 people gathered in Prague to demand the resignation of the government. The police behaved with restraint and the demonstrations were broadcast on television. The government announced that the man who was reputed to have been killed three days earlier was alive, but many were sceptical. Some months after the revolution, it emerged that the KGB had probably been behind the rumour as part of a plan to replace the government with something in line with Soviet *glasnost*.

That there hadn't been a death ultimately made little difference. A committee of opposition groups formed itself into the Civic Forum (Občanské fórum); it was led by Václav Havel, who addressed the masses in Wenceslas Square. On 24 November, 300,000 people assembled to see him, joined by Dubček. With the government having lost control of the media, millions watched the scenes on television, while students from Prague raced out to factories and farms to galvanise the workers into supporting a general strike on 27 November. Workers' militias had put the communists into power in 1948; it was crucial that they chose not to stand by communism in its final hour.

Ladislav Adamec, the acting communist prime minister, also appealed to the crowds and further purges within the Communist Party followed. The party then declared that it felt that the 1968 Soviet invasion had been wrong after all, promising free elections and a multi-party coalition. It was all too late. A new government of reformist communists was proposed, but it was rejected by Civic Forum. Talks between the communists and Civic Forum continued until 27 December, when a coalition of strongly reformist communists and a majority of non-communists – mainly from Civic Forum – took power with Havel as president. Not a single person died; Rita Klímová, Havel's co-revolutionary, called it the Velvet Revolution. But in some ways, given the KGB's involvement in the handover of power, it might as well have been called the Velvet Putsch.

CZECHS GO SHOPPING

For months after the revolution, Prague floated in a dream world as the playwright-president captured the world's imagination. However, the serious issues of economic transformation were not tackled. In summer 1992, the right-of-centre Civic Democratic Party (ODS), led by Václav Klaus, a no-nonsense free-marketeer, was voted into power. But just as Klaus got down to the business of privatisation and decentralisation, calls for Slovak independence were taken up by Vladimír Mečiar's Slovak separatist HZDS party.

Slovaks had always resented what they had felt was a benign neglect by Prague, and Havel had never been popular among them. One of his first acts as president was to abandon the arms trade, dealing a big blow to the Slovak economy. Slovaks complained

Key Events

Prague in brief.

c400 BC The Celtic Boii tribe occupies Bohemia.
AD 600s Slavic tribes settle in the region.
c700 The Přemyslid dynasty begins.
863 Cyril and Methodius bring writing and Christianity to Great Moravia.
929 'Good King' Wenceslas is killed by his brother, and becomes the Czech patron saint.
1235 Staré Město gets a Royal Charter; Jews are forced into the ghetto.
1253 Otakar II becomes king.
1306 The Přemyslid dynasty ends with the murder of Václav III.
1346 Charles IV becomes Holy Roman Emperor and king of Bohemia.
1352 Parler begins St Vitus's Cathedral.
1357 Foundations are laid for the Charles Bridge.
1378 King Wenceslas IV is crowned.
1389 3,000 Jews are killed in pogrom.
1403 Jan Hus begins preaching against Church corruption.
1415 Hus is burned at the stake.
1419 Hussite mobs throw the mayor out of the town hall window; Hussite wars.
1434 Moderate Hussites wipe out the radicals; Pope allows them religious freedom.
1458 Czech noble George of Poděbrady becomes the 'People's king', but is soon excommunicated by the Pope.
1471 Jagellon dynasty rules Bohemia.
1526 Habsburg rule begins with Ferdinand I.
1556 Ferdinand invites the Jesuits to Prague to counter fierce anti-Catholicism in Bohemia.
1583 Habsburg Emperor Rudolf II moves the court to Prague, where it remains for the next 20 years.
1609 Tycho Brahe's work leads to his Laws of Planetary Motion.
1618 Protestants throw two Catholic councillors from a window in the castle, starting the Thirty Years' War.
1621 27 Protestant leaders are executed in Old Town Square.

1648 The Thirty Years' War ends.
1743 The French attack Prague.
1757 Prussians attack Prague.
1781 Emperor Joseph II abolishes the Jesuits and closes monasteries.
1848 Revolutions in Europe; uprisings in Prague against Austrian troops.
1893 The clearing of the Jewish ghetto begins.
1914 World War I; Habsburgs refuse concessions on federalism and Czech soldiers desert to the Allies.
1918 The Czechoslovak Republic is founded; Tomáš Masaryk is president.
1938 Chamberlain agrees to let Hitler take over the Sudetenland.
1939 Hitler takes all Czechoslovakia.
1942 Czech paratroopers assassinate Reichsprotektor Reinhard Heydrich. Nazis destroy the villages of Lidice and Ležáky.
1945 The Prague uprising; the Red Army arrives.
1948 The Communist Party assumes power under Klement Gottwald.
1951 The Slánský show trials and mass purges take place.
1968 Reformist communist Dubček becomes first secretary, but the Prague Spring is crushed troops.
1977 Charter 77 is established to monitor human rights abuses.
1989 Student demos turn into revolution and the communist regime falls.
1990 Poet, writer and anti-communist activist Václav Havel is elected president of Czechoslovakia.
1993 The Slovak Republic and the Czech Republic divide and become separate, independent states.
1998 The largest demonstrations since the Velvet Revolution, as the Czech ice hockey team win an Olympic gold.
2000 Protests demand the ousting of Prime Minister Miloš Zeman and ODS head Václav Klaus.
2003 Havel steps down; next year, the Czech Republic is admitted to the EU.

IN CONTEXT

'With so many skeletons in the closet, it became impossible to untangle the good from the bad.'

that economic reforms were going too fast, but Klaus refused to compromise. Mečiar upped his separatist threats until, with Machiavellian manoeuvring, Klaus called Mečiar's bluff and announced that he would back Slovak independence. The two leaders divided the assets of the state, and the countries peacefully parted ways on 1 January 1993 without so much as a referendum. Havel was elected president of the new Czech Republic, but Klaus had also outmanoeuvred him, forcing Havel into a predominantly ceremonial role.

Klaus indicated that he had little time for a policy of flushing out communists from responsible positions (known as 'lustration'). As such, communists successfully dodged the spotlight amid a blizzard of accusations and counter-accusations. A significant number of Czechs seemed to have skeletons in their cupboards, and it became nearly impossible to untangle the good from the bad. Dissidents watched helplessly while communists remained in charge of the country's largest factories.

However, the first four years of the Czech Republic under Klaus's leadership produced massive privatisation changes, which helped make the Czechs the envy of the East. Foreign investors and businesses, along with a few savvy locals, quickly capitalised on the huge opportunities for profit and development.

ON A WORLD STAGE

Not only has the local economy been transformed since 1992, but the Czech Republic has also taken its place on the world stage. Membership of NATO in 1999 was followed, five years later, by entry into the European Union. Klaus himself was forced out of power in 1997 following a campaign funding scandal, but returned as president in 2004.

With Havel, the country's moral leader, now out of power, attention has shifted to more prosaic questions: foreign investment, still-needed reforms in transparency, modernisation of the courts, and the country's true competitiveness in light of emerging markets to the east. Perceiving little action in the offering of incentives or the reduction of red tape, foreign investors had already started looking beyond the Czech lands before the global financial meltdown of 2008. Finally, it seems, the Czech Republic will have to demonstrate whether it really does offer a strong and disciplined market, or whether it's simply been rising with the tide. Elsewhere, Klaus has emerged as a notorious global warming denier, while the Greens have become a force within the mosaic of major parties.

The Social Democrats, the nation's other major power (aside from an alarmingly strong Communist Party, with whom it sometimes flirts when a parliamentary majority is needed), have lost as much lustre as their conservative rivals of late. Yet they may be headed back for another turn at the wheel following in-fighting on the right fuelled by damaging tabloid TV reports mounted by the largest media conglomerate in the region, the Ron Lauder-owned Central European Media Enterprises, which owns Prague's TV Nova.

As all this plays out, ordinary Czechs who didn't cash in during the wild '90s find themselves having to work harder as they scramble to meet mortgage payments on property for which they paid too much. Healthcare and education remain neglected in the eyes of many, though both remain at least accessible to citizens and to the constantly arriving new residents from the less fortunate countries in Asia and Eastern Europe.

Czech mastery in the world of high-tech, innovation and entrepreneurship remains a bright sign on the horizon, with the country's middle class continuing to grow, and small businesses opening at a rate never dreamed of before. Whether they remain in business in the current chilly economic climate remains to be seen, but one thing is certain: the country is out to prove that its return to the fold of Europe will bring rich rewards, both inside and outside its borders.

IN CONTEXT

Prague Today

Can the local government rebrand its city?

TEXT: IVA SKOCHOVA

In a 2008 commercial designed to tout Prague on foreign TV channels, top model Petra Němcová and former Miss World Taťána Kuchařová demonstrate an apparently ideal holiday in the city. As they dine in a fancy restaurant, clinking champagne glasses, against the kitschy backdrop of Prague Castle, *Eine Kleine Nachtmusik* oozes from the speakers. 'This is Prague,' runs the blurb across the screen. 'An unforgettable experience.'

The commercial makes explicit the city's new attitude to tourism. Prague, it seems, is done with budget travellers, done with cheap and done with dissolute partying. The city fathers now want to focus on wealthy tourists, civilised visitors with cash to splash. And as the cost of living rises for locals, with property prices going through the roof and a new Western-style problem of personal debt, the city is investing in cleaning up its act. But how clean is too clean? Would a homogenised, over-sanitised Prague lose something of its essence?

*Czech writer **Iva Skochovà** splits her time between Prague and New York, publishing features in both English and Czech.*

IN CONTEXT

CH-CH-CH-CH-CHANGES

Prague's wish to push its image upmarket is understandable. No city wants to be a cheap destination forever – and definitely not this one, which paid an estimated $500,000 to assemble the aforementioned 30-second ad. No one noticed that it glorified the same old clichés that have been haunting Prague for the last two decades, simply repackaging them for a wealthier audience. 'Come to Prague!' it winks. 'Beautiful women and plenty of booze for everyone! Oh, and some nice buildings and music as well. (Did we mention the hot chicks?)'

Rebranding Prague from a backpacker's paradise to a luxury destination has not been a smooth transition. Although prices in the centre of town are now comparable to those in other western European cities, the demanding visitor may assert that you don't always get what you pay for. It's still not unusual for taxi drivers to overcharge, for wallets to go missing on the 22 tram, or for a picture-taking tourist to step back into a pile of dogshit.

Still, despite such problems, Prague has been trying to erase its image as a rusty, developing city. Trams now boast posters warning tourists to watch their belongings, while a law that came into effect during spring 2008 made it illegal not just to urinate in public, but also to drink alcohol in the streets and soil public areas with vomit, gum, cigarette butts and animal feed. (The law had outlawed public urinating for some time – at least for adults. Parents are still frequently seen holding their toddlers over pavement curbs when nature calls.) City officials even claim that they regularly perform random taxi checks. But that doesn't mean Prague is in any danger of being confused with Zurich. And the question remains: what does Prague actually want to be when it grows up?

IDENTITY CRISES

Prague has always had a dark, sinister edge to it, which helped make the city a breeding ground for literature and art. Cleaning it up completely would mean washing away some of the good bacteria along with the poisonous ones. Not cleaning it up means attracting the kind of tourists with whom it's rapidly losing patience.

'The economic growth of the last decade has worried economists. As loans and mortgages became more readily available, an increasing number of households spiralled into debt.'

Some 20 years after claiming its post-communist liberties, Prague is suffering the same kind of diagnosis most freedom-obsessed youngsters encounter: an acute identity crisis. She wants to be respected as an adult almost as much as she wants to hang on to her pampered adolescence and, in a nutshell, thinks she can have it all. Maybe she can. But maybe she'll find out that you can't be everything to everybody.

Certainly, the city tries hard to please. High-end cocktail lounges sit next to trashy sex shops, while minimalist designer boutiques rub shoulders with overstocked souvenir stores. Hip sushi joints compete with mediocre restaurants that proudly advertise their English-language, colour-picture menus. And some of the old smoky literary cafés find themselves battling against Starbucks, which opened its first Czech branch in Malostranské náměstí in the spring of 2008. The global chain even had the nerve to move into the building that once housed the famous Malostranská kavárna, a First Republic hangout for authors, philosophers and artists. Somehow, it's hard to imagine Franz Kafka working on *The Metamorphosis* while supping on a skinny caramel macchiato to the soothing stereo accompaniment of Norah Jones.

The whole takeaway coffee concept is still difficult to understand for many from a nation bred on grand Austro-Hungarian cafés, where waiters dress in white, newspapers hang from racks and coffee is served on silver trays. Yet it's catching on. The old-timers can frown all they want, but twentysomething Czechs have every intention of keeping up with their Western counterparts, be it with MP3 players, exotic cocktails, skateboard gear or flavoured coffee in throwaway cups.

INFLATIONARY PRESSURES

In 2008, the Economic Research Institute ranked Prague eighth in its survey of the world's most expensive Western cities, above both Berlin and Brussels. Although such polls might be helpful to someone trying to relocate to the Czech Republic and expecting to lead the same life they did in, say, London, they're generally useless to tourists because they rely on irrelevant comparisons. They might, for instance, compare the price of sushi or a pint of Stella Artois in Brussels and Prague, while neglecting to ask why anyone would drink Stella when visiting the world capital of Czech lager.

Prague used to be full of local pubs carrying different beer brands – big and small, dark, light and mixed, weak and strong – from all corners of the country. In the last couple of years, things have changed, with a majority of pubs in central Prague now carrying one of the two biggest labels: Pilsner Urquell or Staropramen, respectively owned by SABMiller and InBev. Smaller, locally owned breweries have been pushed out of the centre of town, unable to compete. Even so, Czech beer is still cheap. If you're paying the equivalent of £2 for half a litre, you're either in a tourist trap or a strip bar (or possibly both).

Meanwhile, the prices of nearly everything else are catching up with those in the rest of Western Europe. The years when it made economic sense for budget-conscious German families to drive across the border for lunch, or for Brits to come for stag parties because it was cheaper than staying at home, are gone. Sure, you'll still see rowdy stag parties around town, but they're no longer here just because it's cheap. Those looking for a real bargain have moved further east, to Romania and Bulgaria.

IN CONTEXT

Czechs are finally in a position to do the things they used to observe in awe but could never afford. They can travel to other, cheaper countries to make themselves feel wealthy. They can go abroad on shopping sprees. Occasionally, they even tip well. And they love it. After humiliating years spent on the receiving end of the post-revolution 'looting' of their country by bargain-seeking tourists, they're finally experiencing the thrill of being relatively rich. After the Czech crown hit record highs against the euro, the pound and the dollar in 2008, Czechs have started venturing to Germany to shop for clothes, groceries and sometimes even cars that are typically much cheaper than at home. And an increasing number of Czechs are travelling to the US to buy electronics, luxury goods and even property. This latter trend has become so popular that the customs patrols now wait for the direct Czech Airlines flight from New York and bust people for not declaring their new iPods and laptops.

The strong crown has made an incredible difference to how Czechs travel. Only a few years ago, it was standard practice for Czechs on holiday to take all their food with them, earning them the mildly insulting nickname *paštikáři* (pâté people) on the ever-popular coast of Croatia. Just a few years ago, it was unheard of for Czechs to order a cup of espresso in a café in Italy, simply because it was three or more times the cost they would pay at home. Now, though, they're getting used to the idea that they can order a *ristretto* in Rome and pay no more than the price in central Prague.

SCEPTONOMICS

However, the steady economic growth of the last decade has worried some economists. As personal loans and mortgages became more readily available, an increasing number of households have been spiralling into debt, and the overall indebtedness of households has been growing at an average of 30 per cent since 2002. Even before the effects of the global credit crunch were felt in late 2008, with unemployment levels at record lows of around five per cent (and as low as two per cent in Prague), many were wondering how long the country could sustain the joyride.

Václav Klaus.

Revolt! Radar Love

IN CONTEXT

As the US prepares to install a new defence system, the locals are up in arms.

The Czech Republic has found itself at the centre of what some are describing as the dawn of a new cold war. It's all down to a $100 billion missile defence system that the US wants to install in Central Europe, the radar of which will be located in the Czech region of Brdy to the south-west of Prague.

The US argues that the system, designed to shoot down incoming missiles from rogue states such as Iran, is necessary to protect European allies and US forces in Europe. However, the move has riled Moscow, which believes the missiles will in reality be aimed at Russia. As a response, just one day after Barack Obama's victory in 2008, Russian President Dmitry Medvedev announced that his country would base its own missiles in Kalingrad, between Poland and Lithuania on the Baltic coast. The move, claims Medvedev, would neutralise the American system.

The issue has been controversial in the Czech Republic, with polls suggesting that two-thirds of the population may be against the US plan. There have been numerous protests against the proposed system, with some activists even going on hunger strike. There's also been disagreement in parliament, with the leading opposition Social Democrat Party calling for a public debate on the matter.

Ironically, all the fuss could turn out to be purely academic, as the US has yet to prove that the technology it proposes to use actually works. In the event of an attack, missiles fired from a base in Poland would theoretically hone in and destroy the incoming warhead guided by the radar in the Czech Republic. The combined speed of interceptor and missile would be around 24,000 kilometres per hour, or 6.5 kilometres per second. However, critics point out that this means a successful strike would be more difficult than hitting one speeding bullet with another.

The defence system was the brainchild of the Bush administration; it remains to be seen how the saga will play under the Obama regime. In the meantime, for a uniquely local perspective on the issue, look out for *Czech Peace*, a documentary on the issue by Czech film-makers Vít Klusák and Filip Remunda.

Property prices in Prague have skyrocketed at a much higher pace than wages. In 2008, a two-bedroom penthouse apartment in a 1905 art nouveau apartment building went on the market for the equivalent of £1.3 million. Some locals have suggested that charging London prices in a city where the average monthly wage only just reached the equivalent of £900 – and with fewer than a third of residents actually making that much money – is ludicrous.

Meanwhile, the economic gap between Prague and the rest of the country has been widening, with Praguers earning about 150 per cent of the national wage average. In 2007, Eurostat ranked Prague the 12th richest region in the European Union, scoring 157 per cent of the average European Union GDP per person; other Czech regions barely reached 70 per cent. Tied in with this are the fears of inflation that have made Czech economists reluctant to adopt the euro and face the inevitable price rises. The country has pushed the target date for adoption to 2012 at the earliest, even though other countries in the former Eastern bloc have been far quicker (Slovenia in 2007, Slovakia in 2009).

WELCOME TO PRAGUE

Thanks to the rising cost of Czech labour, the push to attract foreign investors has proved challenging. The biggest investment influx has come from the automotive industry: in addition to Škoda (now owned by Volkswagen), Toyota, Peugeot and Citroën have a joint-venture plant in Kolín, and Hyundai is building a new plant in northern Moravia. But the heavy reliance on the automotive industry has raised red flags in a country that's trying to fight its way into the knowledge-based markets.

Because of low unemployment, Škoda has already been forced to recruit from other countries, primarily Vietnam. This isn't the first time that the Vietnamese have been co-opted by Czechs: when Vietnam was under communist rule, Cuba paid for its workers to be sent to Czechoslovakia in return for arms and heavy engineering products. Many Vietnamese stayed on after the fall of communism in 1989 to set up small businesses; and today, most of the city's independent fruit and vegetable stands, as well as small grocery stores, are run by Vietnamese. Despite living in the Czech Republic for years and raising children here, they're still treated as outsiders by most locals.

IN CONTEXT

Roma protestors. *See p40*.

'Suspicion can be an endearing quality here. Praguers are devil's advocates: instead of venturing ways to make something work, they'll give you a million reasons why it should fail.'

Ironically, though, suspicion can actually be an endearing quality here. Praguers are world-class devil's advocates: instead of venturing ways to make something possible, they'll gladly give you a million reasons why it should fail. What some might describe as negativism, Czechs see as critical thinking. They're proud to be thinkers, not 'just doers'. Over-analysing just about everything is a constant habit. Why else would Czechs have elected a philosopher as president after communism ended?

THE WORLD ACCORDING TO KLAUS
Václav Klaus, the current Czech president, was re-elected for his second term in February 2008. Klaus's opponent Jan Švejnar, a Czech-born economist based at the University of Michigan, ran his campaign claiming that he would give up his American citizenship if he won the election in order to keep his loyalties clear. He also said that once his term was over, he would return to the US with his American wife and daughter, neither of whom speak Czech. Needless to say, his unusual situation did not win him points in the election.

Klaus, meanwhile, secured a warm seat at Prague Castle, where he's been busy writing controversial commentaries about global warming. A vehement environmental sceptic, Klaus refutes the notion that global warming is man-made: he claims that environmentalism is like a religion, or a 'modern counterpart of communism' that seeks to change habits and economic systems. Although likening something to the perennially unpopular ideologies of religion and communism still resonates here, most locals will just shrug and tell you that Klaus's global warming agenda is just a harmless piece of narcissism. The 'crotchety old man', as Czech journalists call him, has also been highly critical of the fundamentals of the European Union (beside the dangers of environmentalism, he's sounded alerts about EU bureaucracy) and the controversial design of the newly planned Czech national library. Many wonder if he ever has time for his small-country presidential duties.

Strangely enough, though, Klaus hasn't been so vocal about the biggest foreign policy issue facing the Czech Republic: the US plan to build a radar base on military land about 60 miles south-west of Prague, in addition to an anti-ballistic missile base in Poland (*see p37* Revolt!). The official rhetoric is that the missile shield is there to protect the United States and Europe against a possible attack from Iran or North Korea. Russia, however, has made clear it feels greatly threatened by the plan. And there are few things that Czechs fear more than an angry Russia.

According to surveys, two-thirds of Czechs are opposed to the radar base on their territory. Thousands protested against the planned base right up to the day in July 2008 when Condoleezza Rice and Czech foreign minister Karel Schwarzenberg signed the agreement. Calls for a referendum were dismissed with a statement that defence is far too complicated for ordinary people to understand.

POWER, CORRUPTION AND LIES
In order for the radar-base treaty to take effect, it must be ratified by the Czech parliament. But parliamentary support of the agreement has been in doubt, thanks to the weakness of the coalition government. The current right-leaning government, dominated by the Civic Democratic Party and bolstered by two small parties (the Christian Democratic Union – Czechoslovak People's Party and the Green Party), has been on the verge of

IN CONTEXT

collapse ever since it was elected by a razor-thin margin in 2006. The coalition was an improvement over the period earlier the same year when the Czech Republic had no government at all, but the parties have struggled to get any work done.

What's more, they've made up for their inactivity with a slew of corruption and slander scandals. The most high-profile case concerns Jiří Čunek, the Christian Democratic leader who became popular as a mayor of the south Moravian town of Vsetín because he forced several hundred Roma rent defaulters into primitive container housing outside town. Čunek is currently facing corruption charges after he was unable to explain how he earned the contents of his bank account.

According to the 2007 Country Report on Human Rights Practices, the Czech Republic has had persistent problems with law enforcement and judicial corruption, including high-level political intervention in private lawsuits. Furthermore, what the report describes as 'child abuse and trafficking in persons for sexual exploitation and forced labour' remain enduring problems. Random violence, rallies and vandalism by neo-Nazis and skinhead groups against Roma occurred throughout the year. Discrimination against minorities continues; and, according to the report, there remains a real lack of education, housing, and employment opportunities for Roma.

THE BIG SLEAZY

So what's next for the capital of sleaze, as Prague has been called on more than one occasion? It's certainly changing, but visitors in search of vice needn't worry – they haven't yet missed the boat. Wenceslas Square is still full of touts trying to lure men into clubs. Striptease is widely available and often synonymous with prostitution. *Hernas*, dingy gambling bars that are typically open round the clock, have grown like fungus. And the city is now home to more than 8,000 slot machines. This latter epidemic has chafed middle- and upper-class Czechs for so long that Prague has finally ordered that no new *hernas* can open in the capital. Some districts have banned blinking neon signs in the windows of such venues, while others have decreed that no *hernas* or sex shops can be located within 50 metres of a school.

Smoking bans, though, are still some way off, as is an end to reckless driving and smog-belching traffic. Prague has some of the highest car ownership rates in Europe, with 39 per cent of locals proudly possessing a set of wheels. The cost of public transport increased sharply in 2007, making the choice between a comfortable car and a smelly tram – at least in summer – all the more difficult.

ENDURING APPEAL

It's sometimes hard to explain how a city with so many questionable attributes can continue to draw so many visitors. But there's more to Prague than its infamous vice industry or its fast-rising expense. Try and take a walk along the river right before the sun starts to set, when the city is blanketed in that perfect, soft light that casts a pink hue on the magnificent art nouveau riverfront buildings. It's difficult to resist.

Prague's pull is also rooted in the way that the music echoes in the crooked streets of Hradčany, and the way that girls walk on cobblestones in stilettos. It's in the shadows cast by baroque and nationalist-era statues. It's in the marvellously simple rituals that it seems Czechs will never abandon: the way, for instance, that *nakládaný hermelín* (pickled cheese) tastes after a few beers, which you've sipped at a rough-hewn communal pub table.

Mercifully, the souvenir shop and cheap vice aesthetic is still too weak to steal Prague's real soul. A thousand slot-machines and a government obsessed by ideological debates don't diminish the joy of an afternoon on a Vltava river island with a group of friends. For every Czech in debt up to his eyeballs or chasing you off the pedestrian crossing with his big new BMW (often one and the same person), there'll be ten others inviting you to their family's wine cellar in Moravia for the weekend, or making you sample fresh apricots from Granny's cottage garden. Prague's essence is not found in supermodels clinking champagne on the castle steps. But the 'unforgettable' bit is certainly right.

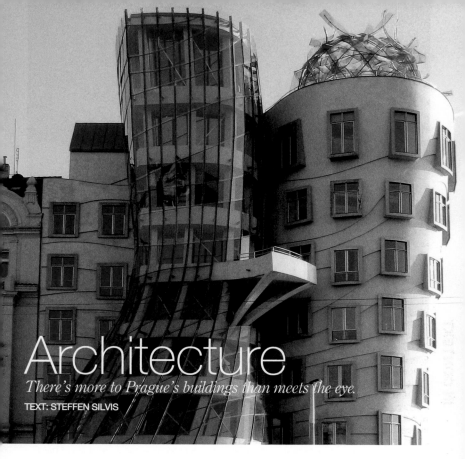

Architecture

There's more to Prague's buildings than meets the eye.

TEXT: STEFFEN SILVIS

There's no mistaking Prague, a mass of extrovert styles knitted together into a glorious and unique cityscape. The Prague of postcards is often described as a meeting of the Gothic and the Baroque, with the fantastical Charles Bridge the most iconic example of this unusual style. But from the gold-roofed National Theatre, embodiment of the National Revival movement, to the Secessionist likes of the grand Municipal Hall, there's more to the city than its biggest landmarks.

Goethe famously described architecture as 'frozen music', an apt definition in the city of Mozart and Dvořák. It's doubtful that the writer meant to suggest lapses into synaesthesia. But as you wander around Prague, and wandering is the only way to know it, the buildings do strike chords and produce vibrations. You can imagine one as an aria from *The Marriage of Figaro,* just as the next hits you like a blast of Coltrane.

Steffen Silvis,
formerly of the
Pulitzer-winning
Willamette Week
in Portland,
Oregon, has been
a film and theatre
critic for the
Prague Post
for three years.

Church of Our Lady Before Týn.

DRAWING CONCLUSIONS

Czech surrealist Vítězslav Nezval wrote that, as seen from the castle's ramparts, Prague was a 'gathering of magicians'. Buildings stand in sorcerers' hats, reminiscent of the Prague seen in the German expressionist film *The Golem*: magical yet strange. Peter Parler, the wizard of Czech Gothic architecture and the father of Prague's architectural eccentricity, even named his style *sondergotik*, which translates as 'odd Gothic'.

Throughout this chapter, we'll try to classify the city's best buildings as representatives of particular styles. Yet the glory of Prague is that many components of its landscape are impossible to slot neatly into files. How do you label Josip Plečnik's **Church of the Sacred Heart** (*see p119*), a glorious pile that can only be described as a Babylonian alarm clock? What about the miniature Ruthenian Orthodox church hidden up the south slope of Petřín Hill – how about Folk Gothic or Forest Baroque? And then there's the villa of symbolist sculptor František Bílek (*see p70*), one of Kafka's favourites, who built a home out of his own febrile imagination.

Czechs are walkers and pilgrims, and Prague is a walker's city. The city's Czech name is Praha, from *práh* – 'threshold'. Czech art and literature is full of the *noční chodec*: the 'night walker', tracing Prague's blind alleys, twisting lanes and lost architecture. Follow in their footsteps and you'll see the city at its best.

FOUNDATION STONES

Celts, Germans and various tribes first inhabited the land surrounding what is now the city of Prague, although the archaeological evidence of permanent settlement within historic Prague proper is sketchy. The national myth of Libuše and the founding of the Přemyslid royal clan aside (*see p17*), it's convenient to nominate Duke Bořivoj I (c852-c888), the grandfather of Wenceslas I, as the founder of Prague: it was Bořivoj who moved the seat of his power from Levý Hradec downriver to the Hradčany outcrop, where Prague Castle now stands.

Three sections of modern Prague were soon developed independently of each other: Hradčany; what is now Staré Město on the opposite side of the river; and Vyšehrad, which eventually came to rival Hradčany. This period is best represented by the odd stacks of fallen bricks and stones unearthed under later structures, some of which can now be seen at various points around the castle. So it's with the Romanesque that a survey of standing architecture in Prague begins, and a handful of exquisite examples remain.

Bazilika sv. Jiří (Basilica of St George; *see p67*), the largest and certainly most striking of them, stands within the castle complex. Although the basilica was founded in 920, the existing basilica dates from 1142, built by what might have been the very first wave of Italian craftsmen in Prague (*see below*).

While it's hidden behind a Baroque wedding cake façade, the basilica's interior is, startlingly, pure Romanesque. Older still are three miniature Romanesque rotundas: **St Longinus** in Nové Město, **Holy Rood** in Staré Město, and Vyšehrad's **Rotunda sv. Martina (Rotunda of St Martin**; *see p119*), the oldest surviving structure in Prague.

GOING GOTHIC

The stereotypical image of Prague is of a city where the Gothic collides with the Baroque. It's a simplistic idea, but contains more than a germ of truth. From Hradčany's ramparts, the Gothic structures sport Nezval's magicians' hats: the twin towers (Adam and Eve) of the **Kostel Matky Boží před Týnem (Church of Our Lady Before Týn**; *see p84*), the **Prašná brána (Powder Gate**; *see p85*), and the town halls of Staré and Nové Město (*see p87 and p108*), which all date from the 14th and 15th centuries.

However, it's the supine **Charles Bridge** that remains Prague's Gothic masterpiece. Peter Parler, then the king's young court architect, was commissioned to build it in 1357; several years later, Parler's workshop also took responsibility for the Staré Město bridge tower, the most impressive of the three towers. Appropriating the flying buttresses and ribbed vaults of the ever-so-stylish French, Parler turned the Gothic into something singular.

Parler's achievements went beyond the bridge. On the death of Matthew of Arras, he took over the construction of **St Vitus's Cathedral** (*see p64*), where he was buried upon his death in 1399. And outside Prague, he built **Karlštejn Castle** (*see p278*), a medieval fantasia for his patron, and Kutná Hora's **Kostel sv. Barbory (Cathedral of St Barbara**; *see p282*), arguably his greatest work.

RENAISSANCE MEN

Historic Prague is often referred to as the city of three peoples: Czechs, Germans and Jews. But there was a fourth people, and a rather important one at that: it would be difficult imagining what Prague would look like had Italian craftsmen never arrived.

Although its absence has more to do with the religious and political turmoil in the Czech lands than to a rejection of the age's tenets, the ideas of the Renaissance can only occasionally be seen in the city's buildings. Other than its obvious influence on the **Pinkas** and **High Synagogues** (*see p96*), both built during the 16th century in Josefov, the primary architectural examples are secular: Hradčany's newly refurbished **Schwarzernberský palác (Schwarzenberg Palace**; *see p71*), for instance, built in 1567 and still replete with its geometric *sgraffito* façade and loggia.

Prague also boasts one of the finest Renaissance pieces in all of Central Europe: the **Belvedere** in Hradčany (*see p69*). Approaching this graceful, arcaded retreat, which Ferdinand I commissioned Paolo della Stella to build for his consort Anne, you'd be forgiven for thinking you've been teleported to Florence. Commanding a geometric garden of box hedges, centred on the famous Singing Fountain, the beautiful Belvedere has taken a beating over the years, but it's now getting a much-needed restoration.

BAROQUE AROUND THE CLOCK

Baroque architecture conjures mixed feelings in Prague. It was a style foisted upon the city by Jesuit fiat, no less brutalist in its way than Soviet architecture. Baroque here is a paradox, somehow managing to be sumptuously severe. There's a menacing coldness in Prague's greatest Baroque monuments: the **Klementinum** (*see p89*), the Jesuits' redoubt in Staré Město, and Malá Strana's **Kostel sv. Mikuláše (Church of St Nicholas**; *see p73*),

IN CONTEXT

built in the early 18th century by the work of father-and-son team Christoph and Kilian Ignaz Dientzenhofer and the masterpiece of the movement. The Dientzenhofers were also responsible for another austere confection named after St Nicholas in Old Town Square (*see p87*). The **Loreto** (*see p70*), a riot of Catholic kitsch at its most gruesome, is another of their Counter-Reformation spectacles.

Toward the end of Kilian Ignaz's life, the stolidness of the Baroque had started to give way to the more feminine curves of the Rococo. One marvellous example is the architect son's lovely pink and white stucco **Kinský Palace** in Old Town Square, although the balcony of this delicious building was used by Klement Gottwald to launch the communist coup in 1948. Given the consequences of that action, a Baroque edifice would have surely lent the more proper air to proceedings.

ARCHITECTURAL REVIVALISM

As they attempted to wrest back their own land in the 19th century, the Czechs used architecture as a weapon. Convincing their Austro-Hungarian overlords that there was a need for a national theatre, the Czech public raised the funds to construct one of the greatest Trojan Horses since *The Aeneid*. The movement toward Czech self-determination became known as the National Revival, and artists from every discipline joined in reconstructing a Czech nationality, whose ultimate aim was independence. The contruction of the **Národní divadlo** (**National Theatre**; *see p244* and *p271*) was pivotal in their attempt to realise their collective goal.

In 1868, 50,000 people were said to have marched in procession behind the theatre's foundation stone as it was wheeled toward the site. Some 13 years later, the theatre opened with a rousing opera by Smetana based on *Libuše*, his people's establishing myth. Two months later, though, the building was gutted by fire.

Looking on at the destruction of the embodiment of their national identity, the Czechs were horrorstruck but not defeated. They threw themselves into more fundraising: the theatre was rebuilt in two years, opening again with Smetana's *Libuše* (the Czechs are not a superstitious people). Carefully lit at night, the burnished gold roof of the theatre remains a beacon for a nation.

The other great National Revival building is the **Národní muzeum** (**National Museum**; *see p101 and p218*), located at the top of Wenceslas Square. Many still mistake this majestic pile for the seat of Czech government, the same error made by the invading Warsaw Pact armies in 1968. Little did they know they were threatening a repository of rocks and stuffed animals.

ART NOUVEAU ARRIVES

As the Austro-Hungarian Empire began to show more cracks, the Czechs became rather gilt-ridden. A new flamboyance emerged from behind the stately revivalist architecture. The artist of the age was, for good or ill, Alfons Mucha, whose sinuous forms and pastellist's aesthetic set a tone of fin-de-siècle excess.

The style known as art nouveau in France and *Jugendstil* in Germany is Secessionism in the Czech lands. One of the reigning Secessionist architects in Prague was Osvald Polívka, who built two of the most charming buildings of the movement: the **Topic Building** and the **Prague Insurance Building**, both on Národní třída in view of the National Theatre (try to see them at night). Polívka joined forces with Antonin Balšánek to construct the jewel box **Obecní dům** (**Municipal Hall**; *see p242*); sensuous filigree, gilt and Tiffany-style stained glass rule the interior, but the outside is no less ornamental.

The Secessionist spirit can be found throughout the city. Wenceslas Square offers the unashamedly florid **Grand Hotel Evropa** (*see p143*). Nearby stands the ruined Secessionist glories of Josef Fanta's once-magnificent **Hlavní nádraží** (train station; *see p102*), butchered by the communists but currently undergoing major renovation (chiefly, alas, to install shops). **Slavín** (*see p119*), the Vyšehrad cemetery where the dead elite of Czech culture are buried, is a Secessionist compound filled with beautiful and bizarre Modernist

IN CONTEXT

Revolt! New for Old

Will two new architectural developments hit the rocks?

Praguers are usually vigilant when it comes to development in their city. It's one thing to close a beloved, cheap caff and install a Starbucks, but it's quite another to demolish an entire building or neighbourhood. Developers mess with the city's fabric at their peril.

Recently, two battles have been waged in Prague over proposed developments. One is the City Development, a privately built array of skyscrapers (*mrakodrapy*, or 'cloud clawers'). The other, a more contentious issue, is the building of a new National Library, designed by a renowned Czech architect who lived in London from 1968 until his death in January 2009.

Created by real estate development firm ECM, the **City Development** scheme allows for the construction of a number of new buildings in the Pankrác district, set downriver from the city's historic core. There are already a number of skyscrapers in place, all neatly cordoned off from the centre in the fashion of La Défense outside Paris.

ECM's plans encompass a combination of office buildings, hotel and luxury flats, and its designs range from inspired to clichéd. The block of apartments, a forked affair, looks like two fingers stuck up at the historic skyline. And it's this building that's inspired a spirited protest against the entire development. Local community groups began a small-scale war, becoming emboldened when UNESCO stepped in on their behalf. In classic Czech fashion, deadlock has set in. ECM is currently ignoring a court order, while the community activists have sworn their undying enmity. At the end of the day, the dodgy economy might finish the whole thing off regardless.

Meanwhile, the attacks on the new **National Library** (or 'the Blob') have raged on for some time. After beating 400 other designs in a stiff competition, London-based Czech architect Jan Kaplický found himself fighting against his own city until his sudden death in early 2009. Kaplický's library certainly bears little or no resemblance to any other structure in the country. Its shape has been likened to an octopus, one that would rise up from Letná park just a short walk from Hradčany.

The National Library director, a supporter, has been fired from his post (although his replacement is also a supporter). Mayor Pavel Bém was an early enthusiast, but he's now playing the outraged populist. President Václav Klaus has let the world know that he'll chain himself to a digger in protest should groundbreaking begin. Kaplický's supporters have been left seething, while Prague shrugs and guts another historic interior for a coffee franchise.

IN CONTEXT

'Czech artists embraced cubism and made it into something strikingly singular, applying its tenets both to furniture and architecture.'

gravestones. And thanks to Mucha's stained-glass windows and the stunning crucifixion by Secessionist-symbolist sculptor František Bílek, the style is even found within the ancient St Vitus's Cathedral.

PRAGUE CUBED

In the spirit of Peter Parler, Czech artists in the early 20th century embraced cubism, another artistic style emerging from France, and made it into something strikingly singular. For the most part, Czech cubist painting is fairly derivative of Gris and Braque (as a side note, though, the French have recently 'discovered' Czech painter Emil Filla, whom they've deemed a genuine kindred spirit). But the uniquely Czech contribution to the movement came when the locals took the tenets of cubism and applied them to furniture and architecture, with astonishing results.

There were two phases of cubist architecture in Prague. The best collection of the first period can be found below Vyšehrad in the form of three buildings designed by Josef Chocal. However, the most famous example is in Staré Město: Josef Gočár's **Dům u Černé Matky Boži** (**House of the Black Madonna**; *see p84*), which fittingly now houses the Czech museum of cubism.

After World War I, Gočár and his colleague Pavel Janák (along with cubist sculptor Otto Gutfreund) launched the second phase of Czech cubist architecture. Rondo-cubism, they called it, inspired by the use of semicircular motifs within their designs. The height of this short-lived movement is their **Adria Palace** on Jungmannova. Le Corbusier dismissed it as 'Assyrian', but its odd mesh of Italian Renaissance and Modernism is nothing less than *sonderkubismus* – literally, 'odd cubism'.

FORM AND FUNCTIONALISM

The building that really floored Le Corbusier was the **Veletržní palác**, the Trade Fair Palace in Holešovice that now houses the National Gallery's collection of modern art (*see p114*). The glass-walled building, by architects Oldřich Tyl and Josef Fuchs, left the great Swiss architect initially unmoved. 'Interesting, but not yet architecture,' was his initial response. Still, he kept pondering over what he'd seen in Holešovice, and soon came to a different final verdict. 'When I first saw the Trade Fair building in Prague, I felt totally depressed. I realised that the large and convergent structures I had been dreaming of really existed somewhere, and at the time I had just built a few small villas.' Appropriately, some of Le Corbusier's paintings now hang there.

But as a new national architectural design, rondo-cubism proved a non-starter. It was functionalism that attracted the serious draftsmen, with even Gočár becoming a convert. This sleek Modernist movement eventually deteriorated into the dull urban boxes of the 1970s, but a number of cooler relics still dot Prague's landscape. Other than the Veletržní palác, perhaps the best are Ludvík Kysela's two glass-walled structures on Wenceslas Square, the **Lindt Building** and the **Baťa** shoe store. Both were built in the late 1920s, and both still look vibrantly new.

A TOUCH OF STALIN

When not busily confecting kitsch, the communists were experts in creating dreariness. About the only thing they knew how to build were expectations. As a consequence, the most prominent architectural legacy of their dutifully dull period is the ring of workers'

IN CONTEXT

Rotunda of St Martin.
See p43.

Danube House.

housing, called the *paneláky*, that girds the city. It's the same grey, utilitarian style that you find choking Krakow, Bucharest and Moscow.

However, the most conspicuous monument of the age, the one at which visitors tend to gasp when they first see it rising above the olde worlde Prague of postcard fame, is the **Žižkov Tower** (*see p121*). This space-age phallus is a structure that grows on you, particularly when you've visited it up close and seen what's growing on it – a legion of hydrocephalic babies, by David Černý, the Czech art world's enfant terrible. Although the communists originally planned that it should block Western European broadcasts, the tower now supports television antennae,

AFTER THE REVOLUTION

With democracy came commercial squalor. Many buildings in Prague have been sadly transformed by signage, or ground-floor spaces in which tat is hawked to the masses under stark fluorescent lights. But the buildings survive. Many of the large shopping centres that have been developed within the old city incorporate existing historic façades: take the recently opened **Palladium** (*see p192*) on Náměstí Republiky, built within the old imperial army barracks.

Outside the centre, there's an outcrop of skyscrapers in the Pankrác district, and there are plans to extend this development further (*see p45* **Revolt!**). The well-appointed **Danube House**, part of the River City office/residential project in Karlín and pre-sold to newly flush Czechs before it was even completed, is a harbinger of what's to come: it's a far cry from concrete-panel apartments.

Still, only one contemporary building has been embraced: **Tančící dům** (**Dancing Building**; *see p107*), also known as Fred & Ginger, which was built by Frank Gehry and Vlado Miluníc. It's a subdued piece of work by Gehry's standards, but the undulating glass and steel structure came as a shock to Praguers. Still, today, it's a point of pride. But how will the city follow it?

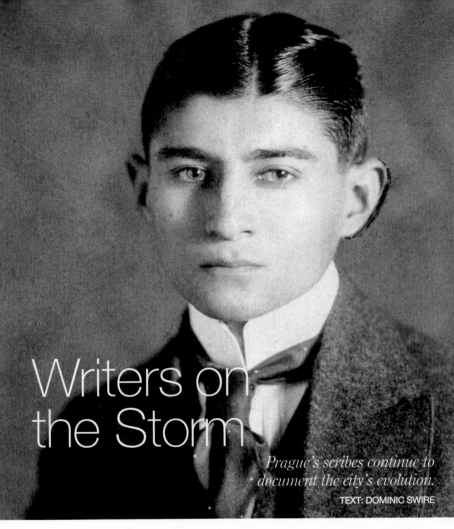

Writers on the Storm

Prague's scribes continue to document the city's evolution.

TEXT: DOMINIC SWIRE

Based in Prague, freelance journalist **Dominic Swire** *covers business and politics across Central and Eastern Europe.*

Prague's reputation as a literary city was boosted by the unusual distinction of having a playwright for president; before taking charge in the wake of the Velvet Revolution, writer Václav Havel had spent the communist era as a dissident. However, the city's shadowy streets and fairytale architecture inspired creative souls long before Havel's political ascent. And when you consider the longtime cross-pollination of culture, the relaxed bohemian lifestyle and the cheap beer, it's obvious why Prague has been tantamount to a mecca for generations of aspiring writers, even if the locals haven't always embraced the talents that their city has spawned.

KAFKA & KUNDERA

Despite the fact that **Franz Kafka** (*pictured left*) was born, buried and lived most of his life in Prague, it wasn't until 2004, some 80 years after his death, that the city acknowledged his achievements by unveiling a weird statue in Old Town's Dušní street. Although fluent in Czech, German was Kafka's mother tongue and the language in which he chose to write. Many scholars even argue that his idiosyncratic style is impossible to appreciate fully in anything other than its original language. Because of this, Kafka has never been entirely accepted by Czechs as one of their own. However, that hasn't stopped a small industry of cafés and restaurants around his old neighbourhood in the tourist-saturated Jewish quarter of Josefov from cashing in on his name.

Milan Kundera, the other great Czech literary celeb abroad, suffers from a similar problem to Kafka's. Most of his works were written in French, and Kundera himself has lived in France since the 1970s. Again, many of his compatriots have looked upon him less than favourably, as they generally do with those lucky few who managed to escape the hard years of communism. *The Unbearable Lightness of Being*, Kundera's most famous work, was published in 1984 but didn't make it into Czech until 2006, due in part to the author's dissatisfaction with all the previous attempts at translation. And then in October 2008, the reclusive writer found himself at the centre of a media scandal after one Czech magazine printed an article suggesting he had worked as an informer for the communist regime. Kundera strenuously denies the accusations.

BEYOND THE BIG NAMES

For a clearer idea of what Czechs view as great Czech literature, it's worth looking out for other, less internationally known works. The troubled Jewish community of the early 20th century from which Kafka emerged also spawned other greats: **Max Brod**, who was instructed to burn Kafka's manuscripts upon his death; and novelists **Paul Leppin** (*Severin's Journey into the Dark*) and **Gustav Meyrink** (*The Golem*), both of whom wrote haunting accounts of the twilight of the Habsburg Empire. Holocaust survivors such as **Jiří Weil** and **Arnošt Lustig**, the latter still active in Prague's rich theatre scene, kept up the tradition. And elsewhere on the spectrum, look out for the politically charged novels of **Ivan Klíma**, the dissident writings of **Ludvík Vaculík** and the experimental poems of **Jiří Kolář**, to name but a few.

Particular mention should also be made of **Jaroslav Hašek**, who created perhaps the most famous character in Czech literature: the Good Soldier Švejk, from the book of the same name published in 1923. Set around the time of World War I, the story recounts the adventures of Švejk, an army veteran who's so keen to follow his orders to the letter that people are unsure if he's cunningly attempting to undermine the ruling Austro-Hungarian Empire or if he's simply an idiot. Czechs have warmed to the subversive nature of the main character, and many pubs and restaurants across the city make reference to his name. Both character and author have even had asteroids named after them: 2734 Hašek and 7896 Švejk.

Of course, the works of dissident, playwright and ex-president **Václav Havel** still inspire. Havel's activities during communism resulted in frequent prison sentences; in later and more enlightened times, his letters to his wife from this period were published as *Letters to Olga*. Since retiring from his job at Prague Castle, the shy and fussy scribe has once again found wide audiences after a return to writing.

SEEING THE SCENE

Prague's strong literary tradition continues today with frequent festivals, poetry slams, readings and book signings. The biggest regular event is the **Prague Writers' Festival** (*see p213*): held each year in spring or early summer, it welcomes illustrious global names such as Salman Rushdie, Irvine Welsh and John Banville alongside talented local scribes. November's **Poetry Days in Prague** (www.volny.cz/denpoezie/english.html) also brings a number of readings and other literary events, showcasing work from the Czech

'Czechs have warmed to the subversive nature of Jaroslav Hašek's character Švejk, and many pubs and restaurants make reference to his name.'

Republic and abroad. And you might also find a gem or two during the **Prague Fringe Festival** (*see p274*) and the **Winter Fringe & Fringe Comedy Nights**.

Away from the festivals, there are well-attended readings and literary happenings throughout the year. One of the best places to search for them is via the **Alchemy** group (www.alchemy-prague.com), which organises monthly readings and performances at the **Globe Bookstore & Coffeehouse** (*see p193*) on the first Monday of every month. The Globe is a particularly good place to find English books and periodicals. To keep your finger on the pulse of contemporary culture in the city, and much further afield, look out for publications such as *Umělec* (www.divus.cz). Elsewhere, the **National Library of the Czech Republic** (*see p306*) hosts, organises and advertises many literary events and exhibitions in the city.

Cafés in Prague with a literary bent include **Shakespeare & Sons** (*see p189*), which even has its own bookstore in the back. Formerly known as Obratnik, **Symbiosa** in Anděl (www.symbiosa.eu) sells books, sports its own wine cellar and stages regular literary happenings, although they're mainly in Czech. And around the corner from Karlovo náměstí, the **Red Room** (www.redroom.cz) can be a little more rowdy, but its regular open mic nights on Sunday have been known to attract the odd poet or two.

IN CONTEXT

Big Ben Bookshop.

Revolt! Havel Sharpens His Pen

The former president returns to his literary roots.

Prior to his 13 years as president, Václav Havel was a well-known political dissident and playwright. Much of his work rubbed the communists up the wrong way, and even earned him five years in jail. Now, following a 20-year break, Havel is back on the literary scene with a new book, *To the Castle and Back*, and a play, entitled *Leaving*.

The retired head of state began writing *Leaving* before he took office in the wake of the Velvet Revolution in 1989, but only completed the play after his tenure ended in 2003. Set in an unnamed European country, *Leaving* follows a president in the last days of his administration, reluctant to hand over the seat of power to his successor. Many observers have drawn comparisons to Havel's stormy relationship with his political arch rival Václav Klaus, although Havel himself denies the connection.

Also available in an English translation by Paul Wilson, *To the Castle and Back* was received more warmly. The cover,

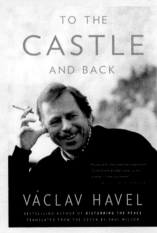

TO THE
CASTLE
AND BACK

VÁCLAV HAVEL

BESTSELLING AUTHOR OF *DISTURBING THE PEACE*
TRANSLATED FROM THE CZECH BY PAUL WILSON

which shows a cheerful portrait of the man laughing with a cigarette in hand, makes it easy to forget that Havel is now 73 years old and slowly dying of lung cancer. (Despite the picture, Havel claims to have given up smoking some 20 years ago, but still admits to the craving.) The book is a compilation of recollections from his presidency, interspersed with a selection of office notes and excerpted interviews. It's full of idiosyncratic details, such as a note to his staff concerning the problem of a bat that's taken up residence in a cupboard that houses the vacuum cleaner.

At home, some Czech readers were disappointed that there weren't more lurid details of clashes with Klaus, but Havel defends the omission. 'I am very much opposed to reducing the last 20 years of our history to personal tiffs between myself and Václav Klaus,' he told the *Financial Times* in 2008. 'And I don't like it when people get the impression that I did nothing but fight with him. I don't like that, and it doesn't reflect reality.'

IN CONTEXT

Of the more traditional bookstores in the city, by far the biggest is the **Neo Luxor** chain, which boasts a sizeable flagship branch just a block outside Old Town (Václavské náměstí 41, www.neoluxor.cz). Aside from holding the city's best collection of Czech literature in English translations, it hosts the most complete offerings of Czech art and photography books in Prague. Keep an eye out for books published by **Twisted Spoon Press** (www.twistedspoon.com), which specialises in translating up-and-coming Czech authors into English for the first time while also providing an outlet for many expat scribblers in town.

Other mainstay English-language bookshops include **Anagram** and **Big Ben Bookshop** (for both, *see p193*), both in Old Town. And the **Prague City Library** (Mariánské námesti 1, www.mlp.cz/english) has a surprisingly rich catalogue of English-language books for browsing. It's worth putting your head around the door, if only to marvel at the Lewis Carroll-esque tower of books in the foyer.

Cheers!

With a pivo in hand, Praguers are always at peace.

TEXT: DOMINIC SWIRE

When faced with what Czechs regard as their real national treasure, you might be tempted to forget the history, the music and the architecture that otherwise define the Bohemian capital. 'Liquid bread', as the locals lovingly call beer, has been brewed, sold and drunk in Czech lands for around 1,000 years. Pilsner, indeed, was invented right here.

Such a rich heritage demands that Czech beer should be pretty decent, but the raw statistics suggest that it's a lot better than that. Per capita, Czechs drink more beer than any nation in the world: an amazing 157 litres of the stuff every year. You can put the popularity of beer down to its ubiquity: it's available more or less any time, any place. You could mark its success down to price: it's still generally cheaper than bottled water. But, ultimately, quality is as responsible as quantity: there are plenty of terrific brews to consider as you bar-hop around this famously boozy town.

THE BREWING COMMENCES

Fermented brewing in Bohemia dates back to the Middle Ages, and proved so inspirational that proverbs were written about its products – 'Unus papa Romae, una cerevesia Raconae', for instance, which translates as 'One pope in Rome, one beer in Rakovnik'. In 1290, King Wenceslas II granted no fewer than 260 families in Pilsen (Plzeň to the locals) the right to brew beer, which set the wheels of beer culture in motion.

However, the golden lager that really put the Czech lands on the map was actually developed in Pilsen several centuries after Wenceslas's remit, using a breakthrough bottom-fermenting process. Invented in 1842 by brewer Josef Groll, the new beer's appealing combination of texture, taste and colour proved so successful that the brew was eventually branded as Pilsner Urquell – Original Pilsner – when German brewers copied the process. Both here and abroad, it remains a hugely popular style.

The pilsner wrangle was merely the first in a series of controversies surrounding Czech beer. One of the longest-running and most famous battles has been between the old Czech label Budvar, or Budweiser in German, and the American mass-market beer of the same name. There's no connection between the two companies. However, the US brand has been demanding exclusive use of the name for many years, despite the fact that the Czech brewer was founded a century before its American rival. Anheuser-Busch, the brewer of American Budweiser, has even tried to buy its Czech rival on occasion. But the state-owned South Bohemian brewery is not for sale. Unlike castles, churches and national park areas, this is one national treasure that Czechs have no interest in selling off.

MARKET FORCES

Despite all the tradition and heritage that beer carries in the Czech Republic, market consolidation has been a problem with the country's beer industry in recent years. Much as they have in many other countries around the world, corporations have been expanding fast and gobbling up small producers, a chain of events that's ultimately resulted in a smaller and more homogeneous range of beers on offer for the casual drinker.

Many Bohemian beer drinkers have been particularly concerned with the way that multinationals have been affecting Czech beer. Staropramen, for instance, is now owned by Interbrew, which has been successful at pushing Stella Artois on to the Czech market. Other foreign brands have also gained in popularity at the same time. The net result is that whereas drinkers were once greeted by beer taps for a whole range of Czech brews when they stepped into any corner pub, they may now find just one major Czech beer on tap alongside a range of increasingly familiar imports.

However, this trend has been countered by the development and increased popularity of microbreweries, which have launched a number of new and more interesting Czech beers. **Pivovarský dům** (*see p185*), a Nové Město microbrewery, serves beers from the Czech Republic and around the world, but it also creates new brews of its own. The **Richter Brewery** at the **Pivovar u Bulovky** pub (Bulovka 17, 284 840 650, www.pivovaru bulovky.cz) offers some excellent varieties of its own. And at **U Medvídků** (*see p162*), a restaurant and brewery with its own museum attached, you can find unpasteurised Budvar.

DRINKING FOR BEGINNERS

In order to appreciate Czech beer in its native environment, it's useful to have a couple of facts in your back pocket. Perhaps most pertinently, it's important to know that the numbers attached to beers in the Czech Republic refer not to alcohol content but to a 'degrees' figure, which represents the amount of malt extract used in the brewing process. A higher degree figure generally means a fuller flavour, and it always results in a stronger brew. The alcohol percentage works out at about a little more than one-third of the stated degree: ten-degree beers are generally at around four per cent alcohol, with 12-degree beers nearer five per cent. Czech beer is available in everything from six-degree to rare and unusually potent 19-degree varieties. But by far the most common are the ten-degree (also known as *desítka*) and 12-degree (*dvanáctka*) beers.

Although the fame of Czech beer means that it's now available across the world, there is one type that you won't find outside the country: unpasteurised beer. Normal beer production involves heating the liquid to 60°C for about half an hour, killing any lurking bacteria and basically giving the product a longer shelf life. However, in Prague, a number of pubs offer beer straight from the tank. These are called *tankovna* pubs (*see right* **Tanked Up**).

WHAT TO DRINK...

'If Czech beer is the best in the world,' ask many visitors as they prop themselves up at a bar in the city, 'what's the best beer in the Czech Republic?' The answer isn't as straightforward as you might hope or expect. Despite the fact that the average pub carries fewer local brands than a few years ago, there's still a pretty broad choice. And with this choice comes a wide range of differing opinions as to which beers lie at the top of the tree.

The most popular beer here is Gambrinus, sponsor of the domestic football league. However, it's not universally recognised as the best. Kozel's Medium, a pale lager, won the prize for the best Czech beer at the Research Institute of Brewing & Malting awards in 2008. Many locals, meanwhile, claim that Pilsner Urquell is the best of the bunch, with Czechs from Pilsen insisting that the water quality in their home city means that their pilsner is superior to those produced anywhere else in the country. And we haven't even mentioned other brands such as Staropramen, Bernard, Budvar and Radogast, all of which have their fans. Nor, for that matter, hundreds of less well-known brewing firms around the country.

... AND WHERE TO DRINK IT

Inevitably, Prague is home to a number of bars that specialise in beer, offering a huge variety or a carefully chosen selection of top-notch brews. In addition to the venues featured in our extensive **Cafés, Pubs & Bars** chapter (*see pp175-190*), both the **Pivovarský Klub** (Křižíkova 17, Prague 8, www.gastroinfo.cz/pivoklub) and the **Pivní Galerie** (U Průhonu 9, Prague 7, www.pivnigalerie.cz) offer around 200 different varieties. A handful of bars, such as those listed earlier in this section, even brew their own. And ultimately, the quest to find the best Czech beer is necessarily subjective. Which is good news, because it necessitates plenty of research.

U Černého vola. *See p56.*

Tanked Up

Beer doesn't have to be pasteurised: at a tankovna, it's as fresh as a daisy.

In Prague, there are pubs, and there are *tankovna* – tank pubs. To know the difference is to understand one of the reasons why, despite plenty of stiff competition, the Czech Republic remains the beer capital of the world.

Most internationally branded beer – and, for that matter, local beer – is pasteurised before export, a process that entails sterilising at high temperatures in order to kill any bacteria that may be present. While this process stabilises the product, making it more suitable for export, it also increases the chance of oxidisation. This can result in the odd duff bottle with a flat taste and an unpleasant flavour, especially if it has been shipped halfway round the world.

Without pasteurisation, beer is liable to go off quite quickly. But to solve this problem, crafty Czech beer-lovers have come up with an ingenious solution. More and more Prague pubs now serve *pivo* from massive steel tubes or tanks that hold ten hectolitres of brew in plastic sacks, at the ideal steady temperature of between 8 and 10°C. Beer is pressed out of the tanks via a high-pressure air compressor, ensuring it stays safe from any risk of contamination but remains fresh. For connoisseurs, the result is immediately obvious: a rounder, more complex flavour full of hops and spices.

For a long time, only a handful of pubs served Pilsner Urquell from the tank. Among them is **U Pinkasů** (*see p171*), hidden around the corner at the bottom of Wenceslas Square. Now, though, the industry has cottoned on to its own best-kept secret: *tankovnas* are popping up all over the place, and many more beer labels getting into the act.

For Budvar, check out the new tank equipment recently installed at **U Medvídků** (*see p162*). For Staropramen, head straight to the brewery (Nádražní 43, Smíchov, http://navstevnicke-centrum.pivovarystaropramen.cz), where you can also learn a little about what you're drinking with a brewery tour. And for Krušovice, head to the **Beograd** pub at Vodičkova 12. The beer itself was a favourite of Emperor Rudolf II in the 16th century. Indeed, he liked it so much that he bought the brewery, hence its slogan: 'the King's beer.'

> *'"If Czech beer is the best in the world," ask many visitors to Prague, 'what's the best beer in the Czech Republic?" The answer isn't as straightforward as you might hope or expect.'*

Despite Prague's gradual gentrification, the city has retained a number of traditional old alehouses in which visitors can sample traditional Czech beers. The most famous is **U Zlatého tygra** (*see p183*), just round the corner from Old Town Square. Czech president Václav Havel took Bill Clinton for a drink here in 1994; apparently, Clinton downed three beers and cancelled his daily run the next morning. Another classic local, or *hostinec*, is **U Černého vola** (*see p175*): just up from the castle, it's one of the best-loved pubs in Prague.

On a similar note, despite all the consolidations and expansions and buyouts across the industry, it's good to see that even the biggest breweries have kept their hands on their heritage. Pilsner Urquell's main brewery is now huge and suitably modern, expanded from humble origins in order to meet demand from home and abroad. But there's also a workshop here where a small team builds and maintains oak barrels, in which beer is then fermented in much the same way as it has been for centuries. If you head out here for a brewery tour, you'll of course get the chance to taste the mass-produced Pilsner Urquell. But you'll also get a rare opportunity to sample pilsner brewed in the old-fashioned oaky way, a simple link to the beer's beginnings nearly 170 years ago. 'Liquid bread', indeed.

If your search for the perfect beer has left you feeling a bit under the weather, don't worry. Journey a couple of hours west of the city to **Chodovar** (www.chodovar.cz), which describes itself as 'your beer wellness land'. For 600 Kč, you can have a plunge in a bath full of the amber nectar, along with a couple of jars to quaff while you're at it. Only in the Czech Republic.

U Zlatého tygra. *See p56.*

Sightseeing

Astronomical Clock.
See p87.

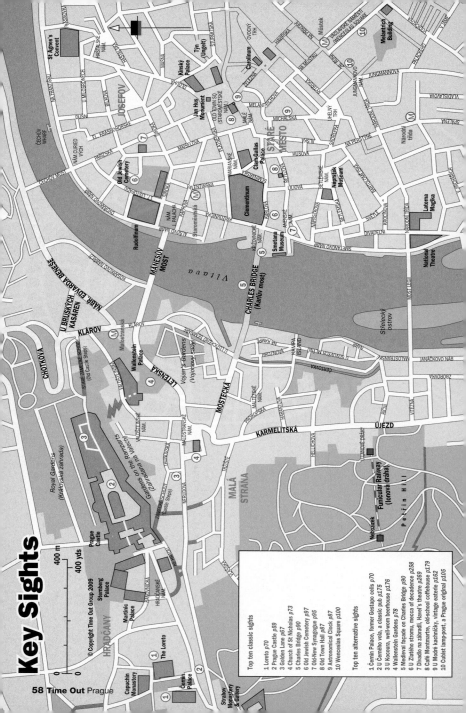

Key Sights

© Copyright Time Out Group 2009

Top ten classic sights

1 Loreto *p70*
2 Prague Castle *p59*
3 Golden Lane *p67*
4 Church of St Nicholas *p73*
5 Charles Bridge *p90*
6 Old Jewish Cemetery *p97*
7 Old-New Synagogue *p95*
8 Old Town Hall *p87*
9 Astronomical Clock *p87*
10 Wenceslas Square *p100*

Top ten alternative sights

1 Černín Palace, former Gestapo cells *p70*
2 U Černého vola, a classic pub *p175*
3 U Kocoura, well-worn beerhouse *p176*
4 Wallenstein Gardens *p78*
5 Medieval facade on Charles Bridge *p90*
6 U Zlatého stromu, mecca of decadence *p258*
7 Divadlo na zábradlí, Havel's theatre *p269*
8 Café Montmartre, old-school coffeehouse *p179*
9 U Modré kachničky, vintage eaterie *p162*
10 Cubist lamp-post, a Prague original *p105*

Hradčany

The high life returns to Prague Castle.

Prague Castle dominates the city's skyline, its jumble of styles and influences perfectly illustrating the shifting demands of its occupants and conquerors over the last millennium. At the centre of the castle, its dramatic Gothic spires and flying buttresses visible from everywhere in town, is the imposing St Vitus's Cathedral; even the most jaded of visitors will be given pause by its grandeur.

Surrounding the castle, stretching north and west across the hilltop, is the elegant Hradčany district. It's quiet, enchanting and less touristy than the castle itself. Wandering its atmospheric streets and squares is a joy; the Nový Svět (New World) pocket of streets is particularly enchanting.

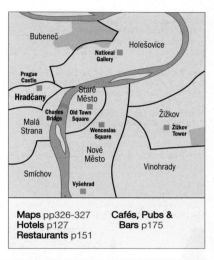

Maps pp326-327
Hotels p127
Restaurants p151

Cafés, Pubs & Bars p175

PRAGUE CASTLE

Founded more than 1,000 years ago by Přemysl princes, the impressive if somewhat sombre Prague Castle complex – including the Old Royal Palace, three churches and a monastery – is an enormous festival of architectural styles: the final touches to the castle's look, including the present shape of **St Vitus's Cathedral** (*see p64*), were not added until the early 20th century. The complex seems strangely quiet these days, but it does still attract a steady stream of students, sketchbook-toting artists and – of course – tourists.

The grandiose façade enclosing the complex is the result of Empress Maria Theresa's desire to bring some coherence to the jumble of mismatched parts that the castle had become by the middle of the 18th century. But the outcome of Nicolo Pacassi's monotonous design concept is uninspiring – 'an imposing mass of building in the factory style of architecture', as one 19th-century commentator put it. After Maria Theresa's son, Joseph II, attempted to turn the castle into a barracks, it was largely deserted by the Habsburgs. Václav Havel chose not to live here, although his presidential office was installed in the castle. However, he did his

best to enliven the palace, opening it to the public and hiring the costume designer from the film *Amadeus* to remodel the guards' uniforms.

The palaces, chapels, museums, galleries and gardens serve as testament to the rise of the Přemyslids, the first documented Bohemian native dynasty, and every bloody, internecine struggle for power within that dagger-happy family and the later rulers and their competitors: the Jagellons, Charles IV, the Habsburgs and the Catholic Church, to name just the major players. The Golden Age of Charles, in the mid 14th century, and the Nazis' march through the gates are just two events in the castle's relatively recent history that indicate its iconic value as the nation's grandest seat of power. Nowhere else in Prague resonates with as much national identity and symbolism, increased by the pride Czechs have taken since having had the castle returned to them in 1989.

The complex is undergoing makeovers and renovations as the Czech Republic's finances improve and the Catholic Church continues to assert its rights over the cathedral. Aside from a dozen rooms newly opened to the public beneath the **Old Royal Palace**, with excellent historic and architectural displays (since 1989 worthy of such a national treasure), the entire

SIGHTS

exterior of the **Basilica of St George** has been renewed, the **Lobkowicz Palace** has opened as a fully fledged museum, the city's best restaurant vista has opened in the **Villa Richter**, and the calendar is swelling with cultural series such as **Jazz at the Castle** (www.jazznahrade.cz).

You can't get away without spending at least half a day exploring the castle. Trouble is, neither can every other visitor to the city. To avoid the worst of the crush, come as early or as late in the day as you can. Another frustration is the almost complete lack of labelling in English, and lacklustre exhibits on the castle tour: the St Vitus crypt looks more

Prague Castle.

like a concrete bunker, despite being the final resting place for the nation's hallowed forefathers. That said, most of the female volunteers installed around the castle and its palaces are friendly and forthcoming to visitors, and speak English.

★ Prague Castle information

Hradčanské náměstí, Prague 1 (224 371 111/ http://www.hrad.cz). Metro Malostranská/tram 12, 22. **Open** *Apr-Oct* 9am-4pm daily. *Nov-Mar* 9am-4pm daily. **Admission** 200-350 Kč; 125-175 Kč reductions; 300-500 Kč family. Tickets valid for 2 days. **Credit** AmEx, MC, V. **Map** p327 E2. There's no charge to enter the grounds of the castle, but you will need a ticket to see the main attractions. One ticket covers entrance to the Old Royal Palace (which now has a large new museum on castle life), the Basilica of St George, the Golden Lane, the Daliborka Tower and the crypt and tower of St Vitus's Cathedral (except Jan-Apr & Oct-Dec, when the tower is closed and the Golden Lane is free). Entrance to the art collection of St George's Convent (*see p67*) and the Prague Castle Picture Gallery (*see p64*) are also included, but not the Toy Museum (*see p68*) or the recently opened Lobkowicz Princely Collections museum (*see p68*).

Be warned that it's a stiff uphill walk to the castle from Malostranská metro station. The least strenuous approach is by tram 22; get off at the Pražský hrad stop. There's a handful of adequate cafés within the castle complex, if you don't mind paying high prices.

The first & second courtyards

The grandest entrance to the Prague Castle complex, through the **Hradčanské náměstí gates**, is overseen from a discreet distance by an approving Tomáš Garrigue Masaryk, the first president of free Czechoslovakia, whose bronze likeness was added during the Praha 2000 cultural festival. The gateway has been dominated since 1768 by Ignatz Platzer's huge sculptures of battling Titans, which make an arresting if not exactly welcoming entrance. The changing of the guard takes place in this courtyard, a Havel-inspired attempt to provide some ceremony. The change is carried out on the hour every day from 5am to 10pm, but the big crowd-pulling ceremony, complete with band, takes place at noon.

To reach the second courtyard, go through the **Matyášova brána (Matthias Gate)**. A Baroque portal dating from 1614, it's topped by a double-headed German Imperial Eagle that pleased Hitler when he came to stay in 1939. A monumental stairway is visible from inside the passage (on the left), which leads up to the magnificent gold-and-white **Španělský sál (Spanish Hall)**. It's open to the general

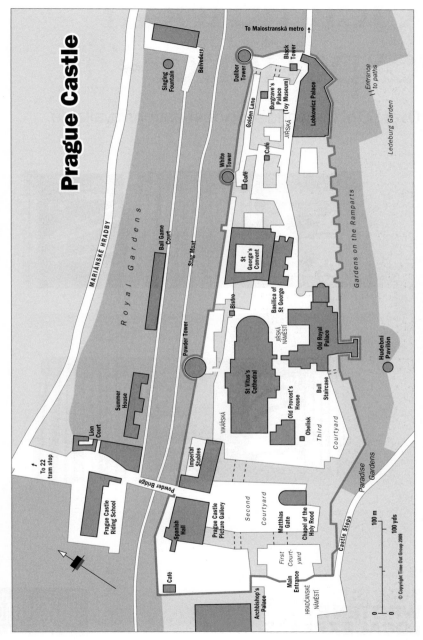

Prague Castle

To Malostranská metro ↑

SIGHTS

Get the local experience

Over 50 of the world's top destinations available.

Revolt! The Presidential Suite

A new book sheds light on Václav Havel's life in Prague Castle.

The Czech presidency is a largely ceremonial post, which allows few opportunities for the incumbent to flex political muscle. As such, it was ironic that when Václav Havel ascended from dissident playwright to president in 1989, he had surprisingly few tools with which to change the system that had imprisoned him. *To the Castle and Back*, Havel's recently-published book, offers some poignant insights into that paradox, along with warm, quirky and painfully honest accounts of the multiple other absurdities of life as the first president of the nation post-Velvet Revolution.

Havel's musings on the Iraq war are characteristic. He recalls warning George W Bush, twice, that the newly liberated nation might well give rise to a new terrorism nation, while adding that it's the US's stated rationale for the invasion that troubles him most, not the ousting of Saddam Hussein. 'Defending human beings,' he writes, 'is a higher responsibility than respecting the inviolability of a state.' But, as Havel points out, Czechs were told before both the Nazi invasion and the Soviet-backed invasion of their own country that these acts were necessary to liberate humans in danger. 'Why didn't they just tell the truth?' he asks of the US.

Daily life within the walls of Prague Castle, and in particular the preparations and often ridiculous levels of ceremony required by his role as head of state, are another favourite subject. In an early version of the award-winning documentary *Citizen Havel*, shot over a decade by Pavel

Koutecký and completed by Miroslav Janek, the reluctant president can be seen wondering if a parade of Arab officials he must greet is actually as large as it appears or whether those at the front are circling back to come around again.

Elsewhere in the book, Havel admits to exploring the inner sanctum of Prague Castle almost as a tourist. At one point, he discovered a secret radio room hidden in a locked, long-abandoned chamber. Another memorable moment was when he wanted to take his guests, the Rolling Stones, out on to the terrace, but no one could find the key to open the door.

Such visits could be a blessing, of course. Havel even admits that during his first year in office, with the first free elections soon to confirm his appointment as president, the young democracy sometimes resembled a vaudeville act. 'At times it was pretty wretched,' he confesses. 'The Pope was able, for a while at least, to direct the public's attention upward and compel it to think about serious matters.'

SIGHTS

public only during occasional concerts; but if one occurs during your stay, it's worth the effort to attend.

The hall was built in the 17th century for court ceremonies but the decor was redone in the 19th century, when the trompe l'oeil murals were covered with white stucco, and huge mirrors and gilded chandeliers were brought in to transform the space into a glitzy venue suitable for the coronation of Emperor Franz Josef I. Franz Josef, though, failed to show up, and it wasn't until the 1950s that the hall was given a new use: it was here that the Politburo came to discuss the latest five-year plan.

Behind the austere grey walls of the second courtyard lies a warren of opulent state rooms

whose heyday dates from the time of Rudolf II. Rarely open to the public, these state rooms housed Rudolf's grand art collection and such curiosities as a unicorn's horn and three nails that were supposedly taken from Noah's Ark.

The bulk of the collection was carried off in 1648 by Swedish soldiers, although some remnants are housed in the diminutive **Prague Castle Picture Gallery** (*see p64*), found on the north side of the courtyard near the Powder Bridge entrance. The yard is now dominated by the 17th-century Baroque fountain and the thick-walled rotunda of the **Chapel of the Holy Rood**, which now houses a box office for castle tours and concert tickets, and rents out audio guides.

Vladislav Hall. *See p66.*

Obrazárna Pražského hradu
Prague Castle Picture Gallery

*Prague Castle (2nd courtyard), Prague 1
(224 373 531/www.obrazarna-hradu.cz). Metro
Malostranská/tram 18, 22.* **Open** *Nov-Mar* 9am-
4pm daily. *Apr-Oct* 9am-6pm daily. *Tours* Tue-
Sun. **Admission** 100 Kč; 50 Kč reductions; 150
Kč family; free under-6s. **No credit cards.**
Map p326 D2.

With a collection spanning three centuries, starting
in the era following Charles IV's golden reign, this
little gallery perhaps tries to do too much. It also
seems overlooked, maybe because it stands next to
so many better collections of the National Gallery at
the castle complex.

Nonetheless, some florid pieces – Bartholomeus
Spranger's *Allegory of the Turkish War*, Lucas
Kranach's portrait of Sts Catharine and Barbara
from the altar of St Vitus's Cathedral – do offer a
glimpse of the splendour that once filled the environs around what is, today, a tidy and all-too-well-
run tourist attraction. The gallery also includes
works by Hans von Aachen, Veronese and lesser-
known masters. And though there's no hope of ever
piecing together Emperor Rudolph II's magnificent
original collection, which has been scattered to the
winds, the castle shows off a handful of works from
the original cache.

Katedrála sv. Víta (St Vitus's Cathedral)

The third courtyard, the oldest and most
important site in the castle, is dominated by
the towers, pinnacles, spires and buttresses of
St Vitus's Cathedral, the Czech Republic's
finest house of worship. The cathedral is in its
third generation. A humble stone rotunda first
stood here, part of the citadel built up from 870
by the Count Bořivoj, founder of the Přemyslid
dynasty; it was then replaced by a rustic
Romanesque chapel nearly two centuries later,
when the city was made a bishopric. Deciding
that the prize real estate, now an archbishopric,
merited something far grander, Charles IV
founded what became St Vitus's Cathedral
in 1344. Entry is free to the nave and chapels,
but a ticket is required for the rest.

Although the cathedral was completed as
recently as 1929, exactly 1,000 years after the
murdered St Wenceslas was laid to rest here,
there's no doubt that the awe-inspiring building
is the spiritual centre of Bohemia. This has
always been a sacred place: Svantovít, the
Slavic god of fertility, was worshipped here
in pagan times, and it was no accident that the
cathedral was dedicated to his near-namesake
St Vitus ('svatý Vít' in Czech), a Sicilian peasant
who became a Roman legionnaire before he was
thrown to the lions (surviving, miraculously,
long enough to be laid on the rack). Up until
the 18th century, young women and anxious
farmers would arrive bearing offerings of wine,
cakes and cockerels.

The cathedral's Gothic structure owes its
creation to Charles IV's lifelong love affair
with Prague. In 1344, he managed to secure
an archbishopric for the city, and work began
on the construction of a cathedral under the
direction of French architect Matthew of Arras.
Matthew died eight years into the project;
Swabian Peter Parler was called in to take up
the challenge, and is responsible for the German
late Gothic design. However, the cathedral
remained unfinished until late 19th-century
nationalists completed the work according to
Parler's original plans. The skill with which the
later work was done makes it hard to tell where
the Gothic ends and the neo-Gothic begins, but
a close look at the nave, the twin towers and
the rose window of the west end will reveal the
newer, lighter-coloured stone. There are also
several tympanums and pedestals that still lack
figures, creating a certain work-in-progress feel.

From outside, as from anywhere you look
in the town below, the **Great Tower** is easily
the most dominant feature. The Gothic and
Renaissance structure is topped with a Baroque
dome that houses Sigismund: the largest bell in
Bohemia, it was made in the middle of the 16th
century and weighs in at a hefty 15,120 kilos

(33,330 pounds). The clapper, which alone weighs more than 400 kilos (880 pounds), fell out in 2002, an event that many said was a forewarning of disaster. Sure enough, the city's worst floods in modern history soon followed. Getting Sigismund into the tower was no mean feat: according to legend, it took a rope woven from the hair of the city's noblest virgins to haul it into position.

Below the tower is the Gothic **Zlatá brána (Golden Portal)**, visible from the courtyard south of the cathedral. It's decorated with a mosaic of multicoloured Venetian glass depicting the Last Judgement that, after years of Getty-funded refurbishment, has been restored to its original lustre. On either side of the centre arch are likenesses of Charles IV and his wife, Elizabeth of Pomerania, whose talents are said to have included being able to bend a sword with her bare hands.

Inside, the enormous nave is flooded with vari-hued light from the gallery of stained-glass windows created at the beginning of the 20th century. All 21 of them were sponsored during a period of nationalist fervour by finance institutions including (third on the right) an insurance company with a motto – 'those who sow in sorrow shall reap in joy' – that was subtly incorporated into the biblical allegory. The most famous is the third window on the left, in the **Archbishop's Chapel**, created by Alfons Mucha. It depicts the struggle of Christian Slavonic tribes; appropriately enough, the artwork was paid for by Banka Slavia.

On the right is the **Svatováclavská kaple (Chapel of St Wenceslas)**, on the site of the original tenth-century rotunda where 'Good King' Wenceslas was laid to rest. Built in 1345, the chapel has 1,345 polished amethysts, agates and jaspers incorporated into its design and contains some of the saint's personal paraphernalia, including armour, chain shirt and helmet. Alas, it's closed to the public – too many sweaty bodies were causing the gilded plaster to disintegrate – but you can catch a glint of its treasure trove over the railings. And occasionally, on state anniversaries, the skull of the saint is put on display, covered with a cobweb-fine veil.

A door in the corner leads to the chamber that contains the crown jewels. A papal bull of 1346 protects the jewels, and legend has it that an early death will befall anyone who uses them improperly. The curse seemed to work on the Nazis' man in Prague: Reichsprotektor Reinhard Heydrich tried on the crown, and was assassinated shortly afterward by the Resistance. The door to the chamber is locked with seven keys, one per seal in the Book of Revelations, and each looked after by a different Prague state or Church official.

The most extraordinary Baroque addition to the cathedral was the silver **tomb of St John of Nepomuk**, the priest who was flung from Charles Bridge in 1393 as a result of King Wenceslas IV's anti-clerical wrath. The tomb, designed by Fischer von Erlach the Younger in 1733-36, is a flamboyant affair (the entry ticket

St George's Convent. See p67.

is now required to get a proper look at it). An astonishing 2,032 kilograms (two tons) of silver was used for the pedestal, the statue of the saint and the fluttering cherubs holding up a red velvet canopy. The phrase 'baroque excess' scarcely does it justice.

Close by is the entrance to the crypt. Below lie the remains of various Czech monarchs, including Rudolf II. Easily the most eye-catching tomb is Charles IV's modern, streamlined metal affair, designed by Kamil Roškot in the mid 1930s. The vault itself, hastily excavated between world wars, has a distinctly cramped, temporary look to it.

After the cathedral, the second most noticeable monument in the third courtyard is the fairly incongruous 17-metre-high (50-foot) granite **obelisk**. It's a memorial to the dead of World War I, erected by Plečnik in 1928.

The rest of the third courtyard

Close to the cathedral's Golden Portal is the entrance to the **Starý královský palác** (**Old Royal Palace**; ticket required). The palace contains three different areas of royal chambers above ground level – all with badly photocopied engravings for displays, most with more Russian text than English – and a wonderful, gorgeously presented new permanent exhibition on palace life, 'The Story of Prague Castle', in the basement. The new displays inhabit the 12th-century Romanesque remains of Prince Soběslav's residence.

Six centuries of kings called the palace home and systematically built new parts over the old; one worthwhile highlight at ground level is the **Vladislav Hall**, designed by Benedict Ried at the turn of the 16th century. The hall, where Václav Havel was sworn in in 1990 as the first democratically elected president since 1948, is notable for its exquisitely vaulted ceiling, representing the last flowering of Gothic in Bohemia; the large, square windows were among the first expressions of the Renaissance in this part of Europe. It's here that the National Assembly elects its new president. The specially designed **Rider's Steps**, at the east end, let knights enter the hall without dismounting.

On the floor above the Vladislav Hall sits the **Bohemian Chancellery**, and the window through which the victims of the defenestration of 1618 were ejected. In the chamber above, the Habsburgs inflicted their payback – 27 Czech nobles were sentenced to death after the Battle of White Mountain in 1621.

The **Diet Chamber**, above the Rider's Steps, is the palace's third attraction. Here's where you'll find the oratory space that once held the forerunner to today's parliament and heraldic crests from all the best families of Bohemia, plus a few editions from the court library, catalogued before numerical systems were invented, using an imaginative system of plant and animal images on the spines. It's clear from the evidence that kings have never had an easy time taxing the landed nobles in the Czech

Golden Lane.

INSIDE TRACK
KAFKA ON GOLDEN LANE

The house at 22 Golden Lane was owned by Franz Kafka's sister Ottla. The writer himself stayed here for a while in 1917, reputedly drawing inspiration from the streets for his novel *The Castle*.

---

lands, though it's also evident that parliament meetings were once smaller-scale affairs that were easier to orchestrate.

Just east of the cathedral is **Jiřské náměstí**, named after **Bazilika sv. Jiří (Basilica of St George)**. If you stand far enough from the basilica's newly restored red-and-cream Baroque façade, you'll see two distinctive Romanesque towers jutting out behind it. The Italian craftsmen who constructed them in 1142 built a fatter male tower (Adam, on the right) standing guard over a more slender female one (Eve).

Founded by Prince Vratislav in 921, the basilica has burned down and been rebuilt several times over the centuries. Its first major remodelling took place 50 years after it was originally erected, when a Benedictine convent was founded next door. A major renovation in the early 20th century swept out most of the Baroque elements and led to the uncovering of the original arcades, remnants of 13th-century frescoes and the bodies of a saint (Ludmila, who was strangled by assassins hired by Prince Wenceslas's mother, Drahomíra) and a saint-maker (the notorious Boleslav the Cruel, who martyred his brother Wenceslas by having him stabbed to death). The basilica's rediscovered simplicity seems closer to God than the Baroque pomposity of most Prague churches. On the left of the main entrance is an opening built to give access for the Benedictine nuns from **St George's Convent** next door (*see right*), in order to minimise their contact with the outside world. The convent now houses part of the National Gallery's vast collections.

Vikářská lane gives access to the 15th-century **Mihulka** or **Prašná věž (Powder Tower)**, which was undergoing reconstruction at press time. Rudolf II employed his many alchemists here in many attempts to distil the Elixir of Life and transmute base metals into gold. Today, the tower hosts exhibits (in Czech only) about alchemy and Renaissance life in the castle. Access to them will resume after reconstruction; in the meantime, visitors will instead be let into the smaller Daliborka tower, which features a much more basic collection of torture instruments and a few theories about how true the legends of Dalibor, its most famous inhabitant, might be.

Klášter sv. Jiří
St George's Convent

Jiřské náměstí 33, Prague 1 (257 531 644).
Metro Malostranská & up the Old Castle steps/tram 18, 22. **Open** 9am-6pm daily.
Admission 150 Kč; 200 Kč family; free under-10s. **No credit cards**. **Map** p327 E2.

With a newly reorganised collection that focuses on Czech 19th-century art, St George's Convent seems much better matched to its task than when it was hosting the best of Baroque. The rise of the Czech middle class and its intelligentsia can be charted in the paintings, glass work and sculpture on display, offering a window into a nation on the rise (and yet still deeply rural and pastoral). Norbert Grund's charming dinner tables balance out landscapes and allegory with a good representation of the realist painters of the day: František Xaver Procházka, Christian Seckel and Ludvík Kohl. *Photo p65.*

Elsewhere on the castle grounds

Downhill from St George's, signposts direct you to the most visited street in Prague, **Zlatá ulička (Golden Lane**; ticket required Mar-Sept). The tiny multicoloured cottages that cling to Prague Castle's northern walls were cobbled together by the poor in the 16th century, from whatever waste materials they could find. Some allege that the name is a reference to the alchemists of King Rudolf's days, who supposedly were quartered here, while others contend that it alludes to a time when soldiers billeted in a nearby tower used the lane as a public urinal. In fact, the name probably dates from the 17th century, when the city's goldsmiths worked in the area.

Both sides of the street were once lined with houses, with barely enough space to pass between them, until a hygiene-conscious Joseph II had some of them demolished in the 18th century. Although the houses look separate, a corridor runs the length of their attics and used to be occupied by the sharpshooters of the Castle Guard. Though the street is atmospheric at night, the lane is clogged with shuffling tourists during the day.

At the eastern end, some steps take you under the last house and out to the **Daliborka (Dalibor Tower)**, named after an inmate who amused himself by playing the violin while awaiting execution – according to legend (and Smetana's opera *Dalibor*), that is, which maintains that he attracted crowds of onlookers who turned up at his execution to weep en masse. Continuing down the hill takes you past a **Lobkovický palác (Lobkowicz Palace)**, one of several in the town. Completed in 1658, it houses a newly renovated museum known as the **Princely Collections** (*see p68*), showing off the muskets, Mozart manuscripts and the odd portrait by Brueghel the Elder. Opposite is Burgrave House, home of the **Muzeum hraček (Toy Museum**; *see p68*). The statue of a naked boy in the courtyard fell foul of Marxist-Leninist ideology when President Novotný decided the boy's genitals were not an edifying sight and had them removed. Happily, the lad and his equipment have since been reunited.

The lane passes underneath the **Černá věž (Black Tower)** and ends at the **Staré zámecké schody (Old Castle Steps)**, which take you to Malá Strana; so do the **Zámecké schody (Castle Steps)** on Thunovská, accessed from the other end of the castle. Before descending, pause at the top for a view over the red tiled roofs, spires and domes of the Lesser Quarter (*see p72*).

An even better view can be had from the **Rajská zahrada (Paradise Gardens**; *see p78*) on the ramparts below the castle walls (enter from the Bull Staircase or from outside the castle, to the right of the first courtyard). This is where the victims of the second and most famous defenestration fell to earth. They were fortunate that it was a favoured spot for emptying chamber pots, as the dung heap surely saved their lives. The site is now marked by an obelisk, signifying ground consecrated by the victorious Habsburgs after putting down the upstart Czech Protestants. Initially laid out in 1562, the gardens were redesigned in the 1920s by Josip Plečnik, whose work includes the huge granite bowl and the spiralling **Bull Staircase** that leads up to the castle's third courtyard.

The restoration of the gardens took many years, but you can now make the descent to Malá Strana via the terraced slopes of five beautiful Renaissance gardens; open, like most gardens in Prague, from April to October only. The highlight of the restoration project is the lovely **Ledeburská zahrada (Ledebour Gardens)**, with its fountains, ornate stone stairways and palace yards; it delivers you to the middle of **Valdštejnská**. Fit hikers might consider ascending to the castle this way, though there's a fee of 60 Kč whichever route you take.

Muzeum hraček
Toy Museum

Jiřská 6, Prague 1 (224 372 294/www.muzeum hracek.cz). Metro Malostranská/tram 12, 18, 22. **Open** 9.30am-5.30pm daily. **Admission** 60 Kč; 120 Kč family; free under-5s. **No credit cards**. **Map** p327 F2.

Part of Czech émigré Ivan Steiger's large collection is displayed on the two floors of this museum in the castle grounds. Brief texts accompany cases of toys, from teddy bears to an elaborate tin train set. Kitsch

fans will love the robots and the enormous collection of Barbie dolls, clad in vintage costumes from throughout the decades. The museum is good for a rainy day but is probably better for the young at heart than the actually young, most of whom prefer playing with toys to looking at them from a historical perspective.

▶ *For attractions with more kid-friendly appeal, see p217.*

Princely Collections

Jiřská 3, Prague 1 (mobile 602 595 998/ www.lobkowiczevents.cz). Metro Malostranská/ tram 12, 18, 22. **Open** 10.30am-6pm daily. **Admission** 60 Kč; 120 Kč family; free under-5s. **No credit cards**. **Map** p327 F2.

The Princely Collections' evocative paintings of happy peasants (a subject about which the historically powerful Lobkowicz clan knows plenty), musical scores, instruments, weapons and decorative art look fresh compared to the somewhat fusty museums run by the castle; the Beethoven and Mozart manuscripts are a particular highlight. But it's unlikely that visitors who've seen all the competing collections in the surrounding complex will feel a yen to tour another one. If that's the case, take comfort in the news that free 1pm concerts and a scenic courtyard café lie within this newly opened palace. There's also a gift shop with a good array of books, posters and other castle-related stuff.

The Royal Garden & the Belvedere

Cross **U Prašného mostu (Powder Bridge)** from the castle's second courtyard and you'll reach the **Královská zahrada (Royal Garden)**, on the outer side of the **Jelení příkop (Stag Moat)**. Laid out for Emperor Ferdinand I in the 1530s, it once included a maze and a menagerie, but was devastated by Swedish soldiers in the 17th century.

INSIDE TRACK
GOING UNDERGROUND

Near the Royal Garden stands the quaint, mustard-coloured **Dientzenhofer Summer House**. When it served as the presidential residence from 1948 to 1989, large sections of the castle were closed to the public, and enormous underground shelters were excavated to connect the house with the remainder of the complex. But no sooner had the shelters been completed than someone pointed out that the subterranean passages could conceal counter-revolutionary saboteurs, so the exits were blocked with massive concrete slabs.

Outside **Dalibor Tower**.

At the eastern end of the gardens is the **Belvedere**, saved from French fire in the 18th century by a canny head gardener's payment of 30 pineapples. The beautiful Renaissance structure was built by Paolo della Stella between 1538 and 1564, though work was interrupted by a devastating fire at the castle in 1541. The strangely shaped green copper roof is supported by delicate arcades and columns.

The Belvedere was the first royal structure in Prague to be dedicated to pleasure-seeking rather than power-mongering: it was commissioned by Ferdinand I as a gift for his wife, Anne, leaving it as a loveshack one remove away from the skulduggery of life in Prague Castle. But the long-suffering Anne never got to see it, drawing her last breath after producing the 15th heir to the throne. The royal couple are immortalised in the reliefs adorning the façade. The Belvedere went on to become the site of all sorts of goings-on: mad King Rudolf installed his astronomers here, and, much later, the communists bricked up the windows of the upper level to prevent assassins from getting too close to the president. People come here today to see occasional art shows.

On the southern side of the garden, overlooking the Stag Moat, is another lovely Renaissance structure, completed by Bonifác Wohlmut in 1563 to house the king's **Míčovna (Ball Game Court)**. The elaborate black-and-white sgraffito has to be renewed every 20 years. The last time this was done, some decidedly anachronistic elements were added to the allegorical frieze depicting Science, the Virtues and the Elements: look at the ladies on the top of the building and you'll see that the woman seated next to Justice (tenth from the right) is holding a hammer and sickle.

HRADČANY

Hradčany owes its grand scale and pristine condition to the fire that swept through the castle and surrounds in 1541, destroying the medieval district. A frenzied period of Counter-Reformation building followed the Protestant defeat at the Battle of White Mountain in 1620; little has changed here in the centuries since.

The area's focal point is **Hradčanské náměstí**. One of the grandest squares in the city, it's lined with august palaces built by the Catholic aristocracy, anxious to be close to the Habsburg court. However, it was cut off from the castle and its temperamental inhabitants by a complicated system of fortifications and moats, which remained until Empress Maria Theresa had a grand spring-clean in the middle of the 18th century. Along with the moat went the tiny Church of the Virgin Mary of Einsedel, which used to stand next to the castle ramp. Lovely as this was said to have been, it's hard to believe that it was lovelier than the superb panorama of **Malá Strana**, the **Strahov Gardens** (*see p71*) and **Petřín Hill** (*see p82*) opened up by the demolition.

Over on the north side of the square, next to the castle, is the domineering **Arcibiskupský palác (Archbishop's Palace)**. It was built in the 16th century, but the frothy rococo façade was added later in 1763-64. Next door, between the palace and a lane of former canons' houses, stands the **Šternberg Palace** (*see p71*), which houses part of the National Gallery's collection of European art. And just opposite stands the heavily restored **Schwarzenberg Palace** (*see p71*): built between 1545 and 1563, its outside exquisitely decorated with 'envelope' sgraffito, it's one of the most imposing Renaissance buildings in Prague. The palace has been added in recent years to the National Gallery's collection of venues, and features masterful Baroque painting and sculpture.

Further up Loretánská is the respected pub **U Černého vola** (*see p175*), a Renaissance building with a crumbling mural on the façade. As a result of some direct action in 1991 – the patrons bought the place – it's one of the few places left in Hradčany where the locals can afford to drink. Its well-worn environs make a just reward after a day of castle-trekking, and you don't have to feel guilty about the amount you drink: all profits from the sale of beer go to a nearby school for the blind.

The pub overlooks **Loretánské náměstí**, a split-level square on the site of a pagan cemetery. Half of the square is taken up by a car park for the Ministry of Foreign Affairs in the monolithic **Černínský palác (Černín Palace)**, an enormous and unprepossessing structure. Commissioned in 1669 by Humprecht Johann Černín, the imperial ambassador to Venice, the palace financially ruined his family. As a result, the first people to move in were hundreds of 17th-century squatters. Gestapo interrogations were conducted here during the Nazi occupation. And the curse of the building struck again in 1948, when Foreign Minister Jan Masaryk, the last major political obstacle to Klement Gottwald's communist coup, fell from an upstairs window a few days after the takeover and was found dead on the pavement below. Few believed the official verdict of suicide, but no culprit has been found.

Rather dwarfed by the Černín Palace is the **Loreto** (*see p70*), a Baroque testimony to the Catholic miracle culture that swept the Czech lands after the Thirty Years' War. The façade (1721) is a swirling mass of stuccoed cherubs, topped with a bell tower. Every hour, the 27 bells ring out the loud melody 'We Greet You a Thousand Times'.

The streets behind the Loreto, known as **Nový Svět (New World)**, are some of the prettiest and quietest in Hradčany. The quarter was built in the 16th century for Prague Castle staff; its tiny cottages are now the most prized property in the city. Going down Kapucínská, you'll pass the **Domeček (Little House)** at no.10; it was once home to the notorious Fifth

Department, the counter-intelligence unit of the Defence Ministry. On nearby Černínská sits **Gambra** (no.5, 220 514 527, open Mar-Oct noon-6pm Wed-Sun, Nov-Feb noon-6pm Sat, Sun), a funky gallery specialising in surrealist art. It's owned by animator Jan Švankmajer, who lives in the attached house. At the foot of the hill is Nový Svět street itself, full of colourful cottages restored in the 18th and 19th centuries. It's all that remains of Hradčany's medieval slums, the rest having been destroyed in the great fire of 1541.

Back up from Loretánské náměstí is **Pohořelec**, Hradčany's last major square. The passage at no.8 leads to the peaceful surroundings of the **Strahovský klášter (Strahov Monastery)**, which contains some magnificent libraries and religious art.

Bílkova vila
Bílek Villa

Mickiewiczowa 1, Prague 1 (224 322 021). Metro Hradčanská/tram 18, 22. **Open** 10am-5pm Sat, Sun. **Admission** 50 Kč. **No credit cards. Map** p332 A4.

Down the hill on the opposite side of Prague Castle, to the north, this building must be the only one in the world designed to look like a wheat field. Built in 1911-12 by mystic sculptor František Bílek as his studio and home, it still contains much of his work. Bílek went to Paris to study as a painter, but discovered that he was partially colourblind and thereafter turned to sculpture and illustration; the wheat field, representing spiritual fertility and the harvest of creative work, was one of his many motifs. His work ranges from the sublime to the repellent, but if the grouping of Hobbit-like wooden figures out front takes your fancy, you should have a look inside.

★ Loreto

Loretánské náměstí 7, Prague 1 (220 516 740/ www.loreta.cz). Tram 22. **Open** 9am-12.15pm, 1-4.30pm Tue-Sun. **Admission** 110 Kč; 90 Kč reductions. **No credit cards. Map** p326 B3.

A sculpture of the bearded St Wilgefortis, the skeletons of another two female saints, the highest concentration of cherubs found anywhere in the city… Built as part of a calculated plan to reconvert the masses to Catholicism after the Thirty Years' War, the Loreto is probably the most outlandish Baroque fantasy you'll see in Prague.

At its heart is the Santa Casa (Holy House), a small chapel with a history that seems too improbable to be true. The story goes that the original Santa Casa was the home of the Blessed Virgin Mary in Nazareth until it was miraculously flown over to Loreto in Italy by angels, spawning a copycat cult all over Europe. This one, dating from 1626-31, boasts two beams and a brick from the 'original', as well as a crevice left on the wall by a divine lightning bolt that struck an unfortunate blasphemer.

INSIDE TRACK
THE STAR-GAZING SCHOLAR

Tycho Brahe, the Danish astronomer known for his missing nose and accurate observations of the planets, lived at no.1 Nový Svět, the Golden Griffin.

However, the red colour scheme makes it look less like a virgin's boudoir and more like a place in which to hold a black mass.

The shrine was a particular hit with wealthy ladies, who donated the money for Baroque maestri Christoph and Kilian Ignaz Dientzenhofer to construct the outer courtyards and the Church of the Nativity (1716-23) at the back. They also sponsored the carving of St Wilgefortis (in the corner chapel to the right of the main entrance), the patron saint of unhappily married women, who grew a beard as a radical tactic to get out of marrying a heathen, and that of St Agatha the Unfortunate, who can be seen carrying her severed breasts on a meat platter (in the Church of the Nativity). The famous diamond monstrance, designed in 1699 by Fischer von Erlach and sporting 6,222 stones, is in the treasury.

Muzeum miniatur
Miniatures Museum

Strahovské nádvoří 11 (grounds of Strahov Monastery), Prague 1 (233 352 371/www. muzeumminiatur.com). Metro Malostranská/ tram 22. **Open** 9am-5pm daily. **Admission** 50 Kč; 30 Kč reductions. **Credit** AmEx, DC, MC, V. **Map** p326 A4.

With magnifying glasses and microscopes, you'll be able to see truly tiny works of art: portraiture on a poppy seed, a caravan of camels painted on a grain of millet, a prayer written out on a human hair, minuscule copies of masterpieces by the likes of Rembrandt and Botticelli. It's just as well you can combine this with a visit to the Strahov Monastery: it's arguably not worth the long walk in itself.

★ Schwarzernberský palác
Schwarzenberg Palace

Hradčanské náměstí 21, Prague 1 (233 081 713/ www.ngprague.cz). Metro Malostranská/tram 22. **Open** 10am-6pm Tue-Sun. **Admission** 180 Kč; 80 Kč reductions; 200 Kč family; free under-10s. **No credit cards**. **Map** p326 D3.

The National Gallery relaunched its permanent display of Bohemian Baroque art in spring 2008 at the sprawling Renaissance-era Schwarzenberg Palace. The museum presents around 160 sculptures and 280 paintings from the late 16th to the late 18th centuries. Mathias Braun, the master of Baroque sculpture who contributed some of the Charles Bridge's best ornaments, takes pride of place, along with Maximilian Brokof; great Bohemian painters of the epoque such as Karel Škréta and Peter Brandl also get special attention. Don't miss the stylised work of Antwerp innovator Bartholomaeus Spranger, whose sophisticated colours, elegant eroticism and obscure themes typify mannerism at its best.

★ Strahovský klášter
Strahov Monastery

Strahovské nádvoří 1, Prague 1 (233 107 711/ www.strahovskyklaster.cz). Tram 8, 22/bus 143,

149, 217. **Open** 9am-noon, 1-5pm daily. **Admission** 80 Kč. **No credit cards**. **Map** p326 A4.

The Premonstratensian Order (or Norbertines) set up house at this monastery in 1140 and soon after embarked upon their austere programme of silent contemplation and celibacy. The complex, which retains its 12th-century basilica ground plan despite 17th-century remodelling, still carries an air of seclusion, with orchard gardens stretching down the hill to Malá Strana. Since 1990, several cowled monks have returned to reclaim the buildings taken from them by the communists in 1948. They can sometimes be seen from Úvoz street walking laps around green fields and meditating; in a pointed rejoinder to their one-time communist overlords, the Mass is again being offered in the Church of Our Lady.

The Strahov Gallery here exhibits part of the monks' collection of religious art, but the complex's real highlights are the superb libraries, which appear on posters in universities all over the world. The frescoed Theological and Philosophical Halls alone contain 130,000 volumes, with a further 700,000 volumes in storage, and together form the most important collection in Bohemia. Visitors aren't allowed to stroll around the libraries, but they are permitted to look through the doors.

The comprehensive acquisition of books didn't begin until the late 16th century. When Joseph II effected a clampdown on religious institutions in 1782, the Premonstratensians managed to outwit him by masquerading as an educational foundation, and their collection was swelled by the libraries of less shrewd monasteries. Indeed, the monks' taste ranged far beyond the standard ecclesiastical tracts, including such highlights as the oldest extant copy of *The Calendar of Minutiae* or *Selected Times for Bloodletting*. Nor did they merely confine themselves to books: the 200-year-old curiosity cabinets house a collection of deep-sea monsters that any landlocked country would be proud to possess.

Šternberský palác
Šternberg Palace

Hradčanské náměstí 15, Prague 1 (233 350 058). Metro Malostranská/tram 22. **Open** 10am-6pm Tue-Sun. **Admission** 130 Kč; free under-10s. **No credit cards**. **Map** p327 C2.

Enlightened aristocrats trying to rouse Prague from provincial stupor founded the Šternberg Gallery in the 1790s. Located just outside the gates of Prague Castle, the palace now houses the National Gallery's European old masters. It's not a large collection, especially since some of its most famous works were returned to their pre-war owners, but some outstanding paintings remain, including a brilliant Frans Hals portrait and Dürer's *Feast of the Rosary*. The gallery's recent renovations made space for more paintings from the repositories, and restored ceiling frescoes and mouldings that had long been covered up. It's now fully dusted off and well worth an hour.

SIGHTS

Malá Strana

Palaces, parks and pubs shelter in the shadow of the castle.

Bounded by green space and river views, the idyllic streets and gorgeous façades of Malá Strana offer a refreshing contrast to the crowds of the Old Town. Neon is still a rarity in the city's left bank district, which lies between the Vltava and Prague Castle, and only a handful of developers have managed to jam commercial ventures among the district's ornate palaces, embassies, characterful pubs and Baroque churches. The characters themselves, descendents of former residents, are also still around: poets, artists, goldsmiths and Italian builders working for the castle.

Whether you're strolling beside the river, exploring the beautiful Kampa Island or taking the funicular up Petřín Hill, it makes for an idyllic afternoon.

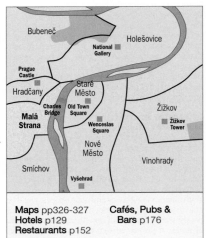

Maps pp326-327	Cafés, Pubs &
Hotels p129	Bars p176
Restaurants p152	

INTRODUCING THE AREA

Malá Strana was founded by the Přemyslid Otakar II in 1287, when he invited merchants from Germany to set up shop on the land below the castle walls. The area was transformed into a sparkling Baroque district by the wealthy Catholic aristocracy, who won huge parcels of land in the property redistribution that followed the Thirty Years' War.

When the fashionable types followed the Habsburg court to Vienna in the 17th century, the poor returned to the area. Indeed, the present-day appearance of the area dates only to the 17th century; precious few Gothic buildings remain. Ever since, for the last 300 years or so, Malá Strana has provided a home for poets, drunks, bohemians and mystics. Near the castle, they've shared unlikely pavement space with diplomats: the British, American, German, Irish, Italian and French embassies are all situated in Malá Strana.

The character of the area is changing rapidly, as accountancy firms, bankers and wine bars set up shop. Still, it's remarkable just how few businesses make their homes in what is one of the city's most central neighbourhoods. Apart from stores selling souvenirs and cut glass,

there's very little shopping in the area. And while Malostranské náměstí now throbs with life into the night, its appeal is mostly down to overt tourism marketing, and the many bars, restaurants and music venues that draw visitors to the capital. This relative lack of development means that Malá Strana has preserved its ancient look, and the locale's backstreets are favoured by film crews shooting period pieces. Local residents are unfazed by the attention, and carry on as if nothing has happened.

MALOSTRANSKÉ NÁMĚSTI

At the very heart of Malá Strana sits broad, open **Malostranské náměstí**, a lively square edged by large Baroque palaces and Renaissance gabled townhouses perched on top of Gothic arcades. It's long been a local landmark, but its armour has lately suffered a few controversial chinks.

Outposts of McDonald's and Subway have been here for years; however, the arrival of a Starbucks, which set up shop in the space known for a century as Malostranská Kavárna and formerly the inspiration for beloved Prague-born writer Jan Neruda, has had many locals fretting.

Bang in the middle of the square, dividing it in two, is the **Kostel sv. Mikuláš (Church of St Nicholas)**, a monumental late Baroque affair with a dome and adjoining bell tower that dominate the skyline of Prague's left bank. Built between 1703 and 1755, it's the largest and most ornate of the city's many Jesuit-founded churches. Local residents fought bitterly against the destruction of the two streets, two churches and various other structures that had to be demolished to make room for the church, but it's now a landmark.

The grim block next door at no.25 is another Jesuit construction, built as a college for the society's priests but now home to harassed-looking maths students. More appealing is the **Lichtenštejnský palác (Lichtenstein Palace)** opposite, completed in 1791. The Lichtensteins used to be major landowners in Bohemia; the Alpine principality has been battling to regain the palace, which was confiscated in 1918 and is currently used as a venue for classical concerts. Also in the square, set in the former town hall at no.21, is the club **Malostranská beseda**, normally home to music of a more raucous bent but undergoing a major retrofit at the time of going to press. Opposite the south side of St Nicholas sits a parade of pubs and restaurants, among them American backpacker haunt **Jo's Bar** (*see 176*).

★ **Kostel sv. Mikuláše**
Church of St Nicholas

Malostranské náměstí, Prague 1 (257 534 215). Metro Malostranská/tram 12, 22. **Open** *Nov-Feb* 9am-4pm daily. *Mar-Oct* 9am-5pm daily. **Admission** 70 Kč; 35 Kč reductions. **Map** p327 F3.

The immense dome and bell tower of St Nicholas, which dominate Malá Strana, are monuments to the money and effort that the Catholic Church sank into the Counter-Reformation. The church was commissioned by the Jesuits, and saw three generations of architects, several financial crises and the demolition of much of the neighbourhood between presentation of the first plans in 1653 and final completion in 1755. The rich façade by Christoph Dientzenhofer, completed around 1710, conceals an interior and dome by his son Kilián Ignaz that's dedicated to high Baroque at its most flamboyantly camp – bathroom-suite pinks and greens, swooping golden cherubs, swirling gowns and dramatic gestures. There's even a figure coyly proffering a pair of handcuffs.

A trompe l'oeil extravaganza, created by the Austrian Johann Lukas Kracker, covers the ceiling, seamlessly blending with the actual structure of the church below. Frescoes portray the life and times of St Nicholas, best known as the Bishop of Myra and the bearer of gifts to small children, but also the patron saint of municipal administration. Maybe this is why St Nicholas's was restored by the

Church of St Nicholas.

Vojan's Gardens. *See p78.*

communists in the 1950s, while the rest of Prague's Baroque churches were left to crumble. The church tower also made a favourite spy roost for teams of secret police.

▶ *For concerts here, see p243.*

West along Nerudova

Nerudova, which heads up from the north-west corner of the square towards Prague Castle, is crowded with restaurants, cafés and shops aimed at the ceaseless flow of tourists. However, it's also a fine street on which to begin deciphering the ornate signs that decorate many of the city's houses: the Three Fiddles at no.12, for example, or the Devil at no.4. This practice of distinguishing houses continued until 1770, when relentless modernist Joseph II spoiled the fun by introducing numbered addresses.

The street is named after 19th-century poet and novelist Jan Neruda, who formerly lived at no.47 (**U Dvou slunců**, or the Two Suns). After Neruda died in 1891, the house was later turned into a pub; during the communist period, it was a favourite hangout of the Plastic People

of the Universe, the underground rock band that was later instrumental in founding the Charter 77 petition carried against restrictions of the regime. Sadly, the place is now pretty joyless and usually chock-full of tourists.

You're also best off ignoring the turquoise drinking establishment at Nerudova 13, where Václav Havel, in an uncharacteristic lapse of taste, once took Boris Yeltsin for a mug of beer. Head, instead, for **U Kocoura** (*see p176*) at no.2. The alley next door leads up to the British Embassy at Thunovská 14, which a diplomatic wag christened 'Czechers'.

Leading up from here are the **Nové zámecké schody (New Castle Steps)**, one of the most peaceful and least strenuous routes up to the castle and a star location in the film *Amadeus*. However, note that Nerudova itself also leads up to Prague Castle, with the route offering the added incentive of a respite from the crowds and a good midway break at mellow pub U zavěšenýho kafe (*see p178*).

There are plenty of embassies on Nerudova itself. At no.20, the Italians occupy the **Thun-Hohenštejnský palác (Thun-Hohenstein**

Palace), built by Giovanni Santini-Aichel in 1726 and distinguished by the contorted eagles holding up the portal – they're the heraldic emblem of the Kolowrats for whom the palace was built. However, the Italians were trumped for a while by the Romanians, who used to inhabit the even more glorious **Morzinský palác (Morzin Palace)** at no.5. Also the work of Santini-Aichel, the 1714 façade sports two hefty Moors – a pun on the family's name – who hold up the window ledge. Their toes have been rubbed shiny by passers-by, who believe that touching them will bring good luck.

East towards the river

The short main drag between Malostranské náměstí and the Charles Bridge is **Mostecká**. A continuation of the Royal Route, the path taken by the Bohemian kings to their coronation, it's lined with elegant Baroque dwellings such as the **Kaunicův palác (Kaunitz Palace)** at no.15. It was built in 1773 for Jan Adam Kaunitz, an advisor to Empress Maria Theresa who sycophantically painted the exterior with the empress's favourite colours of yellow and white. These days it serves as the embassy of Serbia & Montenegro.

Just off Mostecká are the inviting **Blue Light** jazz pub (*see p176*) and **U Patrona** restaurant (Dražického náměstí 4, 257 530 725, www.upatrona.cz), both oases of quality in a stretch otherwise dominated by naff souvenir shops. And by walking north up U Lužického semináře, you'll eventually come to Cihelna, named after the former brick factory but long since converted into a restaurant and library dedicated to the writings of Václav Havel. The road provides an opening on to the river and an almost perfect view of the Vltava and Charles Bridge beyond.

If you instead follow the tram tracks north-east from Malostranské náměstí, you'll reach the **Kostel sv. Tomáše (Church of St Thomas**; *see p78*). Tucked into the narrow side street of Tomášská, its rich Baroque façade is easy to miss, but it's worth the attention. Based on a Gothic ground plan, the church was rebuilt in the Baroque style by Kilián Ignaz Dientzenhofer for the Augustinian monks. The symbol of the order, a flaming heart, can be seen all over the church and adjoining cloisters (now an old people's home). Held tightly in the hand of St Boniface, a fully dressed skeleton who occupies a glass case in the nave, it makes a distinct impression.

Leading by Example

Czech democratic freedoms have caused problems of their own.

Rambling through the **Wallenstein Gardens** (*see p78*), everything seems so calm and respectable. Baroque garden paths lead you past a calming pool that's home to both colourful carp and gliding ducks. A faux grotto covers one wall just next to an open-air stage, where free concerts entertain visitors every summer. And you'll be amazed to see figs growing ripe on an east-facing wall of the building, which also contains the Czech parliament. Visitors have been known to pick the lush fruit and stuff it furtively into their pockets. But it's within the palace walls that the big-time thieves go to work.

Scarcely a month goes by without another parliamentary scandal relating to the dodgy conduct of MPs. One recent affair resulted in a full-page flow chart of relationships between Mafia figures, Czech celebrities, party leaders and members of parliament. And not long before that, parliament's members flatly rejected a proposal from the Czech Senate that would have redefined parliamentary immunity from prosecutions, adopting

the system used in the United Kingdom and in the US Congress. The Senate's proposal would have limited legal immunity to statements and actions made during lawmaking sessions, with crimes or libellous statements made outside parliament subject to prosecution, as they are for any other citizen. However, MPs argued – rather creatively – that the immunity law was needed to protect them from the kind of political persecution they faced from the Austro-Hungarian Empire when the law was first enacted in 1920.

It seems the Habsburgs had a habit of charging upstart Czech MPs with crimes if they spoke out too loudly for the cause of freedom during the days before Czechoslovakia was consolidated as a sovereign state at the close of World War I. And, well, you just never know if an empire like that might rise up again, do you? If that wasn't enough, MPs found reasons to reject immunity limits on no fewer than 17 other occasions. Yes, 17. And people wonder why Czech voters have become so cynical so soon.

Walk Messing About by the River

Praguers may neglect their riverfront, but there's plenty here that appeals.

Though the normally gentle Vltava shapes the heart of Prague, life along its banks is elusive. Sure, rowboats ply the water, and there's a pleasant embankment, but it seems there's little real life centred down by the river these days. The great shipping days have long since passed; Czechs now treat the flood-prone river with a healthy respect, preferring to enjoy it from the streets above or the bridges across it. But an hour-long stroll along the left-bank attractions of Malá Strana shows off the waterway at its best.

Start on the other side of the water in front of the **Rudolfinum** (*see p242*), the city's most respected and elegant concert hall. It's located on Náměstí Jan Palacha, a square named after the student martyr to the Warsaw Pact invasion of 1968. At the intersection of Kaprova and Alsovo nábřezi, turn your gaze from the soaring home of the Czech Philharmonic to the green above the river to the west. Lolling students from the nearby art academy make the most of this spot on fair days, when you can sense the continuity in Bohemian culture.

The arts get paid a further tribute here. This embankment is named for the seminal Czech painter Mikoláš Aleš, while the **Mánesův most**, the bridge across the river, is dedicated to Josef Mánes, another leading light in the Prague arts. Designed by Antonín Balšánek and Josef Šakař, this 1911 art nouveau span marked a considerable improvement over the chain footbridge that stood here from 1869. Even though it permits car traffic, it feels much less crowded than the Charles Bridge upstream: it's relatively free of thronging tour groups, and offers a grand approach to Malá Strana.

Once you've crossed the river, turn left on Klárov, the first intersection. Just before it turns into U Lužického semináře, slip off the road and ramble down to the waterfront once more, from where you can take in Old Town with a swan's-eye view. If you've already got riverside dining on your mind, continue back along the street and then south on U Lužického semináře, where you'll find a host of pubs, cafés, galleries and a graceful walled garden (the **Vojanovy sady**; see p78). However, the finest waterfront views are

offered at **Cihelna** and **Kampa park** (for both, *see p75*).

Continue south, pass under the Charles Bridge and cross the **Čertovka (Little Devil canal)** on to **Kampa**. This lovely left-bank island hosts the splendid Museum Kampa; once you've taken in the modern art and Czech avant-garde sculpture, retire to the fine café terrace.

Continue south to Vitězná and stroll on to the **Most Legií (Legions Bridge)**, named for the Czech battalions in the Great War. At the bridge's midpoint, it leads down to **Střelecký ostrov (Shooters' Island)**, another green escape. In summer, films are shown here alfresco, and there seems to be a music festival every weekend. Even when there are no special events, it's a great place to take in the castle and the Charles Bridge, this time from upstream, while listening to the lapping tides at your feet.

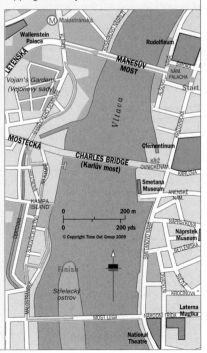

Close by, on the corner of Josefská and Letenská is the Jean-Baptiste Mathey-designed **Kostel sv. Josefa (Church of St Joseph)**, a tiny Baroque gem set back from the road. Since 1989, it's been returned to the much-diminished Order of English Virgins, who were also one-time owners of the very tranquil **Vojanovy (Vojan's Gardens)** just nearby.

Back on Letenská, towards Malostranská metro station, is a door in a wall that leads into the best-kept formal gardens in the city. Along with the adjoining **Valdštejnský palác (Wallenstein Palace)**, the early 17th-century **Wallenstein Gardens** belonged to General Albrecht von Wallenstein, commander of the Catholic armies in the Thirty Years' War and a formidable property speculator. Designed by the Milanese architect Andrea Spezza between 1624 and 1630, the enormous palace once had a permanent staff of 700 servants and 1,000 horses. It's now home to the Czech Parliament.

A little-noticed entrance to the palace gardens, just to the right of the Malostranská metro station exit, provides a wonderful way of cutting through the district and leaving tourists behind. You come out on Valdštejnské náměstí, just west of an even more impressive collection of greenery, terraces and Baroque arches, the **Rajská zahrada (Paradise Gardens)**.

Between the square and Malostranská metro station, much of the neighbourhood is currently sprouting cosy little bars and cafés. One of the best is **Palffy Palác** (*see p158*); meanwhile, just uphill from Parliament and a new favourite of its members sits restaurant **U Zlaté studně** (*see p158*), up the tiny street of the same name.

Kostel sv. Tomáše
Church of St Thomas

Josefská 8, Prague 1 (257 530 556). Metro Malostranská/tram 12, 22. **Open** 11am-1pm Mon-Sat; 9am-noon, 4.30-5.30pm Sun. **Admission** free. **Map** p327 F3.

It's worth craning your neck to get a good look at the curvy pink façade of St Thomas's. The lopsided structure is the legacy of an earlier Gothic church built for the Order of Augustinian hermits. After the structure was damaged by fire in 1723, Kilián Ignaz

Dientzenhofer was employed to give it the Baroque touch. The newly rich burghers of Malá Strana provided enough cash for the frescoes to be completed at breakneck speed (they took just two years) and for Rubens to paint the altarpiece, *The Martyrdom of St Thomas*. They even bought the body of St Boniface. The original altarpiece is now part of the National Gallery's collection on show in the Šternberg Palace (*see p71*) and has been replaced by a copy, but the skeletons of the saints dressed in period costume are still on display. Next door are 17th-century cloisters, where the monks dabbled in alchemy before realising that transforming hops into beer was easier and more lucrative than trying to make gold out of lead. A door on Letenská leads to their former brewery, now a tourist-filled restaurant.

Václav Havel Library

Hergetova Cihelna, Cihelná 2b, Malá Strana, Prague 1 (222 220 112/www.vaclavhavel-knihovna.org). Metro Malostranská/tram 6, 9, 22. **Open** 10am-6pm Tue-Sun. **Admission** 120 Kč; 60 Kč reductions. **No credit cards.** **Map** p327 G5.

The newest location for this library, an evolving project established in 2004, gives it proper prominence and offers the best public access set up thus far to the journals, photos, memoirs and letters of one of the Cold War's most important forces for dissidence and human rights. The former playwright president's humility, his passion for the underdog, his wry humour and his reputation for being persnickety all emerge from this well curated exhibition. Havel's awareness of the historical importance of his cause resulted in a strategic approach to his speeches and journals; his endeavours to address every topic related to that struggle can overwhelm, but are uniquely complete and often moving.

► *For more on Havel, see p30 and p51.*

KAMPA ISLAND

Until 1770, **Kampa Island** was known simply as Ostrov or 'island', which led to confusion with the other islands of the Vltava – especially since Kampa's southern end looks as if it's attached to land. A little fork of the Vltava, the burbling Čertovka ('Little Devil') runs briefly underground at the south end but resurfaces to slice Kampa from the mainland. The communists proposed filling the Čertovka to create a major road but were thwarted by a sudden outbreak of good sense, and this singular place, with its medieval water wheels, has survived. It's an oasis of calm on even the most crowded August day. For more on the island, *see p76* **Walk**.

Attractions here include the revamped **Museum Kampa** and, at the southern end of the island, one of the loveliest parks in the city. It was created in the 19th century, when an egalitarian decision was made to join the gardens of three private palaces and throw them open to the public. Washerwomen once rinsed shirts on the banks; note the **Chapel to St John of the Laundry** (Kaple sv. Jana Na Prádle) near the southern end. Today, it's taken up by snoozing office workers and bongo-beating hippies. However, the river and bridge views are as romantic as they come, and the overhanging chestnut trees make shady spots for reading and recharging. In spring, the park fills with pink blossom.

★ Museum Kampa

U Sovových mlynů 2, Kampa Island, Prague 1 (257 286 147/www.museumkampa.cz). Tram 12, 22, then funicular railway. **Open** 10am-6pm daily. **Admission** 120 Kč; 60 Kč reductions; free under-6s. **No credit cards**. **Map** p327 G5.
One of the most respected art refuges in town, the Kampa Museum enjoys an enviable location on the waterfront of the city's loveliest island, with a gor-geous terrace café. Its impressive modern art collection was amassed over decades by Jan Mládek, an international financier and former Prague student, and his wife, art patron Meda Mládek, both of whom lived in exile before the Velvet Revolution. Sculpture by Otto Gutfreund and work by František Kupka sit alongside a permanent show of modern art from across Central Europe. The programme of temporary exhibitions brings in fresh art from Europe and beyond.

WEST OF KAMPA ISLAND

Across the tiny bridge on Hroznová that leads to tranquil **Velkopřevorské náměstí** sits the **Buquoyský palác (Buquoy Palace)**. A pink stucco creation dating from 1719 , it now houses the French Embassy. The wall nearby has long been dedicated to John Lennon; *see p80* **Dear John**.

For centuries, the Knights of Malta lived around the corner in the quiet and lovely **Maltézské náměstí**. Although the communists dissolved the order, the Knights regained great swathes of property under the restitution laws. Among the buildings now under their control is the **Kostel Panny Marie pod Řetězem (Church of Our Lady Beneath the Chain)**, the square's most notable sight. The oldest Gothic parts of the church were built by a military-religious order with a view to guarding the Judith Bridge, which spanned the Vltava close to where Charles Bridge sits today; parts of the original bridge are visible in the lobby

Kampa Island.

of the **Rezidence Lundborg** (*see p133*). The Hussite wars barred the construction of the church and it was never finished. In place of a nave is an ivy-covered courtyard that leads to a Baroque addition (dating from 1640-50), built in the apse of the original structure. The two heavy towers at the church's entrance now contain some of the most prized apartments in all of Prague.

Opposite the church is the excellent little café-restaurant **Cukrkávalimonáda** (*see p154*); just round the corner on Saska ulička, meanwhile, are the prettiest flower shops and club-clothing boutiques in town. Heading west, Prokopská is home to the **U Maltézských rytířů** restaurant (*see p157*), which occupies a Gothic cellar that was once a hospice operated by the Knights. The Baroque building on the corner has suffered more than its fair share of misfortune: its priceless Flemish tapestries were given to Von Ribbentrop, Hitler's foreign affairs advisor; and in 1990, back when it was still the Museum of Musical Instruments, its collection of priceless Stradivarius violins were stolen. The museum is gone, but the sound of

students diligently practising at the nearby conservatory provides a soundtrack for wandering around the area.

South along Karmelitská & Ujezd

At the western end of Prokopská, at the foot of Petřín Hill, the road meets the north-south street known here as Karmelitská and further south as Ujezd. Head south down Karmelitská from its junction with Prokopská and you'll soon reach the **Kostel Panny Marie Vítězné (Church of Our Lady Victorious)**, the first Baroque church in Prague. The church belongs to the Discalced (Barefoot) Carmelites, an order that returned to the city in 1993 and is now in charge of the church's most celebrated relic: the doll-like, miracle-working Bambino di Praga. Porcelain likenesses of the wonder baby fill nearby shop windows, and pilgrims from across the globe file into the church year-round.

Around 200 yards to the south is the **Michnův palác (Michna Palace)**, another fine Baroque construction. Built between 1640 and 1650, the mansion was designed to rival the

Dear John

Three decades after his death, Prague pays homage to Dr Winston O'Boogie.

In the early 1980s, a previously unnoticed stretch of wall on Velkopřevorské náměstí near the French Embassy quietly began to take on a new appearance. For no good reason, the wall was adopted by fans of John Lennon, who, after the singer's death in 1980, congregated at the wall and scrawled messages – of love, peace and rock 'n' roll, but also of political protest – across it.

Inevitably, the secret police soon got involved. Believing the wall's graffiti to be a subversive plot to undermine the state, the police lost no time in painting over the slogans on what soon became known as the **John Lennon Wall**. But, without fail, John's smiling face always reappeared a few days later.

This state of affairs continued until 1989 when the wall was returned to the Knights of Malta as part of a huge restitution package. The Knights proved even more uptight than the secret police, and were all set to whitewash the graffiti until an unlikely Beatles fan came to the rescue. Claiming to enjoy the strains of 'Give Peace a Chance' wafting through his office window, the French Ambassador almost sparked a diplomatic incident but saved the wall.

The Knights eventually had a change of heart. The scrawled graffiti and the crumbling remains of Lennon's face were removed, before the wall was replastered and the Beatle's portrait was repainted by artist František Flasar. The John Lennon Peace Club now encourages modest graffiti at the site, preferably in the form of little flowers.

Wallenstein Palace, which was itself dreamed up as competition for the majesty of Prague Castle. Francesco Caratti took Versailles as his model in designing the garden wing, but his gardens today contain little but tennis courts. Continuing south to the intersection of Újezd and Vítězná, the border between Malá Strana and Smíchov, you'll often find rock music and college kids spilling out on to the street from the **Újezd** club (*see p258*).

Kostel Panny Marie Vítězné
Church of Our Lady Victorious
Karmelitská 9, Prague 1 (257 533 646). Tram 12, 22. **Open** 8.30am-7pm Mon-Sat; 8.30am-8pm Sun. **Admission** free. **Map** p327 F4.

You'll spot this humble church from the queues of pilgrims from Catholic countries all over the world, all waiting to catch a glimpse of its most famous occupant: Pražské Jezulátko, or Il Bambino di Praga, such a star that Czech children await Christmas presents from him rather than from good old Santa Claus. This 400-year-old wax effigy of the baby Jesus draws admirers, letters and cash from believers, and is also credited with performing innumerable miracles – there are more than 100 stone plaques expressing gratitude. The figure was brought from Spain to Prague in the 17th century and placed under the care of the Carmelite nuns, just in time to protect them from the plague. It was later granted miracle status by the Catholic Church.

A wardrobe of more than 60 outfits befits the dazzling doll's reputation: the babe is always magnificently turned out, his clothes changed by the Order of English Virgins at sunrise on selected days over the past 200 years. Although he's said to be anatomically correct, the nuns' blushes are spared by a specially designed wax undershirt. At the back of the church is a shamelessly commercial gift shop, jostling with miraculous souvenirs.

North-west on Tržiště & Vlašská

If you head left up the hill from near the intersection of Karmelitská and Prokopská, you'll be on Tržiště. Near the corner stands **U Malého Glena** (*see p251*), a convivial jazz pub run by expat American Glenn Spicker; further after-dark diversions are provided by the hip **St Nicholas Café** cellar bar (*see p177*) and, opposite, the cosy, traditional **Gitanes** restaurant (*see p155*).

At Tržiště 15 sits the 17th-century **Schönbornský palác (Schönborn Palace)**. It was built by Giovanni Santini-Aichel, who, despite his Mediterranean-sounding name, was actually a third-generation Praguer and one of the descendants of Italian craftsmen who formed an expat community on Vlašská just up the hill. The building itself now houses the American Embassy.

Maltézské náměstí. *See p79.*

From here, Tržiště becomes a tiny little lane as it winds its way up the hill, giving access to some of the loveliest hidden alleys in Malá Strana. Developers have been busy converting most of the flats here into investment property, but at no.22, you'll find a great survivor: **Baráčnická rychta** (*see p176*), one of the most traditional and insalubrious drinking establishments of the Lesser Quarter.

Running up the hill from Tržiště, Vlašská is home to the **Lobkovický palác (Lobkowicz Palace)** at no.19. Built between 1703 and 1769 to Bernini's unrealised plans for the Louvre, it's one of four Lobkowicz palaces in Prague; until the nationalisation of property in 1948, the family was one of Bohemia's major landowners. In 1989, the gardens sheltered thousands of East Germans, who ignored the '*verboten*' signs and scaled the high walls before setting up camp until they were granted permission to leave for the West.

From here, Vlašská ambles on upwards, fading out as it passes a hospital and chapel founded in the 17th century by the area's Italian community. It finally leads back to Petřín Hill.

PETŘÍN HILL

Rising up in the west of Malá Strana, **Petřínské sady (Petřín Hill)** is the highest, greenest and most peaceful of Prague's seven hills, and is a favourite spot for tobogganing children in winter and canoodling couples in

SIGHTS

summer. The name comes from the Latin word for rock, a reference to the hill's past role as the source for much of the city's Gothic and Romanesque building material. The southern edge of the hill is traversed by the so-called **Hladová zeď (Hunger Wall)**, an eight-metre-high stone fortification that was commissioned by Charles IV in 1362 in order to provide some work for the poor of the city.

At the top of the hill, accessible via a funicular (*see right* **Inside Track**) sits a fine collection of architectural absurdities. Among them is the **Rozhledna (Petřín Tower)**, a fifth-scale copy of the Eiffel Tower. If you ascend the 299 steps, your efforts will be rewarded by spectacular views over the city. The tower was erected in 1891 for the Jubilee Exhibition, as was the neighbouring mock-Gothic castle that houses **Zrcadlové bludiště (Mirror Maze)**, a fairground-style hall of wacky reflectors. There's a café at the base of the tower and a basic refreshment hut nearby. The third and least-frequented of the Petřín attractions is the **Hvězdárna (Štefánik Observatory)** at the top of the funicular.

While children love these hilltop attractions, grown-ups will enjoy Petřín's meandering paths. As you wind through the trees, look out for the statue of Karel Hynek Mácha, the unofficial patron saint of lovers; the shadowy bowers are a favourite of his disciples. **Strahov Monastery** (*see p71*) and the tram 22 stop are just a gentle stroll downhill from here.

Hvězdárna
Štefánik Observatory

Petřín Hill, Prague 1 (257 320 540/www. observatory.cz). Tram 12, 22, then funicular. **Open** *Jan, Feb, Nov-Dec* 6-8pm Tue-Fri; 10am-noon, 2-8pm Sat, Sun. *Mar* 7-9pm Tue-Fri; 10am-noon, 2-6pm, 7-9pm Sat, Sun. *Apr-Aug* 2-7pm, 9-11pm Tue-Fri; 10am-noon, 2-7pm, 9-11pm Sat, Sun. *Sept* 2-6pm, 8-10pm Tue-Fri; 10am-noon, 2-6pm, 8-10pm Sat, Sun. *Oct* 7-9pm Tue-Fri; 10am-noon, 2-6pm, 7-9pm Sat, Sun. **Admission** 40 Kč; 30 Kč reductions; free under-3s. **No credit cards**. **Map** p326 D6.

Some of astronomy's greatest breakthroughs were fuelled by the obsessive accuracy of planetary observations recorded by the temperamental Dane Tycho Brahe, a favourite of Emperor Rudolf II whose work led to the discovery of oblique orbits by his protégé Johannes Kepler. Czech scientists are still at it up here, with one of Štefánik's three domes reserved for research with a 40cm Meade mirror telescope. The other two domes keep inconvenient opening hours, but there are plenty of stellar displays (some in English). By day, there's the chance to see glimpses of sunspots and solar transits by Mercury and Venus; on clear nights, you'll be greeted by panoramas of the moon, planets and the occasional nebula.

INSIDE TRACK
CLIMBING THE HILL

The laziest and most enjoyable way to the top of Petřín Hill is on the funicular from Újezd, which runs roughly every ten minutes during the summer season (Apr-Oct 9am-11.30pm daily) and every 15 minutes in winter (Nov-Mar 9am-11.20pm daily). Your standard 26 Kč metro and tram ticket will get you a ride; alternatively, you can buy one from the machine at the entrance to the funicular.

★ Rozhledna
Petřín Tower

Petřín Hill, Prague 1 (257 320 112). Tram 12, 22, then funicular railway. **Open** *Jan-Mar, Nov, Dec* 10am-5pm Sat, Sun. *Apr, Sept* 10am-7pm daily. *May-Aug* 10am-10pm daily. *Oct* 10am-6pm daily. Closed in poor weather. **Admission** 50 Kč; 40 Kč reductions. **No credit cards**. **Map** p326 C5.

While Parisians were still hotly debating the aesthetic value of their newly erected Eiffel Tower, the Czechs decided that they liked it so much that they'd build their own version out of recycled railway tracks – which they duly did, in a lightning 31 days, for the 1891 Jubilee Exhibition. The tower's fiercest opponent was Adolf Hitler, who looked out of his room in the castle and immediately commanded his forces to remove 'that metal contraption'. Somehow, though, it survived.

The tower is fairly tatty these days, but the climb to the top is made worthwhile by phenomenal views of the city: more than just the usual vista of a set of spires poking over the top of the castle. Just try not to think about the way the tower sways in the wind.
▶ *There are more great views at the Old Town Bridge Tower; see p91.*

Zrcadlové bludiště
Mirror Maze

Petřín Hill, Prague 1 (257 315 212). Tram 12, 22, then funicular railway. **Open** *Jan-Mar, Nov, Dec* 10am-5pm Sat, Sun. *Apr, Sept* 10am-7pm daily. *May-Aug* 10am-10pm daily. *Oct* 10am-6pm daily. **Admission** 70 Kč; 50 Kč reductions. **No credit cards**. **Map** p326 C6.

Still one of the top draws for kids on Prague's most popular hill, the weather-worn Mirror Maze has old-time appeal, thanks to its mock-Gothic castle appearance, complete with drawbridge and crenellations. Inside, you'll find all the props of a good Hitchcock nightmare sequence: bendy mirrors that stretch, compress and warp visitors, usually to the general delight of couples and families. Alongside them sits a wax diorama of one of the proudest historical moments for the citizens of Prague: the defence of Charles Bridge during the Swedish attack of 1648.

SIGHTS

Staré Město

Prague's Old Town isn't quite ready for the 21st century.

From the clip-clop of horses' hooves crossing Old Town Square to the gatherings of old men in backstreet pubs, the long, sordid past of Staré Město ('Old Town') only grudgingly gives way to the modern world.

It's immediately obvious why so many kings preferred to live in this part of town, abandoning Prague Castle as too exposed and too far from the action; in this medieval warren of streets, roughly a square kilometre in size, it's far easier to hide your deeds.

The old centre's soul is most keenly felt at night and on bitingly cold winter days, but it's never short on charisma. Though camera-toting tourists abound in the main thoroughfares and along Charles Bridge, you can always find a quiet corner by ducking down one of the alleyways that wind off the tourist trail and into the old town's underbelly.

Maps pp328-329	Cafés, Pubs &
Hotels p136	Bars p178
Restaurants p158	

CENTRAL STARÉ MĚSTO

Defined by the high streets that run where its walls once stood, with only the Gothic **Prašná brána (Powder Gate**; *see p84*) continuing to demark the former safe haven, the heart of Prague retains its traditions. The old-fashioned Christmas markets, ironmongers and shoe-repair shops continue to hold their ground here; Bohemian teens flock to the **Roxy** (*see p257*), as before, and writers from around the world still meet annually for lectures and signings at the **Big Ben Bookstore** (*see p193*).

That said, the neighbourhood has seen changes. A crop of Czech fashion designers has taken root here, restaurant menus are diversifying, and galleries are both reviving artists suppressed by the pre-1989 regime and nurturing others too young to remember it. All this with the ghosts of bloody martyrs and the still haunted Jewish ghetto in silent witness.

Built in 1475, the Powder Gate marks the border between the Old and New Towns. The gate also signals the start of the **Královská Cesta (Royal Route**): the coronation path

traditionally taken by the Bohemian kings, it's now a tourist track filled with crystal shops manned by sullen students.

Celetná heads east from the Powder Gate, and is lined with freshly restored Baroque and Renaissance buildings. However, there's a more recent revamp at no.34 in the shape of the **Dům u Černé Matky Boží (House of the Black Madonna**; *see p84*). Built in 1911-12 as a department store with a street-level café, the first cubist building in the city now houses the city's first museum of Czech cubism.

On the opposite side of Celetná, an alley leads into **Templová**. Here, the ancient façades are jumbled with fresh new pastel-paint jobs, and restoration has revitalised long-dormant lanes. It's an after-hours hub: backpackers, tourists and foreign residents disappear nightly into its warren of bars, clubs and restaurants, many of which have French names for no particular reason: within a block, you'll find **La Provence** (*see p163*) and the lively **Chapeau Rouge** (*see p179*). Just west on Malá Štupartská is the **Bazilika sv. Jakuba (Basilica of St James**; *see p84*), a typical Baroque reworking of an older Gothic church, and the friendly Big Ben Bookstore, the city's best English-language bookshop.

From Malá Štupartská, you can find a sharp contrast to the sleaze of the neighbourhood's popular bars in the crisply restored, café- and restaurant-lined square of **Týn**. Better known by its German name of Ungelt, the square now houses upscale businesses such as **Botanicus** (*see p206*) and the **Ebel Coffee House** (*see p180*). Continuing west will take you past the ominous **Kostel Matky Boží před Týnem** (**Church of Our Lady Before Týn**; *see p84*), Staré Město's parish church since the 1100s, and on to Old Town Square.

Bazilika sv. Jakuba
Basilica of St James

Malá Štupartská 635, Prague 1 (224 828 816). Metro Náměstí Republiky/tram 5, 14, 26. **Open** 9.30am-noon, 2-4pm Mon-Sat; 2-3.45pm Sun. **Admission** free. **Map** p328 M3.

Known for its spectacular acoustics, best experienced during organ recitals, St James's boasts a grand total of 21 altars, some fine frescoes and a desiccated human forearm hanging next to the door. The latter belonged to a jewel thief who broke into the church in the 15th century and tried to make off with gems from the statue of the Virgin. The Madonna grabbed the thief by the arm and kept him captive; the limb had to be cut off.

★ Dům u Černé Matky Boží
House of the Black Madonna

Ovocný trh 19, Prague 1 (224 211 746). Metro Náměstí Republiky/tram 5, 8, 14. **Open** 10am-6pm Tue-Sun. **Admission** 100 Kč; 150 Kč family. **No credit cards**. **Map** p329 N4.

Renovated and reopened in 2003, this fantastic cubist building and collection of paintings and sculptures strive to present a totally plane-defying environment. Worth a visit for the Josef Gočár-designed building alone, the House of the Black Madonna is perhaps the finest example of cubist architecture you'll find in Prague. Despite its new lease of life under the umbrella of the National Gallery, English-language information on displays remains frustratingly scarce. Nevertheless, it proudly houses a collection of unique works focusing on the feverish cubism period of 1910-19, with an engaging series

House of the Black Madonna.

of paintings by Emil Filla, Bohumil Kubišta, Vincenc Benea, Josef Čapek, Antonín Procházka, Václav Špála and the surrealist Jan Zrzavý.

Kostel Matky Boží před Týnem
Church of Our Lady Before Týn

Staroměstské náměstí 604, Prague 1 (222 318 186). Metro Náměstí Republiky or Staroměstská/tram 17, 18. **Open** *Services* (doors open 30mins before) 6pm Tue, Thur; 3pm Fri; 8am Sat; 9.30am, 9pm Sun. **Admission** free. **Map** p328 M4.

Although you could easily miss the church's entrance, concealed in a courtyard, the Týn is one of the landmarks of Staré Město thanks to its twin towers. The church dates from the same period as much of St Vitus's Cathedral (late 14th century; *see p64*), but whereas St Vitus's was constructed to show the power of King Charles IV, Týn was a church for the people. As such, it became a centre of the Hussite movement in the 15th century before being commandeered by the Jesuits in the 17th.

The Jesuits commissioned the Baroque interior, which blends uncomfortably with the original Gothic structure; they also melted down the golden chalice in the church façade, which was a symbol of the Hussites, before recasting it as the Virgin. At the end of the southern aisle is the tombstone of Tycho Brahe, Rudolf II's personal astronomer, who was famous for his false nose and gnomic utterances. Look closely at the red marble slab and you'll see the former; the lines above, translating as 'Better to be than to seem to be', are evidence of the latter.

INSIDE TRACK
KUBISTA

On the ground floor of the House of the Black Madonna, look out for **Kubista** (*see p207*) a stylish shop selling original cubist pieces and copies made according to the original techniques.

Prašná brána
Powder Gate

U Prašné brány, Prague 1 (mobile 724 063 723). Metro Náměstí Republiky/tram 5, 14, 26. **Open** *Apr-Oct* 10am-6pm daily. **Admission** 70 Kč; 50 Kč reductions. **No credit cards. Map** p329 N4.

The Powder Gate (or Tower) is a piece of late 15th-century flotsam, a lonely relic of the fortifications that used to ring the whole town. The bridge that incongruously connects it to the art nouveau masterpiece of the Municipal House (*see p242*) used to give access to the royal palace that stood on the same site during the tenth century. By the mid-14th century, Charles IV had founded Nové Město, the New Town, and the city's boundaries had changed. The Powder Gate mouldered until it finally gained a purpose, and a name, when it became a store for gunpowder in 1575. Unfortunately, this made it a target for invading Prussian troops, and it was severely damaged during the siege of 1757. The gate was once again left to crumble until the neo-Gothic master Josef Mocker provided it with a new roof and redecorated the sides in the 1870s.

Staroměstské náměstí/
Old Town Square

Edged by an astonishing jumble of Baroque and medieval structures, the beautiful (and much photographed) **Staroměstské náměstí** (Old Town Square) has been attracting newcomers and visitors to Prague since the tenth century. This was the medieval town's main marketplace, and has always been at the centre of the action: criminals were executed here, martyrs were burnt at the stake, and, in February 1948, enormous crowds gathered here to listen to the announcement of the communist takeover.

Most of the houses here are much older than they look, with Romanesque cellars and Gothic chambers hiding behind the toy-town, pastel-coloured Baroque and Renaissance façades. Thank the communists, who spent an unprecedented $10 million smartening up the formerly grimy square for the 40th anniversary of the Czechoslovak Socialist Republic.

The focal point of the square is the powerful **Jan Hus Monument**. Designed by Ladislav Šaloun and unveiled in 1915, when it was received as a passé artistic flop, it is dedicated to the reformist cleric who was burnt at the stake by the Catholic Church in 1415 for heresy. Some 500 years after the event, the Church has formally apologised. At any rate, Hus's fans may at last feel vindicated as they point to the quote on the side of his monument that reads 'Pravda vítězí' ('Truth will prevail'). Those words were also used, perhaps ironically, by President Klement Gottwald, after the

The **Astronomical Clock**. *See p87.*

SIGHTS

The secret is in the ingredients

Angus Aberdeen Beef

We want you to enjoy our Churrasco like in Rio and,
what's more, we want it to do good both to your senses and health.
We believe that there is nothing mysterious about good food; because
all it takes are fresh, all-natural ingredients and the use
of well-proven techniques of hand preparation.

Na Příkopě 22, Praha 1, tel. +420 221 451 200   U Radnice 8, Praha 1, tel. +420 224 234 474

AMBIENTE
RESTAURANTE BRASILEIRO

w w w . a m b i . c z

communist takeover in 1948. However, Hus's proclamation did finally come true during the Velvet Revolution in 1989.

Work on the **Staroměstská radnice (Old Town Hall**; *see below*) began in 1338, after the councillors had spent fruitless decades trying to persuade the king to allow them to construct a chamber for their affairs. John of Luxembourg finally relented, but with the bizarre proviso that all work was to be financed from the duty on wine. He obviously underestimated the high-living inhabitants of Staré Město: within the year, they had collected enough money to purchase the house adjoining the present tower.

The grassy area behind the kitschy souvenir stalls on the west side of the square was provided by the Nazis, who destroyed much of the Old Town Hall on 8 May 1945 while the rest of Europe was celebrating the end of World War II. The town lost most of its archives, but gained a fine vista of the **Church of St Nicholas** (Kostel sv. Mikuláše; *see p243*).

You can still see what remains of the Old Town Hall after the Nazis did their worst, although trying to decipher the extraordinary components of the **Orloj (Astronomical Clock**; *see below*) is a more rewarding way to spend your time. Now a major tourist draw, the clock was constructed in the 15th century, some time before the new-fangled notion that Prague revolves around the sun and not vice versa. Undismayed, the citizens kept their clock with its gold sunburst swinging happily around the globe.

Perhaps the finest of the houses that make up what is left of the Old Town Hall is **U Minuty (Minute House)**, a beautiful black-and-white sgraffitoed structure that stands on the south-west corner and dates from 1611. Franz Kafka lived here as a boy, and the whole area teems with other Kafka sites: the writer was born at U Radnice 5, lived for a while at Oppelt's House on the corner of Pařížská and the square (where *The Metamorphosis* takes place), went to primary school on nearby Masná, and later attended the strict German Gymnasium on the third floor of the Golz-Kinský Palace. This frothy stuccoed affair in the north-east corner of Staroměstské náměstí once contained Kafka's father's fancy goods shop; it now houses the **Franz Kafka Bookshop** (no.12, 222 321 454), which carries numerous translations of his works.

Adjoining the palace is the imposing **Dům U Kamenného zvonu (House at the Stone Bell**; *see p229*). This beautiful old building now houses temporary exhibitions devoted to Czech artists, along with the Zvon biennale. The Baroque cladding that once encased the building was removed in the 1980s to reveal a 14th-century Gothic façade.

★ **Staroměstská radnice & Orloj**
Old Town Hall & Astronomical Clock

Staroměstské náměstí, Prague 1 (mobile 724 508 584). Metro Staroměstská/tram 17, 18. **Open** *Nov-Mar* 11am-5pm Mon; 9am-5pm Tue-Sun. *Apr-Oct* 11am-6pm Mon; 9am-6pm Tue-Sun. **Admission** 70 Kč. **No credit cards. Map** p328 L4.

Established in 1338, the Old Town Hall was cobbled together over the centuries out of several adjoining houses. However, only around half of the original is still standing today, with the present Gothic and Renaissance portions having been carefully restored since the devastation of World War II. Look out for the Old Town coat of arms, adopted by the whole city after 1784, which adorns the front of the Old Council Hall. And if you choose to climb the clock tower, built in 1364, you'll reach a viewing platform that's definitely worth the effort.

The 12th-century dungeon in the basement became the headquarters of the Resistance during the Prague uprising in 1945, when reinforcements were spirited away from the Nazis all over Staré Město via the connecting underground passages. Four scorched beams in the basement remain as a testament to the Resistance fighters who fell there. On the side of the clock tower, you'll find a plaque giving thanks to the Soviet soldiers who liberated the city in 1945. There's also a plaque commemorating Dukla, a pass in Slovakia where the worst battle of the Czechoslovak liberation took place, resulting in the death of 84,000 Red Army soldiers.

The Astronomical Clock has been ticking and pulling in the crowds since 1490, although its party trick is laughably unspectacular. Every hour on the hour, from 8am to 8pm, wooden saints emerge from trap doors, while below them, a lesson in medieval morality is enacted by Greed, Vanity, Death and the Turk. The clock shows the movement of the sun and moon through the zodiac, as well as giving the time in three different formats: Central European Time, Old Czech Time (in which the 24-hour day is reckoned around the setting of the sun) and, for some reason, Babylonian Time. Just below the clock face is a calendar painted by Josef Mánes in 1865, depicting saints' days, the astrological signs and the labours of the months.

A particularly resilient Prague legend concerns the fate of Master Hanuš, the clockmaker. Hanuš was blinded by the vainglorious burghers of the town, in a bid to prevent him repeating his horological triumph elsewhere. In retaliation, Hanuš thrust his hands into the clock and simultaneously ended his life and, briefly, that of his masterpiece. *Photo p85.*

OLD TOWN SQUARE TO CHARLES BRIDGE

The simplest and most direct route from Old Town Square to Charles Bridge is along **Karlova**, the continuation from Celetná of the

SIGHTS

Revolt! Drinking in the Scenery

Cafés or culture? The battle for the soul of Old Town Square continues…

If you're reading this while lounging in one of the many outdoor cafés in Old Town Square, you may be an accessory to vandalism. One of the oldest market spaces in Europe has, in the words of writer Stephen Weeks, been 'turned into an immense dining room'.

The rows of tents and awnings on the square, all touting various beers and spring waters, are relatively new. But so, too, is the outrage that's been generated by their presence. The fight over whether they should stay or go ultimately comes down to the debate about how Prague should present itself to visitors. Should it cater to curious, worldly travellers in search of history and high culture? Or should it aim to please the stereotypically vulgar tourist?

As admittedly cheery as alfresco drinks and dining here can be, this canteen encampment has destroyed the integrity of the square's architecture and, thus, its character. You would be forgiven, for instance, for not knowing that almost the entire south side of Old Town Square is actually an arcade. But although Prague's City Hall has recently been making a few hopeful bleatings on the subject, the problem for protestors is that there are absolutely no rules or regulations regarding such constructions.

The problem is compounded during the annual Christmas and Easter markets, which have begun to metastasise throughout the square. There's hardly room for visitors to walk, squeezed as they are between the barricades of the rogue restaurants and the tacked-up stalls flogging kitsch. This festive setting comes complete with an oversized stage, where Moravian children's choirs and elderly cloggers from Kutná Hora compete for the attention of trapped trinket shoppers. There is, literally, no escape.

The arguments in favour of the status quo hinge on the supposed needs of visitors to the city. Certainly, the fact that the square continually groans with traffic for both markets and cafés lends some credibility to this argument.

Regardless of the guarded noises from City Hall, things will surely stay as they are until visitors begin showing an interest in the architectural fabric of the square. But even so, as annoying as the situation is, it still hasn't quite reached the questionable level of the ice-cream wagon permanently outside the Holocaust museum at Terezín…

Royal Route. Twisting and curling as it does, the lane would not be particularly obvious were it not for the crowds proceeding along it. It's best viewed at night, when the tour groups are all back at their hotels.

Before heading down Karlova, fuel up at **U Radnice** (*see p163*), a traditional cellar restaurant on the west side of the Old Town Hall. To reach Karlova, walk past the Old Town Hall into **Malé náměstí (Little Square)**. In the centre is a plague column enclosed by an ornate Renaissance grille and overlooked by the neo-Renaissance **Rott House**, which was built in 1890 and entirely decorated with wonderfully intricate murals of flowers and peasants by Mikoláš Aleš.

Karlova winds past a succession of souvenir Bohemian glass shops, at the third turn arriving at the massive, groaning giants that struggle to hold up the portal of the **Clam-Gallasıv palác (Clam-Gallas Palace)** on Husova. Designed by Fischer von Erlach and completed in 1719, the mighty palace now houses the city's archives; at least, the portions of it that weren't destroyed by backed-up sewers in the devastating flood of 2002.

You can also stroll to the Charles Bridge along **Řetězová**, a block south of Karlova. This walk, down a narrow lane full of funky smells, takes you past **Café Montmartre** (*see p179*), a historic scene of hedonism that's now been revived as a mellow sipping space with embroidered parlour sofas. It was here during the glory days of the inter-war First Republic that opium, absinthe and jazz mixed into a potent cocktail that, at one point, led to black masses and orgies – or so the owners say, at any rate. A block further west on Anenské náměstí, you'll find the little **Divadlo Na zábradlí (Theatre on the Balustrade**; *see p271*), where a set-builder named Václav Havel first tried his hand at absurdist playwriting and soon landed himself in jail.

Back on Karlova, the vast, looming bulk of the **Klementinum (Clementinum**; *see right*) makes up the right-hand side of Karlova's last stretch. Next to Prague Castle, it's the largest complex of buildings in Prague. The Jesuits, the storm troopers of the Counter-Reformation, set up home here and enthusiastically went about their traditional tasks of pedagogy and casuistry. If you get peckish (and aren't too picky), there's all-night diner **U Zlatého stromu** (222 220 441, www.zlatystrom.cz) in a complex at Karlova 6, which also has a hotel, a disco and a strip show.

At the foot of Karlova, tourists have trouble crossing the road past the continuous stream of trams and cars that race through **Křížovnické náměstí (Knights of the Cross Square)**. The eponymous Knights, a bunch of elderly

---

INSIDE TRACK
SWEET LORRAINE

If you've fallen in love with the city, seek out the bronze **Lorraine cross** located on the wall halfway across the Charles Bridge on the downstream side. Touch it and make a wish – hey presto! It's guaranteed that you'll return to Prague.

---

neo-medieval crusaders, have come out of retirement and reclaimed the **Kostel sv. Františka (Church of St Francis)**. Designed by French arcitect Jean-Baptiste Mathey in the late 17th century, the red-domed church is unusual for Prague, not least because its altar is facing the wrong way.

The gallery next door houses religious bric-a-brac that the Knights extricated from various museums, and a subterranean chapel decorated with stalactites made out of dust and eggshells, an 18th-century fad that enjoyed unwarranted popularity in Prague. On the eastern side of the square is the **Kostel sv. Salvátora (Church of St Saviour**; *see right*), which marks the edge of the Clementinum.

Klementinum
Clementinum

Mariánské náměstí 4, Prague 1 (221 663 111). Metro Staroměstská/tram 17, 18. **Open** *Library Apr, Oct, Nov* 10am-6pm daily. *May, June* 10am-8pm daily. *July, Aug* 10am-8.30pm daily. *Sept* 10am-7pm daily. *Chapel of Mirrors* for concerts only. **Admission** 220 Kč. **Map** p328 K4.

In the 12th and 13th centuries, this enormous complex of buildings was the Prague headquarters of the Inquisition. When the Jesuits moved in during the 16th century, kicking out the Dominicans, they retained some of the Holy Office's less savoury practices, including the forcible baptism of the city's Jews. They also replaced the medieval Church of St Clement with a much grander design of their own (rebuilt in 1711-15 and now used by the Greek Catholic Church), while also gradually constructing the building of today. It's arranged around five courtyards, and several streets and 30 houses were demolished during its construction.

The Jesuits' grandest work was the **Kostel sv. Salvátora (Church of St Saviour)**, which has an opulent but grimy façade that was designed to reawaken the joys of Catholicism in the Protestant populace. Built between 1578 and 1653, it was the most important Jesuit church in Bohemia.

However, it's not the only superb building here. The Jesuits' main tool was education, and their library is a masterpiece. Completed in 1727, it has a magnificent trompe l'oeil ceiling showing the three levels of knowledge, with the Dome of Wisdom

SIGHTS

Charles Bridge.

occupying the central space. However, the ceiling started crumbling; to prevent the whole structure from collapsing, the **Zrcadlová kaple (Chapel of Mirrors)** was built next door in 1725 to bolster the walls. The chapel interior, decorated with fake pink marble and the original mirrors, is lovely, and there are two 18th-century organs.

At the centre of the complex is the **Astronomical Tower**, where Kepler came to stargaze. It was used up until the 1920s for calculating high noon: when the sun crossed a line on the wall behind a small aperture at the top, the castle was signalled and a cannon fired.

▶ *Mozart used to play at the Zrcadlová kaple (Chapel of Mirrors). Appropriate, then, that the room is now only open to the public for chamber concerts; see p244.*

CHARLES BRIDGE

The **Karlův most** (better known as **Charles Bridge**) is the most popular place in the city at which to get your portrait painted, take arty photos of the castle, listen to ropey street entertainment, have your pocket picked or pick up a passing backpacker. The stone bridge was built in 1357 (replacing the earlier Judith Bridge that collapsed in a flood in 1342), and has survived more than 600 years of turbulent city life. However, the 2002 flood did cause significant damage, which has resulted in a major restoration project. The ongoing work has, for the time being, shunted pedestrians to one side only.

Guarding the entrance to the bridge is the early 14th-century **Staroměstská mostecká věž (Old Town Bridge Tower;** *see right*), a Gothic gate topped with a pointed, tiled hat. Climb the tower for bird's-eye views of Prague's domes and spires, the wayward line of Charles Bridge, the naff **Klub Lávka** and **Karlovy Lázně** *(for both, see p254)*, the biggest recent addition to Prague clubbing.

The statues lining the bridge itself didn't arrive until the 17th century, when leading sculptors such as Josef Brokof and Matthias Braun were commissioned to create figures that would inspire the masses as they went about their daily business. The strategy proved more effective than an earlier Catholic decoration: the severed heads of Protestant nobles. More mundane statues were added in the 1800s.

The third statue on the right, from the Staré Město end of the bridge, is a crucifixion bearing a mysterious Hebrew inscription in gold. According to local lore, it was put here in 1696 by a Jew found guilty of blaspheming in front of the statue; his punishment was to pay for the inscription 'Holy, Holy, Holy, Lord God Almighty'. St John of Nepomuk – the most famous figure – is eighth on the right as you walk towards Malá Strana, recognisable by his doleful expression and the gold stars fluttering around his head. Legend has it that John was flung off the bridge after refusing to reveal the secrets of the queen's confession. Actually, he was just in the wrong place at the wrong time

SIGHTS

during one of Wenceslas IV's anti-clerical rages. Placed here in 1683, the statue is the bridge's earliest. Cast in bronze, it has weathered better than the sandstone statues, most of which have been replaced by copies. A bronze bas-relief below the statue depicts the scene; people stop and rub it for luck.

Further towards Malá Strana, fourth from the end on the left, is the Cistercian nun St Luitgard, sculpted by Matthias Braun in 1710 and depicted in the middle of her vision of Christ. The statue is considered by many, including Prince Charles, to be the finest work on the bridge; he pledged the money to save her from the elements, which threatened to wipe the look of wonder off her face.

On the same side, second from the Malá Strana end, is the largest grouping on the bridge. It commemorates the founders of the Trinitarian Order, which built its reputation by ransoming Christians held hostage by the Ottomans: SS John of Matha and Felix of Valois (accompanied by his pet stag) share space with a rogue St Ivan, included for no obviously discernible reason. Below them is a lethargic Turk and his snarling dog.

Staroměstská mostecká věž
Old Town Bridge Tower
Křížovnické náměstí, Prague 1 (224 220 569). Metro Staroměstská/tram 17, 18. **Open** *Jan, Feb* 10am-5pm daily. *Mar* 10am-6pm daily. *Apr, Nov, Dec* 10am-7pm daily. *May-Oct* 10am-10pm daily. **Admission** 70 Kč; 50 Kč reductions. **No credit cards. Map** p328 J4.
Built in 1373, along the shadow line of St Vitus's Cathedral (*see p64*), the Old Town Bridge Tower was badly damaged in 1648 by marauding Swedes, but Peter Parler's sculptural decoration on the eastern side survives. There's a dull exhibit on the tower's history, but the real reason for visiting is to take in the splendid views from the top. Don't miss the medieval gropers on the tower's outer corners, just visible before you go under the tower coming from Staré Město: each depicts a buxom lass being felt up by a gentleman friend.

OVOCNÝ TRH & AROUND

Canny German merchants were the first to develop the area south of Old Town Square, building a church dedicated to St Havel (more commonly known as St Gall) after Charles IV generously donated some spare parts of the saint from his burgeoning relic collection. The onion domes of the existing **Kostel sv. Havla (Church of St Gall)**, on Havelská, were added in 1722 by the Shod Carmelites, the Barefooted Carmelites settled on the other side of the river. The opposite end of Havelská is lined with bowed Baroque houses precariously balanced

on Gothic arcades. Prague's best open market (*see p193*) also stands in this lane.

Between here and Celetná, on Ovocný trh, sits one of Prague's finest neoclassical buildings: the **Stavovské divadlo (Estates Theatre**; *see p245* and *p271*), dubbed the 'Mozart Theatre'. Unlike Vienna, Prague loved Mozart – and Mozart loved Prague. During the composer's lifetime, the theatre staged a succession of his greatest operas, including the première of *Don Giovanni* conducted by the composer himself. The building was paid for by Count Nostitz, after whom it was named when it opened in 1783 with the aim of promoting productions of works in German. By the late 19th century, though, most productions were performed in Czech, and the name was changed to the Tyl Theatre after dramatist JK Tyl. His song 'Where Is My Home?' was played here for the first time and later adopted as the Czech national anthem.

The massive oriel window overlooking the theatre belongs to the **Carolinum**, the university founded by Charles IV (*see p18*). Charles never made a move without consulting the stars and ascertained that Aries was an auspicious sign for the first university in Central Europe, established on 7 April 1348.

Opposite the Estates Theatre is the former Soviet House of Science and Culture. Assorted boutiques, a **Ticketpro** (*see p210*) outpost and a dubious black light theatre occupy the complex these days.

BETLÉMSKÉ NÁMĚSTÍ & AROUND

Once the poorest quarter of Staré Město and a notorious haunt of prostitutes, whose present-day descendants can be seen lining Perlova and Na Perštýně a few blocks away, the area around

SIGHTS

Walk Getting Away from It All

Avoid the crowds with this stroll through quiet Staré Město.

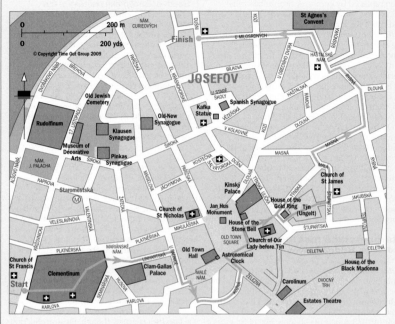

Despite its compact dimensions, Prague's Old Town manages to shield a number of communities that live separate but parallel lives. On the main streets of Karlova and Celetná, you'll find a less than appealing mix of crowds, noise, crystal shops and touts. But just a street or two away, you'll find dozens of tranquil sanctuaries in which to soak up centuries of history. This route of eight such gems should take a little over an hour.

Start by taking the best escape route from the throngs pouring off the Charles Bridge: the **Klementinum** (*see p89*). The outside walls of this vast former Jesuit complex of Baroque libraries, churches and concert halls create a mellow strolling space in the heart of tourist central. Within its confines, you can explore the ornate and little-used **Church of St Clement**, the **Chapel of Mirrors** and the library, a masterpiece inside, before moving on to Mariánské náměstí. City Hall looms, with statues of phantoms guarding its entry.

Head up Linhartská to Radnice and go right on to **Malé náměstí** (**Little Square**; *see p87*), the charming understudy to Old Town Square around the corner. Like a native, head into the passage on the south side to reach Michalská; Praguers regularly use these mouse holes to escape the crowds en route to somewhere else.

Turn left here and cross Melantrichova to once again trump the crowd by moving on to little Kožná, leading to Železná. Turn left again, heading toward the **Orloj** (**Astronomical Clock**; *see p87*) on Old Town Square. If you can squeeze past the mobs gathered to watch it chime the hour, turn right and head through the Baroque arcade in front of the **Church of our Lady Before Týn** (*see p84*) and into its older interior. This unjustly overlooked space provides refuge once again from the madding crowds with its airy, fantastical interiors, storied pipe organ and, of course, the tomb of royal astronomer Tycho Brahe.

SIGHTS

Take a right turn as you exit up the shadowy passage north of the church and continue up **Týnská**. Here, at no.6, is a redoubt well loved by students and locals: the **Týnská literární kavárna** (*see p182*). Rich espresso and strudel are the main offerings. It leads to the excellent **Dům U Zlatého prstenu (House at the Golden Ring**; *see p98*).

Return to Týnská and head through Ungelt on your left to make another left on Malá Štupartská, being sure not to miss the fabulous fresco of St James on your right. Continue to Masná, turning right and then left on Rybná. You'll soon reach the soothing **Dahab** teahouse (*see p179*), where dates and mint tea await. Also here: weird art at the upstairs bar/art space **Gallery NoD**.

Continue north on Rybná across Haštalské náměstí and up Anežská to the **Klášter sv. Anežky České (Convent of St Agnes of Bohemia**; *see p98*). Take in the small but stunning National Gallery collection of medieval art and mull it over in the attached courtyard. And when you're done, head west down U milosrdných and finish your stroll at the **Kostel sv. Šimona a Judy (Church of St Simon & St Jude**; *see p243*), a desanctified church that features intricate trompe l'oeil reliefs and a busy calendar of chamber music.

Betlémské náměstí (Bethlehem Square) was the natural breeding ground for the radical politics of the late 14th century.

On the north side of the square stand the swooping twin gables of the **Betlémská kaple (Bethlehem Chapel**; *see p94*), a reconstructed version of the 1391 building where Jan Hus (*see p19*) and other independent Czech preachers passed on their vision of the true church to the Prague citizenry. Across the courtyard is the **Galerie Jaroslava Fragnera** (Betlémské náměstí, 222 222 157), the best place in town for Czech and English-language design books and magazines. **Klub Architektů** (*see p161*) serves reasonably priced eats in the basement and, in summer, at tables outside.

On the opposite side of the square sits the **Náprstkovo muzeum (Náprstek Museum**; *see p94*). After making his fortune by inebriating the masses, Vojta Náprstek decided to install a collection of ethnological knick-knacks in the family brewery. A 19th-century do-gooder, he didn't just spend his time hunting down shrunken heads, but also founded the first women's club in the country. Untouched for 100 years, the room can still be seen, although the peephole he drilled through from his office perhaps draws into question the purity of his motives.

The **Rotunda sv. Kříže (Rotunda of the Holy Cross)**, one of three Romanesque rotundas in the city, sits on nearby Konviktská. The tiny 12th-century building was constructed entirely in the round so that the devil had no corner to hide in. If you don't manage to get a look inside, try the **Hostinec U Rotundy** (Karoliny Světlé 17, 224 227 227). Covered with lovely sgraffito, it's as authentic a pub as you'll find in Staré Město.

On Husova, just to the north-east, is the **Kostel sv. Jiljí (Church of St Giles)**, an enormous Gothic structure that looks rather like a fortress from the outside. It was built between 1340 and 1370 by the Dominicans, a mendicant order that has now returned to reclaim its heritage and inhabit the monastery next door. Nearby is **U Zlatého tygra** (*see p183*); it was a favourite watering hole of the late Bohumil Hrabal, the author and Nobel Prize nominee who spent half his life inside pubs and the other half writing about what goes on inside them. The pub makes a convenient refuelling stop before a visit to the Romanesque **Dům Pánu z Kunštátu a Poděbrad (House of the Lords of Kunštát & Poděbrady)** on Řetězová.

The river is not far from here. From the west end of the street, you'll have a perfect view across it to Kampa, with the castle high on the hill beyond. Turning right will take you past

SIGHTS

Novotného Lávka, a group of buildings jutting into the river centred around a 19th-century water tower and a scattering of bars, and back to Charles Bridge. Alternatively, turn left (south) at the end of Konviktská to reach the **National Theatre** and start of the Nové Město.

Betlémská kaple
Bethlehem Chapel

Betlémské náměstí 4, Prague 1 (224 248 595). Metro Národní třída or Staroměstská/tram 6, 9, 18, 22. **Open** *Nov-Mar* 10am-5.30pm Tue-Sun. *Apr-Oct* 10am-6.30pm Tue-Sun. **Admission** 50 Kč; 30 Kč reductions. **Map** p328 K5.

A huge, barn-like structure dating from 1391, the Bethlehem Chapel was where proto-Protestant Jan Hus delivered sermons in the Czech language, accusing the papacy of being, among other things, an institution of Satan. Given such remarks, it's perhaps unsurprising that, in 1415, he was burnt at the stake.

Before being thrown to the flames, Hus's last request was for 'history to be kind to the Bethlehem Chapel'. In response, the Jesuits bought the site and turned it into a woodshed. In the 18th century, German merchants moved in and built two houses within the walls. But Hus's wish was finally fulfilled under the communists, who chose to look on him as a working-class revolutionary thwarted by the forces of imperialism and spared no expense in the extensive restoration of the chapel. Three of the original walls remain and still show the remnants of the scriptures that were painted on them to enable people to follow the service. Following the fall of communism, religious services have resumed at the chapel, but secular visitors are also welcome.

Náprstkovo muzeum
Náprstek Museum

Betlémské náměstí 1, Prague 1 (224 497 500/511/www.aconet.cz/npm). Metro Městek or Národní třída/tram 6, 9, 17, 18, 22. **Open** 10am-6pm Tue-Sun. **Admission** 80 Kč; free under-6s; free 1st Fri of mth. **No credit cards**. **Map** p328 K5.

The 19th-century nationalist Vojta Náprstek had two passions: modern technology and primitive cultures. Although the gadgets he collected are now in the National Technical Museum (*see p114*), the ethnographic oddities he acquired from numerous Czech travellers can be seen here in an extension to his house. The displays concentrating on the native peoples of the Americas, Australasia and the Pacific Islands are interesting and arranged in exemplary fashion. Temporary exhibitions tend to favour travelogues of exotic cultures by Czech photographers.

JOSEFOV

The main street of **Josefov** is **Pařížská**. An elegant avenue of designer shops, flash restaurants, expensive cocktail bars and airline offices, it leads from Old Town Square down to the river and is home to swish hangouts such as **Barock** (*see p178*) and **Bugsy's** (*see p179*). However, for all the street's attractions, Pařížská stands in sharp contrast to the rest of what was once Prague's Jewish quarter.

The **Staronová synagoga (Old-New Synagogue**; *see p94*), the spiritual heart of Josefov, stands on a wedge of land between Maiselova and Pařížská. Built around 1270, it's the oldest synagogue in Europe. Legend has it that the foundation stones were flown over by angels from the Holy Temple in Jerusalem on the condition (*al tnay* in Hebrew) that they should be returned on Judgement Day; hence the name Alt-Neu in German, or Old-New in English.

Next door is the former **Jewish Town Hall** (Maiselova 18). Dating from the 1560s, it boasts a rococo façade in delicate pinks and a Hebraic clock with hands that turn anti-clockwise. Ever since its construction, the Town Hall has been the centre of the Jewish community. The **High Synagogue**, built at the same time as the Town Hall and attached to it, was returned to the community early in 1994 and is now once again a working synagogue serving the Jewish community (it's not open to sightseers). The money to build both the Town Hall and High Synagogue was provided by Mordecai Maisel, a contemporary of Rabbi Löw and a man of inordinate wealth and discriminating taste.

Further down Maiselova you'll come to the **Maiselova synagoga (Maisel Synagogue**; *see p96*), home to a permanent exhibition of Jewish history and one of six sites that together comprise the extraordinary **Jewish Museum** (*see p96*). The Maisel Synagogue was originally funded by the wealthy 16th-century money-lending mayor, but the current building is a 1905 replica of the original (apparently, the most splendid synagogue of them all): the first effort burnt down in the great fire of 1689, when all 318 houses of the ghetto and 11 synagogues were destroyed.

Nearby, on U starého hřbitova, is the **Starý Židovský hřbitov (Old Jewish Cemetery**; *see p97*), a small, unruly patch of ground that contains the remains of thousands upon thousands of bodies. Forbidden to enlarge their burial ground, the Jews buried their dead on top of each other in an estimated 12 layers, so that today crazy mounds of earth are jammed with lopsided stone tablets.

To the left of the entrance is the **Klausova synagoga (Klausen Synagogue**; *see p96*), built in 1694 by the same craftsmen responsible for many of Prague's Baroque churches. Inside, the pink marble Holy Ark could almost pass for a Catholic altar, were it not for the gold

Old Jewish Cemetery.

inscriptions in Hebrew. You'll find displayed various religious artefacts and prints as well as explanations of Jewish customs and traditions. And facing the synagogue is the **Obřadní síň (Former Ceremonial Hall**; *see p96*), designed in the style of a Romanesque castle at the beginning of the last century, it now hosts an exhibition of funerary ornaments.

On the other side of the cemetery stands the **Pinkasova synagoga (Pinkas Synagogue**; *see p96*), built as the private house of the powerful Horowitz family in 1607-25. The building is primarily given over to a memorial to the Jewish men, women and children of Bohemia and Moravia who died in Nazi concentration camps. A communist-era 'refurbishment' once obscured the names recorded on the Pinkas walls, but each one was painstakingly repainted in a two-year project undertaken in the 1990s.

Josefov's final synagogue, the **Španšlská synagoga (Spanish Synagogue**; *see p97*), was built just outside the boundaries of the ghetto in 1868, on Dušní. It was constructed for the growing number of Reform Jews, and its façade is of a rich Moorish design. Since being returned to the community, it's been meticulously restored and is now a working synagogue once again. Well worth a visit, it features a permanent exhibition on Jewish history in the Czech lands up to the beginning of World War II.

Precious Legacy Tours
Kaprova 13, Prague 1 (222 321 954/www. legacy tours.net). Metro Staroměstská/tram 17, 18. **Open** *Oct-Mar* 9.30am-6pm Mon-Fri, Sun. *Apr-Sept* 9.30am-6pm Mon-Fri, Sun. **Admission** 300 Kč; *tour with guide* 630 Kč. **No credit cards. Map** p328 L2.

This Jewish travel agency offers tickets for the various Jewish Museum sights, the Old-New Synagogue, tours of Prague and trips to Terezin, a small town that was used in 1941 as a holding camp for Jews destined for concentration camps further east. The English-speaking staff are also able to book boat tours, meals in kosher restaurants and accommodation.

Staronová synagoga
Old-New Synagogue
Červená 2, Prague 1 (no phone). Metro Staroměstská/tram 17, 18. **Open** *Apr-Oct* 9am-6pm Mon-Thur, Sun; 9.30am-5pm Fri. *Nov-Mar* 9am-5.30pm Mon-Thur, Sun; 9am-2pm Fri. **Admission** 200 Kč; 140 Kč reductions; free under-6s. **No credit cards. Map** p328 K3.

The oldest survivor of the ghetto and the spiritual centre of the Jewish community for over 700 years, the Old-New Synagogue is a rather forlorn piece of medievalism that's now been returned to the community and is still used for services. Despite its wealth of historical and religious significance, there's not much to see once you're inside, and little explanation is provided. But the story behind it is an interesting one.

The synagogue's austere exterior walls give no clues to its peculiar Gothic interior. An extra rib was added to the usual vaulting pattern to avoid the symbolism of the cross, and the decor and structure revolve around the number 12, after the 12 tribes of Israel: there are 12 windows, 12 bunches of sculpted grapes, and clusters of 12 vine leaves decorate the pillar bases.

SIGHTS

The interior was left untouched for 500 years as a reminder of the blood spilled here during the pogrom of 1389, when the men, women and children who sought sanctuary in the synagogue were slaughtered. However, 19th-century neo-Gothic enthusiasts couldn't resist the temptation to 'restore' the original look of the building and slapped a fresh coat of paint over the top.

Oak seats line the walls facing the *bema*, or platform, protected by a Gothic grille; with the exception of the Nazi occupation, the Torah has been read aloud every day here for more than 700 years. The tall seat marked by a gold star belonged to Rabbi Löw, the most famous inhabitant of the ghetto. The rabbi lived to the age of 97, and a sculpture by Ladislav Šaloun to the right of the New Town Hall in Mariánské náměstí depicts the manner of his death. Unable to approach the scholar, who was always absorbed in study of the scriptures, Death hid in a rose that was offered to Löw by his innocent granddaughter.

The rabbi's grave can be found in the Old Jewish Cemetery, recognisable by the quantity of pebbles and wishes on scraps of paper that are placed on his tomb even today.

★ Židovské Muzeum
Jewish Museum
U Staré školy 1, Prague 1 (221 711 511/ www.jewishmuseum.cz). Metro Staroměstská/ tram 17, 18. **Open** *Apr-Oct* 9am-6pm Mon-Fri, Sun. *Nov-Mar* 9am-4.30pm Mon-Fri, Sun. Closed Jewish holidays. **Admission** 300 Kč; 200 Kč reductions; free under-6s. *Old-New Synagogue* 200 Kč. **No credit cards**. **Map** p328 L2.
These directions, hours and rates apply to the six museum sites listed below. You can buy tickets at any one for the entire complex.

Klausova synagoga (Klausen Synagogue)
U starého hřbitova 3A, Prague 1 (222 310 302). **Map** p328 K3.
The great ghetto fire of 1689 destroyed the original Klausen Synagogue, along with 318 houses and ten other synagogues. Hastily constructed on the same site five years later, the existing synagogue has much in common with Prague's Baroque churches, as it was built by the same craftsmen. Its permanent exhibition explores the role religion played in the lives of the ghetto's former inhabitants.

The best view of the synagogue is from the Old Jewish Cemetery, where the simple façade rises behind the dense tangle of ancient gravestones, topped by two tablets of the Decalogue with a golden inscription.

Maiselova synagoga (Maisel Synagogue)
Maiselova 10, Prague 1 (224 819 456). **Map** p328 K3.
Mordecai Maisel (1528-1601), mayor of the Jewish ghetto during the reign of Rudolf II, was one of the

richest men in 16th-century Europe. Legend traces Maisel's wealth to a lucky intervention by goblins, but more realistic historians suggest that Rudolf II granted Maisel a lucrative trading monopoly. The original building on this site, funded by Maisel, was apparently the most splendid of all the quarter's synagogues until it burned down along with most of the others in 1689.

The present structure, sandwiched between apartment blocks, has a core dating to the 1690s; the rest was redone between 1892 and 1905. The synagogue houses exhibitions on the Jewish history of Bohemia and Moravia.

Obřadní síň (Former Ceremonial Hall)
U starého hřbitova 3A, Prague 1 (222 317 191). **Map** p328 K3.
The Romanesque turrets and arches of this building at the exit of the cemetery make it appear as old as the gravestones. In fact, the Former Ceremonial Hall was built in 1906 for the Prague Burial Society, which used the building for only 20 years. Today, it hosts fascinating temporary exhibitions on such topics as Jewish customs and traditions, focusing particularly on illness and death.

Pinkasova synagoga (Pinkas Synagogue)
Široká 3, Prague 1 (222 326 660). **Map** p328 K3.
The story goes that a Rabbi Pinkas founded this synagogue in 1479 after falling out with the elders at the Old-New Synagogue. The building was enlarged in 1535, and a Renaissance façade was added in 1625. In the 1950s, the names of more than 80,000 men, women and children of Bohemia and Moravia who died in the Holocaust were inscribed on the synagogue's walls as a memorial.

In 1967, after the Six Day War, the Czechoslovak government expelled the Israeli ambassador and closed the synagogue for 'restoration'. In the ensuing 22 years, the writing became indecipherable. Not until after 1989 could the museum begin carefully restoring the names, a job that was completed in 1994. The Pinkas also houses a particularly powerful exhibition of drawings by children interned in Terezin, the last stop en route to the death camps in the east.

Španšlská synagoga (Spanish Synagogue) *Vězeňská 1, Prague 1 (224 819 464).* **Map** p328 L2.

The Old Synagogue (or Altschul), older still than the Old-New Synagogue, stood on this site as an island in Christian territory, to which Jews could cross from the main ghetto only at certain times. It became a Reform synagogue in 1837, three decades before the prospering congregation rebuilt it in the then-fashionable Moorish style.

After painstaking reconstruction, the long-decrepit building finally reopened in 1998, its lovely domed interior glowing with hypnotic floral designs that are traced in green, red and faux gold leaf and lit by stained-glass windows. The building houses varied and inspired exhibitions on Jewish history and, in its upper-floor prayer hall, an exhibition of synagogue silver. It occasionally hosts concerts; tickets are available in the lobby.

Starý Židovský hřbitov (Old Jewish Cemetery) *Široká 3, Prague 1 (no phone).* **Map** p328 K2.

The Old Jewish Cemetery, where all of Prague's Jewish residents were buried until the late 1600s, is one of the eeriest remnants of the city's once-thriving Jewish community. The 12,000 tombstones that are crammed into this tiny, tree-shaded patch of ground are a forceful reminder of the lack of space accorded to the ghetto, which remained walled until the late 1700s. Forbidden to enlarge the burial ground, the Jews were forced to bury their dead on top of one another. An estimated 100,000 bodies were interred here, piled up to 12 layers deep. Above them, lopsided stone tablets were crammed on to mounds of earth.

Burials began here in the early 15th century, although earlier gravestones were brought in from a cemetery nearby. Decorative reliefs on the ancient, crumbling headstones indicate the name of the deceased or their occupation: a pair of scissors, for example, indicates a tailor. The black headstones are the oldest, carved from 15th-century sandstone; the white ones, made from marble, date from the 16th and 17th centuries.

NORTH ALONG THE RIVER

The area along the banks of the Vltava wasn't incorporated into the new design of Josefov, and the grandiose buildings there have their backs turned upon the old ghetto.

Walking down Kaprova towards the river will bring you to **Náměstí Jana Palacha**, a square named in memory of the first of the students who set themselves on fire in 1969 to protest the Soviet bloc invasion. (The second student to die in the protest, Jan Zajíc, didn't get a square named after him, although he is remembered on the striking memorial found in Wenceslas Square.)

The square itself is dominated by the breathtakingly beautiful **Rudolfinum** (*see p242*), which houses the Dvořák and Suk concert halls. Built between 1876 and 1884 in neoclassical style and entirely funded by the Czech Savings Bank to display its 'patriotic, provincial feelings', it is named after Rudolf II. You can see the bank's corporate logo, the bee of thrift, in the paws of the two sphinxes with ample breasts who guard the building's riverfront entrance.

In 1918, the concert hall became home to the Parliament of the new republic. When Chamberlain returned to England after meeting Hitler in 1938, washing his hands of the 'quarrel in a faraway country between people of whom we know nothing', 250,000 citizens came here to take an oath and pledge themselves to the defence of the republic. But the Nazis, having little use for a parliament, soon turned the building back into a concert hall and called it 'the German House of Arts'. Opposite, with its back to the Old Jewish Cemetery (*see pleft*), is the magnificent **Uměleckoprůmyslové muzeum (Museum of Decorative Arts;** *see p98*).

Few visitors make it over to the streets of art nouveau tenement houses in northern Staré Město. Most have been restored over the last few years, but some are still semi-derelict. However, they're well worthy of inspection, even without the attraction of **Klášter sv. Anežky České (Convent of St Agnes of Bohemia;** *see p98*), the oldest example of Gothic architecture in the city. The building is now home to the National Gallery's fine medieval collection.

Nearby is **Dlouhá**, or 'Long Street'. Back in the 14th century, when beer champion Charles IV forbade the export of hops, it contained no fewer than 13 breweries. These days, though, its main attraction is the **Roxy** (*see p257*), a crumbling cinema that was once the improbable headquarters of the Communist Youth Association and is now, even more

SIGHTS

INSIDE TRACK DE-COMPOSITION

Legend has it that after the Nazis took over, they decreed that a statue of the Jewish composer Mendelssohn should be removed from the **Rudolfinum** (*see p242*). However, the workmen, not knowing what Mendelssohn looked like, took their lessons in racial science to heart and removed the figure with the biggest nose – which turned out to be Richard Wagner.

SIGHTS

Museum of Decorative Arts

improbably, the city's most atmospheric club. Next door is the serene **Dahab** teahouse (*see p179*), replete with belly dancers and Middle Eastern cheap eats; above it lies **Gallery NoD**, a hive of new media artists and one of the city's grooviest internet bars.

In the pleasantly quiet streets between Dlouhá and the river lie several more convivial bars and cafés, including the French-style **Chez Marcel** (*see p160*), the Irish **Molly Malone's** and the über-hip **M1 Secret Lounge** (*for both, see p181*).

Dům U Zlatého prstenu
House at the Golden Ring

Týnská 6, Prague 1 (224 827 022). Metro Náměstí Republiky/tram 5, 8, 14, 26. **Open** 10am-6pm Tue-Sun. **Admission** 90 Kč; 160 Kč family; free under-6s. **No credit cards. Map** p328 M4.

Now reopened after renovation, this beloved, charismatic former Renaissance manor house is set to feature a three- to five-year show of Jiří Příhoda's intriguing architectural art, along with new sculptures in the courtyard and airy, remodelled exhibition spaces. The broad spectrum of 20th-century Czech works showcased here, organised intriguingly by theme rather than by artist or period, is always well curated and fresh. An ever-changing

programme of international shows, often exploring digital media, provides balance.

▶ *For more on the city's galleries, see p228-235*

★ Klášter sv. Anežky České
Convent of St Agnes of Bohemia

U milosrdných 17, Prague 1 (224 810 628). Metro Náměstí Republiky/tram 5, 8, 14. **Open** 10am-6pm Tue-Sun. **Admission** 150 Kč; 200 Kč family; free under-10s. **No credit cards. Map** p328 M2.

This intimate and manageable part of the National Gallery, set in the oldest surviving Gothic building in Prague (worth a visit in its own right), houses a collection of Bohemian and Central European medieval art from 1200 to 1550. Prague, after all, was at the forefront of European artistic development during the reign of Charles IV (1346-78), and one of the greats of the end of the 14th century was the Master of Třeboň. Here you can see his altarpiece featuring the *Resurrection of Christ* and his *Madonna of Roudnice*, an example of the 'Beautiful Style' that prevailed until the outbreak of the Hussite wars. The Gothic style remained popular in Bohemia right up to the 16th century, as seen in the extraordinary wood carvings. The convent is fully wheelchair-accessible.

Uměleckoprůmyslové muzeum
Museum of Decorative Arts

Ulice 17. listopadu 2, Prague 1 (251 093 111/ www.upm.cz). Metro Staroměstská/tram 17, 18. **Open** 10am-7pm Tue; 10am-6pm Wed-Sun. **Admission** 120 Kč; free under-10s; free 5-7pm Tue. **No credit cards. Map** p328 K3.

Built between 1897 and 1900, this neo-Renaissance museum is a work of art in itself, boasting richly decorated halls, stained- and etched-glass windows, and intricately painted plaster mouldings. Exhibits are grouped according to material; in addition to the excellent 20th-century collection, the permanent, pre-20th-century collections comprise lavishly crafted pieces including furniture, tapestries, pottery, clocks, books, a beautifully preserved collection of clothing, and fine displays of ceramics and glass. Check online for details of the latest temporary exhibition: past subjects have ranged from Charles and Ray Eames' iconic furniture designs to Moravian tapestry.

INSIDE TRACK
ST AGNES

St Agnes died a full 700 years before the Pope made her a saint. Popular opinion held that miracles would accompany her canonisation; sure enough, within five days of the Vatican's announcement the Velvet Revolution was under way.

Walk Down from Above

Look up when strolling Staré Město, and you'll be greeted by some odd faces.

On façades throughout the city of Prague, saints vie with secular gods and a few banished pagan ones. And nowhere are the displays more lively than in Staré Město. A walk through the area reveals a concentrated variety of such architectural accretions: plaques, memorials and Catholic decorations, running from Baroque icons to the biomorphic forms of Modernism.

From the **Charles Bridge** (*see p90*), start at **Karlova 3**, where the corner of the **U zlaté studny** (*see p140*) is tiered like an iconostasis. The lower level features two saints: the famously pierced St Sebastian and, to his left, the more obscure St Roc. Few saints commanded more fervent devotion than Roc, though he suffered greatly from lust, something he begged God to cure. He's seen here exposing his thigh, as something oozes down it.

Accompanying the saint is a little mutt that seems to be suffering from mumps. In answering St Roc's prayer, God sent the saint the little dog, which jumped under St Roc's tunic and bit off his testicles. So it's blood we see flowing down St Roc's leg, while the puffy cheeks of the dog each contain a testicle.

Directly across from this holy castration at **Karlova 22** sits enthroned in gold the Czechs' prophetess-queen: Libuše, the royal seer who foretold the founding of Prague. She seems rather bemused by the hordes of tourists below – or perhaps it's just St Roc's predicament to which she's reacting.

From here, take Seminářska (to the right of U Zlaté Studny), which leads to Mariánské náměstí and the **Old Town Hall** (*see p87*). Jutting up from the building's right corner is Ladislav Šaloun's great sculpture of Golem-creator Rabbi Löw, found here grappling with the Angel of Death. Šaloun's works, as influenced by art nouveau as they are by Rodin, are seen throughout Prague.

Across the street at **Platnéřská 17**, you'll find a commemorative marker to the people who fell during the Prague uprising against the Nazis in 1945. The names of the fallen – among them the 21-year-old Bedřich Kůla – are listed underneath a sculpted raised hand.

Around the corner at **Žatecka 1** is the world headquarters of UNIMA, the international union of puppeteers, which was founded in puppet-mad Prague in 1929. The whimsical sculpture, looking a bit *Last Supper*-ish, brings together Punch and Kašpar, his Czech cousin, among a variety of guests.

On the nearby corner of Maiselova and Náměstí Franze Kafky, you'll find a modernist likeness of Kafka marking his birthplace. There are now a few memorials to Kafka dotted around Old Town Square. The best is **Staroměstská náměstí 17**: the site of Berta Fant's famous literary salon, it was here that Fant introduced Kafka to Einstein, whose profile appears on the building's plaque.

The greatest architectural accretion of all is, of course, the famous **Orloj** (**Astronomical Clock**; *see p87*). Nearby, off Melantrichova at the corner of **Kožná**, is the house where Egon Erwin Kisch was born and lived. The famous early 20th-century German-Jewish Praguer was the Hunter S Thompson of his day. He's revered throughout Central Europe, but English-speakers have yet to discover him.

Nové Město

Neon, crystals, sausages, money-making – and Wenceslas Square.

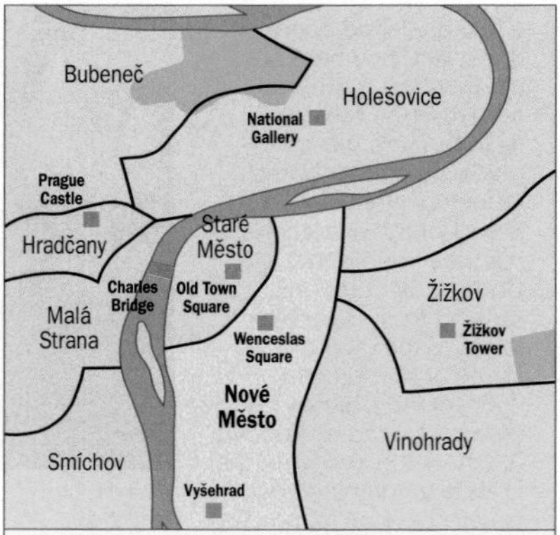

The charms of Nové Město (New Town) are not as immediately apparent as those of Staré Město (Old Town). However, the neighbourhood's characterful pockets more than make up for the noise and bustle. And with Wenceslas Square having long ago replaced Old Town Square as the living heart of the city, it's also the place in which to see the authentic face of modern Prague. With its mix of grand architecture, low streetlife, glitzy stores and crumbling reminders of life under foreign oppressors, Nové Město embodies the zeitgeist of an entire nation seeking to establish its place in 21st-century Europe.

The neighbourhood is bounded roughly to the north and east by Národní, Na Příkopě and Revoluční, which form the border with Staré Město. The busy arterial road Wilsonova (which turns into Mezibranská and Sokolská) forms a natural barrier to the east. Heading west from there along Žitná or Ječná takes you through the backstreets and past some of the more historic buildings and squares in Nové Město and on to the Vltava river.

Map labels: Bubeneč · Holešovice · National Gallery · Prague Castle · Hradčany · Staré Město · Charles Bridge · Old Town Square · Žižkov · Malá Strana · Wenceslas Square · Žižkov Tower · Nové Město · Smíchov · Vinohrady · Vyšehrad

Maps pp330-331
Hotels p141
Restaurants p166

Cafés, Bars & Pubs p183

WENCESLAS SQUARE

The hub of Nové Město – and for that matter, the city – is **Wenceslas Square**, a broad, sloping boulevard that's nearly a kilometre in length. Almost every major event in Prague's last century unfolded here, or at least passed through it. The masses assembled here for the founding of the Czechoslovak Republic in 1918, and again in 1939, when Nazi troops marched in to the city to establish the Protectorate of Bohemia and Moravia. In 1968, the brief hope of the Prague Spring was born and died here. And when the communist regime was finally toppled by the Velvet Revolution in 1989, the world watched crowds celebrating in Wenceslas Square.

Only faint echoes of those events are now discernible, mostly in the form of monuments and plaques that are easy to miss. The tone today is commercial, with a busy mix of hotels, shops, restaurants, clubs and tourist services.

Cabs buzz up and down the boulevard, which is often cluttered with construction work, parked cars and police pulling over traffic offenders. During the day, office workers, shoppers and vendors mingle with the tourist crowds that head here all year round.

After dark, though, the night people emerge: hustlers trying to draw marks into clubs, hookers soliciting startled passers-by, unsteady, boisterous groups of drunken tourists careening from pub to pub. The glow of neon adds to the energy, as do the smell of frying sausages from the food stands and the mix of languages, laughter and come-ons as you walk along the pavements.

It's like a carnival, with crystal shops and brightly lit souvenir arcades glittering along both sides of the main promenade. It's an image that the city's fathers have long disdained; but although plans to clean up the square's tawdrier aspects are announced regularly (*see p183* **Revolt!**), they've so far had little effect.

SIGHTS

A tour of the square

At the top of Wenceslas Square, overlooking the boulevard, sits the **Národní muzeum** (**National Museum**; *see p218*). Built between 1885 and 1890, this neo-Renaissance palace is covered in decades of grime and the street graffiti that has become common in Prague since the Velvet Revolution. Nevertheless, the building merits a visit, as every niche, corner and column-top boasts elaborate nationalist stonework. The soaring lobby and grand staircase inside are also worth a look, unfortunately far more so than the natural history-related contents of the museum.

In front of the blackened edifice, twin mounds in the cobbled street mark the site of two self-immolations. In January 1969, Czech student Jan Palach set himself on fire to protest against Soviet oppression; the following month, another student named Jan Zajíc did the same (*see p28*). To this day, the mounds are usually covered with flowers and candles.

One of the most popular meeting spots in Prague is across **Wilsonova** in the gigantic form of the Czech patron saint: the statue of Wenceslas astride a horse, surrounded by Saints Agnes, Adalbert, Procopius and Ludmila, Wenceslas's grandmother. (The good king takes a satirical ribbing nearby, inside the

Lucerna complex at the corner of Štěpánská, where he hangs from the ceiling in an inverted version, the work of art prankster David Černý.) A few steps below 'the horse', as the stately monument is known, a headstone with the images of Palach and Zajíc stands as a memorial to the victims of communism.

The modern glass and stone structure just east of the National Museum was once the parliament building, where the Federal Assembly met until the Czech and Slovak republics split in 1993. It then became the home of Radio Free Europe, nicknamed 'the Fortress' by station employees owing to the concrete barriers and tight security that surround it. Concerns about terrorism – the station's prime focus now is broadcasting to audiences mainly in Asia, where its programmes presumably provoke extremists – led RFE to agree late in 2005 to move to the suburbs, although the move is awaiting the completion of a new building. The current Czech parliament, meanwhile, is ensconced in the more fashionable Valdštejnský palác (Wallenstein Palace; *see p78*) across the river in Malá Strana.

The next building along is the **Státní Opera** (**State Opera**; *see p245*), which opened in 1888 as the New German Theatre. Red-headed stepchild of the city's performing arts establishment, the theatre is perennially

SIGHTS

Wenceslas Square.

National Museum. *See p101.*

underfunded and perpetually trying to compensate with creativity and enthusiasm. It's worth the price of a ticket just to see the sumptuous neo-rococo performance hall.

Just past the State Opera beauty is the beast: **Hlavní nádraží** (*see p300*), the city's main train station; it's also known as Wilsonovo nádraží (Wilson Station). Way overdue for renovation, the station no longer retains even faded glamour: dirty inside and out, it's a haven for the homeless, junkies and cruising rent boys. The upstairs rotunda, which houses a rough café, offers a few glimpses of bygone glory: dull brass rails, dusty statues and peeling murals that disappear into the dark curve of the dome. The lower level, where escalators connect with the metro, is a prime example of late communist design.

Heading down Wenceslas Square, historical monuments quickly give way to capitalist totems such as McDonald's and KFC. It also hosts a new crop of designer hotels and a crop of gambling dens (*see p110* **Herna Blues**) and adult entertainment venues. There are also a few sports pubs here – but if you feel like a sporting fix, you're better off going around the corner to **Zlatá Hvězda** (*see p187*), which shows more than just hockey and football.

Along with the upside-down horse, the **Lucerna** shopping passage is one of the last survivors of pre-war Czech grandeur. This tattered art nouveau gem is a maze of shops ranging from high-fashion boutiques to a **Ticketpro** (*see p210*). Walk through the passage for a flavour of everyday Prague, the small-scale cafés, second-hand camera shops and wedding dress rentals epitomising the soul of the city. Take the big staircase from the main lobby up to the **Lucerna** cinema bar (*see p223*), a classy, run-down art nouveau relic.

Further along Wenceslas Square, the façades become increasingly ornate. Sit on any bench and look up, and you'll see stone angels, griffins, muscular atlantes and all manner of ornamental filigree. There's a particularly impressive set of murals on the **Wiehl House** (1896) at no.34, and Blecha's **Supich Building** (1913-16) at nos.38-40 has some likeably bizarre Assyrian-style masks. The second-floor balcony of the **Melantrich Building** (no.30) was the venue for one of the most astounding events of the Velvet Revolution: on 24 November 1989, in front of over 300,000 people, Václav Havel and Alexander Dubček stepped forward and embraced, signifying the end of 21 years of 'normalisation'. Within weeks, the entire cabinet had resigned.

For an interior version of gorgeous art nouveau mural and stained-glass work, stop in at the **Grand Hotel Evropa** (*see p143*) at no.25, the hotel time forgot. From here, though, the growing number of Levi's and Nike logos tell you you're approaching the cobbled walkway at the bottom of Wenceslas Square.

NORTHERN NOVÉ MĚSTO

From the end of Wenceslas Square, **Na Příkopě** runs north-east along what was once a moat around Staré Město, though there's no hint of that now. Instead, the street boasts some of Prague's poshest shops and most impressive examples of 'adaptive reuse' – in this case, turning stately Baroque buildings into shopping palaces. **Palác Koruna**, at the junction of Wenceslas Square and Na Příkopě, is a prime example.

Across the way at 28.Října 3 is a dance club that's noteworthy not for its DJs but for the way it illustrates the blithe manner in which former socialist countries expropriate capitalist symbols. Despite first appearances, it's no licensed satellite of the Hard Rock Café chain, though everything about the sign and the drinks menu does its best to suggest it is. In reality, it's an all-Czech stand-alone venture that's appropriated the name; along with a second name, Batalion. As with many such ventures across the city, the owners seem to feel that if business doesn't bloom under the first brand you try, why not add a second or even a third name while keeping the first?

A short walk north at Na Příkopě 20 is the **Prague Information Service** (*see p315*), a good source of leaflets, schedules and maps. Also on Na Příkopě, you'll find the interesting **Muzeum komunismu (Museum of**

Communism; just off Na Příkopě on Panská is the **Muchovo muzeum (Mucha Museum**; *for both, see p104*), devoted to the works of artist Alfons Mucha. There's entertainment at a very different sort at the swanky **Slovanský dům** shopping mall, housed in the former offices of the Gestapo and the Communist Party. Somewhere, totalitarians are spinning in their graves over the sushi bar, multiplex cinema and U2-owned Joshua Tree club.

Opposite Slovanský dům is one of Prague's cultural treasures, the resplendent **Obecní dům (Municipal House**; *see p242*). The city's finest art nouveau orgy, built from 1905 to 1911, it's now a multipurpose facility with galleries, offices, meeting rooms, restaurants and the 1,500-seat performance hall of the Prague Symphony Orchestra (*see p242*). The entranceway is crowned with a dome and arched gable framing *Homage to Prague*, a monumental tile mosaic by Karel Špillar. The walls and floors inside are also covered with fabulous tile work and murals, some of the latter by Alfons Mucha.

The forbidding Gothic structure attached to the Municipal House is the 15th-century **Prašná brána (Powder Gate**; *see p84*), which has been renovated and modified numerous times. Centuries ago, the tower marked the beginning of the Royal Route, which coronation parades took through Staré Město, across the Charles Bridge and up to Prague Castle.

A brief loop around two streets running east from the Obecní dům offers a capsule view of a city in transition. V Celnici could be almost anywhere in Western Europe, with the modern **Marriott** (*see p144*) and **Hilton Prague Old Town** (*see p143*) facing each other across the street. The Hilton holds the **Millennium Plaza** mall, complete with one of the swankiest fitness centres in town.

The street ends at **Masarykovo nádraží**, the Masaryk train station, a smaller and cleaner version of Hlavní nádraží. It's generally only used for domestic trains, but it has a glorious history as one of the city's first major stations in the 19th century. Turn right and south and you'll end up in **Senovážné náměstí**, a square formerly named after President Klement Gottwald (some old-school Praguers still delight in calling it *Gottvaldák*).

Heading north on Havlíčkova, you'll soon reach Na Poříčí. If you take a right, you'll eventually come to the **Muzeum Hlavního môsta Prahy (Museum of the City of Prague**; *see p104*). A left, though, will take you back toward the Municipal House, past newly polished shops and the hip and airy **Café Dinitz** (*see p183*). Consumer fever can be felt as you reach the bottom of the street, where massive new shopping mall **Palladium** (*see*

SIGHTS

p192) has recently replaced a 17th-century barracks. Sharing the building with Dinitz is the YMCA; if it's open, stop in for a look at a working paternoster, a cross between a dumb waiter and a lift that's a thrilling fright to ride.

Muchovo muzeum
Mucha Museum
Kaunický palác, Panská 7, Prague 1 (221 451 333/www.mucha.cz). Metro Můstek/tram 3, 9, 14, 24. **Open** 10am-6pm daily. **Admission** 120 Kč. **No credit cards. Map** p329 N5.

This museum is dedicated to Alfons Mucha (1860-1939), perhaps the most famous of all Czech visual artists. Known for his commercial work such as mass-produced decorative panels and posters for Sarah Bernhardt's theatre performances, Mucha exercised his greatest influence through his *Encyclopaedia for Craftsmen* (1902), a catalogue of art nouveau decorative elements, forms and designs. Mucha created a stained-glass window for St Vitus's Cathedral (*see p64*) and the *Slavonic Epic*, a series of gigantic narrative oil paintings that now reside in Moravský Krumlov castle, south-west of Brno. The museum also displays lithographs, drawings, sketches and notebooks from Mucha's days in Paris.

Muzeum Hlavního města Prahy
Museum of the City of Prague
Na Poříčí 52, Prague 1 (224 816 773/www. muzeumprahy.cz). Metro Florenc/tram 3, 8, 24. **Open** 9am-6pm Tue-Sun. **Admission** 110 Kč; 180 Kč family; free under-6s; 1 Kč 1st Thur of mth reductions. **No credit cards. Map** p329 Q2.

Antonín Langweil spent 11 years during the early 1800s building an incredibly precise, room-sized paper model of Prague. Now this museum's prize exhibit, it's the only complete depiction of what the city looked like before the Jewish ghetto was ripped down. Other displays follow the city's development from pre-history through to the 17th century, with some English labels provided in the rooms devoted to medieval and later events. The upstairs galleries host temporary exhibitions and the original of the Josef Mánes painting reproduced inside the Old Town Hall's Astronomical Clock tower (*see p87*).

★ Muzeum komunismu
Museum of Communism
Na Příkopě 10, Prague 1 (224 212 966/www. muzeumkomunismu.cz). Metro Můstek/tram 3, 9, 14, 24. **Open** 9am-9pm daily. **Admission** 180 Kč. **Credit** AmEx, MC, V. **Map** p328 M5.

Opened in 2001 as the first enterprise of its kind in the country, this museum puts the communist era in historical perspective through its ample archive photographs, each with explanatory texts, as well as hundreds of relics on display. Co-founded by American restaurateur and long-time Prague resident Glenn Spicker, the museum has mock-ups of a schoolroom from the period, with Czechoslovak and Soviet flags hanging side by side and a Russian lesson on the blackboard. More eerie is the interrogation room, just like those used by the Czechoslovak secret police. And to keep Lenin spinning, the museum is directly above a McDonald's and shares a floor in the building with a casino.
▶ *Spicker runs U Malého Glena; see p251.*

Hlavní nádraží. *See p102.*

INSIDE TRACK
CUBISM LIGHTS THE WAY

Elsewhere in the world, cubism was confined to painting. In the Czech Republic, though, it shaped everything from furniture to the bizarre, solitary creation outside the **Kostel Panny Marie Sněžné (Church of Our Lady of the Snows**; *see below*) – the world's only cubist lamp-post.

SOUTHERN NOVÉ MĚSTO

Back at Wenceslas Square, 28.Října stretches from the north end of the square south-west to Jungmannovo náměstí, where you'll find several notable buildings. Built between 1923 and 1925, the **Palác Adria (Adria Palace)** at no.28 is perhaps the city's finest example of rondocubist architecture. And don't miss the **Kostel Panny Marie Sněžné (Church of Our Lady of the Snows)**, especially its towering, awe-inspiring black-and-gold Baroque altarpiece. In the church's side chapel (accessible via a door on the right in the rear), you can gawp at a trio of gruesome crucifixes.

Outside, a path leads to the **Františkánská zahrada (Franciscan Gardens)**, an oasis of green and calm – unless it's a sunny day, when it will probably be full of teens, grannies, kids and couples. Heading west from Jungmannovo náměstí along Národní, meanwhile, will bring you to **Tesco** (*see p191*); expats gather here to forage for non-Czech grocery items. Gather here after clubbing to catch a night tram (*see p301*).

Across Spálená, you'll find **Café Louvre** (*see p185*), accessible via a lobby and staircase entrance from the street. The Louvre was once a hangout for Prague's literary and intellectual crowd. Cleaned up and modernised, it's now an ideal place to people-watch and mix with locals.

Further down the street is another fine café: the **Slavia** (*see p182*), a famous dissident meeting place during the 1970s and '80s, and a haven for literati such as Tolstoy and Kafka for a century before that. There's no plotting now and precious little inspiration – just a pricey menu and one of the best riverside views in town. Grab a window seat for a glamour shot of the castle after dark.

Next to the entrance for Café Louvre, you'll notice photos of Bill Clinton playing saxophone in basement jazz club **Reduta** (*see p251*). Little of that vibe has been left behind, though – the club feels like it's still run by the old regime. For a funkier hangout, try the adjoining **Rock Café** (*see p248*) or the basement club **Vagon** (*see p250*) across the way at no.25.

Národní ends at the Vltava river, where the breathtaking **Národní divadlo (National Theatre**; *see p271*) anchors the nation's culture. Topped by a crown of gold, and with statues of bucking stallions lining the balustrade, the building is a product and symbol of the fervour of 19th-century Czech nationalism. It took 20 years to raise the money to begin construction, and 13 years (1868-81) to build it. The building was gutted by fire almost immediately. However, construction started all over again, and proved a lot quicker second time around: the building eventually opened in 1883 with *Libuše*, an opera written for the occasion by Smetana. The hall is only open for performances, but it's a wonderful place, perfect for a swish night on the town. A recent effort to restore the weather-battered horses and chariots above the entrance has helped keep this gem in good shape.

Just before you reach the National Theatre, you'll see its bastard offspring: the **Laterna Magika (Magic Lantern**; *see p272*). A frosted-glass monstrosity, it was built between 1977 and 1981 as a communist showpiece. The interior is made from expensive imported marble – the floors, walls, even the banisters – and every seat is upholstered in leather, now well worn and patched. The black light shows and other multimedia fare that play here are not worth the admission, perhaps in keeping with an unintentionally ironic socialist relic.

Directly across the street, however, is a high neo-Renaissance delight, in the shape of the **Akademie Věd (Czech Academy of Sciences)**. The building was constructed between 1858 and 1862 as a Czech savings bank; fashioned after St Mark's Library in Venice, the grand façade is crowned with an allegorical figure receiving the savings of the people. Inside, stone lions guard the entrance hall; in the spacious library beyond, ornate female figures of Economy and Thrift watch over the stacks. The academy itself remains a prestigious institution; since 1989, Czech scientists have made major breakthroughs in AIDS and cancer treatment research, as well as in the field of high-tech optics.

INSIDE TRACK
TAKE TO THE WATER

In the days before slacking became an art form, Berlioz came to Slovanský Island and was appalled at the 'idlers, wasters and ne'er-do-wells' who congregated on it. With a recommendation like that, it's hard to resist visiting the outdoor café or spending a few lazy hours in one of the rowing boats for hire.

SIGHTS

Wanted. Jumpers, coats and people with their knickers in a twist.

From the people who feel moved to bring us their old books and CDs, to the people fed up to the back teeth with our politicians' track record on climate change, Oxfam supporters have one thing in common. They're passionate. If you've got a little fire in your belly, we'd love to hear from you. Visit us at **oxfam.org.uk**

Be Humankind ⊗ Oxfam

Slovanský Island & south along the river

Following the river south takes you past **Slovanský ostrov (Slovanský Island)**. Look out for a fine statue of Božena Němcová, as seen on the front of the 500 Kč note. As the author of *pohádky*, a literary form akin to fairy-tales that's still dear to most adult Czechs' hearts, she's one of the most beloved figures in the canon. The island is home to **Žofín** (224 934 880, www.zofin.cz), a cultural centre housed in a large yellow building dating from the 1880s that hosted tea dances and concerts until just before World War II. The schedule offers concerts and lectures; you'll also find one of the sweetest riverside beer gardens in Prague.

At the southern tip of the island is **Galerie Mánes** (*see p232*), a 1930s functionalist building oddly attached to a medieval water tower. Named for Josef Mánes, the 19th-century artist and nationalist, the building also houses a restaurant and dance club. The intelligentsia gathered here between the wars; in 1989, this was where the Civic Forum churned out posters and leaflets. Some of that spirit lives on in the gallery's shows, which mostly feature contemporary Czech artists.

Back on the riverside, continuing south along Masarykovo nábřeži brings you to the corner of Resslova and the **Tančící dům (Dancing Building**; *see p47*), a collaboration between Czech architect Vlado Milunić and American architect Frank Gehry that was completed in 1996. Also known as 'Fred and Ginger' – he's the rigid vertical half, she's the swaying glass partner – the project presaged Gehry's later, more prominent work, such as the Guggenheim Museum in Bilbao. According to the American, the original inspiration for the pinch in the middle of the glass tower came from a desire to protect a neighbour's view of Prague Castle.

Two blocks further south, **Palackého náměstí** is dominated by a huge Stanislav Sucharda sculpture of 19th-century historian František Palacký, who took 46 years to write a history of the Czech people. The solemn Palacký sits on a giant pedestal, oblivious to the beauties and demons flying around him. Behind him rise

National Theatre. *See p105.*

the two modern spires of the altogether more ancient **Klášter Na Slovanech (Emmaus Monastery**), founded by Charles IV. The spires were added after the Baroque versions were destroyed by a stray Allied bomb during World War II.

Around Karlovo náměstí

The streets that lie between the National Theatre and the Dancing Building, moving east back toward Spálená, make up one of the least famous but most entertaining nightlife areas of the city. Sometimes referred to as SONA (an abbreviation of 'South of Národní'), this part of town often pulses with clubbers late into the night. But part of the neighbourhood's charm is its amorphous character – there are interesting pubs and restaurants on almost every street, although they never quite coalesce into a scene. Given that, and the tendency of these places to appear and disappear with alarming regularity, you always feel like you're exploring.

For many years, the **Globe Bookstore & Coffeehouse** on Pštrossova (*see p193*) was the centre of expat life in Prague, but now that's not so true. A quick glance at the menus posted outside the entrances of neighbouring restaurants shows one reason why: most are in both Czech and English, an indication of how English-friendly the central city has become.

SIGHTS

INSIDE TRACK
IT'S A MIRACLE!

Centuries ago, Karlovo náměstí was the site of Charles IV's relic fair. Once a year, Charles would wheel out his collection of sacred saints' skulls, toenails and underwear, causing cripples to throw down their crutches and the blind to miraculously regain their sight. Allegedly.

INSIDE TRACK
CAFÉ IMPERIAL

On Na příkopě, off Senovážné náměstí republiky, you'll find the splendid **Café Imperial**. This lovingly restored, high-ceilinged and high-spirited remnant of First Republic decadence boasts eye-popping, floor-to-ceiling ornamental porcelain tilework.

On the parallel street of Křemencova, **U Fleků** (*see p185*) remains a tourist mainstay, mostly for the busloads of Germans who disembark ready to quaff dark beer and sing along with accordion players. Its entrance is marked by a picturesque old clock hung like a tavern sign. But there are plenty of hip, relaxed and far better-value pubs nearby. Walk north to the corner of Opatovická and you'll see a host of places accommodating a variety of budgets and tastes. Most now cater to the huge numbers of American and Western European students doing semesters in Prague. Several, such as the dullish **H2O** (no.5, no phone) and **Cheers** (Křemencova 17, no phone) feature cocktail menus reflecting how worldly (or globally uniform) Prague has become, at least in its boozing. But the more you walk, the more places you'll discover – including, by day, some entertaining antique shops, such as **Hamparadi Antik Bazar** (*see p207*).

The south-east corner of the area drops you into **Karlovo náměstí**, a sprawling square that was once a cattle market. On the north end of the park that forms the area's spine, the handsome **Novoměstská radnice (New Town Hall)** dates back to the 14th century, though the current version was built during the 19th and early 20th centuries. In 1419 it was the site of Prague's first defenestration (*see p19*).

Across the square is the **Kostel sv. Ignáce (Jesuit Church of St Ignatius)**, a lush early Baroque affair with gold-trimmed cream, pink and orange stucco. Built between 1665 and 1670, it features a wonderful collection of angels in its arches and nave. At the south-west corner of the park sits the **Faustův dům (Faust House)**, an ornate 17th-century building that has more than a few legends attached to it. Edward Kelly, the earless English alchemist, once lived here, as did a poor student who was lured into making a Faustian pact with the Prince of Darkness. The impoverished kid was offered riches in exchange for his soul, which Satan then snatched through a hole in the roof.

Walking east on Ječná will bring you to no.14, where Dvořák died. Rather than staring at the plaque on the wall, go to the nearby **Muzeum**

Antonína Dvořáka (**Dvořák Museum**). It is quartered in a lovely summerhouse that was designed by Kilián Ignaz Dientzenhofer, the Villa Amerika, though these days it's surrounded by incongruous modern bits of concrete. Try to time your visit to coincide with a concert. At the end of the street is a museum of a very different sort – the **Muzeum policie ČR (Police Museum**; *see p110*). Brek, the stuffed wonder dog responsible for thwarting the defection of several hundred dissidents, has been given a decent burial, but there are still plenty of gruesome exhibits to delight the morbid.

If it all gets too much, seek sanctuary in the church next door, dedicated to Charlemagne, Charles IV's hero and role model. The octagonal nave of **Na Karlově** was completed in the 16th century, and for years the superstitious locals refused to enter it for fear that it would collapse. The gilt-frescoed walls inside were restored after the building was partially destroyed in the Prussian siege of 1757, but bullets can still be seen embedded in them. From the garden, there are extensive views across the Nusle Valley to Vyšehrad on the other side.

A few blocks to the west on Vyšehradská is the **Kostel sv. Jana na Skalce (Church of St John on the Rock)**, a fine Dientzenhofer structure built in the 1730s, perched at the top of an impressive double stairway. A little further south from that are the delightful if little-visited **Botanická zahrada (Botanical Gardens)**. Walking the other way on Ječná (west, towards the river), the street turns into Resslova and soon brings you to the Baroque **Kostel sv. Cyrila a Metoděje (Orthodox Cathedral of SS Cyril and Methodius)**.

★ Kostel sv. Cyrila a Metoděje
Orthodox Cathedral of SS Cyril & Methodius

Resslova 9, Prague 2 (224 916 100). Metro Karlovo náměstí/tram 4, 7, 9, 12, 14, 16, 18, 22, 24. **Open** *Nov-Feb* 10am-4pm Tue-Sun; *Mar-Oct* 10am-5pm Tue-Sun. At other times, ring the administrator's bell to be admitted. **Admission** 60 Kč; 30 Kč reductions. **No credit cards. Map** p330 K9.

Built in the 1730s, this Baroque church was taken over and restored by the Czech Orthodox Church in the 1930s. A plaque and memorial outside, together with numerous bullet holes, still attract tributes and flowers today, and are a clue to what happened inside during World War II.

On 29 December 1941, two Czech paratroopers who had trained in England were flown into Bohemia together with five colleagues in order to carry out, among other resistance acts, the assassination of Reinhard Heydrich, Reichsprotektor of Bohemia and Moravia and also the man who chaired the infamous 1942 Wannsee Conference on the Final

SIGHTS

Solution. Josef Gabčik and Jan Kubiš eventually ambushed Heydrich as he drove to work on 27 May 1942. Gabčik's gun jammed, but Kubiš threw a grenade at the car, which seriously wounded the SS man; he died in agony a week later.

Gabčik, Kubiš and their co-conspirators were given sanctuary in the crypt of the church, but they were eventually betrayed to the Germans. In the early hours of 18 June, 350 members of the SS and Gestapo surrounded the church and spent the night bombarding it with bullets and grenades. The men, who managed to survive until dawn, used their final bullets to shoot themselves. However, the incident didn't end there: the recriminations were swift, brutal and arbitrary. Hundreds of people, many of them Jews, were rounded up in Prague and shot immediately, and five villages and most of their inhabitants were liquidated, the most famous being Lidice.

The events brought about a turning point in the war, as Britain repudiated the Munich Agreement and Anthony Eden declared that Lidice had 'stirred the conscience of the civilised world'. The story of the assassination and its aftermath is movingly told in the crypt of the church, where the paratroopers made their last stand. You can also see the tunnel through which the assassins tried to dig their way out in a bid to reach the city sewer, coming within centimetres of reaching their goal.

Muzeum Antonína Dvořáka
Dvořák Museum
Villa Amerika, Ke Karlovu 20, Prague 2 (224 923 363). Metro IP Pavlova/tram 4, 6, 11, 16, 22, 34. **Open** *Apr-Sept* 10am-5.30pm Tue-Sun. *Oct-Mar* 9.30am-5pm Tue-Sun. **Admission** 50 Kč. **No credit cards. Map** p331 N10.

New Town Hall.

SIGHTS

Hidden away behind wrought-iron gates, the Dvořák Society's well-organised tribute to the most famous Czech composer is housed in an elegant early 18th-century Baroque summer palace, a red-and-ochre villa built by Kilián Ignaz Dientzenhofer in 1720 for Count Jan Václav Michna but later used as a cattle market.

Memorabilia and photographs make up the ground-floor display; upstairs are further exhibits and a recital hall, decorated with frescoes by Jan Ferdinand Schor. However, the concerts held here are the best way to appreciate the building's past as a retreat for the composer, with outdoor recitals in warm weather particularly evocative. Ironically, Dvořák actually spent very little time here: the composer's career was mainly established in the grand concert halls of Western Europe.

▶ For more on Prague's great composers, see p240.

Muzeum policie ČR
Police Museum
Ke Karlovu 1, Prague 2 (224 923 619/www. mvcr.cz/ministerstvo/muzeum.htm). Metro IP Pavlova/tram 6, 11. **Open** 10am-5pm Tue-Sun. **Admission** 30 Kč; 50 Kč family. **No credit cards. Map** p331 N11.

Prague's surprisingly interesting Police Museum resides in a former convent attached to the Karlov Church. The final room of the museum contains an arsenal of home-made weaponry that would please James Bond: sword sticks, makeshift pistols, pen guns and even a lethal lighter. Beforehand, in the section on crime detection techniques, you can take your own fingerprints or try to reconstruct events at a creepy scene-of-the-crime mock-up. Children love it, though parents are warned that some of the photographs are quite graphic. Most of the texts, unfortunately for visitors from abroad, are in Czech.

Revolt! Herna Blues

The death knell sounds for Prague's seedy drinking subculture.

If you keep your eyes open while walking through the streets of Prague, you may notice dozens of small and rather dingy-looking bars with neon lights and the word 'Herna' glowing dully in the window. These unattractive watering holes are a uniquely Czech institution – but they may be in danger of dying out before long.

The creation of the *herna* bar (literally, 'gambling house' in English) addressed a fundamental concern that has blighted the Czech psyche for years – where is it possible to drink and gamble any time of the day or night? Herna bars are open 24 hours a day, apart from on the occasions when they're briefly closed for cleaning. Some have been known to stagger their closing times, presumably so that punters can stagger themselves out of one and into another.

Still, if you enter one of these places, you may be surprised to hear that they're cleaned at all. Usually dark, smoky, full of fruit machines and populated by a gruff clientele, they don't exactly support the image that the Czech authorities want to project. As a consequence, there's been an ongoing battle in recent years between regulators and bar owners, and it seems the regulators may be slowly winning.

There are around 3,500 *herna* bars nationwide, many of which have been blamed for increasing levels of crime, late-night disturbances and a host of other gambling-related problems. Their existence drags down the image of the neighbourhood in which they sit, and house prices come down with it.

In 2006, the Czech Senate attempted to do something about the problem of *herna* bars with an amendment that would have restricted the prevalence of gambling nationwide. The bill failed, effectively leaving individual municipalities to deal with the issue themselves. And so at the start of 2008, Prague City Hall made its own attempt to tackle the problem in its own backyard by passing legislation to limit the amount of time and locations slot machines can be operated in town.

New legislation has meant that it's no longer possible for any company to operate gambling machines inside public buildings, within 100 metres of schools or within 50 metres of municipal buildings. They've also been banned in locations with 'special significance', meaning historical places – basically, anywhere tourists are likely to find themselves.

The result of these new laws has had a major impact, virtually halting the growth of the *herna* trade. Buoyed by the results of this move and the growing popularity of Prague as a tourist destination, it seems the future for low-rent gaming bars looks bleak. However, intrepid tourists can still experience this uniquely Czech institution in Nové Město at such venues as **Happy Day** (Václavské náměstí 35) and **Tipgames** (Václavské náměstí 56).

SIGHTS

Further Afield

Parks to loll in, art on the rise, and urbanites gaining ground.

Although the visual pull of Prague Castle and the commercial attractions of Wenceslas Square keep most visitors on the same well-worn tracks, the city's outlying districts provide a welcome glimpse behind the tourist clichés as a reward to people stepping off the tram lines. **Holešovice** has all the social and cultural amenities a modern urbanite could want; **Dejvice** offers some of the last remnants of communist decor in Prague; **Smíchov** is where Mozart stayed (yes, there's a museum); and **Vyšehrad** is closely tied with the mythic past of the city.

A trip off the beaten path and across to where the crowds don't go can be an instructive and fascinating way to get under the city's skin.

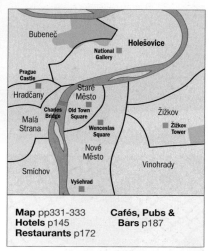

Map pp331-333	**Cafés, Pubs &**
Hotels p145	**Bars** p187
Restaurants p172	

HOLEŠOVICE, LETNÁ & TROJA

Lying across the Vltava river north of Staré Město, the rapidly transforming **Holešovice** district is the logical place to be for savvy apartment-buyers and all the gallerists, restaurateurs and bar owners that follow in their wake. Defined by a bend of the river, the locale has long had commercial and artistic gravitas, but it's currently coming alive as a magnet for urbanites who shy away from the main tourist tracks.

Many of its 19th-century buildings are still grimy, and Nádraží Holešovice, the bustling international train station, is as sleazy and feral as it gets in Prague. But a big, rambling park offers fresh air and shady trees that inspire workouts and slow-paced Sunday strolls. Meanwhile, former industrial spaces such as the Holešovická tržnice, once a rendering and slaughterhouse complex, are now transforming into commercial and cultural spaces; the nearby arts centre DOX (*see p116* **Industrial Art**) forms the leading edge of the revolution.

One of the area's main attractions sits towards the river on Kostelní: the **Národní technické muzeum (National Technical**

Museum; *see p114*). Its rather dull name belies a fascinating collection of Czechnology that instantly wows children. Housed in a constructivist building dating from 1938-41, it's currently undergoing a massive renovation that's due for completion in 2010 – part of the city's general upgrade to its enormous collection of museums.

Five minutes' walk east is Holešovice's main drag, **Dukelských hrdinů**. On it stands a sleeker constructivist building, the modern-looking **Veletržní palác**. Built in the mid 1920s to house the trade fairs that had long outgrown Výstaviště, it was gutted by fire in 1974, but has been splendidly restored. The white atrium rises seven storeys and is lined with sweeping guard rails, giving it the feel of a massive ocean liner. It's now home to the main building of the **Sbírka moderního a současného umění (National Gallery Collection of 19th-, 20th- and 21st-Century Art;** *see p114*).

A couple of minutes' walk to the north is **Výstaviště** (*see p117*), a fairground fronted by an unusual wrought-iron pavilion erected for the Jubilee Exhibition of 1891 and considered the first expression of art nouveau in the city. Tragically, its south wing was gutted by fire

Time Out Prague **111**

Vyšehrad. *See p118*.

Lofty Ambitions

Holešovice's revival continues with the emergence of industrial living.

The **První Pražský Měšťanský Pivovar** brewery in Holešovice was set up in 1895 to compete with the established beer-making enterprises in Pilsen and Velké Popovice, another historic brewing town in South Bohemia. The success of the upstart brewery was far from guaranteed, but it soon cemented its place in the city's drinking lives. Before and after World War I, the brewery put out millions of gallons of popular 15-degree Ležák Primátor beer and the sweeter, darker Kardinál.

After the communist coup in 1948, the brewery was consolidated into a large, centrally planned collective of breweries, which did no favours to fans of the famous beers. For a few brief salad years after the Velvet Revolution in 1989, the dark beer flowed once again from the mammoth Holešovice plant, but the free market proved too treacherous. The brewery closed in the 1990s – and the hulking industrial space has now been converted in order to allow a new generation of Prague homebuyers a shot at cool urban living.

Loft apartments are nothing new in Central Europe, of course. Berlin was at the forefront of the trend in the '70s, at the same time that New Yorkers were discovering the wonders of the Bowery (once they could work out how to heat the cavernous spaces, of course). Fashion-conscious young Czechs have shunned industrial spaces until recently, perhaps because of scarcity of modern apartments under the old regime. But they now seem to be waking up to the idea of moving into spaces with such inherent charisma.

The city's Karlín district, another once-bleak industrial zone, has seen more and more such conversions, although few have successfully incorporated as many elements of the original buildings and its atmosphere as the brewery conversion. Star architects Frank Gehry and Jean Nouvel, who designed the Zlatý Anděl building in Smíchov, have both been involved in the reconstruction of the landmark complex, part of a concept that called for three new buildings alongside renovations that integrated the original structures and gave rise to offices, retail space, apartments and lofts.

Perhaps convinced by the computer-animated apartment dweller seen lounging contentedly in one of the new units at www.holesovickypivovar.cz, contemplating the meaning of 'freedom' and 'good light' in his personal life, eager customers have been queuing up and making downpayments for the 155 spaces. That would seem to make it official: in Prague, at long last, concrete's cool again.

in late 2008, but workers were scrambling to get it rebuilt fast in order that it could be returned to its role as host to trade fairs of every description. In the Lapidárium, and fortunately undamaged, you'll find an intriguing collection of reject monuments that once stood around the city. But don't go expecting much laughable communist-era public art: the collection is mainly made up of historic Baroque and Gothic statuary, including most of the original statues from Charles Bridge (those there now are almost all copies; *see p90*) that were moved here years ago to protect them from the elements.

Beyond the pavilion is **Lunapark**, where you'll find a rollercoaster and a Ferris wheel. During February's traditional St Matthew's Fair, some serious rides that offer the latest technologies in propelling riders skyward roll in from abroad too. It's always a favourite with local teens. The rides provide fine views over the woody environs of **Stromovka**, a park to the west that was laid out by Rudolf II in the 16th century as a place where he could commune with nature. Rudolf's favoured companion was English alchemist John Dee, who got the job when he claimed to understand the language of the birds and the one Adam and Eve spoke in Eden. Today, the leafy park makes a wonderful spot for a stroll or picnic, though you may have to dodge the hordes of speeding in-line skaters.

A 20-minute walk north of Stromovka (or bus no.112 from Metro Nádraží Holešovice) brings you to the elaborate **Trojský zámek** (**Troja Château**; *see p114*), restored after suffering massive damage from the floods of 2002. The inmates of **Prague Zoo** (*see p217*) across the road, rebuilt and expanded since the floods, can only curse their historical mistiming – at Troja, the count's horses were provided with a vast, sumptuous stable block with marble floors, decorated with frescoes of their noble forebears.

Just south of Stromovka, meanwhile, lie two of the city's hotbeds of late-night lifestyling: **Fraktal** (*see p187*), a thriving art bar where you'll find media artists and affable international drunks sitting around hand-carved furnishings, and **La Bodega Flamenca** (*see p187*), a Czech-owned cellar-haven of sangria-sipping and one of the area's best after-hours refuelling options. For some of Prague's best clubbing, try **Mecca** (*see p255*), on the eastern side of the district, after warming up at groovy art bar the **Cross Club** (*see p254*).

If you need a breath of fresh air, take a half-hour walk back to Staré Město via the sedate embassy-land of **Bubeneč**, just to the west of these bars and clubs, then ramble on past the **AC Sparta** stadium (*see p261*) and through **Letenské sady** (**Letná park**). This was where the biggest demonstration of 1989 took place, attended by nearly a million people. Its location is currently a massive construction site, where the city is working on underground traffic and parking relief. Letná features its own hot hangout: **Výletná** (*see p187*), which masquerades as a great garden barbecue pub.

Národní technické muzeum
National Technical Museum
Kostelní 42, Holešovice, Prague 7 (220 399 111/www.ntm.cz). Metro Hradčanská or Vltavská/tram 8, 25, 26. **Open** closed until 2010. **Admission** call for details. **No credit cards.** **Map** p332 D3.

Don't let the mundane name put you off. When it reopens in 2010, this unexpected treasure trove will feature the latest technology. Before its closure it contained a fascinating collection, enjoyable for children and adults, tracing the development of technology and science in Czechoslovakia – which, until the stultifying communist era, was among Europe's most innovative and industrially advanced nations. The Transport Hall contains steam trains, vintage motorcycles, racing cars and biplanes, while the claustrophobic 'mine' in the basement has sinister coal-cutting implements in place in mock tunnels. Guided tours of the mine are available in English. There's also an extensive photography and cinematography section, and a collection of rare astronomical instruments. Call or check online for precise details of its reopening date.

★ Sbírka moderního a současného umění
National Gallery Collection of 19th-, 20th- & 21st-Century Art
Veletržní palác, Dukelských hrdinů 47, Holešovice, Prague 7 (224 301 111/www.ngprague.cz). Metro Vltavská/tram 5, 12, 17. **Open** 10am-6pm Tue-Sun. **Admission** 160 Kč; *all 4 floors* 250 Kč. *Temporary exhibitions* 50 Kč; free under-10s. **No credit cards. Map** p332 E3.

This surprisingly modern-looking building, in reality a functionalist wonder designed by Oldřich Tyl and Josef Fuchs and opened in 1929, was designed to host trade fairs. It hasn't hosted any such events for more than 50 years, though; since its 1995 reconstruction, it's housed the National Gallery's collections of modern and contemporary art.

Highlights of the 19th-century collection include the paintings of Karel Purkyně, informed by close observation and a thorough knowledge of old master techniques, and the mystical strain of 19th-century Czech art, represented by symbolists Max Švabinský and František Bílek. There's also an impressive collection of Czech art from 1900 to 1930: groundbreaking abstract artist František Kupka is well represented, along with Czech cubists, surrealists and social art from the 1920s. It's hard to imagine a better collection of Bohemian art from 1930 to the present, including surrealist works by Toyen and Jindřich Štýrský. And elsewhere, there are many chilling but sometimes amusing works of Stalin-era socialist realism and the existentialist Art Informel pieces from around the same period.

The museum is the venue for the International Triennial of Contemporary Art (*see p235*). It also hosts a show of finalists for the NG 333 Prize for artists under the age of 33, which the gallery started in 2007 as a counterpart to the well-established Jindřich Chalupecký Award for under-35s.

Trojský zámek
Troja Château
U Trojského zámku 1, Holešovice, Prague 7 (283 851 614). Metro Nádraží Holešovice/bus 112. **Open** *Apr-Oct* 10am-6pm Tue-Thur, Sun; 1-7pm Fri; 10am-7pm Sun. *Mar-Nov* 10am-5pm Sat, Sun. **Admission** 120 Kč; 60 Kč reductions. **No credit cards.**

You'd be hard-pressed to envisage the riches contained within this amazing pile from the wrong side of its sizeable walls. And indeed, it's too often eclipsed by the more obviously appealing zoo next door. But the megalomaniacal Count Šternberg, a major beneficiary of spoils after the Thirty Years' War, created a monument here that still competes with its surroundings fairly well. An 18th-century Czech nobleman, Šternberg was anxious to demonstrate his loyalty to the Habsburg emperor and literally moved mountains to do so. The hillside had to be dug out to align his villa with the royal hunting park of Stromovka, still accessible via a footbridge from the embankment, and the distant spires of St Vitus's Cathedral. The result, built by a French architect and Italian craftsmen, is a paean to the Habsburgs, modelled on a classical Italian villa and surrounded by formal gardens in the French style.

The interior is replete with beautiful trompe l'oeil murals. On the massive external staircase, classical gods hurl the rebellious titans down into a dank and dreary grotto. In the Grand Hall, meanwhile, the Habsburgs enjoy a well-earned victory over the

SIGHTS

Akropolis. *See p119*.

Industrial Art

DOX places modern-day art in Prague firmly on the bleeding edge.

Although **Veletržní Palace** (*see p111*) was built as a trade fair showplace, its role as an important art venue actually dates back to its earliest years. Following glowing reviews in New York for the *Slav Epic*, his collection of 20 massive historic tableaux portraying great pan-Slavic myths, the acclaimed Czech art nouveau painter Alfons Mucha put the panels on show here in 1928.

The event should have been a high point of Czech culture in a newly formed sovereign state that was enjoying its first decade. Instead, as Derek Sayer explains in *The Coasts of Bohemia*, the reception was lukewarm. Mucha, a fixture of fin-de-siècle Czech and, later, Parisian art, was apparently not modern enough. Prague audiences preferred more forward-looking pieces, such as Otto Gutfreund's streamlined sculpture and Jan Zrzavý's surrealist portraits.

That the Palace eventually became the home of the Czech Republic's modern art collection would have surely pleased all those progressives back in the inter-war years. But one can only imagine what they would have to say about the group of still more contemporary artists who've moved into yet another industrial space in Holešovice and declared it the territory of the kind of art that even the National Gallery isn't ready to exhibit.

DOX (*see p229*), as the new arts centre at Osadní and Vojtěšská streets is known, is leading a transformative art movement that is reshaping the city's most rapidly evolving district. Judging by the success of its hit opening in late 2008 with a show titled 'Welcome to Capitalism!', there's no question that Czech art audiences are as eager for fresh ideas as they ever were. The centre's manifesto sets out its ideals with admirable clarity: 'Today, when more and more people tend to think dangerously alike, art's capacity to suspend, even for a moment, our habitual ways of seeing may be its greatest value.'

First conceived in 2002 by Leoš Válka, along with partners Robert Aafjes, Richard Fuxa and Václav Dejčmar, the 6,250-square-metre building is the work of architect Ivan Kroupa, who transformed the former metal factory into a bold, glass-walled collection of exhibition and meeting spaces. The sense of celebration six years later when DOX threw open its doors and christened itself a 'living arts centre', a platform for Czech and international contemporary art, has been infectious. Poor old Mucha is surely spinning in his fabulously ornamental grave.

infidel Turks, a fascinating though slightly ludicrous example of illusory painting that constitutes Troja's main attraction. To see it, you'll have to don huge red slippers to protect the marble floors.
► *For the zoo next door, see p217.*

Výstaviště

U Výstaviště, Prague 7 (220 103 111/484/ www.incheba.cz). Metro Nádraží Holešovice/tram 5, 12, 17. **Open** 2-9pm Tue-Fri; 10am-9pm Sat, Sun. **Admission** 20 Kč Sat, Sun; free under-6s; free Tue-Fri. **No credit cards. Map** p332 D1.

Built from curvaceous expanses of wrought iron and designed to house the Jubilee Exhibition of 1891, Výstaviště played a key role in Prague's art nouveau movement. During the late 1940s, the building served as the site of various communist congresses, but it's now mainly used for trade shows for industries that range from information technology to pornography.

In early 2009, the main hall collapsed at one end. For the time being, you'll be deprived of the interior's vivid stained glass and floral decorations, but the fairgrounds are still worth a visit if you're not troubled by the pounding pop music on the loudspeakers. The best view of what remains of the main hall's exterior is from the back, where a monumental modern fountain gushes kitschily at night in time to popular classics and accompanied by a light show. Nearby sit architectural oddities such as the Lapidárium and the delightfully dilapidated funfair Lunapark, which pulls in weekend crowds of Czech families.

DEJVICE & FURTHER WEST

Some of the most exclusive residences in the city are located in **Prague 6**, the suburbs that lie beyond Prague Castle. The area is filled with embassies and the former residences of court and republic retainers of all stripes. However, you'd be forgiven for assuming the worst from a quick visit to **Vítězné náměstí**, the rather desolate hub of the area.

Leading north from the square is the wide **Jugoslávských partyzánů (Avenue of Yugoslav Partisans)**, at the end of which you'll find the **Crowne Plaza Hotel** (Koulova 15, 296 537 111). Formerly known as the Hotel International, this monumental piece of 1950s socialist realism is one of the last remaining bastions of Marxist-Leninist decor in the city. The façade over the main entrance features Russian war heroes being greeted by grateful Czech peasants. However, juxtaposed with the bars inside the lobby, frequented by yuppies and well-heeled foreign business folk, the entrance is now a little out of place.

On the hill above the hotel are the **Přírodní památka Baba (Baba Villas)**, a colony of constructivist houses built after, and inspired by the huge success of, the 1927 Exhibition of Modern Living in Stuttgart. Under the guidance

INSIDE TRACK
URBAN ESCAPISM

North of the Hvězda Hunting Lodge, off Evropská, is the extensive and wonderfully wild **Divoká Šárka** nature park – a fine place to stroll, swim or cycle, away from the city crowds and fumes. In summer, there's a nude sunbathing area by the murky lake.

of Pavel Janák, all 33 houses were designed to provide simple but radical living spaces for ordinary families. However, they were quickly snapped up by leading figures of the Czech avant-garde. Many still retain their original fixtures and fittings; none, alas, are open to the public, but their exteriors are a must-see for any fans of modern architecture. To reach the estate, take bus 131 to U Matěje and walk up Matějská.

On the western fringe of the city, just north of Patočkova, set at Bělohorská, is the **Benediktinské arciopatství sv. Vojtěcha a sv. Markéty (Břevnov Monastery)**, inhabited by Benedictine monks since 993 and modelled on 'God's perfect workshop'. Since the Velvet Revolution, the monks have purged most traces of the Ministry of the Interior, which for the preceding four decades used the **Bazilika sv. Markéty (Basilica of St Margaret)** as a warehouse for its files on suspicious foreigners. The Romanesque church was remodelled by the Dientzenhofer father-and-son act in the early 18th century and is one of their most triumphant commissions, with a single high nave and unfussy interior.

Close by, near the terminus of tram route 22, a small stone pyramid marks the site of **Bílá Hora (White Mountain)**, the decisive first battle of the Thirty Years' War that was fought in 1620. In the park is the **Letohrádek Hvězda (Hvězda Hunting Lodge)**, a product of the Renaissance that was built in the 1550s for Archduke Ferdinand of Tyrol. Ferdinand was obsessed with numerology, and the building was conceived as an intellectual conundrum – the angular walls and roof are arranged in the pattern of a six-pointed star (*hvězda* in Czech).

SMÍCHOV & BARRANDOV

Since Mozart stayed here in 1787, **Smíchov** has undergone some substantial changes. Rapid industrialisation spoiled the ambience of the aristocracy's summer houses, and the area after 1989 was dominated by factories such as the still-busy Staropramen Brewery. In recent years, it has exploded with new developments – malls, multiplexes and office complexes.

However, a few remnants of proletarian glories are commemorated in a couple of surviving socialist realist murals in Anděl metro station. To get an idea of what Smíchov was once like, visit **Bertramka**, the house with lilac gardens that belonged to František and Josefína Dušek. It's now a museum to their most famous house guest, Wolfgang Amadeus Mozart.

South of Smíchov is **Barrandov**, the Czech version of Hollywood. On the cliffs below, there are even white Hollywood-style letters that spell out 'Barrande' – though this is actually in homage to the 19th-century geologist after whom the quarter takes its name. The vast movie studios built here in the 1930s have been the centre of the Czech film industry ever since.

Bertramka
Mozart Museum

Mozartova 169, Smíchov, Prague 5 (257 318 461/ 465/www.bertramka.com). Metro Anděl/tram 4, 7, 9, 10. **Open** *Apr-Oct* 9am-6pm daily. *Nov-Mar* 9.30am-4pm daily. **Admission** 110 Kč; free under-6s; concerts 390-450 Kč. **No credit cards**.
The lovely, almost pastoral Villa Bertramka, a former vineyard manor house that has now been restored to its 18th-century glory, seems a world apart from the modern hustle and bustle of the district in which it sits. It's easy to imagine Mozart strolling the two-tiered garden on the hill behind it, as the strains of *Don Giovanni*'s overture popped into his head the night before its 1787 première in the Nostitz Theatre (now the Estates Theatre; *see p245*). And indeed, Mozart stayed here several times as a guest of the villa's owners, composer František Dušek and his wife Josefína. These days, Bertramka showcases memorabilia relating to Mozart and the Dušeks, including personal keepsakes, musical instruments, manuscripts and letters. His music still inhabits the place, an invariable feature of the many concerts here; those in the open air, in particular, are something to savour. The courtyard café remains relatively undisturbed by tour groups.
▶ *For concerts at Bertramka, see p242.*

Zámek Zbraslav
Zbraslav Château

Bartošova 2, Zbraslav, Prague 5 (257 921 638). Metro Smíchovské nádraží, then 129, 241 or 243 bus to Zbraslavské náměstí. **Open** 10am-6pm Tue-Sun. **Admission** 80 Kč; 120 Kč family. **No credit cards**.
This Baroque house showcases the National Gallery's surprisingly extensive collection of Asian art. The Chinese and Japanese holdings are particularly good, but there's also a smattering of Indian, South-east Asian and Islamic pieces, plus a handful of Tibetan scrolls. It's a 30-minute bus ride from the metro, but the grounds of the museum, housed in another former palace, make the trip worthwhile. There are also a few interactive art activities for kids.

VYŠEHRAD

The rocky outcrop south of Nové Město, **Vyšehrad** is where all the best Prague myths were born. It's where Libuše, the mythic mother of Prague, fell into a trance and sent her horse out into the countryside to find a suitable spouse – the ploughman called Přemysl, after whom the early Bohemian kings take their name. The more prosaic story is that a castle was founded here in the first half of the tenth century, and enjoyed a period of importance when King Vratislav II (1061-92) built a royal palace on the rock. Within 50 years, though, the Přemyslid rulers had moved back to Prague Castle and Vyšehrad's short-lived period of political pre-eminence was over.

The easiest way to reach Vyšehrad is to take the metro to the Vyšehrad stop, under the enormous road bridge spanning the **Nusle Valley**. Built in the 1970s, the bridge was hailed as a monument to socialism, a description that was hastily dropped when chunks of concrete began falling on passing pedestrians and it became the most popular spot for suicides in the city. Walk away from the towering **Corinthia** (Kongresová 1, Prague 4, 261 191 111) and past the unappealing, monolithic **Kongresové centrum** (**Congress Centre**; *see p247*), completed in 1980 as the supreme architectural expression of the Soviet-imposed 'normalisation' years, then head through the Baroque gateway into the park. The information centre (V pevnosti, no phone) to the right can provide maps of the area. One of the first sights you'll pass is the over-restored **Rotunda sv. Martina** (**Rotunda of St Martin**). Dating from the second half of the 11th century, the Rotunda is the oldest complete Romanesque building in Prague.

There's been a church at Vyšehrad since the 14th century, but the original was apparently irrevocably damaged when Lucifer, angered by an insubordinate cleric, threw three large rocks through the roof. The granite slabs (known as the Devil Pillars) can be found close to the Old Deanery, but the holes are gone. Joseph Mocker's neo-Gothic **Kostel sv. Petra a Pavla** (**Church of SS Peter & Paul**) dates from the beginning of the 20th century. Restoration has brought out the best of the splendid polychrome interior, decked out with art nouveau-style saints and decorative motifs.

Next door is **Slavín**, Vyšehrad's cemetery. Conceived by the 19th-century National Revival movement, it's the last resting place of the cream of the country's arts worthies: composers Dvořák and Smetana, writers Karel Čapek and Jan Neruda, painter Mikoláš Aleš. The Slavín (meaning 'pantheon') was designed by Antonín Wiehl and jointly commemorates further artistic big cheeses such as painter Alfons Mucha and sculptor Josef Václav Myslbek. Surrounded by Italianate arcades, the cemetery contains an abundance of fine memorials, many displaying art nouveau influences. On the south side of SS Peter & Paul are four monumental sculptural groups by Myslbek depicting mythological heroes from Czech history; the couple nearest to the church are Přemysl and Libuše. The park extends to the cliff edge overlooking the Vltava, affording lovely views across to Prague Castle.

If you continue down the hill from Vyšehrad along Přemyslova, you'll find one of the city's most outstanding pieces of cubist architecture, a corner apartment block designed by Josef Chochol at Neklanova 30 (1911-13).

VINOHRADY & ŽIŽKOV

Vinohrady came into existence in what the communist guidebooks called the period of Bourgeois Capitalism, and its magnificent fin-de-siècle tenements have been extensively restored (and sold off by developers).

The heart of the neighbourhood is **Náměstí Míru**, a round 'square' spiked by the twin spires of the neo-Gothic **Kostel sv. Ludmily (Church of St Ludmila)** and faced by the **Divadlo Na Vinohradech (Vinohrady Theatre)**. The **Radost FX** café, gallery and nightclub complex (*see p257*), still one of the city's premier clubs, is nearby on Bělehradská; on a different note, the **Café Medúza** (*see p188*) on quiet Belgická is one of the city's cosiest – if most threadbare – winter hideouts.

The area south of Náměstí Miru has become a centre of Prague's gay scene, with bars, clubs and pensions (*see p237*). The main artery of Vinohrady, however, is **Vinohradská**, a little further north. Formerly called Stalinova třída, after one of history's greatest mass-murderers, it saw some of 1968's fiercest street battles against Warsaw Pact troops. Art nouveau apartment blocks line Vinohradská, looking on to the **Nejsvětější Srdce Páně (Church of the Sacred Heart)** on Nàměsti Jiřího Z Poděbrad. The church was built between 1928 and 1932 by Josip Plečnik, the pioneering

Slovenian architect who also redid Prague Castle; dominated by its huge glass clock, it's still one of the most inspiring pieces of modern architecture in the city. Fans of ecclesiastical modernism, if such creatures exist, might also appreciate Pavel Janák's 1930s **Husův sbor (Hussite Church)** on the corner of U Vodárny and Dykova, as well as Josef Gočár's functionalist **Kostel sv. Václava (Church of St Wenceslas)** on Náměstí Svatopluka Čecha.

Near Plečnik's church is the scary **Žižkov Tower** (*see p121*), completed in 1989. A couple of nearby venues worthy of note are **Hapu**, a contender for top living-room cocktail bar, and cheap and Czech **U Sadu** (*for both, see p190*), which offers well-located outside seating in summer. Nearby, you'll also find the ever-popular **Akropolis** (*see p247*).

Down the hill to the north and east is **Žižkov**. Notorious for its rowdy pubs and large Romany population, the area has also become known for quirky outlandishness. More surprising, perhaps, is that this working-class district became a popular interment place for post-war communist presidents. The massive **Národní památník (National Memorial;** on top of **Vítkov Hill** is a mausoleum with the largest equestrian statue in the world, a 16,764-kilogram (37,000-pound) effigy of Hussite hero Jan Žižka. Weaknesses in the bronze have been detected, so restoration was in progress at the time this guide went to press. The corpses of the communist presidents were ejected from the mausoleum in 1990 and reburied elsewhere or cremated; it's now an eerie place that sometimes hosts raves (consult www.techno.cz/party for advance information).

Further east on Vinohradská are two cemeteries. **Olšanské hřbitovy (Olšany Cemetery**; *see p121*) is the largest in Prague, extending from the Flora metro station to Jana Želivského; it includes a Garden of Rest, where the Red Army soldiers who died liberating Prague are buried. Since 1989, the cemetery has suffered from graffiti and grave-robbing. Next door is the **Židovské hřbitovy (Jewish Cemetery**; not to be confused with the Old Jewish Cemetery, *see p97*). Fans of Kafka come to pay respects at his simple grave (follow the sign at the entrance by Želivského station; it's 200 metres down the row by the southern wall). Though the cemetery was founded in 1890, only a fraction of the space has been used since World War II, and the neglect is obvious.

Národní památník
National Memorial

U památníku 1900, Prague 3 (222 781 676).
Metro Florenc/bus 133, 168, 207. **Open** times vary (advance booking required, min 20 people). **Admission** varies. **Map** p333 C1.

SIGHTS

Although its interiors are closed until October 2009 for restoration, you'll get a vivid sense of the National Memorial simply from walking around this impressive monument. A hulking mass of concrete that's one of the city's best-known and least-liked landmarks, the immense constructivist block and enormous equestrian statue high up on Vitkov Hill can be seen from around the city.

The memorial was built in 1925 by Jan Zázvorka as a dignified setting for the remains of the legionnaires who fought against the Austro-Hungarian Empire in World War I. In 1953, though, the communist regime turned it into a mausoleum for Heroes of the Working Class. The mummified remains of Klement Gottwald, the first communist president, were kept here, tended by scientists who unsuccessfully tried to preserve his body for display (Lenin-style) before the project was abandoned and the decaying remains were fobbed off on Gottwald's family in 1990. In front of the memorial stands the massive equestrian statue of one-eyed General Žižka; he was the scourge of 14th-century Catholics and the darling of the communists, who subsequently adopted him in an effort to establish genuine Bohemian credentials.

Olšanské hřbitovy
Olšany Cemetery
Vinohradská 153 at Jana Želivského, Prague 3 (272 011 113). Metro Flora or Želivského. **Open** dawn-dusk daily. **Map** p333 E3.

The overgrown yet beautiful Olšany Cemetery contains grand memorials to two unlikely bedfellows: Klement Gottwald, the first communist president, who died after catching a cold at Stalin's funeral; and Jan Palach, the most famous anti-communist martyr, who set fire to himself in Wenceslas Square in 1969. In death their fates have been oddly linked, as neither has been allowed to rest in peace. Palach was buried here in 1969, but his grave became such a focus of dissent that the authorities disinterred his body and reburied it deep in the Bohemian countryside. In 1990, though, he was dug up and brought back to Olšany. His grave is to the right of the main entrance.

Gottwald, too, travelled in death. His remains were first housed in the National Memorial (*see p119*), where scientists tried to mummify him. But following the Velvet Revolution, his corpse was removed and returned to his family. His current resting place is harder to locate, hidden away as it is in section five and sharing a mass grave with various other discredited party members.

★ Žižkov Tower
Mahlerovy sady, Prague 3 (267 005 775/www.tower.cz). Metro Jiřího z Poděbrad/tram 5, 9, 26. **Open** 10am-11.30pm daily. **Admission** 60 Kč; free under-5s. **No credit cards. Map** p333 C2.

This huge, thrusting, three-pillared television tower has long been dubbed the *Pražský pták*, or 'Prague Prick', by local admirers. Seemingly modelled on a Soyuz rocket ready for blast-off, or maybe something out of *Thunderbirds*, it's been more of a hit with space-crazy visitors than with the locals. In recent years, it made a guest appearance in *Blade II*.

The tower was planned under the communists (who tore up part of the adjacent Jewish Cemetery to make room for it) and completed in early 1990. However, no sooner had it started operating in 1990 than it came under attack from nearby residents who claimed it was guilty of, among other things, jamming foreign radio waves and giving their children cancer. More than 20 TV channels broadcast from behind the white plastic shielding that defends against the elements, while transmitters lower down deal with radio stations and emergency services.

You can take a lift up to the eighth-floor viewing platform or have a drink in the fifth-floor café. However, in many ways standing at the base and looking up the 216m (709ft) of grey polished steel is an even more scary experience. The tower is also now the home of some public art, with several large black babies crawling on its exterior. The intriguing, rather disturbing *Miminka* are the work of Czech bad-boy artist and satirist David Černý.

JIŽNÍ MĚSTO & HÁJE

To the south and east of the city centre lies the wilderness of **Prague 4**. Though parts of the area are very old and beautiful, the postcode has come to mean only one thing for Praguers: *paneláky*. The Czech word *panelák* refers to tower blocks made from prefabricated concrete panels, erected in Prague 4 in the 1960s and '70s as a cheap solution to the post-war housing crisis. **Jižní Město (Southern Town)** has the greatest concentration. While there have been intermittent efforts to individualise the buildings with pastel exteriors, this has only made the district look like a nightmarish toy town.

Háje, the last metro stop on the red Line C, is a good place in which to see the best of the worst. Before 1989, Háje used to be known as Kosmonautů, a nod in the direction of the USSR; a rather humorous sculpture of two cosmonauts stands outside the metro station. Nearby is **Hostivař Reservoir** (Prague 15; take tram 22 or 26 to the end of the line), a popular swimming spot that's full of sun-seekers in summer.

INSIDE TRACK
CINEMATIC SNACKS

In Háje, the nine-screen **Galaxie** (Arkalycká 877, Háje, Prague 4, 267 900 540, www.cinemacity.cz) is Central Europe's first multiplex cinema. It's also possibly the only place in the world that sells pork-flavoured popcorn.

Consume

Art Deco.
See p207.

Hotels

History and modernity are on the menu, but only if you book ahead...

Over recent years, Prague hotel prices have grown into a sizeable bubble. The good news for visitors is that it finally seems to have burst. Although the strength of the crown continues to make the high life in the Czech capital less attainable than it once was, increased competition has led to a number of noticeable improvements in the city's hotels. The notoriously erratic Prague service remains a catch, of course, but many respected operations have slashed room rates while simultaneously improving decor, amenities (Wi-Fi is now pretty much standard) and eating options. Notwithstanding the recent economic instability, it's a good time to visit the city.

STAYING IN PRAGUE

A majority of tourists come to Prague in search of history, and many find it in the city's grand old hotels. However, it's not all about tradition. The Czechs are well ahead of their Central and Eastern European counterparts in the style stakes, with modern, sometimes outlandishly 'designer' lodgings throughout the capital. The **Hostel Rosemary** appeals to latte-loving backpackers, while the **Ventana** lets those with more cash live out magazine-spread fantasies. Other, pricier new entries such as the **Savic** and the **Riverside** combine old-world elegance with modern appointments. And the flagship hotels such as the **Savoy** and **Le Palais** continue to refine their appeal.

After years of slim pickings, finding a room that sits somewhere between opulence and austerity is now an enjoyable and rewarding pursuit. Families can find deals at big names such as the **Mövenpick** and the **Marriott**, or family-owned inns including the **Residence Řetězova**; while couples can nestle without breaking the bank at cosy charmers such as the **Julian** and the **Hotel Anna**. Independent innkeepers are being squeezed by competitive forces, but those same forces also keep drawing new entrants to the game.

❶ Red numbers given in this chapter correspond to the location of each hotel on the street maps. *See pp326-333.*

Service at the city's higher-end hotels is comparable to that of any European capital, and all deluxe hotels have English-speaking staff. Many hotels can also arrange airport pick-ups for a fixed price. However, service is less impressive at some of the city's more modest hotels, where staff – not all of whom speak English – sometimes give the impression that it's your privilege to stay with them rather than their responsibility to look after their guests.

Booking a hotel

Prices and availability in Prague hotels can vary hugely with the seasons. Rooms are generally 20 to 40 per cent cheaper off-season, and many deluxe hotels give similarly sizeable discounts in July and August. A relative lack of business conferences and some chilly weather

INSIDE TRACK TAXI!

Prague's often-dubious service extends to the taxis that cluster around the entrances to many hotels, which often rip off tourists. If the hotel has its own fleet of cabs, it's a better option, but their charges may still be double those set for city taxis. The best bet of all is to call an honest taxi service yourself, such as AAA or Profi. For more on taxis and getting around in the city, *see pp300-302.*

Residence Hotel Green Lobster. *See p132.*

CONSUME

Domus Henrici.

CONSUME

combine to make the months from October to March, plus a few weeks in later summer, the most competitive times of the year for the city's top hotels. Hostels, meanwhile, tend to stay full from May to September. Regardless of your preferred price bracket,
aim to book well ahead in summer.

If you want to maximise your buying power at hotels around the city, regardless of their style and budget, a little knowledge goes a long way. Smaller places may offer a significant reduction for cash payment; try to establish this, preferably with hard-copy confirmation, before you arrive. Internet booking discounts are also plentiful, so check the web frequently for special deals. And many hotels give discounts to groups and for longer stays of around ten days or more.

Information & prices

Hotels in this section have been classified first by neighbourhood, and then by the price of their cheapest double rooms. Note, though, that these prices are usually only available off-season. Also, be aware that most hotels in Prague now fix their room rates in euros, even though the country is not yet in the euro zone. For the sake of consistency, we've converted all prices into Czech crowns. However, exchange-rate fluctuations may affect all prices listed here, especially given the fragile state of the global economy.

In this section, a 'Deluxe' hotel is one in which the cheapest double room costs 8,000 Kč or more per night. Doubles in 'Expensive' hotels cost 6,000-8,000 Kč; in operations labelled 'Moderate', you can expect to pay around 3,000-6,000 Kč; and doubles in 'Budget' hotels go for under 3,000 Kč. There's a separate category covering hostels. We've listed only prices for double rooms, but cheaper single rates are available at many properties. As, for that matter, are more expensive suites. And some hotels are also able to provide an additional bed for family rooms.

All the rooms listed in the 'Deluxe' and 'Expensive' categories have an en suite bathroom. The same goes for hotels in the 'Moderate' category, unless otherwise stated. Facilities in other categories vary – it's always best to check exactly what you'll be getting when you book. A selection of hotels that are particularly welcoming to gay guests is listed in the Gay & Lesbian chapter; see p237.

Agencies

See also p146 **At Home Abroad**.

Agentura Kirke

271 725 898/www.agentura-kirke.cz.
British expat Nicholas Kirke's eponymous agency offers rentals on flats, with a minimum lease of one year. All flats are unfurnished.

Alchymist Grand Hotel & Spa. *See p129.*

Prague Accommodations

mobile 608 228 999/
www.pragueaccommodations.com.
The properties kept on the books of Prague Accommodations include some of the most centrally located and elegant historic buildings available to the public. Prices range from cheap to moderate, depending on how many people plan to stay in any given apartment.

Stop City

222 521 233/www.stopcity.com.
Helpful staff at Stop City can book you into a pension, a hotel, a private room or an apartment, starting at around 480 Kč per person. Rooms range from the slightly dodgy to slightly above average, with a wide range of price options ensuring there's something for every traveller's budget. The agency doesn't handle hostel bookings but staff are willing to make reservations for callers from abroad, provided a credit card number is given via fax.

Hotels
HRADČANY

Staying within the shadow of Prague Castle does limit your culinary and nightlife options, and not everyone is up for a hike up the hill at the end of the day. But rooms here come with bragging rights, and the backstreets hold some treasures.

Deluxe

Hotel Savoy

Keplerova 6, Prague 1 (224 302 430/www.
hotel-savoy.cz). Tram 22. **Rooms** 61. **Rates**
4,778-8,550 Kč double. **Credit** AmEx, MC, V.
Map p326 A3 ❶
The Savoy's restaurant (*see p151*) was ranked as one of the country's top ten in a recent survey, and its parent hotel rates just as highly. Stepping into the quietly dignified lobby, complete with its reading room and fireplace, it may seem hard to imagine stars such as Tina Turner and Princess Caroline of Monaco staying here; but it's a peaceful bastion of first-class service, with tasteful, modern rooms. The standard rooms are spacious, while the deluxe rooms almost qualify as suites (Sean Connery required the vast Presidential Suite during a two-month movie shoot). The concierge service is top-notch, and breakfast, a newspaper and a shoe-shine are included in the room rate.
Bar. Business centre. Concierge. Disabled:
adapted rooms. Gym. Internet (cable, 290 Kč/hr).
Parking (€25). No-smoking rooms. Restaurant.
Room service. Spa. TV: DVD/pay movies.

Expensive

Domus Henrici

Loretánská 11, Prague 1 (220 511 369/www.
domus-henrici.cz). Metro Malostranská/tram 12,
20, 22. **Rooms** 8. **Rates** 3,000-5,250 Kč double.
No credit cards. Map p326 C3 ❷

Just eight rooms, but the mix of high-standard doubles and suites is charming indeed, each individually done in old-fashioned, homely decor and all just a four-minute walk from the gates of Prague Castle. Top service and management adds appeal and, if it happens to be booked full, the Hidden Places group also owns a similar hotel just west of the Charles Bridge, Domus Balthasar. Touches such as polished wood floors and ceiling-high ceramic wood stoves, plus free Wifi, laptop-ready LCDs in rooms and a cosy dining area have won over many. *Photos p126. No-smoking rooms. Internet (wireless, free). TV: Satellite.*

★ Romantik Hotel U raka

Černínská 10, Prague 1 (220 511 100/www. romantikhotel-uraka.cz). Tram 12, 22. **Rooms** 6. **Rates** 3,480-4,080 Kč double. **Credit** AmEx, DC, MC, V. **Map** p326 A2 ❸

Dating from 1739, this small, rustic pension is run by photographer Alexandr Paul and his artist family, and is ideal for couples. Its cottage-like building is situated just up the hill from the castle and within earshot of the bells of the Loreto. The hotel has tons of personality, but it still boasts the polish and service you'd expect for these prices. There are just six rooms available, two in the main house and four adjacent cottages, plus a beautiful breakfast room/café/reading room with a brick hearth. Reserve well in advance. Children under 12 aren't allowed, but staff welcome pets. *Internet (wireless, free). Parking (360 Kč). Room service.*

Moderate

Hotel Questenberk

Úvoz 15, Prague 1 (220 407 600/www. questenberk.cz). Tram 22. **Rooms** 30. **Rates** 2,040-3,820 Kč double. **Credit** AmEx, MC, V. **Map** p326 B4 ❹

The baroque building that houses the Questenberk was established in the 1660s as the Hospital of St Elisabeth and St Norbert. Keep the address handy when you're looking for the hotel – you may walk right by the place, with the dramatic stone crucifix at the entrance perhaps causing you to mistake it for a cathedral. Inside, the rooms are standard for this category of hotel, but you're paying for the location: it's just 500m from the castle. *Bar. Internet (cable, free). No-smoking rooms. Parking (300 Kč). Restaurant.*

MALÁ STRANA

The Lesser Quarter feels like a small town in its own right. If you book well ahead, it's entirely feasible that you'll be able to score a bargain room on a cobbled, hilly lane straight out of a Dickens tale – or, if you prefer, a Jan Neruda story.

Deluxe

Alchymist Grand Hotel & Spa

Tržiště 19, Prague 1 (257 286 011/www. alchymisthotel.com). Metro Malostranská/tram 12, 20, 22. **Rooms** 46. **Rates** 14,585 Kč double. **Credit** AmEx, MC, V. **Map** p327 E4 ❺

Prague's most decadent Habsburg days are still on tap at the Alchymist, with its antique furniture, frescoes, marble baths, ornately carved ceilings and sweeping, gauzy curtains. Formerly the Ježišek Palace and built in the 16th century, the hotel is a short walk from the throngs on the Charles Bridge, but the on-site spa boasts an experienced team of Indonesian masseuses who can rub out any stresses caused by the crowds. Finish the day with a dip in the hotel's indoor pool, or a glass of top-drawer Cabernet from the hotel restaurant. *Photo p127. Bar. Concierge. Gym. Internet (cable, free). No-smoking rooms. Parking (off-site, 650 Kč). Pool. Restaurant. Room service. Spa. TV: DVD.*

★ Aria Hotel

Tržiště 9, Prague 1 (225 334 111/www.aria hotel.net). Metro Malostranská/tram 12, 20, 22. **Rooms** 52. **Rates** 7,040-9,300 Kč double. **Credit** AmEx, MC, V. **Map** p327 E4 ❻

It's fair to say that the music-themed Aria, established by Henry Callan of New York's Library Hotel, substantially raised the bar in Prague hospitality when it opened a few years ago. Floors are divided by musical genre (classical, opera, contemporary,

The view from the **Aria Hotel**.

CONSUME

Hotel Mandarin Oriental.

CONSUME

jazz) and each of the cool, comfortable rooms is dedicated to an artist: the in-room PCs, DVD players, fresh orchids and custom-designed furniture from Spatium are joined by a full soundtrack of the theme artist's work. The music lending library in the lobby supplements those collections with more specialised discs, plus books and performance DVDs. The roof terrace vies for the honour of best view in the city; the skylit lobby restaurant Coda excels; and the amenities, service and location are all tremendous. Request a room facing the Vrtba Gardens.
Bar. Business services. Concierge. Disabled-adapted rooms. Gym. Internet (cable, free). No-smoking rooms. Parking (580 Kč). Restaurant. Room service. TV: DVD.

Expensive

★ Alchymist Residence Nosticova

Nosticova 1, Prague 1 (257 312 513/www. nosticova.com). Metro Malostranská/tram 12, 20, 22. **Rooms** 16. **Rates** 7,920-16,340 Kč suite. **Credit** AmEx, MC, V. **Map** p327 E4 ❼
Standing in quiet elegance on a cobbled lane just off Kampa Island and recently acquired by the Alchymist (*see p129*) just up the street, this classy little 17th-century villa with modernised rooms appeals to visitors who plan to stay longer in town. The suites range from ample to capacious and come

with antique furniture, baths big enough to swim in and, best of all, fully equipped kitchenettes. Two have working fireplaces, and one boasts a rooftop terrace. Continental breakfast is served for an extra €15, and bringing pets costs another €20 (though kids under 11 are free).
Bar. Internet (wireless, free). Parking (650 Kč). Restaurant. Room service. TV: DVD.

★ Hotel Mandarin Oriental

Nebovidská 1, Prague 1 (233 088 888/ www.mandarinoriental.com/prague). Metro Malostranská/tram 6, 9, 12, 20, 22. **Rooms** 99. **Rates** 7,900-19,280 Kč double. **Credit** AmEx, MC, V. **Map** p327 F5 ❽
Gracious and hip, the Mandarin has won raves since its 2006 opening for its fabulously textured and draped rooms and for the Asian cuisine served at its restaurant, Essensia. Ensconced in a former 14th-century monastery right next to the Czech Museum of Music, the hotel stands discreetly on a little-trafficked lane that's just a ten-minute walk from the Charles Bridge. In mild weather, thick walls protect the designer terrace amid blooming lavender; inside, the Barego bar (*see p176*) is a smart hangout for Prague's arty and media types. Other facilities include a first-class gym and spa.
Bar. Gym. Internet (wireless). Parking (750 Kč). Restaurant. Spa.

Hotel Neruda

Nerudova 44, Prague 1 (257 535 557/ www.hotelneruda.cz). Metro Malostranská/ tram 12, 20, 22. **Rooms** 42. **Rates** 3,100-5,700 Kč double. **Credit** AmEx, DC, MC, V. **Map** p326 D3 ❾

A recent arrival in the market, the Neruda has been quick to build its reputation. As you might guess from its discreet baroque façade, it's a hotel with history: the main building dates from 1348. And the Neruda's success has resulted in the addition of a wing designed by Bořek Šípek, the Czech Republic's top glass artist and architect, who's added free-floating curves galore. The rooms in the older building are comfortable but a little plain, so be sure to ask for one with a view of Nerudova street. Service is friendly and attentive.

Bar. Internet (cable or wireless, free). No-smoking rooms. Parking (650 Kč). Restaurant. Room service. Spa.

★ Riverside Hotel

Janáčkovo nábřeží 15, Prague 1 (234 705 155/ www.riversideprague.com). Metro Malostranská/ tram 6, 9, 12, 20, 22. **Rooms** 81. **Rates** 3,770-8,420 Kč double. **Credit** AmEx, MC, V.

A nicely appointed venture set up by the MaMaison group, the Riverside offers surprisingly good deals on its basic rooms, which are anything but basic. The historic building on the city's riverfront has been restored to its original state of elegance and comes with commanding views. All of the rooms contain modern but plush furnishings and tiled bathrooms that invite a soak. Wooden cabinets and floors balance out the cream and ivory walls to wonderfully calming effect. Although there's no restaurant or gym, service is top-notch, and returning here after a meal may rate as highly on the pleasure scale as the feast itself.

Bar. Concierge. Disabled: adapted rooms. Internet (cable, free). Room service.

Moderate

Hotel Čertovka

U lužického semináře 2, Prague 1 (257 011 500/ www.certovka.cz). Metro Malostranská/tram 12, 22. **Rooms** 21. **Rates** 3,470-4,120 Kč double. **Credit** AmEx, MC, V. **Map** p327 G4 ❿

Located on a little winding street near the Charles Bridge, the Čertovka is named after the canal on which it sits. Formerly a baroque mansion, it was developed into a comfortable hideaway in 2000, then badly hit by the floods of 2002. Now, though, it's back on top, and reasonably priced to boot. Some rooms look on to Prague Castle or the Charles Bridge tower (no.10 has the best view), but the most romantic room fronts the canal. The furnishings are tastefully modern with hints of 18th-century poshness, and staff are warm and attentive.

Disabled: adapted rooms. Internet (wireless, free). Parking (off-site, 600 Kč).

★ U Červeného Lva

Nerudova 41, Prague 1 (257 533 832/www.hotel redlion.com). Metro Malostranská/tram 12, 22. **Rooms** 8. **Rates** 2,600-5,100 Kč double. **Credit** AmEx, MC, V. **Map** p326 D3 ⓫

CONSUME

Riverside Hotel.

The Renaissance-era Red Lion is one of the few small hotels on the Royal Route leading up to the castle that boasts authentic 17th-century decor, including hand-painted vaulted ceilings. This reconstructed burgher's house provides guests with a sense of Renaissance Prague. Service has improved of late. There's no parking at the hotel, but you can park nearby for 550 Kč.
Bar. Restaurant.

Hotel Waldstein
Valdštejnské náměstí 6, Prague 1 (257 533 938/ www.hotelwaldstein.cz). Metro Malostranská/ tram 12, 18, 20, 22. **Rooms** 36. **Rates** 2,565-5,380 Kč double. **Credit** AmEx, MC, V. **Map** p327 F3 ⑫
From the hearty buffet breakfasts served in a vault to the stone floors and handsome arched ceilings, the Renaissance-style Hotel Waldstein offers good value for your doubloons, especially in the off-season. The rooms have antique furniture and 17th-century frescoes, but there are no lifts. Budget travellers can opt for the Waldstein annexe next door, with 11 apartment rooms and a suite that are rather plainer but still classy. Staff are exceptionally friendly and helpful.
Internet (wireless, free). No-smoking rooms. Parking. Room service.

U Karlova mostu
Na Kampě 15, Prague 1 (257 531 430/www. archibald.cz). Metro Malostranská/tram 12, 20, 22. **Rooms** 26. **Rates** 2,510-5,400 Kč double. **Credit** AmEx, DC, MC, V. **Map** p327 G5 ⑬
Formerly named Na Kampě 15, this hotel 'At the Charles Bridge' affords some fine views of the bridge and Old Town, yet it's situated at a sufficient distance to provide its guests with some peace and quiet. The management has done a sensitive restoration job on what used to be a 15th-century tavern (which, at the time, brewed one of the city's pioneering beers): the rooms are attractive, with wood floors, exposed beams and garret windows alongside modern furnishings. The two cellar pubs and the beer garden at the back offer a reasonably varied menu, a good assortment of Czech and French wines and, of course, excellent Czech beer. Service is very welcoming.
Bar. Internet (shared terminal, free). Parking (400 Kč). Restaurants (2).

★ U krále Karla
Úvoz 4, Prague 1 (257 532 869/www.romantic hotels.cz). Metro Malostranská/tram 12, 22. **Rooms** 19. **Rates** 3,000-4,000 Kč double. **Credit** AmEx, MC, V. **Map** p326 D3 ⑭
Although it continues to generate buzz on some online Prague discussion boards, the King Charles remains its stolid, lovely self, with no visible ego boost. Ornamental oak furnishings, painted vaulted ceilings, stained-glass windows and various baroque treasures lend this hotel the feel of an aristocratic country house. In fact, though, it was once owned by the Benedictine Order.
Bar. Parking (call ahead to reserve). Restaurant. Room service.

U Kříže
Újezd 20, Prague 1 (257 312 272/www.ukrize. com). Tram 6, 9, 12, 20, 22. **Rooms** 22. **Rates** 2,260-3,900 Kč double. **Credit** MC, V. **Map** p327 F6 ⑮
A popular choice, U Kříže provides great value for money in this price category. Although the rooms won't win any design awards, they are clean, and the hotel's location is a winner: it's across the street from Petřín Hill, a quick walk from Kampa Island, one tram stop from the National Theatre and two stops from Malostranské náměstí. Be sure to ask for a room facing the atrium – other rooms face Petřín Hill but are above a noisy tram route.
Bar. Internet (wireless, free). Parking (350 Kč). Room service. Restaurant.

Residence Hotel Green Lobster
Nerudova 42, Prague 1 (257 532 158/ www.green-lobster-prague-hotel.com). Metro Malostranská/tram 12, 22. **Rooms** 20. **Rates** 4,150-5,532 Kč double. **Credit** AmEx, MC, V. **Map** p326 D3 ⑯
This neighbour of U Červeného Lva (*see p131*) offers both romantic rooms and excellent service. Originally built in the 1460s, the house was badly damaged in the great fire of 1541 and then reconstructed several times; but despite the damage, it still features beamed ceilings and four-poster beds. These days, breakfast on the lovely terrace (included with the room rate) is so appealing that the locals may even join you. *Photo p125.*
Internet (wireless, free). Restaurant.

Rezidence Lundborg
U lužického semináře 3, Prague 1 (257 011 911/www.lundborg.se). Metro Malostranská/ tram 12, 20, 22. **Rooms** 13. **Rates** 4,020-18,860 Kč double. **Credit** AmEx, DC, MC, V. **Map** p327 G4 ⑰
Built on the site of the older Juditin Bridge and now boasting prime views of the Charles Bridge, this luxurious Scandinavian-owned hotel exudes charm. An example of the executive residence/hotel hybrid, the Lundborg pampers its guests with 13 suites, each a distinct and tasteful blend of reconstructed Renaissance decor and modern business amenities. It's a major splashout, but every conceivable need has been anticipated, from the wine cellar to the jacuzzis in every newly redone bathroom. The front desk can efficiently arrange anything else you desire, right down to the golf programmes in Karlštejn or Konopiště resorts during summer.
Bar. Concierge. Internet (cable or wireless, free). Parking. Room service. TV: DVD.

CONSUME

Castle Steps. *See p135.*

★ Zlatá Hvězda

Nerudova 48, Prague 1 (257 532 867/www.stars hotelsprague.com). Tram 12, 20, 22. **Rooms** 26. **Rates** 2,600-5,100 Kč double. **Credit** AmEx, MC, V. **Map** p326 C3 ⓲

The Golden Star dates from 1372, but a reconstruction in 2000 added lifts and modern bathrooms to the five-storey house's original architectural elements (vaulted ceilings and a spiral staircase, for instance). Room numbers ending with '5' are spacious and have huge bathrooms. Discounts for longer stays can sometimes be negotiated via the website, but rates are also pretty good for shorter stays. There's a tour desk on site.
Bar. Internet (cable, free). No-smoking rooms. Parking (off-site, 550 Kč). Restaurant.

★ U Zlaté Studně

U Zlaté studně 4, Prague 1 (257 011 213/www. zlatastudna.cz). Metro Malostranská/tram 12, 22. **Rooms** 19. **Rates** 2,515-6,765 Kč double. **Credit** AmEx, DC, MC, V. **Map** p327 F2 ⓳

The former residence of court astronomer Tycho Brahe is now an improbably classy, comfortable old-world hotel with knockout views. Nestled on a secluded street in Malá Strana, U Zlaté Studně offers tasteful, high-end rooms with wood floors and ceilings with ornamental appointments. If you love to soak, ask for one of the rooms with a huge tub. Breakfast on the terrace comes with a gobsmacking vista of the city below; the outlook from the dining area, where the award-winning Pavel Sapík presides, goes well with the Moravian wine on hand.
Concierge. Internet (wireless, free). No-smoking rooms. Parking (off-site, 580 Kč). Restaurant. TV: DVD.

Budget

Castle Steps

Nerudova 7, Prague 1 (257 216 337/www.castle steps.com). Metro Malostranská/tram 12, 20, 22. **Rooms** 84. **Rates** 1,580-3,970 Kč double. **Credit** AmEx, DC, MC, V. **Map** p327 E3 ⓴

Actually a collection of rooms, suites and apartments in a group of nearby buildings, Castle Steps is part of a growing trend in great-value Prague accommodation that breaks with traditional hotels and pensions. Rooms feature antiques, some have Castle views, some share a bath, others are pure luxe. Service is on call but it's essentially self-catered, which makes for deep discounts. Considering the amazing location and elegance, it's well worth considering. *Photo p133.*
Internet (dataport).

★ Golden Horse House

Úvoz 8, Prague 1 (257 532 700/www.goldhorse. cz). Metro Malostranská/tram 12, 20, 22. **Rooms** 10. **Rates** 800-1,400 Kč double. **No credit cards. Map** p326 C3 ㉑

Considering the great rates, the remarkably friendly staff and the excellent location, you'd probably be happy to do without an authentic 15th-century address – but you don't have to do so at this gorgeous, hard-to-beat old hotel. The rooms here are on a par with the better pensions or hostels in town. Breakfast costs 100 Kč and is served in an atmospheric wine vault.
Internet (wireless, free). No-smoking rooms. Parking (off-site, 250 Kč).

Hotel William

Hellichova 5, Prague 1 (257 320 242/www. euroagentur.cz). Tram 12, 20, 22. **Rooms** 42. **Rates** 1,300-2,760 Kč double. **Credit** AmEx, MC, V. **Map** p327 F5 ㉒

Open since 2001, the William is an inconspicuous hotel set in a great location, a quick walk to the funicular up Petřín Hill. The interior is very memorable, with the decorators having gone overboard trying for a 'castle feel'. Part of the Euroagentur agency, it trades off some individual character for efficiency, and the first floor is immersed in kitchen smells, but the rooms are comfortable and great value for money. Ask for a room at the back of the hotel, away from the noise of the trams.
Internet (wireless, free). No-smoking rooms. Parking (450 Kč).

★ Pension Dientzenhofer

Nosticova 2, Prague 1 (257 311 319/www. dientzenhofer.cz). Metro Malostranská/tram 12, 20, 22. **Rooms** 9. **Rates** 2,700-4,800 Kč double. **Credit** AmEx, DC, MC, V. **Map** p327 G5 ㉓

This 16th-century house is the birthplace of baroque architect Kilian Ignaz Dientzenhofer, whose work fills this quarter of the city. The calming courtyard and back garden of this pension offer a lovely respite in the midst of Malá Strana. The rooms aren't tremendously posh, but they are bright and airy, and the staff are friendly. Book well ahead, as the hotel invariably fills up for summer.
Bar. Disabled-adapted rooms. Internet (cable, free). Parking (320 Kč).

Hostels

Hostel Sokol

Nosticova 2, Prague 1 (257 007 397). Metro Malostranská/tram 12, 20, 22. **Beds** 104. **Rates** Per person 300-350 Kč shared room; 700-900 Kč double. **No credit cards. Map** p327 G5 ㉔

Find Hostel Sokol, hidden in the yard behind the Sokol sports centre (follow the signs to reception), and you've found the thirsty student travel nexus of Prague. Many of the bunks are located in a large gymnasium; escape to the great beer terrace, or to the nearby castle and the Charles Bridge. Book rooms ahead via the phone number above, or via email to hostelsocool@seznam.cz.
No-smoking rooms. Parking (100 Kč).

CONSUME

STARÉ MĚSTO

Sleeping in the heart of things won't necessarily break the bank, though you'll pay more for food and drink. New inns are always opening, and major hotels often offer discounts.

Deluxe

Four Seasons Hotel Prague

Veleslavínova 2a, Prague 1 (221 427 000/ www.fourseasons.com/prague). Metro Staroměstská/tram 17, 18. **Rooms** 161. **Rates** 7,920-18,735 Kč double. **Credit** AmEx, MC, V. **Map** p328 J4 ㉕

Expectations were high for the Four Seasons' long-awaited arrival in Prague a few years back, and the hotel has matched or bettered them all. The well-located property offers a sort of all-in-one preview of Prague's best architecture, but although the hotel is a seamless melding of restored Gothic, baroque, Renaissance and neoclassical buildings, guests will be hard-pressed to catch even a whiff of musty history. Moneyed visitors will want to reserve the top-flight rooms with sweeping views of Prague Castle and Charles Bridge before dining in Allegro, proud possessor of the nation's first Michelin star.

Bar. Concierge. Disabled: adapted rooms. Gym. Internet (cable or wireless, free). No-smoking rooms. Parking. Restaurant. Room service. TV: DVD.

Iron Gate.

Iron Gate

Michalská 19, Prague 1 (225 777 777/www. irongate.cz). Metro Staroměstská or Národní třída/tram 6, 9, 18, 21, 22, 26. **Suites** 43. **Rates** 5,255-11,190 Kč studio. **Credit** AmEx, MC, V. **Map** p328 L5 ㉖

Antiquarians wanting authentic places to stay, take note: in 2003, the Prague Municipality recognised the Iron Gate as the best historic reconstruction. The two buildings date from the 14th and 16th centuries; management has preserved the original painted ceiling beams and frescoes, and, to maintain the Gothic look, the suites' kitchenettes are discreetly tucked inside antique armoires. The Tower Suite is over the top in more ways than one: on three floors of the building, it features a heart-shaped bed, a jacuzzi built for two, and a study suitable for the astronomer Johannes Kepler, with views of the Old Town Hall, Prague Castle and acres of orange roof tiles.

Bar. Concierge. Gym. Internet (wireless). Restaurant. Room service.

Expensive

Grand Hotel Bohemia

Králodvorská 4, Prague 1 (234 608 111/ www.grandhotelbohemia.cz). Metro Náměstí Republiky/tram 5, 8, 9, 14. **Rooms** 78. **Rates** 4,526-6,161 Kč double. **Credit** AmEx, MC, V. **Map** p329 N4 ㉗

The Bohemia was an officially non-existent address under the pre-1989 regime – this is where the Central Committee members lived it up in secret. Nowadays, though, it's an understated, Austrian-run art deco masterpiece that goes quietly about its task of providing top-notch service with Habsburg-like stateliness, and you'd never guess that the hotel's subterranean ballrooms also hosted scandalous Jazz Age excesses. Today's guests are mainly preoccupied with business and the odd moment of serenely gazing down on the city from the upper floors. Children aged up to nine stay free of charge.

Bar. Concierge. Disabled: adapted rooms. Internet (wireless, free). No-smoking floors. Restaurant.

Pachtův Palace

Karolíny Světlé 34, Prague 1 (234 705 111/www. pachtuvpalace.com). Metro Můstek/tram 6, 9, 17, 18, 22. **Rooms** 50. **Rates** 4,249-10,687 Kč studio. **Credit** AmEx, DC, MC, V. **Map** p328 J5 ㉘

With 50 deluxe and just-modernised apartments, and managers for various big-town corporations already moving in, you'll be in some powerful company during a stay at the Pachtův Palace. The former residence of Count Jan Pachta is now a swanky hotel, where a classy bar and in-house babysitting go nicely with the timbered rooms and the stunning palatial public areas. The buzz about this grand villa is persistent among Prague's elite.

Bar. Gym. Internet (cable, free). Restaurant. Room service.

Backpacker Chic

A new wave of enterprises has reinvigorated hostel culture in Prague.

The sofas aren't trashed. The walls in the common room aren't peeling. And, most shockingly, the toasters work. It's almost as if they want to take all the fun out of no-budget travel...

The sacred traditions of hostel accommodation are on the way out in Prague. The old ways have been replaced by a new generation of Prague hostels, which come with designer interiors, private suites, nice bathrooms, no curfews, free Wi-Fi, cable TV and all kinds of amenities that have, until now, rarely been found in local hostels. Staff will happily arrange tours, provide free maps and show you where to park your car. And perhaps most unexpected of all is the general sense of pleasant quietude and cleanliness that pervades new establishments such as **Hostel Rosemary** (*see p145*).

Located in the swinging Holešovice district, the **A&O Hostel** (*see p149*) is more in the traditional mould than some of its competitors. However, its cellar cocktail bar is far from the cheerless canteen you might expect. Known as

Brick, this intimate hangout with old brick vaulting is the kind of space that makes hostel-surfing feel more like hotel-hopping.

Elsewhere, the **Hostel Boathouse** (*see p149*) is almost an athletics club, with canoeing, tennis and bikes for rent (breakfast included, of course). **Sir Toby's Hostel** (*see p149*), the neighbourhood's other hostel option, has recently invested in a cool retrofit, with a cosy red-accented common room and a lovely brick-decked terrace for milder weather. It's also got its own brick-arched cellar eatery and bar, this one with Asian-inspired floor seating.

However, it's **Miss Sophie's Prague** (*see p149*) in fashionable Vinohrady that's recently been generating the most backpacker buzz. The operation includes apartments, which come with kitchens and are all in a separate building from the dorms, so you can keep your distance from the Dylan singalongs. Private suites with decor touches worthy of an interior designer with great antique shop connections add extra appeal.

Moderate

Bellagio Hotel Prague

U milosrdných 2, Prague 1 (221 778 999/www.bellagiohotel.cz). Metro Staroměstská/tram 17/133 bus. **Rooms** 46. **Rates** 5,000-6,261 Kč double. **Credit** AmEx, MC, V. **Map** p328 L2 ㉙
This newish Italian-style hotel in Josefov features a grand, winding stairwell that leads guests into fine rooms that boast modular, sensible furniture, and brown and burnished gold touches. The management has poached talented chefs from places such as Kampa Park for Isabella, its Italian and world cuisine restaurant. A no-nonsense cocktail bar and conference room and appeal; so does the location, a five-minute walk from the Old Jewish Cemetery.
Bar. Internet (wireless, free). Restaurant.

★ Černá Liška

Mikulášská 2, Prague 1 (224 232 250/www.cernaliska.cz). Metro Staroměstská/tram 17, 18. **Rooms** 12. **Rates** 3,244-4,526 Kč double. **Credit** MC, V. **Map** p328 L4 ㉚
Now partnered with the nearby Metamorphis, the Black Fox pulls off the seemingly impossible feat that's only attempted by a half-dozen competitors: it remains a charming, personable and good-quality hotel with a front door that opens on Old Town

Square. The neat rooms offer excellent value; wake to the sound of the Týn bells (and the rumble of tourist traffic), then stumble out for some gallery-hopping, pubbing and clubbing without ever needing to take a taxi. Note: the lifts are tiny.
Disabled: adapted rooms. Internet (wireless, free). Restaurant.

Cloister Inn

Konviktská 14, Prague 1 (224 211 020/www.cloister-inn.com). Metro Národní třída/tram 6, 9, 18, 22. **Rooms** 75. **Rates** 2,489-3,244 Kč double. **Credit** AmEx, DC, MC, V. **Map** p328 K5 ㉛
The Cloister Inn has a lot going for it: attentive staff, great location, good prices and, if you're in need of redemption, a nearby house that's chock-full of nuns. The rooms are bright and cheery; in the lobby, you'll find a computer with free internet access, free coffee and tea, and a lending library. Prices have risen of late, so keep your eye on its website for deals.
Concierge. Internet (shared terminal, free). No-smoking rooms. Parking.

Euroagentur Hotel Royal Esprit

Jakubská 5, Prague 1 (224 800 055/www.hotel mejstrik.cz). Metro Náměstí Republiky/tram 5, 14, 26. **Rooms** 29. **Rates** 3,948-5,557 Kč double. **Credit** AmEx, DC, MC, V. **Map** p329 N3 ㉜

CONSUME

Founded in 1924 and formerly known as the Mejstřík, this great find is handily located a block from Old Town Square (not so handy if you don't care for packs of late-night singing stag parties, of course), and is something of a revived classic. The individually decorated rooms are a hybrid of standard modern decor and 1920s style (art deco elements, wood trim). Corner rooms offer great vantage points from which to spy on streetlife and gables. *Bar. Business service. Disabled: adapted rooms. Internet (cable, free). No-smoking rooms. Parking. Restaurant.*

★ Floor Hotel
Na příkopě 13, Prague 1 (234 076 300/www. floorhotel.cz). Metro Můstek. **Rooms** 43. **Rates** 3,093-6,035 Kč double. **Credit** AmEx, MC, V. **Map** p328 M5 ③③
Floor offers luxury digs on Prague's marquee shopping promenade. Half the rooms are designed with traditional luxury in mind, while the remainder go for the sleek, modern look. Only four storeys high, it features an upmarket Italian restaurant with an impressive menu, and a large, crystal-chandeliered conference room for the business traveller. *Bar. Internet (cable, free). Restaurant.*

★ Hotel Josef
Rybná 20, Prague 1 (221 700 111/www.hotel josef.com). Metro Náměstí Republiky/tram 5, 8, 9, 14. **Rooms** 109. **Rates** 4,878-5,381 Kč double. **Credit** AmEx, MC, V. **Map** p329 N3 ③④
Definitely the hippest – and, perhaps, the only – designer hotel in Old Town, the Josef opened in 2002. The flash interiors, unique fabrics and handsome glass bathrooms (superior-class rooms only) are the work of London-based designer Eva Jiřičná. The hotel is in the thick of the historic centre, with the top-floor rooms in the 'Pink House' having the best views. Children under six stay free. *Bar. Business services. Concierge. Gym. Internet (wireless, free). No-smoking floors. Parking. Room service.*

Hotel U Klenotníka
Rytířská 3, Prague 1 (224 211 699/www. uklenotnika.cz). Metro Můstek/tram 6, 9, 11, 18, 22. **Rooms** 11. **Rates** 2,400-3,100 Kč double. **Credit** AmEx, DC, MC, V. **Map** p328 L5 ③⑤
A burgher house from the 11th century situated on a narrow street lined with historic façades, U Klenotníka is perfect for night owls, situated as it is right between Wenceslas and Old Town Squares. The rooms are sparse but tidy and clean, and the bathrooms have been thoroughly renovated. The quietest rooms face the back of the hotel: doubles 11 and 21, and singles 12 and 22. The tiny lift is only for luggage, so the hotel's not a good choice if you're uncomfortable climbing stairs. *Bar. Internet (wireless, free). Parking (off-site). Restaurant.*

Hotel Metamorphis
Malá Štupartská 5 (Ungelt Square), Prague 1 (221 771 011/www.metamorphis.cz). Metro Náměstí Republiky/tram 5, 14, 26. **Rooms** 24. **Rates** 2,741-5,457 Kč double. **Credit** AmEx, DC, MC, V. **Map** p328 M3 ③⑥
The former Pension Metamorphis has metamorphosed into not a beetle but a fully fledged and very approachable hotel. Each room is different, but all are tastefully designed, with wood floors and an array of comforts; some ceilings have beams that date from the end of the 15th century. The once-empty square on which the hotel stands has become a tourist paradise, jammed with craft shops, a respectable bookstore and cafés; one of the best cafés, though, is on the ground floor of the Metamorphis itself. Ask for a view of Týn Church. *Bar. Internet (wireless, free). Parking. Restaurants (2). TV: pay movies.*

Hotel Paříž Praha
U Obecního domu 1, Prague 1 (222 195 195/ www.hotel-pariz.cz). Metro Náměstí Republiky/ tram 5, 8, 9, 14. **Rooms** 95. **Rates** 5,250-6,500 Kč double. **Credit** AmEx, DC, MC, V. **Map** p329 N3 ③⑦
If any hotel captures the spirit of Prague's belle époque, it's the Hotel Paříž, immortalised by Bohumil Hrabal's *I Served the King of England*. Visitors weary of cookie-cutter hotels will appreciate the patina of the historic rooms and the preserved Jazz Age dining room and Sarah Bernhardt café (*see p165*). Is money no object? Then be sure to reserve – far in advance, mind – the Royal Tower Suite, which boasts a 360-degree view of the city. *Bar. Internet (cable, free). No-smoking rooms. Restaurant. Room service. Spa.*

Inter-Continental Praha
Náměstí Curieových 43-45, Prague 1 (296 631 111/www.intercontinental.com). Metro Staroměstská/tram 17, 18. **Rooms** 372. **Rates** 6,412-8,250 Kč double. **Credit** AmEx, MC, V. **Map** p328 K2 ③⑧
Celebrating its 35th anniversary in 2009, the Inter-Continental Praha may at last be getting it right. Although visual traces of communist design were expunged during a $50 million refurbishment in the 1990s, only now does the transformation seem to have taken hold in earnest, with courteous service and no reminders of the c-word in sight. All rooms have Wi-Fi; elsewhere, the fitness centre (*see p264*) is one of the best in town, much favoured by non-guests with expense accounts. The negative? One side of the hotel faces a garish neon-lit casino, and there's an extra charge if you want a room facing the river. Children eat for free. *Bar. Business services. Disabled: adapted rooms. Gym. Internet (wireless, free). No-smoking floors. Pool. Restaurants (2). Room service. TV: pay movies.*

Metropol

Národní třída 33, Prague 1 (246 022 100/ www.metropolhotel.cz). Metro Národní třída/ tram 6, 9, 18, 22. **Rooms** 65. **Rates** 2,489-6,035 Kč double. **Credit** AmEx, MC, V. **Map** p328 L6 ③

This slick, centrally located bargain has won praise for its newly completed modern architecture. Prices are competitive, and the rooftop Bella Vista restaurant offers amazing views of the spires all around. The crimson-carpeted rooms are clean and come with cool, glassy bathrooms that could be fun in a sci-fi sort of way. But the hotel tends to attract large groups of Mediterranean package tourists and you may feel like a sheep, especially when you squeeze into the rooms.

Bar. Internet (wireless, free). Restaurants (2).

★ Residence Řetězova

Řetězova 9, Prague 1 (222 221 800/www. residenceretezova.com). Metro Staroměstská/tram 17, 18. **Rooms** 9. **Rates** 3,394-7,292 Kč double. **Credit** AmEx, MC, V. **Map** p328 K5 ④

The Residence Řetězova features nine bright and airy apartments on one of the city centre's quieter, tourist-friendly streets. Just a stone's throw from Charles Bridge, the doubles have more character than most hotel rooms in town, with warm wood accents and soft, neutral tones. Fireplaces and vaulted ceilings are the norm for the suites, as are bidets and comfy sitting areas.

Internet (cable, free). No-smoking rooms. Parking (off-site). TV: DVD.

Savic Hotel

Jilska 7, Prague 1 (224 248 555/www.savic.eu). Metro Staroměstská/tram 17, 18. **Rooms** 27. **Rates** 2,489-4,000 Kč double. **Credit** AmEx, MC, V. **Map** p328 L5 ④

An elegant and thorough restoration of a collection of former townhouses, with some parts dating back to 1319, the Savic offers impressive value and a great location for the price. Rooms include timbered and floral-painted ceilings, parquet floors, and Italian marble running throughout the bathrooms. Staff are gracious and the skylit courtyard is a calming spot – for that matter, so is the quiet street on which it sits, just off the main tourist track in Old Town. *Internet (cable, free; wireless, €10/hr). No-smoking rooms. Parking (off-site). Restaurant.*

Ventana Hotel

Celetna 7, Prague 1 (866 376 7831/www.epoque hotels.com). Metro Náměstí Republiky/tram 5, 8, 9, 14. **Rooms** 29. **Rates** 4,023-6,412 Kč double. **Credit** AmEx, V. **Map** p328 M4 ④

The Italian marble, elegant detailing, soft lighting and high, stuccoed ceilings show a sense of understated style at this charming new entry just off Old Town Square. The library and bar are welcoming, and rooms have Philippe Starck touches, café au lait colour schemes and big beds. Service is also sharp, as at other Epoque Hotel properties. *Bar. Concierge. Internet (cable, free). Room service.*

★ U zlaté studny

Karlova 3, Prague 1 (222 220 262/www. uzlatestudny.cz). Metro Staroměstská/tram 17. **Rooms** 6. **Rates** 2,500-3,550 Kč double. **Credit** AmEx, MC, V. **Map** p328 K4 ④

Fans of the arcane will delight in this 16th-century building, historically known as 'At the Golden Well', and the ornate water hole that still stands in its cellar. Exquisitely decorated and furnished with Louis XIV antiques and replicas, the four suites and two double rooms are positively cavernous by Old Town standards. Once they get their bearings, sightseers will appreciate the hotel's location halfway between Charles Bridge and Old Town Square on the Royal Route. Children under 16 stay for free. *Photo p142. Internet (shared terminal, free). Restaurant.*

Budget

Botel Albatross

Nábřeží Ludvíka Svobody (adjacent to Štefáník Bridge), Prague 1 (224 810 541/www.botel albatros.cz). Metro Náměstí Republiky/tram 5, 8, 14, 26. **Rooms** 86. **Rates** 1,800-3,080 Kč double. **Credit** AmEx, MC, V. **Map** p329 O1 ④

Essentially a floating prefab apartment, this boat-hotel is an unusual place to stay. It's not luxurious, but it has at least been recently renovated, and pretty successfully at that. For a quiet room in Old Town, the prices are great, especially if you're going to spend most of your time ashore away from the modest, ocean-liner-sized facilities and the rather salty staff.

Bar. Parking. Restaurant.

Červené Židle

Liliová 4, Prague 1 (296 180 018/www. redchairhotel.com). Metro Národní třída/ tram 6, 9, 18, 22. **Rooms** 15. **Rates** 1,750-4,400 Kč double. **Credit** AmEx, MC, V. **Map** p328 K5 ④

Disarmingly friendly staff and a prime location on one of Old Town's loveliest squares mean that you may be happy to settle for the somewhat spartan rooms at this property. Still, although they're basic, they're done up quite nicely with green-stained wood, some with ceiling rafters and, naturally, red chairs. Bathrooms are as good as those at hotels three times the price.

Internet (cable, free). Parking.

Hotel Černy Slon

Tynská 1, Prague 1 (222 321 521/www.hotel cernyslon.cz). Metro Staroměstská/tram 17, 18. **Rooms** 16. **Rates** 3,100-5,300 Kč double. **Credit** AmEx, MC, V. **Map** p328 M3 ④

Ventana Hotel.

With an incredible location in the shadow of the Týn Church just off Old Town Square, this cosy 16-room inn is ensconced in a 14th-century building that is on the UNESCO World Heritage list. Gothic stone arches and wooden floors go along with the small-ish but comfortable rooms, which have been laid out with basic amenities. Windows look out on the cob-bled mews of Old Town, with a constant parade of characters. Fortunately, it's on one of the district's quieter lanes, though that can change fast if one of the city's howling stag parties careens through. *Bar. Internet (cable, free). Parking (off-site). Restaurant.*

U Medvídků

Na Perštyně 7, Prague 1 (224 211 916/ www.umedvidku.cz). Metro Národní třída/tram 6, 9, 18, 22, 26. **Rooms** 33. **Rates** 2,300-4,500 Kč double. **Credit** AmEx, MC, V. **Map** p328 L6 ㊼

The Little Bears hearkens back to a number of Dark Ages. The iron doors on some rooms may remind you of Gothic dungeons, while the rudimentary bathrooms evoke the benighted years of communism. The traditional inn's pub, one of the first to serve Budvar, keeps a constant stream of tourists and locals fed on roasted pig, and there's also an attached bar that's hopping until 3am (fortunately, the thick walls make for good soundproofing). *Bar. Restaurant.*

Hostels

Travellers' Hostel

Dlouhá 33, Prague 1 (224 826 662/224 826 663/www.travellers.cz). Metro Náměstí Republiky/ tram 5, 14, 26. **Rates** *Per person* 300-530 Kč bed in shared room; 590-800 Kč double. **Credit** MC, V. **Map** p329 N2 ㊽

The two constants at the Travellers' Hostel on Dlouhá are good value and English-speaking back-packers. In addition to dorm beds, this location also now features five apartments (1,900-3,200 Kč/night) and a surprisingly romantic double suite complete with beamed ceilings; all six of these add-ons have kitchens and offer great value. You'll find internet access, drinks and sandwiches for sale in the lobby. The hostel also functions as a booking office con-necting travellers to a whole network of hostels (www.czechhostels.com).
Internet (shared terminal). No-smoking hotel. **Other locations** throughout Prague.

NOVÉ MĚSTO

Prague's New Town lacks the medieval charm of Old Town, but more than makes up for it with lower prices, more rooms and better dining. And you're still only streets away from the centre, but also near the happening neighbourhoods of Vinohrady and Žižkov.

CONSUME

U zlaté studny. *See p140.*

Deluxe

Hotel Palace Praha

Panská 12, Prague 1 (224 093 111/www.
palacehotel.cz). Metro Můstek/tram 3, 9, 14,
24, 26. **Rooms** 124. **Rates** 5,607-6,965 Kč
double. **Credit** AmEx, MC, V. **Map** p329 N5 ⑲
Off Wenceslas Square yet still close to everything,
especially the city's smarter Na příkopě, the Palace
almost seems to belong in another part of Prague.
The rooms are understated and tasteful; as, for that
matter, are the staff. You won't be oohing and
ahhing, but you won't miss anything either.
Bar. Business services. Disabled: adapted rooms.
No-smoking rooms. Restaurant. Room service.
Spa.

Expensive

Hotel Yasmin

Politických vězňů 12, Prague 1 (234 100 100/
www.hotel-yasmin.cz). Metro Mustek/tram 3,
9. **Rooms** 209. **Rates** 5,532-7,041 Kč double.
Credit AmEx, DC, MC, V. **Map** p329 O6 ㉚
This ultra-modern hotel opened in early 2006,
bolstered by its location (just off Wenceslas Square)
and the easy access to public transit. Rooms come

with clean lines and cutting-edge design; the lobby
and the restaurant, Noodles, combine high fashion
and a retro 1970s flair via lots of glass and geometric shapes. The property includes more than 100
non-smoking rooms and several rooms for people
with disabilities.
Bar. Business services. Disabled: adapted rooms.
Gym. Internet (wireless, free). No-smoking rooms.
Restaurant.

Radisson SAS Alcron

Štěpánská 40, Prague 1 (222 820 000/
www.radisson.com/praguecs). Metro Muzeum/
tram 3, 9, 14, 24, 26. **Rooms** 211. **Rates** 5,000-
7,519 Kč double. **Credit** AmEx, DC, MC, V.
Map p331 N7 ㉛
The Radisson SAS Alcron was known as a jazz hotel
when it was built in 1930. It's kept that part of its
history preserved, despite since morphing into one
of the city's first luxury hotels. The higher your
room, the more beautiful the views, but the towering ceilings and period furnishings in all the rooms
make each one a gem. There's also a worthwhile
restaurant here, for which *see p166*.
Bar. Concierge. Disabled: adapted rooms. Gym.
No-smoking floors. Parking. Restaurant. Room
service. TV: pay movies.

Moderate

987 Prague

Senovážné náměstí 15, Prague 1 (255 737 100/
www.designhotelscollection.com). Metro Hlavní
Nádraží/tram 3, 9, 14, 24. **Rooms** 80. **Rates**
2,480-3,740 Kč double. **Credit** AmEx, DC, MC, V.
Map p329 P4 🔢

A recent development that's operated by the Spanish
hotel chain Design Hotels Collection, 987 Prague
owes its übercool look and feel to Philippe Starck. It
was built as an apartment building in the 19th
century; during the renovations, the architects
left the outside untouched but let Starck infuse the
interior with contemporary brightness. There's a
bit of a '70s feel, but it's brought off in a more effective, sleek and comfortable way than many other
hotels in Prague have managed. Check the website
for deep discounts.

Bar. Concierge. Internet (wireless, free).
Restaurant. TV: pay movies.

Carlo IV

Senovážné náměstí 13, Prague 1 (224 593
111/www.boscolohotels.com). Metro Hlavní
nádraží/tram 5, 9, 26. **Rooms** 152. **Rates**
6,010-8,520 Kč double. **Credit** AmEx, DC,
MC, V. **Map** p329 P4 🔢

The Carlo IV offers slightly misplaced Italian opulence. The incongruity comes from its location in a
well-placed but not particularly pretty street, while
the luxury comes courtesy of the Boscolo Hotels
chain, which did a lot of work on this former
bank/post office in order to turn it into the decadent
hotel it is today. There's a cigar bar, an indoor swimming pool, wooden floors and a soothing colour
palette of sage, gold and mahogany. It's a cushy
place to stay, even if some rooms might benefit from
more space and less poshness. *Photos pp144-145.*
Concierge. Internet (cable, free). Gym. No-smoking
rooms. Parking (500 Kč). Pool (indoor).
Restaurant. Spa. TV: pay movies.

Grand Hotel Evropa

Václavské náměstí 25, Prague 1 (224 228
117/www.evropahotel.cz). Metro Můstek/
tram 3, 9, 14, 24, 26. **Rooms** 92. **Rates**
2,200-4,000 Kč double. **Credit** AmEx, MC, V.
Map p329 N6 🔢

The art nouveau façade of the building that houses
the Grand Hotel Evropa sticks out like a sore thumb
among the souvenir shops of Wenceslas Square.
Once inside, though, you'll appreciate the exterior.
Some rooms still come in tattered Louis XVI style,
although the renovated ones are more pleasant. If
you want a laugh, and a chance to snap some inside-
and-out photos to show pals back home, try 'economy class' accommodation: rooms have a basin but
share a bathroom. (However, 52 of the 92 rooms do
have en suite facilities.)
Concierge. Parking. Restaurant.

Hilton Prague Old Town

V celnici 7, Prague 1 (221 822 111/www1.
hilton.com). Metro Náměstí Republiky/tram 5, 8,
9, 14. **Rooms** 310. **Rates** 5,250-7,500 Kč double.
Credit AmEx, MC, V. **Map** p329 P3 🔢

This corporate satellite has long built its reputation
on consistency. But since converting from a
Renaissance to a Hilton, its status has been elevated
by the addition of Gordon Ramsay's Maze restaurant, the chef's first venture into the Czech Republic.
With its high-tech meeting rooms and high-speed
Wi-Fi, the hotel is an excellent choice for business
travellers. Guest rooms are well kept and nicely decorated, offering a bit more warmth than others
within this price band. Amenities include well-hyped
new beds featuring custom duvets, big pillows and
luxurious linens. Breakfast, though, is not included.
Bar. Business services. Disabled: adapted rooms.
Gym. Internet (wireless). No-smoking rooms.
Parking (750 Kč). Pool. Restaurants (2). TV:
pay movies.

Hotel Adria Prague

Václavské náměstí 26, Prague 1 (221 081 111/
www.hoteladria.cz). Metro Můstek/tram 3, 9, 14,
24, 26. **Rooms** 88. **Rates** 3,770-4,650 Kč double.
Credit AmEx, DC, MC, V. **Map** p328 M6 🔢

Once a Carmelite convent but now in the heart of Sin
City on Wenceslas Square, the Adria offers decent
value for its in-the-thick-of-it location. A complete
renovation has brought it up to modern snuff in
recent years, modernising this veteran nicely with
cool designer tones. Other perks include the attached
Fransiscan Gardens and, in the cellar, a faux grotto
cellar restaurant.
Bar. Concierge. Disabled: adapted rooms. Gym.
Internet (cable). No-smoking rooms. Parking (450
Kč). Restaurant. Room service. TV: pay movies.

★ Hotel Elite

Ostrovní 32, Prague 1 (224 932 250/www.
hotelelite.cz). Metro Národní třída/tram 6, 9, 18,
21, 22, 26. **Rooms** 79. **Rates** 2,310-4,950 Kč
double. **Credit** AmEx, MC, V. **Map** p330 L7 🔢

The Elite is a member of the Small Charming Hotels
group; for once, the name of the parent group is an
accurate description. The 14th-century building has
been carefully renovated and retains many ancient
architectural features; the suite is even protected by
the Town Hall as a historical monument. The location is slightly off the beaten path but by no means
inconvenient; it's a good base from which to explore
the restaurants and bars of the neighbourhood.
Bar. Concierge. Internet (wireless, free). Parking
(400 Kč). Restaurant.

Hotel Opera

Těšnov 13, Prague 1 (222 315 609/www.hotel-
opera.cz). Metro Florenc/tram 8, 24. **Rooms** 67.
Rates 3,000-5,300 Kč double. **Credit** AmEx, DC,
MC, V. **Map** p329 Q2 🔢

CONSUME

You can't miss the towering pink building of the Hotel Opera, just steps from the Florenc metro station. Everything's been redone following severe damage in the floods of 2002. It's not a charmer, really, but it offers good-value rooms in an emerging neighbourhood close to Old Town.
Bar. Gym. Internet (cable, free). Parking (400 Kč). Restaurant.

Marriott

V celnici 8, Prague 1 (222 888 888/www. marriothotels.com). Metro Náměstí Republiky/ tram 5, 8, 9, 14. **Rooms** 293. **Rates** 4,200-5,300 Kč double. **Credit** AmEx, DC, MC, V. **Map** p329 P3 ⑨
You know what to expect for the money, and – sure enough – you'll get the same excellent service here that you would at any other Marriott. A good location and solid amenities make it a fine choice for business travellers, but there are also good deals for families and an amazing fitness centre on site.
Bar. Business services. Concierge. Disabled: adapted rooms. Gym. Internet (cable, free). No-smoking floors. Parking (450 Kč). Pool. Restaurant. Room service. TV: pay movies.

Mercure Prague Centre Na Poříčí

Na poříčí 7, Prague 1 (221 800 800/www. mercure.com). Metro Náměstí Republiky/tram 5, 8, 9, 14. **Rooms** 174. **Rates** 4,140-5,280 Kč double. **Credit** AmEx, DC, MC, V. **Map** p329 O3 ⑩
The bright white lobby and sweeping staircase inside the Mercure will match any expectations born of the building's beautiful neo-baroque exterior. The rooms themselves are basic, but efficient staff ensure a pleasant stay. Literary tourists should note that Franz Kafka worked in the building when it housed an insurance company, and the bar/library is a tribute to him and other Czech writers.
Bar. Concierge. Disabled: adapted rooms. Internet (wireless, free). No-smoking rooms. Restaurant. Room service.

Budget

Hotel 16 U sv. Kateřiny

Kateřinská 16, Prague 2 (224 920 636/224 919 676/www.hotel16.cz). Metro IP Pavlova/tram 4, 6, 10, 11, 16, 22. **Rooms** 14. **Rates** 2,900-3,500 Kč double. **Credit** MC, V. **Map** p330 M10 ⑪
A little way off the beaten path, this small hotel is good value for travellers looking for a quiet bargain within walking distance of Wenceslas Square. Located right next to the Botanical Gardens, it's a peaceful place with friendly staff, and even offers some big-hotel amenities (babysitting and airport transfers, for instance). The rooms are straightforward and hardly modish, but it's really all about the wallet-friendly rates.
Bar. Parking (350 Kč).

Jerome House

V jirchářích 13, Prague 1 (224 933 207/www. hoteljeromehouse.cz). Metro Národní třída/tram 6, 9, 18, 21, 22, 26. **Rooms** 65. **Rates** 1,300-3,300 Kč double. **Credit** MC, V. **Map** p330 K7 ⑫
Having grown into a travel agency with several other bargain properties in town, the Jerome is worth calling even if this location's full. The hotel's interiors are as basic as they come, but they're clean and modern. For a cheaper deal if you're travelling in a group, ask about the special rates for the nine rooms that offer shared facilities. The location isn't typical for tourist hotels; still, Wenceslas Square is nearby, which means there are plenty of restaurants and shops waiting to be discovered.
Business services. Disabled: adapted rooms.

U Šuterů

Palackého 4, Prague 1 (224 948 235/www. usuteru.cz). Metro Můstek/tram 3, 9, 14, 24, 26. **Rates** 2,490-4,190 Kč double. **Credit** MC, V. **Map** p330 M7 ⑬
The building in which it's housed dates all the way back to 1383, but the rooms that comprise U Šuterů were renovated in handsome and surprisingly stylish fashion as recently as 2004. The interior is tastefully decorated with understated elegance, and the pub downstairs is famed throughout the city for its affordable goulash and old-fashioned service. A good-value option for the area.
Bar. No-smoking rooms. Restaurant.

CONSUME

Carlo IV. See p143.

Hostels

Charles University Dorms

Voršilská 1, Prague 1 (224 933 825). Metro Národní třída/tram 6, 9, 18, 22, 26. **Rates** *Per person* 250-500 Kč double. **No credit cards.** **Map** p330 K7 ⓺

Budget travellers should check out the possibility of staying in the university's dormitories, which are open to visitors out of academic termtimes. However, some locations are a bit out of town, and you'll be roughing it at others. The central office arranges accommodation in hundreds of dorm rooms scattered throughout the city; prices vary according to location.

★ Hostel Rosemary

Růžová 5, Prague 1 (222 211 124/www.prague citycityhostel.cz). Metro Můstek. **Rates** *Per person* 350-850 Kč bed in shared room; 600-800 Kč double. **Credit** AmEx, MC, V. **Map** p329 O5 ⓺

The Rosemary has been winning over backpackers in droves, and for good reason: prices are keen and services are sound. Alongside the shared rooms, there are some private rooms with en suite baths. Facilities include free internet access, a kitchen and laundry facilities, and the location (just off Wenceslas Square) is great for the price. There are more beds available at the nearby sister hostel U Melounu. *See also p137* **Backpacker Chic.**
Internet (shared terminal, free).

Klub Habitat

Na Zderaze 10, Prague 2 (224 918 252). Metro Karlovo náměstí/tram 4, 10, 16, 22. **Rooms** 7. **Rates** *Per person* 300-450 Kč bed in shared room. **No credit cards.** **Map** p330 K8 ⓺

The rooms are spick and span, all proceeds go to charity and you get free lemonade and a complimentary breakfast. Suspicious? Don't be: Klub Habitat offers outstanding value, great service and a very worthwhile location. Book well ahead, mind: understandably and unsurprisingly, it gets very busy. Beds are in quadruple rooms.
Bar.

FURTHER AFIELD

Staying towards the edge of the city (which is small, so all of the hotels below are within a ten- to 15-minute public transport ride from the centre) can mean fresher air, lots more neighbourhood character and a chance to mix with locals. It can also save you a lot of money.

Deluxe

Le Palais

U Zvonařky 1, Vinohrady, Prague 2 (234 634 111/www.palaishotel.cz). Metro IP Pavlova or Náměstí míru/tram 4, 10, 16, 22. **Rooms** 72. **Rates** 4,770-10,830 Kč double. **Credit** AmEx, DC, MC, V. **Map** p331 P12 ⓺

At Home Abroad

A new wave of enterprises allows visitors a taste of apartment life in Prague.

CONSUME

For roughly the price of a night in a smartish mid-range hotel, savvy Prague visitors could find themselves right at home. Or, to be precise, in someone else's home, thanks to a number of operations that deal in short-term apartment rentals in the city. Major agencies charge almost as much as budget hotels for such a service, and sometimes a fair bit more. However, longtime Praguers such as photojournalist David Brauchli have had a different idea.

Having seen a string of guests and visiting friends overcharged for fairly standard rooms over the years, Brauchli decided to launch **Apartments in Prague** (http://apartments-in-prague.org) in 2000. A natural at ferreting out privileged information, Brauchli has done a great job in tracking down homely crash-pads, cosy niches and historic apartments throughout the city.

At one point, Apartments in Prague had 24 apartments, but Brauchli has downsized to a more manageable 16 this year. All of them come with the usual amenities (such as Wi-Fi, a kitchenette and reading room), and range in size from studios to two-bedroom affairs. One, on Zborovská street, just three blocks south of the Malá Strana district in Smíchov, was designed by the owner with cool modernist touches such as sand-coloured bathroom tilework, an extra deep tub and a heated floor, with hardwood underfoot and both European- and American-standard electric currents. Others, such as a two-bed apartment by the Charles Bridge (with a third sofabed for flexibility), supplement incredible access to the sights with wonderful antique furniture.

With a little more than a dozen apartments, **Amazing Prague** (www.amazing-prague.com) is another good resource for down-home Prague living. One of its apartments, a two-minute walk from Prague Castle, features satellite TV, a washing machine, free internet access and space for five guests. Another building in Malá Strana overlooks a formal garden with a fountain, some ten minutes from the Charles Bridge.

Toucan Apartments (www.toucan apartments.com) has been operating in Prague since 1997, while simultaneously running operations in Amsterdam and Gran Canaria. Particularly gay-friendly, Toucan offers a full range of lodgings, from affordable studios to a seven-room 'mansion' that's just a short walk from the Charles Bridge. Nightly rates run a bit higher than the competition, but visitor reviews are routinely glowing.

Situated in an idyllic corner of Vinohrady, this beautiful belle époque palace is one of the best insider tips in town. The building was originally decorated by renowned Czech artist Luděk Mařold in exchange for rent, and many of his original touches remain; check out, in particular, the frescoed ceilings and staircase. Service is excellent, and amenities include a large and well-equipped fitness centre, a fine restaurant, a summer terrace and the newly added Pure Spa. The bedrooms themselves are nicely decorated, but some could still benefit from a bit more renovation.

Bar. Concierge. Disabled: adapted rooms. Gym. No-smoking rooms. Parking (660 Kč). Restaurant. Room service. Spa.

Expensive

Diplomat Hotel Praha

Evropská 15, Dejvice, Prague 6 (296 559 111/ www.diplomatpraha.cz). Metro Dejvická/tram 2, 20, 26. **Rooms** 398. **Rates** 6,580-8,250 Kč double. **Credit** AmEx, MC, V.

Thanks to a thorough renovation in 2007, the Diplomat is an even better choice than before for visitors who prefer to stay a little distance from the hustle of tourist central (it's a short ride on the metro), but not so far away that they can't take advantage of the centre's benefits. The hotel is only 20 minutes by car from the airport, and its excellent meeting rooms and other amenities make it a positive choice for business travellers. It's also popular with families, thanks to its periodic specials and the ample room to roam outside. Helpful and friendly staff add to the recommendation.

Bar. Business services. Concierge. Disabled: adapted rooms. Gym. Internet (cable). No-smoking rooms. Parking (500 Kč). Restaurants (3). Room service. TV: pay movies.

Moderate

Bohemia Plaza

Žitná 50, Prague 2 (224 941 000/www. bohemiaplaza.com). Metro IP Pavlova or Muzeum/tram 4, 6, 10, 11, 16, 22. **Rooms** 20. **Rates** 4,480-5,600 Kč double. **Credit** MC, V. **Map** P330 L8 ⑬

The quiet elegance inside the Bohemia Plaza, located between Wenceslas Square and Vinohrady, fortunately overshadows the noisy street outside. Some 15 of the hotel's 20 guestroom options are suites, each of which is decorated in a different theme: take no. 9, with its Chinese wedding theme and shockingly pink walls, or the Russian Imperial design of no.14, decorated with original oil paintings. Most of the rooms aren't as fancy as those, but the owners have taken care with the antique furniture in each one. Monthly rates are available.

Bar. Concierge. Internet (wireless). No-smoking rooms. Parking. Restaurant. Room service.

Corinthia Towers

Kongresová 1, Vyšehrad, Prague 4 (261 191 111/www.corinthia.cz). Metro Vyšehrad. **Rooms** 544. **Rates** 3,470-7,500 Kč double. **Credit** DC, MC, V.

This high-rise is a little way outside the centre, but it is adjacent to Vyšehrad. The Corinthia group has a reputation for outstanding service, and its Prague operation is no exception. The 24-storey building offers five non-smoking floors and a range of suites, as well as many more run-of-the-mill rooms with pretty basic hotel-room decor. Amenities include a bowling alley, a casino and, on the 26th floor, a swimming pool.

Bar. Concierge. Disabled: adapted rooms. Gym. Internet (cable, free). No-smoking floors. Pool. Restaurant.

Hotel Villa Schwaiger

Schwaigerova 3, Bubeneč, Prague 6 (233 320 271/www.villaschwaiger.cz). Metro Hradčanská/ bus 131. **Rooms** 22. **Rates** 3,020-5,530 Kč double. **Credit** AmEx, MC, V.

Villa Schwaiger is a peaceful, elegant option, located close to a beautiful park. The hotel has been designed for comfort and style, with new designer rooms and a mini-spa; the overall effect is simple but tasteful, and you'll be sleeping in the heart of ambassador row. Sizzling Brazilian-style steaks are the restaurant's speciality.

Bar. Internet (wireless, free). Parking (350 Kč). Restaurants (3). Spa. TV: pay movies.

Mövenpick Hotel

Mozartova 1, Smíchov, Prague 5 (257 151 111/ www.moevenpick-prague.com). Metro Anděl/ tram 4, 7, 9. **Rooms** 442. **Rates** 2,140-4,020 Kč double. **Credit** AmEx, MC, V.

The Mövenpick is the exception that proves the old rule about location, location, location. The hotel is out of the city centre, but the combination of surrounding natural beauty, excellent service and top-class amenities has helped it overcome its situation. The hotel is made up of two buildings, with the executive wing only accessible by cable car; its breathtaking views and fine dining attract many a Czech celebrity. Rooms are comfortable, although they're also a little nondescript. The peaceful park that lies below the hotel is a relaxing place in which to stroll.

Concierge. Disabled: adapted rooms. Gym. Internet (cable, free). No-smoking floors. Parking. Restaurants (2). Room service. TV: pay movies.

Budget

1. Alpin Penzion

Velehradská 25, Žižkov, Prague 3 (222 723 970/www.alpin.cz). Metro Jiřího z Poděbrad/ tram 11. **Rooms** 24. **Rates** 1,370-1,710 Kč double. **Credit** MC, V. **Map** p333 C3 ⑬

CONSUME

Contrary to what its name suggests, this is no half-timbered cottage with a flaxen-haired shepherdess tending the hearth. It's actually a bare-bones, institutional-looking pension, but the staff are friendly and the prices reasonable. Oddly, there's 10% off for aviators (the management runs a flying school). The hotel is located in the heart of Žižkov's pavement café district; breakfast is included.
Disabled: adapted room. Internet (cable, free). Parking.

★ Botel Admiral
Hořejší nábřeží, Smíchov, Prague 5 (257 321 302/www.admiral-botel.cz). Metro Anděl/tram 4, 6, 7, 9, 10, 12, 14, 20, 26. **Rooms** 87. **Rates** 2,160-3,130 Kč double. **Credit** AmEx, DC, MC, V.
The Botel Admiral offers the joy of staying on the high waters of the Vltava, always a thrill during summer flood season. The boat-hotel offers excellent views across and down the river, plus a fun restaurant topside and a bar; the rooms, meanwhile, are comfortable and clean. A decent and decidedly unusual place to stay.
Bar. No-smoking rooms. Parking (400 Kč). Restaurant. Room service.

Hotel Abri
Jana Masaryka 36, Vinohrady, Prague 2 (722 811 097/www.abri.cz). Metro Náměstí Míru/tram 4, 10, 16, 22. **Rooms** 25. **Rates** 1,800-2,800 Kč double. **Credit** AmEx, MC, V.
The Abri is a small but tidy hotel with a nice location in a residential Vinohrady neighbourhood, about five minutes from the metro and two minutes from a tram stop. Don't expect many designer flourishes in the rooms, which are large, airy and simply done with salmon-coloured accents. The lobby is spacious, and the terrace is a restful respite in warm weather. The staff, too, are excellent.
Disabled: adapted rooms. Parking (250 Kč). Restaurant.

Hotel Anna
Budečská 17, Vinohrady, Prague 2 (222 513 111/www.hotelanna.cz). Metro Náměstí Míru/tram 4, 10, 16, 22. **Rooms** 24. **Rates** 2,740 Kč double. **Credit** AmEx, MC, V. **Map** p333 B4 ⑩
Thanks to its late-1800s building and its art nouveau interior, not to mention its location on a quiet, tree-lined street in Vinohrady, the Anna brings the traveller back to yesteryear. The guestrooms are a bit on the small side, but they're nicely furnished, and the rates are good value.
Internet (Wi-Fi, free). Parking (350 Kč/day). TV: satellite.

Hotel City Bell
Belgická 10, Vinohrady, Prague 2 (www.hotel-city-bell-prague.com). Metro Náměstí Míru/tram 4, 10, 16, 22. **Rooms** 24. **Rates** 2,050-2,500 Kč double. **Credit** AmEx, MC, V. **Map** p333 A4 ⑪

Formerly known as Hotel City, this property has undergone extensive renovations of late. Now renamed for the second time in three years, it offers friendly, helpful service in a quiet, tucked-away corner of Vinohrady. Everything is new, including the light wood furniture and colourful painted walls. There are 'classic' and 'economy' rooms; economy class entails sharing a bathroom with another room.
Internet (cable, free). No-smoking rooms. Parking (350 Kč). TV.

Hotel Ibis Praha Malá Strana
Plzeňská 14, Smíchov, Prague 5 (221 701 700/ www.accorhotels.com). Metro Anděl/tram 6, 9, 20. **Rooms** 225. **Rates** 1,630-2,260 Kč double. **Credit** AmEx, MC, V.
Despite the optimistic name, this branch of the Ibis chain isn't really in Malá Strana, but in the bordering Smíchov district. Still, it's within a five-minute tram ride of the centre, and offers some of the best value rooms in the area if you're not bothered by staying in a honeycomb. Certainly, it's a good back-up plan if all the charmers are full and you're heading here on short notice but don't fancy shelling out for a Marriott or Hilton. The staff know their customer service.
Bar. Gym. Internet (wireless, free). Parking (400 Kč). Restaurant. Room service. TV: pay movies.
Other locations Kateřinska 36, Nove Mesto, Prague 2 (228 65 777); Šaldova 54, Karlín, Prague 8 (222 332 800).

Hotel Tosca
Blanická 10, Vinohrady, Prague 2 (221 506 111/www.hotel-tosca.cz). Metro Náměstí Míru/ tram 4, 10, 16, 22. **Rooms** 27. **Rates** 2,800-3,900 Kč double. **Credit** AmEx, MC, V. **Map** p333 A4 ⑫
If you can forgive the location on a noisy road, you may well enjoy the Hotel Tosca. There's a huge and welcoming bar area when you enter, whereupon you'll be greeted by friendly staff. The rooms won't win any decorating prizes, but they are comfortable and contain all the usual necessities. A good-value option.
Bar. Concierge. Disabled: adapted rooms. Internet (wireless, free). No-smoking rooms. Parking (480 Kč).

Hotel Tříska
Vinohradská 105, Žižkov, Prague 3 (222 727 313/www.hotel-triska.cz). Metro Jiřího z Poděbrad/tram 11. **Rooms** 57. **Rates** 1,700-2,500 Kč double. **No credit cards. Map** p333 C3 ⑬
The Tříska's combination of Czech murals, art deco and whitewashed empire furnishings is a style all its own. The rooms each have their own decorating scheme, but it's obvious that the owners took time over the interior and pride in what they've done. If possible, request a courtyard-facing room, as the street can get quite noisy. The location is a

good one, an ideal base from which to explore the city at large.
Bar. Disabled: adapted room. Parking (free). Restaurant. TV: satellite.

★ Julian
Elišky Peškové 11, Smíchov, Prague 5 (257 311 150/www.julian.cz). Tram 6, 9, 12, 20.
Rooms 33. **Rates** 2,900-3,320 Kč double.
Credit AmEx, MC, V.
A bit of luxury in up-and-coming Smíchov, the Julian features a drawing room with a fireplace and a library, both wonderful places in which to relax and unwind after a day spent about town. The hotel has a separate breakfast room for smokers but its lobby bar is non-smoking, a rarity here. All rooms are decorated in a light, understated style; there are apartments with kitchenettes as well as a family room, complete with toys. It's not dead in the centre, but it's only a ten-minute tram ride away.
Bar. Gym. Disabled: adapted rooms. Internet (cable, free). No-smoking rooms. Parking (350 Kč). TV: pay movies.

Pension Vyšehrad
Krokova 6, Vyšehrad, Prague 2 (241 408 455/ www.pension-vysehrad.cz). Metro Vyšehrad.
Rooms 5. **Rates** 1,700 Kč double. **No credit cards.**
If you want to live like a local, the Vyšehrad is a very good bet. Located in a residential area, the family-run pension is full of home-style hospitality. The rooms are lovingly decorated, and there's a beautiful green garden in which to while away sunny days. It's just two metro stops from the centre, but you'll have the luxury of staying away from the crowds. Pets stay free.
Parking (200 Kč).

Hostels

A&O Hostel Prague
U vystaviště 1, Holešovice, Prague 7 (220 870 252/www.aohostels.com). Metro Holešovice/tram 5. **Beds** 140. **Rates** *Per person* 330-450 Kč bed in shared room; 400-660 Kč double. **No credit cards. Map** p332 E1 ❼❹
The Prague branch of this small German hostel chain offers dormitory, single and double rooms in a great location in the Holešovice area, with good tram and metro services to the city centre. There's no curfew, 24-hour service, big American breakfasts (good value at 150 Kč) and a bar in an 18th-century cellar. *See also p137* **Backpacker Chic.**
Bar. Internet (shared terminal). No-smoking rooms. Parking (200 Kč).

Clown & Bard
Bořivojova 102, Žižkov, Prague 3 (222 716 453/www.clownandbard.com). Metro Jiřího z Poděbrad/tram 5, 9, 11, 26. **Beds** 143. **Rates**

Per person 250-300 Kč bed in shared room.
Per room 780-1,000 Kč double. **No credit cards. Map** p333 B2 ❼❺
Set in the colourful Žižkov neighbourhood, the Clown & Bard certainly does its best to contribute to the local fun factor. Its popularity means that it's not really the place for a quiet stay. But if you want to party, this is the hostel for you: no lockout, no reservations, music jams and one double even has an en suite bath – luxury! Breakfast is available.
Bar.

Hostel Boathouse
Lodnická 1, Modřany, Prague 4 (241 770 051/ www.hostelboathouse.com). Tram 3, 17, 21.
Beds 56. **Rates** *Per person* 350-420 Kč bed in shared room. **No credit cards.**
Set on the banks of the Vltava, the Hostel Boathouse is a great place for those who want to escape to the country while visiting the city. Amenities include all the usual bits and pieces; friendly staff can organise golf, tennis, bikes for rent, canoeing and hiking trips. Breakfast and bed linens are included in the rates.
See also p137 **Backpacker Chic.**
Internet (shared terminal, 1 Kč/min). Parking (200 Kč).

★ Miss Sophie's Prague
Melounova 3, Vinohrady, Prague 2 (296 303 530/www.miss-sophies.com). Metro Karlovo náměstí/tram 4, 6, 10, 16, 22. **Beds** 25.
Rates *Per person* 410 Kč bed in shared room.
Per room 1,500-1,800 Kč double. **Credit** MC, V.
Map p331 N9 ❼❻
Miss Sophie's covers the spectrum in style, with dorms, private rooms and apartments in smart Vinohrady. The dorm rooms are sparse with wooden floors; private rooms have elegant marble bathrooms; and the apartments, located across the street, have full kitchens. The owners have done an admirable job with antique touches; in particular, the staircase is a marvel. Boasting a terrace and a brick cellar lounge, this is a stylish addition to the Prague hostel scene. *See also p137* **Backpacker Chic.**
Bar. Internet (shared terminal).

Sir Toby's Hostel
Dělnická 24, Holešovice, Prague 7 (283 870 635/ www.sirtobys.com). Metro Vltavská or Nádraží Holešovice/tram 1, 3, 9, 12, 15, 25. **Beds** 70.
Rates *Per person* 250-470 Kč bed in shared room. *Per room* 1,100-1,600 Kč double. **Credit** AmEx, DC, MC, V. **Map** p312 E2 ❼❼
Accommodating staff make Sir Toby's a sure winner. The art nouveau building has been stylishly redecorated, and the interior almost makes you forget you're staying in a hostel. The Holešovice neighbourhood is happening, and there's easy access to the centre of town. Shared and private rooms are available. *See also p137* **Backpacker Chic.**
Bar. Internet (wireless, free). Parking (200 Kč).

CONSUME

Restaurants

Times – and tastes – are changing on the city's restaurant scene.

It sometimes seems as if Czechs would be happy eating the same old *guláš*, dumplings and sauerkraut all their lives. Understandable, perhaps, once you've tasted these hearty classics done to perfection. But if Prague's new crop of dining rooms is any indication, the locals are slowly starting to enjoy more exotic tastes.

You'll find everything from sushi to four-cheese ravioli these days, occasionally mingling on menus with traditional Czech food straight from granny's cookbook. It's far from a food capital, Prague: pick a restaurant at random, and the odds are it will be a humdrum pizzeria or a design-obsessed place that relies heavily on its microwave. But it's getting better.

DINING IN PRAGUE

The prevailing logic on the Prague dining scene is that locals need a trump card in order to persuade their party to try a new place that offers foreign cuisine. 'Don't worry, Honza,' offers the host. 'Of course, they can also do *guláš*.' The hold of robust Bohemian meats and potato pancakes is so strong that while many young Czech chefs have mastered lobster liquorice foam and Moroccan tagine, many restaurateurs still feel a need to offer trad Czech fare alongside their less familiar dishes.

Traditions remain intact, not least of which is the classic overlit, nicotine-stained local pub. Many are mere drinking dens; for those, *see pp175-188*. But those that serve food, such as **Pivnice u Pivrnce** (*see p163*), are a treat. At these old-school *hospoda* or *hostinec*, you can expect to sit at communal tables munching on hearty dishes (*see p167* **Profile**). Most such places close their kitchens at 10pm, and may tell you that food isn't available after 9pm.

Further up the scale, some restaurants have dug deeper into the traditional cookbooks and come up with dishes that are both familiar and unique. And location can also be key. Although

many restaurants offer masterful *svíčková* (Czech beef in cream sauce), the winner is, or should be, the one that serves it in a Gothic bell tower, as at **Zvonice** (*see p172*).

The French and Italians have felt no need to expand on their own classic repertoires, of course, and have proudly added **Brasserie M** (*see p166*) and **Giardino** (*see p173*) to the Prague scene. Others have found you don't need non sequiturs on the menu if you're good at blending: **Allegro** (*see p158*), the city's first Michelin star winner, makes no compromises with its Tuscan delights, yet also offers classic Mitteleuropa conceptions. **Villa Richter** (*see p151*), meanwhile, has solved the problem by doing incredible Argentine steak upstairs and a stunning Bohemian duck one level down.

Essential information

Prague still dines with a relaxed dress code, and reservations are necessary at only the new generation of upmarket spots. Although you

❶ Blue numbers given in this chapter correspond to the location of each restaurant on the street maps. *See pp326-333.*

INSIDE TRACK
SHARING A TABLE

At restaurants where tables are shared, patrons should ask '*Je tu volno?*' ('Is it free?') before sitting down. It's also polite to wish your fellow diners '*dobrou chuť*' ('bon appetit') before tucking in.

should have little trouble making a phone booking in English at modern establishments, it might otherwise be easier to reserve in person.

Many waiters still record diners' tabs on a slip of paper, which translates into a bill at the end of the meal. Pay the staff member with the folding wallet in his or her waistband, not your waiter; the phrase '*Zaplatím, prosím*' means 'May I pay, please?'). Speaking of service, you may well run up against some of the city's famously negligent and testy waiters, even at the smartest restaurants. But that's all part of the post-communist transformation.

A small cover and extra charges for milk, bread and even frightful accordion music are still observed at many pubs, as is tipping by rounding the bill up to the nearest 10 Kč. At nicer places, ten to 15 per cent tips have become the rule.

HRADČANY

U Císařů

Loretánská 5, Prague 6 (220 518 484/www. ucisaru.cz). Metro Malostranská, then tram 22, 23. **Open** 9am-1am daily. **Main courses** 300-550 Kč. **Credit** MC, V. **Map** p326 C3 ❶ **Czech**
A long-favoured location for traditional Czech food within a short walk of Prague Castle, At the Emperor's has platters of smoked meats, hearty roasts, decadent desserts, classy service and ye olde Bohemian interiors. Other attractions include a good-sized wine cellar and street tables.

Kč Malý Buddha

Úvoz 46, Prague 6 (220 513 894/www.maly buddha.cz). Metro Malostranská, then tram 22, 23. **Open** noon-10.30pm Tue-Sun. **Main courses** 100-250 Kč. **No credit cards.** **Map** p326 B4 ❷ **Asian**
Little Buddha is a teahouse with a difference: great vegetarian spring rolls and noodle dishes go hand in hand with the dozens of teas brewed by the laid-back owner, who's always on hand. Sit in the soft candlelight and inhale heady whiffs of incense with your eggrolls. Mellow doesn't go halfway towards describing this place.

Restaurant Hradčany

Keplerova 6 (224 302 430/www.savoyhotel.cz). Metro Malostranská, then tram 22, 23. **Open** 6.30am-10.30am, noon-3pm, 6-11pm daily. **Main courses** 350-750 Kč. **Credit** AmEx, MC, V. **Map** p326 A3 ❸ **European**
The classy gourmet dining room at the Savoy has won several awards of late, with its mix of Czech classics and hip conceptions of Euro cuisine, from lamb shank with veal tarragon sauce to smoked trout with egg gnocchi. Service is of a high calibre and hotel guests get menu deal discounts.
▶ *For the hotel, see p127.*

Villa Richter.

★ U Ševce Matouše

Loretánské náměstí 4, Prague 6 (220 514 536/ www.usevcematouse.cz). Metro Malostranská, then tram 22, 23. **Main courses** 150-350 Kč. **Credit** AmEx, MC, V. **Map** p326 B3 ❹ **Czech**
The classic steakhouse, Czech style, with done-to-order tenderloins in traditional sauces such as green peppercorn or mushroom. A short walk east of Prague Castle, it's housed in a cosy former shoe-maker's workshop where it was once possible to get your boots repaired while lunching. Prices are reasonable given the prime location.

★ Villa Richter

Staré Zamecké Schody 6 (257 219 079/www.villa richter.cz). Metro Malostranská/tram 22, 23. **Open** 10am-11pm daily. **Main courses** 210-710 Kč. **Credit** AmEx, MC, V. **Map** p327 G2 ❺ **Czech/International**
Come to the best terrace location in the city for this exciting new restaurant – or, to be precise, trio of restaurants: there's expertly wrought gourmet cuisine from monkfish to Argentine beef up top at Piano Nobile; masterful Czech classics in the middle at Piano Terra; and lighter, delicate tastes from tagliatelle to Dijon pork neck at Panorama Pergola at the lower level. The three overlook the city and the Malá Strana district from a graceful vineyard just outside the east gate of Prague Castle, and are extensions of a creamy-toned palace with a wine cellar that has won rave reviews.

What's on the Menu?

Don't let the Czech carte get lost in translation.

English-language menus are common at most Czech restaurants and pubs these days, and most even offer the same prices as the Czech versions. But when visiting an old-school pub or eatery, it's useful to know that there are two categories of main dishes: *minutky*, cooked to order (which may take ages); and *hotová jídla*, ready-to-serve fare.

The usual accompaniments to these dishes are rice, potatoes and the fried béchamel dough known as *krokety*, all of which should be ordered separately.

When dining in pubs, the closest thing served to fresh vegetables is often *obloha*: a garnish of pickles, or a tomato on a single leaf of cabbage. Tasty appetisers to try include *polévka,* Prague ham with horseradish, or various rich soups; *bramborová polévka* (potato soup) is a classic. Dessert staples include *palačinky*, pancakes filled with ice-cream, fruit or jam, and *jablečný závin*, apple strudel.

MEALS (JÍDLA)
snídaně breakfast; **oběd** lunch; **večeře** dinner.

PREPARATION (PŘÍPRAVA)
bez masa/bezmasá jídla without meat; **čerstvé** fresh; **domácí** home-made; **dušené** steamed; **grilované** grilled; **míchaný** mixed; **na roštu** roasted; **pečené** baked; **plněné** stuffed; **smažené** fried; **špíz** grilled on a skewer; **uzené** smoked; **vařené** boiled.

BASICS (ZÁKLADNÍ)
chléb bread; **cukr** sugar; **drůbež** poultry; **karbanátek** patty of unspecified content; **máslo** butter; **maso** meat; **ocet** vinegar;

olej oil; **omáčka** sauce; **ovoce** fruit; **pepř** pepper; **rohlík** roll; **ryby** fish; **smetana** cream; **sůl** salt; **sýr** cheese; **vejce** eggs; **zelenina** vegetables.

DRINKS (NÁPOJE)
čaj tea; **káva** coffee; **mléko** milk; **pivo** beer; **pomerančový džus** orange juice; **sodovka** soda; **víno** wine; **voda** water.

APPETISERS (PŘEDKRMY)
boršč Russian beetroot soup (borscht); **chlebíček** meat open-sandwich; **hovězí vývar** beef broth; **kaviár** caviar; **paštika** pâté; **polévka** soup; **uzený losos** smoked salmon.

MEAT (MASO)
biftek beefsteak; **hovězí** beef; **játra** liver; **jehně** lamb; **jelení** venison; **kančí** boar; **klobása, párek, salám, vuřt** sausage; **králík** rabbit; **ledvinky** kidneys; **slanina** bacon; **srnčí** roebuck; **šunka** ham; **telecí** veal; **tlačenka** brawn; **vepřové** pork; **zvěřina** game.

POULTRY & FISH (DRŮBEŽ A RYBY)
bažant pheasant; **husa** goose; **kachna** duck; **kapr** carp; **křepelka** quail; **krocan** turkey; **kuře** chicken; **losos** salmon; **pstruh** trout; **úhoř** eel.

MAIN MEALS (HLAVNÍ JÍDLA)
guláš goulash; **řízek** schnitzel; **sekaná** meat loaf; **smažený sýr** fried cheese; **svíčková** beef in cream sauce; **vepřová játra na cibulce** pig's liver stewed with onion; **vepřové koleno** pork knee; **vepřový řízek** fried breaded pork.

MALÁ STRANA

Alchymist
Hellichova 4, Prague 1 (257 312 518). Metro Malostranská/tram 12, 20, 22, 23. **Open** noon-3pm, 7-11pm daily. **Main courses** 900-1,400 Kč. **Credit** AmEx, MC, V. **Map** p327 F5 **6 Central European/French**
Renovated in 2008, this over-the-top venue has gone more boldly than ever into designer fantasy – though red velvet, alchemical symbols, statues and gilt mirrors remain part of the scheme. Its look is still a stronger suit than the French-influenced menu, which – admittedly – is also wild and varied.

Kč Bar Bar
Všehrdova 17, Prague 1 (257 312 246/www.bar-bar.cz). Tram 6, 9, 12, 20, 22, 23. **Open** noon-midnight Mon-Thur, Sun; noon-2am Fri, Sat. **Main courses** 115-300 Kč. **Credit** MC, V. **Map** p327 F6 **7 Crêperie**
On a curving little backstreet near Kampa Island, Bar Bar has been a local secret for years. The open sandwiches, salads and grill dishes will pass, but the savoury crêpes are the real highlights. Run by a group of artists and animators, this cellar bar and restaurant serves a host of savoury pancakes, plus English-style dessert ones with lemon and sugar. Waiters are reasonably flexible about substitutions.

CONSUME

SIDE DISHES (PŘÍLOHY)
brambor potato; **bramborák** potato pancake; **bramborová kaše** mashed potatoes; **bramborový salát** potato salad; **hranolky** chips; **kaše** mashed potatoes; **krokety** potato or béchamel dough croquettes; **obloha** small lettuce and tomato salad; **rýže** rice; **salát** salad; **šopský salát** cucumber, tomato and curd salad; **tatarská omáčka** tartar sauce; **zelí** cabbage.

CHEESE (SÝR)
balkán feta; **eidam** hard white cheese; **hermelín** soft cheese, similar to a bland brie; **Madeland** Swiss cheese; **niva** blue cheese; **pivní sýr** beer-flavoured semi-soft cheese; **primátor** Swiss cheese; **tavený sýr** packaged cheese spread; **tvaroh** soft curd cheese.

VEGETABLES (ZELENINA)
česnek garlic; **chřest** asparagus; **cibule** onion(s); **čočka** lentils; **fazole** beans; **feferonky** chilli peppers; **hrášek** peas; **kukuřice** corn; **květák** cauliflower; **mrkev** carrot; **okurka** cucumber; **petržel** parsley; **rajčata** tomatoes; **salát** lettuce; **špenát** spinach; **žampiony** mushrooms; **zelí** cabbage.

FRUIT (OVOCE)
ananas pineapple; **banány** banana; **borůvky** blueberries; **broskev** peach; **hrozny** grapes; **hruška** pear; **jablko** apple; **jahody** strawberries; **jeřabina** rowanberries; **mandle** almonds; **meruňka** apricot; **ořechy** nuts; **ostružina** blackberry; **pomeranč** orange; **rozinky** raisins; **švestky** plums; **třešně** cherries.

DESSERTS (MOUČNÍK)
buchty traditional curd-filled cakes; **čokoláda** chocolate; **dort** layered cake; **jablečný závin** apple strudel; **koláč** cake with various fillings; **ovocné knedlíky** fruit dumplings; **palačinka** crêpe; **pohár** ice-cream sundae; **šlehačka** whipped cream; **zákusek** cake; **závin** strudel; **žemlovka** bread pudding with apples and cinnamon; **zmrzlina** ice-cream.

USEFUL PHRASES
Mohu vidět jídelní lístek? May I see the menu?
Máte...? Do you have...?
Jsem vegetarián/vegetariánka (m/f) I am a vegetarian
Jak je to připravené? How is it prepared?
Říkal jste 'pivní sýr'? Did you say 'beer cheese'?
Páni, to smrdí! Wow, that smells!
Mohu mít bez...? Can I have it without...?
Nechci kečup na pizzu, prosím No ketchup on my pizza, please
Neobjednal jsem si to I didn't order this
Jak dlouho to ještě bude? How much longer will it be?
Účet, prosím The bill, please
Nedá se to jíst a nezaplatím to I can't eat this and I won't pay for it! (use with extreme caution)
S sebou Takeaway/to go
Pivo, prosím A beer, please
Dvě piva, prosím Two beers, please
Ještě jednou, prosím Same again, please
Co si dáte? What'll you have?
Dám si... I'll have...
Pro mě ne, děkuji Not for me, thanks
Bez ledu, děkuji No ice, thanks
Je totálně namazaný He's really smashed

CONSUME

★ El Barrio de Ángel
Lidická 42, Prague 5 (mobile 725 535 555/ www.elbarrio.cz). Metro Anděl/tram 6, 9, 12, 20. **Open** 11.30am-midnight Mon-Wed; 11.30am-1am Thur-Sat; noon-midnight Sun. **Main courses** 160-330 Kč. **Credit** AmEx, MC, V. **Americas**
Descend into this hip, dark, wood-planked shrine to Argentine beef. Start with a chimichanga *de pollo* or a light rocket salad, but whatever you do, don't leave without sampling a burger or steak: finely scorched, tender as the night, and complemented by reasonably priced, full-bodied wines. Save room for the *dulce de leche*. Service can be spotty, but this is Prague so you'll probably be used to it by now. *Photo p154.*

Kč Bohemia Bagel
Lázeňská 19, Prague 1 (257 218 192). Metro Malostranská/tram 12, 20, 22, 23. **Open** 7.30am-7pm daily. **Main courses** 100-300 Kč. **No credit cards.** **Map** p327 G4 **❽** **Americas**
With a newly expanded menu, this American-owned chain continues to grow. After bringing the first true bagel café to post-1989 Prague, it moved on to free coffee refills, fresh muffins, delicious breakfast bagels and bagel sandwiches. For innovative, good-value dinner specials, try the Holešovice branch.
▶ *The owners also operate U Malého Glena, a fine local jazz club; see p251.*

El Barrio de Ángel. See p153.

Other locations Masná 2, Staré Město, Prague 1 (224 812 560); Dukelských hrdinu 48, Holešovice, Prague 7 (220 806 541).

Café El Centro

Maltézské náměstí 9, Prague 1 (257 533 343/ www.elcentro.cz). Metro Malostranská/tram 12, 22, 23. **Open** noon-midnight daily. **Main courses** 150-280 Kč. **Credit** MC, V. **Map** p327 F4 **❾ Mediterranean**

This easily overlooked Malá Strana bar, just a block off the main square, specialises in mambo soundtracks and tropical cocktails. Efforts to expand into a full restaurant specialising in paella for two and assorted hot and cold tapas aren't winning over the daiquiri-lovers, but the postage-stamp patio at the rear is a boon.

★ Café Savoy

Zborovská 68, Smíchov, Prague 5 (251 511 690/ www.ambi.cz). Tram 6, 9, 12, 22. **Open** 8am-10.30pm Mon-Fri; 9am-10.30pm Sat, Sun. **Main courses** 300-600 Kč. **Credit** AmEx, MC, V. **Map** p327 G6 **❿ Mediterranean/seafood**

Now part of the thriving Czech restaurant group Ambiente, this high-ceilinged, 19th-century café is elegant, airy and expert, offering an excellent menu of seafood and other Mediterranean fare, plus classy service. It attracts a fashionable crowd and is just out of the way enough to merit a walk across the Most Legii from Staré Město.

C'est la Vie

Říční 1, Prague 1 (721 158 403/www.cest lavie.cz). Tram 6, 9, 12, 22, 23. **Open** 11.30am-1am daily. **Main courses** 300-1,200 Kč. **Credit** AmEx, MC, V. **Map** p327 G6 **⓫ Central European/Italian**

Self-billed as a 'trendy restaurant for those who want to be in', this improbably upmarket place is geared toward Czuppies, but it may be worth cutting through the attitude for a river embankment table, baked butterfish with mushroom risotto or *filet mignon* with a good cabernet. Service doesn't keep up with the ambitious menu.

Cowboys

Nerudova 40, Prague 1 (800 152 672/www. kampagroup.com). Metro Malostranská/tram 12, 22, 23. **Open** noon-2am daily (meals served until 10.30pm). **Main courses** 250-500 Kč. **Credit** AmEx, MC, V. **Map** p326 D3 **⓬ Americas**

You might not believe it when you see the stetsons, kinky leather vests and hottie servers, but Cowboys is a lot classier than the restaurant that previously inhabited this labyrinth of brick cellars. For the location, service and T-bones, not to mention occasional live rock and folk, it's incredible value, all topped off by a terrace with enviable views of the city.

Cukrkávalimonáda

Lázeňská 7, Prague 1 (257 530 628). Metro Malostranská/tram 12, 20, 22, 23. **Open** 8.30am-8pm daily. **Main courses** 100-300 Kč. **No credit cards**. **Map** p327 F4 **⓭ Light meals**

Best for salads, cakes and coffees, this calming, characterful caff just off the main drag from Charles Bridge is situated on a lovely, quiet corner of Maltézské náměstí. The short list of wines and daily light lunch specials make for handy open-air refreshment in summer. Expect tall lattes, casually alert service, designer benches, hanging greenery and slick magazines to peruse.

David

Tržiště 21, Prague 1 (257 533 109/www. restaurant-david.cz). Metro Malostranská/tram 12, 20, 22, 23. **Open** 11.30am-11pm daily. **Main courses** 350-1,450 Kč. **Credit** AmEx, MC, V. **Map** p327 E4 **⓮ Czech/Central European**

Another backstreet Malá Strana district gem, David has a long history of serving quiet, excellent meals for patrons who eschew publicity. The strong suit is definitive Bohemian classics such as roast duck with red and white sauerkraut or rabbit fillet with spinach leaves and herb sauce. Booking is essential.

Il Giardino

Mozartova 1, Smíchov (257 154 262/www. movenpick-prague.com). Metro Anděl/tram 4, 7, 9. **Open** 5.30am-10.30am, noon-11pm daily. **Main courses** 350-1,200 Kč. **Credit** AmEx, MC, V. **Mediterranean**

CONSUME

The Mövenpick's international chefs, top-drawer reputation, family-friendly service and fine views complement the very fair Mediterranean cuisine. Excellent lunch specials and swift service (meals served in 20 minutes, with free parking) appeal to the business crowd. The chef's renditions of *saltimbocca alla romana* and bouillabaisse have won cheers from all and sundry.

★ Gitanes

Tržiště 7, Prague 1 (257 530 163/www.gitanes.cz). Metro Malostranská/tram 12, 20, 22, 23. **Open** noon-11.30pm daily. **Main courses** 150-350 Kč. **Credit** MC, V. **Map** p327 D3 **⑮ Balkan**

Offering a bracing taste of spice in traditional, safe Central Europe, this two-room place just off the district's main square serves Balkan favourites such as sweet corn *proja* with cheese, stuffed peppers and home-made bread with paprika milk-fat spread, all washed down with hearty red wine. Warm service, cosy gingham and doilies give you the feeling you're visiting your Balkan granny's house, only with much cooler music (emanating from speakers hidden in the birdcages). There's a private table for curtained-off dalliances.

Hergetova Cihelna

Cihelna 2b, Prague 1 (257 535 534/reservations 800 152 692/www.kampagroup.com). Metro Malostranská/tram 12, 22, 23. **Open** 11.30am-midnight daily. **Main courses** 250-450 Kč. **Credit** AmEx, MC, V. **Map** p327 H4 **⑯ Americas/International**

Impressive value and creative culinary efforts, two signature qualities of owner Nils Jebens, ensure that Hergetova Cihelna remains a hot reservation, even in winter. The combination of great Belgian beers, killer casual chow and knock-out riverside tables (complete with blankets for when it's chilly) is a winner. The local obsession with the celebs gathering in the upstairs bar is a perfect insight into what makes Prague tick.

▶ *Jebens also owns Kampa Park next door; see below.*

★ Kampa Park

Na Kampě 8b, Prague 1 (257 532 685/ www.kampa group.com). Metro Malostranská/ tram 12, 20, 22, 23. **Open** 11.30am-1am daily; kitchen closes at 11pm. **Main courses** 435-995 Kč. **Credit** AmEx, MC, V. **Map** p327 H4 **⑰ Central European/seafood**

Gourmet seafood and the best tableside views of Charles Bridge have been winning this place rave reviews from heavy-hitter foreign critics for over a decade. After the likes of lobster tail or seared scallops and capers for starters, it only gets better with the mains, from turbot and pumpkin purée to wild mushroom risotto with garlic foam. A slick bar-room scene happens inside, which dependably acts as a celeb lightning rod while drawing presidents and Hollywood heart-throbs. The gorgeous riverside terrace is open all year.

U Karlova mostu

Na Kampě 15, Prague 1 (257 531 430/ www.nakampe15.com). Metro Malostranská/ tram 12, 22, 23. **Open** 11am-11pm daily. **Main courses** 90-200 Kč. **Credit** AmEx, DC, MC, V. **Map** p307 F4 **⑱ Czech**

CONSUME

Kampa Park.

Our team of chefs and pâtissiers led by Oldřich Sahajdák prepares three tasting menus consisting of seven courses supplemented with seven amuse-bouches.

In the menu Dégustation Bohême Bourgeoise we present traditional meals of Czech culinary art from the end of the 19th century inspired by masterful techniques of the Czech culinary personality Marie B. Svobodová.

The light and fresh menu Terre et Eau is composed of fish and vegetable courses prepared from carefully selected ingredients according to traditional Czech and Mediterranean recipes following modern culinary techniques.

The menu Sélection du Chef offers you a selection of both menus animated with the distinctive style and inspiration of the chef.

The courses vary according to seasonal changes and current offers of Czech producers and organic farms.

Our sommeliers headed by Klára Kollárová set up daily a wine menu well-matched with single courses.

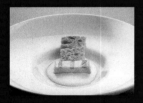

LA DEGUSTATION
BOHÊME BOURGEOISE

La Degustation Bohême Bourgeoise
Haštalská 18 | 110 00 Praha 1
reservation: +420 222 311 234 | www.ladegustation.cz

What's going on? An unpretentious pub-restaurant serving potato thyme soup and *topinka* (Czech fried toast with raw garlic) this close to Charles Bridge? Just don't tell the tourists – and mind that you don't accidentally wind up in the pricey restaurant at this same address. Instead, swing around the corner to the pub with the mustard walls for the real thing. The scattering of outdoor tables on the edge of Kampa Park is among the perks.

U Malé Velryby

Maltézské náměstí 15, Prague 1 (257 214 703/ www.umale velryby.cz). Metro Malostranská/ tram 12, 20, 22, 23. **Open** 11am-midnight daily. **Main courses** 255-315 Kč. **Credit** AmEx, MC, V. **Map** p327 F5 ⑲ Central European/seafood

Owner Jason Le Gear oversees the most exciting culinary addition to this district in a while. The veteran chef of several hit Prague restaurants has now launched his own operation, whipping up delicate seafood (a speciality) and light, perfectly wrought steaks, lamb shanks and duck. Hearty home-made breads and tapas, plus a great wine list (all at impressive prices), start things off in the small, homely, open-kitchen dining room.

U Malířů

Maltézské náměstí 11, Prague 1 (257 530 318/ www.umaliru.cz). Tram 12, 22, 23. **Open** 11.30am-11.30pm daily. **Main courses** 500-790 Kč. **Credit** AmEx, MC, V. **Map** p327 F4 ⑳ Central European

No longer one of Prague's most expensive restaurants, a status it held for years among the business crowd, this quaint 16th-century house with original painted ceilings has shifted its menu from French to Central European but still ladles on the decadence in its conceptions of venison, duck and pork. A bottle will, of course, still double the cost of a meal.

U Maltézských rytířů

Prokopská 10, Prague 1 (257 533 666/www. umaltezskychrytiru.cz). Tram 12, 22, 23. **Open** 11am-11pm daily. **Main courses** 300-1,050 Kč. **Credit** AmEx, MC, V. **Map** p327 F4 ㉑ Czech/Central European

The Knights of Malta once offered this as an inn for the crusader monks. Now a restaurant has been set up in the candlelit, Gothic cellar; and it's a fine one at that, with a noteworthy venison chateaubriand. Mrs Černiková, whose family runs the place, does a nightly narration on the house's history, then harasses you to eat the incredible strudel. Booking is essential.

Nagoya

Stroupežnického 23, Smíchov (251 511 724/ www.nagoya.cz). Metro Anděl/tram 6, 7, 9, 10, 12, 14, 20. **Open** 11.30am-2pm, 6-11pm Mon-Sat. **Main courses** 200-450 Kč. **Credit** AmEx. Sushi

In the sushi craze that still holds Prague in its grip, a few leaders have clearly emerged. Nagoya is one of them. This is one of the few foodstuffs that will set you back more in Prague than in many Western capitals, but if you do shell out, the sashimi, agemono and bento platters are worth the investment.

Nebozízek

Petřín Hill, Petřínské sady 411, Prague 1 (257 315 329/www.nebozizek.cz). Metro Malostranská/ tram 12, 20, 22. **Open** 11am-11pm daily. **Main courses** 230-790 Kč. **Credit** AmEx, MC, V. **Map** p326 D6 ㉒ Central European

Set just next to the middle stop of the funicular railway that runs up Petřín Hill, this touristy restaurant can still be worthwhile on a fine, temperate day for its patio view of Old Town across the river. Prices for the traditional Czech grub are elevated with the view, but a meal here still won't break the bank.

★ Noi

Újezd 19, Prague 1 (257 311 411/www.noi restaurant.cz). Metro Malostranská/tram 20, 22, 23. **Open** 9am-midnight daily. **Main courses** 100-300 Kč. **Credit** AmEx, MC, V. **Map** p327 F6 ㉓ Thai

The most engaging venue for indulging in Prague's growing obsession, Thai food, is better than its tagline, 'the art of taste'. There's cheery service, relaxed Zen style, a lovely patio, and, er, complimentary condoms in the washrooms. Not that your mind will be on much besides the fiery duck *phad kra-prao*.

Noi

CONSUME

CONSUME

Pálffy Palác

*Valdštejnská 14, Prague 1 (257 530 522/
www.palffy.cz). Metro Malostranská/tram 12, 20,
22, 23.* **Open** 11am-11pm daily. **Main courses**
495-850 Kč. **Credit** AmEx, MC, V. **Map** p327 F2
㉙ **Central European**
Set in a wonderfully atmospheric Baroque palace
owned by the Ministry of Culture (it also hosts a classical music academy), Palffy is something to remember in your old age. Originally founded by Prague
clubbing mogul Roman Rezníček, this gem built its
reputation in the early '90s with offerings such as
expertly done rabbit in wine sauce and roebuck marinated in honey and juniper. The crêpes and salads
are generous and delicate affairs.

U Patrona

*Dražického náměstí 4, Prague 1 (257 530 725/
www.upatrona.cz), Metro Malostranská/tram
12, 22, 23.* **Open** 11.30am-1am daily. **Main
courses** 350-600 Kč. **Credit** AmEx, MC, V.
Map p327 G4 ㉕ **Central European**
U Patrona is an oasis of quality in an area dominated
by naff souvenir shops, serving delicate conceptions
of Czech game classics at just a few tables. The country's first glass-walled kitchen lets the clientele know
just what's going into the soup.

Petřínské Terasy

*Seminářská zahrada 13, Prague 1 (257 320 688/
www.petrinsketerasy.cz). Metro Malostranská/
tram 12, 22, 23.* **Open** noon-11pm Mon-Fri;
11am-11pm Sat, Sun. **Main courses** 250-550 Kč.
No credit cards. Map p326 D5 ㉖ **Czech**
One of two tourist traps on Petřín Hill, the 'Petřín
Terraces' offer exquisite views of Prague Castle and
the city, unfortunately alongside expensive
Krušovice beer and indifferent service. Still, if you're
starved and on the hill on a fine day, you may be
able to forgive and enjoy.

U Sedmi Švábů

*Jánský vršek 14, Prague 1 (257 531 455). Metro
Malostranská/tram 12, 22, 23.* **Open** 11am-
11pm daily; kitchen closes at 10pm. **Main
courses** 150-250 Kč. **Credit** AmEx, MC, V.
Map p326 D3 ㉗ **Czech**
Another cellar maze of stone-walled, torch-lit rooms,
this *krčma*, or Czech medieval tavern, has a name
that translates as the Seven Swabians. It's a trippy
if borderline-tacky experience, with occasional trou-
badours, traditional sweet honey liqueur behind the
bar and salty platters of pork knuckle on the tables.
Only in Prague.

Střelecký ostrov

*Střelecký ostrov 336, Prague 1 (224 934 026/
www.streleckyostrov.cz). Metro Národní třída,
then tram 6, 9, 22, 23.* **Open** noon-midnight
daily. **Main courses** 250-450 Kč. **Credit** AmEx,
MC, V. **Map** p327 H6 ㉘ **Czech/Mediterranean**

Sitting on a lovely Vltava river island in the centre
of town, this terraced spot caters to the casual with
decent pizzas, but also manages crispy steaks, Czech
trad food and a decent wine list. Previous endeavours at this location have been ruined by floods, but
the current management is banking on better luck.

U Zlaté studně

*U Zlaté studně 166, Prague 1 (257 533 322/
www.zlatastudna.cz). Metro Malostranská/tram
12, 22, 23.* **Open** 7am-11am, noon-11pm daily.
Main courses 400-750 Kč. **Credit** AmEx, MC,
V. **Map** p327 F2 ㉙ **Central European**
In mild weather, a stop here is the perfect reward for
tramping about Prague Castle – you can walk right
in from the castle gardens. Now run by the management of the Aria hotel, At the Golden Well offers
spectacular views of Malá Strana below, sharp service and a menu that starts off with decadent choices
such as duck livers marinated in Armagnac.
▶ *For the Aria hotel, see p129.*

STARÉ MĚSTO

★ Allegro

*Veleslavínova 2a, Prague 1 (221 426 880/
www.fourseasons.com/prague). Metro
Staroměstská/tram 17, 18.* **Open** 6.30am-11pm
daily. **Main courses** 650-1,800 Kč. **Credit**
AmEx, MC, V. **Map** p328 J4 ㉚ **Czech/Italian**
The winner of the Czech Republic's first Michelin
star, the Four Seasons' flagship was brought up to
world-class speed by chef Vito Mollica, who has
since passed on the mantle. The menu, an inspired
Tuscan-meets-Czech list, features delights like veal
fillet, pan-fried foie gras and truffles or monkfish
saltimbocca. The wine list is just as great, and the
terrace looks out on Prague Castle across the Vltava.
▶ *For the hotel, see p136.*

Amici Miei

*Vězeňská 5, Prague 1 (224 816 688/www.amici
miei.cz). Metro Staroměstská/tram 17, 18.* **Open**
11.30am-11pm daily. **Main courses** 250-650 Kč.
Credit AmEx, MC, V. **Map** p328 L2 ㉛ **Italian**
Amici Miei offers outstanding cuisine in a slightly
overlit hall, discreetly curtained off from the street.
Highlights include veal scallops, simple, comforting
tagliata with parmesan and rocket, and unusually
warm and attentive service, plus an excellent Italian
wine list. The dark, old wood interiors and white
linen service never suffocate, thanks to genial staff.

★ Angel

*V kolkovně 7 (mobile 773 222 422/www.angel
restaurant.cz). Metro Staroměstská/tram 17, 18.*
Open 11.30am-midnight Mon-Sat; 11am-4pm
Sun. **Main courses** 180-450 Kč. **Credit** AmEx,
MC, V. **Map** p328 L3 ㉜ **Asian fusion**
This fresh new entry into the Old Town dining scene
is already buzzing, thanks to its engaging menu of

Angel Delight

Local chef Sofia Aziz on the local culinary scene.

Sofia Aziz has been known to Praguers since the mid '90s. Drawing on Asian influences but extending to decadent desserts, her fine cooking could once be tasted at a long-defunct restaurant called Angel. Now there's a new **Angel** (*see left*) in town – but this time, instead of owning and running the restaurant, Aziz is content simply to rule the kitchen.

Time Out Prague (TOP): Creative menus are rare in Prague. What's the problem?
Sofia Aziz (SA): I don't know if it's such a challenge to create good food. But it's a challenge to achieve consistency and to get chefs to care about what they're doing and not treat the profession as just a job. I think perhaps the profession isn't viewed the same way as in other countries, though this is changing.

TOP: Is it still a challenge to get Czechs to move beyond the traditional?
SA: Not really, which is quite a change from when I started. Now, Czech diners are more adventurous, travelling more widely and becoming more open to trying different foods and flavours.

TOP: Supply must be much easier than it was years ago too.
SA: It's definitely much easier than in the past. Not perfect at times, but most of what I need can be found here with a little bit of legwork. Being in the EU helps.

TOP: So how did you get talked into this again?
SA: This incarnation of Angel is not actually mine – past experiences have made me realise that it's pretty tough to run a business and be a chef at the same time, and my heart and soul belong in the kitchen. It's owned by my two friends from the old Atelier in Vršovice and an investor. I was approached by them to be the head chef: they wanted a restaurant with great food that was based on a chef's name and track record.

TOP: Which dish sells best?
SA: Our taster platter has a selection of four of our starters, and is the obvious choice for customers who are trying the restaurant out for the first time. Also,

black pepper prawns, marinated veal fillet steak – a 'safe' choice, but one that comes with a twist and kick – and, of course, our cheesecake.

TOP: What's the most rewarding aspect of your work?
SA: There are many moments: to see so many Czechs coming in to give us a try and coming back again; when the more unusual dishes, such as the black rice pudding, start to sell; when a (Czech) customer told me, 'You must really love what you do'; my small crew of young chefs producing fantastic food on my days off and clients telling me that they thought I was in the kitchen...

TOP: What's your guiding culinary mantra?
SA: Spice – Asian food can be spicy but isn't always. Balance is crucial.

TOP: What are your main inspirations?
SA: Previous lives, travel, books, talking to other chefs, tasting. I 'taste' food in my head first, then put it all together on a plate – with some trial and error, of course – and eventually work towards a final product.

TOP: Tell us more about your desserts.
SA: Desserts should be sexy, irresistible and naughty. You've already taken diners to the heights of taste and smell, so you want them to groan with pleasure rather than with sensory overload when it comes to the dessert. I tend to keep them simple yet decadent.
Take my favourite dessert: a perfect creme brulée. No need for razzle-dazzle and over-the-top presentation, which I'm not very good at anyway. And we haven't got the space or budget for a dedicated pastry chef. You have to think 'sexy' to accomplish this... It's hard to describe.

TOP: Why the name and the groovy gilt decor?
SA: The owners chose the name Angel because it's recognised in Prague from my previous work... As for the decor, we didn't want either the clichéd Asian restaurant look or over-the-top poshness, but something simple yet warm. Kind of like the food – not over-fussy and over-presented, but still sexy.

CONSUME

Angel.

South-east Asian delights. Prawns in coconut chutney, Javanese slow-cooked lamb shank and scallops with laksa and pineapple are all conceived by veteran chef Sofia Smith in a simple, Zen-like space. Book well ahead for the popular brunch menu. *See also p159* **Angel Delight**.

★ Ariana

Rámová 6, Prague 1 (222 323 438/www.sweb.cz/kabulrest). Metro Náměstí Republiky/tram 5, 8. **Open** 11am-11pm daily. **Main courses** 220-460 Kč. **Credit** AmEx, MC, V. **Map** p328 M2 ❸❸ Afghan

Ariana is a comfortable little Afghan restaurant with excellent, tender, spiced lamb and sumptuous vegetarian *chalous*. Familial service goes with the straightback chairs, rugs and brass lamps. You'll find yourself lingering longer than expected and needing a walk through Old Town after the feast.

Bellevue

Smetanovo nábřeží 18, Prague 1 (222 221 443/www.pfd.cz). Metro Národní třída/tram 6, 9, 18, 22, 23. **Open** noon-3pm, 5.30-11pm Mon-Sat; 11am-3.30pm, 7-11pm Sun. **Main courses** 350-1,250 Kč. **Credit** AmEx, MC, V. **Map** p328 J6 ❸❹ Central European

An early leader on the Prague dining scene, the formal and traditional Bellevue still delivers, although service can be inconsistent and the menu hasn't

evolved in years. But veal loin in black truffle sauce and fallow venison in juniper reduction still go mighty well with Sunday jazz brunch. There are wonderful views of Prague Castle, one reason why booking is essential.

Brasileiro

U Radnice 8, Prague 1 (224 234 474/www.ambi.cz). Metro Staroměstská/tram 17, 18. **Open** 11am-midnight daily. **Main courses** 495-625 Kč. **Credit** AmEx, MC, V. **Map** p328 L4 ❸❺ Americas

In the authentic tradition of Brazilian butchery, this hit locale in the Old Town Hall building serves all the fine cuts of meat you can eat for the fixed price of 495 Kč until 6pm, upping the ante to 625 Kč thereafter. Czech meat-lovers can't seem to get enough of its hearty goodness.

Le Café Colonial

Široká 6, Prague 1 (224 818 322). Metro Staroměstská/tram 17, 18. **Open** 10am-midnight daily. **Main courses** 350-1,250 Kč. **Credit** AmEx, MC, V. **Map** p328 K3 ❸❻ French

An airy restaurant, Le Café Colonial comes with teak accents, miniature quiches, delicate pork and delightful salads. There's more formal dining on the left side in a darker setting, and a veranda with rattan furniture and Matisse colour tones fills out the right side. Its location, opposite the Jewish Cemetery, makes it a draw with tourists, but you won't find buses here. Resolutely French.

Casa Andina

Dušní 15, Prague 1 (224 815 996/www.casaandina.cz). Metro Staroměstska/tram 17, 18. **Open** 11am-11pm Mon-Wed, Sun; 11am-2pm Thur, Fri; 2pm-2am Sat. **Main courses** 260-430 Kč. **Credit** AmEx, MC, V. **Map** p328 L3 ❸❼ Americas

Casa Andina offers Latin American fare cooked with real flair in a warm, new setting – an altogether surprising find in Old Town. Try the *escabeche* or chicken skewer in Aji Panca sauce for a taste of the house speciality: savoury Peruvian cuisine. An excellent Chilean wine list matches the culinary concept. *Photo p163*.

Chez Marcel

Haštalská 12, Prague 1 (222 315 676). Metro Náměstí Republiky/tram 5, 8, 14. **Open** 8am-1am Mon-Sat; 9am-1am Sun. **Main courses** 200-350 Kč. **No credit cards. Map** p328 M2 ❸❽ French

As French as it gets in Prague, Chez Marcel attracts a local crowd drawn by its appealing brass accents, copies of *Le Monde* and views on to a lovely Old Town square. It also makes the deepest quiche in town, which goes well with the big baskets of crispy fries, dappled with Dijon mustard. By night, it's quieter, but still a good hangout in which to enjoy a glass of burgundy and a long conversation.

CONSUME

Kč Country Life

Melantrichova 15, Prague 1 (224 213 366/
www.countrylife.cz). Metro Můstek/tram 3, 9,
14, 24. **Open** 9am-8.30pm Mon-Thur; 8.30am-
2.30pm Fri; 11am-8.30pm Sun. **Main courses**
75-180 Kč. **No credit cards. Map** p328 L4 **39**
Vegetarian
This Czech neo-hippie cafeteria specialises in dirt-
cheap, wholesome, organically grown vegetarian
fare. Menu highlights include massive DIY salads,
fresh carrot juices, delectable lentil soups and
crunchy wholegrain breads. It's best to go at off-
peak times if you can, as there's something of a
lunchtime crush.

La Dégustation

Haštalská 18, Prague 1 (222 311 234/www.la
degustation.cz). Metro Náměstí Republiky/tram
5, 8, 26. **Open** 6pm-midnight Mon-Sat. **Meals**
945-2,650 Kč. **Credit** AmEx, MC, V. **Map** p328
M2 **40 Czech/Central European**
The seven-course menu offered here will take up
most of an afternoon or evening, promising 'the
flavours and tastes of molecular cuisine'. That the
restaurant generally pulls it off is no mean feat –
and makes the pretension forgiveable. Choose from
three fixed-price meals: Bohemian Bourgeoise,
Earth & Sea or Traditional Bohemian, featuring
Wagyu beef, organic Argentine ribs, sweetbreads,
tongue, truffles, and Valrhona Jivara chocolate. Not
all at once.

Francouzská Restaurace

Náměstí Republiky 5, Prague 1 (222 002 770/
www.francouzskarestaurace.cz). Metro Náměstí
Republiky. Metro Národní třída/tram 6, 9, 18,
22, 23. **Open** noon-11.30pm daily. **Main courses**
250-650 Kč. **Credit** AmEx, MC, V. **Map** p329 N4
41 French/Central European
With the city's finest art nouveau pile as a backdrop,
this absurdly ornate dining room, recently featured
in Jiří Menzel's film *I Served the King of England*,
also happens to be a consistent award winner for
cuisine. Try a classic roast duck or let the chefs go
wild with a prawn saffron risotto.
▶ *Book a table here on Sunday for the lovely*
jazz brunch.

★ Kč Himalaya

Soukenická 2, Prague 1 (233 353 594/
www.himalayarestaurant.cz). Metro Náměstí
Republiky/tram 5, 8, 26. **Open** 11am-11pm
Mon-Fri; noon-11pm Sat, Sun. **Main courses**
120-280 Kč. **Credit** AmEx, MC, V. **Map** p329 O2
42 Indian
Easily the most affordable, credible Indian option
for a relaxed dinner in the Old Town area, this cosy
little split-level spot is good for the soul of many
an expat who feels starved of spice. Samosas, vin-
daloo, rogan and korma are among the stalwarts on
its well-thumbed menu.

Kabul

Karolíny Světle 14, Prague 1 (224 235 452/
www.kabulrestaurant.cz). Metro Národní třída/
tram 6, 9, 18, 22, 23. **Open** 10am-11pm daily.
Main courses 80-280 Kč. **Credit** AmEx, MC, V.
Map p328 J6 **43 Afghan**
Done up in Persian rugs and hanging lanterns,
Hasib Saleh's cosy little eatery is a local fave, serving fine specialities such as ashak pastry parcels and
okra fingers, all with fresh flatbread. The place soon
fills up at lunchtime, so you're more likely to get a
table later in the day or evening.

King Solomon

Široká 8, Josefov, Prague 1 (224 818 752/
www.kosher.cz). Metro Staroměstská/tram 17, 18.
Open noon-11pm Mon-Thur, Sun (kitchen closes
10.30pm); 11am-90mins before sundown Fri; open
by request with reservation Sat. **Main courses**
450-950 Kč. **Credit** AmEx, MC, V. **Map** p328 L3
44 Jewish
Just a block from the Jewish Museum, King Solomon
is a congruous and solid addition to the area: an
upmarket restaurant with Hebrew-speaking staff
and certified kosher cuisine unavailable elsewhere
in town. With an atrium in the back, a long and
authoritative Israeli wine list and austere sandstone-
and-iron decor, it may be an odd setting for traditional comfort food such as gefilte fish, chicken soup
and carp with prunes, but Solomon's a hit with visiting groups. And the portions, darling!

Kč Klub Architektů

Betlémské náměstí 5a, Prague 1 (224 401 214).
Metro Národní třída/tram 6, 9, 18, 22, 23.
Open 11.30am-midnight daily. **Main courses**
120-350 Kč. **Credit** AmEx, MC, V. **Map** p328 K4
45 Central European
You'll find this intimate, great-value restaurant
down in the cellar of an architecture and design
gallery next door to the Bethlehem Chapel. The
cusine is credible and creative European, the waiters are gracious and friendly, and the speed is just
right. Just don't trip on the steep stairs leading down
into it. In mild weather, try to nab one of the tables
at the front.

Kogo Pizzeria & Caffeteria

Havelská 27, Prague 1 (224 214 543/www.
kogo.cz). Metro Můstek/tram 6, 9, 18, 22, 23.
Open 8am-11pm daily. **Main courses** 420-910
Kč. **Credit** AmEx, MC, V. **Map** p328 M4 **46**
Mediterranean
Prices have gone up of late at this wildly popular
local chain of fashionable Mediterranean restaurants, but a visit is still a treat. Fortunately, there
are heaps of salads, soups and starters to provide
cheaper, lighter options – not that anyone could call
the mains heavy. Scampi, bruschetta, bean soup and
focaccia are served fast and stylishly by foxy staff,
as are nicely topped pizzas.

CONSUME

Other locations Na Příkopě 22, Nové Město, Prague 1 (221 451 259); L'Angolo by Kogo Restaurant Lounge, Dlouhá 7, Prague 1 (224 829 355).

★ Kolkovna

V Kolkovně 8, Prague 1 (224 819 701/www. kolkovna.cz). Metro Staroměstská/tram 17, 18. Open 9am-midnight daily. Main courses 180-450 Kč. Credit AmEx, MC, V. Map p328 L3 **47** Czech

An art nouveau interior and trad pub grub – potato pancakes, beer-basted goulash – attracts the bright and beautiful local patrons to a re-creation of old Prague. And it's licensed by the brewery Pilsner Urquell, so you know the beer will be good. If it's packed, the sister location on V Celnici generally has more space (and a hopping basement disco). Other locations V Celnici 4 (224 212 240); Vítězná 7 (251 511 080).

Maestro

Křižovnická 10, Prague 1 (222 320 498). Metro Staroměstská/tram 17, 18. Open 11am-11pm daily. Main courses 180-350 Kč. Credit AmEx, DC, MC, V. Map p328 J4 **48** Italian

Wicker chairs, baroque trompe l'œil on the walls and, yes, proper wood-fired pizzas… But Maestro is more than just a standard corner pizza palace. Service is generally right on target, and the food is a bargain. The chicken cacciatore is inspiring if the pizzas don't appeal.

★ Kč U Medvídků

Na Perštýně 7, Prague 1 (224 211 916/www. umedvidku.cz). Metro Národní třída/tram 6, 9, 18, 22, 23. Open 11am-11pm Mon-Fri; 11.30am-11pm Sat; 11.30am-10pm Sun. Main courses 150-350 Kč. Credit AmEx, MC, V. Map p328 K6 **49** Czech

Five centuries of cred as a beerhall have made the Little Bears a mecca for Budvar drinkers. The menu goes well beyond pub grub, with pork in plum sauce and fillets in dark beer reduction, among other treats. Hardcore diners might care for *tlačenka*, or head cheese. It's invariably packed with locals.

Metamorphis

Malá Štupartská 5, Prague 1 (221 771 068/ www.metamorphis.cz). Metro Náměstí Republiky/ tram 5, 8, 26. Open 9am-midnight daily. Main courses 420-910 Kč. Credit AmEx, MC, V. Map p328 M3 **50** Mediterranean

Sedate and capable, this family-run pasta café and pension has just one disadvantage: it's directly on a main tourist route to Old Town Square. The cellar restaurant within is enhanced by live jazz at night, though, and there's enough competition around these days that it's not necessarily overrun. It's the only place within a few blocks of Old Town Square to eat alfresco after 10pm.

Kč Modrá Zahrada

Národní třída 37, Prague 1 (224 239 055). Metro Národní třída/tram 6, 9, 17, 18, 22, 23. Open 11am-11.30pm daily. Main courses 120-280 Kč. Credit AmEx, MC, V. Map p328 L6 **51** Pizza

A popular and utilitarian pizza joint with moody blue decor and an art deco theme. At street level, you'll find a futuristic bar, with vanity tables in the window for exhibitionists. One level up (stairs hidden at the back), regulars gather for cheap, pleasant pies, nearly all of which contain some kind of meat. It's a relaxing place and a bargain given the location. Service can be somewhat dizzy.
Other locations Široká 114, Josefov, Prague 1 (222 327 171); Vinohradská 29, Vinohrady, Prague 2 (222 253 829).

U Modré kachničky

Michalská 16, Prague 1 (224 213 418/www.u modrekachnicky.cz). Metro Staroměstská/tram 6, 9, 18, 22, 23. Open 11.30am-11.30pm daily. Main courses 350-750 Kč. Credit AmEx, MC, V. Map p328 L5 **52** Czech

One of the most successful little dining rooms opened since the Velvet Revolution occupies a granny's house-style setting on a narrow side street. The kitchen offers hearty, slightly modernised classics, such as roast duck with pears and boar steak with mushrooms.
Other locations Nebovidská 6, Prague 1 (257 320 308).

Nostress

Dušní 10, Prague 1 (222 317 007/www. nostress.cz). Metro Staroměstská/tram 17, 18. Open 8am-11pm Mon-Fri; 10am-11pm Sat, Sun. Main courses 250-550 Kč. Credit AmEx, MC, V. Map p328 L3 **53** Central European/French

Staff at this elegant café-cum-lifestyle shop encourage patrons to have a good look around at the wrought-iron furnishings and hanging lamps, which are all for sale. The couches and tables could be a bit much for hand luggage, but much of the good stuff is portable and locally made by hand. It's a great, tranquil spot for lunch or an afternoon drink.

INSIDE TRACK JITRNICE

In the admittedly slightly unlikely event that you're invited to a traditional pig slaughter while you're here, you'll have the opportunity to try *jitrnice*: sausage made with pig's intestine, stuffed on the spot after the pig is killed. If your constitution can take it, you can try an alternative version, with blood and grain mixed in. There's nothing that satisfies like a good *jelito*.

CONSUME

Casa Andina. *See p160*.

Pivnice u Pivrnce

Maiselova 3, Josefov, Prague 1 (222 329 404).
Metro Staroměstská/tram 17, 18. **Open** 11am-
midnight daily; kitchen closes at 11.30pm. **Main
courses** 120-230 Kč. **Credit** MC, V. **Map** p328
K3 ⑤④ **Czech**
Rough, ready and looking all set to stare down the
next century unchanged, this pub prides itself on
traditional, rib-sticking Czech pork and dumplings,
served with above-average presentation. *Svíčková*
(beef in a lemon cream sauce), duck with sauerkraut
and walls covered with crude cartoons are guaranteed to offend. Radegast here is well tapped and
nicely priced.

Pizza Nuova

Revoluční 1, Prague 2 (221 803 308/www.ambi.cz).
Metro Karlovo Náměstí/tram 4, 6, 10, 22. **Open**
11.30-11.30pm daily. **Main courses** 180-370 Kč.
Credit AmEx, MC, V. **Map** p329 N3 ⑤⑤ **Pizza**
This new property of the Czech chain Ambiente
meets its usual standards for service, decor and
food, which generally set the pace for such ventures.
That pace isn't particularly pulse-quickening and
certainly not risky, but it does produce dependable
pizzas and pastas with quickish service at reasonable prices. The zesty house tomato sauce and
cheeses have won stellar reviews, and the location's
handy if you need to refuel after a morning's shopping on Dlouhá street.

Pravda

Pařížská 17, Prague 1 (222 326 203/www.
pravda restaurant.cz). Metro Staroměstská/
tram 17, 18. **Open** noon-11pm Mon-Thur,
Sun; noon-midnight Fri, Sat; kitchen closes

1hr before closing times. **Main courses** 250-850
Kč. **Credit** AmEx, MC, V. **Map** p328 L3 ⑤⑥
International
Owner Tommy Sjöö, who helped bring fine dining
to post-1989 Prague, now runs a nicely airy and elegant restaurant. Chicken in Senegal peanut sauce
vies with Vietnamese nem spring rolls and borscht,
all done credibly. Further appeal is provided by high
ceilings, an Old Europe atmosphere, aproned waiters and graceful service.

La Provence

Štupartská 9, Prague 1 (222 324 801/www.
kampa group.com). Metro Náměstí Republiky/
tram 5, 8, 14. **Open** 11am-11pm daily. **Main
courses** 350-670 Kč. **Credit** AmEx, MC, V.
Map p328 M4 ⑤⑦ **French**
Under the management of Nils Jebens, the Czech
Republic's answer to Terence Conran, La Provence
is a comfy rural French restaurant that does fine foie
gras, tiger prawns, roast duck and monkfish. It's
also a comfortable tourist attraction, just a block off
Old Town Square.

U Radnice

U radnice 2, Prague 1 (224 228 136). Metro
Staroměstská/tram 17, 18. **Open** 10am-11pm
daily. **Main courses** 50-100 Kč. **Credit** AmEx,
DC, MC, V. **Map** p328 L4 ⑤⑧ **Czech**
U Radnice is one of the last places around Old Town
Square that offers traditional food served at prices
meant for the locals. The tasty Czech specialities
such as goulash or beef in cream sauce go for a pittance. Alas, a recent restoration cleaned it up a bit
too much, but the communal tables still create a comfortable pub atmosphere.

CONSUME

Red Hot & Blues

Jakubská 12, Prague 1 (222 314 639). Metro Náměstí Republiky/tram 5, 14, 26. **Open** 9am-11pm daily. **Main courses** 120-230 Kč. **Credit** AmEx, MC, V. **Map** p309 K3 ⑤⑨ **Americas**
Perhaps best on Sunday mornings for brunch on the patio (assuming you're not trumped by a stag party), this requisite expat institution first brought Cajun and Mexican platters to Bohemia. With the requisite blues player seated on a stool by night, and the patio now conveniently heated and enclosed for winter, the restaurant is reliable and relaxed. You're best off avoiding the overpriced drinks specials.

Kč Restaurance po Sečuánsku

Národní třída 25, Prague 1 (221 085 331). Metro Národní třída/tram 6, 9, 17, 18, 22, 23. **Open** 10am-11pm daily. **Main courses** 79-220 Kč. **No credit cards. Map** p328 K6 ⑥⓪ **Chinese**
Tucked away in the Palác Metro shopping passage, this is a handy, clean, bright option for Chinese food, with a vast list of *rychlé*, or quick, items priced well under 100 Kč. *Kung pao*, sweet-and-sour chicken and fried rice all come in this size, perfect for a snack.

U Sádlů

Klimentská 2, Prague 1 (224 813 874/www. usadlu.cz). Metro Náměstí Republiky/tram 5, 8, 14. **Open** 11am-midnight Mon-Sat; noon-midnight Sun. **Main courses** 180-450 Kč. **Credit** MC, V. **Map** p329 N2 ⑥① **Czech**
OK, it's medieval kitsch – but efficient, tasty and affordable medieval kitsch. And a good quantity of mead with pepper steak or boar can make for a great Friday night out. Reading the illuminated menu by torchlight can be a challenge, but there is nice armour in the bar.

Sarah Bernhardt

U Obecního domu 1, Prague 1 (222 195 900/ www.hotel-pariz.cz). Metro Náměstí Republiky/ tram 5, 8, 26. **Open** 6.30-10am, noon-4pm, 6-11pm daily. **Main courses** 280-650 Kč. **Credit** AmEx, MC, V. **Map** p329 N3 ⑥② **Central European**
The favourite model for Alfons Mucha has lent more than her name to this fabulously gilded lobby restaurant of the Hotel Paříž. The chef has revived the place of late, and a series of tasting menus overseen by celebrity guest chefs, a serenaded Sunday brunch and a vinotheque complete with takeaway foie gras have built up further buzz. It's worth a splash even if staying at the hotel is not within your budget.
▶ *For the hotel, see p139.*

Siam-I-San

Valentinská 11, Prague 1 (224 814 099/ www.arzenal.cz). Metro Staroměstská/tram 17, 18. **Open** 10am-midnight daily. **Main courses** 250-650 Kč. **Credit** AmEx, MC, V. **Map** p328 K3 ⑥③ **Thai**

This chic Thai restaurant sits above a designer glassware shop, and has the biggest selection of fiery South-east Asian appetisers in town. It's a favourite among well-heeled expats: eating here is a bit like being in a display case, but it's handy for Old Town, and fairly priced for the district.

★ Kč Siam Orchid

Na poříčí 21, Prague 2 (222 319 410/www.siam orchid.cz). Metro Náměstí Republiky/tram 5, 8, 26. **Open** 10am-10pm daily. **Main courses** 120-320 Kč. **Credit** AmEx, MC, V. **Map** p329 P3 ⑥④ **Thai**
An easy-to-miss family joint up the stairs in a shopping passage, Siam Orchid has the most authentic and unpretentious Thai food in town. Look out in particular for chicken satay and delicious mains of fried tofu with mung beans, fiery chicken and cod curries, plus Thai beer.

Století

Karolíny Světlé 21, Prague 1 (222 220 008/ www.stoleti.cz). Metro Národní třída/tram 6, 9, 18, 22, 23. **Open** noon-midnight daily (kitchen closes 10.30pm). **Main courses** 180-299 Kč. **Credit** AmEx, MC, V. **Map** p328 J6 ⑥⑤ **Central European**
A comfortable, capable and imaginative eaterie, Století doesn't waste effort on empty flourishes, but just delivers the goods without fuss. Encompassing a good choice of dishes for vegetarians, including a delicate spinach soufflé, the list of remarkably affordable mains otherwise favours roast chicken, pork and beef with interesting sauces (cold orange curry and cayenne). There's soothing old-world decor and swift service too.

Sushi Point

Na příkopě 19, Prague 2 (222 211 013/www. sushi-point.cz). Metro Náměstí Republiky/tram 5, 8, 26. **Open** 11am-10pm daily. **Main courses** 180-350 Kč. **Credit** AmEx, MC, V. **Map** p329 N4 ⑥⑥ **Sushi**
Sushi Point is the latest place in which to be seen tossing back raw tuna and slivers of pickled ginger, with a crowd of spendy young Czech consumers fresh from the shopping malls nearby. It's one of the better reasons to duck into this otherwise retail-heavy complex.

La Veranda

Elišky Krásnohorské 2, Prague 1 (224 814 733/ www.laveranda.cz). Metro Staroměstská/tram 17, 18. **Open** noon-midnight Mon-Sat; noon-10pm Sun. **Main courses** 295-495 Kč. **Credit** AmEx, MC, V. **Map** p328 L2 ⑥⑦ **Central European**
Once a bit obnoxiously trendy, this top-rated dining room and cellar has morphed into a more comfortable, capable and affordable gem with excellent-value lunch specials. Taking pride in using only local beef, rabbit and lamb from South Bohemia,

CONSUME

La Veranda serves up approachable modern conceptions of the Czech classics, along with al dente pastas and engaging specialities such as quail and coffee crème brûlée.

V Zátiší
Liliová 1, Betlémské náměstí, Prague 1 (222 221 155/www.pfd.cz). Metro Národní třída/tram 6, 9, 18, 22, 23. Open noon-3pm, 5.30-11pm daily. Main courses 400-600 Kč. Credit AmEx, MC, V. Map p328 K5 ⑱ International
Celebs and foodies are often spied slipping into this old townhouse on a narrow lane, seduced by the call of delicate gourmet risottos, sashimi, monkfish and saffron sauce, venison with rosehip sauce or a maple and herb-crusted rack of New Zealand lamb. This was for years considered one of the city's most elegant dining rooms, with expert chefs and some fine French vintages. It's since been surpassed but is still a contender.
▶ The management runs the Bellevue; see p160.

NOVÉ MĚSTO

★ Alcron
Štěpánská 40, Prague 1 (222 820 038). Metro Můstek/tram 3, 9, 14, 24. Open 5.30-10.30pm Mon-Sat. Main courses 400-1,850 Kč. Credit AmEx, MC, V. Map p331 N7 ⑲ Seafood
Before World War II, the Alcron was a byword for a top-class night on the town. The name was borne by the predecessor to what is now the Radisson, where the restaurant lurks in a side room off the lobby. Over just seven tables, seafood master Roman Paulus casts lobster bisque and smoked eel with black truffles and savoury sauces. Lunch is by prior arrangement only.
▶ For the hotel, see p142.

Banditos
Melounova 2, Prague 2 (224 941 096/www.banditosrestaurant.cz). Metro IP Pavlova/tram 6, 10, 11, 22, 23. Open 9am-12.30am daily. Main courses 180-380 Kč. Credit AmEx, MC, V. Map p331 N9 ⑰ Americas
There's an expat-friendly, café-style atmosphere to Banditos, where the food runs to Tex-Mex and Southwestern favourites. Try the spicy chicken sandwich, the Caesar salad or the cheeseburgers. Although it's off the beaten path, it's a great gathering point for margarita and bull sessions.

Brasserie M
Vladislavova 17, Prague 1 (224 054 070/www.brasseriem.cz). Metro Národní třída/tram 6, 9, 18, 22, 23. Open 11am-11pm Mon-Fri; noon-midnight Sat. Main courses 125-645 Kč. Credit AmEx, MC, V. Map p330 L7 ⑰ French
This big room has earned praise and crowds for its delectable French grills, which include tender steaks in tangy sauces, and an impressive but reasonably

priced wine list. Sunday brunches are the toast of expat families; at other times, the beef tartare à l'Armagnac is the kind of inspired French twist that has helped make this place such a success.

Bredovský Dvůr
Politických vězňů 13, Prague 1 (224 215 428/www.bredovskydvur.unas.cz). Metro Můstek/tram 3, 9, 14, 24. Open 11am-midnight Mon-Sat; 11am-11pm Sun. Main courses 140-360 Kč. Credit AmEx, MC, V. Map p329 O6 ⑰ Czech
An open secret among the office workers around Wenceslas Square, this resolutely Czech dining room has gruff waiters and some of the finest Pilsner in town thanks to the beer tank, which preserves body and flavour. Come here for pork knuckle, sauerkraut and dumplings; productivity in local workplaces probably plummets after lunch. Photo p168.

Café Lamborghini
Vodičkova 8, Prague 1 (222 231 869/www.Ambi.cz). Metro Můstek/tram 3, 9, 14, 24. Open 8am-10pm Mon-Sat; 10am-10pm Sun. Main courses 250-450 Kč. Credit AmEx, DC, MC, V. Map p330 M8 ⑰ Italian
Burning rubber in the race to be Prague's hottest café, Lamborghini is a clean, streamlined space with slate grey accents, where you'll be served with killer Italian coffee, imaginative salads with tropical fruit and gorgonzola, and the best pappardelle carbonara in town. Grind your own fresh parmesan as you take in the colourful cast of casual-cool patrons.
Other locations Vězeňská 1 (224 813 257).

Kč Cafeterapie
Podskalská 3, Prague 2 (224 916 098/www.cafe terapie.o1.cz). Metro Karlovo náměstí, then tram 7, 16, 17, 21. Open 10am-10pm Mon-Fri; noon-10pm Sun. Main courses 100-350 Kč. No credit cards. Mediterranean
Cafeterapie offers fine Mediterranean fare, with a strong vegetarian showing on the menu. Highlights include big, crisp salads, tempeh and a selection of good-value specials that make the most of seasonal ingredients. Situated just off the Vltava, this genial spot makes for a handy stop-off on an outing up to nearby Vyšehrad.

Červená Tabulka
Lodecká 4, Prague 2 (224 810 401/www.cervena tabulka.cz). Metro Náměstí Republiky/tram 8, 26. Open 11.30am-11pm daily. Main courses 120-300 Kč. Credit AmEx, MC, V. Map p329 P2 ⑰ Central European
Amid whimsical play-school decor, Tabulka offers lava-grilled lamb, comforting poultry dishes and other robust favourites: baked duck leg with bacon dumplings, apple and sauerkraut, for instance, cheerily served alongside tasty skewered rabbit with cream and lime sauce. Service is above-par and prices are fair.

Profile Pub Food

Stomach-lining pub grub in Prague offers plenty of unexpected flavour.

Prague's old-school pubs are national treasures. Although drink is the thing, many give more than a passing nod to food, serving hungry diners at communal tables. Despite the emergence of chic, modish restaurants in this increasingly forward-looking city, they look set to stay for the long haul.

Perhaps the most classic pub dish of all is roast pork knuckle – you'll find it in any pub worth

its salt. But there's plenty more to sample on the traditional menu. Try *matjes* (smoked mackerel), the blackened, dried-up pub favourite that's eaten cold. And if that's not quite smelly enough, consider ordering *Olomoucké syrečky*, the cheese so rancid it put the town of Olomouc on the culinary map. It can be fried, though the cooking won't do much to dampen its pong.

Tlačenka, by contrast, is basically odourless. However, it makes up for its absence of aroma with a most unusual composition: composed of mysterious morsels of meat held together with aspic, it can only be translated, roughly but appositely, as 'head cheese'.

If *tlačenka* seems a bit much to tackle, many pub kitchens can throw together a plate of raw beef topped with an egg and served with deep fried toast, raw garlic, paprika, mustard, pepper and salt. This is known as *tatarák* – the Czech version of beef tartare. The technique is to rub the toast with the raw garlic, then top that with the raw beef, into which you've mixed the egg and the spices. *Dobrou chuť*!

CONSUME

PUBS WITH GRUB

Pivnice u Pivrnce (*see p163*). Good beer, soaked up by meaty, no-nonsense local fare.

U Medvídků (*see p162*). Get stuck into a dish of head cheese, if you dare.

U Radnice (*see p163*). Take a seat at the shared tables for a feast; prices are a steal.

Bredovský Dvůr. *See p166.*

Cicala

*Žitná 43, Prague 2 (222 210 375/www.trattoria.
cicala.cz/cz). Metro IP Pavlova/tram 4, 6, 10, 16,
22, 23.* **Open** 11.30am-10.30pm Mon-Sat. **Main
courses** 250-550 Kč. **No credit cards. Map**
p331 O8 🕖 Italian

Still considered a substitute for home by the local
Italian community, this hospitable, low-key cellar
venue features the freshest weekly specials the
owner can create or import, presented like works of
art. An easily missed two-room restaurant on an
otherwise rather unappealing street, Cicala is
worth seeking out.

Deminka

*Škretova 1, Prague 2 (224 224 915/www.
deminka.com). Metro IP Pavlova/tram 6, 10, 11,
22, 23.* **Open** 11am-11pm daily. **Main courses**
140-550 Kč. **Credit** AmEx, MC, V. **Map** p331 P9
🕖 Czech

This celebrated café has changed several times since
opening in 1886, and at least twice since 1989. These
days, though, it seems to have settled on its classically renovated space and a menu of upmarket
Bohemian classics mixed with quality Italian cuisine. It's been known recently as Il Conte Deminka,
but seems to have reverted to its old moniker.
There's free Wi-Fi.

Don Pedro

*Masarykovo nábřeží 2, Prague 2 (224 923 505).
Metro Národní třída/tram 6, 9, 18, 22, 23.*
Open 5-11pm Tue-Fri; noon-11pm Sat, Sun.
Main courses 180-350 Kč. **No credit cards.
Map** p330 J9 🕖 Americas

You won't find many Colombian restaurants in
Prague, so it's just as well that Don Pedro is the real
deal. Authentic zesty empanadas, spicy beef and
potato soup and gorgeously grilled meats are served
up amid bright southern-hemisphere colours. The
oxtail *cola guisada* with yuca root is a firm
favourite, and makes it well worth enduring the
South American-speed service.

Dynamo

*Pštrossova 220-229, Prague 2 (224 932 020/
www.mraveniste.cz). Metro Národní třída/tram
6, 9, 18, 22, 23.* **Open** 11.30am-midnight daily.
Main courses 180-350 Kč. **Credit** AmEx, MC,
V. **Map** p330 J7 🕖 Central European

This sleek designer diner typifies the renaissance
that's swept through the area to the south of the
National Theatre. Steaks and pasta just about keep
up with the decor; don't miss the wall of single-malt
scotches, but maybe don't try and mix them with the
lunch specials if you want a productive afternoon.
Service is friendly and speedy.

Kč Govinda

*Soukenická 27, Prague 2 (224 816 631/
www.govinda.cz). Metro Náměstí Republiky/
tram 5, 8, 26.* **Open** 11am-5pm Mon-Fri.
Main courses 75-180 Kč. **No credit cards.**
Map p329 O2 🕖 Vegetarian

Cheap but not so cheerful, this Krishna restaurant
offers a basic self-service vegetarian Indian meal for
a mere 85 Kč. Although it's not the most handsome
place in town, it's a clean spot in which to share a
table while seated on floor cushions (there are also
real tables and chairs).

▶ *One of the city's most popular vegetarian
restaurants is Country Life; see p161.*

Hot

*Václavské náměstí 45, Prague 1 (222 247 240).
Metro Muzeum/tram 11.* **Open** 6.30am-1am
daily. **Main courses** 180-450 Kč. **Credit** AmEx,
MC, V. **Map** p331 🕖 Central European

Hot offers a cool if not exactly peaceful refuge on
Wenceslas Square in the lobby of the remade classic Hotel Jalta. The programme's changed from Thai
and seafood, but the place is still run by capable
Prague restaurateur Tommy Sjöö, who now offers
a menu high on ribs and steaks.

Hybernia

*Hybernská 7, Prague 1 (224 226 004/www.
hybernia.cz). Metro Náměstí Republiky/tram 3,
5, 8, 14, 24, 26.* **Open** 9.30am-11.30pm Mon-Fri;
11am-11.30pm Sat, Sun. **Main courses** 120-310
Kč. **Credit** AmEx, MC, V. **Map** p329 O4 🕖
Central European/Mediterranean

Hybernia has earned itself a regular lunchtime
crowd of wheeler-dealers with its large portions of
hearty fare. It's next to the headquarters of the
Social Democrat party, but bodyguards and heads

of government are less frequent visitors now that the conservatives are in power. The menu includes pastas with nice touches, and the ginger-marinated duck breast is a star pick.

★ Kč Jáma

V jámě 7, Prague 1 (224 222 383/www.jamapub. cz). Metro Můstek/tram 3, 9, 14, 24. **Open** 11am-1am Tue-Sat, 11am-midnight Sun. **Main courses** 100-300 Kč. **Credit** AmEx, MC, V. **Map** p331 N7 ❸❷ **Czech/Americas**

Still a lunch and brunch fave after all these years, American-owned and -outfitted Jáma has kept the loud college vibe that made its name, drawing Czech scenesters by day and young business types by night. Lunch specials and happy-hour deals are a big pull, as is the Czech-Mex menu. There's a prime patio space and a children's playground out back, and a bank of internet terminals by the door.

JB Club

Kateřinská 7, Prague 2 (224 918 425). Metro Karlovo Náměstí/tram 4, 6, 10, 22. **Open** 11.30am-11.30pm Mon-Fri; noon-11.30pm Sat. **Main courses** 180-440 Kč. **Credit** AmEx, MC, V. **Map** p330 M10 ❸❸ **Czech/Americas**

In the stately house where Czech opera legend Ema Destinnova was born, American chef Steven Trumpfheller offers a menu that's rich in Czech classics. At JB, however (also known as Restaurant U Emy Destinnové), the fare is leavened with inspiration and wider European influences. Why not start with aubergine stuffed with goat's cheese and move on to duck breast in port, apricots and walnuts?

Lemon Leaf

Na Zderaze 14, Prague 2 (224 919 056/ www.lemon.cz). Metro Karlovo náměstí/tram 7, 16, 17, 21. **Open** 11am-11pm Mon-Thur; 11am-12.30am Fri; 1pm-12.30am Sat; 1-11pm Sun. **Main courses** 180-320 Kč. **Credit** AmEx, MC, V. **Map** p330 K8 ❸❹ **Thai**

Well-cooked Thai and Burmese food, with bargain lunch specials, is served in a warm, yellow and dark-wood setting. A number of other Prague eateries now offer Thai food that's just as tasty, but the Lemon Leaf still serves the real deal with no compromises for the many spice-phobic Czechs. Street tables may appeal, but be warned that the street itself is trafficky.

★ Maze

V Celnici 7, Prague 1 (221 822 300/www. gordon ramsay.com/mazeprague). Metro Náměstí Republiky/tram 5, 8, 26. **Open** 6.30am-10.30am, noon-3pm, 6-11pm daily. **Main courses** 600-700 Kč. **Credit** AmEx, MC, V. **Map** p329 P3 ❸❺ **Czech/Central European**

Gordon Ramsay's first Prague beachhead has lived up to its fanfare with admirable aplomb so far, offering stunning little dégustations of lamb loin and garlic purée or glazed pork belly with tempura of black pudding in a newly made-over Secessionist dining room conceived by David Collins. The setting might be super-stylish, but the atmosphere is casual. Enjoy the same delights you'd find at the original London version, but at surprisingly reasonable Prague prices. At lunch, there are inspired tasting menus to sample.

Jáma.

Žofín Garden. *See p172.*

Metropol Music Café

Na poříčí 12, Prague 1 (222 314 071/
www.metropol-prague.com). Metro Náměstí
Republiky/tram 3, 5, 8, 14, 24. **Open** 9am-2pm
daily. **Main courses** 150-350 Kč. **Credit** AmEx,
MC, V. **Map** p329 O3 ❸ **Central European**
The Metropol Music Café is actually an entire com-
pex of eateries and bars set in a neo art deco space
with great balconies and windows on to the street.
The food and cocktails can be somewhat unpredictable, but it's worth taking a chance on a meal
here. There's regular live jazz.

Millhouse Sushi

Slovanský dům, Na příkopě 22, Prague 1 (221
451 771/www.millhouse-sushi.cz). Metro Náměstí
Republiky/tram 5, 8, 14. **Open** 11am-11pm daily.
Main courses 400-800 Kč. **Credit** AmEx, DC,
MC, V. **Map** p329 N4 ❺ **Sushi**
Millhouse Sushi is handy if you happen to be in the
mall catching a film, but prepare for your travel funds
to be rapidly depleted. This is one of the trendiest
sushi bars in town, and few diners deny that its
maki and nagiri are very decent. But cheap it ain't.
Other locations Sokolovská 84-86, Karlín,
Prague 8 (222 832 583).

Kč Modrý Zub

Jindřišská 5, Prague 1 (222 212 622/www.
modryzub.com). Metro Můstek/tram 3, 9, 14,
24. **Open** 11am-11pm Mon-Fri (kitchen closes

10.30pm); noon-11pm Sat, Sun (kitchen closes
10pm). **Main courses** 120-320 Kč. **Credit**
AmEx, MC, V. **Map** p329 N6 ❽ **Thai**
Modrý Zub is a popular, reasonably priced, quick
and non-Czech lunch option for the Wenceslas Square
crowd, who flock here for spicy Thai noodles, a modern casual streetside setting and takeaway service
at the back. If you're eating here in the evening, note
the kitchen's relatively early closing times.

Novoměstský Pivovar

Vodičkova 20, Prague 1 (222 232 448/www.
npivovar.cz). Metro Můstek/tram 3, 9, 14, 24.
Open 10am-11.30pm Mon-Fri; 11.30am-11.30pm
Sat; noon-10pm Sun. **Main courses** 210-650 Kč.
Credit AmEx, MC, V. **Map** p330 M7 ❾ **Czech**
One of surprisingly few brewpubs in Prague,
Novoměstsky Pivovar is a sprawling underground
warren with great beer and pub grub, but also busloads of tourists and all the slack service and dodgy
maths that go with them. Still, some people swear
its pork knuckle is the definitive form of this classic
dish, and the massive goose platters (order ahead)
are a hit with groups.

★ Oliva

Plavecká 4, Prague 2 (222 520 288/www.oliva
restaurant.cz). Metro Karlovo náměstí, then tram
7, 16, 17. **Open** 11.30am-3pm, 6pm-midnight
Mon-Sat. **Main courses** 355-485 Kč. **Credit**
AmEx, MC, V. **Map** p330 K12 ❿ **Mediterranean**

From Moroccan lamb couscous to veal in mathurini sauce, the Mediterranean accents at Oliva are sumptuous, confident and a wake-up call to the senses, especially good in Prague's long grey season. Zingy starters such as mango gazpacho set the tone, and desserts including *pain d'épices* are hard to resist. The wine list is just as engaging, with affordable, quality choices. What's more, the decor and staff are fresh, classy and welcoming.

Pigy Pizza & Gyros

Spálená 47, Prague 2 (no phone). Metro Národní třída/tram 6, 9, 18, 22, 23. **Open** 24hrs daily. **Main courses** 60-120 Kč. **No credit cards.** **Map** p330 L6 ⑤ **Fast food**

Pigy Pizza & Gyros is what the name implies and, sadly, is still a good indicator of Prague's late-night options for the hungry. The ever-cheerful (or brusque and sweaty) guys here do roast chicken, falafel, kebabs and just-edible mini pizzas, but they do them fast, cheap and all night long for people waiting for a night tram home – the stand stands where all the lines meet.

★ Kč U Pinkasů

Jungmannovo náměstí 16, Prague 1 (221 111 150/www.upinkasu.cz). Metro Můstek/tram 6, 9, 18, 22, 23. **Open** *Restaurant* 10am-11am daily. *Pub* 4pm-4am Tue-Sat. **Main courses** 120-300 Kč. **Credit** AmEx, MC, V. **Map** p328 M6 ⑫ **Czech**

If you're here for the beer, then make a pilgrimage to the first Pilsner pub, first opened in 1843. Over a century and a half later, it's still smoky, packed and a dependable source of brusque, authentic service and classic meat platters: leg of hare, for instance, and duck served with red and white cabbage and potato dumplings. The place has several rooms: some are just pubs but others have a food menu, so it's worth exploring.

Pizza Coloseum

Vodičkova 32, Prague 1 (224 214 914/www. pizzacoloseum.cz). Metro Můstek/tram 3, 9, 14, 24. **Open** 11am-11.30pm daily. **Main courses** 180-320 Kč. **Credit** AmEx, MC, V. **Map** p330 M7 ⑬ **Pizza**

Just off Wenceslas Square, this cellar is a top Prague pizzeria. The excellent bruschette and big, saucy pastas come with good wines; there's also a familiar range of steak and fish. The pizzas themselves are typical of the Prague style, with thin crusts but a wide range of zesty toppings, from grilled aubergine to classic sausage and tomato sauce.

Pizzeria de Carlo

Karlovo náměstí 30, Prague 2 (222 231 381/ www.dicarlo.cz). Metro Karlovo Náměstí/tram 4, 6, 10, 22. **Open** 11-10.30pm Mon-Fri; 10.30-10.30pm Sat-Sun. **Main courses** 125-380 Kč. **Credit** MC, V. **Map** p330 L9 ㉞ **Pizza**

A popular, convenient lunch favourite for office workers in the district, this family-run place has an appealing courtyard that's a tranquil refuge in clement weather. With seating for 180 in comfortable *junque shoppe* style and warm, attentive service, it's a affordable boon any time of year. It's not the place for culinary flights of fancy, but it's dependable for oven-fired pizzas and a decent array of Northern Italian wines.

Kč Radost FX Café

Bělehradská 120, Prague 2 (224 254 776/ www.radostfx.cz). Metro IP Pavlova/tram 4, 6, 10, 16, 22, 23. **Open** *Restaurant* 11.30am-3am daily. *Club* 10pm-4am Thur-Sat. **Main courses** 180-350 Kč. **No credit cards.** **Map** p331 P9 ㊿ **Vegetarian**

Prague's first vegetarian restaurant, serving pastas, couscous and meatless Mexican food, has the latest opening hours in town. Dishes are of variable quality and the ornamental tables bash your knees, but it's still as popular as ever. There's a change of scenery in its groovy, tassled backroom lounge.

Rio's Vyšehrad

Štulcova 2, Prague 2 (224 922 156/www.rio restaurant.cz). Metro Vyšehrad/tram 7, 18, 24. **Open** 11am-midnight daily. **Main courses** 180-320 Kč. **Credit** AmEx, MC, V. **Mediterranean**

The cuisine and service at Rio's pass muster: the menu offers good selections of salads, seafood dishes and pastas, and there's a reasonable wine selection. But the main draw is the view from Prague's oldest hilltop castle ruins, a 12-minute metro ride south of the centre after a short walk.

Samurai

Londýnská 120, Prague 2 (222 515 330/www. sushi-restaurace-samurai.cz). Metro IP Pavlova/ tram 6, 10, 11, 22, 23. **Open** 10am-10pm daily. **Main courses** 120-320 Kč. **Credit** AmEx, MC, V. **Map** p331 P10 ㊈ **Japanese**

Taking the Prague sushi craze one step beyond, Samurai wins bonus points for its teppanyaki grill. The decor also goes all the way to the max, with tatami mats and sliding paper panels. It's not just about good looks, though: the seafood and sashimi are both excellent.

Soho Restaurant & Garden

Podolské nábřeží 1, Prague 2 (244 463 772/ www.sohorestaurant.cz). Tram 3, 16, 17. **Open** 11.30am-1am daily. **Main courses** 250-650 Kč. **Credit** AmEx, MC, V. **International**

Trendy, well outfitted for barbecue or sushi, and just a short trek south of the centre, Soho is a new hotspot in this part of town. Chefs throw butterfish or American-style rib-eye steak on the grill; eat them on the modernist river terrace for a real treat. Gracious staff and a thoughtful wine list complete the positive picture, but prices have risen of late.

★ Universal

V Jirchářích, Prague 2 (224 934 416). Metro Národní třída/tram 6, 9, 18, 22, 23. **Open** 11.30am-midnight Mon-Sat; 11am-11.30pm Sun. **Main courses** 180-320 Kč. **Credit** MC, V. **Map** p330 K7 ❻❼ **Czech/French**

With old French advertisements displayed in pride of place on the wine-coloured walls, an interior inspired by train cars, servers who know their stuff, and appealing daily specials (cod in white sauce, flank steak and rolled veggie lasagne), Universal is hard to fault. The sides are as impressive as the mains: delectable fresh spinach or roasted gratin potatoes, cooked with real flair.

Zahrada v opeře

Legerova 75, Prague 2 (224 239 685/www. zahradavopere.cz). Metro Muzeum/tram 11. **Open** 11.30am-midnight daily. **Main courses** 220-480 Kč. **Credit** AmEx, MC, V. **Map** p331 P7 ❾❽ **International**

The entrance to the Opera Garden is hard to find – it's at the back of the office building in which the restaurant is housed. However, the food at this Czech and international dining room makes it worth the effort. Tuna steak in filo is a delight, and is entirely in keeping with the airy minimalist decor and the quietly gliding waiters.

Žofín Garden

Žofín 226, Slovanský Island, Prague 1 (mobile 774 774 774/www.zofingarden.cz). Metro Národní třída/tram 17, 18, 22, 23. **Open** 11am-midnight daily. **Main courses** 300-450 Kč. **Credit** AmEx, MC, V. **Map** p330 J8 ❻❾ **Czech/Central European**

An ideal setting on the Vltava's prettiest island, opposite the National Theatre, is a good match for Zofin Garden's grill menu of spicy shrimp and rib-eye steak. The wine list is just as impressive; less so the sometimes inconsistent service. But if you visit with children on a fine summer day, you may find the kids' menu and activities (on weekend afternoons) mean you don't mind the wait too much. *Photo p170.*

Zvonice

Jindřišská věž, Prague 1 (224 220 009/ www.restaurantzvonice.cz). Metro Můstek/tram 3, 9, 14, 24. **Open** 11.30am-midnight daily. **Main courses** 180-450 Kč. **Credit** AmEx, MC, V. **Map** p329 O5 ❶⓿⓿ **Central European**

Věž means tower in Czech, and that's exactly what you get here. Dining amid the ancient belfry timbers, with the St Maria bell (which dates from 1518) hanging overhead, certainly makes for a unique experience. It's more than just a gimmick, though: the restaurant earns its culinary stripes with the likes of delicate rump steak and bacon-wrapped asparagus spears, and there are good-value lunch specials as well.

FURTHER AFIELD

Kč Akropolis

Kubelíkova 27, Vršovice, Prague 3 (296 330 913/www.palacakropolis.cz). Metro Jiřího z Poděbrad/tram 11. **Open** 11am-12.30am daily. **Main courses** 100-190 Kč. **No credit cards**. **Map** p333 C2 ❶⓿❶ **International**

As an eating destination, the Akropolis is no Michelin-star contender, but if you're clubbing here or rocking out in the attached concert space, a Czech chicken curry may be just what you fancy. Or maybe a fried, battered mushroom as a vegetarian option? Whatever you choose, drown them out with beer and focus on the surrounding environment, a dining room designed by surrealist artists. The service is laid-back, to say the least.

▶ *For more on the musical agenda here, see p247.*

★ Aromi

Mánesova 78, Prague 2 (222 713 222). Metro Jiřího z Poděbrad/tram 11. **Open** 11am-10pm Mon-Thur, Sun; 11am-11pm Fri, Sat. **Main courses** 280-680 Kč. **Credit** AmEx, MC, V. **Map** p333 B3 ❶⓿❷ **Italian/seafood**

One of Prague's best Italian restaurants is located in quiet Vinohrady, mercifully off the tourist radar. Inside, the rough wood and brick interiors bely authoritative kitchen staff, offering fine presentation of everything from the six-seafood antipasti platter to veal on saffron risotto with thyme. There's also a list of excellent wines, fairly priced and drawn from all around the boot.

Barracuda

Krymská 2, Vinohrady, Prague 2 (271 740 599/ www.barracuda-cafe.cz). Metro Náměstí Míru/tram 4, 22. **Open** *Upstairs* 11.30am-midnight Mon-Fri; 5pm-midnight Sat, Sun. *Downstairs* 5-11.30pm Mon-Fri. **Main courses** 130-270 Kč. **Credit** AmEx, MC, V. **Americas**

Once a top draw for Mexican food in Prague, Barracuda is now ultimately only worth a visit if you're in the neighbourhood. Still, the service remains improbably friendly; highlights of the menu include a popular, sizzling fajitas platter, and some generously stuffed tacos.

Kč La Crêperie

Janovského 4, Prague 7 (220 878 040). Metro Vltavská/tram 1, 5, 8, 12, 14, 25. **Open** 9am-11pm Mon-Sat; 9am-10pm Sun. **Main courses** 110-250 Kč. **No credit cards**. **Map** p332 E3 ❶⓿❸ **Crêperie**

The French-owned La Crêperie serves sweet and savoury crêpes for a pittance. Seating is in a comfortable but closet-sized basement, so it's probably not ideal for coach parties. Still, while the room is small, the portions are large. There's an above-average wine list, and fresh croissants.

Giardino.

CONSUME

Kč Efes

Vinohradská 63, Prague 2 (222 250 015). Metro Náměstí Míru/tram 11. **Open** 11.30am-11pm Mon-Sat. **Main courses** 110-280 Kč. **No credit cards. Map** p333 B3 ⓾ **Middle Eastern**

Efes offers Prague's finest Anatolian chow. Check out exotic, warming dishes such as *ayvar*, a red pepper, chilli and garlic paste you spread on fresh sourdough bread; *sonbahar kisiri*, a flavour-packed mixture of cracked wheat with walnuts and olives; and the *kizartma* of caramelised aubergine and peppers, which seduces quite a bit faster than the relaxed service. The meat dishes are also enjoyable, with fine minced meats with Turkish spices featuring in the meze.

Giardino

Záhřebská 24, Prague 2 (222 513 427). Metro Náměstí Míru/tram 4, 6, 10, 16, 22. **Open** noon-3pm, 5.30pm-midnight Mon-Thur; 5.30pm-midnight Fri-Sun. **Main courses** 280-880 Kč. **Credit** AmEx, MC, V. **Map** p331 Q11 ⓾ **Italian**

Giardino offers an excellent garden setting for its fine Italian food. Start with creamy, decadent mozzarella Burrata before moving on to risotto *frutti di mare* or salt-baked sea bass accompanied by a bottle of crisp pinot grigio, and you should be all set for a fine evening.

▶ *Another spot to eat alfresco is the river terrace at the Soho Restaurant; see p171.*

Grosseto Pizzeria

Jugoslávských partyzánů 8, Dejvice, Prague 6 (233 342 694/www.grosseto.cz). Metro Dejvická/tram 2, 20, 25, 26. **Open** 11.30am-11pm daily. **Main courses** 120-310 Kč. **No credit cards. Pizza**

With several booming locations in Prague and beyond, Grosseto specialises in flame-cooked pizzas. Most notable among them is the four-cheese version: beware of lesser imitations elsewhere using anything called *eidam* or *hermelín* (generic Czech cheeses). The minestrone is wonderfully hearty, too, and carpaccio in rich tomato sauce is perfect for sopping up with the complimentary fresh, hot peasant bread.

Other locations Náměstí Míru (224 252 778).

Mailsi

Lipanská 1, Žižkov, Prague 3 (222 717 783/www.pakistani-restaurant-mailsi.eu). Tram 5, 9, 26. **Open** noon-3pm, 6pm-midnight daily. **Main courses** 250-350 Kč. **Credit** AmEx, MC, V. **Map** p333 C2 ⓾ **Pakistani**

Mailsi is simply a comfortable, friendly neighbourhood Pakistani restaurant – but it's the district's only one. There's not much atmosphere, but the good, solid Pakistani food goes down well in one of Prague's few truly ethnically mixed districts. The kebabs, dahls and other traditional dishes are all expertly prepared, then served with fast and friendly gusto by competent waiting staff.

Masala

Mánesova 13, Vinohrady, Prague 2 (222 251 601/ www.masala.cz). Metro Muzeum/tram 11. **Open** 11.30am-11pm Mon-Fri; 12.30-11pm Sat, Sun. **Main courses** 130-270 Kč. **No credit cards. Map** p333 A3 **107 Indian**

Masala is a bit out of the way. Still, it's worth seeking out for its homely atmosphere and capably created Indian cuisine, served speedily and at reasonable prices. Tender kebabs, tikka, Tandoori and chicken fenugreek have been quietly drawing in locals for ages. Book ahead – then explore the magic combination of Czech beer and Indian cooking.

★ Mozaika

Nitranská 13, Prague 2 (224 253 011). Metro Jiřího z Poděbrad/tram 11. **Open** 11.30am-midnight Mon-Fri; noon-midnight Sat; 4pm-midnight Sun. **Main courses** 180-380 Kč. **Credit** AmEx, MC, V. **Map** p333 C4 **108 International**

A favourite among locals, friendly and casual Mozaika offers solid value. It's known for its above-average comfort food: praise-worthy hamburgers with fresh mushrooms, home-made pâté and Philly cheesecake are equally well done. It's all served with speed and cheer, earning Mozaika a loyal following.

Passepartout

Americka 20, Prague 2 (222 513 340/www. passepartout.cz). Metro Náměstí Míru/tram 4, 6, 10, 16, 22. **Open** noon-midnight daily. **Main courses** 250-60 Kč. **No credit cards. Map** p333 A4 **109 Czech/French**

An elegant but casual island of tasty Francophile fare, Passepartout caters to French property investors who are doing up Vinohrady at present. Come here for quality bistro food, from Moroccan lamb stew to duck confit, preceded by fresh and varied salads and followed by a tempting dessert cart and espresso.

Ristorante da Emanuel

Charles de Gaulla 4, Dejvice, Prague 6 (224 312 934). Metro Dejvická/tram 2, 20, 25, 26. **Open** noon-11pm daily. **Main courses** 180-480 Kč. **Credit** AmEx, MC, V. **Italian**

Thanks to a focus on interesting dishes such as swordfish carpaccio and *pappardelle al cinghiale* (mildly spiced ground boar), this little neighbourhood pasta joint always requires reservations. Expatriate Italians commute across Prague to eat at the tiny tables in an atmosphere defined by doting servers and terrible seaport decor.

Roca

Vinohradská 32, Prague 2 (222 520 060/www. trattorialarocca.cz). Metro Náměstí Míru/tram 11. **Open** 10am-midnight daily. **Main courses** 160-320 Kč. **Credit** AmEx, MC, V. **Map** p333 A3 **110 Italian**

Roca is a grand little Italian restaurant, complete with family and *paisano* regulars in the corners. Overall, it's a fine hole in the wall, with a great assortment of pastas and delicately flavoured, creamy pasta sauces and soups. In particular, the superbly tender chicken scallopini and unctuous squid risotto nero are a treat. Just beware the occasional midweek crooner.

Kč Sonora

Radhoštská 5, Prague 3 (222 711 029/www. sonoras.cz). Metro Flora/tram 11. **Open** 11am-midnight daily. **Main courses** 120-260 Kč. **Credit** MC, V. **Map** p333 D3 **111 Americas**

Some of the city's most inspired efforts in Mexican cuisine are offered at bargain prices at Sonora: mole, taco salads, beef burritos and tasty quesadillas. All are complemented perfectly by cheap Czech beer and an intriguing wall-size map of North American Indian tribes.

Svatá Klára

U Trojského zámku, Troja, Prague 7 (233 540 173/www.svataklara.cz). Metro Nádraží Holešovice, then bus 154, 191. **Open** 6pm-midnight daily. **Main courses** 280-480 Kč. **Credit** AmEx, MC, V. **Czech**

This upmarket, high-quality restaurant doles out traditional Czech game dishes with a flair that rewards the adventurers who've trekked out to the adjoining Troja Château to take in the historic frescoes and formal gardens. Affordable cinematic decadence, pretty much.

Včelín

Kodaňská 5, Vršovice, Prague 10 (271 742 541). Tram 4, 22, 23. **Open** 11am-midnight Mon-Fri; 11.30am-1am Sat; 11.30am-11pm Sun. **Main courses** 250-400Kč. **Credit** AmEx, MC, V. **Czech/Mediterranean**

The Beehive is an appropriately named gathering spot for up-and-coming Prague creatives, but comes without the attitude that spoils most places of a similar ilk. The quick, amiable servers hustle from table to table bearing any of three great Czech beers on tap, beneath walls done up with hip, graphic-design magazine covers. Foodwise, the house special is gnocchi in spinach sauce is the hit of this little room.

Kč Žlutá pumpa

Belgická 12, Prague 2 (mobile 608 184 360/www. zluta-pumpa.info). Metro Náměstí Míru/tram 4, 6, 10, 16, 20, 22. **Open** noon-12.30am daily. **Main courses** 110-280 Kč. **No credit cards. Map** p331 Q11 **112 Czech**

The latest Prague trend, new angles on trad pubbing, finds Czech-Mex expression down at the Yellow Pump. It's buzzy, colourful and inexpensive, but don't go expecting great service or outlandishly memorable chow.

Cafés, Pubs & Bars

Prague's pace is faster these days, but life still revolves around the local.

Drinkers, you have the weight of history on your side. Beer has been brewed in what's now the Czech Republic since the Middle Ages, with pilsner originating here in 1842. Almost 150 years later, the Velvet Revolution was fomented in the cafés and bars around the National Theatre.

Drinking, then, has long been embedded in local culture, and it remains a key part of life for many Praguers. Despite a higher cost of living and more demanding working lives, you'd be hard-pressed to find a single block in any Prague district that doesn't have at least one unreformed, no-nonsense neighbourhood pub, or *hostinec*, serving cheap beer without ceremony to a band of loyal regulars.

WHAT TO DRINK

Beer may be the country's greatest national cultural treasure, but its popularity is under siege. So few of the Czech Republic's small, independent breweries are still in business that you'd be forgiven for thinking 500 years of brewing has produced only Pilsner Urquell, Gambrinus and Staropramen.

Although Czechs are loyal to their favourite brands, the crisis has been worsened by the younger generation's growing passion for cocktails. However, lovers of beer are still well looked after at **U Medvídků** (*see p162*), **U Černého vola**, **U Houdků**, **U Provaznice**, **U Vejvodů**, and dozens of other places with names that start with 'U'. Beer tastes even better when accompanied by traditional food such as smoked meat platters, pickled mackerel and the magnificently smelly *pivní sýr* (beer cheese).

Cocktail bars continue to crop up and die off almost like juniper berries. Veteran favourites such as **Tretter's** have shown staying power, but others have fallen. Hopefully, **Barego** and **Papas** will survive in this risky sector, as the lovely wine bars **Monarch** and **Le Terroir** have. Some brilliant all-night bars, such as

> ❶ Green numbers given in this chapter correspond to the location of each café, pub and bar on the street maps. *See pp326-333.*

Bukowski's and **Le Clan** (for both, *see p253*), seem like born survivors, the kind of places that people ask after when returning to the city.

Café culture in Prague still means pre-war decadence and old Vienna-style settings (bring your own poodle), and one of the grandest of the grandes dames is back in action: the impossibly ornate **Café Imperial**. The cosy **Café Montmartre** and almost oppressively old-world **Franz Kafka Café** are also great for time travel, while the opulent **Kavárna Obecní dům** is an art nouveau wonder.

Meanwhile, dressy expat caffeine addicts often drop by to get their fix at **Le Patio**; artistic types flock to **Duende**; and the **Globe Bookstore & Coffeehouse** holds the middle ground, as does the **Ebel Coffee House**.

HRADČANY

★ U Černého vola

Loretánské náměstí 1, Prague 1 (220 513 481). Tram 22. **Open** 10am-10pm daily. **No credit cards. Map** p326 B3 ❶

The Black Ox is one of the last authentic neighbourhood pubs in this district, with murals that make it look as if it's been here forever when it was actually built after World War II. Its superb location above the castle made it a prime target for redevelopment in the post-1989 frenzy, but the rugged regulars bought it in order to ensure that bearded artisans would have at least one place where they could afford to drink. The Kozel beer is perfection; snacks are pretty basic, but they do their job.

MALÁ STRANA

Baráčnická rychta

Tržiště 23, Prague 1 (257 532 461). Metro Malostranská/tram 12, 22. **Open** noon-1am daily. **Credit** MC, V. **Map** p327 E3 ❷

Incredibly, a purely local, old-time Czech pub is still standing just downhill from the castle, complete with fried cheese, dark wood interiors and grumpy waiters. Like something out of Jan Neruda's *Prague Tales*, this former hall of barons and landlords has thrived in Malá Strana since the 19th century and has made only grudging nods to the present day, with designer lamps illuminating its heavy, communal tables. Behind a series of archways, the pub is split into a small beerhall frequented by hardcore *pivo* drinkers, and a music hall downstairs.

★ Barego

Nebovidská 19, Prague 1 (233 088 888/ www.mandarinoriental.com/prague). Metro Malostranská/tram 12, 22. **Open** 6.30-10.30am, noon-2.30pm, 6pm-2am daily. **Credit** AmEx, MC, V. **Map** p327 F5 ❸

The epitome of the smart cocktail scene in Malá Strana, the Mandarin Oriental's gorgeous little design bar is a great place in which to witness the city's new chic ethic. The Monastery Smoky Martini, the house special, goes well with the sophisticated atmosphere, as the international elite meet to pull up a sleek red leather seat and trade notes on the latest crazes.

▶ *For more on checking in at the Mandarin Oriental, see p132.*

Blue Light

Josefská 1, Prague 1 (257 533 126/www.bluelight bar.cz). Metro Malostranská/tram 12, 22 ,23. **Open** 6pm-midnight daily. **No credit cards.** **Map** p327 F3 ❹

This pleasant, dark jumble of a bar attracts local cognoscenti, who gather for cocktails under the jazz posters plastered over the dilapidated walls; perhaps they should have gone all the way and called it the Blue Note instead. By day, it's a good spot in which to loiter with a friend, especially when there's room at the bar. At night, it gets more rowdy and conversation becomes nigh-on impossible, but the vibe is certainly infectious. There's a decent range of malt whiskies too.

Jo's Bar

Malostranské náměstí 7, Prague 1 (257 531 422). Metro Malostranská/tram 12, 22. **Open** 11am-midnight daily. **No credit cards.** **Map** p327 F4 ❺

A street-level adjunct to a basement bar and sometime-club, Jo's Bar & Garáž, Jo's Bar was once renowned for being every backpacker's first stop in Prague and the original source of nachos in the Czech Republic. Founder Glen Emery has moved on and Jo's new owner has less charisma, but it's still a good place in which to meet fellow travellers.

▶ *For Jo's Bar & Garáž, see p254.*

U Kocoura

Nerudova 2, Prague 1 (257 530 107). Metro Malostranská/tram 12, 20, 22. **Open** 10am-2am daily. **No credit cards.** **Map** p327 E3 ❻

Long since granted iconic status in the Prague pubbing world, this smoky, well-worn place was briefly owned by the Friends of Beer, a former political party that has morphed into a civic association. Although its manifesto is a bit vague, the staff's ability to pour a good, cheap pint is beyond question.

★ Latin Art Café

Jansky Vršek 2, Prague 1 (mobile 774 343 441). Metro Malostranská/tram 12, 22. **Open** 11am-1am daily. **No credit cards. Map** p326 D4 **7**
It's worth finding the stone steps of this backstreet for this lively little caff, which is just as its name implies. Live jam sessions of Latin music go with the strong coffees and warm hideout atmosphere, helped along by cunning Botero paintings.

U Malého Glena

Karmelitská 23, Prague 1 (257 531 717/www.maly glen.cz). Metro Malostranská/tram 12, 20, 22. **Open** 10am-2am daily. **Credit** MC, V. **Map** p327 F4 **8**
From a glance at the rowdy pub at street level, you'd never guess that the downstairs bar is one of Prague's top jazz holes. Tall mugs of Bernard beer are swung with gusto by expats and Czechs, and the large tables and benches are perfect for groups. There's always an easygoing, affable vibe, but it's less noisy in the afternoons.

St Nicholas Café

Tržiště 10, Prague 1 (257 530 204). Metro Malostranská/tram 12, 20, 22. **Open** noon-2am daily. **Credit** AmEx, MC, V. **Map** p327 E4 **9**

An atmospheric vaulted cellar decked out with steamer trunk tables and painted arches, St Nick's comes with Pilsner Urquell on tap. A mellow but lively crowd gathers in the nooks for late-evening conversation, keeping the pizza oven busy. It's also good if you fancy giving the beers a rest and taking up a glass of Havana Club rum.

Starbucks

Malostranské náměstí 28 (257 214 725/www.starbuckscoffee.cz). Metro Malostranská/tram 12, 22. **Open** 7am-9pm Mon-Fri; 8am-9pm Sat, Sun. **Credit** AmEx, MC, V. **Map** p327 F3 **10**
The first Czech beachhead of the global chain has proved a hit with tourists and locals seeking a branded coffee experience; particularly members of the nearby Czech parliament, who think it's the height of cool to tote a coffee thermos with a Starbucks logo on it. Most other residents are staying well clear, despite the fluffy muffins and early opening hours.

★ Tato Kojkej

Kampa Park, Prague 1 (no phone). Metro Malostranská/tram 22. **Open** 10am-midnight daily. **No credit cards. Map** p327 G6 **11**
A wonderfully run-down gallery café hidden on the shore side of Kampa Park, this former millhouse still features a wooden water wheel. There's a long list of cocktails – though the staff are not expert at making them – and a short one of cheap red wines. Sofas, second-hand chairs, abstract sculpture and a terrace are the trump cards. Sunday-night movies are fun.
▶ *For more on Kampa Park, see p79.*

Latin Art Café.

U Zavěšenýho kafe

Úvoz 6, Prague 1 (257 532 868/www.
uzavesenyhokafe.com). Metro Malostranská/
tram 12, 22. **Open** 11am-midnight daily. **No**
credit cards. Map p326 C3 ⓬
The Hanging Coffee Cup is a mellow, thoroughly
Czech spot with plank flooring, traditional grub
(onion soup and duck with sauerkraut) and a long
association with artists and intellectuals. The name
comes from a tradition of paying for a cup of coffee
for someone who may arrive later without funds.

STARÉ MĚSTO

★ Bakeshop Praha

Kozí 1, Prague 1 (222 316 823/www.bakeshop.
cz). Metro Staroměstská/tram 17, 18. **Open** 7am-
7pm daily. **Credit** MC, V. **Map** p328 M3 ⓭
Steadily growing in floor space and menu length,
this comfort-food emporium has been buzzing since
San Franciscan Anne Feeley first opened its doors.
The reason for its success, aside from the zesty
quiches, traditional nut breads, muffins and peanut
butter cookies, is the Northern Californian vibe.
Grab a copy of the *Guardian* and hang out on a
bench while you savour your java and croissants.

Bar & Books

Týnská 19, Prague 1 (224 808 250/www.bar
and books.cz). Metro Staroměstská/tram 17, 18.
Open 5pm-4am daily. **Credit** AmEx, MC, V.
Map p328 M3 ⓮

Small, dim, hushed and oddly formal, this bar, patterned after a New York model, offers top-drawer
cocktails, brandy, cigars and service in a library-like
setting. Red leather benches and seats go along with
red-jacketed hostesses who make a show of taking
your coat and helping you with any booze-related
query you might have. Old James Bond movies loop
quietly on monitors above the bar; other perks
include free Wi-Fi.

Barock

Pařížská 24, Prague 1 (222 329 221/www.
barockrestaurant.cz). Metro Staroměstska/tram
17, 18. **Open** 10am-1am daily. **Credit** AmEx,
MC, V. **Map** p328 L2 ⓯
While you have to wonder what was behind the
promo line for this all-too-stylish caff ('Delicious
meal and beautiful women'), Barock makes for an
amusing perch. You probably won't rub shoulders
with the trendiest local Czuppies here, but the location on Prague's glitziest boulevard remains a coup.
These days, the Russians ordering Sex on the Beach
cocktails while cavorting under enormous framed
fashion photographs are just as revealing about the
state of the city. An upbeat Latin music soundtrack
adds to the fun.

La Bodeguita del Medio

Kaprova 5, Prague 1 (224 813 922/www.lab
delm.cz). Metro Staroměstská/tram 17, 18.
Open 10am-2am daily. **Credit** AmEx, MC, V.
Map p328 K3 ⓰

Speaking the Language

Drunk in Prague? Your vocabulary should expand with your stomach.

The Czech repertoire of words and
phrases dedicated to describing states
of drunkenness is seemingly bottomless.
If you've overdone it, you may be referred
to as **zpumprdlíkovanej**; or made into
a **pumprdlík**, which is basically a runt.
Getting drunk is also not unlike being
hit – in fact, 'hit pretty well', which is one
translation of **ztřískanej**.

When you've really had enough, tell
your co-drinkers that **mam vopici** ('I have
a monkey'). If someone's already nabbed
that line, there's always **zpitý pod čáru**
('drunk under the line'), **zlitej jak dán**
('drunk as a Dane'); **zlitej jak doga** ('drunk
as a Great Dane'), **být pod vobraz** ('under
the picture') or, a real teenager's favourite,
být na kaši ('turned to mush').

This sorry state of affairs is often a result
of **nasávat jak houba**, or 'drinking like a
mushroom'. If you're really far gone, you
may find yourself **hodit šavli** ('throwing a

sabre') – or, if you prefer, **hodit kosu**
('throwing a scythe'). Throwing up.

Hopefully, before that stage one can
at least enjoy being **zkouřenej** ('smoked
out'), **zmalovanej** ('painted') or **mít hlavu**
jako pátrací balón ('having a head like a
searching balloon'). Do try to maintain
some degree of composure, however,
lest you **nadávat jako dlaždič** ('swear like
a cobblestone layer').

You should be careful not to **zaseknout**
sekeru hluboko ('stick the axe in') lest you
run up a big tab. Better to call it quits while
you can still **plazit se jako šnek** ('slither
like a snail'). Just don't be surprised the
following morning when your mind is
found to be **být mimo** ('outside') .Worse
still, you could find you have your
nametený ('brain swept up like leaves')
or, if you've really overdone it, **mít hlavu**
jako střep ('have a head like a piece of
broken glass'). You have been warned…

Pretty much packed with revellers since its opening in 2002, the Czech branch of the 60-year-old Havana institution that claims credit for inventing the mojito (and hooking Hemingway on it, of course) is a jumping joint. Attractions include salsa bands, Cuban and creole seafood, and oceans of good rum.

Bugsy's

Pařížská 10 (entrance on Kostečná), Josefov, Prague 1 (224 810 287/www.bugsysbar.cz). Metro Staroměstská/tram 17, 18. **Open** 7pm-2am daily. **Credit** AmEx, MC, V. **Map** p328 L3 ⑰

Once the only source for proper cocktails in town, Bugsy's today attracts an older crowd, many suits and not a few hustlers, all soaking up its swish Pařížská location. Its main claim to fame is the impressive drinks list, including 200 cocktails, and bar staff good enough to mix them properly. Prices prohibit all but flush tycoons, but it's still packed out most evenings.

★ Café Angelato

Rytířská 27, Prague 1 (no phone). Metro Můstek/tram 6, 9, 18, 21, 22. **Open** 10am-10pm daily. **No credit cards. Map** p328 M5 ⑱

Thick, creamy Italian ice-creams and sorbets can be found in this small shop, whose owners have earned local plaudits since its opening. The reason: the incredible flavours, particularly the mango, chocolate, coffee and forest fruit, all at surprisingly reasonable prices. Service is friendly; street tables are deployed in warm weather.

Café Imperial

Na poříčí 15, Prague 1 (246 011 440/www.cafe imperial.cz). Metro Náměstí Republiky/tram 5, 8, 26. **Open** 7am-11pm daily. **Credit** AmEx, MC, V. **Map** p329 P3 ⑲

Entering the Imperial is a little like stepping into a Stanley Kubrick film. Its walls and ceiling covered with sculpted porcelain, this incredibly ornate art nouveau shrine has been restored to the opulence it had when it opened in 1914. Now attached to the nearly-as-posh Hotel Imperial, the old-world dining room serves elegant renditions of trad schnitzels and rump steak, but seems more suited to lighter fare, conversation and crisp white wine.

Café Indigo

Platnéřská 11, Prague 1 (mobile 731 216 035/www.indigospace.cz). Metro Staroměstská/tram 17, 18. **Open** 9am-midnight daily. **No credit cards. Map** p328 J4 ⑳

Student heaven, and – despite its industrial art theme and front room like a fish tank – a comfortable café. With a limited menu and cheap wine, the Indigo has an upbeat and easygoing vibe and serves as a community centre for scholars from the nearby Charles University. Service is above average for this genre, though the smoke does get thick – less so in the children's corner at the back.

★ Café Montmartre

Řetězová 7, Prague 1 (no phone). Metro Staroměstská/tram 17, 18. **Open** 9am-11pm Mon-Fri; noon-11pm Sat, Sun. **No credit cards. Map** p328 K5 ㉑

One of the last great, old-style coffeehouse bars, this buzzy spot is where Czech literati such as Gustav Meyrink and Franz Werfel tippled before it became a Jazz Age hotspot. Creative miscreants still gather around the threadbare settees and battered tables for late-night talk and dodgy red wine.

La Casa Blů

Kozí 15, Prague 1 (224 818 270/www.lacasa blu.cz). Metro Staroměstská/tram 5, 8, 14. **Open** 11am-midnight Mon-Thur, Sun; 11am-2am Fri, Sat. **No credit cards. Map** p328 M2 ㉒

Feeling like an island of Latin American flavours and warmth, this long, rustic room has folk rugs draped over chairs, street signs in Spanish, tequila specials and an authentic Mexican menu. Try the buzzer even if the door is locked: people often wheedle their way in after closing time. There's free Wi-Fi.

Chapeau Rouge

Jakubská 2, Prague 1 (222 316 328/www.chapeaurouge.cz). Metro Náměstí Republiky/tram 5, 14, 26. **Open** noon-3am Mon-Thur; noon-6am Fri; 4pm-4am Sat; 4pm-2am Sun. **No credit cards. Map** p328 M3 ㉓

Although it's certainly not suitable for claustrophobics, the Red Hat does attract hordes of ebullient young Americans and travelling twentysomethings of all stripes and nationalities. It's always loud and always happening. *Photo p181.*
▶ *For more, see p253.*

Čili

Kožná 8, Prague 1 (mobile 777 945 848). Metro Staroměstská/tram 17, 18. **Open** 5.30pm-2am daily. **No credit cards. Map** p328 L4 ㉔

A quiet but decisive hit on the competitive Prague bar scene, this narrow room is notable for its hidden location on a skinny backstreet off Old Town Square, and for its outsize mojitos, G&Ts and comfortably broken-in living-room vibe. The overstuffed leather armchairs are the prize spots.

Dahab

Dlouhá 33, Prague 1 (224 827 375/www.dahab.cz). Metro Náměstí Republiky/tram 5, 8, 14. **Open** noon-11pm Mon-Thur, Sun; noon-2am Fri, Sat. **No credit cards. Map** p329 N2 ㉕

With a newly developed menu of Middle Eastern treats served in its dimly lit back tearoom (the greasy spoon on the Dlouhá street end is only for the adventurous), Dahab is more appealing than ever. Try a tagine or couscous with mint tea and settle into pillow seating in what resembles a candlelit harem. Turkish coffees and occasional belly dancing add to the fun. Otherwise, it's thoroughly calming.

CONSUME

CONSUME

Duende

Karoliny Světlé 30, Prague 1 (mobile 604 269 731/www.barduende.cz). Metro Národní třída/ tram 6, 9, 17, 18, 22. **Open** 1pm-1am Mon-Fri; 3pm-1am Sat; 4pm-1am Sun. **No credit cards.** **Map** p328 J5 **㉖**

Duende is Prague-new-Bohemian in a nutshell, attracting low-budget intellectuals from the publishing and film scenes alongside other affable regulars. The Latin-flavoured café-bar is a good deal more than the sum of its parts: various events pop up at random on its weekly calendar, from folk nights to bizarre video projections. Smoking is almost compulsory, the tattered sofas and fringed lampshades add character and the walnut liqueur (Ořechovka) is a rare treat.

Ebel Coffee House

Týn 2, Prague 1 (224 895 788/www.ebel coffee.cz). Metro Náměstí Republiky/tram 5, 8, 14. **Open** 9am-8pm daily. **Credit** AmEx, MC, V. **Map** p328 M4 **㉗**

Ebel's serious coffees come courtesy of journalist and designer Malgorzata Ebel, who was one of Prague's first suppliers of good beans. Alongside the 30-plus prime arabica varieties, there are passable quiches, bagels and brownies, served in a lovely cobbled courtyard or in a cosy wood-trimmed room. A caffeine-junkie's heaven.

Érra Café

Konviktská 11, Prague 1 (222 220 568). Metro Národní třída/tram 6, 9, 18, 22. **Open** 10am-midnight Mon-Sat; 11am-midnight Sun. **Credit** AmEx, MC, V. **Map** p328 K6 **㉘**

Érra's whimsical but not obnoxious designer interiors attract a collection of media and IT types to this little cellar bar, which adds appeal with zesty salads and Mediterranean snacks that will do for lunch or a light dinner. The service is great by Prague standards, but the chairs are less comfortable. There's a gay-friendly scene by night, with a permanent house-music soundtrack.

Franz Kafka Café

Široká 12, Prague 1 (222 318 945). Metro Staroměstská/tram 17, 18. **Open** 10am-9pm daily. **No credit cards.** **Map** p328 L3 **㉙**

Dim, old-world and almost austere, this little coffeehouse is a trip back in time: there's frosted glass, dark wooden booths, old engravings of the Jewish Quarter (it's just around the corner from the Jewish Cemetery) and, naturally, lots of Kafka portraits. The decent coffee and convivial tables on the street make it a convenient stop when touring Josefov.

Au Gourmand

Dlouhá 10, Prague 1 (222 329 060/www. augourmand.cz). Metro Staroměstská/tram 17, 18. **Open** 8am-7pm Mon-Fri; 8.30am-7pm Sat; 9am-7pm Sun. **Credit** MC, V. **Map** p328 M3 **㉚**

Pretty as an art nouveau postcard, Au Gourmand is also the richest little French bakery in town, with savoury baguette sandwiches and quiches on one side, luscious pear tarts and sumptuous Black Forest cakes on the other. Sit down at a wrought-iron table in the middle, surrounded by the unique, fin-de-siècle tile interior, and watch half of Prague slip in for a bite of sin.

★ Grand Cafe Orient

Ovocný trh 19, Prague 1 (224 224 240/www. grandcafeorient.cz). Metro Náměstí Republiky/ tram 5, 14, 26. **Open** 9am-10pm Mon-Fri; 10am-10pm Sat, Sun. **Credit** AmEx, MC, V. **Map** p329 N4 **㉛**

Probably the most stylish caff in Old Town, which is saying something, the Orient provides an unmissable opportunity to sip cappuccino in a cubist building. The café is a bit on the tourist track, but it's worth negotiating the crowds to see this historic building returned to its original use. Surprisingly, both service and breakfast are decent. *Photo p184.*
▶ *The café is attached to the House of the Black Madonna, for which see p84.*

Hostinec U Templáře

Masná 7, Prague 1 (222 325 296/www.amos restaurant.cz). Metro Náměstí Republiky/tram 5, 14, 26. **Open** 11am-11pm daily. **Credit** AmEx, MC, V. **Map** p328 M3 **new㉜**

One of the few remaining neighbourhood locals that seem untouched by Old Town's tourist hordes, this old-fashioned pub serves up unpasteurised Pilsner Urquell. Many have dubbed this bitter lager the Czech Republic's finest; a more fitting place to sample three or four would be hard to find in the old centre. Amos, the attached restaurant, is handy if the taste of authentic *pivo* brings on a yen for Bohemian duck or pork with sauerkraut. Service is classically gruff.

★ Kavárna Obecní dům

Náměstí Republiky 5, Prague 1 (222 002 763/ www.vysehrad2000.cz). Metro Náměstí Republiky/ tram 5, 14, 26. **Open** 7.30am-11pm daily. **Credit** AmEx, MC, V. **Map** p329 N4 **㉝**

Easily the most epic café space in town, this balconied, art nouveau sipping space (with a grand piano, no less) is situated at street level in the magnificently restored Municipal House. Replete with elaborate Secessionist brass chandeliers, odd characters and always a few grandes dames, there's no more memorable venue for an espresso in all of Prague. Highly recommended.
▶ *For more on the Municipal House, see p242.*

Kozička

Kozí 1, Prague 1 (224 818 308/www.kozicka.cz). Metro Náměstí Republiky/tram 5, 8, 14. **Open** noon-4am Mon-Fri; 6pm-4am Sat; 7pm-4am Sun. **Credit** AmEx, MC, V. **Map** p328 M3 **㉞**

Chapeau Rouge. *See p179.*

Although it's looking a bit threadbare these days, the Little Goat is still a popular, unpretentious local scene that dwells in a subterranean labyrinth down some metal stairs from the street. The place has homely nooks and crannies, mighty steaks are served until 11pm and Krušovice is available on tap.

M1 Secret Lounge

Masná 1, Prague 1 (227 195 235/www.m1 lounge.cz). Metro Staroměstská/tram 17, 18. **Open** 7pm-3am Mon-Thur; 7pm-5am Sat, Sun. **No credit cards. Map** p328 M3 ③⑤

Long a late-night oasis on the quiet northern end of Old Town, M1 can be a bit too hip for its own good, although it does get points for its original, sculpted metal work and the stock behind the bar. It does well earlier in the evening if you're after a more mellow sipping space; but in later hours, it gets intensely raucous. A wild crowd, including many from the film business, gathers on the red velour seats.

Molly Malone's

U Obecního dvora 4, Prague 1 (224 818 851/ www.mollymalones.cz). Metro Náměstí Republiky/

tram 5, 14, 26. **Open** 11am-1am Mon-Thur,
Sun; 11am-2am Fri, Sat. **Credit** AmEx, MC, V.
Map p328 M2 ㊱
Prague's first Irish bar started an invasion that has
never slowed. It's kitted out with a roaring log fire,
mismatched chairs, and tables constructed out of old
beds and sewing machines. There's incessant
Pogues in the background and 'traditional Irish
food', and it attracts backpackers and rowdy
English businessmen. But the bar is great for prop-
ping up, the Guinness is excellent, and there's a
warm and welcoming atmosphere in winter.

Monarch

Na Perštýně 15, Prague 1 (224 239 602/
www.monarchvinnysklep.cz). Metro Národní
třída/tram 6, 9, 18, 21, 22. **Open** 11am-7pm
Mon-Sat. **Credit** AmEx, MC, V. **Map** p328 K5 ㊲
With a touch of sophistication, a great sense for
lighting, discreet back corners and racks and racks
of great wines, this is a place for connoisseurs. The
Monarch is the place to come for South American or
Californian imports, the best local bottles, and
knowledgeable, friendly service. A good selection of
regional sausages and more than 25 varieties of
cheese are available to go with the vintages.

Papas

Betlemské náměstí 8, Prague 1 (222 222 229/
www.papasbar.cz). Metro Národní Třída/tram 6,
9,18, 22. **Open** 8am-1am Mon-Thur; 8am-2am
Fri; noon-2am Sat; noon-midnight Sun. **Credit**
AmEx, MC, V. **Map** p328 K5 ㊳
A lively cocktail specialist with deep maroon red
interiors, Papas is bold and popular with expat students and Czuppies. Caipirinhas are mixed with
gusto by the energetic staff, and the bar food is
colourful and varied enough for a nice lunch. Quieter
by day, it's dependably raucous by night.

★ U Provaznice

Provaznická 3, Prague 1 (224 232 528/
www.uprovaznice.cz). Metro Můstek/tram 6,
9, 18, 21, 22. **Open** 11am-midnight daily.
No credit cards. Map p328 M5 ㊴
Incredibly, this classic pub is convivial and reasonably priced, yet within spitting distance of the
Můstek metro and tourist crowds. The drinks and
typical Bohemian fare (duck, dumplings, smoked
meat) attract a pleasantly global yet nonetheless
chiefly local mix. It's understaffed, but the waiters
and waitresses do their best to make up for it.

Slavia

Smetanovo nábřeží 2, Prague 1 (224 218 493/
www.cafeslavia.cz). Metro Národní třída/tram 6,
9, 17, 18, 22. **Open** 8am-11pm daily. **Credit**
AmEx, MC, V. **Map** p328 J6 ㊵
A struggling Václav Havel and pals once tippled
here as they plotted the overthrow of communism
at the Slavia. They wouldn't recognise it now: the

new, art deco fixtures and crisp service were long
overdue, but they're not the stuff of Jaroslav
Seifert's classic poem *Café Slavia*. Still, it has fine
castle views, free Wi-Fi and a decent salmon toast.
Watch your bags.

Le Terroir

Vejvodova 1, Prague 1 (222 220 260/www.
leterroir.cz). Metro Národní třída/tram 6, 9, 18,
22. **Open** 11am-11pm Tue-Sat. **Credit** AmEx,
MC, V. **Map** p328 L5 ㊶
With a massive wine list, strong on Spanish and
French labels, this cosy, stone-walled cellar doubles
as an upscale restaurant, with delicate, nouvelle
treatments of rabbit, venison and lamb. It's evolved
nicely since opening as a smart wine bar a few years
back, but it can still be a bit stiff, like many such
places in the city, from trying too hard to be chic.

Tretter's

V Kolkovně 3, Prague 1 (224 811 165/www.
tretters.cz). Metro Staroměstská/tram 17, 18.
Open 7pm-3am Mon-Sat; 7pm-2am Sun. **Credit**
AmEx, MC, V. **Map** p328 L3 ㊷
With bar staff who've all graduated from Miloš
Tretter's academy, you won't find any slouching
here. The maroon colour scheme and retro decor create a classy vibe; blues singers occasionally provide
entertainment. The drinks list includes 50 cocktails
created by the owners; try the Moncheri, a coffee,
cherry liqueur and cream confection, or just stick to
a classic dry martini.

▶ *If you're here for the blues, you'll also like*
U Malého Glena; see p251.

Týnská literární kavárna

Týnská 6, Prague 1 (224 826 023/www.knihy
tynska.cz). Metro Staroměstská/tram 17, 18.
Open 9am-11pm Mon-Fri; 10am-11pm Sat, Sun.
No credit cards. Map p328 M3 ㊸
Its red wine may be vinegary, but the much-
improved coffees and a few pastries straight from
the old Czech kitchen tradition have helped make
this a mecca for students and literary types from
abroad, who file in to smoke, cavort, sit on the patio
in summer and get steadily wasted. An arty location, with spacey staff.

U Vejvodů

Jilská 4, Prague 1 (224 219 999/www.restaurace
uvejvodu.cz). Metro Můstek/tram 3, 9, 14, 24.
Open 10am-3am Mon-Thur; 10am-4am Fri,
Sat; 10am-2am Sun. **No credit cards. Map**
p328 L5 ㊹
Another brewery-owned mega beerhall (it's licensed
by Pilsner Urquell), this vast, multilevel pub caters
to big tour groups; stick to the smaller front room if
you want to avoid them. There's quick service and
old-style wood interiors, accented by the obligatory
huge copper beer vat lids. For an olde pub feel, fine
brews and traditional pub fare, it's hard to beat.

Revolt! The Drinking Ban

The beer-drinking capital of the world clamps down on rowdiness.

If you're planning a few alfresco beers in Prague, be careful where you do it. In summer 2008, a new law was introduced that banned the consumption of alcohol in a number of public places across the city. Drinking alcohol outside has now been banned within 100 metres of schools, children's playgrounds and other educational establishments, healthcare facilities, subway entrances and public transport stops. It's also been outlawed in Hradčanské náměstí, by the castle; on Na Kampě, Kampa Island; near the National Theatre, along Národní třída; in Betlémské náměstí and nearby Uhelný trh; behind the Old Town Hall on Old Town Square; on Na příkopě; and in Wenceslas Square.

Despite being home to the biggest beer drinkers on the planet, Prague is no stranger to strict drinking laws. For years, many establishments in residential areas have been forced to close at 10pm in order to keep the noise levels acceptable. But these laws are aimed not at the bar but at the drinker. If you're caught, you're likely to be landed with a 1,000 Kč on-the-spot fine, which could rise to 30,000 Kč if legal proceedings ensue. However, the ban won't apply to beer gardens or food stands that are permitted to sell alcohol, or during festivals and celebrations such as New Year's Eve.

The new legislation has been introduced alongside a number of other measures – tougher laws against littering, for instance – as part of an experiment by Prague City Hall designed to clean up the city. Similar laws have recently been introduced in the smaller cities of Ústí nad Labem and Mladá Boleslav. It may also be prudent for those planning drinking activities in the capital to be vigilant, and to try and avoid being too rowdy outside. Prague police are not known for their high levels of tolerance when faced with a crowd of foreign drunks.

'Citizens should not be afraid of this law,' Prague City police spokeswoman Radka Bredlerová told the *Prague Post* newspaper. 'It aims to solve problems connected with drinking in certain public spaces, especially those places where a number of citizens who are not socially integrated hang out... who, after they drink, tend to bother other citizens, litter or use the street as a bathroom.'

The new drinking law was originally scheduled to be introduced as part of a series of citywide bans across the country. However, the idea didn't make it very far, after the Constitutional Court deemed that such a move would be an infringement of human rights. So it appears that the Czech's basic human right to drink beer still counts for something.

CONSUME

U Zlatého tygra
Husova 17, Prague 1 (222 221 111). Metro Staroměstská/tram 17, 18. **Open** 3-11pm daily. **No credit cards. Map** p328 K5 ⑮

Small, full of cranky old locals and equally testy staff, At the Golden Tiger was once the second home of Prague's favourite writer, the famously crotchety Bohumil Hrabal. It's lost virtually all its appeal since its famous patron fell to his death from a hospital window in 1997. Tourists still flock here, which may explain why the Pilsner Urquell is no bargain.

NOVÉ MĚSTO

Café Archa
Na poříčí 26, Prague 1 (221 716 117). Metro Náměstí Republiky or Florenc/tram 3, 24. **Open** 9am-10.30pm Mon-Fri; 10am-10pm Sat; 1-10pm Sun. **No credit cards. Map** p329 P3 ⑯

Theatre cafés are some of the best spots in Prague in which to surf the culture wave, owing to the city's long-held passion for the stage. This glass fishtank, with dangling lamps as bait, has hooked a young, laid-back clientele with cheap drinks, pristine surfaces, and posters and photos from the theatre and rock worlds. It was recently refurbished.

Café Dinitz
Na poříčí 12, Prague 2 (222 314 071/www. metropol-prague.com). Metro Náměstí Republiky/tram 3, 8, 24, 26. **Open** 9am-3am Mon-Fri; 11am-3am Sat, Sun. **Credit** AmEx, MC, V. **Map** p329 O3 ⑰

Still clearly marked as Café Dinitz but in the process of a name-change to Metropol, this stylish café is a local secret, with small, quality menus that match the classy retro decor. It's a favoured hangout among local writers, who appreciate the well-shaken cocktails, the regular jazz trios and the venue's long history.

★ Café Louvre
Národní třída 20, Prague 1 (224 930 949/www.kavarny.cz/louvre). Metro Národní třída/

CONSUME

Grand Café Orient. *See p180.*

tram 6, 9, 18, 22. **Open** 8am-11.30pm Mon-Fri; 9am-11.30pm Sat, Sun. **Credit** AmEx, DC, MC, V. **Map** p330 K6 ④⑧
Popular since the 19th century, this lofty café somehow manages to get away with a garish cream-and-turquoise colour combination, perhaps because it leads to a fine backroom with pool tables. Other attractions include weekend breakfasts, vested waiters, a non-smoking room (off to the left side of the bar) and a more modern terrace one level below with free Wi-Fi. *Photo p188.*

U Fleků
Křemencova 11, Prague 1 (224 934 019/www. ufleku.cz). Metro Národní třída/tram 3, 6, 14, 18, 24. **Open** 9am-11pm daily. **Credit** AmEx, DC, MC, V. **Map** p330 H7 ④⑨
Yes, it's the city's most famous pub, and it has indeed been brewing fine 13-degree dark beer on the premises for centuries. Unfortunately, the world and his wife know this, and invariably troop in when visiting Prague. The long tables will most likely be filled with Germans swinging glasses to oompah music; never take the too-expensive Becherovka when it's recommended by your smiling waiter. Try the picturesque courtyard, shaded by cherry trees and enclosed by a graffitied wall and leaded windows.

French Institute Café
Štěpánská 35, Prague 1 (222 231 782/www. ifp.cz). Metro Můstek/tram 3, 9, 14, 24. **Open** 8.30am-8pm Mon-Fri; 10am-2pm Sat. **No credit cards. Map** p331 N8 ⑤⓪
An island of Left Bank *esprit*, this convivial, smoky café is a crucial source of croissants, philosophy and strong espresso (plus, of course, free Wi-Fi). The French Institute is a Gallic nerve centre, with an unapologetically Francophile art gallery downstairs and an adjoining cinema. It's an elegant, prime posing space, with an open courtyard that offers a fair chance of starting an intellectual romance.

★ Globe Bookstore & Coffeehouse
Pštrossova 6, Prague 1 (224 934 203/www. globebookstore.cz). Metro Národní třída/tram 6, 9, 18, 22. **Open** 9.30am-midnight daily. **Credit** AmEx, MC, V. **Map** p330 K8 ⑤①
Far more than a bookstore with coffee, the city's original expat bookshop-café has been pegged as the literary heart of post-revolutionary Prague – and blamed for encouraging all the wannabe Hemingways. The Globe still carries the burden graciously, offering a cosy reading room and comfortable café surroundings to scribblers of novellas and postcards. Passable pasta salads and suchlike do for food, but they're easily surpassed by the tall lattes and enormous brownies. The internet terminals and bulletin board are lifelines for expats.
▶ *For more on the Globe, see p193.*

Jazz Café č.14
Opatovická 14, Prague 1 (no phone). Metro Národní třída/tram 6, 9, 18, 22. **Open** 10am-11pm Mon-Fri; noon-11pm Sat, Sun. **No credit cards. Map** p330 K7 ⑤②
Filled with second-hand knick-knacks, and always both smoky and busy with struggling students, the Jazz Café makes for a snug winter hideaway. The service is patchy and jazz is only heard via CDs, while very basic snacks do for victuals: *medovník*, or honey cake, is about it. But the *svařák*, or mulled wine, is warming indeed.

U Kruhu
Palackého 6, Prague 1 (mobile 605 258 978). Metro Národní třída/tram 3, 9, 14, 24. **Open** 10am-10pm Mon-Fri; 1-10pm Sat, Sun. **No credit cards. Map** p330 M7 ⑤③
This dyed-in-the-wool Czech pub offers well-poured beer and a small patio space (surprisingly tranquil, considering it's only a block from Wenceslas Square). For an easy taste of authentic Prague pub culture, presided over by genial staff, it's hard to beat.

Le Patio
Národní třída 22, Prague 1 (224 934 375/ www.lepatio.cz). Metro Národní třída/tram 6, 9, 18, 22. **Open** 8am-11pm Mon-Fri; 10am-11pm Sat, Sun. **Credit** AmEx, MC, V. **Map** p330 K6 ⑤④
Opulent and well-stocked, with decadent sweets and serious coffee, this French-owned emporium of imported and locally made decorative art doubles as an atmospheric café. Wonderful hanging lamps provide a Middle Eastern/Asian feel, and there's free Wi-Fi for surfers.

★ Pivovarský dům
Lipová 15, Prague 2 (296 216 666/www.gastro info.cz/pivodum). Metro Karlovo náměstí/tram 4, 10, 16, 22. **Open** 11am-11.30pm daily. **Credit** AmEx, MC, V. **Map** p330 M9 ⑤⑤
This modern microbrewery should be on the agenda for any serious beer fan. It makes and sells excellent traditional lager plus possibly Prague's best *pivo*, and the various wheat, cherry, champagne and coffee varieties are novelties that are actually worth trying. There's an affordable menu of Czech cuisine, in case you need something to soak up the suds.

Propaganda
Pštrossova 29, Prague 1 (224 932 285/www. volny.cz/propagandabar). Metro Národní třída/ tram 6, 9, 17, 18, 22. **Open** 3pm-2am Mon-Fri; 5pm-2am Sat, Sun. **Credit** AmEx, MC, V. **Map** p330 K7 ⑤⑥
Propaganda is ultimately just a friendly neighbourhood café and bar, but it's invariably jumping with a lively young Czech crowd and occasional local celebrities. Alas, it has no street tables and can get rather fuggy on humid nights, but spirits remain ever-high.

CONSUME

The Wild Frontier

There's more to Czech beer than the perfect pilsner.

With few exceptions, Czechs accept as a simple fact of life that their country's beer is the finest in the world. Certainly, a number of international experts agree that the traditional golden lager crafted from West Bohemian Žatec hops, a process perfected with the advent of bottom-fermenting in 1842, is awfully good. But the best in the world? To the exclusion of all else? *Really?*

That's a debate for another time and place. Elsewhere, though, a handful of Czech brewers have set out to prove that their national drink need not be limited to the much-heralded classics, and have dared to move beyond the *světlé* (light) and *tmavé* (dark) flavours of traditional lager. They're not out to create a Bohemian stripe of Apache Fat Tire or the light Mexican all-star Corona. They

wouldn't take much interest in a Czech version of a Belgian-style fruit beer. And they're certainly not among the heretics who dare to put Heineken and Stella taps in their Prague beerhalls. Rather, these pioneers have brought together the best old-school brewing science and infused it with a bit of whimsy.

Founded by returning Czech émigrés in the mid-90s, **Pivovarský dům** (*see p185*) has never shied away from trying new flavours, textures and colours in its brews. Of course, the pub/microbrewery offers an in-house *ležák* (premium lager). But it was also the first place in town to introduce coffee, banana and champagne beers, all of which are much more subtle and appealing than they sound, and has since developed a pleasantly tart nettle beer. In recent times, staff have even installed one of the Czech Republic's only hand-pumps.

However, if you're on a quest for the Platonic perfection of *pivo*, there's no need to get too radical. The new generation of brewmasters are all about innovation, sure, but they see no need to abandon the classics. Beers from Pivovar Kout na Šumavě and the delectable Kocour, or Tomcat, from Pivovar Varnsdorf are both generating a buzz in more ways than one, but without deviating too far from tradition.

The drive for quality has become more urgent with the consolidation of the market. Global giant SABMiller bought out Pilsner Urquell, the greatest Bohemian beermaker, years ago; Staropramen, founded in 1869, is now owned by Inbev and exports to 37 countries. Such mass-production is hardly conducive to the kind of character once offered by more than a hundred small local breweries, most of which are now defunct. Fortunately, though, a few brave Czech beer loyalists have continued on their never-ending quest for the perfect brew.

Solidní nejistota

Pštrossova 21, Prague 1 (224 933 086/ www.solidninejistota.cz). Metro Národní třída/tram 6, 9, 17, 18, 22. **Open** 6pm-6am daily. **No credit cards. Map** p330 K8 ⑤⑦
A shrine to posing and pick-ups, Solid Uncertainty comes equipped with the now-standard blood-red interior and grill bar. Occasional rock shows draw in the crowds, as do parties for local celebrities and their entourages.

U Sudu

Vodičkova 10, Prague 1 (222 232 207/www. usudu.cz). Metro Karlovo náměstí/tram 3, 9, 14, 24. **Open** 8am-3am Mon-Fri; 9am-4am Sat; 9am-3am Sun. **No credit cards. Map** p330 M8 ⑤⑧
Very local, very trashed and very worthwhile, U Sudu started life as a small, dark wine bar tucked away on the ground floor of its current premises. Over the years, though, it's gradually expanded to fill three Gothic cellars; they've been claimed by the

student crowd, while the upstairs area plays host to everyone from scruffily-clad artists to business types to little old ladies.

▶ *The wine is nothing special, except when the* *burčák (a half-fermented, traditional Czech wine* *punch) arrives in September; see p214.*

Ultramarin

Ostrovní 32, Prague 2 (224 932 249/www.ultra marin.cz). Metro Národní třída. **Open** 10.30am-4am Mon-Sat; 2pm-4am Sun. **Credit** AmEx, DC, MC, V. **Map** p330 L7 ⑨

A cool combination of ancient townhouse and modern art bar, Ultramarin is one of the city's most stylish bars. The atmospheric retro jazz on the sound system, the Santa Fe chicken salad on the menu, and the blonde wood and mottled paints on the walls would all be better complemented by real cocktails and decent wines. Still, it's just about the best option for mellow late-night refuelling.

Velryba

Opatovická 24, Prague 1 (224 931 444/ *www.kavarnavelryba.cz). Metro Národní třída/* *tram 6, 9, 18, 22.* **Open** 11am-midnight daily. **No credit cards. Map** p330 L7 ⑥

With rock blasting out from the sound system, a fog of cigarette smoke, greasy, cheap grub and barely drinkable wine, the Whale is starving-student heaven. In the loud front room there are pastas and chicken steaks to be devoured; elsewhere, there's chess in the back room plus a cellar gallery specialising in fringe art and photography shows. The bar serves bottled Gambrinus.

Vesmírna

Ve Smečkách 5, Prague 1 (222 212 363/ *www.vesmirna.cz). Metro Muzeum/tram 11.* **Open** 8.30am-10pm Mon-Fri; 2-10pm Sat. **No credit cards. Map** p331 N8 ⑥

Hidden away on a backstreet but well worth seeking out, this calming, low-key coffeehouse serves fresh juices and tasty light meals, using healthy ingredients and organic produce. The organic couscous, served with cheese and vegetables, and the excellent apple pie are both hits with the lunchtime crowd. Service, which includes special-needs staff, is also impressive.

Zlatá Hvězda

Ve Smečkách 12, Prague 1 (296 222 292/ *www.sport bar.cz). Metro Muzeum/tram 4, 6,* *10, 16, 22.* **Open** 11am-11pm Mon, Tue, Sun; 11am-11.30pm Wed, Thur; 11am-midnight Fri, Sat. **No credit cards. Map** p331 N8 ⑥

A tattered interior, terrible service and just-edible pizzas don't discourage the sports fans who gather here to watch the games on the battered big screens. There are better sports bars closer to Wenceslas Square, of course, but none can match the character of this old favourite.

FURTHER AFIELD

Dejvice

Café Orange

Puškinovo náměstí 13, Dejvice, Prague 6 *(mobile 603 894 499). Metro Hradčanská.* **Open** 10am-11pm Mon-Sat; 11am-3pm Sun. **No credit cards.**

This out-of-the-way café is ideal for a secret rendezvous. Set on a quiet, hard-to-find square, with street tables coming into play during summer, it was the first daytime venue in Prague 6 to serve such exotic luxuries as lattes and mozzarella ciabattas.

Holešovice

La Bodega Flamenca

Šmeralova 5, Prague 7 (233 374 075/www.la bodega.cz). Metro Vltavská/tram 1, 8, 25, 26. **Open** 4pm-1am Mon-Thur, Sun; 4pm-3am Fri, Sat. **No credit cards. Map** p332 C3 ⑥

The easily missed entrance to this cellar tapas bar conceals a perpetual sangria party. Owner Ilona oversees the bar, serving tapas such as marinated olives and garlic mushrooms. Bench-style seats line the walls and fill up fast. In true Spanish style, things only really start hotting up after 1am.

★ Fraktal

Šmeralova 1, Prague 7 (mobile 777 794 094/ *www.fraktalbar.cz). Metro Vltavská/tram 1, 8,* *25, 26.* **Open** 11am-midnight daily. **No credit cards. Map** p332 C3 ⑥

This comfy, well-worn art bar is a trashy, convivial place where pretty much anything goes. Mojitos and tequila gold with orange and cinnamon cocktails make notable accompaniments to the improved menu of the inevitable Czech-Mex dishes, while the burger has been voted the best in town. Free Wi-Fi and Sunday brunch are other attractions.

★ Letenský zámeček

Letenské sady 341, Letná Park, Prague 7 *(233 375 604/www.letenskyzamecek.cz). Metro* *Hradčanská/tram 1, 8, 25, 26.* **Open** *Beer garden* 11am-11pm daily. *Restaurants* 11am-11.30pm daily. **No credit cards. Map** p332 D4 ⑥

A leafy enclave on the hill above the Vltava, this bar is home to what's arguably the city's finest summer beer garden. A local crowd gathers under the chestnut trees for cheap beer in plastic cups late into the evening during the warmer months. The adjoining Brasserie Ullman and Restaurant Belcredi have gone upscale, with modern designer interiors, a dressy crowd and excellent Bernard beer on tap.

Výletná

Letenské sady 32, Prague 7 (no phone). Metro *Hradčanská/tram 1, 15, 25, 26.* **Open** 11am-1am daily. **No credit cards. Map** p312 C3 ⑥

CONSUME

Situated just off the tennis courts in Letná Park, this rustic little pub serves bargain barbecue fare on its terrace in summer and often gets taken over for parties and events, sometimes stretching to literary readings, at other times of the year.

Smíchov

U Buldoka

Preslova 1, Prague 5 (257 329 154/www.ubuldoka.cz). Metro Anděl/tram 6, 9. **Open** 8pm-4am Mon-Sat. **No credit cards**.
At once olde-worlde and modern, At the Bulldog is one of the last classic pubs in the district. Good Staropramen beer and excellent traditional grub go with an international sensibility, quick service and a cool dance club below deck; all-day specials of *halušky* (Slovak gnocchi with bacon) and *guláš* soup accompany the light and dark beer. There's a good collection of Czech herbal liqueurs at the bar.

Káva Káva Káva

Lidická 42, Prague 5 (257 314 277/www.kava-coffee.cz). Metro Anděl/tram 4, 7, 10, 14. **Open** 7am-10pm Mon-Thur; 7am-midnight Fri; 9am-midnight Sat; 9am-10pm Sun. **No credit cards**.
An LA-style coffee and muffin shop, Káva Káva Káva satisfies caffeine cravings with beans ranging from Guatemalan arabica to Sumatra dark roast. It's refreshingly laid-back for this upmarket district, but you'll pay as much as you would at Starbucks.

Kavárna v sedmém nebi

Zborovská 68, Prague 5 (257 318 110). Tram 6, 9, 12, 22. **Open** 10am-1am Mon-Fri; 2pm-1am Sat, Sun. **No credit cards**.
A peaceful, arty café-bar, with a whimsical loft from which to spy on those in the comfy junk-shop chairs below, this meeting place for the local film community is half work of sculpture, half living room. The menu is limited to coffee and tea, along with *bábovka*, a spongy Czech cake, toasted sandwiches and crisps. Laptop-toters enjoy the free Wi-Fi.

Vinohrady

Café Medúza

Belgická 17, Prague 2 (222 515 107/www.meduza.cz). Metro Náměstí Míru/tram 4, 22. **Open** 10am-midnight Mon-Sat; noon-midnight Sun. **No credit cards**. **Map** p331 Q11 ⑥⑦
On a quiet Belgická street, you'll find one of the city's most serene if threadbare winter hideouts, run by two sisters who serve warming soups and mulled wine to bookish regular patrons, along with a few light snacks and herbal liqueurs. The free Wi-Fi is a boon.

Café Sahara

Náměstí míru 6, Prague 2 (222 514 987/www.saharacafe.cz). Metro Náměstí Míru/tram
4, 16, 22. **Open** 11am-12.30am Mon-Sat; 11am-midnight Sun. **No credit cards**. **Map** p331 Q9 ⑥⑧
Capacious rooms in cool sandstone tones, with big wicker chairs and waiters out of a fashion spread: this is a handsome café experience. Add a new Middle Eastern menu of small plates and views of Vinohrady's main square, and it's bound to appeal to style fans. It's definitely not the cheapest option around, but it's top quality.

★ Kaaba

Mánesova 20, Prague 2 (222 254 021/www.kaaba.cz). Tram 11. **Open** 8am-10pm Mon-Fri; 9am-10pm Sat; 10am-10pm Sun. **No credit cards**. **Map** p333 A3 ⑥⑨
Filled with second-hand furniture, most of it fabulous and repainted in pastels, this neighbourhood café is a haven for local creative idlers. The great windows on to the Vinohrady street and decent wines by the glass from well-known domestic producers make it a good choice for long mornings of lazing with magazines and cheap coffee.

Park Café

Riegrovy sady 28, Prague 2 (no phone). Metro Jiřího z Poděbrad/tram 11. **Open** 11am-11pm daily. **No credit cards**. **Map** p333 B3 ⑦⓪
One of the liveliest beer gardens in the district is always crowded with old-timers, children, dogs and expats. The beer is cheap and copious, and rock bands liven up the place during summer. Just watch where you step, as the dogs leave deposits.

Passion Chocolat

Italská 5, Prague 2 (222 524 333/www.musso-praha.com). Metro Náměstí Míru/tram 11.
Open 8am-7pm Mon-Sat. **No credit cards.**
Map p333 A4

Chocoholics throughout Prague have been whispering the name of this lovely little place, set up by French couple Nadine and Jean-François. Top-drawer Valrhona chocolate is a key ingredient in the sweets and pastries – millefeuille with espresso is a slice of heaven. Call or check the website before visiting, as a change of premises may be afoot.

Pastička

Blanická 25, Prague 2 (222 253 228/www.pasticka.cz). Metro Náměstí Míru/tram 4, 10, 16, 22. **Open** 11am-1am Mon-Fri; 5pm-1am Sat, Sun. **Credit** AmEx, MC, V. **Map** p333 A3

The Little Mousetrap is a beloved neighbourhood hangout that's always jumping with a mixed crowd that goes in for gab, grub, beer and cigarettes. The rustic ceramics and rough-hewn wood interiors can get a bit close in winter, but the back garden is hard to resist in milder seasons.

Popocafepetl

Italská 2, Prague 2 (777 944 672/www.popocafe petl.cz). Metro Náměstí Míru/tram 11. **Open** 11am-1am Mon-Fri; 3pm-1am Sat; 3pm-midnight Sun. **Credit** AmEx, MC, V. **Map** p333 A3

A sister café to a thriving operation in Malá Strana, this is the quieter, gentler Popo – but not by much. Regulars flock here until the wee small hours; they're not here for the fine service or superior beers, but somehow the place always has a buzz, thanks in part to the vibrant mix of local bohemians and decadent expats.

▶ *For the Malá Strana branch, see p256.*

Potrefená husa

Vinohradská 104, Prague 3 (267 310 360/www.pivo.cz). Metro Jiřího z Poděbrad/tram 11. **Open** 11.30am-1am daily. **Credit** AmEx, MC, V. **Map** p333 D3

The kind of place that you'd find in every suburb of many Western cities, the Wounded Goose is a runaway success in Prague. It offers a better menu and service than a lot of Prague restaurants – but that's not terribly difficult. Part of a national chain, it's nearly always packed with young professionals sipping Velvet beer and noshing on chicken wings and ribs while taking in sports on cable TV.
Other locations Bilkova 5, Prague 1 (222 326 626)

Shakespeare & Sons

Krymská 12, Prague 10 (271 740 839/www.shakes.cz). Metro Náměstí Míru/tram 4, 22. **Open** noon-midnight daily. **Credit** MC, V.

An elegant bookstore and café located just a stone's throw from the Vršovice–Vinohrady border, Shakespeare & Sons offers a wide selection of mind fodder, as well as Bernard beer and good coffee. Readings and book launches help draw a page-turning bohemian crowd.

▶ *For more on the city's bookshops, see p193.*

CONSUME

Café Louvre. *See p183.*

CONSUME

Zvonařka

Šafaříkova 1, Prague 2 (224 251 990/www.
restauracezvonarka.cz). Metro IP Pavlova/tram
6, 11. **Open** 11am-midnight daily. **No credit**
cards. Map p331 Q12 ⑦
This stylish bar, in a graceful old building, has been
popular for years and still justifies the trip out to the
end of little Šafaříkova. With fine views of the Nusle
valley, the terrace at the back is a godsend. There's
a traditional Czech menu for the hungry, but most
people come here to sip and chin-wag.

Žižkov

Akropolis

Kubelíkova 27, Prague 3 (296 330 911). Metro
Jiřího z Poděbrad/tram 11. **Open** 11.30am-1am
daily. **No credit cards. Map** p333 C2 ⑦
Still the most popular bar in the district among the
post-1989 generation, the Akropolis is a Žižkov
institution of drinking, networking and gig-going.
It has four separate pubs on site, each with its own
crowd and vibe. The street-level Akropolis restaurant serves cheap and decent food with passable
beer (*see p172*); the Kaaba Café is a small, well-lit
place to meet up and get a caffeine fix; the Divadelní
Bar is a hot, intense vortex of DJ action and surreal
woodcarvings; and the Malá Scena is a red-washed
chill-out space with a post-industrial look and battered tables. Take your pick.

Blind Eye

Vlkova 26, Prague 3 (no phone/www.blindeye.cz).
Metro Jiřího z Poděbrad/tram 11. **Open** 11am-
5am daily. **No credit cards. Map** p333 B2 ⑦
A late-night hideout for sleep-starved bohemians of
all nationalities, the open but ever-unfinished Blind
Eye offers rambling conversations at the wavy iron-
top bar, beer at booth tables, the occasional loud rock
jam and more than a few student parties.

Clown & Bard

Bořivojova 102, Prague 3 (222 716 453/
www.clownandbard.com). Metro Jiřího z
Poděbrad/tram 5, 9, 26. **Open** 5pm-midnight
daily. **No credit cards. Map** p333 B2 ⑦
A lively spot for a few bottles of Budvar, cheap shots
or a chess game, the Clown & Bard is about as entertaining as hostel bars get. And that can actually be
quite entertaining, if you come on a night when one
of the undiscovered bands that regularly plays here
is any good.
▶ *For details of the hostel, see p149.*

Hapu

Orlická 8, Prague 3 (222 720 158). Metro Jiřího
z Poděbrad/tram 11. **Open** 6pm-2am Mon-Sat.
No credit cards. Map p333 D3 ⑦
Not easy to find yet invariably full, this one-room
cellar with beaten-up sofas and a small bar has been
a living-room bar to the neighbourhood for years.

That's because it whips up the best cocktails around
but mixes in none of the pretence usually found in
Prague's cocktail bars. A fun crowd of international
raconteurs can always be found on site.

U Houdků

Bořivojova 110, Prague 3 (222 711 239). Metro
Jiřího z Poděbrad/tram 11. **Open** 11am-11pm
daily. **No credit cards. Map** p333 B2 ⑧
U Houdků is just a cheap, neighbourhood pub
untouched by time, where you can sit out in the garden behind and sip away in the sunshine. It's also a
blast of South Bohemia: Eggenberg and Budvar,
hearty brews from the Český Krumlov area, are
served in light and dark versions, alongside mounds
of typical Czech pub grub for pocket change. Every
student and worker in the district seems hooked.

Infinity

Chrudimská 7, Prague 3 (272 176 580/www.
infinitybar.cz). Metro Flora/tram 9, 11, 26.
Open 6pm-1am Mon, Sun; 6pm-4am Fri, Sat.
No credit cards. Map p333 E3 ⑧
Newly toned up, Infinity draws a dressy crowd for
parties and general carousing, and has added a light
menu of antipasti and treats such as lamb carpaccio. Meanwhile, its nooks, recessed lighting, brick
and red-washed interiors make for mellow sipping,
with DJ action (of varying quality) after 10pm.

U Sadu

Škroupovo náměstí 5, Prague 3 (222 727 072/
www.usadu.cz). Metro Jiřího z Poděbrad/tram 11.
Open 8am-2am Mon, Sun, Wed; 8am-4am Thur-
Sat. **No credit cards. Map** p333 C3 ⑧
A classic Czech pub-restaurant in the heart of old-
style Žižkov, U Sadu is popular with students, and
holds its own against the hundreds of earthy pubs
around. The chilli goulash, schnitzels and fried
cheese are marvellously unhealthy treats, the Pilsner
and Gambrinus are good, and service is thoroughly
gruff. It doesn't get any more authentic than this.
And what's more, the kitchen stays open late – for
Prague, at any rate.

U vystřelenýho oka

U božích bojovníků 3, Prague 3 (222 540 465/
www.uvoka.cz). Metro Florenc, then bus 135,
207. **Open** 4.30pm-1am Mon-Sat. **No credit**
cards. Map p333 C1 ⑧
Žižkov has more pubs than any other area of
Prague, but this is one of the best, at least for fans
of garage rock and weird art. The Shot-Out Eye sits
beneath the ominous giant statue of General Jan
Žižka, the renowned warrior whose battle injury
inspired the gory name. A three-level outdoor beer
garden serves bargain-basement Měšťan, while the
taps indoors flow non-stop to a soundtrack of local
anarcho-rockers Psí Vojáci and a backdrop of
grotesque paintings by the artist Martin Velíšek.
There's free Wi-Fi.

Shops & Services

Designers, craftsmanship and a slow improvement in service.

If retail therapy is high on your list of holiday activities, you'll need to think strategically when you visit Prague. Flexibility and good humour are essential skills when dealing with counter service in the Czech capital, as people from other Czech cities and towns will confirm. Every year, things improve, with wider selections of goods and a greater interest in customer needs. But the quaint idiosyncrasies that only a former communist country can possess are far from extinct. You can usually get what you need, but selection and quality can vary wildly from store to store and day to day. Focus on Prague specialities, on the other hand, and there are worthwhile deals almost everywhere.

PRACTICALITIES

Many shop attendants in the centre now speak some English, and more and more shops will take plastic without looking at you as if you have a second head. Longer opening hours have also come into effect, and not just in the more tourist-friendly areas. But straying even a little further out from the centre may still bring you up against shops that close at noon on Saturdays and don't open at all on Sundays.

The majority of the big stores here are multinationals. They've found a welcoming, shopping-crazed new generation of Czuppies waiting for them, especially eager for the clothing shops that sell inexpensive but trendy wares. The mall concept has taken off all too well: one new monolith is the **Palladium** (*see p192*) on the edge of Old Town, and other large malls are concentrated on the outskirts of the town.

These days, Czech fashion buffs don't have to visit Paris or Milan for their dose of couture. A stroll down Old Town's most conspicuously commercial streets, Celetná and Pařížská, will supply all the requirements of a properly tailored lifestyle. But the real rewards of Prague shopping are to be found off the main drags, hidden away down quiet alleyways and

in dusty old shops. This is where you may still come across vintage prints and books, quaint lace and glass, or other treasures.

General

DEPARTMENT STORES

Kotva
Náměstí Republiky 8, Staré Město, Prague 1 (224 801 111). Metro Náměstí Republiky/tram 5, 8, 14. **Open** *Department store* 9am-8pm Mon-Fri; 10am-7pm Sat; 10am-6pm Sun. *Supermarket* 7am-8pm Mon-Fri; 9am-6pm Sat; 10am-7pm Sun. **Credit** AmEx, MC, V. **Map** p329 O4.
Kotva is a historically protected building, but its 1970s design will only charm die-hard fans of the form. It's centrally located and strangely arranged – almost like a market. The items get more varied as you move upwards, with cosmetics and luggage on the first floor, and clothing, sports equipment and furniture on the upper floors.

Tesco
Národní třída 26, Nové Město, Prague 1 (222 003 111). Metro Můstek or Národní třída/tram 6, 9, 18, 21, 22. **Open** *Department store* 8am-9pm Mon-Sat; 9am-8pm Sun. *Supermarket* 7am-9pm Mon-Sat; 8am-8pm Sun. **Credit** AmEx, MC, V. **Map** p328 L6.
Always packed out and occasionally headache-inducing, Tesco nonetheless probably has what you need. You'll need to purchase your items separately

About the author
Jacy Meyer is a freelance writer who has lived in Prague for five years. She works for the Prague Post *and various other publications.*

CONSUME

on each floor: the basement is a grocery store, while the ground floor has cosmetics and beauty supplies, along with a small *potraviny*, or grocer's, and some souvenirs and other gift items. Ascending through the building, you'll find men's, women's and children's clothing, kitchenware and electrical goods.

MALLS

A mall is a mall, and once you're inside you could be anywhere in the world. The newest is out in Chodov, a bit outside the centre but easily reached by metro. Dedicated mall rats should try the shopping centres that line Na příkopě: they may not offer inspired shopping, but there's certainly plenty of it.

Myslbek Centre

Na příkopě 19-21, Staré Město, Prague 1 (224 239 550). Metro Můstek/tram 3, 9, 14, 24. **Open** 8.30am-8.30pm Mon-Sat; 9.30am-8.30pm Sun. **Credit** AmEx, MC, V. **Map** p329 N5.
It's small, but the Myslbek Centre makes up for its size with an excellent location and a couple of decent, large-ish shops. If you're looking for the basics, it'll probably do you fine.

Nový Smíchov Centrum

Plzeňská 8, Smíchov, Prague 5 (251 511 151/ www.novysmichov.eu). Metro Anděl/tram 4, 6, 7, 9, 10, 14. **Open** 7am-midnight daily. **Credit** AmEx, MC, V.
This mall is pleasant enough, with Datart, H&M, Clinique and Sephora among its international chains. A massive (for Prague) branch of Carrefour

has been taken over by Tesco, with the great cheese collection remaining intact; there's also a third-level games arcade, food court and cinema.

Palác Flóra

Vinohradská 149, Vinohrady, Prague 3 (255 741 712/www.palacflora.cz). Metro Flóra/tram 5, 10, 11, 16. **Open** 8am-midnight daily. **Credit** AmEx, MC, V. **Map** p333 C3.
Less crowded than Nový Smíchov Centrum, Palác Flóra is also directly accessible from the metro station. There's something for most shoppers here, with fashionable shops, big chain stores, a supermarket and a dry cleaner, as well as decent food offerings of both the fast and sit-down type. There are no inspiring shops, but fashion-conscious Czechs clearly enjoy spending afternoons here – in fact, it's a popular date destination. Prague's IMAX theatre is also found here.

Palladium

Náměstí Republiky 1, Nové Město, Prague 1 (225 770 250/www.palladiumpraha.cz). Metro Náměstí Republiky/tram 5, 8, 26. **Open** *Mall* 9am-10pm Mon-Sat; 9am-9pm Sun. *Supermarket* 7am-10pm Mon-Fri; 8am-10pm Sat; 8am-9pm Sun. *Restaurants* 11am-midnight daily. **Credit** AmEx, MC, V. **Map** p329 O3.
It's not a mall, it's an entertainment centre. Well, that's how Palladium likes to style itself. It has tons of restaurants (including conveyor belt sushi) and bars, and admittedly did bring some hip new names to Prague. It's huge and bang in the centre of Náměstí Republiky, so you can't miss it even if you want to.

CONSUME

Havelský Market.

INSIDE TRACK
SHOP TALK

When you enter a shop, the clerk will ask, '*Máte přání?*' ('Do you have a wish?'). While ringing up your purchases, he may ask, '*Ještě něco*?' ('Anything else?') or '*Všechno*?' ('Is that all?'). If you want to know the price of an item, say, '*Kolik to stojí*?'

MARKETS

Prague doesn't have much in the way of outdoor markets, except around holiday time. For most of the year, it's mainly just fruit and vegetables, along with the odd wooden or woven item.

Christmas and Easter, however, see the squares come alive with a variety of holiday goodies. The Christmas markets in Old Town Square or Václavské náměstí are the best; since it will be chilly, you'll have a perfect excuse to warm up with a nice cup of steaming mulled wine (*svařené víno* or *svařák*).

★ Havelský Market

Havelská, Staré Město, Prague 1 (no phone). Metro Můstek or Národní třída/tram 6, 9, 18, 22. **Open** 7.30am-6pm Mon-Fri; 8.30am-6pm Sat, Sun. **No credit cards. Map** p328 L5.
Fruit and vegetables have mostly been squeezed out by souvenirs at this central market, but there is still some fresh produce to buy – and an abundance of wooden toys, puppets and other tourist trinkets. Be sure to check out the sweet booths as well as the fresh flowers.

Market at the Fountain

Spálená 30, Nové Město, Prague 1 (no phone). Metro Národní třída/tram 6, 9, 18, 22. **Open** 7.30am-7pm daily. **No credit cards. Map** p330 L8.
Tiny but well stocked, this market behind Tesco will ensure you get your quota of those vitamins not found in beer. There are also some clothing options like scarves and sweaters, the variety of which increases as the weather gets warmer. Talk of reconstruction at the time of going to press has cast doubt on this institution's long-term future.

Specialist
BOOKS & MAGAZINES

Prices and choice still aren't marvellous. However, if you have to have a home-country newspaper or you've just finished your last

paperback, the following places will definitely be able to help out. You may even make a friend among the stacks.

English-language

Anagram Bookshop

Týn 4, Staré Město, Prague 1 (224 895 737/ www.anagram.cz). Metro Náměstí Republiky/ tram 5, 8, 14. **Open** 10am-8pm Mon-Sat; 10am-7pm Sun. **Credit** DC, MC, V. **Map** p328 M3.
A good place for books on Prague and Central Europe, especially second-hand publications.

★ Big Ben Bookshop

Malá Štupartská 5, Staré Město, Prague 1 (224 826 565/www.bigbenbookshop.com). Metro Náměstí Republiky/tram 5, 8, 14. **Open** 9am-7pm Mon-Fri; 10am-6pm Sat; noon-5pm Sun. **Credit** AmEx, MC, V. **Map** p328 M3.
Big Ben probably has the widest selection in town, with fiction, non-fiction, an excellent children's section and a very good range of English papers and magazines. If your title isn't in stock, the shop is able to order it. The staff are friendly and knowledgeable.

Globe Bookstore & Coffeehouse

Pštrossova 6, Nové Město, Prague 2 (224 934 203/www.globebookstore.cz). Metro Národní třída/tram 6, 9, 18, 22. **Open** 9.30am-midnight daily. **Credit** AmEx, MC, V. **Map** p330 K8.
The Globe probably isn't as iconic as it once was, but it's still going and still happening. It stocks a mix of second-hand and new books (heavier on the new), plus the international papers. It also has internet access and a restaurant at the back. *Photos p195.*

Trafika Můstek

Václavské náměstí, Nové Město, Prague 1 (no phone). Metro Můstek/tram 3, 9, 14, 24. **Open** 8am-10pm daily. **No credit cards. Map** p331 O7.
If it's an English-language periodical you're looking for, this kiosk at the bottom of Wenceslas Square should have it in stock.

Used & antiquarian

Prague's second-hand bookshops are known as *antikvariáty*. If you have the time and are passing, go in for a browse. You'll never know what you'll find – communist coffee-table books or cheap prints by unknown Czech artists. These shops are also good for second-hand novels in English.

Antikvariát Dlážděná v Růžové

Růžová 8, Nové Město, Prague 1 (222 243 911/ www.adplus.cz). Metro Můstek/tram 3, 9, 14, 24. **Open** 9am-6pm Mon-Fri; 9am-1pm Sat, Sun. **Credit** AmEx, MC, V. **Map** p329 O6.

Tons of illustrations on the walls, more drawings filed away by topic in drawers, and scores of books – including many in English.

Antikvariát Galerie Můstek

Národní 40, Nové Město, Prague 1 (224 949 587). Metro Národní třída/tram 6, 9, 18, 22. **Open** 10am-7pm Mon-Fri; noon-4pm Sat; 2-6pm Sun. **Credit** AmEx, MC, V. **Map** p328 L6.
At this discriminating *antikvariát*, you'll find a fine selection of antiquarian books and a reliable stock of the major works on Czech art.

Antikvariát Kant

Opatovická 26, Nové Město, Prague 1 (224 934 219/www.antik-kant.cz). Metro Národní třída/tram 6, 9, 18, 22. **Open** 10am-6pm Mon-Fri. **Credit** AmEx, MC, V. **Map** p330 K8.
Its impressive variety makes Kant an enjoyable place in which to waste time. The entry room is filled with tomes priced at 5 to 15 Kč, drawings and English books. Also interesting are the photographs in boxes by the counter; their subject matter is random – such as an operating theatre with victim on the table.

CHILDREN

Toys

You won't find many local children shopping at the stores listed below: they're at home busy with computers and iPods, just like their counterparts in much of the rest of the world. But for a selection of unique Czech toys, try the following places.

Art Dekor

Ovocny trh 12, Staré Město, Prague 1 (221 637 178/wwwartdekor.cz). Metro Metro Náměstí Republiky/tram 5, 8, 26. **Open** 10am-7pm Mon-Sat; 10am-6pm Sun. **Credit** MC, V. **Map** p329 N4.
Whimsical designs and patterned materials make for unique gifts. The beautifully crafted stuffed animals, all made with hypoallergenic materials, are perfect for babies.

Beruška

Vodičkova 30, Nové Město, Prague 1 (no phone). Metro Můstek/tram 3, 9, 14, 24. **Open** 10am-6pm Mon-Fri. **No credit cards. Map** p329 N6.
Beruška is a small shop that's filled with toys for young and older children: you'll find a good selection of stuffed animals, clever wooden toys, and all sorts of puzzles and games.

Sparky's Dům hraček

Havířská 2, Staré Město, Prague 1 (224 239 309/www.sparkys.cz). Metro Můstek/tram 3, 9, 14, 24. **Open** 10am-7pm Mon-Sat; 10am-6pm Sun. **Credit** AmEx, MC, V. **Map** p328 M5.
The House of Toys is really more of a mansion, holding three levels of desirable playthings. 'Czech' toys as well as stuffed animals can be found on the

---

Where to Shop

Prague's best shopping neighbourhoods in brief.

HRADČANY & MALÁ STRANA

The **Hradčany** district around Prague Castle holds lots of overpriced junk shops, selling precious little of interest. However, there are worthwhile antique shops and *antikvariáts* in **Malá Strana**.

STARÉ MĚSTO

Antique shops and the institution known as *antikvariát* (old book shop) remain popular in Prague, especially along some of the streets between **Old Town Square** and **Náměstí Republiky**. Take time to browse, and you'll find delicate porcelain, antique glass, communist-era prints, vintage photographs and old books.

The big streets directly off Old Town Square, among them **Celetná** and **Karlova** (the street leading to Charles Bridge), are best if you're looking for for traditional souvenirs. However, more interesting possibilities will present themselves on

any of the smaller streets in the area, while heading toward Nové Město will also broaden your prospects.

For fashion, hit **Pařížská** for Gucci and Louis Vuitton. But if you want some true Czech fashion, browse the local designer shops in the **Josefov** neighbourhood.

NOVÉ MĚSTO

In Nové Město, **Na příkopě** has a large selection of mini-malls. They're generally packed, at least at weekends, by newly flush locals; unfortunately, they're mostly composed of multinational chains, and finding anything unique, or even slightly different, is nigh on impossible. **Spálená** is where the hip young locals go for their threads, with better prices than the malls. The same can be said for Wenceslas Square. Some of the streets on either side can be interesting, but are best visited during the day.

CONSUME

ground floor; as you go higher up, the age range rises. The lower floor has lots of wooden toys and games, while the top stocks action figures, dolls and more advanced gadgets.

ELECTRONICS & PHOTOGRAPHY

If you need a hairdryer or similar basic appliance, **Tesco** (*see p191*) will probably stock it. If you need something more advanced or hard to find, check out one of the venues detailed below.

General

Datart

Národní 60, Prague 1 (225 991 000/www. datart.cz). Metro Národní třída/tram 6, 18, 19, 22. **Open** 9am-8pm Mon-Fri; 9am-7pm Sat; 10am-6pm Sun. **Credit** AmEx, MC, V. **Map** p328 L6.

This consumer electricals chain is a convenient option for flash drives and digital video tape, camera batteries, or any other appliances you may have forgotten to bring. Service, though, is generally brusque or evasive.

Globe Bookstore & Coffeehouse. *See p193.*

Airline flights are one of the biggest producers of the global warming gas CO_2. But with **The CarbonNeutral Company** you can make your travel a little greener.

Go to **www.carbonneutral.com** to calculate your flight emissions then 'neutralise' them through international projects which save exactly the same amount of carbon dioxide.

Contact us at **shop@carbonneutral.com** or call into the office on **0870 199 99 88** for more details.

CarbonNeutral®flights

Electro World
Řevnická 1, Zličín, Prague 5 (235 002 852).
Metro Zličín. **Open** 10am-9pm daily. **Credit**
MC, V.
Electro World is the big one for silicon geeks: computers, digital cameras, HD TV, audio gear, and all the requirements for our electronic age. If anywhere in Prague stocks it, Electro World does.
Other locations Česlice, Obchodní 117, Prague (267 227 700); Černý Most, Chlumecká 1531, Prague 9 (281 028 555).

Cameras

Foto Škoda
Palác Langhans, Vodičkova 37, Nové Město,
Prague 1 (222 929 029/www.fotoskoda.cz).
Metro Můstek/tram 3, 9, 14, 24. **Open** 8.30am-
8.30pm Mon-Fri; 9am-6pm Sat. **Credit** AmEx,
MC, V. **Map** p328 J6.
Sales, repairs, developing, supplies: everything camera-related you could possibly want, need or think you may have a use for. It's excellent for the professional, but amateurs will also find what they need with an impressive collection of lights, bags and second-hand lenses. The best pick of things photographic in Prague.

Fotoplus
Charvátová 58, Nové Město, Prague 1 (224
213 121/wwww.fotoplus.cz). Metro Náměstí
Republiky/tram 5, 14, 26. **Open** 8.30am-8pm
Mon-Fri; 9am-4pm Sat. **Credit** AmEx, MC, V.
Map p329 N5.
Photo shops are rife in the tourist areas; even your local *drogerie* will probably do photos. Quality is sometimes an issue, though, so if your snaps need to be picture-perfect, it might be worth taking them to Fotoplus. The pros come here for the one-hour photo and digital service (outsize prints included). Note that it's moved from its previous address to a passage off Národní.

Jan Pazdera obchod a opravna
Lucerna, Vodičkova 30, Nové Město, Prague 1
(224 216 197). Metro Můstek/tram 3, 9, 14, 24.
Open 10am-6pm Mon-Fri. **No credit cards**.
Map p329 N6.
This is practically a camera museum, full of beautiful old antique cameras and lenses. There's a small supply of film, batteries and the like, but it's best for the old stuff. Simple camera repairs can be carried out on site.

Computers

Apple Center Anděl
Nadrážní 23, Smíchov, Prague 5 (257 210 493/
www.appleobchod.cz). Metro Anděl/tram 6, 12,
20. **Open** 10am-10pm Mon-Fri; 10am-7pm Sat;
2-7pm Sun. **Credit** AmEx, MC, V.

The main Apple centre in town offers a complete line-up of all things Mac, including sleek iPods, peripherals, software, MacBooks and the rest. The shop is staffed by trained and helpful English-speaking assistants.

HSH Computer
Nádražní 42, Smíchov, Prague 5 (257 310 910/
www.hsh.cz). Metro Anděl/tram 6, 12, 20. **Open**
9am-6pm Mon-Fri. **Credit** MC, V.
Sales, service and rentals of a variety of big-name international brands, including Compaq, HP, IBM and Toshiba.

FASHION
Designer

Prague isn't a high-fashion destination, but local designers can be creative; styles tend to be bolder and more distinctive than the clothes you'll find in many of the chain stores.
These low-key designers continue to make names for themselves at home and abroad, and it's worth visiting to see what's new. And where else but Prague could you get designer items at such prices?

Atelier Tatiana
Dušní 1, Staré Město, Prague 1 (224 813 723/
www.tatiana.cz). Metro Staroměstská/tram 17,
18. **Open** 10am-7pm Mon-Fri; 11am-4pm Sat.
Credit AmEx, MC, V. **Map** p328 L3.
Tatiana Kovářiková's clothing is a mixture of high-fashion elegance and practicality. Garments are perfectly cut and beautifully styled, with lovely details.

Fashion Galerie No.14
Opatovická 14, Nové Město, Prague 1 (no phone).
Metro Národní třída/tram 6, 9, 18, 22. **Open**
noon-7pm Mon-Sat. **Credit** AmEx, MC, V. **Map**
p330 K8.
This store is not for the budget-conscious, but is definitely one for the fashion hound to seek out. Each item is an original, and the quality and designs are beautiful. Dresses are the speciality, but some casual items are available, as well as jewellery to help complete the look.

> ### INSIDE TRACK
> ### FASHION IN STARÉ MĚSTO
>
> In a bid to capitalise on their individual successes, some local designers have teamed up in a bid to win even greater publicity for their clothes. Many are in Staré Město: see www.czechfashion.cz for a round-up of locally run boutiques in the neighbourhood.

CONSUME

From the Catwalk to the Car Plant

One Prague designer is making waves – and in the unlikeliest of places.

Not many fashion designers can boast Miss World and Škoda on their client list. But for **Hana Havelková** (*see below*), they're just two more satisfied customers. Although she says her greatest success was designing the dress that Taťána Kuchařová, Miss Czech Republic, was wearing when she won Miss World in 2006, it's only one of many design coups that have studded her career.

Havelková describes her personal style as sophisticated, simple and verging on the minimalist, but livened up with little details. She recently bought a length of velvet material with embroidered designs and 'just had to have it and make something out of it'. There was a lot of silk and wool fabric in her 2008 autumn and winter collection; she also plays around with chequered prints. The softly spoken star of Prague's demanding fashion world says she draws most of her inspiration from architectural lines, surfaces and façades. She's partial to

functionalism and minimalism because 'everything is for a specific purpose'.

'When I work for myself, I can present myself as an artist, be more daring and creative,' says Havelková. 'When I work for someone else, I'm expected to present a certain style.' So how did the fashion designer end up working for Škoda, staging a fashion show to accompany the presentation of a new model of car?

She admits that the job was a challenge. 'It's not just the company's expectation. You also have to consider the viewers who may not be familiar with "fashion" and just want to see something pretty.'

Havelková is generous and optimistic when discussing her fellow designers. 'I think Czech fashion designers are freer to be more artistic because it isn't so commercialised here. Boutiques aren't a big business, so people are collecting the designs – or it's something special. It's important to reach for change, but still keep your style.'

★ Flamingo Park

Vlkova 11, Žižkov, Prague 3 (no phone/www. flamingopark.cz). Metro Můstek/tram 5, 9, 26. **Open** noon-6.30pm Mon-Fri. **No credit cards. Map** p333 B2.

Founded by a Czech-Australian couple, this shop is an inspired original. The stock runs from clothes by local designers to outré accessories, toys, decor and crafty kitsch – just the thing for spicing up your home or wardrobe. *Photos p200.*

★ Hana Havelková

Dušní 10, Staré Město, Prague 1 (222 326 754/ www.havelkova.com). Metro Staroměstská/tram 17, 18. **Open** 11am-6pm Mon-Fri. **Credit** AmEx, MC, V. **Map** p328 L3.

Unique cuts and clean lines make these outfits perfect for a wide variety of occasions. The range of ensembles goes from smart dresses to more casual looks. *See above.*

Klára Nademlýnská

Dlouhá 3, Staré Město, Prague 1 (224 818 769/ www.klaranademlynska.cz). Metro Staroměstská/ tram 17, 18. **Open** 10am-7pm Mon-Fri; 10am-6pm Sat. **Credit** AmEx, MC, V. **Map** p328 M3.

Cutting-edge but wearable styles for women. The tailored items are terrific, while the suits and separates wonderfully made. All in all, the store is enjoyable for almost anyone.

Kreibich Kožešiny & Rukavice

Michalská 14, Staré Město, Prague 1 (224 222 522/www.kreibich.cz). Metro Staroměstská or Národní třída/tram 6, 9, 17, 18, 22. **Open** 9.30am-6pm Mon-Fri. **Credit** AmEx, MC, V. **Map** p328 L5.

If it came from an animal and you can wear it, this place has it. Nicest of all are the leather items in all styles and colours, including hats, coats and gloves. It also offers the best selection of fur in town. **Other locations** Hybernská 30, Staré Město, Prague 1 (224 222 924).

Discount

Pour Pour

Voršilská 6, Nové Město, Prague 1 (777 830 078/ www.pourpour.com). Metro Národní třída/tram 6, 9, 18, 22. **Open** 11am-7pm Mon-Fri; noon-4pm Sat, Sun. **No credit cards. Map** p330 K6.

One-of-a-kind treasures: bags, colourful skirts, lots of prints, and all of them happy and bright.

General

★ Evergreen Boutique

Slezská 28, Vinohrady, Prague 2 (mobile 725 740 615/www.etique.cz). Metro Náměstí Míru/tram 10, 11, 16. **Open** 11am-8pm Mon-Fri; noon-8pm Sat. **Credit** AmEx, MC, V. **Map** p333 B4.

This boutique specialises in organic yet utterly hip fashion: the motto is fashion first, then organic, so rest assured you'll look fab in your hemp top and smart cotton skirt. It's ethical, green, non-allergenic and attractive. *Photos p203.*

Leeda

Bartolomějská 1, Staré Město, Prague 1 (mobile 608 210 244/www.leeda.cz). Metro Můstek/tram 6, 9, 18, 22. **Open** 11am-7pm Mon-Sat. **Credit** AmEx, MC, V. **Map** p328 K6.
Leeda offers trendy styles for the young and fit, with some cool mix-and-match choices. Fun dresses and other fresh styles make it a store to remember.

Madeo Boutique

Vodičkova 28, Nové Město, Prague 1 (no phone). Metro Můstek/tram 3, 9, 14, 24. **Open** 10am-7pm Mon-Fri; 10am-3pm Sat. **Credit** AmEx, MC, V. **Map** p329 N6.
Constantly rotating stock helps keep Madeo bang on trend. The store offers primarily casual wear, and can be somewhat pricey – but check the sales racks for some good bargains.

Modes Robes

Benediktská 5, Staré Město, Prague 1 (224 826 016). Metro Náměstí Republiky/tram 5, 8, 14. **Open** 10am-7pm Mon-Fri; 10am-4pm Sat. **Credit** MC, V. **Map** p329 N3.
The interior of this tiny shop is as much a reason to visit as the stock. Designed by a local artist, Modes Robes has been selling unique clothing, accessories and art for more than ten years. Check out the wide selection of dresses: every body and every age will find something flattering.

Vivienne Boutique

Rytířská 25, Staré Město, Prague 1 (221 094 314). Metro Národní třída/tram 6, 9, 18, 22. **Open** 10am-5.30pm Mon-Fri; 10.30am-3pm Sat. **Credit** AmEx, MC, V. **Map** p328 L5.
Tailored suits, casual tops, sweaters and jackets are the mainstay at Vivienne's, but some sexy see-through items slip in as well. The selection is varied and unusual enough to ensure that you should find something special.
Other locations Královodvorská 5, Staré Město, Prague 1 (222 323 837).

Used & vintage

Senior Bazar

Senovážné náměstí 18, Nové Město, Prague 1 (224 235 068). Metro Náměstí Republiky/tram 3, 5, 9, 14, 24, 26. **Open** 9am-5pm Mon-Fri. **No credit cards. Map** p329 P4.
You may get the evil eye from the regulars, but Senior Bazar is a Prague institution. It's one of the best second-hand clothes shops in the city, and the variety and the quality on offer are excellent. Head

here for something unusual that won't break the bank; sharp eyes can find rich pickings amid the closely-packed rails.
Other locations Karolíny Světlé 18, Staré Město, Prague 1 (222 333 555).

FASHION ACCESSORIES & SERVICES

Cleaning & repairs

There's not much difference in price at these laundries, so go to the most convenient.
Maintaining a classic pre-1989 tradition, there are shoe repair shops in **Baťa** (*see p201*) as well as the **Tesco** and **Kotva** supermarkets (for both, *see p191*). Failing that, check the *Zlaté stránky* (*Yellow Pages*) under *Obuv-opravy*.

CleanTouch

Dlouhá 20, Staré Město, Prague 1 (224 819 257). Metro Náměstí Republiky/tram 5, 8, 26. **Open** 8am-7pm Mon-Sat. **No credit cards. Map** p328 M3.
A sound option for dry-cleaning, CleanTouch is centrally located and well regarded by locals.
Other locations Na Rybníčku 1329, Vinohrady, Prague 2 (296 368 500); Supermarket Delvita, Jeremiášova 7A, Stodůlky, Prague 5.

Jan Ondráček

Navrátilova 12, Nové Město, Prague 1 (222 231 960). Metro Národní třída/tram 3, 9, 14, 24. **Open** 8am-6pm Mon-Thur; 8am-5pm Fri. **No credit cards. Map** p330 M8.
This central shoe repair shop offers all the services that you need to make your favourite pair last out that little bit longer.

Prague Laundromat

Korunní 14, Vinohrady, Prague 2 (222 510 180/ www.volny.cz/laundromat). Metro Náměstí Míru/ tram 4, 10, 16, 22. **Open** 8am-8pm daily. **No credit cards. Map** p333 A4.
Service here runs a bit hot and cold, but the washing temperature is always correct.

Clothing hire

Prague is a pretty dressed-up city, architecturally speaking, so you never know when the urge to do likewise with your attire may strike. Be sure, however, to make a booking several days in advance, and to take along proof of identity.

Barrandov Studio, Fundus

Kříženeckého náměstí 322, Barrandov, Prague 5 (251 815 598/www.fundus.barrandov.cz). Metro Smíchovské nádraží, then bus 246, 247, 248. **Open** 7am-3pm Mon-Fri. **No credit cards.**

CONSUME

Flamingo Park.
See p198.

This is the big daddy of dressing up: there are 240,000 costumes, 20,000 pairs of shoes and 9,000 wigs in stock. If you can't find something here, you should be staying at home. It's not cheap, but the selection and quality are outstanding.

Ladana Costume Rental
Opatovicka 20, Nové Město, Prague 1 (224 930 234/www.kostymy-ladana.cz). Metro Můstek or Národni třída/tram 6, 9, 18, 22. **Open** 9am-6pm Mon, Wed, Thur; noon-4.30pm Tue, Fri. **Credit** MC, V. **Map** p330 K8.
If you're lucky enough to be invited to a *ples* (ball) in Prague, Ladana has what you need to make a grand entrance. There are all sorts of wedding and evening gowns in stock, as well as period costumes, masks and Czech folk outfits.

Jewellery

Garnets and amber are the most popular jewels, but other unique and interesting gemstones can be found as well. The prices tend to be pretty much the same everywhere. However, quality can vary widely between stores, so it pays to shop around and ask questions.

★ Belda Jewelry Design
Mikulandská 10, Nové Město, Prague 1 (224 933 052/www.belda.cz). Metro Národni třída/tram 6, 9, 18, 22. **Open** 10am-6pm Mon-Thur; 10am-5pm Fri. **Credit** AmEx, MC, V. **Map** p330 K7.
Belda's history is a long one, and its unique, well-crafted goods are testament to its creativity and

style. The small selection includes pieces you won't find anywhere else, with prices to match – but it's a refreshing change from the garnet- and amber-stuffed jewellery stores elsewhere.

Frey Wille
Havířská 3, Staré Město, Prague 1 (272 142 228/www.frey-wille.com). Metro Národni třída/ tram 6, 9, 18, 22. **Open** 10am-7pm Mon-Sat; 11am-6pm Sun. **Credit** AmEx, MC, V. **Map** p328 M5.
It's not Czech, but Frey Wille does have collections that give a nod to the beloved Alphons Mucha, and art nouveau-inspired styles that make classy souvenirs. Its trademark pieces are gold, elaborately enamelled affairs.

Lingerie & underwear

Chez Parisienne
Pařížská 8, Staré Město, Prague 1 (224 817 786). Metro Staroměstská/tram 17, 18. **Open** noon-7pm Mon-Sat. **Credit** AmEx, DC, MC, V. **Map** p328 L3.
If you're looking for some deliciously slinky smalls, Chez Parisienne is the place to head for. Everything is lovely, well made and worth every crown you'll be paying for it.

Dessous-Dessus
Kráľodvorská 7, Staré Město, Prague 1 (222 316 915). Metro Náměstí Republiky/tram 5, 8, 14. **Open** 10am-7pm Mon-Fri; 10am-6pm Sat. **Credit** AmEx, MC, V. **Map** p329 N3.

Dessous-Dessus carries just about everything in the underclothes department – bras, knickers, chemises and more – as well as tights and pyjamas. Lingerie ranges from nearly naughty to nice.
Other locations Železná 547/3, Staré Město, Prague 1 (224 217 854).

Shoes

It's a bit disconcerting to see some of the shoes to which Czech women subject their feet – and on cobblestones, no less. Luckily for footwear buffs, the number of shops is seemingly endless. Much of the stock is imported, but there are some decent Czech brands – and even a few shoes without stiletto heels.

ART
Narodni 36, Staré Město, Prague 1 (224 948 828). Metro Národni třída/tram 6, 9, 12, 18, 22. **Open** 9.30am-7pm Mon-Fri; 9.30am-5pm Sat. **Credit** AmEx, MC, V. **Map** p328 L6.
This place specialises in women's shoes, especially the spiky stiletto heels that Czech women love to wear in any kind of weather. It also carries global brands such as Xti, Doc Martens, Adidas, Camper, Skechers and Crocs.

Baťa
Václavské náměstí 6, Nové Město, Prague 1 (221 088 472/www.bata.cz). Metro Můstek/tram 3, 9, 14, 24. **Open** 9am-9pm Mon-Fri; 9am-8pm Sat; 10am-8pm Sun. **Credit** AmEx, MC, V. **Map** p329 N6.
Baťa is a true Czech original, stocking affordable (if notoriously quick to wear out), sporty and fashionable men's, women's and kids' shoes. It offers shoe repairs on the third floor, and there's also a selection of luggage.
Other locations throughout the city.

Humanic
Národní třída 34, Nové Město, Prague 1 (224 999 590/www.humanic.cz). Metro Národní třída/tram 9, 18, 22. **Open** 9am-8pm Mon-Sat; 10am-6pm Sun. **Credit** MC, V. **Map** p328 L6.
This standard chain store should carry the footwear you need and can afford. There's nothing overly stylish, but the shoes are well made. There are also purses, wallets and hosiery.
Other locations throughout the city.

FOOD & DRINK

The food shops detailed below offer more choice and higher quality than you'd get in many restaurants across the city. If you're looking to play in the kitchen, or have been invited to a dinner party, one of these should satisfy. You might also want to try **Country Life** (*see p161*) for vegetarian goods.

Bakeries

Bakeshop Praha
Kozí 1, Staré Město, Prague 1 (222 316 823/ www.bakeshop.cz). Metro Staroměstská/tram 17, 18. **Open** 7am-7pm daily. **Credit** AmEx, MC, V. **Map** p328 M3.
Is there any more evocative smell than freshly baked bread? Bakeshop Praha has a variety of baked goodies in unique flavours and styles. All are suitable to take away; alternatively, you can sit down here and have a coffee. Sandwiches, quiches and to-die-for muffins and cakes may also tempt your taste buds.

Drinks

Blatnička
Michalská 6, Staré Město, Prague 1 (224 233 612). Metro Národní třída/tram 6, 9, 18, 22. **Open** 10am-6pm Mon-Fri. **No credit cards**. **Map** p328 L5.
A tiny place offering some tasty wines, this Old Town establishment is a local favourite. You can even bring your own plastic bottle for staff to fill. (Indeed, many places in Prague keep *sudova vina* or table wine in big barrels ready for dispensing into any container.)

Cellarius
Lucerna Passage, Štěpánská 61, Nové Město, Prague 1 (224 210 979/www.cellarius.cz). Metro Můstek/tram 3, 9, 14, 24. **Open** 9.30am-8pm Mon-Sat; 2-8pm Sun. **Credit** AmEx, MC, V. **Map** p331 N8.
A huge selection of wines is crammed into this small, maze-like space. There are local labels and some enticing imports, including wines from France, Bulgaria and Chile.

Galerie piva
Lazeňská 15, Malá Strana, Prague 1 (257 531 404). Metro Malostranská/tram 12, 18, 22. **Open** 10am-6pm Mon-Sat. **Map** p327 F4.
A shrine to the country's proud beer-brewing (and quaffing) heritage, the Beer Shop stocks all the major Czech beers and dozens of the more interesting minors in bottles, as well as just about every beer-imprinted mug. It's good for the collector as well as the *pivo*-lover back home.

★ Monarch
Na Perštýně 15, Staré Město, Prague 1 (224 239 602/www.monarchvinnysklep.cz). Metro Národní třída/tram 6, 9, 18, 22. **Open** noon-midnight Mon-Sat. **Credit** AmEx, MC, V. **Map** p328 L6.
Not only an excellent shop but a wine bar as well, Monarch offers more than 25 varieties of cheese to accompany its various offerings to Bacchus. It's a good place to come if you're looking for South American or Californian imports.

CONSUME

La Vinothéque
U Lužického semináře 42, Malá Strana, Prague 1 (257 531 231). Metro Malostranská/tram 3, 9, 14, 24. **Open** 11am-8pm daily. **Credit** AmEx, MC, V. **Map** p327 H3.
An appealing little shop, La Vinothéque offers a large selection of wines from around the world. There are excellent Spanish and French wines, along with fine Czech vintages.

General

Supermarkets can also be found in **Tesco** (*see p191*) and **Palác Flóra** (*see p192*).

Albert
Václavské náměstí 21, Nové Město, Prague 2 (224 232 810/www.ialbert.cz). Metro Můstek/tram 3, 9, 14, 24. **Open** 8am-8pm Mon-Sat; 9am-7pm Sun. **Credit** AmEx, MC, V. **Map** p329 N6.
Conveniently located inside a handful of metro stations (including Námésti Republiky and Můstek) and elsewhere around town, Albert will take care of all your meal or emergency snack needs.
Other locations throughout the city.

Billa
Karlovo náměstí 10, Nové Město, Prague 2 (222 562 292). Metro IP Pavlova/tram 9, 16, 22. **Open** 7am-9pm Mon-Sat; 8am-8pm Sun. **Credit** MC, V. **Map** p330 L9.
Billa now owns the chain formerly known as Delvita. The shops do the job, but with less choice and feel-good factor. Even so, the bakery and meat counters are still well stocked, and there are some good wine deals.
Other locations throughout the city.

Specialist

La Bretagne
Široká 22, Staré Město, Prague 1 (224 819 672). Metro Staroměstská/tram 17, 18. **Open** 9.30am-7.30pm daily. **No credit cards**. **Map** p328 L3.
The Czech Republic may be a landlocked country, but piscivores take heart – fresh seafood can be found in Prague, and La Bretagne is your best bet. A decent variety of ice-packed, fresh imported fish

---

INSIDE TRACK
A GENEROUS BUNCH

Giving flowers is an important Czech tradition, and there's no shortage of florists in Prague. A *květinařství* can be found on every block and near metro stations, and is likely to have the goods for most occasions.

---

is available for baking, grilling or frying; other imported goodies on offer here include wines.

Culinaria Praha
Skořepka 9, Staré Město, Prague 1 (224 231 017/www.culinaria.cz). Metro Národní třída/tram 6, 9, 18, 21, 22. **Open** 8.30am-8pm Mon-Fri; 10am-7pm Sat; noon-5pm Sun. **Credit** AmEx, MC, V. **Map** p328 L5.
Homesick expats flock here to pick up Ben & Jerry's ice-cream, Pop Tarts, Marmite and all sorts of baking ingredients, Asian cooking products and kosher items. Added appeal comes courtesy of the lunch counter and juice bar, plus Indian and Italian cookery lessons (run in English).

Farah Oriental Market
Myslíkova 5, Nové Město, Prague 2 (224 930 704/www.ita.cz/farah). Metro Národní třída/tram 6, 9, 18, 22. **Open** 9am-7pm Mon-Fri; 9am-5pm Sat. **No credit cards**. **Map** p330 J8.
Bags, jars, bins and bottles of goodies; falafel, houmous and tahini: the Middle Eastern and South Asian staples are all here. Farah also offers quality coffees, teas and spices.

★ Interlov Praha
Jungmannova 25, Staré Město, Prague 1 (224 949 516/www.interlov.cz). Metro Národní třída/tram 6, 9, 18, 22. **Open** 9am-5.30pm Mon-Fri. **No credit cards**. **Map** p328 M6.
Fancy a spot of fresh boar, pheasant or rabbit? You don't need a gun: just visit this game butcher for exotic meats and the spices and wine to go with them. For the less knowledgeable cook, Interlov also sells recipe books; for the less adventurous, there's a good choice of sausages.

Koruna Pralines Chocolaterie
V Jámě 5, Nové Město, Prague 1 (mobile 606 222 651). Metro Můstek/tram 3, 9, 14, 24. **Open** 9am-8pm Mon-Fri; 9am-6pm Sun, Sat. **Credit** MC, V. **Map** p330 M7.
The smell will envelop you as you enter the shop. Go there for a nice sniff, sure, but be sure to pick up a little something for your taste buds as well – with all manner of milk, dark and white chocolate, there's something for everyone. Try the Becherovka-filled chocolates, perhaps accompanied with something from the small but pleasant wine selection.

La Vecchia Bottega
Na Perštýně 10, Staré Město, Prague 1 (224 219 488/www.bottega.cz). Metro Národní třída/tram 6, 9, 18, 22. **Open** 9am-8pm daily. **Credit** AmEx, MC, V. **Map** p328 L6.
All manner of Italian specialties – wines, pestos, cheeses, pastas, vinegars and sweets – can be found here. Meanwhile, a separate department down in the basement stocks all the kitchen utensils you can shake a whisk at.

CONSUME

★ U Zavoje Cheese Shop

Havelská 25, Staré Město, Prague 1 (226 006 120). Metro Můstek/tram 6, 9, 12, 18, 22. **Open** 10am-7pm Mon-Sat. **Credit** AmEx, MC, V. **Map** p328 L5.

This foodie's paradise offers the best cheeses in town, and adjacent cognac, cigar and wine shops. French, Swiss, Italian, Greek and Czech cheeses are among the offerings, along with Italian sausages, Greek olives and dried tomatoes and spices.

Food delivery

Food Taxi

mobile 777 171 394/603 171 394/www.food taxi.cz. **Open** 10am-3.30pm, 5.30-10pm Mon-Fri; 11am-10pm Sat. **No credit cards**.

Order online or by phone from nearly 30 local restaurants. Chinese, Mexican and Italian are just a few of the choices.

Pizza Go Home

283 870 000/www.pizzagohome.cz. **Open** 24hrs daily. **No credit cards**.

It's unlikely to win any culinary awards, but this Prague institution has a decent range of pies, offers free delivery on orders over 200 Kč between 11am and 11pm, and reliably makes it to your door within an hour of ordering (still considered a neat feat in the Czech Republic).

GIFTS

Garnets, crystal and wooden toys fairly jump out at you from every tourist shop you pass, but determined souvenir-seekers will find more varied and original swag elsewhere.

Agentura pro vás

Rybná 21, Staré Město, Prague 1 (224 819 359/www.agenturaprovas.cz). Metro Náměstí Republiky/tram 5, 8, 26. **Open** 9am-6pm Mon-Fri. **No credit cards. Map** p329 N2/3.

Agentura pro vás is a good source for a wealth of striking Czech posters, including old adverts and totalitarian dogma. The shop stocks large and small posters, but for variety and appeal, the post-cards are best.

CONSUME

Evergreen Boutique. *See p198.*

CONSUME

All Strung Up

In Prague, puppets aren't just for kids.

The art and craft of puppetry tends to suffer in Prague, thanks to the ubiquitous grinning faces and floppy arms of the low-quality marionettes that are hawked all over the tourist areas. It's a real shame: the form has a long and sometimes subversive history in the Czech Republic, and a number of creative Bohemian carvers are keeping the art form alive. Mass-produced marionettes dominate the shops, but an original hand-carved piece is a collector's treasure.

The history of puppets in the region dates from the 17th century. Originally brought to the Czech lands by Italian and English showmen, they caught on quickly in the Czech countryside, their performances entrancing the wide-eyed locals. Marionettes had their heyday at the end of the 19th century and beginning of the 20th: several professional theatres were established, and the art form was equally popular among children and adults. Nearly every family had their own home theatre in which to create shows on long winter nights.

'It's an interesting art form,' says Karolína Truhlářová, co-owner of **Truhlář Marionety** (www.marionety.com; *see right*). 'Many artists are involved because it's a broad field for creativity and imagination.'

The company has two shops in Prague, plus a studio that guests can visit to watch how marionettes are made – or have a go at making one themselves. Although it has roughly 60 artists working for it, the company is ultimately a family affair: Truhlářová's husband, Pavel, is co-owner; Truhlářová and her mother paint many of the marionettes; and Pavel's brother is a carver.

Although most of the marionettes produced by the firm are hand-carved and painted, with outfits designed and sewn on site, Truhlář Marionety also sells smaller, mass-produced marionettes, as well as wildly popular marionette kits that purchasers assemble themselves. And the production of the marionettes is not just an exercise in creativity: there's a strong technological aspect to it. Take the strings, says Truhlářová: 'We use a special Czech design that allows for more movement and is easier for the operator. We often design them to do a specific activity, like ride a bike or do a backflip.'

If it looks like child's play, that's just down to the hidden mastery that belies a complex operation. 'We have to discuss shape, form, technology, painting and design. Even the faces are painted with different expressions.'

★ Annie's Tulip

Bílkova 8, Staré Město, Prague 1 (222 311 013/ www.anniestulip.cz). **Open** 10am-7pm Mon-Fri; 11am-6pm Sat. **No credit cards. Map** p328 L2.
Annie's does indeed stock a lot of tulips, but also has other cut flowers, wreaths and plants. English-speaking staff are available to advise and create that perfect arrangement.

★ Artěl Style

Celetná 29, Staré Město, Prague 1 (224 815 085/www.artelstyle.com). Metro Metro Náměstí Republiky/tram 5, 8, 26. **Credit** AmEx, MC, V. **Map** p329 N4.
For an attractive memento of Prague, try Artěl Style: it has glass baubles and bangles, many in unusual designs, as well as jewellery, books and other interesting Czech items. *Photos p207.*

Charita Florentinum

Ječná 4, Nové Město, Prague 2 (224 921 501). Metro Karlovo náměstí/tram 4, 6, 16, 22, 34. **Open** 8am-6pm Mon-Fri; 9am-1pm Sat. **No credit cards. Map** p330 J9.
Charita Florentinum sells all kinds of religious goods, including rosaries, candles, crucifixes, and tapes and CDs. Near Christmas, it also offers a small but attractive selection of Nativity scenes.

Květinařství U Červeného Lva

Saská ulička, Malá Strana, Prague 1 (257 535 276/www.cervenylev.cz). Metro Malostranská/ tram 12, 22. **Open** 9am-7pm Mon-Sat; 11am-7pm Sun. **Credit** MC, V. **Map** p327 G4.
This crowded little florist is bursting with colour and variety. Dried flowers hang from the ceiling, while plants, cut flowers and wreaths cover every available space.

Manufaktura

Karlova 26, Staré Město, Prague 1 (221 632 480/ www.manufaktura.biz). Metro Staroměstská/tram 17, 18. **Open** 10am-8pm Mon-Thur, Sun; 10am-9pm Fri, Sat. **Credit** AmEx, MC, V. **Map** p328 K4.
For a truly Czech gift, one that's natural to boot, try the chain with a motto reading 'inspired by nature'. There are blue print items, which incorporate a fabric dyeing technique used in Bohemia in the late 18th century, plus tablecloths, handkerchiefs and more.

Terryho ponožky

Vodičkova 41, Nové Město, Prague 1 (244 946 829/www.terryhoponozky.cz). Metro Můstek/tram 3, 9, 24. **Open** 10am-8pm daily. **Credit** AmEx, MC, V. **Map** p329 N6.
The name, 'Terry's socks', is derived from the leggings Terry Gilliam once left to the attached art film club (the shop is in the Světozor cinema). The place doesn't sell hosiery, but does offer lots of posters and lobby cards of films both Czech and international, new and vintage.

★ Truhlář Marionety

U Lužického semináře 5, Malá Strana, Prague 1 (mobile 602 689 918). Metro Malostranská/tram 12, 22. **Open** 10am-7pm Mon-Fri. **No credit cards. Map** p327 G4.
There are no cheesy souvenir marionettes here: these are works of art. More than 40 Czech puppet designers contribute to the stock, helping to make the shop a museum to craftsmanship. Choose from a range of small plaster replicas or a unique original. *See left* **All Strung Up**.

Včelařské potřeby

Křemencova 8, Nové Město, Prague 2 (224 934 344/www.beekeeping.cz). Metro Karlovo náměstí/ tram 4, 6, 16, 22, 34. **Open** 9am-5pm Mon, Wed; 9am-6pm Tue, Thur; 9am-2pm Fri. **No credit cards. Map** p330 K8.
Bees are not included. However, just about everything else that an apiarist either produces or needs is, from gloves and headgear to honey and cosmetics.

HEALTH & BEAUTY

Hairdressers & barbers

Looking for a basic trim? A *kadeřnictví* (hairdresser) or *holičství* (barber) should do the job, and the price is usually right. For a more classy cut, try the salons listed below. You'll pay a bit more, but you'll still be cutting a bargain by Western standards.

James Hair

Malá Štupartská 9, Staré Město, Prague 1 (224 827 373/www.jameshair.cz). Metro Náměstí Republiky/tram 5, 8, 26. **Open** 8am-8pm Tue-Fri; 9am-5pm Sat. **No credit cards. Map** p328 M3.
The mostly English-speaking staff and generally excellent cuts have combined to help make this a popular salon.

Libor Šula the Salon

Dušní 6, Staré Město, Prague 1 (224 817 575/ www.liborsula.cz). Metro Staroměstská/tram 17, 18. **Open** 9am-9pm Mon-Fri; 11am-6pm Sat. **No credit cards. Map** p328 L2.
This salon has won numerous awards, including Czech and Slovak Hairdresser of the Year. The English-speaking staff will make sure you leave looking like a winner yourself.

Opticians

Eiffel Optic

Na příkopě 25, Nové Město, Prague 1 (224 234 966/www.eiffeloptic.cz). Metro Můstek/tram 3, 9, 14, 24. **Open** 8am-8pm daily. **Credit** AmEx, MC, V. **Map** p329 N5.
Eiffel almost always has some sort of sale running. There are thousands of frames to chose from, along

CONSUME

with a full contact lens service. There's an on-site optician and a one-hour express service, which is useful for emergencies.
Other locations throughout the city.

GrandOptical
Myslbek Centre, Na příkopě 19-21, Staré Město, Prague 1 (224 238 371/www.grandoptical.cz). Metro Můstek/tram 3, 9, 14, 24. **Open** 9.30am-8pm Mon-Fri; 10am-7pm Sat; 10am-6pm Sun. **Credit** AmEx, MC, V. **Map** p329 N5.
Designer brands, at a price. They're fast, they're good and they're all over the place, making it easy to find a branch. You can occasionally find English-speaking staff.
Other locations throughout the city.

Pharmacies

Many central pharmacies (*lékárna* or *apothéka*) have been doing business in exactly the same locations for centuries, and have gorgeous period interiors that are worth seeking out even if you're bursting with good health. Over-the-counter medicines are available only from pharmacies; they're usually open from 7.30am to 6pm on weekdays, although some of them operate extended hours.

All pharmacies are supposed to post directions to the nearest 24-hour pharmacy in their window, though this information will be in Czech. Ring the bell for after-hours service, for which there will usually be a surcharge of approximately 30 Kč.

24-hour pharmacies
Belgická 37, Vinohrady, Prague 2 (222 513 396). Metro Náměstí Míru/tram 4, 6, 16, 22. **No credit cards. Map** p331 M9.
Palackeho 5, Nové Město, Prague 1 (224 946 982). Metro Můstek. **No credit cards. Map** p331 Q11.

Shops

Most department stores will have a cosmetics counter these days, but the addresses below are a little more specialised.

Body Basics
Myslbek Centre, Na příkopě 21, Staré Město, Prague 1 (224 236 800). Metro Můstek/tram 3, 9, 14, 24. **Open** 9am-8pm Mon-Sat; 10am-7pm Sun. **Credit** AmEx, MC, V. **Map** p329 N5.
Bathing emergency? Body Basics has you covered, with tons of shower and bath gels, lotions, and some cosmetics. There are lots of fun animal- and fruit-shaped bath gels for young and old, as well as poufs, body scrubbers and bath salts. Branches are dotted across town.
Other locations throughout the city.

★ Dr Stuart's Botanicus
Týn 3, Staré Město, Prague 1 (224 895 446/www.botanicus.cz). Metro Náměstí Republiky/tram 5, 8,14, 26. **Open** 10am-8pm daily. **Credit** AmEx, MC, V. **Map** p328 M3.
As well as a wide range of soap, lotions, candles and bathing salts and gels, Botanicus also has herb-inspired cooking oils, vinegars, teas, honey and other food stuffs. Botanicus is entirely Czech, with its fragrant natural ingredients grown on a farm just outside Prague.
Other locations throughout the city.

Spas & salons

Mystic Buddha
Dlouhá 39, Staré Město, Prague 1 (221 779 510/www.mysticbuddha.cz). Metro Náměstí Republiky/tram 5, 8, 26. **Open** *Massage* 10am-10pm daily. *Cosmetics & hair salon* 9am-9pm Mon-Fri; 9am-8pm Sat, Sun. **No credit cards. Map** p329 N2.
Mystic Buddha offers Thai and classic massages and also a variety of skin treatments, hairdressing, manicures and pedicures. A good restorative after a day on the cobblestones.

HOUSE & HOME
Antiques

★ Alma Mahler
Valentinská 7, Staré Město, Prague 1 (222 325 865/www.almamahler.cz). Metro Staroměstoská/tram 17, 18. **Open** 10am-6pm daily. **Credit** MC, V. **Map** p328 K3.
This quaint, family-run shop collects items from homes all over the country, specialising in Bohemian glass, porcelain, textiles and furnishings. It has a good range of stock and is great for a browse.

Antic Aura
Vyšehradská 27, Nové Město, Prague 1 (224 922 575). Metro Karlovo Náměstí/tram 3, 7, 17. **Open** 11am-6pm Mon-Fri. **Credit** AmEx, MC, V. **Map** p330 K12.
Its limited weekdays-only opening hours are the worst thing about Antic Aura; otherwise, it's one of the best shops in town, with a fine selection of purses and jewellery. You can also get your hands on ceramics and art.

Antique
Kaprova 12, Staré Město, Prague 1 (222 329 003). Metro Staroměstská/tram 17, 18. **Open** 10am-7pm Mon-Sat; 10am-6pm Sun. **Credit** AmEx, MC, V. **Map** p328 J3.
Antique offers some very impressive pieces, but you will pay for the quality. Stock includes some lovely glass and jewellery, fascinating religious items, and a variety of pocket watches.

CONSUME

Art Deco

Michalská 21, Staré Město, Prague 1 (224 223 076/www.artdecogalerie-mili.com). Metro Staroměstská or Národní třída/tram 6, 9, 17, 18, 22. **Open** *2-7pm Mon-Fri.* **Credit** *AmEx, MC, V.* **Map** *p328 L5.*
Art Deco offers dress-up fun galore: vintage clothing and lots of jewellery, as well as an interestingly varied mix of other goodies. The prices are fair.

Bazar Antik Zajímavosti

Křemencova 4, Nové Město, Prague 1 (no phone). Metro Národní třída/tram 6, 9, 18, 21, 22. **Open** *10am-6pm Mon-Fri.*
Heavy on the glass, this is your typical bazaar. Teacup collectors will think they've found paradise, while other shoppers will appreciate the linens and small collection of paintings and unique lamps.

Hamparadi Antik Bazar

Pštrossova 22, Nové Město, Prague 2 (224 931 162). Metro Národní třída/tram 6, 9, 18, 21, 22. **Open** *10.30am-6pm daily.* **No credit cards.** **Map** *p330 K8.*
Take your time to sift through the goods here: it can resemble a charity shop, but that's half the fun.

The stock tends to be heavy on porcelain and glass, but occasionally includes fun finds such as antique toys and adverts.

Kubista

Dům u Černý Matky Boží, Celetná 34, Staré Město, Prague 1 (224 236 378/www.kubista.cz). Metro Náměstí Republiky/tram 5, 8, 14. **Open** *10am-6pm daily.* **Credit** *MC, V.* **Map** *p329 N4.*
Czech cubism is a quintessentially Prague thing, and Kubista offers a variety of items in this unique style. For a true piece of Bohemian culture, check out the original cubist porcelain and furniture, as well as the excellent replicas and art books. *Photos p208.*

★ Modernista

Celetná 12, Staré Město, Prague 1 (224 241 300/ www.modernista.cz). Metro Můstek or Národní třída/tram 6, 9, 18, 21, 22. **Open** *11am-7pm daily.* **Credit** *AmEx, MC, V.* **Map** *p328 K6.*
Don't know what you want but know it when you see it? Sleek, modern Modernista is happy to introduce you to its selection of cubist, art deco and functionalist art. You'll find restored items from the early to mid 20th century, as well as reproductions from Czech artists and designers.

Artěl Style. *See p205.*

CONSUME

General

Bauhaus

Budějovická 1a, Pankrác, Prague 4 (255 715 111/www.bauhaus.cz). Metro Pankrác. **Open** 7am-8pm Mon-Thur; 7am-9pm Fri; 8am-9pm Sat; 8am-8pm Sun. **Credit** AmEx, MC, V.

Keen DIYers will find themselves in handyman heaven here: Bauhaus stocks everything you need for home repair jobs, plus plants, art and a variety of household items.

Le Patio

Národní třída 22, Nové Město, Prague 1 (224 934 402/www.lepatio.cz). Metro Národní třída/tram 6, 9, 17, 18, 22. **Open** 10am-7pm Mon-Sat; 11am-7pm Sun. **Credit** AmEx, MC, V. **Map** p328 L6.

Le Patio's eclectic stock includes colonial, leather and iron furniture, amazing light fixtures and excellent table settings.

Other locations Pařížská 20, Staré Město, Prague 1 (222 320 260); Týn 640, Staré Město, Prague 1 (224 895 773).

Potten & Pannen

Václavské náměstí 57, Nové Město, Prague 1 (224 214 936/www.pottenpannen.cz). Metro Muzeum/tram 3, 9, 14, 24. **Open** 10am-7pm Mon-Sat. **Credit** AmEx, MC, V. **Map** p329 N6.

As its name suggests, this place sells products for cooks and decorators. Gourmets will find lots to get their cooking juices flowing, while people who want a good-looking kitchen will find pretty, colourful appliances and tableware.

MUSIC & ENTERTAINMENT

CDs & records

★ Bontonland Megastore

Palác Koruna, Václavské náměstí 1, Nové Město, Prague 1 (224 235 356/www.bontonland.cz).

> ### INSIDE TRACK
> ### BAZAAR HUNT
>
> There are dozens of antique shops in Prague, but there are also numerous junk shops, selling everything from old irons and typewriters to prints by Alfons Mucha. If an antique shop is on a main tourist route, you can be fairly sure that the prices are adjusted for foreigners. For cheaper and more unusual items, seek out a bazaar. Some are listed here, but more can be found in the *Zlaté stránky* (*Yellow Pages*) – look for the index in English at the back.

Metro Můstek/tram 3, 9, 14, 24. **Open** 9am-8pm Mon-Sat, 10am-7pm Sun. **Credit** AmEx, MC, V. **Map** p329 N6.

Two floors of musical entertainment and one of video games makes Bontonland a top shop. All the newest releases, as well as huge sections of rock, country and jazz. There's a separate room for classical music, which includes a large opera section.

Disko Duck

Karlova 12, Staré Město, Prague 1 (221 213 696/www.diskoduck.cz). Metro Staroměstská/tram 17, 18. **Open** noon-7pm daily. **Credit** MC, V. **Map** p328 K4.

Aspiring DJs can get their groove on at Disko Duck. More than 5,000 records span the musical worlds of hip hop, techno, jungle and beyond; there's also a selection of DJ equipment, including turntables, mixers and CD decks.

Maximum Underground

Jilská 22, Staré Město, Prague 1 (222 541 333/www.maximum.cz). Metro Můstek, Národní třída or Staroměstská/tram 3, 9, 18, 22. **Open** 11am-7pm Mon-Sat; 1-7pm Sun. **No credit cards.** **Map** p328 L5.

Maximum Underground sells heavy music and the appropriate bodily modifications to go with it – namely tattoos and piercings.

Music shop Antikvariát

Národní třída 25, Nové Město, Prague 1 (221 085 268). Metro Národní třída/tram 6, 9, 18, 22. **Open** 10.30am-7pm Mon-Sat. **Credit** AmEx, MC, V. **Map** p328 L6.

Worth the climb up the stairs, this shop has a huge record selection, and some great used CDs from 50 Kč; jazz and classical discs start at 95 Kč.

DVDs

Planet DVD

Rumunská 20, Vinohrady, Prague 2 (224 250 397/www.planetdvd.cz). Metro Náměstí míru/tram 16, 22. **Open** 8am-11pm daily. **Credit** MC, V. **Map** p330 L8.

Peruse and reserve movies online; if the store is out of what you're looking for, staff will send you a text message when it's arrived. Everything's done by computer: you can view your account and remind yourself what movies you've rented in the past.

Video Gourmet

Jakubská 12, Staré Město, Prague 1 (222 323 364). Metro Náměstí Republiky/tram 5, 8, 14. **Open** 11am-11pm daily. **Credit** AmEx, MC, V. **Map** p329 N3.

Inside the lobby of American restaurant Red Hot & Blues (*see p165*), you can pick up a movie along with Duncan Hines cake and frosting mixes or Orville Redenbacher popcorn.

CONSUME

Hitched Without a Hitch

For better or for worse, weddings are big business in Prague.

Perhaps you've dreamed of your wedding day since you were five years old. Maybe you just want to get it over with as quickly as possible. But whatever sort of bride or groom you hope to be, you'll be in good company in Prague, a popular wedding venue among couples from abroad looking to do something a little different for their special day. The city is well accustomed to hosting glitzy and romantic destination weddings, vow-renewal ceremonies and even organised elopements.

Religious ceremonies, garden weddings, exchanging vows in a castle: all can be arranged in the city or its immediate surroundings. The variety of venues and services available, and the still-reasonable costs, would make Prague an excellent place in which to tie the knot even if Baroque church bells weren't pealing on every other enchanted lane.

According to Petra Hofman, who runs the thriving **White – Prague Wedding Agency** (www.destination-wedding.cz), three of the most popular places in Prague to get married are the Old Town Hall (*see p87*), the New Town Hall (see p108) and the Church of St Nicholas (*see p243*). Both town halls offer couples the chance to pair up in a historic Gothic building, while St Nicholas's Baroque elegance will definitely wow the guests. Elsewhere, though, Prague's historic buildings provide endless photo opportunities. Imagine a wedding snap on Charles Bridge with Prague Castle in the background, or in front of an 18th-century church or Gothic château.

However, the city's wedding planners – among them **PragueWeddings.com** (www.pragueweddings.com) and **Prague**

Wedding Planners (www.praguewedding planners.com) – can help with a lot more than simply securing a venue. They can also arrange accommodation, find the perfect spot for your reception, book horse-drawn carriage rides and boat trips for you and your guests, source the cake, book a photographer and, perhaps most importantly, help with the formalities.

While marriages performed in the Czech Republic are legally valid elsewhere, there's nonetheless an array of paperwork and red tape involved that's best handled by a local expert. Because there's nothing worse than spending all that time, energy and money, only to then arrive home and find you've got to do it all over again…

CONSUME

Musical instruments

Hudební nástroje

Náprstkova 10, Staré Město, Prague 1 (222 221 110/www.nastroje-hudebni.cz). Metro Můstek or Staroměstská/tram 17, 18. **Open** 10am-6pm Mon-Fri; 10am-4pm Sat. **Credit** MC, V. **Map** p328 J5.

Invest in an old Bohemian squeezebox, or clarinet, bongos, xylophone, sax, tuba or drums at this remarkably varied and well-organised second-hand instrument shop. Staff are extremely helpful.

Praha Music Centre

Soukenická 20, Nové Město, Prague 1 (226 011 111/www.pmc.cz). Metro Náměstí Republiky/tram 5, 14, 26. **Open** 9am-6pm Mon-Fri. **Credit** MC, V. **Map** p329 O2.

The PMC is a little more high-tech than your average music shop. In addition to various musical instruments, it sells speakers, pickups, amps and cables. Note the weekdays-only opening hours before paying a visit.

Other locations Revoluční 14, Staré Město, Prague 1 (222 311 693).

U zlatého kohouta

Michalská 3, Staré Město, Prague 1 (224 212 874). Metro Můstek or Národní třída/tram 3, 9, 14, 24. **Open** 10am-noon, 1.30-6pm Mon-Fri. **Credit** AmEx, MC, V. **Map** p328 L5.

Fancy a fiddle? This place has them by the dozen, and even if you aren't a player, you should stop by to take a look at the beautiful craftsmanship that went into each violin. In addition to new instrument sales, the shop also undertakes restoration work.

SPORTS & FITNESS

Rock Point

Martinská 2, Staré Město, Prague 1 (224 228 060/www.rockpoint.cz). Metro Můstek/tram 9, 18, 22. **Open** 10am-8pm Mon-Fri; 10am-6pm Sat, Sun. **Credit** AmEx, MC, V. **Map** p328 L6.

This hip and friendly Czech-owned chain stocks everything for skiing, hiking, rock climbing and just about every other outdoor sport. Sales bring good deals on nifty accessories.

TICKETS

Ticketpro

Old Town Hall, Staré Město, Prague 1 (224 223 613/www.ticketpro.cz). Metro Staroměstská/tram 17, 18. **Open** 9am-6pm Mon-Fri; 9am-5pm Sat, Sun. **Credit** AmEx, MC, V. **Map** p328 L4.

Advance booking for events. The automated free number works for all branches, most of which are found at Prague Information Service offices (*see p315*) and hotels.

Other locations Štěpánská 61, Lucerna, Nové Město, Prague 1 (224 818 080); Rytířská 31, Staré Město, Prague 1 (2161 0162); Václavské náměstí 38, Rokoko, Prague 1 (224 228 455).

TRAVELLERS' NEEDS

Shipping

Most crystal and gift shops will ship your purchases directly, which will save hassle. Otherwise, try UPS.

UPS

K Letišti 57, Ruzyně Airport, Prague 6 (toll-free 800 181 111/www.ups.com). **Open** *Telephone bookings* 9am-6pm Mon-Fri. **Credit** AmEx, MC, V.

Pick-up service with two hours' notice required. Or if it works out to less than the cost of taking an extra parcel with you on your flight home, UPS has a drop-off centre at the airport.

Travel agents

Čedok

Na příkopě 18, Nové Město, Prague 1 (224 197 699/800 112 112/www.cedok.cz). Metro Můstek/tram 3, 5, 8, 9, 14, 24. **Open** 9am-7pm Mon-Fri; 9.30am-1pm Sat. **Map** p329 N5.

The former state travel agency is still the biggest in the Czech Republic. It's a handy place to obtain train, bus and air tickets, along with information on accommodation options.

Kubista. *See p207.*

Arts & Entertainment

Calendar

Witches to poets, beer to potent wine: there's an event for every taste.

Many visitors to Prague say they like it best in winter: despite the short, grey days and long, cold months, it's a mellow kind of season, with endless traditions and plenty of ways to warm up. Still, the coming of spring is a truly joyous event in Prague, and Czechs know, almost to the day, when each new blossom will appear.

They also plan their favourite summer weekend with 12 sets of friends months in advance, hunt down the mushrooms of autumn with alacrity, and never miss a St Nicholas's Eve street party when winter rolls around again. It's a different city with each season. Prague's crowning glory, though, is its calender of musical events, the highlight of which is the inimitable Pražské jaro (Prague Spring).

SPRING

In April and May, people seem to blossom with the lilacs and chestnut trees, and emerge like moles into the sunlight; beer gardens fill up even when the crowd is shivering at dusk. Off come the layers as Stromovka park fills with runners, in training for the **Prague International Marathon**. Soon after that, the **Prague Spring Festival** heralds the warm weather, as it has done for half a century.

Matejská pouť
St Matthew's Fair
Výstaviště, Holešovice, Prague 7 (220 103 204). Metro Vltavská/tram 5, 14, 25. **Admission** 25 Kč. **Date** Feb-Mar.

INSIDE TRACK
THE HOT TICKET

You can book for most ticketed events through **Ticketpro** (see p210), which accepts payments by credit card. Tickets are sometimes also available on the door, but it's advisable to phone ahead; do note that credit cards are unlikely to be accepted at venues. For up-to-the-minute listings of what's on, check the Prague Post (www.praguepost.cz) or Prague TV (www.prague.tv), and look at organisers' websites for any special, one-off events.

St Matthew's Fair marks the arrival of warm weather with cheesy rides for children at a run-down funfair at Prague's exhibition grounds, Výstaviště (*see p111*). Dodgem cars at 10 Kč a pop and the Ferris wheel bring out the juvenile in everyone.

Easter
Date Mar/Apr.
Men rush around the country beating women on the backside with willow sticks; women respond by dousing the men with cold water, and by giving them painted eggs. Then everyone drinks a lot. This ancient fertility rite is rarely seen in Prague these days, but painted eggs and willow sticks (*pomlázka*) are on sale all over the city.

★ Pálení čarodějnic
Witches' Night
Date 30 Apr.
A tradition that rolls the best of Halloween and Bonfire Night into one package, Pálení čarodějnic marks the death of winter and the birth of the new spring. Bonfires are lit to purge the winter spirits, an effigy of a hag is burnt – a relic of real witch hunts – and the more daring observers of the custom leap over the flames.
▶ *Most fires are lit in the countryside, but there's sometimes a pyre in the city: check Petřín Hill in Malá Strana (see p82).*

Labour Day
Date 1 May.
There's little danger of being run over by a tank in Wenceslas Square these days, but May Day is still

a good excuse for a demonstration. The communists, in an attempt to keep the faith alive, usually have a small rally in Letná park (*see p114*) and encourage pensioners to moan about the rigours of the free market. Prague's anarchists also sometimes hold an uncharacteristically orderly parade.

May Day
Petřín Hill, Malá Strana, Prague 1. Metro Malostranská/tram 6, 9, 12, 22. **Map** p326 D6. **Date** 1 May.
Czech lovers of all ages, their sap rising, make a pilgrimage to the statue of Karel Hynek Mácha on Petřín Hill (*see p82*), to deposit bunches of flowers and have a snog. Mácha, a 19th-century Romantic poet, generated many myths, several bastards and the epic poem *Máj* ('May'); it's actually a melancholy tale of unrequited love, but nobody lets that spoil the fun.

VE Day
Date 8 May.
The Day of Liberation from fascism is actually 9 May, which was the day when the Red Army reached Prague in 1945. In its eagerness to be a good European nation, however, the Czech government moved the celebration to 8 May in line with the rest of the Continent. In commemoration, flowers and wreaths are laid on Soviet monuments such as Náměstí Kinský in Smíchov, where a Soviet tank used to stand.

Khamoro
Various venues (222 518 554/www.khamoro.cz). **Admission** free-300 Kč. **Date** May.
A festival that features concerts, seminars and workshops on Roma culture, focusing on the traditional side of Gypsy music, customs and art. The concerts, which are the biggest draw for visitors, run a surprisingly wide gamut from swing guitar jams to a Hungarian all-violin Roma orchestra.
► *For Gipsy.cz, who fuses Gypsy culture with hip hop, see p249.*

★ Prague International Marathon
Throughout the city, route varies (224 919 209/ www.pim.cz). **Registration fee** 1,380-2,500 Kč. **Credit** (online registration only) MC, V. **Date** May.
This event has a new owner and corporate sponsors aplenty; entry fees have more than tripled for the main event in this massive annual run, which draws hundreds of marathon addicts from around the world. Lots of shorter events are held at other times in the year.

★ Festival spisovatelů Praha
Prague Writers' Festival
Various venues (224 931 053/www.pwf.cz). **Admission** varies. **Date** May/June.
An impressive collection of Czech and international literati gathers in Prague to read extracts from their latest works, hobnob and compare royalty contracts.

ARTS & ENTERTAINMENT

St Matthew's Fair.

This is your chance to observe Ivan Klíma's improbable hairdo and spot the quirks of other local literary lions at close range.

▶ *For bookshops in Prague, see p193.*

Mezi ploty
Ústavní 91, nr Bohnice Psychiatric Hospital, Prague 8 (272 730 623/www.meziploty.cz). Metro Nádraží Holešovice, then bus 200. **Admission** 200 Kč/day; 370 Kč/wknd. **Date** last wknd in May.

A unique festival, Mezi ploty brings together professional, amateur and mentally or physically disadvantaged artists, dancers and musicians for two days of events and performances in the grounds of the city's main psychiatric hospital.

★ Pražské jaro
Prague Spring
www.festival.cz. **Date** mid May-early June.
Arguably the cultural highlight of the year. For full details, *see p245.*

SUMMER

With the hot days of June and July, locals (including the staff of most cultural institutions, which go dark until September) tend to clear out to avoid the flood of tourists and head for the country. If you can get an invitation, you may get to experience the joy of the *chata* (cottage) and blueberry picking. The city bears its own sweet fruit during the summer months, though, with music festivals such as the hip **United Islands of Prague** and the **Tanec Praha** modern dance performances.

9 Bran
Nine Gates
Various venues (www.9bran.cz). **Admission** free. **Date** June.
Nine Gates is a decade-old festival of Czech-German Jewish culture that features a week of great music from the likes of 17 Hippies, plus dance and classical music performances in such amazing venues as the Wallenstein Gardens.

Respect
http://respect.inway.cz. **Date** June.
A tremendous world music festival. For full details, *see p251.*

Tanec Praha
Dance Prague
www.tanecpha.cz. **Date** June.
For details of this terrific dance festival, *see p274.*

★ United Islands of Prague
www.unitedislands.cz. **Date** June.
Big names in rock from home and abroad. For full details, *see p251.*

Letní slavnosti staré hudby
Summer Festival of Old Music
www.tynska.cuni.cz. **Date** July.
Renaissance and baroque music galore, *see p245.*

AUTUMN

In autumn, symphonies, operas and balls return to town. With them comes **Prague Autumn**, and not a little of the sneak-attack libation known as **burčák**. And, of course, with the tourists finally gone, Prague's citizens get their beautiful city back to themselves, just as it begins to fill with ice and smog.

★ Pražsky podzim
Prague Autumn
www.pragueautumn.cz. **Date** Sept-Oct.
The next best thing to Prague Spring, *see p245.*

Arrival of burčák
Date late Sept-early Oct.
Burčák – a cloudy, half-fermented, early-season wine – arrives in Prague some time in autumn. It's

a speciality of Moravia, where the inhabitants apparently don't have the patience to wait for their booze to finish ageing. Served straight from the barrel into special jugs, *burčák* looks like murky wheat beer, tastes like cherryade and – drinker, beware – will sneak up on you if you don't treat it with due respect.

Anniversary of the birth of Czechoslovakia
Date 28 Oct.
The country no longer exists, but that's no reason to cancel a public holiday, so the people still get a day off. There are lots of fireworks – as on every other occasion – and it takes forever to get a tram.

All Saints' Day
Date 1 Nov.
If there's one day in the year when you should visit one of the city's cemeteries, All Saints' Day, when people pray for deceased relatives, is it. Whole families turn out to light candles, lay wreaths, remember and pray. The best place to go to is the enormous Olšany Cemetery (*see p121*).

Anniversary of the Velvet Revolution
Národní třída & Václavské náměstí, Nové Město, Prague 1. Metro Národní třída or Můstek/tram 3, 6, 9, 14, 18, 22, 24. **Map** p328 L6. **Date** 17 Nov.
Surprisingly understated rituals commemorate the demonstration that began the Velvet Revolution: flowers are laid and candles lit in Wenceslas Square near the equine statue and on the memorial on Národní třída near no.20.

WINTER

Miserable though winter can be, it has its own rewards: the glorious spires that tower above Staré Město, Old Town, are an incomparable sight in the snow. The city may be a sleepy, grog-guzzling, grey and melancholy place, but its **Christmas markets** are enchanting. And, once the carp have been bashed into submission at the fishmongers' stands for the traditional festive supper, fireworks have people diving for cover in the same square on **New Year's Eve**.

Prague Jazz Festival
www.agharta.cz. **Date** Feb-Oct.
Local favourites and big names from abroad. For full details, *see p251*.

★ St Nicholas's Eve
Around Charles Bridge & Staroměstské náměstí, Staré Město, Prague 1. Metro Staroměstská/tram 17, 18. **Map** p328 J4. **Date** 5 Dec.
Grown men spend the evening wearing frocks, drinking beer and terrorising small children. They

wander the streets in threes, dressed up as St Nicholas, an angel and a devil, symbolising confession, reward and punishment. Rather than a red cloak, St Nicholas usually sports a long white vestment, with a white mitre and staff; the angel hands out sweets to children who have been good, and the devil is on hand to dispense rough justice to those who haven't.

Christmas
Date 24, 25 Dec.
In the week leading up to the Vánoce (Christmas) holiday, the streets sport huge tubs of water filled with carp, the traditional Czech Christmas dish, and there are Christmas markets in Old Town Square and Wenceslas Square. The feasting and exchange of gifts happen on the evening of 24 December, when pretty much everything closes down. Things don't start opening up again until the 27th.
▶ *The finest midnight Mass on Christmas Eve is at St Vitus's Cathedral; see p64.*

New Year's Eve
Václavské náměstí & Staroměstské náměstí, Staré Město & Nové Město, Prague 1. Metro Můstek or Staroměstská/tram 3, 9, 14, 17, 18, 24. **Map** p329 N6. **Date** 31 Dec.
Bring your helmet? On New Year's Eve, or Silvestr, the city's streets are packed with a ragtag crowd of tipsy Euro-revellers, with much of the fun centred on Wenceslas Square and Old Town Square. Fireworks are let off everywhere and flung around with frankly dangerous abandon, then champagne bottles are smashed.

Anniversary of Jan Palach's death
Václavské náměstí, Nové Město, Prague 1. Metro Muzeum/tram 11. **Map** p329 N6. **Date** 16 Jan.
Jan Palach set himself ablaze in Wenceslas Square on 16 January 1969, to protest against the Soviet occupation that killed off the promise of cultural freedom during the brief Prague Spring of 1968. His grave at Olšany Cemetery (*see p121*) is adorned with candles and flowers all year round. Many people visit Olšany or the memorial to the countless victims of communism (*see p101*) near the St Wenceslas statue to lay a few more.

Masopust
Akropolis, Kubelíkova 27, Žižkov, Prague 3 (www.palacakropolis.cz). Metro Jiřího Z Poděbrad/ tram 11. **Map** p333 C2. **Date** mid Feb (7th Sun before Easter).
Traditionally, groups of 12 carollers accompanied by people in masks parade about in this whimsical celebration of what the rest of the world knows as Shrove Tuesday, the eve of Ash Wednesday (the original tradition seen in the Czech lands has the holiday on Sunday). According to custom, everyone who meets this procession should be invited to the

evening feast, which is a great opportunity to stuff yourself with a freshly slaughtered pig and wash it down with rivers of beer.

▶ *There's also a version of a Masopust street party centred around Prague's Žižkov district, especially around the Akropolis club; see p247.*

OUT OF TOWN

★ Mezinárodní filmový festival Karlovy Vary
Karlovy Vary International Film Festival
www.kviff.cz. **Date** July.
A genteel Bohemian spa town briefly becomes the Czech version of Cannes. *For full details, see p226.*

Barum Rally
Start/finish line: Interhotel Moskva, Práce náměstí 2512, Zlín (www.barum.rally.cz). **Admission** free. **Date** Aug.

A classic road race dating back decades, the Barum Rally still attracts thrill-seeking drivers from across Europe, and has recently been ranked one of the best. Moravian roads roar into life as daredevil amateur and pro drivers compete for the big *pohár*, the winner's cup. Ralley Zlin sponsors the event, and an entry form in English can be downloaded from the website above.

Velká Pardubická
Pražská 607, Pardubice (www.pardubice-race course.cz). **Admission** 200-2,000 Kč. **No credit cards. Date** 2nd wknd in Oct.

The star steeplechase event in Prague's annual calendar is also a controversial one: horses and riders alike are often injured on the difficult course. Celebrity horse people pour in from all over Europe, putting box seat prices at a premium. The website has ticket details.

▶ *For more on horse racing, see p263.*

That's All Folklore!

Tradition provides some of Prague's more interesting, and peculiar, festivals.

The government has finally declared Good Friday a public holiday in the Czech Republic, but don't expect to see devout mobs at church doors. It's really just another excuse for the natives to get plastered at their local *pivnice*. Some Christian trappings are difficult to lose, particularly at Christmas, but the primary energy behind all Czech celebrations is pagan in origin. Indeed, for a country of staunch agnostics and atheists, the Czech Republic enjoys a bizarre variety of saints' days (true holy days).

Like most Central and Northern European cultures, the Czechs also have their own *Walpurgisnacht*, or witches' night, called **Pálení čarodźjnic**. On 30 April, effigies of hags or witches are burned in bonfires across the land. In Prague, head to **Petřín Hill** (*see p82*) to see this weird blend of Guy Fawkes Night and Halloween.

In the days following, a distinctly Czech salute to sexuality is quietly celebrated, also on Petřín Hill. Couples trek to the statue of the great Czech Romantic poet **Karel Hynek Mácha**, whose epic poem *Máj* ('May') is still read – almost all Czechs can quote the opening lines. There the lovers lay flowers at Mácha's feet, then retire together to a nearby park bench, or the nearest thicket.

Endearingly, this same erotic intensity is seen in the Czech Easter, which, unlike Christmas, is almost wholly pagan. The now officially recognised **Good Friday** (Velký pátek) is preceded by **Ugly Wednesday** (Škaredá středa) and **Green Thursday** (Zelený čtvrtek), the latter giving roving gangs of young men the excuse to take to the streets and shake a special wooden rattle called a *řehtačka*.

It's on **Easter Monday** (Pondůlí velikonoční), however, that things take a decidedly carnal turn, as these same boys return to the streets with switches of pussywillow twigs, called *pomlázka*, which they use to whip the legs and backsides of young damsels. Said damsels are then required to hand their flogging suitors a painted egg, or tie a ribbon around his *pomlázka* (did we mention that Freud was born in Bohemia?). Although these symbolic high jinks are largely confined to smaller towns and villages, you'll very likely catch sight of the occasional Prague youth wielding his *pomlázka* against squealing shop girls in the centre of town.

Elsewhere in Prague, Easter markets take over the main squares just as the yearly Christmas ones do; but instead of festive firs decked with ornaments and lights, birch trees are set up in the markets garlanded with bright ribbons and colourful wooden or papier mâché eggs. Replicas of these eggs can be bought at any souvenir shop; so can *pomlázkas*, if you're feeling frisky.

Children

Storybook Prague entrances younger visitors.

Grown Czechs melt at the sight of children, and seem especially fascinated by foreign ones – so having one in tow can prove very handy indeed. The city's child-specific offerings are strangely limited, even at the major museums. However, most kids will be fascinated by Prague's picturesque old centre, and its fairytale qualities will be obvious to any little princes and princesses. From the dramatic gates of Prague Castle to the winding medieval streets of Staré Město and Josefov, it's a city that fires the imagination.

SIGHTSEEING

Prague has always been a city that appeals to children. Thankfully, these days it is also becoming more geared to their particular needs. Some of its child-friendly diversions are quaint and low-tech: take the **Zrcadlové Bludiště (Mirror Maze)** on handsome Petřín Hill, which has been a favourite for generations of Czech children; or a ride on historic tram 91 or in a horse-drawn carriage. Other attractions include lovely parks, outdoor playgrounds, boat rides, a trip to **Prague Zoo** and the new **Sea World**.

Some attractions, such as the celebrated **Orloj (Astronomical Clock;** *see p87*), and climbable towers such as the **Rozhledna (Petřín Tower;** *see p82*), **Staroměstská mostecká věž (Old Town Bridge Tower;** *see p91*) and the **Prašná brána (Powder Gate;** *see p85*), are as suitable for children as they are for adults. Note that most towers are closed during winter.

Attractions

★ **Mořský svět**
Sea World
Výstaviště, Holešovice, Prague 7 (220 103 275/ www.morsky-svet.cz). Metro Nádraží Holešovice/ tram 5, 12, 17. **Open** *10am-7pm daily.*
Admission 240 Kč; 145 Kč children; 100 Kč reductions; 670-540 Kč family. **No credit cards.**

About the author
Former managing editor of the Prague Post, **Will Nessmith** *is now chief operating officer of international golf and travel site WorldGolf.com.*

Prices have nearly doubled at Sea World in recent years, but it's worth remembering that this is a venue with a big impact. The aquarium has a collection of over 300 species, and the popular shark and barracuda tanks have great views for visitors and are a big hit with children. A soundtrack of waves crashing and seagulls crying gives the impression you've left this land-locked country. *Photos p218.*

★ **Zoologická zahrada v Praze**
Prague Zoo
U Trojského zámku 3, Trója, Prague 7 (296 112 111/www.zoopraha.cz). Metro Nádraží Holešovice, then bus 112. **Open** *Jan, Feb, Nov, Dec* 9am-4pm daily. *Mar* 9am-5pm daily. *Apr-May, Sept-Oct* 9am-6pm daily. *June-Aug* 9am-7pm daily.
Admission 150 Kč; 100 Kč reductions; 450 Kč family; free under-3s. **No credit cards.**
With nearly 5,000 animals and 652 species in residence, Prague Zoo is often ranked among the best in the world. Since it was hit by floods in 2002, the zoo's inmates have benefitted from numerous improvement projects that had been on the shelf

---

INSIDE TRACK
ROW, ROW, ROW
YOUR BOAT...

If your kids are suitably adventurous and well behaved, hire a boat – it's a great and novel way to see the city. Rowing or paddle boats can be rented at **Novotného lávka**, south of the Staré Město end of Charles Bridge, or at **Slovanský Island**, near the National Theatre. Expect to pay around 80-120 Kč for an hour.

until the floods made them obligatory. In addition, successful breeding programmes add plenty of new animal babies to coo over.

▶ *Stromovka park is nearby, accessible via a pedestrian bridge across the Vltava; see p113.*

Zrcadlové bludiště
Mirror Maze

Petřín Hill, Malá Strana, Prague 1 (257 315 212). Tram 12, 22, then funicular to Petřín Hill. **Open** *Jan-Mar, Nov, Dec* 10am-4.45pm Sat, Sun. *Apr* 10am-7pm daily. *May-Aug* 10am-10pm daily. *Sept* 10am-8pm daily. *Oct* 10am-6pm daily. **Admission** 50 Kč; 40 Kč reductions. **No credit cards. Map** p326 C6.

The mirror maze has been a staple of Czech childhoods for decades, and it might well be the high point of your children's visit. After all, children are the only ones who enjoy seeing themselves distorted into silly shapes. There's also a wax diorama of the Swedes' unsuccessful 1648 attack on Charles Bridge.

▶ *While you're on the hill, check out the Štefánik Observatory; see p82.*

Museums

Národní muzeum
National Museum

Václavské náměstí 68, Holešovice, Prague 7 (224 497 111/www.nm.cz). Metro Muzeum. **Open** *Jan-Apr, Oct-Dec* 9am-5pm daily. *May-Sept* 10am-6pm daily. Closed 1st Tue of mth. **Admission** 120 Kč; 150 Kč family; free under-6s, to all 1st Mon of mth. **No credit cards. Map** p331 P8.

Many of the displays in this natural history museum are a little dull, but children still seem to be fascinated by the stuffed animal exhibits on the top floor.

▶ *For more on the museum, see p101.*

Národní technické muzeum
National Technical Museum

Kostelní 42, Holešovice, Prague 7 (220 399 111/www.ntm.cz). Metro Hradčanská or Vltavská/tram 1, 8, 25, 26. **Open** 9am-5pm Tue-Fri; 10am-6pm Sat, Sun. **Admission** 70 Kč; 150 Kč family. **No credit cards. Map** p332 D3.

Though it's closed for 2009 for major renovations, this fantastic venue for the transport-obsessed child should then reopen its door with more appeal than ever. It's full of original vehicles, some of which can be climbed on to afford a good look at the interiors, and the temporary exhibitions are interesting. A popular coal mine replica tunnels through the basement, and English-speaking tours can be arranged.

▶ *For a full review, see p114.*

EATING & DRINKING

It's getting easier to eat out with children in Prague. More restaurants have high chairs, and many even offer nappy changing areas.

However, be warned that despite non-smoking hours at lunch and dinner, many restaurants still come with a nicotine haze. One eatery with a proper no-smoking section is **Pizzeria Rugantino** (Dušní 4, Staré Město, Prague 1, 222 318 172). Minutes from Old Town Square, it has friendly staff, crayons and paper, and serves child-sized portions; from 4pm to 6pm, children are even allowed to make their own pizzas. Booking is essential.

The Staré Město branch of Bohemia Bagel (*see p153*), with its play corner and quick, child-friendly food, remains a favourite of English-speaking parents. For dessert, treat your kids to a pilgrimage to fruit-ice heaven – also known as **Ovocný Světozor** (Vodičkova 39, Nové Město, Prague 1, 224 946 826), located in the Světozor passage just off Wenceslas Square. Don't be deterred by the crowds: the service is wonderfully speedy.

ARTS & ENTERTAINMENT
Activities & events

Historic Tram 91

296 124 901. **Rides** hourly, noon-6pm Sat, Sun & public holidays. Closed Dec-Mar. **Tickets** 35 Kč; 20 Kč reductions. **No credit cards.**

Sea World. See p217.

This quaint, wood-framed tram travels a loop from Výstaviště, trundling along the banks of Malá Strana, across the Legionnaires' Bridge to the National Theatre, up through Wenceslas Square and then back to Výstaviště via Náměstí Republiky. Hop on the veteran at any stop along the route and see most of the city's sights in one go.

► For more on trams, see p301.

Horse-drawn carriages

Staroměstské náměstí, Staré Město, Prague 1 (no phone). Metro Staroměstská/tram 17, 18. **Rides** 10am-6pm daily. **Tickets** 900-1,000 Kč/20mins. **No credit cards**. **Map** p328 L4.

Hitch a ride on an old-fashioned horse-drawn carriage and see the sights. Rides begin near the clock tower on Old Town Square and run during peak tourist months.

Matějská pouť

Výstaviště, Holešovice, Prague 7 (220 103 204). Metro Vltavská/tram 5, 14, 25. **Date** Feb-Mar. **Admission** 25 Kč. **No credit cards**. **Map** p332 D1.

This popular springtime carnival is generally a big hit with children. For a month, the grounds of Výstaviště fairground (*see p116*) are jam-packed with thrill rides, which complement the bumper cars, Ferris wheel and shooting galleries that are there all year round. The air has the same unmistakeable, evocative fairground smells of doughnuts and candyfloss, of course.

► For other carnivals and events, see pp212-216.

★ O2 Žluté Lázně

Podolské nábřeží, Prague 4 (244 463 777). Tram 3, 15, 17, 21. **Open** 9am-7pm daily. **Admission** 50 Kč/90mins (accompanying adults free); 25 Kč reductions. **No credit cards**.

Prague, like so many European capitals, now has a sandy beach. This riverside complex on the right bank of the Vltava also has spas, football pitches, a half pipe for skateboarders, volleyball, table tennis, watersports, and food and drink concessions.

★ Pražská paroplavební společnost
Prague Steamship Company

Embankment below Palackého náměstí, Nové Město, Prague 1 (224 931 013/www.paroplavba. cz). Metro Karlovo náměstí/tram 3, 4, 10, 16, 17, 21. **Open** times vary Apr-Oct (check website). **Tickets** 220 Kč; 100 Kč reductions; free under-3s. **Credit** MC, V. **Map** p330 J10.

Great in combination with a trip to the Prague Zoo (*see p217*), which this steamship serves via the Vltava river, the PPS offers a leisurely 75-minute ride. The boat plies this route between late March

ARTS & ENTERTAINMENT

INSIDE TRACK
PUPPET PALS

If your little darling wants a marionette of his or her own, make for top puppet shop **Truhlář Marionety** (*see p204*); nearby is another good outlet, **Marionety** (Nerudova 51, 257 533 035). Several more generic sellers can be found along Jilská and Karlova streets in Staré Město.

and November, but the company also offers 55- and 90-minute sightseeing rides elsewhere throughout the year. There are several cruises each day.

Outdoor playgrounds

Prague has a good number of playgrounds fitted out with the latest swings, slides, merry-go-rounds and more; most have equipment suitable for toddlers too. Below are some of the more central ones, all of which are open daily from 8am until sunset.

Kampa

Malostranské nábřeží 1, Malá Strana, Prague 1. Metro Malostranská/tram 6, 9, 12, 20, 22. **Map** p327 G6.
The walled playground on the side of Kampa park closest to the river (not to be confused with the nearby restaurant of the same name) is a consistent hit with local children.

Kinského zahrada

Újezd 1, Smíchov, Prague 5. Metro Anděl/tram 6, 9, 12, 20.
Located just off Naměsti Kinský. To reach the playground, enter the park via the arched iron gate, then follow the pavement to the right.

Petřín Hill

Újezd & Vítězná streets, Malá Strana, Prague 1. Metro Malostranská/tram 6, 9, 12, 20, 22. **Map** p326 C5.
Walk up Petřín Hill past the funicular stop (lanová dráha), then take the pedestrian bridge to the right. That path leads directly to the playground.

Puppet theatre

Puppet theatre has a rich history in Bohemia, having played a key role in the 19th-century National Revival movement. The **National Marionette Theatre** (*see p274*) stages regular child-pleasing shows for foreigners, and a handful of other theatres also host puppet performances. Another option is a non-verbal multimedia performance at the **Magic Lantern** (*see p274*); check listings in the *Prague Post*.

PRACTICALITIES

Baby requirements

As in other European capitals, disposable nappies and baby food are widely available. Any larger, full-service supermarket will stock all your basic baby supplies. For these essentials, along with items such as bottles, teats, nursing supplies, formula, lotions and so on, head to a hypermarket such as **Tesco** (*see p191*), or to a pharmacy (*lékárna*). For late-night emergencies, each district in Prague has a 24-hour pharmacy. The Prague 1 *lékárna* is at Palackého 5 (224 946 982).

If you're in need of clothes and other supplies for your sprog, try Mothercare. Ajuty offers pushchair and car seat hire.

Ajuty

Plzeňská 20, Smíchov, Prague 5 (257 320 032/ www.ajuty.cz). Metro Anděl/tram 4, 6, 7, 9, 10, 12, 14, 20. **Open** 9.30am-6pm Mon-Fri; 9am-noon Sat. **Credit** MC, V.
Ajuty offers pushchair hire for 600-700 Kč per week, while child car seats go for 300-400 Kč per week. A deposit is required.

Mothercare

Myslbek Pasáž, Na příkopě 19-21, Staré Město, Prague 1 (222 240 008). Metro Můstek/tram 3, 9, 14, 24. **Open** 9am-8pm Mon-Fri; 9am-6pm Sat; 10am-7pm Sun. **Credit** AmEx, MC, V. **Map** p329 N5.
Everything for little ones, from pushchairs to clothes. There's also a spacious baby changing area.

Childminding

Large hotels usually offer a babysitting service. Otherwise, try the following, whose rates tend to be cheaper than hotel rates. These agencies all provide sitters who speak English, but be prepared to pay transport costs for sitters who stay after midnight. www.expats.cz has forum posts and tips from expat parents.

Agentura Admina

Americká 10, Prague 2 (mobile 608 281 280/ www.admina.cz). **Rates** 140-200 Kč/hr. **No credit cards.** **Map** p331 Q10.
Apart from the usual babysitting options, Agentura Admina also offers the useful possibility of an indoor play area for short-term childminding.

Agentura Aja

Mobile 603 886 736. **Rates** 180 Kč/hr; 1500 Kč/day. **No credit cards.**
Aja will book a sitter for any schedule and send one to you; rates depend on the time of day and the number of children to be looked after.

Kampa.

Agentura Pohoda
274 772 201/602 252 873/www.agpohoda.cz.
Rates 130-180 Kč/hr. **No credit cards**.
Pohoda specialises in looking after non-Czech children, with a particular sideline working for the local film studios; the agency looked after Bruce Willis's son and daughter when he was filming here.

Health

For sore throats, scuffed knees or worse, call the English-speaking care providers listed below.

Medical
Pankrác House, Lomnického 5, Pankrác, Prague 4 (234 630 111/emergencies 603 555 006/
www.medicover.com). Metro Pražského povstání Náměstí/tram 3, 16, 17, 21. **Open** 7am-7pm Mon-Fri. **Credit** AmEx, MC, V.
A clinic that specialises in paediatrics.

Poliklinika na Národní
Národní třída 9, Nové Město, Prague 1 (222 075 120/emergencies 720 427 634/www.poliklinika. narodni.cz). Metro Národní třída/tram 6, 9, 18, 21, 22. **Open** 8.30am-5pm Mon-Fri. **Credit** AmEx, MC, V. **Map** p328 L6.
Highly professional staff, including a paediatrician, and a central Nové Město location. Handy for crises.

Transport

In Prague, children up to six years old travel free on public transport, and six to 15s travel for half price. On the metro, many stations lack escalators or lifts from ground level down to the entrance vestibule; Czechs are accustomed, however, to helping mums carry pushchairs up or down stairs. They may approach you to offer help, but don't be shy about asking – just say *'Pomoc, prosím'* ('Help, please').

If you're at a busy tram stop, it's a good idea to wave to the approaching driver to let him know you'll be getting on with a pram. People with prams must enter and exit by the tram's rear door; on buses, look for the pram sticker indicating which door to use. As you reach your stop, push the button above the door (not the red emergency one) to signal that you'll need a little extra time disembarking.

INSIDE TRACK
TIME FOR A CHANGE

Finding a spot for nappy changing is fairly straightforward these days. Many restaurant toilets have facilities; and **Mothercare** has one on the first floor, with two changing tables, a sink and a bottle warmer. The **Nový Smíchov** shopping centre (*see p192*) also has facilities on the first floor near the lifts and adult toilets, but be prepared to wait, as the mall is popular with mums. **Tesco** (*see p191*) has a changing table on the first floor – to use it, ask for a key from any cashier.

Film

If it's a moving picture, Czechs will turn out for it.

Although cinema attendance in Prague is in decline, people willing to plunk down for tickets will find the screens here plusher than ever. Not long ago, there was just one multiplex in the city, Galaxie. Now there are a dozen, plus a popular IMAX screen at Palác Flora. And while many of the single-screen cinemas that were once sold out for the weekend by Friday afternoon are struggling to keep a handful of customers, a few movie palace gems remain. The art nouveau interior at the Lucerna, for instance, makes for a welcome break from the assembly-line sterility of the multiplexes.

CINEMA IN PRAGUE

Foreign commentators observing the throngs of Czech teens who pack into Prague cinemas to see low-budget arthouse movies from around the world often say that they dream of having such audiences at home. The flipside to this scenario is that these film-lovers often have to trek out to small-town film festivals for the latest independent film: the fare in most Prague cinemas is too commercial and uninspiring.

This may explain why young Czechs have a reputation for downloading pirate films. In one episode not long ago, a copy of Jan Svěrák's *Empties* appeared on the internet with a clearly visible title indicating that the copy had been sent to the Ministry of Culture – and no one else – in order to qualify for funding. An enraged Svěrák told reporters what he thought of the ministry's respect for artists' rights.

That said, demand for non-Hollywood fare has spawned dozens of festivals, many in Prague. And Czechs are working to ensure that the movies at these events are not just foreign ones. State funding has recently doubled the number of local feature films made per year. There has also been a rise in movies in all genres: one recent animated comedy, *Goat Story*, even came out in 3D.

Tickets & information

Tickets for the multiplexes run at around 150 Kč, or more for special seating. The smaller theatres try to hold the line at 100 Kč. Tickets have assigned seat numbers; you can usually pick your spot from a computer screen at the box office. To prevent arguments, be sure to find the row (*řada*) and seat (*sedadlo*) that are printed on the ticket. By and large, foreign films are screened with original soundtrack and Czech subtitles.

Movie schedules are available in the *Prague Post*, as well as in a number of smaller but ever-changing Czech publications, usually available for free. Big posters at many tram stops and kiosks have fairly complete schedules. All the multiplexes and many of the smaller arthouse theatres have schedules online.

COMMERCIAL CINEMAS

Bio-Illusion

Vinohradská 48, Vinohrady, Prague 2 (222 520 379). Metro Muzeum/tram 11. **No credit cards.** **Map** p333 C3.

Majoring mostly in recent Czech films, usually without English subtitles, this old-time movie palace has had a considerable facelift, with comfortable new seats and a full-service bar for ticket-holders. In an interesting twist, the bar uses furniture left over from a liquor company's advertising campaign, while the fairly comfortable seats in the theatre were recycled from the now-shuttered original Galaxie. When not showing new Czech titles, recent art hits and better Hollywood films fill the schedule.

Blaník

Václavské náměstí 56, Nové Město, Prague 1 (224 032 172). Metro Muzeum/tram 11. **No credit cards.** **Map** p331 N7.

Still hanging on thanks to its prime location, this pleasant if plain single-screen theatre has undergone an extensive renovation and alternates between recent hit films and live theatrical productions.

★ Lucerna

Vodičkova 36, Nové Město, Prague 1 (224 216 972/www.lucerna.cz). Metro Můstek/tram 3, 9, 14, 24. **Credit** DC, MC, V. **Map** p329 N6.

Although it shows mainly Hollywood fare, the Lucerna also is a hub for Czech indie and art cinema. It's also an art nouveau wonder that reminds you how magical movies once were. The elevated lobby bar has large windows that let you watch the 1920s-era shopping arcade. The coat-check is still functioning, and you can watch the films from the balcony. There's even a real curtain in front of the screen. The theatre has been steadily moving to fewer Hollywood and more European films in its programming, which also covers the Music on Film/Film on Music fest in October. *Photo p224.*

▶ *For the music venues here, see p248.*

Perštýn

Na Perštýně 6, Nové Město, Prague 1 (221 668 432). Metro Národní třída/tram 6, 9, 17, 18, 22. **No credit cards.** **Map** p328 L6.

The fairly large basement cinema here has movable tables and chairs, so seating is actually rather limited. The atmosphere is relaxed, but it can be hard to see the screen if people sit on the tables when it's full. The café has a limited selection of packaged snacks and beverages, but no real food.

MULTIPLEXES

Cinema City Flora

Vinohradská 149, Vinohrady, Prague 3 (255 741 002/www.cinemacity.cz). Metro Flora. **No credit cards.**

This shopping-mall film theatre is home to the city's only IMAX screen, capable of 3D screenings.

Cinema City Galaxie

Arkalycká 877, Háje, Prague 4 (reservations 267 900 567/schedule 296 141 414/www. cinemacity.cz). Metro Háje. **No credit cards.**

New management built a more modern Galaxie alongside the old one, which sits abandoned next door. The new Galaxie offers downtown ticket prices and programming.

Multikino Ládví

Burešova 4, Kobylisy, Prague 8 (286 587 027/ www.multikinoladvi.cz). Metro Ládví/tram 24. **No credit cards.**

The new metro stop at Ládví has made this fairly cheap multiplex much easier to access from downtown. Still, its location means that it seldom sells out. The café, one of the few places to go in its housing project neighbourhood, is popular.

★ Palace Cinemas Nový Smíchov

Plzeňská 8, Smíchov, Prague 5 (257 181 212/ www.palacecinemas.cz). Metro Anděl/tram 6, 9, 12. **No credit cards.**

This is the most popular multiplex in town. If the 12 screens and 2,702 seats are sold out, Village Cinemas Anděl City (*see below*) is across the road.

▶ *The multiplex is the new venue for Febiofest; see p226.*

Palace Cinemas Park Hostivař

Švehlova 32, Hostivař, Prague 10 (257 181 212/www.palacecinemas.cz). Tram 22, 26. **No credit cards.**

The first multiplex in the new wave of multiplex building has a slightly less ambitious schedule than its downtown cousins.

Palace Cinemas Slovanský dům

Na příkopě 22, Nové Město, Prague 1 (257 181 212/www.palacecinemas.cz). Metro Náměstí Republiky/tram 5, 8, 14. **No credit cards.** **Map** p329 N5.

The most centrally located of Prague's multiplexes sometimes shows recent Czech films with English subtitles, or original-language versions of animated films that play elsewhere dubbed. The theatre also boasts a high-tech digital projector that can simulcast live concerts or show digital films. Candy counters here are impressive: you choose as much as you want of any of dozens of kinds, all cheerfully bagged. Salt-loaded popcorn is another story.

Village Cinemas Anděl City

Radlická 3179, Smíchov, Prague 5 (251 115 100/ www.villagecinemas.cz). Metro Anděl/tram 6, 9, 12. **Credit** AmEx, DC, MC, V.

It's easy to miss this competing complex near Palace Cinemas Nový Smíchov, but it tends to be less crowded. The Gold Class screens offer reclining seats with a button to summon beverages from the concession stand. The tickets for the luxury seating are the priciest in town.

ARTHOUSE CINEMAS

★ Aero

Biskupcova 31, Žižkov, Prague 3 (271 771 349/ www.kinoaero.cz). Metro Želivského/tram 1, 9, 10, 16. **No credit cards.**

The 70-year-old Aero sets the standard for indie and art cinema fans in Prague. It programmes the best of festivals and other gems rather than relying on the dross that's pushed on to other cinemas by the handful of powerful local distributors. Luckily, the imports often have English subtitles (with Czech translations broadcast into headsets). On occasion, film-makers come along to introduce their films. The theatre is also an apt venue for several festivals. The cinema's bar has become a popular local hangout, but the downside is that noise sometimes filters into the theatre. Tickets can be booked in advance online.

Bio Oko

Františka Křížka 15, Holešovice, Prague 7 (233 382 606/www.kinooko.cz). Metro Vltavská/tram 5, 12, 17. **No credit cards.** **Map** p332 D3.

One of the few theatres with anything resembling a marquee, Oko has made a real stab at becoming one of the city's leading arthouses. Recently, it has become the offical Prague screening home for the Jihlava International Documentary Festival (www.dokument-festival.cz), which just adds to its pedigree. The pre-revolution feel has been replaced with the addition of a café; there are improved, padded seats in the theatre.

★ Evald

Národní třída 28, Staré Město, Prague 1 (221 105 225/www.evald.cinemart.cz). Metro Národní třída/tram 6, 9, 18, 22. **No credit cards.** **Map** p328 L6.

You'll need to get here early for any hope of getting a seat if the film is a good title: this downtown arthouse is one of the best, but it's seriously space-challenged. The owners distribute films and often

Lucerna. *See p223.*

Children of the Night

Meet one of the bright young things of 21st-century Czech cinema.

Irena Hejdová, a film journalist for the Czech online newspaper *Aktuálně*, penned the screenplay for *Děti Noci* (*Night Owls*) five years ago while a student at FAMU, the Czech film academy previously attended by two Oscar-winners. It's a tale of life in the streets of Prague 8, a rapidly transforming district where life seems to centre on nocturnal minimart shopping. We caught up with her, and asked about her inspirations.

Time Out Prague (TOP): What inspired you to write the story? Were these characters that you felt were not being seen in Czech movies up to now?
Irena Hejdová (IH): I wanted to write something about night-time Prague and something tragic – I had a feeling that in Czech cinema, you don't have too many characters who are tragic. I wanted to tell a story about lethargy too: it's in opposition to drama or comic movies.
TOP: How did you go about developing the characters? Did you spend a lot of time in Karlín minimarkets?
IH: I developed the characters from my imagination and intuitively. I've worked in the past as a night bartender at Batalion, so maybe I was able to draw some feelings and experiences from it.
TOP: Is there a danger that some Czech filmmakers make films that will only really appeal to the local mentality? How do you get beyond that as a writer?
IH: Lots of Czech film-makers shoot films only for local audiences, as they know that it is not as exacting as an international audience. But I want to write scripts that will be internationally successful.

TOP: How did the script evolve during shooting with director Michaela Pavlovska?
IH: We wanted to intensify dramatic elements of the script and the relationship between Ofka and Ubr. It was a very nice co-operation; Michaela is a very empathetic and intuitive person.
TOP: Are you working on another script?
IH: I'm working on a script called *Nohama nahoru*, another school script from FAMU. It's a comedy about consumerism. Barrandov Studios will produce it, and shooting should start in spring 2009.
TOP: Where do you do your writing, and what is your routine?
IH: I don't drink coffee – maybe I'm not a typical screenwriter in that way! – and I don't like listening to music when writing. I write my scripts at home by the table on my laptop; I can't imagine I could write it by hand.
TOP: What's the most important thing that needs to happen for Czech independent film-making to develop?
IH: Scripts are very important, but so is courage on the part of the producers who are earning money from them.

ARTS & ENTERTAINMENT

have exclusive bookings on various European art movies, independent American films and Czech flicks, which are sometimes shown with English subtitles. There's no snack bar on the premises, but the theatre does share its basement space with a popular restaurant and bar.

French Institute
Štěpánská 35, Nové Město, Prague 1 (221 401 011/www.ifp.cz). Metro Můstek/tram 3, 9, 14, 24. **No credit cards. Map** p331 N8.
New and classic French films are shown in a full-scale, fairly comfortable basement cinema. Around half of the films have English subtitles. The tickets

are incredibly cheap. Don't even think of bringing food or beverages into the screening room.

MAT Studio
Karlovo náměstí 19, Staré Město, Prague 1 (224 915 765/www.mat.cz). Metro Karlovo náměstí/tram 3, 4, 6, 14, 16, 18, 22, 24. **No credit cards. Map** p330 L9.
The smallest theatre in town shows a fair mix of offbeat films, Czech classics with English subtitles and rare selections from the vaults of Czech TV. The cinema's bar has some movie props and old posters from Czech films. Buy your tickets early – performances inevitably sell out.

Ponrepo

*Bio Konvikt Theatre, Bartolomějská 11, Staré
Město, Prague 1 (224 233 281 ext 31). Metro
Národní třída/tram 6, 9, 18, 22.* **Tickets** 40-60
Kč; annual membership 150 Kč. **No credit
cards. Map** p328 K6.

For some reason, the management at the screening
room for the Czech Film Archive acts like it doesn't
want you to see and enjoy old films. A photo ID is
required, no exceptions, to see films. The schedule
has Czech and Slovak films plus selected world classics. Be sure to check that the movie doesn't have a
live Czech translation announced directly into the
hall (denoted by *s překl*), since it will be impossible
to hear the original soundtrack.

★ Světozor

*Vodičkova 41, Nové Město, Prague 1 (224 946
824/www.kinosvetozor.cz). Metro Můstek/tram
3, 9, 14, 24.* **No credit cards. Map** p329 N6.

A new partner of the respected Aero rep house, the
Světozor books consistently engaging and off-beat
indie and global cinema, and has built up a loyal following in the process. This adds major convenience
since the Aero is out of the centre, and the kino bar
is invariably full of colourful characters.

FESTIVALS & EVENTS

For a country of this size, the number of film
festivals is astounding. Some, in typical Prague
fashion, float a bit in terms of time and location,
so be on the lookout for the occasional embassy-
sponsored event; most of these offer English-
subtitled versions when possible. Interest in
summer outdoor cinema is waning – the one
at Střelecký Island (www.strelak.cz) has been
going it alone of late – but it's worth looking
for posters during the summer months.

Projekt 100
Project 100

www.artfilm.cz. **Date** Jan-Feb.

The programmes at the arthouses are made up in
part of films that come from this travelling festival.
Around ten noted local film critics and scholars each
choose what they think is an important film, either
recent or classic, and the package then plays in
Prague theatres in January and February before
touring the country. After that, they turn up on arthouse schedules as often as their popularity allows.

★ Febiofest

221 101 111/www.febiofest.cz. **Date** late winter.

The largest of the local festivals, in terms of titles,
has moved from its former home at the multiplex at
Slovanský dům to the one at Nový Smíchov. It's also
retooled under the direction of new programmers,
who have moved the focus from quantity to quality.
The most recent winning film, the hip Estonian indie
Magnus, illustrates the improved state of things,

although the programme still features films both old
and new, from all over the globe and on select topics. Famous guests add star pull.

Dnů evropského filmu
Days of European Film

224 215 538/www.eurofilmfest.cz.
Date early Mar.

More than a decade old, this approximately ten-day
festival displays films from European Union members and candidates in Lucerna (*see p223*) and Aero
(*see p224*). Many of the offerings have English
subtitles, and a number of film-makers come to
introduce their works. A few of the films have gone
into local distribution, but most are just screened
once or twice.

One World International Human Rights Documentary Film Festival

www.oneworld.cz. **Date** early spring.

This popular festival of documentaries and features
focusing on human rights issues has grown bigger
and stronger than ever. Talks and interviews have
been added and programming includes some hot
new work each year on timely topics – the struggle
of small Eastern European countries for viability,
say. The venues are spread out, but usually at least
one of the theatres has films in English or with
English subtitles.

★ Mezinárodní filmový festival Karlovy Vary
Karlovy Vary International Film Festival

www.kviff.com. **Date** early July.

Held in the West Bohemian spa town of Karlovy
Vary, this is the only film festival in the country
accredited by the FIAPF, the organisation that sanc-
tions the Cannes, Berlin and Venice festivals. But
unlike those festivals, the Karlovy Vary event is
skewed towards audiences, offering thousands the
chance to see films otherwise impossible to catch
over here. High-profile guests have included Robert
De Niro, Robert Redford and Elijah Wood, but the
real joy is in the gathering of indie film-makers.
Many films sell out, but if space allows they'll fit you
in. Note that tickets can only be bought on site and
only go on sale a day before the screening.

International Aviation Film

www.leteckefilmy.cz. **Date** Sept.

A relatively new event that largely concentrates on
classic war and action films; guests have included
famous pilots and war heroes. The festival seems to
have settled at Village Cinemas Anděl (*see p223*).

Festival francouzského filmu
French Film Festival

221 401 011/http://fff.volny.cz. **Date** late Nov.

This isn't as arty as you might expect: mainstream
French comedies and crime films do appear, along
with French stars introducing their films.

Profile Czech Cinema

Czech movie-making has a patchy past, but there are diamonds in the rough.

The first international splash made by Czech film-making came in 1932 with *Ecstasy*, which featured a nude bathing scene with a young Hedy Lamarr. Over the following few decades, only a couple of Czech films – Karel Zeman's *The Fabulous World of Jules Verne* (1958), for instance – earned international attention.

Little Girl Blue.

Things changed with the Czech New Wave between 1963 and 1968, which brought Miloš Forman, Jiří Menzel and Ivan Passer to prominence. In 1967, Menzel's *Closely Observed Trains* even won an Oscar. However, the Soviet-led invasion in 1968 put a damper on creativity, and it would be another 30 years before matters improved once more.

Since 1989, a number of new film-makers referred to as the Velvet Generation have been credited with reviving Czech cinema's global appeal with films such as *Kolya*, the Oscar-nominated *Divided We Fall* and *Loners*. The likes of Jiří Vejdelek's *Václav* and Karin Babinská's *Pusinky* have won over audiences, critics and festival prize juries, just as character-driven films such as Bohdan Sláma's *Something Like Happiness* and Jan Hřebejk's *Beauty in Trouble* play in arthouse cinemas at home and develop a small but loyal following abroad.

Czech playwright and filmmaker Alice Nellis has won attention for her offbeat tales of family life, and the unique way the post-1989 changes have turned it upside down. She recently won the Golden Kingfisher, the top prize for Czech film, for the superb *Little Girl Blue*, the story of a day from hell for a Prague wife and mother who thought she had everything.

Such successes have been unusual, though – and according to many in the business, there really isn't the need for them. Like many audiences around the world, Czech filmgoers are fascinated to see themselves on screen, so local films don't need to aim much higher than TV fare to generate a decent return. Take films such as Tomáš Vorel's *Gympl*, a potboiler set in a secondary school, or *Bestiář*, a study of rich Praguers, their affairs and their hairdos.

Glimpses of Prague continually turn up in Western fare, even though cheaper locations to the east are stealing its screen time these days. In 2006, *Casino Royale* put the city on the map. With a few exceptions, the movies that followed turned out to be scrappy bargain-basement films that achieved the look of much more expensive rivals: *Hostel*, *Last Holiday*, *Young Hannibal: Behind the Mask* and *The Illusionist*.

But there's also another tier to film-making in Prague: the echelons occupied by the producers of *Wanted*, *GI Joe* and *Prince Caspian*, whose productions tend to take over the city's Barrandov Studios for months at a time. Ironically, that's something that no Czech film-maker could afford to do.

THREE TO SEE

Closely Observed Trains (1966)
A classic portrayal of adolescent angst, set during the occupation.

Kolya (1996)
Jan Sverák's tale of a womanising cellist and an abandoned Russian boy is sweet but never sickly.

Loners (2000)
A wry black comedy that follows the fortunes of seven young Praguers.

Galleries

Reshuffles, renovations, revivals – and, for the art-lover, big rewards.

Prague's art scene is undergoing a rapid and fascinating period of change. Many of the major spaces have revamped to a greater or lesser extent. Commercial galleries are joining together to rebuild the tradition of art collecting in this country, which was going strong during the First Republic but fizzled out under communism. A few non-profit spaces, the funding of which doesn't hinge on appealing to mainstream tastes, are bringing a lot of the most interesting work to public attention. And a small but growing group of private galleries is endeavouring to nurture the market for Czech contemporary art.

THE LOCAL SCENE

There's been a reshuffle of major proportions at Prague's main art institutions. Works that show the 19th-century roots of European modernism have been moved from the National Gallery's Veletržní Palace to the remodelled **St George's Convent** (*see p67*) inside the Prague Castle complex, while the masters of Bohemian baroque have taken up residence in the renovated **Schwarzenberg Palace** (*see p71*), just outside the castle gates. As a result, lovers of European art now have only steps to negotiate between centuries and styles: it's all now held within three buildings in the immediate vicinity of Castle. This is also where you'll find the **Prague Castle Picture Gallery** (*see p64*), which holds many important examples of European art.

Major changes are also afoot at the Prague City Gallery, which was preparing to reopen the House at the Golden Ring (*see p98*) after a year-long closure. With its reopening, Old Town Square has resolidified its position at the centre of the city's art map, but it's getting some serious competition from Holešovice.

The imposing **Veletržní Palace** (*see p111*), the National Gallery's constructivist cathedral, has sharpened its focus on 20th-century art and embraced the 21st century. The neighbourhood is also home to private galleries such as the excellent **Hunt Kastner Artworks** (*see p232*) and the sister spaces **Vernon Gallery** and **Vernon Project** (www.galerievernon.com). And then there's the **DOX Centre for**

Contemporary Art (*see right*), a sprawling new artistic hub that's devoted to contemporary art and culture.

Information

For information on exhibitions, consult the *Prague Post*, *Kultura v Praze* ('Culture in Prague', a listings booklet available in English from newsstands at some central locations) or *Atelier*, a Czech fortnightly broadsheet with an English summary and listings of exhibitions. *Umělec* ('Artist') magazine features reviews of recent shows and articles on the contemporary scene; it's now available in separate English and Czech editions in some galleries and newsstands. Websites with art listings include those run by the Prague Information Service (www.pis.cz) and Prague TV (www.prague.tv).

Most galleries and museums in Prague are closed on Mondays, and some smaller galleries take a holiday in August. It's always best to check that the one you want to visit hasn't closed temporarily for 'technical reasons'.

MAJOR SPACES

The city's main exhibition organisers remain the **National Gallery** (*see p114*), **Prague City Gallery** and **Prague Castle** (*see p64*). The National Gallery is best known for showcasing key artists in the nation's art history (Václav Špála, for instance) at the **Wallenstein Riding School** (*see p230*) and turning over the stately halls of **Veletržní**

Palace (*see p111*) to a varied mix of shows (retrospectives by the likes of Jiří Kolář, exhibits by emerging and more-established Czech artists, occasional shows by foreign artists). The Prague City Gallery, meanwhile, supports the upcoming generation of painters, not only through the Zvon biennale (*see p235*) but also by giving them solo shows at the **Old Town Hall** (*see p230*).

České muzeum výtvarných uměni v Praze
Czech Museum of Fine Arts

Husova 19-21, Staré Město, Prague 1 (222 220 218/www.cmvu.cz). Metro Staroměstská/tram 17, 18. **Open** 10am-6pm Tue-Sun. **Admission** 50 Kč; free students, under-6s. **No credit cards.** **Map** p328 K4.

Housed in a block of renovated Renaissance townhouses, the Czech Museum of Fine Arts exhibits mainly 20th-century Czech art, with an increasing number of exhibitions by foreign artists such as Karen LaMonte and overviews of contemporary art from countries including Slovakia and Northern Ireland. The gallery also hosts big exhibitions with overarching themes such as people, nature or technology, and special shows that are aimed at children around Christmas. The ongoing 'Alternatives' cycle is held in the atmospheric Romanesque cellar.

★ DOX centrum současného uměni
DOX Centre for Contemporary Art

Osadní 34, Holešovice, Prague 7 (224 930 927/ www.doxprague.cz). Metro Vltavská/tram 5, 12, 15. **Open** 10am-6pm Mon, Sat, Sun; 11am-7pm Wed-Fri. **Admission** 100 Kč; free students, under-6s. **No credit cards.**

After years in the making, this shiny new centre for contemporary art opened in autumn 2008 under the auspices of programme director Jaroslav Anděl, who once headed the National Gallery's Veletržní Palace. DOX has ambitious plans to present a changing roster of large and smaller exhibitions that will expose local art-lovers to contemporary trends from abroad, placing Czech and international art in direct confrontation and sparking dialogue among artists and disciplines. The complex has stunning renovated industrial spaces as well as newly constructed rooms; amenities include a bookshop, a café and a restaurant.

▶ *For more on DOX, see p111.*

★ Dům U Kamenného zvonu
House at the Stone Bell

Staroměstské náměstí 13, Staré Město, Prague 1 (224 827 526/www.citygalleryprague.cz). Metro Staroměstská/tram 17, 18. **Open** 10am-6pm Tue-Sun. **Admission** 100-120 Kč; 10 Kč reductions; free under-6s. **No credit cards.** **Map** p328 M4.

The House at the Stone Bell is an atmospheric, Gothic sandstone building on the east side of Old Town Square. It takes quite a show to outweigh the space itself, featuring as it does a gorgeous Baroque courtyard and three floors of exhibition rooms, some of which have their original vaulting. It favours retrospectives of Czech artists such as Toyen and Adolf Hoffmeister, and is also the venue for the Zvon biennale (*see p235*). *Photos p230.*

▶ *The venue is operated by the Prague City Gallery; see p230.*

★ Galerie Rudolfinum

Alšovo nábřeží 12, Staré Město, Prague 1 (227 059 346/www.galerierudolfinum.cz). Metro Staroměstská/tram 17, 18. **Open** 10am-6pm Tue-Sun. **Admission** 120 Kč; 60 Kč reductions; free under-15s. **No credit cards.** **Map** p328 J3.

The only exhibition space in the city that follows a European Kunsthalle model, this gallery in the 19th-century Rudolfinum concert building remains one of the best venues for Czech and international contemporary and modern art. It leans toward retrospectives of enigmatic modernists such as Alén Diviš and Mikuláš Medek, major shows by artists of the middle generation including Petr Nikl and František Skála – and, because the director is an expert, shows of Chinese art. The Rasart series forges links between music, theatre and art.

▶ *The Rudolfinum is also one of Europe's most important concert venues; see p242.*

Městská knihovna
Municipal Library

Mariánské náměstí 1 (entrance on Valentinská), Staré Město, Prague 1 (222 310 489/www.city galleryprague.cz). Metro Staroměstská/tram 17, 18. **Open** 10am-6pm Tue-Sun. **Admission** 100-120 Kč; free under-6s. **No credit cards.** **Map** p328 K4.

Another space run by the Prague City Gallery, the rooms above the Municipal Library provide an excellent showcase for large exhibitions of historical importance, such as a show of Czech 20th-century photography and another charting the medium's development in Germany.

Obecní dům
Municipal House Exhibition Hall

Náměstí Republiky 5, Staré Město, Prague 1 (222 002 101/www.obecni-dum.cz). Metro Náměstí Republiky/tram 5, 8, 14. **Open** 10am-6pm daily. **Admission** *Exhibitions* 120-200 Kč. **Credit** AmEx, MC, V. **Map** p329 N4.

Even if you're not interested in any of the exhibitions here, it's worth coming just to see the building – a masterpiece of Czech art nouveau, fusing diverse influences into a harmonious whole. The exhibition rooms present shows devoted to topics such as decadent art in the Czech lands, and retrospectives – recently, German photojournalist Werner Bischof.

ARTS & ENTERTAINMENT

House at the Stone Bell. *See p229.*

ARTS & ENTERTAINMENT

Palác Kinských
Kinský Palace

Staroměstské náměstí 12, Staré Město, Prague 1 (224 810 758/www.ngprague.cz). Metro Staroměstská/tram 17, 18. **Open** 10am-6pm Tue-Sun. **Admission** 100 Kč; 150 Kč family; free under-6s. **No credit cards. Map** p328 L3.

The National Gallery's renovated pink and white stucco-fronted Kinský Palace, recently at the centre of a much-publicised restitution case, opened in 2000. It currently houses a long-term display of Czech landscape painting from the 17th to the 20th centuries, along with photography from the 19th century to the present.

Staroměstská radnice
Old Town Hall

Staroměstské náměstí 1, Staré Město, Prague 1 (224 810 036/224 482 751/www.citygallery prague.cz). Metro Staroměstská/tram 17, 18. **Open** *Ground floor* 11am-6pm Mon; 9am-6pm Tue-Sun. *City Gallery* 10am-6pm Tue-Sun. **Admission** 40 Kč; free under-6s. **No credit cards. Map** p328 L4.

There are two separate spaces for exhibitions in the Old Town Hall. The one entered on the ground floor shows a mixed bag of predominantly photographic shows, including the annual Czech Press Photo competition, celebrity portraiture and photojournalism. Up on the second floor, behind a forbidding-looking door, is a more adventurous space that's operated by the Prague City Gallery; it specialises in the youngest wave of Czech painters to emerge, with some interesting solo shows.

▶ *For more on the Old Town Hall, see p87.*

★ Valdštejnská jízdárna
Wallenstein Riding School

Valdštejnská 3, Malá Strana, Prague 1 (257 073 136/www.ngprague.cz). Metro Malostranská/ tram 12, 18, 22. **Open** 10am-6pm Tue-Sun. **Admission** 150 Kč; 200 Kč family; free under-6s. **No credit cards. Map** p327 G2.

Part of the Wallenstein Palace complex and operated by the National Gallery (*see p114*), the Wallenstein Riding School space plays host to some of Prague's most popular exhibitions – overviews of celebrated Czech artists such as National Revival-era patriot František Ženíšek, modernist Václav Špála and symbolist Max Švabinský always go down a storm.

COMMERCIAL, INDEPENDENT & PRIVATE GALLERIES

★ AM 180

Bělehradská 45, Vinohrady, Prague 2 (mobile 605 407 320/mobile 731 177 641/www.am180.org). Metro Náměstí Míru/tram 6, 11. **Open** 3-7pm Mon-Fri & by appointment. **Admission** free. **No credit cards. Map** p331 P10.

and a Projekt Room presenting experimental shows by up-and-coming artists. It's a great place in which to see established Czech artists such as Jiří David and Veronika Bromová and bright stars of European contemporary art. A provocative David Černý installation stands in the gallery's courtyard.

Galerie České pojišťovny
Spálená 14, Nové Město, Prague 1 (261 383 111/www.galeriecpoj.cz). Metro Národní třída/ tram 6, 9, 18, 21, 22. **Open** 10am-6pm daily. **Admission** free. **No credit cards**.
Map p330 L8.
Finding Galerie České pojišťovny is half the fun: follow one of three passages (from Spálená, Purkyňova or Vladislavova streets) through a quiet courtyard with a pleasant café until you find the gallery. Opened in 2004 in an art nouveau building that was designed by Osvald Polívka, the venue shows contemporary Czech photography, and painting by the likes of Tomáš Císařovský, Jaroslav Rona and Richard Konvička.

Galerie Display
Bubenská 3, Holešovice, Prague 7 (mobile 604 722 562/www.galerie.display.cz). Metro Vltavská/tram 1, 3, 8, 14, 25. **Open** 3-6pm Wed-Sun. **Admission** free. **No credit cards**.
Map p332 A2.
Display's graffiti-splashed shopfront blends in perfectly with its urban surroundings, and the gallery is a suitably energetic player on the art scene. Open since 2001, it's already a veteran among indie art spaces. In addition to risk-taking exhibitions, which often connect Prague audiences with young artists from other European countries, it also holds screenings and discussions with the artists themselves.

Galerie Gambit
Mikulandská 6, Nové Město, Prague 1 (mobile 602 277 210/www.gambit.cz). Metro Národní třída/tram 6, 9, 18, 21, 22. **Open** noon-6pm Tue-Sat. **Admission** free. **No credit cards**.
Map p328 K6.
You might have to squeeze to get into this tiny gallery, but the beefed-up exhibition programme is worth it: small shows of new works by well-known Czech names such as Michael Rittstein, Petr Nikl and Bedřich Dlouhý, as well as younger or foreign artists and exhibitions of contemporary design.

Galerie Jelení
Drtinova 15, Smíchov, Prague 5 (mobile 737 407 353/www.fcca.cz). Metro Anděl/tram 2, 12, 20. **Open** 3-6pm Tue-Thur. **Admission** free. **No credit cards**.
The Jelení kept its name when it moved from its previous location on Jelení to new quarters in Smíchov. Operated by the Foundation and Centre for Contemporary Art, it puts on a steady stream of experimental shows, including student exhibitions.

This young space is the collective effort of a dynamic group of up-and-coming artists. Shows tend to be imaginatively titled, and even when the art is a tad unpolished, the artists exhibiting here often show great promise. Recently, more established Czech artists including Vacláv Stratil, Vladimír Skrepl and Tomáš Vaněk have been flocking to the gallery.

c2c
Za Strahovem 19, Strahov, Prague 6 (mobile 777 817 774/www.c2c.cz). Metro Hradčanská/ tram 22. **Open** 4-7pm Thur-Sat. **Admission** free. **No credit cards**.
Situated in the neighbourhood up behind the enormous Strahov stadium, c2c opened in late 2005 and is establishing a reputation for experimental group shows focused on complex themes. The name stands for 'Circle of Curators and Critics', and its shows often concentrate on curatorship and critical theory.

★ Futura
Holečkova 49, Smíchov, Prague 5 (251 511 804/ www.futuraprojekt.cz). Metro Anděl/tram 4, 7, 9. **Open** noon-7pm Wed-Sun. **Admission** free. **No credit cards**.
Futura has fast risen to the top rank of the Prague gallery circuit. The brilliantly renovated building houses exhibition spaces that range from white cubes to atmospheric cellar rooms, with a labyrinthine series of nooks devoted to video works

ARTS & ENTERTAINMENT

Galerie Kritiků

Jungmannova 31, Nové Město, Prague 1 (224 494 205/www.galeriekritiku.com). Metro Národní třída/tram 6, 9, 18, 21, 22. **Open** 10am-6pm Tue-Sun. **Admission** 40 Kč; 20 Kč reductions. **No credit cards**. **Map** p328 M6.

An elegant space in the Adria Palace with a grand pyramid skylight, Kritiků has proven itself to be a class act. It is particularly strong when it comes to group shows, and its international contributions often come from Japan.

Galerie Mánes

Masarykovo nábřeží 250, Nové Město, Prague 1 (224 930 754/www.galeriemanes.cz). Metro Karlovo náměstí/tram 17, 21. **Open** 10am-6pm Tue-Sun. **Admission** varies; free children. **No credit cards**. **Map** p330 J8.

The largest and most prominent of the Czech Fund for Art Foundation's network of galleries, Mánes is a beautiful (if run-down) piece of 1930s functionalist architecture by Otakar Novotný. The riverside gallery hosts anything from travelling shows to contemporary Czech artists such as Lukáš Rittstein.

Galerie Miro

Strahovské nádvoří 1, Strahov, Prague 1 (233 354 066/www.galeriemiro.cz). Tram 22. **Open** 10am-5pm daily. **Admission** varies. **No credit cards**. **Map** p326 A4.

Housed in a deconsecrated church in the Strahov monastery complex, the Miro specialises in work by well-known artists (Goya and Dalí, say) but also shows lesser-known contemporary European artists. Owner Miro Smolák shot into the spotlight when he convinced star architect Daniel Libeskind to design a Dalí museum for Prague; the model of the yet-to-be-built museum is on display at the gallery.

★ Galerie Montanelli

Nerudova 13, Malá Strana, Prague 1 (257 531 220/www.galeriemontanelli.com). Metro Malostranská/tram 12, 18, 22. **Open** noon-6pm Mon-Fri. **Admission** free. **No credit cards**. **Map** p326 D3.

The Montanelli gallery specialises in established blue-chip Czech artists including Běla Kolářová and Jitka and Květa Válová, and boosts the younger generation with group shows.

Galerie Václava Špály

Národní třída 30, Nové Město, Prague 1 (224 946 738/www.spalovka.nadace-cfu.cz). Metro Národní třída/tram 6, 9, 18, 21, 22. **Open** 10am-noon, 12.30-6pm Tue-Sun. **Admission** free. **No credit cards**. **Map** p328 L6.

Until recently, visitors found an interesting programme at this place, run by the Czech Fund for Art Foundation. Sadly, it's now in the same boat as fellow foundation gallery Mánes: only shows able to afford the high rent get space on the roster.

Galerie Zdeněk Sklenář

Smetanovo nábřeží 4, Staré Město, Prague 4 (224 218 528). Metro Národní třída/tram 6, 9, 17, 18, 21, 22. **Open** 1-6pm Wed-Sat. **Admission** free. **No credit cards**. **Map** p328 J5.

This gallery shows the works of still-active senior artists such as Zdeněk Sýkora and Karel Malich; but younger names (Federico Díaz, say) are also shown.

Gallery Art Factory

Václavské náměstí 15, Nové Město, Prague 1 (224 217 585/www.galleryartfactory.cz). Metro Můstek/tram 3, 9, 14, 24. **Open** 10am-6pm Mon-Fri. **Admission** 50 Kč. **No credit cards**. **Map** p329 N6.

Set in the old printing house of the main communist-era newspaper, the spacious Art Factory keeps its industrial feel with painted cement floors and some of the old hardware. One speciality is Slovak art; the gallery also runs the annual Sculpture Grande outdoor exhibition of large-scale sculptures up and down Wenceslas Square and Na příkopě.

★ Hunt Kastner Artworks

Kamenická 22, Letná, Prague 7 (233 376 259/www.huntkastner.cz). Metro Vltavská/tram 1, 8, 15, 25, 26. **Open** noon-5pm Thur, Fri & by appointment. **Admission** free. **No credit cards**.

This new private gallery in a blossoming art neighbourhood was established to nurture the careers of more than a dozen Czech contemporary artists such as Tomáš Vaněk and Michael Thelenová.

Jiří Švestka Gallery

Biskupský dvůr 6, Nové Město, Prague 1 (222 311 092/www.jirisvestka.com). Metro Náměstí Republiky/tram 5, 8, 14, 24. **Open** noon-6pm Tue-Fri; 11am-6pm Sat. **Admission** free. **No credit cards**. **Map** p329 P2.

Returned émigré Jiří Švestka has been specialising since 1995 in bold, internationally recognised Czech artists (Milena Dopitová, Krištof Kintera, Jiří Černický) and also exhibits international names such as Tony Cragg in this former photography studio.

★ Karlín Studios

Křižíkova 34, Karlín, Prague 8 (no phone). Metro Křižíkova/tram 8, 24. **Open** noon-6pm Tue-Sun. **Admission** free. **No credit cards**.

A vast complex in a renovated former factory building, Karlín Studios runs its own public gallery in addition to housing two private galleries, Entrance and Behémót; it also gives studio space to artists. It plans to hold a day of open doors twice a year, inviting the public into the normally off-limits studios.

Nová síň

Voršilská 3, Nové Město, Prague 1 (224 930 255). Metro Národní třída/tram 6, 9, 18, 21, 22. **Open** 11am-6pm Tue-Sun. **Admission** free. **No credit cards**. **Map** p330 K7.

Galerie Mánes.

In the skylit space of this formerly venerable gallery – the proverbial white cube – the quality of shows has declined in recent years, with many artists renting out the space and curating themselves. Still, the space is a draw for artists such as Otto Placht, who selected it for his month-long mural project.

PHOTOGRAPHY GALLERIES

Photography is on the up in the Czech art world (*see p234* **Revolt!**). In 2006, a new annual prize called FRAME was established for young photographers; and in April 2008, the organisers of Art Prague held Prague Foto (www.prague foto.cz), a hugely successful photography fair. The Czech photographic tradition is upheld by snappers including Jindřich Štreit, Pavel Baňka and, among the younger generation, Markéta Othová and duo Martin Polák & Lukáš Jasanský.

Galerie Velryba

Opatovická 24, Nové Město, Prague 1 (224 233 337). Metro Národní třída/tram 3, 6, 9, 18, 21, 22. **Open** noon-9pm Mon-Fri; 11am-9pm Sat. **Admission** free. **No credit cards**. **Map** p330 K8.

Handily set in the basement of the trendy Velryba café, the gallery is the showcase for students in the photo department of Czech film academy FAMU, and photo departments at other schools.

★ Josef Sudek Atelier

Újezd 30, Malá Strana, Prague 1 (251 510 760/ www.sudek-atelier.cz). Metro Malostranská/tram 9, 22. **Open** noon-6pm Tue-Sun. **Admission** 10 Kč; 5 Kč reductions. **No credit cards**. **Map** p327 F6.

This little gallery, where father of modern Czech photography Josef Sudek had one of his two photography studios, is accessible through a residential courtyard. Quality art photography is shown in the cosy exhibition room, and Sudek memorabilia is on view in a separate room.

Josef Sudek Gallery

Úvoz 24, Hradčany, Prague 1 (257 531 489/ www.upm.cz). Metro Malostranská/tram 22. **Open** 11am-5pm Wed-Sun. **Admission** 10 Kč; 5 Kč reductions. **No credit cards**. **Map** p326 B3.

Sudek's other studio: he lived and worked here from 1959 to 1976, and it once held a collection of his own photography. These days the programme is run by the Museum of Decorative Arts (UMPRUM) and draws from the museum's vast archives for shows of historical interest in the house's cosy rooms.

Josef Sudek House of Photography

Maiselova 2, Staré Město, Prague 1 (224 819 098/ www.czechpressphoto.cz). Metro Staroměstská/ tram 17, 18. **Open** 11am-6pm daily. **Admission** 20 Kč; 10 Kč reductions. **Credit** DC, MC, V. **Map** p328 K3.

The third of three photo galleries bearing Sudek's name (although he didn't actually work here), this space leans towards documentary pictures and reportage by Czech photographers, with a steady stream of fresh talent from abroad.

Langhans Galerie

Vodičkova 37, Nové Město, Prague 1 (222 929 333/www.langhansgalerie.cz). Metro Můstek/ tram 3, 9, 14, 24. **Open** noon-6pm Tue-Fri; 11am-4pm Sat. **Admission** 60 Kč; 30 Kč reductions. **No credit cards. Map** p329 N6.
This beautifully renovated building was once home to the Jan Langhans Atelier, where anyone who was anyone in interwar Prague had his or her portrait taken. The emphasis now is on historic shows, especially drawing on the Langhans archives, mixed in with work by established and emerging photographers. A recurring theme is memory.

Leica Gallery Prague

Školská 28, Nové Město, Prague 1 (251 614 316/ www.leicagallery.cz). Metro Můstek/tram 3, 9, 14, 24. **Open** 11am-9pm Mon-Fri. **Admission** 60 Kč; 30 Kč reductions. **No credit cards. Map** p330 M7.
When this progressive gallery for documentary photography found itself homeless in the wake of renovations at its original space at Prague Castle, staff handled its fate with trademark creativity – it took its act on the road and became a 'travelling gallery', inviting Sebastião Salgado back to Prague to show his 'Workers' series on a renovated train that rolled throughout the Czech Republic and across the border. It now has a fine new address by Wenceslas Square.

★ Prague House of Photography

Václavské náměstí 31, Nové Město, Prague 1 (222 243 229/www.php-gallery.cz). Metro

Revolt! Picture This

The revival of Czech photography is upon us, and not a moment too soon.

While Czech photographers such as Josef Sudek and Jan Saudek have long made their mark on the international scene, photography has taken a back seat at home for almost two decades. That's set to change with the renewal of a trio of prominent Prague photography galleries, the arrival of an ambitious newcomer, and the creation of a new annual photo prize for under-35s.

The **Prague House of Photography** (*see p234*), founded in the euphoric atmosphere after the Velvet Revolution, has been an institution without a permanent home for the last five years, after it was washed out of its Haštalská space by the floods of 2002. It's finally set to open in a new space, bigger and better than ever, on the street dividing Old Town from New Town. It plans to mix classic modern Czech photography with more recent local trends.

Another venerable photo gallery with new digs is **Leica Gallery Prague** (*see p234*). After losing its lease at Prague Castle, it made the bold move of taking its shows to the people, by installing exhibitions of major figures such as Sebastião Salgado, Antonín Kratochvíl and Wim and Donata Wenders in a set of refurbished train cars that travelled the country. When it opens in its new home on Školská in the New Town, it aims to continue to expose the public to the very best local art photographers

and photojournalists, and will also host shows by international stars, such as fashion photographer Sarah Moon.

Meanwhile, gallerist Jiří Jaksmanický has set up a new space called **Greisen** (Hybernská 7a, 257 534 584, www. greisen.cz). Jaksmanický is a low-key figure on the local photography scene, better known among the international auction set than gallerygoers, but over the years he has run various galleries that have concentrated on Czech classics such as Sudek, František Drtikol and Jaromír Funke, and at Greisen he's taking up the baton of his former Czech Centre of Photography.

Some of the most interesting photography exhibitions in town, though, can be found just downstairs from the venerable Café Louvre (*see p183*). The new **Galerie Fotografie Louvre** has started life with a bang, with impressive shows by ever-mutable Václav Stratil and always-subtle Pavel Baňka.

With all this camera-centric activity going on, it's no wonder the photography world now has its own annual art fair: the first Prague Foto was held in April 2008 at **Galerie Mánes** (*see p232*). The annual FRAME Prize was founded in 2005 to encourage photographers under 35, much in the same way the Jindřich Chalupecký Award – which, incidentally, doesn't exclude photographers – has been doing since 1990.

Muzeum/tram 3, 9, 14, 24. **Open** 11am-6pm daily. **Admission** 30 Kč; 15 Kč reductions. **Credit** AmEx, MC, V. **Map** p329 N6.
The peripatetic PHP seemed to have settled down in a Staré Město courtyard until the devastating floods in 2002 drowned its showroom. After a few years on Wenceslas Square, it has been planning a move to a new permanent space on Revoluční street; when it reopens it will be reborn as an institution with state funding, with vast capacity in two separate halls to stage major retrospectives and group shows.

FESTIVALS & EVENTS

Veletržní Palace is home to what is now the **International Triennial of Contemporary Art** (www.ngprague.cz/itca), held for the first time in summer 2008 under its new label. The locals have grown weary of the bickering between IBCA, as it was previously known, and the **Prague Biennale** (www.prague biennale.org), but the fact that Prague can now host two major gatherings of international contemporary art shows just how far this city has moved toward becoming a bona fide art destination.

The ITCA and the Prague Biennale don't stand alone. The city is also home to Zvon ('Bell'), a roughly biennial exhibition organised by the Prague City Gallery, held at the House at the Stone Bell and designed to provide a platform for emerging artists from the Czech Republic and Central Europe. For the sixth event in 2008, the curator invited back the artists who had participated in the previous edition, including Josef Bolf and Kateřina Šedá, aiming to chart individual artists' development.

Vernon Gallery is the organiser of **Tina B** (www.tina-b.eu). Short for 'This Is Not Another Biennial', Tina B is an annual festival of contemporary art that hasn't yet anchored in one space. In 2006, the bulk of its exhibits were displayed in Veletržní Palace; in September 2008, though, it opened in an alternative space in a run-down building right across the street.

Finally, there's the increasingly popular **Art Prague** (www.artprague.cz), an art fair held every spring. Its gallerists banded together in 2006 into the new Association of Gallerists of the Czech Republic, which grew out of the art fair and aims to educate the art-buying public and nurture the careers of contemporary artists.

ARTS & ENTERTAINMENT

International Triennial of Contemporary Art.

Gay & Lesbian

Be out and proud in this gay-friendly town.

Gay men and lesbians will find themselves right at home in Prague. However, they may also notice that things are a little on the quiet side. People seem content to remain in their own particular orbits, heading to mainstream venues without the need to be out and proud. Although the buzzers and metal doors on some underground cellar bars bring the fun of pretending, no one takes much trouble to hide his or her preferences. Provocative gay guides to the city are on sale at many newsagents, and polls show that 90 per cent of Czechs are just fine with homosexuality.

GETTING OUT AND ABOUT

A number of gay bars are staffed with big but harmless men at the door. Despite the build-up, they're usually just bars. It's worth venturing in: along with some of Prague's gay cafés, many of these venues hold warm-up parties for big gay nights. Elsewhere, some straight clubs hold regular gay nights; in particular, try **Mecca** (*see p255*) and **Radost FX** (*see p257*).

One aspect of the scene that many find offputting is prostitution, which sometimes involves youthful practitioners. The legal age of consent in the Czech Republic is 15, whether straight or gay – but if money changes hands, it's 18, and arrests have been made. Most clubs with 'butterflies' (prostitutes) are run with discretion and supervision – **Drake's** and **Escape** are two examples. But other clubs near the main station attract both a less salubrious clientele and the attentions of the police. Most gay clubs are also home to a varying number of prostitutes. Always discuss financial matters and boundaries before striking a deal.

Prague's lesbian scene has been a slower starter in comparison, perhaps because it hasn't been driven by the engine of prostitution. However, the scene seems to be maturing, and friendly gay bars such as **TERmix** are as welcoming to lesbians as to boys.

The Czech Republic has a relatively low AIDS and HIV infection rate, owing mainly to the country's closed borders until 1989. Recent reports have put the number of HIV-infected people in the country at 807, but the infection rate is probably higher. Condoms are widely

available in supermarkets, select clubs and in vending machines at some metro stations. For more information on health and helpful organisations, *see p304*.

International gay guide **Spartacus** is useful for planning, as are **www.planetout.com** and **http://prague.gayguide.net** (which has up-to-date listings on Prague's gay scene). The community is well served by networks such as the amazingly helpful **www.praguesaints.cz**; discussion boards at **www.expats.cz** cover all the big topics, and the Gay Prague Yahoo group is also good. Czech-language pick-up sites such as **www.xko.cz** and **www.xchat.cz** have some English-speaking users; so does the more

---

INSIDE TRACK
CRUISING THE CITY

Prague's long, hot summers tempt everyone to outdoor escapades, and the metronome atop **Letná park** (*see p114*) beckons men and women with its rhythmic movements. Petřín Hill is no longer a big cruising area, although the terrace at the hill's **Petřínské Terasy** restaurant (Seminářská zahrada 13, 290 000 457) remains a favoured spot. The nudist beach at the lake in **Šárka park** (*see p265*) has a gay section – the area nearest the dam. The **Podolí** swimming pool (*see p267*) is a hot spot for hooking up, with nude sunbathing galore, but do note that families also use the grounds.

mainstream **www.rande.cz**, which has active sections for gays and lesbians. An online escort service for men is at **www.callboys.cz**.

ASSOCIATIONS

Feminismus Gender Studies
Gorazdova 20, Nové Město, Prague 1 (224 913 350/www.genderstudies.cz). Metro Karlovo náměstí/tram 3, 6, 14, 18, 22. **Open** noon-6pm Tue-Fri & by appointment. **Map** p330 J9.
The organisation's English website has been 'under construction' for three years, but may yet become a useful resource for lesbian activities. Meanwhile, in-person visits are best, and the staff speak English.

ACCOMMODATION

Agencies

Prague Center Guest Residence
www.gaystay.net/PragueCenter. **Rates** 1,400-2,880 Kč. **No credit cards**.
Book via the website with Bob, the American owner, who rents some IKEA-inspired rooms and apartments; one has a fireplace. Some have shared bathrooms and living rooms, but service and locations are above average. Reservations are required.

Toucan Apartments
www.toucanapartments.com. **Rates** 1,800-5,800 Kč. **Credit** AmEx, MC, V.

This Dutch-owned agency has more than 30 apartments in Prague 1, 2, 3 and 10, all of which can be booked via the website listed above. Some apartments are wood-beam attic niches, others are studios, and a number have a washing machine – but all are simple, clean and comfortable. The website offers information on nearby nightlife options; all staff are gay. Book ahead.

Hotels

Arco Pension
Voroněžská 24, Vršovice, Prague 10 (271 740 734/fax 271 740 734/www.arco-guesthouse.cz). Metro Náměstí Míru/tram 4, 16, 22. **Rates** (incl breakfast) 1,100 Kč double; 1,700 Kč apartment. **Credit** AmEx, MC, V.
Occupying various addresses on the same street, Arco consists of a comfortable and relaxed collection of apartments, ranging from fairly basic to quite luxurious. The main appeal is the location, along with the friendly restaurant, bar and internet café. Reservations are essential.

Ron's Rainbow Guest House
Bulharská 4, Vršovice, Prague 10 (271 725 664/mobile 604 876 694). Metro Flóra/tram 6, 7, 22, 24, 34. **Open** 9am-9pm daily. **Rates** 600-1,000 Kč. **Credit** MC, V.
The Rainbow comprises four comfortable rooms – one with a whirlpool – in residential Prague next to gay-centric Žižkov. Reservations are required.

Friends. *See p238*.

ARTS & ENTERTAINMENT

ARTS & ENTERTAINMENT

BARS

Non-Czech-speaking visitors may feel a tad neglected in the more local venues listed here – however, the younger the crowd, the more likely you are to find English spoken. If you're given a drinks card upon entering a bar, don't lose it, or you'll be charged at least 1,000 Kč. Listed closing times generally tend to be ignored, depending on how much fun is being had.

Alcatraz

Bořivojova 58, Žižkov, Prague 3 (222 711 458/ www.alcatraz.cz). Metro Jiřího z Poděbrad/ tram 10, 11, 16, 51. **Open** 9pm-4am daily. **Admission** 50 Kč; 100 Kč party nights. **No credit cards. Map** p333 B2.

This hardcore leather and rubber venue is housed in an appropriately dark though well-maintained cellar, with run-off troughs, slings, cages, darkrooms, cabins, videos, glory holes – everything you could imagine and then some, plus the occasional hardcore theme party.

Drake's

Zborovská 50, Smíchov, Prague 5 (no phone). Metro Anděl/tram 6, 9, 12, 22, 57, 58. **Open** 24hrs daily. **Admission** 500 Kč. **No credit cards.**

Drake's is popular with an older and beefier crowd. Pay the high admission price and enjoy the many services and entertainments that are provided 24 hours a day. Drake's may not be a happening clubbar (it can be slow at times), but it's certainly a popular after-hours place – this is, after all, the grande dame of the Prague scene. There are video booths, daily strip shows at 9pm and 11pm, glory holes and an S&M dungeon.

Escape

V jámě 8, Nové Město, Prague 1 (mobile 606 538 111/www.escapetoparadise.cz). Metro Mùstek/ tram 3, 9, 14, 24, 58. **Open** *Disco* 9.30pm-3am daily. *Restaurant* 8pm-2am daily. **Admission** 50 Kč Fri, Sat. **No credit cards. Map** p330 M7.

Escape has wall-to-wall hustlers, but you generally won't be bothered by them if you enter as a couple. What's more, they're well behaved (because they're on the staff), although some visitors still find the place a bit dubious. Strippers, body paint and live sex shows regularly make appearances.

★ Friends

Bartolomějská 11, Staré Město, Prague 1 (224 236 772/www.friends-prague.cz). Metro Národní třída. **Open** 4pm-5am daily. **Admission** free. **Credit** MC, V. **Map** p328 K6.

Friends is a relaxed, comfortable, grown-up sort of place, a great spot in which to get acclimatised to Prague's scene. It was originally located around the corner, but this new address revives one of the

longest-established gay bars in Prague. The setting takes the original atmosphere and adds room for proper dancing (there are DJ parties Wed-Sat); other attractions include Wi-Fi. *Photo p237.*

Street Café

Blanická 28, Vinohrady, Prague 2 (222 013 116). Metro Náměstí Míru/tram 4, 10, 16, 22, 51, 57. **Open** 9am-11pm Mon-Thur; 9am-4am Fri, Sat; 1-10pm Sun. **Admission** free. *Party nights* 50Kč. **No credit cards. Map** p333 A3.

A nondescript door leads to a cellar bar devoted to ladies (though no one is barred entry). Everyone seems to know each other or is getting to know each other, and fun pervades the slow grooves or the raunchy gyrations of table-top dancers – there's even a pole to cavort with. It's a welcome addition to the city's lesbian scene.

Tingl Tangl

Karolíny Světlé 12, Staré Město, Prague 1 (224 238 278/www.tingltangl.cz). Metro Národní třída/tram 6, 9, 18, 21, 22, 51, 54, 57, 58. **Open** *Cabaret* 9pm-5am Wed, Fri, Sat. *Restaurant* 11am-10pm Mon-Fri; 5-10pm Sat. **Admission** 150 Kč. **No credit cards. Map** p328 J5.

The free Wednesday shows are a laugh at this newish venue. Tingl Tangl serves a short menu of international cuisine upstairs and in the quiet courtyard; downstairs you'll find the borderline cliché cabaret and transvestite shows, which trade off with more unusual performers until the DJ takes over. Reservations are recommended.

CLUBS

All the clubs listed in our nightlife chapter (*see pp252-260*) host cool nights, and gay clubbers won't feel out of their element. But for decidedly gay options, try the following spots.

Angel

Kmochová 8 (corner of Grafická), Smíchov, Prague 5 (257 316 127/www.clubangel.cz). Metro Anděl/tram 4, 7, 9, 10, 58. **Open** 7pm-3am Mon-Thur, Sun; 7pm-6am Fri, Sat. **Admission** free Mon-Thur, Sun; 35 Kč Fri, Sat. **No credit cards.** This mirrorballed, LP-decorated 1980s throwback of a dance club is a very local hangout – hence the Czech and Slovak hits played on Friday nights. It's also rather difficult to find, so if Thursday's Karaoke Night appeals, take a taxi. Angel also does a popular weekend-long dance party.

★ Saints

Polská 32, Vinohrady, Prague 2 (222 250 326/www.praguesaints.cz). Metro Náměstí Míru/tram 4, 10, 16, 22, 51, 57. **Open** 5pm-2am Fri; 5pm-4am Sat; 5pm-1am Sun. **Admission** free. **No credit cards. Map** p333 A3.

Valentino.

Saints is a friendly, casual gay bar, with a welcoming, open atmosphere (dykes like it, too) and a small but amusing dance space. Saints is run by British owners who excel at cocktails. The club also doubles as an information hub for the community in Prague (the website provides a lot of gay accommodation and entertainment listings).

★ TERmix

Třebízského 4a, Vinohrady, Prague 2 (222 710 462/www.club-termix.cz). Metro Jiřího z Poděbrad/tram 10, 11, 16, 51. Open 8pm-5am daily. Admission free. No credit cards. Map p333 B3.

Dedicated to the straightforward ideal of gay and lesbian drinks, dancing and sex, TERmix fulfils its brief beautifully. Ring the bell and descend into the sleek and chic club, past a long glass bar, a widescreen TV, sofas and, naturally enough, a car parked in the wall. The dancefloor is regularly packed, especially when DJs spin music at one of several themed nights: Latin and Czech hits are popular, and Thursday's Hot Night is a relaxed get-together of candles and easy music. A chill-out room, make-out room and two darkrooms, cabins and a shower complete the facilities.

Valentino

Vinohradská 40, Vinohrady (222 513 491/ www.club-valentino.cz). Metro Náměstí Míru/ tram 11, 51. Open 9pm-5am daily. Admission varies. No credit cards. Map p333 A3.

Prague's biggest gay disco is a big production indeed, at least on the scale of Czech clubbing. The Red Bar, with oldies tunes and Czech classics, is open nightly; while the Star Bar, blasting house and pop, opens at weekends. Monthly parties are equally over-the-top, but a mellower street level bar offers quieter space for chats and chat-ups. A welcoming yet ebullient party palace.

CAFES

See also **Érra Café** (*see p180*) and **Pálffy Palác** (*see p158*), both popular with gays.

Café Café

Rytířská 10, Staré Město, Prague 1 (224 210 597/www.cafe-cafe.cz). Metro Můstek/tram 6, 9, 18, 22, 51, 54, 57, 58. Open noon-11pm Mon-Fri; 10am-11pm Sat, Sun. Main courses 150-350 Kč. Credit MC, V. Map p328 L5.

This jam-packed café has mirrors to improve the opportunities for scrutiny between the absurdly beautiful people who frequent it. Café Café pulls in a gay crowd, but its Staré Město location makes it popular with all-comers (as long as they're handsome). Large windows and pavement tables make it a handy spot for assignation, planned or impromptu.

SAUNAS

Sauna Babylonia

Martinská 6, Staré Město, Prague 1 (224 232 304/http://babylonia.aspweb.cz). Metro Můstek/ tram 3, 9, 14, 25. Open 2pm-3am daily. Admission 300 Kč full use. Gym only 80 Kč. No credit cards. Map p328 L6.

Babylonia is the most popular gay sauna in Prague, but some of the men here are clearly too young and too beautiful to be just hanging around.

Sauna Marco

Lublaňská 17, Nové Město, Prague 2 (224 262 833). Metro IP Pavlova/tram 4, 6, 11, 16, 22. Open 2pm-3am daily. Admission 180-200 Kč. Credit MC, V. Map p331 O10.

Marco remains highly popular and busy, with cabins, whirlpool and video room. A well-known meeting spot, it's also handy for the main gay clubbing options in the Vinohrady district.

Music

Mozart and Dvořák meet jazz and hip hop in the most tuneful of towns.

For centuries, Prague has had a reputation as
the conservatoire of Europe. The sheer amount
of classical music in the city is astonishing, with
major festivals and concerts joined by a wealth
of excellent chamber ensembles and faculty and
student recitals. Even at the city's biggest concert
halls and opera houses, a good portion of tickets
are still priced for students and pensioners, as if
the ability to hear a Dvořák concerto is considered
a constitutional right. But it's not all about the
classics: there's also a healthy and affordable rock
scene in the city, and a jazz circuit that surprises
as much as it impresses.

Classical & Opera

Locals who struggle to hold down two jobs
while they finish their MBA will nonetheless
always find time to go to a concert at the
Rudolfinum. Every available space in
otherwise sleepy palaces and churches is used
for rehearsal or performance, and the sight of
sweating men manoeuvring double basses on
to trams is so common that no one raises an
eyebrow. Yep, Prague is a city that treasures
its long and impressive musical heritage.

However, despite this history, the Czech
government doesn't offer adequate funding
to the musical arts. The State Opera now gets
just 140 million Kč (£4.3 million) in annual
funding, less than a third of the sum paid
to the **National Theatre**; the shortfall is
a serious hindrance to the opera house's
programming. And as you'd expect, many
of the best singers and musicians emigrate
to countries where their training and skills
command much higher wages.

Still, the band plays on, and much of what
remains in Prague is first-rate. As well as the
five major orchestras and three opera houses,
the city's prestigious musical heritage attracts
a steady stream of international guests, such
as the Vienna Philharmonic and the London
Symphony. Mainstream classical music takes
up a large chunk of the schedule, but there
are also strong and developing baroque and
modern music scenes. When you add it all
together, your main problem will be figuring
out how to fit in everything during your stay.

Tickets & information

Prague has a strong subscription-concert
tradition, and some concerts may be a tough
ticket for non-subscribers. Having said that,
Ticketpro (*see p210*) sells tickets for most
of the major classical venues, with a small
surcharge that's far less than many other
agencies levy on foreigners. If you choose
to buy directly from a venue, usually more
complicated because of odd box office hours
and harassed staff, you might still succeed
even if a show is advertised as 'sold out': touts
buy many seats for popular shows, so just wait
around the entrance until the last minute when
they have to sell or lose their investment. Prices
for concerts vary: some (in smaller churches)
are free, but the cost is usually between 250 Kč
and 600 Kč.

Information can be patchy, but **Bohemia
Ticket International** (*see below*) has an
online calendar prepared months in advance,
and accepts bookings and credit card payments
from abroad. Keep an eye on the *Prague Post*
(www.praguepost.com) for listings of current
and forthcoming events.

Bohemia Ticket International
*Malé náměstí 13, Staré Město, Prague 1 (224
227 832/fax 224 237 727/www.ticketsbti.cz).*
*Metro Můstek or Národní třída/tram 6, 9, 18,
22.* **Open** 9am-5pm Mon-Fri; 9am-1pm Sat.
No credit cards. Map p328 L4.
This is the best non-travel agency if you want to buy
tickets in advance from abroad for opera and for

Walk Melody March

Hooked on classics? Walk the streets that spawned them.

Prague has many temples at which classical music devotees can worship. There are the individual museums dedicated to Prague's holy trinity: **Dvořák** (*see p109*), **Smetana** (Novotného lávka 3) and **Mozart** (*see p117*). And there's the informative and eclectic **Czech Museum of Music** (Karmelitská 2, Malá Strana). But there are also many other noteworthy spots in the city associated with these and other demigods of the classical world.

Walking from Hradčany to Old Town, the first address of interest is **Nerudova 33**. While in Prague working on *Don Giovanni*, Mozart met the famous Venetian roué Giacomo Casanova, who was later one of the renowned first-night attendees of the opera. In his notes, Casanova indicated that he made a number of suggestions to the opera's librettist, Lorenzo Da Ponte (*see below*).

At **Malostanské náměstí 23**, a bust of soprano Ema Destinnová, better known to the world as Emmy Destinn, juts out from the façade. While a Czech patriot, Destinnová committed an unpardonable crime as far as her fellow countrymen were concerned: she was popular elsewhere, performing as Covent Garden's first Madame Butterfly and the world's first Minnie in Puccini's *La Fanciulla del West*. In both instances, she sang opposite the great Caruso, who was long rumoured to be her lover. Back in her native city, she was never invited to sing at the **Národní divadlo** (**National Theatre**; *see p271*) – but then that theatre didn't invite Smetana to the première of one of his own operas. All was forgiven in death, though, and Destinnová now graces the Czech 2,000 Kč note.

A five-minute walk from Destinnová's house takes you to the city's one Beethoven shrine, at **Maltézské náměstí 9**. Beethoven stayed in Prague briefly, in 1796 – long enough, apparently, to affix this stern stone portrait at the site. It's now used by the building's owners, rather shamelessly, as a marketing tool.

Mere steps away, at **Na Kampě 11**, is a rare acknowledgement of Bohuslav Martinů, the Czech composer who lived here as a student. Martinů's reputation is still rising, so expect more than this protruding bust in years to come.

In Staré Město, the primary place of pilgrimage is the **Stavovské divadlo** (**Estates Theatre**; *see p272*), where Mozart premièred *Don Giovanni* and *La Clemenza di Tito* (after a private palace performance). Less well known is the end of **Uhelný trh**, down from the Estates – this is where the opera was actually created. At no.1, Mozart slaved away composing the music; at no.11, directly across the short street, Da Ponte wrote the libretto. With little distance separating composer and librettist, they were said to have communicated by shouting out of their respective windows. There's no plaque to the unjustly ignored Da Ponte, and he's been upstaged at no.11 by a bust of Liszt, who stayed there later. At no.1, however, you can now dine at the **Wolfgang Pizzeria**.

concerts at the National Theatre, Estates Theatre and State Opera, along with other big orchestral and chamber events.
Other locations Na příkopě 16, Nové Město, Prague 1 (224 215 031).

Čedok

Na příkopě 18, Nové Město, Prague 1 (224 197 242/www.cedok.cz). Metro Můstek or Náměstí Republiky/tram 5, 8, 14, 26. **Open** 9am-7pm Mon-Fri; 9.30am-1pm Sat. **Credit** AmEx, MC, V. **Map** p329 N5.
Tickets for various events, including some concerts.
Other locations Václavské náměstí 53, Nové Město, Prague 1 (221 965 243); Rytířská 16, Staré Město, Prague 1 (224 224 461).

ENSEMBLES

Although its members, like many top classical musicians here, have to moonlight in order to make ends meet, the **České filharmonie** (**Czech Philharmonic**; 227 059 352, www.ceskafilharmonie.cz) still leads the pack of Prague's resident orchestras. Czech classics are a paticular speciality, but general manager Václav Riedlbauch recently launched spring's **Prague Premieres** festival of new music (www.prazskepremiery.cz) to ensure the orchestra doesn't get too bogged down. The august ensemble will again have a permanent conductor in 2009, when Eliahu Inbal comes straight from his joint posts at Teatro La Fenice in Venice and Tokyo Metropolitan Symphony Orchestra. Most concerts are held at the Rudolfinum's Dvořák Hall (*see below*).

Next to them, the **Symfonický orchestr hl m Prahy (Prague Symphony Orchestra**; 222 002 336, www.fok.cz) is sometimes considered second string, but that's hardly a put-down here. Run by the City of Prague, the respected ensemble has a strong Russian repertoire – it has recorded the complete Shostakovich symphonies, led by Dmitri's son Maxim – and a long list of international collaborating artists. The orchestra is based at the Municipal House (*see below*).

The **Pražská komorní filharmonie (Prague Philharmonia**; 224 811 258, www.pkf.cz) is the hardest-working orchestra in town, backing most of the visiting opera stars and running an ambitious schedule of chamber and orchestra concerts. With expert assistance from visiting French conductor Michel Swierczewski, a protégé of Pierre Boulez, the Philharmonia has developed adventurous modern music programming. The Philharmonia performs regularly at the Rudolfinum's Dvořák Hall (*see below*), and at the Church of St Simon & St Jude (*see p243*).

The **Český národní symfonický orchestr (Czech National Symphony Orchestra**; 267 215 576, www.cnso.cz) has also pioneered interesting new paths, playing with unorthodox guests such as American jazz musician Chris Brubeck. You can find them at the Municipal House's Smetana Hall (*see below*). And although the **Czech Radio Symphony Orchestra** (www2.rozhlas.cz/socr) is the least ambitious of the city's major ensembles, its longevity alone – the orchestra marked its 80th anniversary at the 2006 Prague Spring Festival – makes its Rudolfinum concerts worth a listen.

VENUES

Major concert halls

★ **Obecní dům**
Municipal House
Náměstí Republiky 5, Nové Město, Prague 1 (222 002 101/www.obecni-dum.cz). Metro Náměstí Republiky/tram 5, 14, 26. **Open** *Box office* 10am-6pm daily. **Tickets** 150-800 Kč. **Credit** AmEx, MC, V. **Map** p329 O4.

An architectural treasure, the Municipal House was restored in the mid 1990s to its stunning original art nouveau state. It's built around the Smetana Hall, home to the Prague Symphony Orchestra; the PSO launches Prague Spring (*see p245*) here most years, a tradition that dates back half a century. Listen to Smetana variations on folk tunes while gazing at the ceiling mosaics of old Czech

myths (and the president sitting in his box at stage right) for an authentic Bohemian reverie.

▶ *For more on the Municipal House, see p103; for its gallery, see p229.*

★ **Rudolfinum**
Alšovo nábřeží 12, Staré Město, Prague 1 (227 059 352/www.rudolfinum.cz). Metro Staroměstská/tram 17, 18. **Open** *Box office* 10am-6pm Mon-Fri. Closed mid July-mid Aug. **Tickets** 200-1,100 Kč. **Credit** AmEx, MC, V. **Map** p328 J3.

Stately and commanding, this former parliament building is one of Europe's finest concert venues. It was built in the neoclassical style at the end of the 19th century, and has two halls: the Dvořák Hall, for orchestral works and major recitals, and the Suk Hall, for chamber, instrumental and solo vocal music. Opinion is divided about the acoustics of the former, but the grandeur of the building's interior and the high standard of musicianship make an evening here eminently worthwhile.

▶ *There's also a gallery here; for details, see p229.*

Smaller venues

The repertoire is largely baroque and classical with a Czech emphasis; performances are usually of a high standard. Tickets for concerts can generally be bought from the venue one to two hours before a performance is due to start; **Bohemia Ticket International** (*see p240*) also sells tickets for some events.

Bazilika sv. Jakuba
Basilica of St James
Malá Štupartská 6, Staré Město, Prague 1 (224 828 816). Metro Náměstí Republiky/ tram 5, 14, 26. **Open** *Box office* 1hr before performance. **Tickets** 250-400 Kč. **No credit cards. Map** p328 M3.

The opulent soaring vaults at the Basilica are typical of Czech Baroque architecture, and produce resounding organ acoustics. In addition to large-scale sacred choral works, the music for Sunday Mass (usually 10am) is impressive. Concerts are held from Easter until September.

▶ *The basilica is also open to the public during the day; see p84.*

★ **Bertramka**
Mozartova 169, Smíchov, Prague 5 (257 318 461/www.bertramka.cz). Metro Anděl/tram 4, 7, 9, 10, 12, 14. **Open** 9.30am-5pm daily. **Tickets** 110-450 Kč. **No credit cards.**

In a dignified, park-like setting, ideal for outdoor summer concerts but with restored interiors that are just as good, the house where Mozart stayed is now a museum devoted to him that stages regular performances. Nearly all include at least one work by

the Austrian, who's been adopted as a favourite son in the Czech musical pantheon. Musical seasons such as 'Beethoven versus Mozart' and 'Divertimenti in Prague' fill out the schedule.
▶ *For the museum itself, see p117.*

Chrám sv. Mikuláše
Church of St Nicholas
Malostranské náměstí, Malá Strana, Prague 1 (224 190 991). Metro Malostranská/tram 12, 22. **Open** *Box office* 2hrs before performance. **Tickets** 250-450 Kč. **No credit cards. Map** p327 E3.
This is one of Prague's most celebrated churches, where blatantly over-the-top Baroque interiors provide a backdrop for performances of music from the same period. Irregular choral concerts and organ recitals are generally of high quality, and can be as grand as the setting itself.
▶ *For details on visiting the church outside of its concert schedule, see p74.*

Klášter sv. Anežky české
Convent of St Agnes of Bohemia
U milosrdných 17, Staré Město, Prague 1 (221 879 270). Metro Staroměstská or Náměstí Republiky/tram 5, 14, 26. **Open** 10am-6pm Tue-Sun. **Tickets** 250-550 Kč. **No credit cards. Map** p328 M2.
The acoustics here may have their critics, but St Agnes's Convent, which also features the medieval

collection of the National Gallery, has a Gothic atmosphere for concerts. Programming is focused on high-quality chamber music, with an emphasis on Smetana, Dvořák and Janáček.
▶ *It's also open during the day; see p98.*

Kostel sv. Mikuláše
Church of St Nicholas
Staroměstské náměstí, Staré Město, Prague 1 (no phone). Metro Staroměstská/tram 17, 18. **Open** noon-4pm Mon; 10am-4pm Tue-Sat.
No credit cards. Map p328 L4.
The other St Nicholas can't compete with its namesake across the river in Malá Strana, but still hosts regular organ, instrumental and vocal recitals in a plainer yet still pretty setting. Most tend to focus on popular classics, but the main emphasis is on the baroque period.

Kostel sv. Šimona a Judy
Church of St Simon & St Jude
Dušní & U milosrdných, Staré Město, Prague 1 (222 321 352). Metro Staroměstská/tram 17. **Open** *Box office* 1hr before performance. **Tickets** 200-600 Kč. **No credit cards. Map** p328 L2.
Renovated with cunning trompe l'oeil work, this deconsecrated church is now a full-time venue for chamber music. It serves as an extra hall for some of the major ensembles and orchestras in the city, and is a popular venue during festivals.

ARTS & ENTERTAINMENT

Rudolfinum.

Lichtenštejnský palác
Lichtenstein Palace
*Malostranské náměstí 13, Malá Strana, Prague 1
(257 534 205). Metro Malostranská/tram 12, 22.*
Open 10am-7.30pm daily. **Tickets** 30-100 Kč.
Credit MC, V. **Map** p327 F3.
The Lichtenstein Palace is the striking, formal and
elegant home of the Czech Academy of Music.
Concerts, which usually start at about 7.30pm, are
given in the Gallery and in the Martinů Hall; watch
for summer recitals in the lovely courtyard.

Lobkovický palác
Lobkowicz Palace
*Jiřská 3, Hradčany, Prague 1 (233 312 925/
www.lobkowiczevents.cz). Metro Malostranská/
tram 22.* **Open** 10.30am-6pm daily. **Tickets**
390 Kč. **No credit cards. Map** p327 E2.
Concerts of baroque and Romantic chamber works
are held in the imposing banquet hall of the
Lobkowicz Palace, which is also a historical museum
of princely collections. The palace boasts stunning
frescoes by Fabián Harovník. Concerts are held
daily at 1pm.
▶ *There's more about the palace on p67.*

Zrcadlová kaple
Chapel of Mirrors
*Klementinum, Mariánské náměstí, Staré Město,
Prague 1 (222 220 879/www.klementinum.com).
Metro Staroměstská/tram 17, 18.* **Open** *Box
office* 10am-8pm daily. **Tickets** from 650 Kč.
No credit cards. Map p328 K4.

This pink marble chapel in the vast Clementinum
complex hosts all manner of Romantic, baroque and
original chamber and organ recitals – oddly enough,
along with regular Gershwin – and is seemingly a
world away from the tourist hordes outside.
Concerts usually start at 6pm.
▶ *For more on the Clementinum, see p89.*

OPERA

Prague's opera houses concentrate on the
Czech repertoire, but they've become more
cosmopolitan in recent years. The **State
Opera** continues to reinvigorate work that's
been left in the shadows: Camille Saint-Saëns'
one-act opera *Hélène*, for instance, which hadn't
had a public airing in a century. Although
National Theatre operas are usually performed
with English subtitles, those at the State Opera,
sung in the original language, generally are not.

Národní divadlo
National Theatre
*Národní 2, Nové Město, Prague 1 (224 901 448/
www.narodni-divadlo.cz). Metro Národní třída/
tram 6, 9, 17, 18, 22.* **Open** *Box office* 10am-
6pm daily. Closed July & Aug. **Tickets** 30-1,400
Kč. **Credit** AmEx, MC, V. **Map** p330 J7.
Smetana was a guiding light behind the establishment of the National Theatre, which opened in 1883
with a performance of his opera *Libuše*. But although
the building is almost sacred, performances are vital.
The theatre concentrates on Czech opera, the core of

Prague Spring.

the repertoire being works by Smetana and Dvořák (including lesser-known works such as Dvořák's *The Devil and Kate*). Operas by non-Czech composers and impressive ballets are also performed; there are generally five or six major new productions a year year.
▶ *Read more about the theatre on p105; for its theatrical performances, see p271.*

★ Státní Opera
State Opera
Wilsonova 4, Nové Město, Prague 2 (224 227 266/www.opera.cz). Metro Muzeum/tram 11. **Open** *Box office* 10am-5.30pm Mon-Fri; 10am-noon, 1-5.30pm Sat, Sun. **Tickets** 200-900 Kč. **No credit cards. Map** p331 P7.
The State Opera (originally the German Theatre) opened in 1887, and was regarded as one of the finest German opera houses outside Germany until World War II. After the war, it changed its name to the Smetana Theatre, and became an outpost of the National Theatre; today, it's a separate organisation, and presents consistently bold contemporary opera alongside standards from the Italian, German, French and Russian repertoires.

Stavovské divadlo
Estates Theatre
Ovocný trh 1, Staré Město, Prague 1 (information 224 228 503/box office 224 215 001/www.estates theatre.cz). Metro Můstek or Staroměstská/tram 3, 9, 14, 17, 18, 24. **Open** *Box office* 10am-6pm daily. **Tickets** 700-1,050 Kč. **Credit** MC, V. **Map** p328 M4.
As you might expect at this shrine for Mozart lovers – where, as they'll endlessly remind you, *Don Giovanni* and *La Clemenza di Tito* had their premieres – there's a steady stream of the Austrian's works. But the theatre, built by Count Nostitz in 1784 and now fully restored, also offers interesting lesser-known work: Gaetano Donizetti's *Don Pasquale* and Theodor Veidl's *Die Kleinstädter*, for instance. Much of the programming is given over to theatre, but there's still regular opera – including, of course, *Don Giovanni*.
▶ *For more on the theatre, see p91 and p272.*

FESTIVALS

The best news of late on the festival circuit has been the improvement of the summer programme. Although major orchestras and opera companies still shut down for July and August, the Prague Philharmonia and the Czech National Symphony Orchestra now run mini-festivals in summer, a nice mix of the standard classical repertoire and the Czech masters.

Another winning summertime fest is the baroque concert series staged by **Collegium Marianum** (224 229 462, www.tynska.cuni.cz), Prague's premier baroque ensemble, in some of the city's most ornate and atmospheric small halls. Several summer festivals are also held

out of town; for more information, contact the **Prague Information Service** (*see p315*).

In the autumn, visit the annual **Modern Music Marathon** at the Archa Theatre (www.archatheatre.cz), and the **Martinů Festival** in early December (www.martinu.cz), which honours the excellent 20th-century Czech composer Bohuslav Martinů.

Events are listed in chronological order.

★ Pražské jaro
Prague Spring
257 310 414/www.festival.cz. **Tickets** from 200 Kč. **Credit** AmEx, MC, V. **Map** p327 F5. **Date** May, June.
Now into its seventh decade, Prague Spring is still the heavyweight among local music festivals. It's had a stronger international flavour since the Velvet Revolution, and attracts first-class international performers such as violinist Gil Shaham and pianist Garrick Ohlsson. The festival typically opens with *Má Vlast* (*My Country*), Smetana's patriotic cycle of symphonic poems, and concludes with Beethoven's Ninth. However, it's also kept up with the times, expanding its parameters in recent years to include contemporary musicians such as jazz pianist Herbie Hancock and young sitar star Anoushka Shankar.
Many of the big events sell out quickly; it's best to get tickets from the festival office rather than from ticket agencies, which add a mark-up. The office opens a month before the festival, and there are two price ranges: one for tickets sold in Prague and one for those booked from abroad.

Letní slavnosti staré hudby
Summer Festival of Old Music
Collegium Marianum, Melantrichova 19, Staré Město, Prague 1 (224 229 462/www.tynska. cuni.cz). Metro Staroměstská/tram 17, 18. **Admission** from 120 Kč. **Date** July.
This increasingly popular gala of Renaissance and baroque music, performed on period instruments and in historic settings, is one of the few native musical offerings during the summer holidays. It also attracts some of the finest performers around.

Pražsky podzim
Prague Autumn
222 540 484/www.pragueautumn.cz. **Tickets** from 90 Kč. **Credit** AmEx, MC, V. **Map** p333 B1. **Date** Sept-Oct.
Prague Autumn seems to be gaining on its bigger brother, with an increasingly diverse programme and headliners from the Bamberger Symphony to the Vienna Radio Symphony Orchestra.

Struny podzimu
Strings of Autumn
224 901 247/www.strunypodzimu.cz. **Tickets** 80-1,100 Kč. **Credit** AmEx, MC, V. **Map** p330 J7. **Date** Oct, Nov.

ARTS & ENTERTAINMENT

With bold new ideas and concerts at the National Theatre and the Rudolfinum, this well-established festival is known for lining up international performers in a wide range of genres. Recent stars have included Czech rocker Lenka Dusilová and top baroque ensemble Les Arts Florissants.

Rock, Roots & Jazz

In Prague, as many people admire Václav Havel for his friendship with the Rolling Stones as they do for his moral leadership. Indeed, rock was at the centre of the dissident movement: it was mainly for their right to party and be left alone by the authorities that many students and hippies got involved in politics after the Soviet-led invasion of 1968. After 1989, the revelry resumed, and hasn't let up since.

Czech rock doesn't always export well: many of the country's iconic bands, such as Už jsme doma and Psí vojáci, are acquired tastes. Still, there is some approachable music being made: modern acts focus on interesting alchemies, skillfully fusing electronica, Latin, Middle Eastern, acoustic and funk elements with Czech and traditional rock.

Tickets & information

Ticket prices are aimed at the Czech market, so seeing megastars in Prague is often a bargain. Book ahead for big-name concerts, especially at small venues – though at the funkier ones, you'll need to buy directly from the venue.

The *Prague Post*'s pullout section 'Night & Day' (online at www.praguepost.com) lists the hippest shows, and carries a handy calendar of those coming in the next week. The expat website **PragueTV** (http://prague.tv) shows events for the next month, as does **ticketpro.cz**. Otherwise, fliers with the latest information are invariably piled up at clubs such as **Radost FX**, **U Malého Glena** and the **Globe Bookstore & Coffeehouse**. For sounds with a digital bent, **www.techno.cz/party** still has the best gen around, usually with a bit of English text to help with directions and contacts.

ROCK & POP

Major shows

Prague's largest venue, the 200,000-capacity **Stadium Strahov**, has been played in the past by President Havel's mates, the Rolling Stones. Shows are more frequent at **T-Mobile Arena**, though the sound quality at both is poor.

Abaton

Na Košince 8 (off Povltavská), Libeň, Prague 8 (no phone/www.prostorabaton.cz). Metro Palmovka/tram 12, 14, 24.
Not many places these days offer the thrill of early 1990s Prague, when revelry happened in disused industrial spaces and licences were a non-issue. Located in the former Interplast factory and running a big programme of concerts and parties, Abaton still delivers that rush. Events vary greatly, from the recent Get Punked confab to hip hop nights, but two

Lucerna Music Bar. *See p248.*

Sound Czech

Venture off the beaten musical path and seek out some local bands.

Although there are far fewer venues for live music than there were in the '90s, rock music continues to thrive in Prague. During the Velvet Revolution, the **Plastic People of the Universe** were made into unintentional martyrs. Events such as this are still a decent measure of the importance of music to young Czechs.

The acts that pack local concert halls don't always have universal appeal. Take folk/pop **Divokej Bill**, whose fairly silly softcore video for 'Malování' (on YouTube) is representative of his style. Part of the reason is that Czech fans delight in lyrics with double meanings, irony and riffing on their native tongue that's impossible to translate. Other acts are more mainstream. With a following dating to the mid '80s, **Lucie** is led by David Koller, a singer/songwriter still held in high regard for his anthems to change.

Elsewhere, **Sto Zvířat** (100 Animals) have been firing up ska parties for over a decade, and are always worth a look. **Monkey Business**, a hugely popular brassy funk band, also offers a guaranteed good time. **JAR**, staffed by some of the county's top rockers and jazz players, is more nuanced, with a nice palette of tones and moods (if few concert dates these days).

Moody, intellectual **Psí Vojáci** (Dog Soldiers), led by pianist/songwriter Filip Topol with lyrics co-written by his novelist brother Jachym, has issued standout recordings over the past 15 years and still delivers transcendent shows on those rare dates when the group still performs. Another long-respected fave is the band **Čechomor**, which combines Moravian folk rhythms and traditional arrangements and songs with modern rock.

mainstays are the top-drawer sound and lights. Dance, chill, cavort at one of the bars or just explore the caverns. Concerts generally start around 8.30pm.

Kongresové centrum
Congress Centre
5 května 65, Vyšehrad, Prague 4 (261 171 111/ www.kcp.cz). Metro Vyšehrad/tram 18, 24.
Shows in the 2,764-capacity hall of the Congress Centre always feel a bit odd, thanks to the ghosts of its former life as the locus of Communist Party congresses. Still, even when seated on outsized auditorium chairs designed for bureaucratic backsides, you're likely in for a remarkable show: BB King, Tom Waits, Lou Reed and Björk have all played here. Many touches of Old Guard faux cool still remain – the bar areas, for one thing, are a wonder.

O2 Arena
Ocelářská 460, Vysočany, Prague 9 (266 121 122/ www.sazkaticket.cz). Metro Českomoravská/tram 3.
The city's newest major arena usually offers performers that are markedly less inspiring than the impressive, soaring hall. But if you must see what's left of Queen, or Holiday on Ice, this is the place. At least the beer stands are fuelled by high-power pumps.
▶ *The arena is also home to the Slavia Praha hockey team; see p261.*

Stadium Strahov
Diskařská 100, Břevnov, Prague 6 (233 014 111). Metro Karlovo náměstí, then bus 176 or tram 22 to Újezd, then funicular. Map p326 A6.

The biggest concert venue in town is a concrete monstrosity built before World War II without much to offer besides its ability to accommodate epic rock shows – which, these days, are booked more rarely than ever. Getting here is a bit of a trek; a special bus service is laid on for larger gigs.

Tesla Arena
Výstaviště, Za elektrárnou 319, Holešovice, Prague 7 (266 727 411). Metro Nádraží Holešovice/tram 5, 12, 17. Map p332 E1.
Prague's corporate fortunes can be gauged in the name of this ice hockey rink-cum-concert hall. Once the Paegas Arena and then the T-Mobile Arena, it's still an old, drafty and sonically challenged venue, but it's charming in its own way – especially when the resident Sparta Praha play.

Smaller venues

★ Akropolis
Kubelíkova 27, Žižkov, Prague 3 (296 330 911/www.palacakropolis.cz). Metro Jiřího z Poděbrad/tram 5, 9, 11, 26, 55, 58. **Open** *Divadelní Bar* 7pm-5am daily. *Malá Scená Bar* 7pm-3am daily. **Concerts** 7.30pm. **Admission** from 90 Kč. **No credit cards. Map** p333 C2.
Still the city's most soulful venue, this 1927 art deco theatre and coffeehouse is alive and more than kicking in the heart of Žižkov. The Akropolis lives up to its official billing as a cultural centre, with avant-garde stage plays, indie rock and world music. The main basement stage boasts lights and sound as

good as any in Prague, but stages groups you won't witness anywhere else in the city. The Divadelní (theatre) Bar has nightly DJs and occasional MCs, all for free, while the Malá Scena features live jams and red-lit sofas. The former street-level coffeehouse is now a restaurant and pub.

Batalion Music Club

28 Řijna 3, Staré Město, Prague 1 (220 108 148/www.batalion.cz). Metro Můstek/tram 3, 9, 14, 24. **Open** 24hrs daily. **Concerts** times vary. **Admission** free. **No credit cards**. **Map** p328 M5.

When nothing else is open and no one in your party can be bothered to leave the centre of town, you may find yourself considering Batalion. Think twice: it's warm, dry and open all night… but so is the main train station, which may be more fun. The programme consists of loud rock DJs and the occasional 'revival' act doing Doors covers in heavy accents.

Futurum

Zborovská 7, Smíchov, Prague 5 (257 328 571/ www.musicbar.cz). Metro Anděl/tram 6, 9, 12. **Open** 8pm-3am daily. **Concerts** 9pm. **Admission** from 100 Kč. **No credit cards**.

Forming a clubbing beacon for the Smíchov district, Futurum is a remade community centre, with a formal exterior that belies the hip and groovy space within. Though it's given over to pop DJs on Fridays and Saturdays, concerts here are the real appeal. Fun local rockers such as Traband play midweek; otherwise, odd American and Brit punk bands alternate with ska and electronica acts, among other genres. Take it in while perched at the mosaic-tiled long bar.

Klub 007

Vaníčkova 5, Koleje ČVUT dorm 7, Strahov, Prague 6 (257 211 439). Metro Dejvická, then bus 143, 149, 217. **Open** 7pm-midnight Mon-Sat. **Concerts** 9.30pm. **Admission** 40-100 Kč. **No credit cards**.

Student heaven – or, perhaps, hell. If you can find this place in the concrete basement of dorm 007, you'll never believe it could be a must on any international ska tour of Central Europe. But it is, as you'll discover when the bands start up. As authentic a youth vibe as you'll find, complete with cheap beer in plastic cups.

Lucerna Great Hall

Vodičkova 36, Nové Město, Prague 1 (224 225 440/www.lucpra.com). Metro Můstek/tram 3, 9, 14, 24, 52, 53, 55, 56. **Concerts** 7-8pm. **Admission** 200-900 Kč. **Credit** AmEx, MC, V. **Map** p329 N6.

Run independently from the Lucerna Music Bar (*see below*), this vast, pillared, underground hall hosts big-time acts from Maceo Parker to the Cardigans. Its art nouveau ballrooms, balconies, grand marble stairs and wooden floors add a palatial feel to rock

shows. Though it feels big and the sound can echo, you're always reasonably close to the band. There are no regular box office hours, so book ahead through an agent such as Ticketpro (*see p210*).
► For the Lucerna's cinema, see p223.

★ Lucerna Music Bar

Vodičkova 36, Nové Město, Prague 1 (224 217 108/www.musicbar.cz). Metro Můstek/tram 3, 9, 14, 24, 52, 53, 55, 56. **Open** 8pm-3am daily. **Concerts** 9pm. **Admission** 80 Kč; 80-300 Kč concerts. **No credit cards**. **Map** p329 N6.

You might not guess it from the threadbare and scuffed interiors of this hot club beneath Wenceslas Square, but this is a great spot. Jazz acts join local blues groups and the likes of Ladytron to further heat up this soulful spot when they raise the stage and everyone leans over the balconies to catch a better look. Enter the venue from the faded 1920s Lucerna Passage. One word of warning: '80s disco nights take over on Fridays and Saturdays, when there isn't a touring artist passing through town.

Malostranská beseda

Malostranské náměstí 21, Malá Strana, Prague 1 (257 532 092). Metro Malostranská/tram 12, 22, 57. **Open** 5pm-midnight daily. **Concerts** 8.30pm or 9.30pm. **Admission** 80 Kč. **No credit cards**. **Map** p327 F3.

Following a massive reconstruction, this venerated local rock venue is set to reopen in mid 2009. When it does, some of the most beloved Prague bands will once again return to their home venue, an imposing former lecture salon on Malá Strana's main square. It's also a gallery space with fantastic views through the windows that overlook palaces and churches.

Meloun

Michalská 12, Staré Město, Prague 1 (224 230 126/www.meloun.cz). Metro Můstek/tram 3, 9, 14, 24, 51, 52, 53, 54, 55, 56, 57, 58. **Open** 11am-3am daily. **Concerts** 9pm. **Admission** 80-100 Kč. **No credit cards**. **Map** p328 L5.

Strictly local, smoke-filled and loud, the Mellon is often packed with Czech pop and disco fans, but occasionally breaks the bad DJ habit with a good blues night. More often, though, it's album tracks better left in the pre-1989 community hall of a small Bohemian village. The cellar pub also offers occasional film screenings; during summer, the attached garden pub offers Czech schnitzels and the like.

Rock Café

Národní třída 20, Nové Město, Prague 1 (224 933 947/www.rockcafe.cz). Metro Národní třída/ tram 6, 9, 18, 22, 51, 54, 57, 58. **Open** 10am-3am Mon-Fri; 5pm-3am Sat; 5pm-1am Sun. **Concerts** 9pm. **Admission** 90-150 Kč. **No credit cards**. **Map** p328 L6.

With a programme that ranges from the Frames to local cult talents such as Roe-Deer, this spacious

Profile Gipsy.cz

How Radoslav Banga is bringing a 21st-century sensibility to Gypsy culture.

Fusing traditional Gypsy (or Roma) rhythm and instruments with contemporary hip hop, rap and a political edge, Gipsy.cz is starting to make waves outside his homeland. In a nutshell, he's the Czech Republic's answer to Eminem – except that he's multilingual, and isn't shy about rapping in most of the languages he speaks.

Radoslav Banga was born in Prague, where he lived on the streets until the age of 13, when he discovered a love for music. After collaborating with local hip hop groups, he started working on his own, developing a distinctive style that introduced Roma language and instruments such as violins, accordions and double basses alongside more modern streetwise sounds.

'I feel myself like a new generation of tradition,' Gipsy explained in an interview with Radio Prague. 'Hip hop's already been done. Black people from the States, from France, white people from Europe – everybody's already said what had to be said. Now I'm here and I'm trying to do something completely new.'

Gipsy's music comes with a political message, but it's not one you might expect. While his songs are often critical of the discrimination that many of the Roma community experience in the Czech Republic, Gipsy isn't averse to poking fun at his own people. Take the very stylishly produced video to *Čekuj*, which starts with a group of Gypsies breaking into a car. But the scene is a comic one, which, says Gipsy, is important. 'I believe that the point must be radical and also funny. That way, people can't judge you. They smile, but feel that there is something deeper.'

Gipsy's musical talent was first recognised on the national stage in 2006, when he won the title of Best New Artist at the Angel awards (the Czech equivalent of the Grammies). Since then, he's toured Europe and played at both the Notting Hill Carnival and Glastonbury, and his two albums have both made it into the top ten of the World Music Charts Europe. It seems that there's a bright future ahead for this rising star.

FURTHER LISTENING
Check out either of Gipsy.cz's albums, *Romano Hip Hop* and *Reprezent*.

ARTS & ENTERTAINMENT

U Malého Glena.

underground hall is one of the bastions of live rock and blues in the city. Rock Café has an impassioned local following, folk who appreciate its embrace of the strange, and its unpretentious bunker-like qualities. It's regained its pioneering mettle of late, and a new dawn seems to be breaking for this old favourite.

★ Roxy

Dlouhá 33, Staré Město, Prague 1 (224 826 296/ www.roxy.cz). Metro Náměstí Republiky/tram 5, 14, 26, 51, 53, 54. **Open** 7pm-2am Mon-Thur; 7pm-4am Fri, Sat. *DJ events* from 10pm. *Live acts* from 8pm. **Admission** *DJs events* 100-250 Kč. *Live acts* 150-450 Kč. **No credit cards**. **Map** p328 L3.

Although dominated by club culture, the Roxy also hosts live acts, generally to accompany the digital stuff but occasionally standing alone. The space itself is a wonder of a crumbling former movie house that attracts and sponsors artists of all genres, with the main proviso that they're weird.

▶ *For the clubbing side of the operation, see p257.*

★ Vagon

Národní třída 25, Nové Město, Prague 1 (221 085 599/www.vagon.cz). Metro Národní třída/ tram 6, 9, 17, 18, 22. **Open** 6pm-5am Mon-Sat; 6pm-1am Sun. **Concerts** 9pm. **Admission** 60 Kč. **No credit cards**. **Map** p328 L6.

This smoky little cellar hosts bands playing fresh, unrecorded rock, jam nights and reggae, live and on the sound system. It's just a student bar, but one with a love for chilled-out, dreadlocked hanging-out. The entrance is hidden in a shopping passage.

JAZZ & BLUES

Prague's jazz history stretches back to the 1930s, when Jaroslav Ježek led an adored big band while colleague RA Dvorský established a standard of excellence that survived Nazi and communist oppression. Karel Velebný, of the renowned Studio 5 group, continued that tradition after the war, and Czech-Canadian novelist Josef Škvorecký chronicled the eternal struggle of Czech sax men in book after book.

These days, the jazz scene occupies a lower echelon, but a corps of talented players works the city circuit to such an extent that you often find the same dozen top players in most of the venues. The clubs are far more affordable than their counterparts in Western Europe, even if it means that the musicians, and sometimes the clubs themselves, are often struggling to get by.

AghaRTA

Železná 16, Staré Město, Prague 1 (222 211 275/ www.agharta.cz). Metro Můstek/Národní třída/ tram 6, 9, 18, 22. **Open** *Club* 7pm-1am daily. *Concerts* 9pm. *Jazz shop* 5pm-midnight Mon-Fri; 7pm-midnight Sat, Sun. **Admission** 200 Kč. **No credit cards**. **Map** p331 O8.

Named after one of Miles Davis's most controversial LPs, this dyed-in-the-wool jazz mecca has moved to Old Town from its old digs off Wenceslas Square, but has kept its following intact. The owners run the AghaRTA fest, which has brought the likes of Chic Corea and John McLaughlin to town, but regular local acts such as saxman Franta Kop bassist Robert Balzar are well worth catching. Look out for releases on the club's own ARTA label.

Blues Sklep

Liliova 10, Staré Město, Prague 1 (221 466 138/ www.bluessklep.cz). Metro Můstek/tram 3, 9, 14, 24. **Open** 7pm-midnight daily. **Concerts** 9pm. **Admission** free. **No credit cards**. **Map** p328 K5.

A steady line-up of local artists and the occasional touring band draw regular crowds to the Blues Cellar. It's an intimate, relaxed space, which suits the music well – but don't go expecting top-flight performances. Still, with shows running 9pm to midnight, it won't take up the whole night.

Charles Bridge Jazz Club

*Saská 3, Malá Strana, Prague 1 (257 220 820/
www.jazzblues.cz). Metro Můstek or Náměstí
Republiky/tram 3, 5, 9, 14, 24, 26.* **Open** 7pm-
midnight daily. **Concerts** 9.15pm. **Admission**
150-300 Kč. **No credit cards. Map** p327 G4.
The highest-priced jazz club in town (drinks
included) doesn't catch much of a local crowd, but it
does offer a solid line-up of jazzers and funkers in a
groovy stone-walled space, with programming by
owners who know their stuff – they also organise
shows by the likes of Bill Frisell and Mike Stern.

★ U Malého Glena

*Karmelitská 23, Malá Strana, Prague 1 (257 531
717/www.malyglen.cz). Metro Malostranská/
tram 12, 22, 57.* **Open** 8am-2am daily. **Concerts**
9pm. **Admission** 100-150 Kč. **No credit cards.
Map** p327 F5.
A nice little double act, Little Glenn's is a relaxed,
dimly lit bar and restaurant at street level, and a
downstairs club that heats up fast with primo local
players and a few talents from abroad. Blues
Wednesday with the Rene Trossman Band is an
institution; Groove with Jan Kořínek delivers retro
Hammond sounds; Sunday jams let you try out
your own riffs.
▶ *You can also stay here: the new Uncle Glenn's
apartments start at 1,950 Kč a night.*

Reduta

*Národní třída 20, Nové Město, Prague 1 (224
933 487/www.redutajazzclub.cz). Metro Národní
třída/tram 6, 9, 18, 22, 51, 54, 57, 58.* **Open**
Box office 5-9pm daily. *Club* 9pm-12.30am daily.
Concerts 9pm. **Admission** 200 Kč. **No credit
cards. Map** p328 J6.
Part of Prague history since 1958, Reduta is not generally home to the young Turks, but it does have a
distinctive vibe (even if it's a bit sad that it still touts
Bill Clinton's visit with sax of so many years ago).
The cramped bench seating hasn't changed in years,
and the venue charges tourist prices. Still, the acts
are as talented as any in Prague, if decidedly older
and softer; and you'll be seeing them up close and
personal. Just mind the coat-check guy who asks for
your jacket, presumably in hopes of a tip.

U staré paní

*Michalská 9, Staré Město, Prague 1 (224 228
090/www.ustarepani.cz). Metro Můstek/Národní
třída/tram 6, 9, 18, 22.* **Open** 7pm-2am daily.
Concerts 9pm. **Admission** 150 Kč. **Credit**
AmEx, MC, V. **Map** p328 L5.
In the cellar of the hotel of the same name (with
good soundproofing, obviously), this is one of Old
Town's top venues for local talents. It's a dark
space, with modern decor and a few decent wines
at the back bar. The Old Lady forms a club in more
ways than one, with players and audiences well
known to each other. This can be good and bad: a

bit more competitive pressure might improve some
of the more self-indulgent acts that take to the
stage. But it's all in good fun.

FOLK & COUNTRY

Many visitors seem surprised by the Czech
obsession with cowboy culture. But Bohemian
settlers in Mexico and Praha (Texas) fired up
a passion back home that's still red hot, and
'trampers' – avid hikers and campers – still
won't leave their block housing without a
battered guitar and a list of campfire songs.

U Bocmana

*Korunní 101, Vinohrady, Prague 2 (224 256
131). Metro Náměstí Míru/tram 4, 10, 16, 22.*
Open 11am-11pm Mon; 11am-midnight Tue-Fri;
5pm-midnight Sat; 6-11pm Sun. **Admission** 20
Kč. **No credit cards. Map** p333 B4.
Formerly known as Country Saloon Amerika, which
seems to have now been relegated to nickname status, this downhome pub is still every Czech cow-
punch's dream, with big steaks on the grill and
regular bluegrass fiddle jams on the programme.

FESTIVALS

Festivals are staged all year round in Prague.
In summer, almost every weekend sees blues,
world, soul or rock bands performing under
trees, in palaces or at other incongruous venues.

Prague Jazz Festival

Various venues (222 211 275/www.agharta.cz).
Admission varies. **Date** Feb-Oct.
One of the hottest jazz fests in Central Europe, the
Prague Jazz Festival features world-class players
like John Scofield and Marcus Miller. Sponsored by
the AghaRTA club (*see p250*), the festival is small
but persistent, carrying on throughout the spring,
summer and autumn, with performances mainly at
the Lucerna Music Bar (*see p248*).

Respect

*Various venues (222 710 050/mobile 603 461
592/www.respectmusic.cz).* **Admission** from 120
Kč. **Date** June.
The world and ethnic music high point of the year
features Balkan folk and Gypsy music, with performers such as Taraf de Haidouks. The organiser
is Prague's main underground and ethnic music
label, Rachot; concerts are usually staged at the
Akropolis (*see p247*).

United Islands of Prague

Various venues (www.unitedislands.cz).
Admission varies. **Date** June.
Concerts and beer stands take over the Vltava riverfront; performers include musicians local and global,
and names as big as Iggy Pop and Placebo.

Nightlife

Welcome to Bohemia after dark.

Prague has always been liveliest at night, with after-dark venues acting as both the social glue and the social balm that lifts the morale of Czech society. Things start to get interesting after the traditional pubs close (most shut at 11pm), and the crowd changes dramatically. The city isn't known for its dance clubs, but the scene is uninhibited; a welter of casinos (*see p259*) and adult clubs (*see p260*) offer further after-hours naughtiness. Prague's city fathers have become concerned about the town's clubs in recent years. But other than fretting about the amount of neon and sleaze on Wenceslas Square, no one seems to do much to change things, and the scene remains loud and popular.

ARTS & ENTERTAINMENT

CLUBS

Prague's dance clubs can get pretty tacky unless you stick to the venues that are clearly about the music and the good-time crowds. The **Roxy** and **Akropolis** have won and kept clubbers' hearts over the years, while ventures such as **Matrix** and **Cross Club** are deeply devoted to the underground scene. Elsewhere, the likes of **Vertigo**, **Duplex**, **Celnice** and **Mecca** are good bets if you want to watch the newly wealthy show off their winter tans, hair gel and chat-up lines.

The scene is changing all the time. Clubs are even more ephemeral in Prague than elsewhere, in part because they tend to share buildings with residential spaces, and Czechs are early risers – thus making for uneasy relationships between clubs and their neighbours.

The other unique aspect of Prague clubbing is a feeling of anarchy that could only be found in a place with virtually no safety regulations or political correctness. Bar-top stripping, crumbling walls and rampant stimulant use can all be found in Staré Město on any Friday night. That said, you're on your own if you're caught with drugs. Czech police may arrest anyone in possession of what they deem 'more than a little' of a controlled substance, and your embassy may take little interest in your story.

U Bukanýra

Na Františku embankment (nr Štefánik Bridge), Staré Město, Prague 1 (mobile 777 891 348/ www.bukanyr.cz). **Open** 7pm-3am Thur; 9pm-6am Fri, Sat. *Metro Staroměstská/tram 17, 18, 51, 54.* **Admission** free-100 Kč. **No credit cards**. **Map** p329 M1.

The programme at this floating barge party can be iffy. House DJs hold sway when At the Buccaneer is operating, but it's not unheard of for the club to go dark for weeks at a time. Still, it's good fun when it's open, and has a very central location.

★ Bordo

Vinohradská 40, Žižkov, Prague 3 (mobile 733 165 166/www.bordo.cz). Metro Náměstí Republiky/tram 5, 8, 14, 51. **Open** *Restaurant* 11am-2am daily. *Club* 10pm-4am Thur; 11pm-4am Fri, Sat. **Admission** 50-200 Kč. **Credit** AmEx, MC, V. **Map** p333 A3.

Inside this multipurpose building, your quarry is upstairs. Bordo seems to be permanently in a state of renovation but always generates a buzz, booking the coolest underground DJs and occasional live bands. Inside its black-washed walls, you'll find infectiously fun nights organised by groups such as

---

INSIDE TRACK
GETTING HOME

Any tram with a number in the 50s is a night tram, which you'll need after the metro shuts down at midnight. At the end of a long evening, a night tram is an experience in itself.

Hats Off!

At long last, Prague welcomes the relaunch of a clubbing stalwart.

A jam-packed club where backpackers cross swords with hip locals and clubbing expats, the **Chapeau Rouge** (*listings below*) has always been more about reputation than actual appeal. But while its credibility has never been in doubt, long-term patrons will scarcely believe their eyes when they next head to the old place. A stunning renovation has transformed the Chap, as the local indie 'zines invariably call it, into a three-storey party palace, with three stages, four bars and a nightly line-up of powerhouse DJs and live acts. And in a city where clubs seem to die off even faster than the industry standard, this transformation has come just in time.

As ever, the street-level bar is a free-entry, red-walled space in which to cavort, flirt, drink and confuse the bartenders, who never seem to count up totals. (They've traditionally thrown the take into a lock-box, an old tradition whose origins

have long since been lost.) Dubbed the Dance Club, the first-level underground doubles the bar space with bench seating, a cooler colour scheme, a powerful sound system, monitors, impressive light racks and its own drinks counter. And the second level down, officially known as Chateau Underground, offers another sound stage, another bar and all the technical add-ons you can imagine (in classic Czech fashion, a full description of the technical spec is posted on the club's website).

Programming runs from a night called Blackmania (Czechs are fond of saying 'I love black music', a phrase that generally covers anything from blues to soul to funk to hip hop) to shows from bands such as Dorian Gray's Prostitutes. All in all, it adds up to the hottest news to hit Prague clubbing in years – and not a moment too soon.

www.hiphopfest.cz. In short, it's how clubbing used to be in Prague's mid-'90s salad days.

Bukowski's

Bořivojova 86, Žižkov, Prague 3 (no phone). Metro Náměstí Míru/tram 9, 11, 26, 51, 55, 58. **Open** 8pm-2am daily. **Admission** free. **No credit cards. Map** p333 C2.

Launched as an alternative to the Žižkov district's countless beer pubs, this self-billed dive bar is a magnet for mischievous expats, bohemians and pretty much everyone else for whom the name might hold some appeal. Owner Glen Emery, a Prague bartending legend, makes good times just about guaranteed at this rollicking little joint, done out in the classic British pub style (plus the odd glass art light fixture).

U Buldoka

Preslova 1, Smíchov, Prague 5 (257 329 154/ www.ubuldoka.cz). Metro Anděl/tram 4, 6, 7, 9, 10, 12, 14, 20, 54. **Open** 11am-4am Mon-Thur; 11am-5am Fri; noon-5am Sat. **Admission** 30-50 Kč. **No credit cards.**

With Staropramen beer and excellent traditional grub, the Bulldog is a classic cheap Czech pub with the twist that it manages to conceal a groovin' club below. The space is done up in the prevailing retro style, with the usual Czech DJs. Nights such as Mojito Mania and Shake Weekends are notable for the barmen's displays of flying bottles that seem to obsess Praguers.

Celnice

V celnici 4, Nové Město, Prague 1 (224 212 240/ www.clubcelnice.com). Metro Náměstí Republiky/ tram 5, 8, 14, 51, 54. **Open** *Restaurant* 11am-2am daily. *Club* 10pm-4am Thur; 11pm-4am Fri, Sat. **Admission** *Men* 100 Kč. *Women* free. **Credit** AmEx, MC, V. **Map** p329 O3.

Old Town's former customs house is unrecognisable these days, as lithe, slick clubbers scrum for VIP area reservations or turn out for the cheesy Moscow Night. It's good for a sociology survey, possibly, or a pick-up if you're sufficiently buffed and bankrolled; otherwise, it's about the last place in Prague in which to experience memorable mixing or meet someone interesting. You have to love the space-age gold mosaic interior, and the upstairs trad Czech restaurant is pretty capable.

Chapeau Rouge

Jakubská 2, Prague 1 (222 316 328/www. chapeaurouge.cz). Metro Náměstí Republiky/ tram 5, 14, 26. **Open** noon-3am Mon-Thur; noon-6am Fri; 4pm-4am Sat; 4pm-2am Sun. **No credit cards. Map** p328 M3.
See p179 and above **Hats Off!**.

Le Clan

Balbínova 23, Žižkov, Prague 3 (no phone/ www.leclan.cz). Metro Náměstí Míru/tram 11, 51. **Open** 2am-10am Thur, Fri; 2am-noon Sat, Sun. **Admission** varies. **Credit** MC, V. **Map** p333 A3.

Offering that thrill of insider exclusivity yet with a surprisingly democratic ethic, Le Clan only advertises itself at street level with a small glowing crescent moon and a red-lit buzzer. However, it's no den of illicit activity, just a comfortable, surprisingly old-fashioned lounge bar hidden on two levels below a quiet street. Capable at cocktails, it makes a lovely late-night hangout.

★ Cross Club

Plynární 23 (mobile 736 535 053/www.cross club.cz). Metro Nádraží Holešovice/tram 5, 15, 53, 54. **Open** 4pm-3am Mon-Fri; 4pm-5am Sat, Sun. **Map** p332 F4.

It may look like a car spares shop, but don't be deceived as you hike north from the Metro station to find it. This magnet for arty types is a centre for music, film, dance and drink, and every surface has been welded or moulded, gallery-style, into what is the city's hippest art bar – and a raw and laid-back one at that, altogether unpretentious. *Photo p256.*

Double Trouble

Melantrichova 17, Staré Město, Prague 1 (221 632 414/www.doubletrouble.cz). Metro Můstek or Staroměstská/tram 3, 6, 9, 14, 18, 22, 24, 51, 52, 54, 55, 56, 58. **Open** 7pm-4am Mon-Thur, Sun; 7pm-5am Fri, Sat. **Admission** free-180 Kč. **No credit cards. Map** p328 L4.

Were it not for geography and the relentless spread of Brit stag parties, this might have had a shot at being a decent club. As it is, you're more than likely to be sharing the place with three Kevs and a Nigel stripping off on the bar to the delight of their mates. If you're not one of them, best move on. Trouble indeed.

★ Duplex

Václavské náměstí 21, Nové Město, Prague 1 (mobile 732 221 111/www.duplexduplex.cz). Metro Můstek/tram 3, 9, 14, 24, 51, 52, 54, 55, 56, 58. **Open** *Café* 10am-midnight daily. *Restaurant* noon-midnight daily. *Club* 9.30pm-2am Tue-Thur; 9.30pm-5am Fri, Sat. **Admission** 150 Kč. **Credit** AmEx, MC, V. **Map** p329 N6.

With themes such as Dirty Dancing and Love Parade, it's clear that Duplex isn't a place in which to find inspiringly original DJ programming. That said, the crisp sound system and eyrie of bars and dancefloors in a glass box high over Wenceslas Square make for a unique night out. Tuesdays are reserved for Afro-Latin sounds (like many Prague clubs, the genre changes nightly), and usually offer good sets and live music by the likes of local faves Son Caliente. There's dining on site and a chillout space on the terrace. *Photo p257.*

La Fabrique

Uhelný trh 2, Staré Město, Prague 1 (224 233 137). Metro Můstek or Národní třída/tram 6, 9, 18, 22, 53, 57, 58, 59. **Open** 5pm-2.45am Wed, Thur, Sun; 5pm-3.45am Fri, Sat. **Admission** free. **Credit** AmEx, MC, V. **Map** p328 L5.

Disco-lovers cram into this subterranean Staré Město club to hear nightmarish DJs who love to announce things over the tunes. Done up in factory decor, it's a maze of rooms with a narrow entrance just off the Havelská fruit market.

Guru Club

Rokycanova 29, Žižkov, Prague 3 (mobile 777 155 103/www.guru-club.cz). Metro Jiřího z Poděbrad/tram 5, 9, 26, 52. **Open** 2pm-2am Mon-Thur; 3pm-5am Fri-Sun. *Shows* 8pm or 9pm. **Admission** 30-200 Kč. **No credit cards.**

The Guru Club has a very irregular programme and, in that sense, is very Žižkov. With the right act in place, it can offer a brilliant dive-bar experience, but do some research before coming here unless you enjoy a gamble. It's a strange, worn-out, subterranean space with a split-level dancefloor, balconies and dazed bartenders. Staff ask for a deposit on glass beer mugs, which gives you an idea how rowdy the crowds get.

Jo's Bar & Garáž

Malostranské náměstí 7, Malá Strana, Prague 1 (257 530 162/www.josbar.cz). Metro Malostranská/tram 12, 20, 22, 57. **Open** 9pm-2am daily. **Admission** 50-100 Kč. **Credit** AmEx, MC, V. **Map** p327 F3.

Once a key venue on the expat clubbing scene, Jo's is pretty sleepy these days, but occasionally rouses itself for amusing parties for backpackers and students. It's another stone cellar club, two levels down from the once legendary bar that served the Czech Republic's first nachos to a crowd that's since grown up or fled the country. Worth a look if you happen to be in the area.

Karlovy Lázně

Novotného lávka 1, Staré Město, Prague 1 (222 220 502/www.karlovylazne.cz). Metro Staroměstská/tram 17, 18, 53. **Open** *Café* 11am-4am daily. *Club* 9pm-5am daily. **Admission** 50-120 Kč. **No credit cards. Map** p328 J5.

If you're drawn to the kind of club where teens line up for an hour to get in, this place is for you. It's the city's megaclub, set up in a former public baths building with five floors of clubbing action (a different genre on each); it's next to the Charles Bridge, which makes navigation easier when you're, like, totally wasted, dude. And it's every bit as spontaneous as you'd expect from its location.

Klub Lávka

Novotného lávka 1, Staré Město, Prague 1 (222 222 156/221 082 278/www.lavka.cz). Metro Staroměstská/tram 17, 18, 53. **Open** *Bar* 24hrs daily. *Disco* 9.30pm-5am daily. **Admission** 50-100 Kč. **Credit** AmEx, MC, V. **Map** p328 J5.

Le Clan. *See p253.*

Yes, it's more pop disco fever, but compared to the hulking commercialism of the next-door Karlovy Lázně (*see left*), it seems almost charming. There's a lovely river terrace at the back, go-go dancers, funk and disco sounds, and views of the Charles Bridge. In a town that still retires relatively early, the open-all-night aspect is quite an attraction.

Mánes

Masarykovo nábřeží 250, Nové Město, Prague 1 (224 931 112). Metro Karlovo náměstí/tram 17, 18, 53, 57, 58, 59. **Open** 11am-11pm daily. **Admission** 50-150 Kč. **No credit cards.** **Map** p330 J8.

This classy 1930s functionalist gallery combines art (it's the Czech Fund for Art Foundation's most important exhibition space) with another, living, culture: it's a run-down riverside dance venue with an amazing location. For a while, it specialised in Tropicana nights on Friday and Saturday; these days, the programme is unpredictable, but a beer on the terrace (open until 11pm) is never a bad idea.

Matrix

Koněvova 13, Žižkov, Prague 3 (mobile 776 611 042/www.matrixklub.cz). Metro Florenc, then bus 133, 207/tram 52. **Admission** free-120 Kč. **No credit cards.** **Map** p333 D1.

As underground as Neo himself, this former frozen meat plant knows its jungle and drum 'n' bass, booking hip DJs and other acts. It draws a young crowd of aficionados and adventurers, who seem to appreciate the noise, the shadows and the Gambrinus beer on tap. Occasional local heroes such as Babe LN play, as do international bands willing to do nearly-free shows, but generally it's a fringe line-up.

Mecca

U průhonu 3, Holešovice, Prague 7 (283 870 522/www.mecca.cz). Metro Vltavská/tram 1, 3, 12, 25, 54. **Open** *Club* 10pm-6am Fri, Sat. *Restaurant* 10am-11pm Mon-Thur; 10am-6am Fri; 8am-6am Sat. **Admission** 100-300 Kč. **No credit cards.** **Map** p332 F2.

These days, Mecca is a bit too slick for its own good, but it's still fun at times for its excesses. It was the first big club to set up in the burgeoning Holešovice district. Under new management, it still draws improbably beautiful people, but it all seems rather forced and posed. But it's still the biggest modern dance palace in the district, and does deliver powerful, clean sounds.

Misch Masch

Veletržní 61, Holešovice, Prague 7 (mobile 603 272 227/www.mischmasch.cz). Metro Vltavská/tram 1, 5, 15, 25, 26, 56. **Open** 8pm-6am daily. **Admission** 80-150 Kč. **No credit cards.**

This big, glittery club on the edge of the city centre is where locals who love mixing Malibu into their drinks come out to play. If the pounding pop tracks get tiresome (fairly likely), there are other clever entertainments such as the Barmaid Flair Challenge or the annual Miss Misch Masch (which, of course, is fairly naughty). Fascinating in its way, but be aware what you're getting into.

N11

Národní třída 11, Nové Město, Prague 1 (222 075 705/www.n11.cz). Metro Národní třída/tram 6, 9, 18, 22, 53, 57, 58, 59. **Open** 8pm-4am Tue-Thur; 7pm-5am Fri, Sat. **Admission** 80-150 Kč. **No credit cards.** **Map** p330 K6.

Cross Club. *See p254.*

With a fairly tame programme of pop, rock and reggae tracks laid down by skilled DJs, N11 doesn't set out to challenge. In fact, its owner – a doctor, social critic and sometime Senate candidate – set this place up to be a smoke- and drug-free party place (with decent food and reasonable prices). The club features a great sound system and light racks, and occasional live acts.

Nebe
Křemencova 10, Nové Město, Prague 1 (mobile 777 800 411/www.nebepraha.cz). Metro Národní třída/tram 6, 9, 18, 22, 53, 57, 58, 59. **Open** 8pm-4am Tue-Thur; 7pm-5am Fri, Sat. **Admission** 80-150 Kč. **No credit cards.** **Map** p330 K8.

It may not live up to its claim to have 'inimitable' atmosphere and 'delicious cocktails at very attractive prices', but Heaven provides a generally good time for clubbers on a budget, many of whom are foreign students. The bar has 50 drinks under 100 Kč, and the DJs know how to send out a good beat; no one's going to object to you snogging in a corner.

Občanská plovárna
U plovárny 8, Malá Strana, Prague 1 (257 531 451/www.obcanskaplovarna.cz). Metro Malostranská/tram 12, 17, 51, 56. **Open** 8pm-4am Tue-Thur; 7pm-5am Fri, Sat. **Admission** 80-150 Kč. **No credit cards. Map** p328 J1.

'You can do whatever you want,' reckons Prague's newest club, clearly a believer in the scattergun approach. Typical Fridays and Saturdays deliver live acts followed by '80s and '90s disco; at other times, you might get the Prague Poker Palooza cards festival or the So Pretty 'provocative fashion show'. Set in the former municipal pool on the Vltava's left bank, it's an appealing venue, with a well-stocked bar and wine cellar.

★ Popocafepetl
Újezd 19, Malá Strana, Prague 1 (mobile 602 277 226/www.popocafepetl.cz). Metro Malostranská/tram 12, 17, 58. **Open** 4pm-2am daily. **Admission** 80-150 Kč. **No credit cards.** **Map** p327 F6.

Student parties linked to Prague's Radio 1 pack the kids into this stone cellar: Friday and Saturday Dance Fever nights are clearly aimed at paying the rent. That said, Popocafepetl also puts on live Latin and world music acts during the week and on Sundays, so the overall mix is interesting. It's all very informal, loud and tipsy. Not to be confused with the same company's bar/restaurant in Vinohrady, for which *see p189.*

Punto Azul
Kroftova 1, Smíchov, Prague 5 (no phone/ www.puntoazul.cz). Tram 6, 9, 12, 20, 58, 59. **Open** 7pm-2am daily. **Admission** free-50 Kč. **No credit cards.**

Punto Azul is so far underground that you'll need canaries just to test the air. Despite the name, there's nothing Spanish about the place: it's just a student dive on every wirehead's map, with a dance space that isn't much bigger than a circuit board. Still, a

bad

consistent groove is achieved through a line-up of the city's more avant-garde house DJs.

★ Radost FX

Bělehradská 120, Nové Město, Prague 2 (224 254 776/www.radostfx.cz). Metro IP Pavlova/ tram 4, 6, 10, 11, 16, 22, 51, 56, 57, 59. **Open** 8.30am-4am Mon-Fri; 11am-6am Sat, Sun. *Club* 10pm-4am Thur-Sat. **Admission** 120-250 Kč. **No credit cards. Map** p331 P10.

Prague's original house party is going strong after more than a decade, with the best all-night mix you'll find in the city: a combination of creative veggie café, spaced-out backroom lounge and a small but slick downstairs club, which provides a first-class venue for fashion shows and local house and techno stars. *Photo p258.*

▶ *Radost FX also serves one of the best Sunday brunches in town; see p171.*

Retro Music Hall

Francouzská 4, Vinohrady, Prague 2 (mobile 603 476 747/www.retropraha.cz). Metro Malostranská/tram 12, 17, 51, 57, 59. **Open** 4pm-2am daily. **Admission** 80-150 Kč. **No credit cards. Map** p333 A4.

With a capacity of 1,200, Retro has revived a former party palace that went dark for years. The bar has been raised a bit, but the programme is still largely made up of student parties (sometimes with foam) and the occasional promise of 'the real rock concert' at weekends. One for the curious, bored or brave.

Roxy

Dlouhá 33, Staré Město, Prague 1 (224 826 296/www.roxy.cz). Metro Náměstí Republiky/ tram 5, 8, 14, 51, 54. **Open** 7pm-2am Mon-Thur; 7pm-4am Fri, Sat. *Party nights* 10pm-5am. **Admission** *DJ nights* 100-250 Kč. *Live events* 150-450 Kč. **No credit cards. Map** p328 L3.

The run-down Roxy is Prague's top destination for house, R&B and jungle, thanks largely to party organiser David Urban. Star acts no other club could afford get talked into doing shows here, as do local kings of the decks. Meanwhile, the Galerie NoD fills out the venue with multiple floors of cutting-edge, non-commercial culture and fringe art. Free Mondays pack the place with kids.

▶ *For live music at the Roxy, see p250.*

Sedm vlků

Vlkova 7, Žižkov, Prague 3 (222 711 725/ www.sedmvlku.cz). Metro Jiřího z Poděbrad/ tram 5, 9, 26, 51. **Open** 5pm-3am Mon-Sat. **Admission** free. **No credit cards. Map** p333 B2.

Newly redone with surrealist art, low light and bendy ironwork, the Seven Wolves remains an appealing art bar and club space in the party heaven of the Žižkov district. The decks dispense hot and cold running jungle, but there's really only beer to slake a thirst. The crisp sound system is another reason this club has stolen some of the thunder from more established venues such as the neighbouring Akropolis (*see p247*).

ARTS & ENTERTAINMENT

Duplex. *See p254.*

Solidní nejistota

Pštrossova 21, Nové Město, Prague 1 (224 933 086/www.solidninejistota.cz). Metro Národní třída/tram 6, 9, 17, 18, 22, 53, 57, 58, 59. **Open** 6pm-6am daily. **Admission** free. **No credit cards. Map** p330 K8.

Solid Uncertainty is the most shameless meat market in Prague. World-weary bar staff man the taps at the centre of the room, surrounded by hopeful creatures scanning the possibilities. If the Prague aquarium (*see p217*) is closed, this is the next best place in which to see sharks. The grill stays open late into the night, but it looks like the beefy doormen are the only ones who use it.

Tropison

Náměstí Republiky 8, Staré Město, Prague 1 (224 801 276). Metro Náměstí Republiky/tram 5, 8, 14, 51, 54. **Open** 8pm-3am Mon-Wed; 8pm-5am Thur, Fri; 7pm-5am Sat; 6pm-3am Sun. **Admission** free-100 Kč. **No credit cards. Map** p329 O4.

Granted, the service and uninspiring menus aren't likely to tempt you, but wait until you see the view from Tropison's terrace. Other highlights include the chance to boogie down on the grave of communism (this was once a communist department store) at the silly Latin dance parties. Put it down as a 'maybe'.

★ Újezd

Újezd 18, Malá Strana, Prague 1 (no phone). Metro Malostranská/tram 6, 9, 12, 20, 22, 58, 59. **Open** *Bar* 2pm-4am daily. *Café* 6pm-4am daily. *Pub* 8pm-4am daily. **Admission** free. **No credit cards. Map** p327 F6.

In its earlier incarnation as Borát, this three-storey madhouse was an important venue for the alternative music crowd. Today, with a young Czech crowd in dreads and a thick, smoky atmosphere, Újezd is home to some loud, badly amplified Czech rock music, with battered wooden chairs in the café upstairs and shouted conversation in the bar below. Despite it all, it's not a jot less popular.

Ultramarin

Ostrovní 32, Nové Město, Prague 2 (224 932 249/www.ultramarin.cz). Metro Národní třída/tram 6, 9, 17, 18, 22, 53, 57, 58, 59. **Open** 10.30am-4am daily. **Admission** free. **Credit** AmEx, MC, V. **Map** p330 J7.

Lesser-known DJs rock this small stone cellar, an engaging place in which to stay up late and get sweaty. However, in true Prague style, it seems there's often nothing on, and the dance crypt below the bar is empty. At street level, it's an art pub with a small menu of salads, Czech and Thai food, and seating made from designer materials such as layered cardboard. In a handy location, just streets from Staré Město, it draws a grown-up crowd.

U zlatého stromu

Karlova 6, Staré Město, Prague 1 (222 220 441/www.zlatystrom.cz). Metro Staroměstská/tram 17, 18, 53. **Open** *Club* 8pm-6am daily.

Radost FX. *See p257.*

Restaurant 24hrs daily. **Admission** 80 Kč.
Credit AmEx, MC, V. **Map** p328 K4.

Here's one of the strangest combinations in the Staré Město area: a non-stop disco, strip club, bar, restaurant and hotel. Descend into the cellar labyrinth of bad pop and strippers, and you could end up in a peaceful outdoor garden or a recessed nook ideal for that profound conversation about God and sex. The upstairs café has a full menu, plus coffee and drinks.

Vertigo

Havelská 4, Staré Město (mobile 774 744 256/ www.vertigo-club.cz). Metro Můstek/tram 3, 6, 9, 14, 18, 22, 24, 53, 57, 58, 59. **Open** 9pm-4am Thur-Sat. **Admission** free. **Map** p328 L5.

Vertigo offers three levels of capable café and clubbing space, with decent DJs, decor, lights and sound, plus the obligatory LCD displays. It's easily overlooked and can be quietish, though it seems to be attracting more lively crowds these days with scratchers such as Funky Vibes and Audiosex. Don't try to make sense of marketing gambits such as 'Sexy look… you feel the thirst'. Eh?

Wakata

Malířská 14, Holešovice, Prague 7 (233 370 518/ www.wakata.cz). Metro Vltavská/tram 1, 8, 25, 26, 56. **Open** 5pm-3am Mon-Thur; 5pm-5am Fri, Sat; 6pm-3am Sun. **Admission** free. **No credit cards. Map** p332 D2.

A down-and-dirty teenage wasteland, Wakata can deliver great jungle, but more often it feels like you've unwittingly stepped out of Prague and on to the set of a cheap horror film. At least it stays open way past official hours, has motorcycle seats for bar stools, and is, er, away from it all.

XT3

Pod plynojemem 5, Libeň, Prague 8 (no phone/ www.xt3.cz). Metro Palmovka/tram 1, 3, 8, 10, 12, 19, 24, 54. **Open** 4pm-2am daily. **Admission** free. **No credit cards**.

XT3 dishes up breakbeat, lots of smoke and cheap beer, all in a venue unlikely to be stumbled upon by foreigners. Mixing starts at eight, and there's always someone new trying out his or her collection of samples. Don't forget your skateboard, and bring Czech teen friends if you want to blend in.

Zvonařka

Šafaříkova 1, Vinohrady, Prague 2 (224 251 990). Metro Náměstí Míru/tram 6, 11, 56. **Open** 11.30am-midnight Mon-Fri; noon-midnight Sat, Sun. **Admission** free-200 Kč. **Credit** MC, V.

What was once a popular Czech pub has had a makeover, and now looks a bit like a cruise ship. The circular bar and blue and silver motifs set the stage for high-energy parties when the place is busy; should you pine for old Prague, there's a terrace that looks out over the city's southern suburbs. Even if the DJs aren't up to much, the food is reliable.

GAMBLING

Gambling is completely legal, and high rollers will find the city has no shortage of casinos. It's big business, and seems to get bigger every year. First came the *hernas* or 'gambling halls', essentially bars full of one-armed bandits (*see below*). Then came the bigger casinos that line Wenceslas Square. Regulation is patchy; if you want to roll some dice, it's generally best to stick to the respectable international chains, which are geared towards tourists, encourage small-time betting, and have fairly relaxed atmospheres.

Casinos

Banco Casino

Na příkopě 27, Nové Město, Prague 2 (221 967 380). Metro Náměstí Republiky/tram 5, 8, 14, 24, 26, 51, 52, 54, 55, 56, 58. **Open** 24hrs daily. **Credit** MC, V. **Map** p329 N5.

Classy enough to have appeared in *Casino Royale*, the Banco is a reputable, plush establishment with private salons and high-tech slots for people not attracted to green felt.

Millennium

V celnici 10, Nové Město, Prague 1 (224 231 886). Metro Náměstí Republiky/tram 5, 8, 14, 24, 26, 51, 54. **Open** 3pm-4am Mon-Thur, Sun; 3pm-5am Fri, Sat. **Credit** MC, V. **Map** p329 O3.

Plush, classy and palatial, the Millennium looks like an appropriate playground for any passing superspies. It's part of a spick and span hotel and retail complex just east of Staré Město; free drinks for players add to the fun if you can keep your head.

★ Palais Savarin

Na příkopě 10, Nové Město, Prague 1 (251 177 888/www.czechcasinos.cz). Metro Můstek/tram 3, 5, 8, 9, 14, 26, 51, 52, 54, 55, 56, 58. **Open** 1pm-4am daily. **Credit** DC, MC, V. **Map** p329 N5.

INSIDE TRACK
HERNA BARS

Would-be beatniks and Bukowskis will find a feast of material in Prague's ubiquitous *herna* bars, smoky dives lined with one-armed bandits. The *hernas* cater mostly to locals, pay a maximum of 300 Kč for a 2 Kč wager, and operate on a legally fixed ratio of 60 to 80 odds. Most herna bars are pretty seedy; **Herna Můstek** (inside Můstek metro station and open 24 hours) is not too threatening, but it probably doesn't pay to look like a tourist. For more, *see p110* **Revolt!**

Run by Casinos Austria International, the Savarin is one of the most established operations in town, with candelabras and Baroque frescoes up stone stairs. It's a world apart from most of the betting rooms on Wenceslas Square, and worth a look even if you don't gamble; if you do, drinks are on the house. American roulette and stud poker are offered along with all the standard games of chance. Bets run from 20 Kč to 5,000 Kč.

ADULT CLUBS

Czech lawmakers enjoy skirting the issue of prostitution: although pimping is illegal, the law doesn't address prostitution directly. Clubs and hundreds of patrons certainly do, however: women in most strip clubs work legally as independent contract entertainers, and 'private dances' in private rooms are widely available. It's all pretty safe and hygienic, and most of the clubs these days will refund your entry fee if you opt for the extra services packages. But as in similar clubs anywhere, the drinks prices are hugely inflated, and strippers are encouraged to ask for them from customers. Stag party favourites include **Darling Club Cabaret** and **Hot Peppers**.

Big Sister
Nádražní 46, Smíchov, Prague 5 (257 310 043/ www.bigsister.net). Metro Smíchov/tram 12, 54. **Open** 6pm-4am daily. **Admission** 290 Kč; couples free. **Credit** MC, V.
The most astounding new wave in Prague's booming sex business, Big Sister nakedly cashes in on the Big Brother phenomenon, but puts its live internet cameras inside a free brothel (excluding admission) at which all the punters agree to appear on the web in exchange for an hour of gratis action.

Cabaret Atlas
Ve Smečkách 31, Nové Město, Prague 1 (296 326 067/www.atlas-cabaret.cz). Metro Muzeum/ tram 4, 6, 10, 16, 22, 51, 52, 54, 55, 56, 58. **Open** 7pm-7am daily. **Admission** 250 Kč. **Credit** MC, V. **Map** p331 N8.
Atlas offers striptease, a business crowd that can expense the drinks, and whirlpools or 'private shows' at a mere 2,500 Kč per half-hour. And that's just for starters.

Captain Nemo
Ovocný trh 13, Staré Město, Prague 1 (224 211 868). Metro Náměstí Republiky/tram 5, 8, 14, 51, 52, 54, 55, 56, 58. **Open** 8pm-5am Mon-Thur, Sun; 4pm-6am Fri, Sat. **Admission** 300 Kč. **Credit** MC, V. **Map** p328 M4.
Captain Nemo is a handy Staré Město club that employs mainly local talent and goes for a nautical theme, though it's not clear whether anyone has noticed yet.

Carioca
Václavské náměstí 4, Nové Město, Prague 1 (296 325 314). Metro Můstek/tram 3, 9, 14, 24, 51, 52, 54, 55, 56, 58. **Open** 9pm-4am daily. **Admission** 200-500 Kč. **Credit** AmEx, MC, V. **Map** p329 N6.
Deep under Wenceslas Square in what looks like an imperial bedroom, Carioca was one of the city's best jazz joints in a previous and altogether rather different life. The baroque red and gold setting remains, but the new management has installed a cabaret: dancers with top hats and canes alternate with strippers in what could almost be entertainment for a date (with the usual high drink prices).

★ Darling Club Cabaret
Ve Smečkách 32, Nové Město, Prague 1 (mobile 775 021 971/www.kabaret.cz). Metro Můstek/ tram 3, 9, 14, 24, 51, 52, 54, 55, 56, 58. **Open** noon-5am Mon, Thur, Sun; 8pm-5am Tue; noon-6am Fri, Sat. **Admission** 200 Kč. **Credit** AmEx, MC, V. **Map** p331 N8.
The biggest bacchanalia in town and a stopover for travelling 'entertainers' from all over the place, Darling attracts hordes patrons with three plush bars and loads of improbably beautiful women. It wins out over Cabaret Atlas (*see left*) among aficionados of this sort of thing, even though it offers the same prices and services.

Goldfingers
Václavské náměstí 5, Nové Město, Prague 1 (224 193 571). Metro Můstek/tram 3, 9, 14, 24, 51, 52, 54, 55, 56, 58. **Open** 9pm-4am daily. **Admission** 450 Kč. **Credit** AmEx, MC, V. **Map** p329 N6.
Welcome to Prague's version of a Vegas revue, with a theatrical setting and dizzy dancers. It's strictly dancing and so is all fairly innocent in the end – perhaps to the disappointment of the stag parties.

Hot Peppers
Václavské náměstí 5, Nové Město, Prague 10 (mobile 724 134 011/www.hotpeppers.cz). Metro Můstek/tram 3, 9, 14, 24, 51, 52, 54, 55, 56, 58. **Open** 8pm-5am daily. **Admission** 500 Kč. **No credit cards**.
A recent addition to Wenceslas Square's increasingly tawdry reputation, Hot Peppers is just for striptease and drinks extortion. For more, customers will have to look elsewhere.

Showpark
Bubenské nábř 306, Holešovice, Prague 7 (261 314 151/www.redlight.cz). Metro Vltavská/ tram 1, 25, 26, 56. **Open** 3pm-3am daily. **Admission** 100 Kč. **No credit cards**.
Formerly known as Red Light, this Amsterdam-style complex is the city's bargain-basement fleshpot, with a bar that attracts Marines and rooms upstairs where girls await your custom.

Sport & Fitness

Prague gave you a beer belly, Prague can help you shift it…

Czechs now regard health and eternal youth to be as much a part of their New Europe life as a great career and holidays in Thailand. And visitors are able to reap the benefits of this change in attitude. Prague's sporting facilities were once a closed shop, catering mainly to clubs of serious athletes. However, there's now a wide range of facilities across the city, open to everyone. And we're not just talking about gyms and pool: being curious, intellectual sorts, Praguers are also deeply fascinated by the more technical sports, and many test the extremes of rock climbing, parachuting or bungee jumping.

SPECTATOR SPORTS

Although the Czech Republic has no world-class football teams, turnout at matches is still robust, and a few new facilities have breathed fresh life into the game. But if you really want to see what Czechs can do, spend a day down at the ice rink.

During the communist era, the state pumped millions into training tennis stars in a bid to win glory and gold for this small nation, and there are still courts all over the city; but since funding dried up, the roost is ruled by the hockey teams. Hockey now has the city's best facilities, complete with eager corporate sponsors, cheerleaders and regular scandals. Young Czech players continue to flood into the NHL in America, and the national team is a force to be reckoned with.

The country no longer boasts tennis success stories to rival Ivan Lendl and Martina Navrátilová, and the days of running legend Emil Zátopek are long gone. However, there's talk of a bid for the 2020 Summer Olympics, while the country still manages to pick up a medal or two at the Winter Olympics in skiing or jumping. And if sporting victories are following the course of the nation as a whole into diverse, individualistic pursuits, that's probably only fitting.

About the author

Sam Beckwith *is a Prague-based writer and editor. He writes for praguetv.com and www.stumpymoose.com.*

Football

AC Sparta Praha

Toyota Arena, Milady Horákové 98, Holešovice, Prague 7 (296 111 400/www.sparta.cz). Metro Hradčanská/tram 1, 8, 15, 25, 26. **Admission** 100-2,300 Kč. **No credit cards. Map** p332 B3.
Though its dominance of the domestic league is periodically challenged by provincial upstarts such as Slovan Liberec and Baník Ostrava, AC Sparta remains the Czech football league's top team. Though it compares poorly to European teams such as Barcelona and Juventus, this hasn't stopped the team from pulling off some mighty upsets against wealthier opponents. Its 18,500-capacity stadium, known locally as Letná, hosts big international matches.

FK Viktoria Žižkov

Stadion FK Viktoria Žižkov, Seifertova 130, Žižkov, Prague 3 (222 722 045/www.fkvz.cz). Tram 5, 9, 26. **Admission** 90-150 Kč. **No credit cards. Map** p333 B2.
Despite dismal support, 'Viktorka' has enjoyed several impressive seasons in the past, along with significant redevelopment of its compact stadium. For the time being, it's struggling, and seems to spend as much time overcoming scandals as taking on opponents. Fans can get particularly rowdy as well – indeed, they're the most notorious in Prague.

SK Slavia Praha

Stadion Eden, Vladivostocká 10, Vršovice, Prague 10 (mobile 731 126 104/www.slavia.cz). Tram 22, 24. **Admission** 70-200 Kč; free children under 140cm. **No credit cards.**

Profile Bohemians

Now owned and run by its fans, Prague's beloved football team battles on.

Bohemians was founded in 1905 as AFK Vršovice, named after the unfashionable west Prague area in which the club is based; the name changed in 1927, following a historic tour of Australia during which they represented Czechoslovakia. During their time down under, the team was given two kangaroos, which it donated to Prague Zoo. But the fun didn't end there: the team also changed its logo to a kangeroo and gained the nickname of *Klokani* (the Czech plural for the hopping marsupials).

The club generated further support after the war from fans who didn't support the ruling communist regime. The two big clubs were Sparta Prague and Dukla, a military team; both were funded by the government at the time. Bohemians, though, had no connection to the ruling elite and even played in green, which itself seemed to be defiantly opposed to the communist red.

A century after its inception, though, the club found itself with a serious problem: $2 million worth of debts, which left the club bankrupt and resulted in a demotion to the third division. Czech football was suffering from a corruption scandal at the time, and the club found it impossible to find investors.

However, all was not lost: the team's loyal fans clubbed together and collected enough money to save it from going under. The resurrection was led by Antonín Jelínek, chairman of the Bohemians Supporters' Trust, and club coach Antonín Panenka, who scored the penalty against Germany that resulted in Czechoslovakia winning the European Championship in 1976. So far so good, but the beleaguered fans may soon face another challenge, following speculation that the club may be moved from its historic home in order to sell the land. There may be trouble ahead...

The fascinating story of Bohemians has been recorded in a documentary called *Kangaroo Confidential*, the work of filmmaker and lifelong Bohemians fan Filip Šebek. With classic Czech offbeat irony, the film includes not just the expected fan and player interviews but several guest appearances from zoologists.

FURTHER READING
For more on the team and Šebek's film, see www.fc-bohemians.cz or check out www.duse klokani.cz.

Finally settled into their newly renovated, five-storey Eden stadium in Vršovice, both team and fans are chuffed indeed, and newly fired up for their permanent goal of catching up with Sparta.

Horse racing

Chuchle
Radotínská 69, Radotín, Prague 5 (242 447 036/ www.velka-chuchle.cz). Metro Smíchovské nádraží, then bus 129, 172, 241, 243, 244, 255. **Tickets** 100-200 Kč. **No credit cards.**
Chuchle is for flat racing. The season runs from April to October, but takes a summer break for the months of July and August. The races start at 2pm on Sundays.

Dostihový spolek
Pražská 607, Pardubická, 110km (68 miles) east of Prague (466 797 111/www.pardubice-racecourse.cz). Metro Florenc, then ČSAD bus to Pardubice. **Tickets** 110-1,200 Kč. **No credit cards.**
The facilities are basic, with outdoor seating and indoor monitors for watching the action, and a handy selection of dilapidated bars and restaurants. Regular race meetings are also held every Saturday from May to October.
► *The Velká Pardubická steeplechase, a highlight of the Czech sporting calendar, is held here on the second Sunday in October; see p216.*

Ice hockey

★ HC Slavia Praha
O2 Arena, Ocelářská 460, Vysočany, Prague 9 (www.o2rena.cz). Metro Českomoravská. Tram 8, 19. **Open** *Box office* 90mins before games. **Admission** 100-1,150 Kč; 40 Kč children under 135cm. **No credit cards.**
Slavia has come a long way from its former cramped, weatherbeaten stadium to this state-of-the-art, designer behemoth, the largest indoor sports venue in the Czech Republic. The fans have shared in the spoils, with an average attendance of 7,000 per game, and more than 11,000 for playoffs – more than double the turnout at their former digs in the pre-reconstruction Eden stadium.
► *For the arena's music programme, see p247.*

HC Sparta Praha
Tesla Arena, Za elektrárnou 419, Holešovice, Prague 7 (266 727 443/www.hcsparta.cz). Tram 5, 12, 14, 15, 17. **Open** *Box office* 1-6.30pm Mon-Fri. **Admission** 50-170 Kč. **No credit cards.**
Sparta's home ice rink was state-of-the-art when it was built. It's now showing signs of wear and tear, but the team itself is well financed and always competitive. The large arena doesn't come alive until the playoffs; regular season games are often poorly

---

INSIDE TRACK
PLACE YOUR BETS

Betting at Prague racetracks works in a similar way to the British system, with two agents accepting minimum bets of 20 Kč and 50 Kč respectively. You can bet to win (*vítěz*) or place (*místo*), or you can bet on the order (*pořadí*).

---

attended, yet the Sparta boys were the 2006 champs. Tickets can be bought in advance from the box office at entrance 30 or from Ticketpro (*see p210*).

ACTIVE SPORTS

Climbing

Boulder Bar
U výstaviště 11, Holešovice, Prague 7 (233 313 906/www.boulder.cz). Metro Vltavská/tram 5, 12, 17. **Open** 8am-11pm Mon-Fri; noon-11pm Sat, Sun. **Rates** 60-80 Kč/2hrs. **No credit cards. Map** p330 M7.
Prague's only bar with a climbing wall has moved to a more roomy, modern space in the Holešovice district, from which it operates not just the pub and practice room, but also runs climbing courses in the field. Bring your rock boots, or pick some up. Enthusiastic staff are always happy to discuss the latest gear and techniques.

Sport Centrum Evropská
José Mártiho 31, Vokovice, Prague 6 (220 172 309/www.sportcentrumevropska.cz). Metro Dejvická, then tram 20, 26. **Open** 7am-11pm daily. **Rates** 60-80 Kč/2 hrs. **No credit cards.**
A popular and impressive indoor climbing wall within the environs of Charles University's sports faculty. Booking is essential; you can rent harnesses, carabiners and ropes.

Cycling

See p302.

Fitness centres

In addition to the venues below, the central **Marriott** (*see p144*) has a good gym.

Cybex
Hilton Prague, Pobřežní 1, Karlín, Prague 8 (224 842 375/www.cybexprg.cz). Metro Florenc/ tram 8, 24. **Open** 6am-10pm Mon-Fri; 7am-10pm Sat, Sun. **Admission** 900 Kč/day; 250 Kč under-15s. *Squash* 600 Kč/hr. **Membership** 3,900 Kč/mth; 19,900 Kč/6mths; 29,900 Kč/yr. **Credit** AmEx, MC, V.

ARTS & ENTERTAINMENT

Cybex is based in the Hilton, so you know what to expect: a swanky, state-of-the-art fitness centre that also offers spa and beauty treatments.

Delroy's Gym

Zborovská 4, Smíchov, Prague 5 (257 327 042/ www.delroys-gym.cz). Metro Anděl/tram 4, 7, 10, 14. **Open** 7am-9pm Mon-Fri; 9am-9pm Sat, Sun. **Admission** *Gym* 75 Kč/90mins; 990 Kč/mth. *Taebo* 150 Kč/class. *Thai kick boxing* 150 Kč/class. *Karate* 150 Kč/class. *Thai kick boxing for children* 170 Kč/class. **No credit cards**.

Delroy Scarlett has been around since Thai boxing became all the rage in the Czech Republic, and this is the place in which to learn the discipline. Though Scarlett's gym specialises in martial arts, it also offers a wide variety of other courses, ranging from aerobics to self-defence.

★ Fitness Club Inter-Continental

Náměstí Curieových 43, Staré Město, Prague 1 (296 631 525/www.intercontinental.com/prague). Metro Staroměstská/tram 17. **Open** 6am-11pm Mon-Fri; 8am-10pm Sat, Sun. **Admission** *Gym* 290 Kč/90mins. *Pool, sauna & hot tub* 400 Kč/ 2hrs. *Turbo solarium* 20 Kč/min. *Yoga, Pilates, aqua aerobics* 250 Kč/class. **Credit** AmEx, MC, V. **Map** p328 K2.

This newly renovated fitness centre, health club and spa is popular among the rich and moderately famous. This is a posh workout palace in a similarly posh hotel, and it features good cardio machines and eager trainers.

▶ *For the hotel itself, see p139.*

HIT Fitness Flora

Chrudimská 2, Žižkov, Prague 3 (267 311 447/www.hitfit.net). Metro Flora/tram 5, 10, 11, 16. **Open** 7am-11pm Mon-Fri; 8am-11pm Sat, Sun. **Admission** *Gym* 110 Kč. *Solarium* 10 Kč/min. *Squash* 280-340 Kč. *Aerobics, Pilates, boxing, spinning* 150-180 Kč/class. **No credit cards**.

The HIT Fitness Flora is a well-equipped, modern and reasonably priced gym that is conveniently located not too far from the centre of town.

Go-karting

Kart Centrum

Výpadová 1335, Radotín, Prague 5 (mobile 774 002 001/www.kart-centrum.cz). Bus 172 or 244 from Smíchovské nádraží to Přeštínská. **Open** 3pm-midnight Mon-Fri; 11am-midnight Sat, Sun. **Rates** 200 Kč/10min.; *under-15s* 150 Kč/10min. **No credit cards**.

A colourful and cheerfully tacky indoor go-karting centre set in converted glasshouses in far-flung Radotín, Kart Centrum claims to be Europe's largest. There's even a water feature. Children can race round on a smaller track.

> ## INSIDE TRACK
> ## JUMPING FOR JOY?
>
> Come to Prague, jump off a bridge. Obvious, right? Well, during the summer, **KI Bungee Jump** (777 250 126, 608 768 168, www.bungee.cz) will let you do just that: from June to September (though at weekends only), there are regular weekend plummeting sessions from Zvíkovské podhradí, a bridge high over the Vltava. Expect to pay 900-1,000 Kč per jump, and be sure to book ahead.

Golf

Once shunned by communists, golf continues to rise in popularity among the country's business classes – but Prague itself has only one course, the Golf Club Praha. Outside the city, in Central Bohemia, there are 18-hole courses in **Poděbrady** (Golf Club Poděbrady, 325 610 982, www.golfpodebrady.cz), **Karlštejn** (Golf Resort Karlštejn, 311 604 999, www.karlstejn-golf.cz) and **Konopiště** (Golf Resort Konopiště, 317 784 044, www.gcko.cz).

Erpet Golf Centrum

Strakonická 4, Smíchov, Prague 5 (296 373 111/ www.erpet.cz). Metro Anděl, then tram 12, 14, 20. **Open** 8am-11pm daily. **Rates** *Golf simulators* 300-500 Kč/hr. *Squash* 150-330 Kč/hr. *Tennis* 200-600 Kč/hr. **Membership** 11,900 Kč/yr. **Credit** AmEx, MC, V.

An indoor golf centre catering to the city's newly wealthy elite. The golf simulators here offer the only 18-hole course (virtual, of course) inside Prague's city limits. There are also squash courts, and tennis in the summer.

Golf Club Praha

Plzeňská 401, Smíchov, Prague 5 (257 216 584/ www.gcp.cz). Metro Anděl, then tram 7, 9, 10. **Open** 8am-dusk daily. **Rates** 450-550 Kč/9 holes; 800-1,000 Kč/18 holes. **Credit** MC, V.

A nine-hole course and driving range on a hilltop. The course can get very dry in the summer.

Horse riding

Velkostatek Tetín
Equestrian Centre

Tetín, Central Bohemia (mobile 602 633 775). **Rates** *Group lessons up to 4 people* 520 Kč/hr . *Private lessons* 600 Kč/30mins. *Trail riding* 600 Kč/hr. **No credit cards**.

This Canadian-Austrian riding centre offers English-language group and private lessons, plus trail riding. Phone ahead.

Ice skating

Zimní stadion Štvanice

Ostrov Štvanice 1125, Holešovice, Prague 7
(mobile 602 623 449/www.stvanice.cz). Metro
Florenc or Vltavská/tram 5, 8, 12, 14, 17.
Open 10.30am-noon Mon; 10.30am-noon, 3.30-
5pm, 5.30-7pm Tue, Thur; 10.30am-noon, 3.30-
5pm Wed, Fri; 10.30am-noon, 3.30-5pm, 8-9.30pm
Sat; 9-11am, 2.30-5pm, 8-10pm Sun. **Admission**
100 Kč. *Skate rental* 80 Kč. **No credit cards**.
This somewhat rickety-looking structure houses
two ice rinks, with reasonably generous opening
hours, on an island in the Vltava. It provides a taste
of true old-school Prague, complete with eccentric,
inconvenient hours.

Zimní stadion USK Praha Hotel Hasa

Sámova 1, Vršovice, Prague 10 (271 747 128).
Tram 6, 7, 24. **Open** 9-11am Mon, Tue, Thur,
Fri; 9-11am, 4-5.30pm Wed; 10am-noon Sat, Sun.
Admission 30 Kč. **No credit cards**.
The future of this big ice skating hall remains uncer-
tain. It would be a great pity if it did close, since the
facilities, and the large expanse of ice, are good
enough to attract figure skaters and ice hockey
teams. The rest of the time it's available to the public to try out jumps and spins.

In-line skating

Ladronka In-Line Park

Ke Kotlářce & Plzeňska streets, Břevnov, Prague
6 (no phone/www.ladronka.cz). Metro Anděl,
then bus 191 to stop U Ladronky. **Open** 2-9pm
Mon-Fri; noon-9pm Sat, Sun. **Rates** 120 Kč/hr
incl pads. **No credit cards**.
The best spot for in-line skating in the city.

Letná K2

Kamenická 19, Holešovice, Prague 7 (776 057
783/www.inlinespecial.cz). Tram 1, 8, 25, 26.
Open noon-6pm Mon-Fri; 11am-1pm Sat. **Rates**
50Kč/hr. **No credit cards**.
A good selection of in-line rentals just across from
Letná, a popular skating park.

Jogging

Prague's infamous pollution makes jogging,
even in the parks of the central part of the city,
a relatively serious health hazard. But if you
must run, try one of the following areas, which
are far enough from the worst of the pollution
to make the endeavour a little less risky.

Divoká Šárka

Nebušice, Prague 6. Metro Dejvická, then tram
20, 26 or bus 119, 218.
Challenging, hilly trails for joggers, with bulbous
rock formations and thick forests. The reservoir at
the west end of the park attracts hordes of people in
summer. Šárka is most easily accessible from
Evropská, towards the airport.

Stromovka

Holešovice, Prague 7. Metro Nádraží Holešovice,
then tram 5, 12, 14, 15, 17. **Map** p332 C1.
The most central of Prague's large parks. After the
initial sprint to avoid the Výstaviště crowds, you can
have the meadows to yourself.

ARTS & ENTERTAINMENT

Divoká Šárka. *See p267.*

Parachuting

★ **Paraškola Impact**

Dolní 12, Nusle, Prague 4 (261 225 431/www. paraskolaimpact.cz). Metro Muzeum, then tram 11. **Open** 10am-7pm Mon-Fri. **Rates** *Basic course* 2,000 Kč. *Tandem jumps* 3,500 Kč. *Jump & video* 5,100 Kč. **No credit cards.**

Notwithstanding its unfortunate name, Impact is an established parachuting school that offers basic and advanced courses, along with tandem jumps (which require no training).

Skyservice

Kunětická 2, Nové Město, Prague 2 (mobile 724 002 002/www.skyservice.cz). Metro Muzeum, then tram 11. **Rates** *Basic course* 2,000 Kč. *Tandem jumps* 3,800 Kč. **No credit cards.** Map p333 A2.

You can't skydive in New Town: the listing above is for the Prague office of a firm that organises jumps from airfields in Příbram or Prostějov.

Pool

★ **Billard Centrum**

Šmeralova 5, Holešovice, Prague 7 (233 375 236/ www.billardcentrum.cz). Metro Vltavská/tram 1, 25, 26. **Open** 11am-midnight daily. **Rates** *Pool* 100 Kč/hr. *Snooker* 120 Kč/hr. **Credit** MC, V. **Map** p329 N5.

This popular spot has plenty of tables that draw a mellow, neighbourhood crowd. It also has a handy bar, and a few video games with which to pass the time if there's a wait for a table (unlikely).

Shooting

AVIM Praha

Sokolovská 23, Karlín, Prague 8 (222 329 328/ www.avim.cz). Metro Florenc/tram 8, 24. **Open** 10am-10pm daily. **Rates** 100 Kč/30mins; 150 Kč/hr. **No credit cards.**

Try out a Glock, Ruger or even a pump-action shotgun in this shooting range close to the centre of town. If you want English-language assistance, phone in advance and ask for George.

Skateboarding

Aside from the Mystic Skate Park, skaters can use the pavilion next to the National Theatre ticket office (*see p271*) and the area around the metronome in Letná park (*see p114*).

Mystic Skate Park

Ostrov Štvanice 38, Holešovice, Prague 7 (222 232 027/www.mysticskates.cz). Metro Florenc or Vltavská/tram 5, 8, 12, 14, 17. **Open** *Oct-Apr* noon-9pm daily. *May-Sept* 9am-10pm daily. **Rates** *BMX, in-line skates* 80-120 Kč. *Skateboard* 50-80 Kč. **No credit cards.** **Map** p332 E4.

This popular skate park, on Štvanice Island in the Vltava, also hosts the internationally known Mystic Skate Cup every July.

Skiing & snowboarding

Although the scenery isn't ideal for skiers (there's a distinct lack of mountains), the Czech winter is sufficiently cold to guarantee snow at higher altitudes. Most of the Czech Republic's winter resorts offer equipment rental, but it's also possible to secure skis and boards in advance in the capital.

★ **Happy Sport**

Národní obrany 16, Dejvická, Prague 6 (224 325 560/www.happysport.cz). Metro Dejvická/tram 2, 8, 20, 26. **Open** 9am-6pm Mon-Fri; 9am-1pm Sat. **No credit cards.**

Snowboard rentals start at 250 Kč per day, with ski rentals at 100 Kč per day; you'll also have to pay insurance of 50-80 Kč, and leave a deposit of 1,500-3,500 Kč. Happy Sport also does repairs. **Other locations** Beranových 127, Letňany, Prague 9 (286 920 113); Na Pankráci 1598, Pankrác, Prague 4 (241 403 961).

Squash

Squash can also be played at **Erpet Golf Centrum** (*see p264*).

Squash & Fitness Centrum Arbes

Arbesovo náměstí 15, Smíchov, Prague 5 (257 326 041/www.squasharbes.cz). Metro Anděl, then tram 6, 9, 12, 20. **Open** 7am-10.30pm Mon-Fri; 9am-10pm Sat, Sun. **Rates** 150-340 Kč/hr. **No credit cards.**

A smart fitness centre with four squash courts and a reasonably central location.

Squashové centrum

Václavské náměstí 13-15, Nové Město, Prague 1 (224 232 752/www.asbsquash.cz). Metro Můstek/ tram 3, 9, 14, 24. **Open** 7am-11pm Mon-Fri; 8am-11pm Sat, Sun. **Rates** 160-380 Kč/hr. **No credit cards.** **Map** p329 N6.

Three courts and a central location draw Prague's business community to this underground facility.

Swimming

Pool facilities have markedly improved since 1989. These days, a more significant problem is selecting a pool that isn't block-booked by clubs or packed with hysterical children and amorous teenagers. If you prefer open-air swimming, dam reservoirs are usually murky as soup but wildly popular among the locals, especially the one at Šárka park. Other options are hotels that have fitness centres with pools (*see pp124-149*).

Tenisový klub Slavia Praha.

★ Divoká Šárka
Nebušice, Prague 6 (no phone). Metro Dejvická, then tram 20, 26 or bus 218, then 5min walk. **Open** *May-mid Sept* 9am-7pm daily. **Admission** 40 Kč; 10 Kč children. **No credit cards**.
An outdoor pool in an idyllic setting, with a comfortable lawn area on which to lounge. *Photo p265*.

Hotel Axa
Na poříčí 40, Nové Město, Prague 1 (222 323 967/www.hotelaxa.com). Metro Florenc or Náměstí Republiky/tram 3, 8, 24, 26. **Open** 7-9am, noon-1pm, 5-10pm Mon-Fri; 9am-9pm Sat, Sun. **Admission** 1 Kč/min (100 Kč deposit). **No credit cards**. **Map** p329 O3.
The pool in this hotel is of a good length, and free from hordes of shrieking children in the morning. There are decent sauna facilities (mixed and women's, 100 Kč/hr; 200 Kč deposit).

Plavecký Stadion Podolí
Podolská 74, Podolí, Prague 4 (241 433 952/www.pspodoli.cz). Metro Palackého náměstí, then tram 17, 21. **Open** 6am-9.45pm (last entry 9pm) Mon-Fri; 9am-7.45pm (last entry 7pm) Sat, Sun. **Admission** 110-150 Kč; 80 Kč children. **No credit cards**.
Prague's biggest (and perpetually packed) swimming centre is a survivor from the old regime. It has outdoor lap swimming all year round, and a 50m indoor pool that attracts serious swimmers.

Ten-pin bowling

Bowling centrum RAN
V celnici 10, Nové Město, Prague 1 (221 033 020). Metro Náměstí Republiky/tram 3, 5, 14, 24, 26. **Open** noon-2am daily. **Rates** 270-390 Kč/hr. **No credit cards**. **Map** p329 O3.
Eight professional AMF lanes are discretely tucked away underneath the Marriott hotel (*see p144*).

Tennis

The Czech Republic has long been renowned for its stellar tennis stars. Although Navrátilová and Lendl both defected to the West, they are still national heroes. Czech tennis has struggled to come to terms with post-communist economics, but although it no longer inspires the fanaticism of the communist era, there's plenty of interest.

1. ČLTK
Ostrov Štvanice 38, Holešovice, Prague 7 (222 316 317/www.cltk.cz). Metro Florenc or Vltavská/tram 5, 8, 12, 14, 17. **Open** 7am-midnight daily. **Rates** 360-600 Kč/hr. **No credit cards**.
Founded in 1893, this venerable but modernised facility has 14 outdoor clay courts, three of which are floodlit, and sparkling indoor facilities (four hard courts, two clay courts). It has been newly reconstructed since the devastating floods of 2002. Booking is essential.

Tenisový klub Slavia Praha
Letenské sady 32, Holešovice, Prague 7 (233 374 033). Metro Hradčanská, then tram 1, 8, 15, 25, 26. **Open** *Jan-Mar, Nov, Dec* (indoor only) 7am-10pm daily. *Apr-Oct* 7am-9pm daily. **Rates** *Indoor* 600 Kč/hr. *Outdoor* 200-250 Kč/hr. **No credit cards**.
Eight floodlit outdoor clay courts, and a tennis bubble for the winter months on Letná plain.

Yoga

Jógacentrum Blanická
Blanická 17, Vinohrady, Prague 2 (224 253 702/www.joga.cz/praha). Metro Náměstí Míru/tram 11. **Open** 10am-9pm Mon, Thur. **Rates** from 150 Kč/4 lessons. **No credit cards**. **Map** p333 A4.
The Blanická centre offers a huge range of yoga classes, mainly in Czech, as well as information on other yoga centres across Prague.

Prague Yoga Studio & Teacher Training
Plavecká 12, Nové Město, Prague 2 (mobile 777 028 371/www.prayoga.cz). Metro Karlovo náměstí/tram 3, 7, 16, 17, 21. **Rates** 150-200 Kč/hr. **No credit cards**.
Drop-in classes in English and Czech make this calming but busy studio a hit. It holds intermediate and advanced Ashtanga Vinyasa, Viniyoga, Vinyasa flow, Yin/Yang, Yoga elements, oriental dance and shamanic healing classes several times a day, every day – and also runs weekend retreats.

ARTS & ENTERTAINMENT

Theatre & Dance

Raising the curtain – and the roof.

The Czech affection for the stage is rooted in history. When the Czech lands were being Germanised, theatre – particularly puppet theatre – became a repository for the Czech language, and for the myths and history of a near-vanquished people. Unlike the Poles and Russians, who adopted the word 'theatre', the Czechs clung doggedly to their own old word, *divadlo*. Czech nationalism eventually rose under the same scaffolding of the National Theatre (Národní divadlo). Indeed, *nazdar*, the friendly Czech word for 'hello', has in it the echoes of '*Na zdar du, stojneho Národního divadla*' – or 'For the accomplishment of a dignified National Theatre', a 19th-century fund-raising slogan. As a result, theatre retains a firm hold on the nation's cultural scene. Even Czechs who don't regularly attend the theatre maintain an interest in the actors, playwrights and directors slaving away on their behalf. *Nazdar*, and enjoy the show.

PRAGUE IN STAGES

A quick glance at the daily theatre listings will prove that there's plenty to see in Prague. Every evening offers a wealth of options, and many performances sell out well in advance. There's excellent work being done in theatres such as **Divadlo Na zábradlí**, **Divadlo Komedie**, **Divadlo Alfred ve Dvoře** and the **Divaldo Archa**. The universal language of dance and movement is fluently spoken at **Ponec**, **Gallery NoD** and the new **Prostor Preslova 9** space. Then there are the puppets, those wooden saviours of Czech culture; a terrific variety of festivals; and the **Narodní divadlo** (**National Theatre**), a cornerstone of Czech identity.

Tickets & information

Theatre websites rarely have ticket-purchasing options, and many theatres don't accept credit cards. However, most websites will direct you to ticket agencies such as Ticketpro (*see p210*), where you can use your credit card.

Buying tickets in person at a theatre box office (*pokladna*) can be tricky. If the person behind the counter is under 30, the chances are that their English is better than yours. But if the person is over 50, you'd better be good at charades – at one of the medium-sized theatres,

the staff includes a matronly lady who simply won't believe that a non-Czech speaker would want to see a show at her theatre, and will refuse to sell you a ticket.

Ticket touts cluster at the National Theatre, Estates Theatre and State Opera. You can often get into sold-out (*vyprodáno*) performances, at a price. Wait until the last bell for the best deal.

Ask the locals what's worth seeing, as some productions have exceeded their shelf life. Information can be found at Prague's **Theatre Institute** (Divadelní ústav, Celetná 17 in Old Town); it's also home to Prospero, an excellent theatre bookshop that includes many titles in English (among them the institute's own magazine of criticis and scholarship). For the latest theatre and dance listings, and occasional reviews, pick up the *Prague Post* or drop into the **Prague Information Service** (*see p315*; there's also help online at www.pis.cz).

CZECH THEATRES

Divadlo Alfred ve Dvoře
Alfred ve Dvoře Theatre
Františka Křížka 36, Holešovice, Prague 7 (233 376 985/www.alfredvedvore.cz). Metro Vltavská/tram 1, 5, 8, 12, 17, 25, 26. **Open** *Box office* 1hr before performance. **Tickets** 100 Kč; 60 Kč students. **No credit cards. Map** p332 D3.

The Alfred's fare tends toward movement and non-verbal work; if something text-based is featured, the theatre provides English programme notes. The venue serves as the primary organiser for the Malá Inventura Festival (www.malainventura.cz), and also co-produces new work with such groups as Chicago's Goat Island. One resident company to catch is Handa Gote: Research & Development.

★ Divadlo Archa
Archa Theatre

Na poříčí 26, Nové Město, Prague 1 (221 716 111/www.archatheatre.cz). Metro Náměstí Republiky or Florenc/tram 3, 8, 24, 26. **Open** *Box office* 10am-6pm Mon-Fri; 2hrs before performance. **Tickets** 100-300 Kč. **Credit** AmEx, MC, V. **Map** p329 O3.

Arguably the most important centre for new and experimental work in the Czech Republic, Archa covers everything: dance, music, theatre, film and puppetry. It's also the stomping grounds for such acclaimed Czech artists as Iva Bittová, Petr Nikl and the SKUTR group. The importance of Archa in the Czech theatre landscape is best shown by the fact that Václav Havel's new play, *Odcházení* (*Leaving*), premièred here, not at the National Theatre.

Divadlo Bratři Formanů
Forman Brothers Theatre

*Loď Tajemství, Kotviště, under the lighthouse on the Vltava, Holešovice, Prague 7 (222 326 843/*www.formanstheatre.cz). Trams 1, 12, 25.* **Open** times vary. **Tickets** 50-290 Kč.
See p274 **Like Father, Like Sons**.

Divadlo Komedie

Jungmannova 1, Nove Mesto, Prague 1 (224 222 734/224 238 271/www.divadlokomedie.cz). Metro Můstek/tram 3, 9, 14, 24. **Open** *Box office* 10am-6pm daily. **Tickets** 70-300 Kč.
No credit cards. **Map** p328 M6.

Fans of German theatre should know the Komedie: Pražské komorní divadlo (Prague Chamber Theatre), the resident company, specialises in contemporay German-language work, albeit in Czech translations. This is where Czechs come to see work by the likes of Thomas Bernhardt, Elfreide Jelinek and Peter Handke. The Komedie is also a theatre for directors. But unlike at Švandovo divadlo (*see p271*), they possess vision. Try and catch Jan Nebeský's production of *Kabaret Ivan Blatný*, a startling vaudeville on the Czech poet who died mad in an English asylum.

Divadlo Na zábradlí
Theatre on the Balustrade

Anenské náměstí 5, Staré Město, Prague 1 (222 868 868/www.nazabradli.cz). Metro Staroměstská/tram 17, 18. **Open** *Box office* 2-8pm Mon-Fri; 2hrs before performance Sat, Sun. **Tickets** 100-290 Kč. **No credit cards**.
Map p328 J5.

ARTS & ENTERTAINMENT

Prague Fringe. *See p274*.

Black Light Theatre
IMAGE

BLACK THEATRE
PANTOMIME
MODERN DANCE

Pařížská 4, Praha 1
GPS: N 50° 05'17", E 14° 25'12"

Performance daily at 8.00 p.m.

tel.: (+420) 222 314 448, (+420) 222 329 191, fax: (+420) 224 811 167
www.imagetheatre.cz   e-mail: image@imagetheatre.cz

Founded in 1958, the Theatre on the Balustrade lay the groundwork for Czech Theatre of the Absurd. It was the focus of much secret police attention prior to 1989, when it harboured such dissidents as Václav Havel (whose works are still part of the repertoire) and New Wave film-maker Jiří Menzel. More recently, the theatre was commanded by exciting director Petr Lébl, who hanged himself in the theatre's rafters after the première of his bold *Uncle Vanya*; it remains in the repertoire as a memorial. Though Na zábradlí has yet to find a replacement of Lébl's calibre, the work remains strong, and the resident company of actors (Jiří Ornest, Magdaléna Sidonová, Igor Chmela, Pavel Liška) is unbeatable.

Galerie NoD

1st Floor, Dlouhá 33, Prague 1 (224 826 296/ www.roxy.cz). Metro Staroměstská or Náměstí Republiky/tram 5, 8, 14. **Open** 1pm-1am Mon-Sat. **Tickets** 60-80 Kč. **No credit cards.** **Map** p328 L3.

Galerie NoD is a proper artists' hangout, decked out in surrealist decor, that stages off-centre theatre events, experimental music and comedy nights. Supported by the Linhart Foundation, a major funder of Czech alternative culture, it offers radical but hit-or-miss work. The venue also houses an art gallery and a hip internet café-bar.

Národní divadlo
National Theatre

Národní 2, Nové Město, Prague 1 (224 902 312/www.nd.cz). Metro Národní třída/tram 6, 9, 17, 18, 22. **Open** Box office 10am-6pm daily. **Tickets** 50-1,400 Kč. **Credit** AmEx, MC, V. **Map** p330 J7.

A separate Czech nation began to be built, literally, on the foundation stone of this landmark. As such, it would be nice to say that the opera, drama and ballet presented within it were the best of the best, but they're pretty inconsistent. For every brilliant interpretation of Chekhov or Dvořák, there's some tatty, musty old warhouse trundled out from the wings, trailing exhausted performers hitting their lines or notes by rote. The ballet, under the artistic direction of Petr Zuska, fares best. Still, this bedrock institution may soon improve under recently appointed director Ondřej Černý, a man of some vision. He may yet make the National matter again. *Photo p273.*

▶ *For more on the National Theatre, see p44 and p244.*

★ Ponec

Husitská 24A, Žižkov, Prague 3 (222 721 531/ www.tanecpha.cz). Metro Florenc, then bus 133 or 207. **Open** Box office 5-8pm Mon-Fri. **Tickets** 140-250 Kč. **No credit cards.** **Map** p333 A1.

As you walk toward Ponec, and you will be walking, you may wonder whether you're heading into Prague's Senseless Killing District. But persevere.

First, Prague is one of the safest cities in Europe. And second, your destination will be worth it: Ponec is the most important dance theatre in the Republic, a venue where terpsichorean careers are made and broken. Performances feature native dancers and choreographers, as well as international visitors.

Státní Opera
State Opera

Wilsonova 4, Nové Město, Prague 2 (224 227 232/www.opera.cz). Metro Muzeum/tram 11. **Open** Box office 10am-5.30pm Mon-Fri; 10am-noon, 1-5.30pm Sat, Sun. **Tickets** 200-900 Kč. **No credit cards. Map** p331 P7.

Next to the Estates (*see below*), the State Opera offers the second most dazzling theatre interior in Prague, which will come in handy when you want to avert your eyes from the stage. The quality of the work here is similar to the National, and the misses really will have you counting the cupids and caryatides. Just as at the National, the ballet bills are the strongest, particularly those geared towards children. Programmes are available in English.

▶ *For more on the State Opera, see p101 and p245.*

Stavovské divadlo
Estates Theatre

Ovocný trh 1, Staré Město, Prague 1 (information 224 901 448/box office 224 902 312/www.nd.cz). Metro Můstek/tram 3, 9, 14, 24. **Open** Box office 10am-6pm daily. **Tickets** 100-1,400 Kč. **Credit** MC, V (for advance sales only). **Map** p328 M4.

If you've seen Miloš Forman's film *Amadeus*, you've seen the Estates. This Baroque gem, which appears to be made from marzipan, was where Mozart's *La Clemenza di Tito* and *Don Giovanni* premièred, with the composer conducting. Today, it's one of the three performance venues under the National Theatre's umbrella. Opera is still performed here, along with dance and drama. Although the opera offers surtitles in English and German, plays are very rarely accompanied by translations.

▶ *There's more on the theatre's history and Mozart connection on p91.*

★ Švandovo divadlo
Švandovo Theatre

Štefánikova 57, Smíchov, Prague 5 (257 318 666/www.svandovodivadlo.cz). Metro Anděl/tram 6, 9. **Open** Box office 11am-2pm, 2.30-7pm Mon-Fri; 5pm-7pm Sat, Sun; or until 9pm performance days. **Tickets** 150-400 Kč. **No credit cards.**

There's no more accessible theatre in Prague for anglophones than Švandovo, which offers surtitles in English for all its productions. This is a boon for anyone wanting to explore otherwise untranslated Czech work, particularly classics by František Langer and Gabriela Preissová (whose play *Její pastorkyňa* served as the basis for Janáček's *Jenůfa*). The

ARTS & ENTERTAINMENT

theatre is also home to the marvellous puppet company Buchty a Loutky (Cakes & Puppets). Unfortunately, the theatre's directors, who fancy themselves auteurs, are at best acceptable and at worst uniquely unqualified.

▶ *The theatre has an impressive third space at Prostor Preslova 9, home to the performance troupe Farma v jeskyni (Farm in the Cave).*

BLACK LIGHT THEATRE

Black light theatre (*Černé divadlo*) was the brainchild of Jiří Srnec (*see below*), who cleverly combined elements of Japanese hooded bunraku puppetry with modern lighting techniques. It was a great hit at the Brussels World Expo in 1958 and the following year at the Edinburgh Festival. However, what began as a magical theatrical style of movement has become sclerotic: it's now primarily a tourist trap, the equivalent of going up to London to catch *The Mousetrap*. Praguers dismissively label the myriad theatres that specialise in it as *opičárny* (monkey houses).

Černé divadlo Jiřího Srnec
Black Light Theatre of Jiří Srnec
Reduta, Národní třída 20, Staré Město, Prague 1 (257 921 835/www.blacktheatresrnec.cz). Metro Národní třída/tram 6, 9, 18, 22. **Open** *Box office* 9am-7.30pm daily. **Tickets** 490 Kč. **No credit cards. Map** p328 L6.
Jiří Srnec, the inventor of Czech black light theatre, is still alive, and has lent his name to one of the more reputable of black light emporia. It's an institution, but some of the work has been around a while and is now looking a bit tatty.

Divadlo Image
Image Theatre
Pařížská 4, Staré Město, Prague 1 (222 314 448/222 314 548/www.imagetheatre.cz). Metro Staroměstská/tram 17, 18. **Open** *Box office* 9am-8pm daily. **Tickets** 400 Kč. **No credit cards. Map** p328 K2.
With more dancing, modern jazz and pantomime than some black light theatres, the shows at the Image epitomise the modern style. There are daily performances, and clips from all the shows are medleyed in a monthly 'Best of Image' production.

Laterna Magika
Magic Lantern
Nová Scéna, Národní třída 4, Nové Město, Prague 1 (224 931 482/www.laterna.cz). Metro Národní třída/tram 6, 9, 17, 18, 22. **Open** *Box office* 10am-8pm Mon-Sat. **Tickets** 300-600 Kč. **No credit cards. Map** p328 L6.
This company's glossy, high-tech multimedia productions are certainly professional, though no longer at the cutting edge; more slick modern dance than

traditional black light theatre, but still with an emphasis on visual tricks. The company's home is the Nová Scéna, the glass addition to the National Theatre (*see p105*).

PUPPET THEATRE

Puppetry is not just for children in Bohemia – it formed an intrinsic part of the Czech National Revival in the 1800s. Although much puppet theatre is aimed at tourists, high-quality Czech puppeteers and productions appear frequently. The **Divadlo Drak (Dragon Theatre)** and **Buchty a Loutky (Cakes & Puppets)** troupes put on particularly inspired shows.

★ Divadlo Minor
Minor Theatre
Vodičkova 6, Nové Město, Prague 1 (222 231 351/www.minor.cz). Metro Karlovo náměstí/tram 3, 9, 14, 24. **Open** *Box office* 10am-1.30pm, 2.30-8pm Mon-Fri; 11am-6pm Sat, Sun. **Tickets** 80-120 Kč. **No credit cards. Map** p329 N6.
A lively and progressive Czech puppet theatre for children and young adults. All directors and designers are contemporary guest artists invited from the worlds of opera and film as well as puppet theatre. Clown performances and productions are without words and therefore good for foreigners.

Národní divadlo marionet
National Marionette Theatre
Žatecká 1, Staré Město, Prague 1 (224 819 322/www.mozart.cz). Metro Staroměstská/tram 17, 18. **Open** *Box office* 10am-8pm daily. **Tickets** 490 Kč. **Credit** AmEx, MC, V. **Map** p328 K3.
The touristy National Marionette Theatre presents unchallenging but popular and skilful productions of *Don Giovanni*.

FESTIVALS

Every Czech city has a theatre scene, and it's not uncommon to find their companies setting up in the capital for a week to show what's happening in the hinterlands. If the Brno-based theatre **Husa na Provázku (Goose on a String)** is playing, go, particularly if Vladimír Morávek is directing. Festivals are listed in chronological order.

Česká tanečni platforma
Czech Dance Platform
Various venues (224 817 886/www.divadlo ponec.cz). **Tickets** 100-400 Kč. **No credit cards. Date** Apr.
Now into its second decade, Czech Dance Platform collects the best in Czech and Slovak dance and movement theatre every spring. Events take place in venues across town.

ARTS & ENTERTAINMENT

National Theatre.
See p271.

Mezi ploty

Areál PL Bohnice, Ústavní 91, Bohnice, Prague 8 (271 721 361/www.meziploty.cz). *Metro Nádraží Holešovice, then bus 152, 200.* **Tickets** 100-200 Kč. **No credit cards. Date** late May, Oct.
This two-day theatre, music and art festival is staged in the grounds of the Bohnice mental hospital on the outskirts of Prague. It features top Czech theatre companies, but nothing for English speakers.

★ Prague Fringe

Various venues (www.praguefringe.com). **Tickets** 100-200 Kč. **No credit cards. Date** June.
The city's newest theatre festival combines the best of Czech and international companies in a host of standard and unusual venues, and has now expanded into comedy nights in November and December. Any company is welcome to apply, so the result is an unpredictable cocktail – anything from cabaret to multimedia. There are some English language productions and a full English programme. *Photo p269.*

★ Tanec Praha
Dance Prague

Various venues (www.tanecpha.cz). **Tickets** 150-250 Kč. **No credit cards. Date** June.
Dance Prague is the biggest and longest-running dance event in Prague, featuring world-renowned companies alongside lesser-known Czech and international dance and dance-theatre troupes. Shows run alongside workshops and symposiums.

Čtyři dny v pohybu
Four Days in Motion

Various venues (www.ctyridny.cz). **Tickets** 100-200 Kč. **No credit cards. Date** Oct.
This annual festival of dance and visual theatre brings practitioners of experimental international movement theatre and multimedia performance to an assortment of makeshift theatres inside industrial spaces around Prague. Recent festivals have been located creatively in spaces such as a former sewerage plant and an ancient sports complex. There are some English-language productions.

Like Father, Like Sons

Two inventive creatives take their art to the people – by boat.

When film director Miloš Forman was forced to leave Czechoslovakia, he left behind his family. After he'd gone, twin sons Matěj and Petr began their own film careers as child actors in Czech cinema. In 2008, a public family reunion took place when the three Formans staged Jiří Suchý and Jiří Šlitr's charming '60s musical *A Walk Worthwhile* (*Dobře placená procházka*) at the National Theatre. It's still playing in rep there, and worth seeing, but the twins also work elsewhere in the Republic's theatre and movie industry. When they're not working in front of the cameras or backstage, the siblings can be found on the **Mystery Boat** (http://formanstheatre.cz), where they create their greatest work.

Every summer and autumn for nearly a decade, the Formans have cruised the narrow, landlocked coasts of Bohemia, primarily on the Vltava and Labe rivers, bringing their brand of theatre to the hinterlands by inviting the locals to step on board their craft and see shows in its 170-capacity theatre (every seat comes equipped with a life vest).

Their growing reputation is such that the Mystery Boat has also successfully anchored in far-flung ports of call such as Antwerp. It's understandably popular, so be sure to buy tickets in advance.

Barokní opera, the brothers' most famous piece, is one of the first examples of Czech opera, written by an 18th-century organist called Karel Loos. Bearing the catchy subtitle *A Czech Opera about a Comically Small Crooked-Looking Chimney Built by Masons, or The Quarrel Between the Landlord and the Masons*, the piece follows the struggle between an entrepreneur and a gang of slipshod masons responsible for putting up a dodgy chimney.

In the hands of the Formans, the opera becomes a slapstick epic for puppets and live performers. The playing area itself is a miniature mock-up of a classic Baroque stage, populated by a variety of puppets, from antique marionettes to hand puppets; masked actors continually intrude upon the grotesqueries that ensue. Film director Míra Janek made a movie of the piece, which serves as a documentary on the Formans' creation and as a stunning small film in its own right.

When the brothers are off touring, the Boat is still afloat with kindred companies: the staged punkery of Divadlo Aqualung and the excellent Husa na Provázku (Goose on a String). But with its cosy hull bar and charming Formanesque touches, such as stained-glass tables in the theatre, the boat merits a visit in its own right.

Escapes & Excursions

Karlovy Vary.
See p281.

Getting Started

Take off and hit the cesta.

Like most capitals, Prague is a world unto itself. So if you want to get a feel for what Czechs are really about, you'll need to get out of town. The gregariousness, practicality and beauty of the Czech Republic's smaller towns and countryside are affecting. Rolling up to an ancient castle town in an almost-as-ancient train is an experience to savour. It's an easily accessible land of rolling hills, ruins and hamlets that look as if they haven't changed for centuries. So leave behind the growing noise, exhaust fumes and stress of Prague – if only for a short break – and hit the highway, or *cesta*, to check out greater Bohemia and Moravia.

THE HIGHLIGHTS

Divided into the provinces of **Bohemia** in the north-west and **Moravia** in the south-east, the terrain of the Czech Republic offers surprisingly diverse countryside. Graced with wooded hills and little valleys, Moravia is prettiest in autumn, when a leisurely week could be spent vineyard-hopping, combing through caves and getting a culture fix in **Brno**, the Czech Republic's second city (*see p288*).

Despite inheriting a sad legacy of pollution from heavy industry, North Bohemia offers the beautiful **Český ráj (Czech Paradise**; *see p295*), a playground for hikers. Here, striking sandstone cliffs line the banks of the **Labe (Elbe)** river. Green, mountainous South Bohemia, with its carp ponds and dense woods, attracts pilgrims from spring to autumn, and quaint, ancient towns such as **Kašperské Hory** (*see p296*) and **Český Krumlov** (*see p290*) make great jumping-off points for hikes, road trips and mushrooming expeditions.

In West Bohemia, the stars still shine as they touch the earth during the **Karlovy Vary International Film Festival** (*see p226 and p280*). However, the hilly landscape around the famed spa towns is enchanting at any time of year, with spruce forests and hot springs.

ABOUT THE CHAPTERS

Our selection of trips out of town is split into two parts. **Excursions** (*see pp278-285*) covers destinations that are feasible day trips, with no

overnight stays required. As well as some picturesque towns, we've also included a selection of classic Central Bohemian castles.

The destinations featured in **Escapes** (*see pp286-298*), meanwhile, will all require an overnight stay. If you're thinking of staying overnight at any of these destinations, the tourist offices should be able to help you book lodgings. Private houses all over the country also offer rooms for tourists, offering a chance to savour something of real small-town life.

GETTING AROUND

Most destinations that are listed have been included with ease of access by public transport in mind. The main exception is the Czech Republic's wine country, which lies in the eastern province of Moravia and is well suited to a driving tour. If you want a city break with minimal effort, try one of the trips to **Terezín** (*see p284*), **Karlštejn** (*see p278*) or **Karlovy Vary** (*see p281*), available through **Čedok** (*see p311*). Rafting and cycling trips can also be arranged through **Central European Adventures** (Jáchymova 4, Staré Město, Prague 1, 222 328 879, www.members.tripod. com/cea51).

The trains of the former Eastern bloc are an excellent resource: a survivor of communist times, they may be a bit shabby and overheated, but they're also cheap, efficient and scenic, and they go just about everywhere. Alternatively, cars can be hired for around 800Kč a day if you shop around (*see p302*).

And buses, also very cheap, go everywhere that the trains don't – though their drivers may cost you in other ways if you're prone to nerves.

By bus

The state bus company **ČSAD** (Křižikova 4, Karlin, Prague 8, 900 144 444, www.idos.cz) covers most destinations. It's best to pick up tickets a day beforehand for popular weekend trips. Also, note that you'll need a local friend to get any use out of the Czech-only information line, which is open 24 hours a day but costs 14 Kč per minute.

Many intercity bus services depart from **Florenc** coach station (*see p300*). Services are more frequent in the morning. It's worth checking the return times before you leave, as the last bus back may depart disappointingly early (often before 6pm). A few buses also leave from **Nádraží Holešovice** station (*see p300*).

A number of private bus services now offer competitive prices and times, and, as in the case of the **Student Travel Agency** (www. studentagency.cz), far better service and coaches. Don't be put off by the name: this friendly, helpful company is priced for students but intended for anyone on a budget.

By car

There are just a few motorways in the Czech Republic, and drivers are often confined to local roads. Prices for car hire vary depending on whether you're renting from an international or local company (*see p302*). The speed limit is 50kph (31mph) in built-up areas, 130kph (81mph) on motorways, and 90kph (56mph) everywhere else. If you have an accident, call the **Emergency Road Service** on 1240.

Petrol stations, some marked by a big *benzín* sign, are ubiquitous these days, and now come fully stocked with microwaveable junk food and coffee machines. Petrol comes in two grades, super and special; the latter is recommended for most West European cars. Unleaded is called 'natural' and diesel is *nafta*.

By train

Czech train travel is priced by the kilometre and, despite recent price hikes, is still a bargain. Trains often follow more scenic routes than buses but cover less ground and usually take longer. There are four main railway stations in Prague, but no fixed pattern as to which domestic destinations they serve. **Hlavní nádraží** (*see p300*) is the most central station and one of two principal departure points for international services, as well as some domestic services. Timetables can be obtained at the

information windows (don't queue at a *mezinárodní* information window unless you want an international train). **Nádraží Holešovice** (*see p300*) is also principally used for international services. As a rule, **Masarykovo nádraží** serves most destinations in northern and eastern Bohemia. Domestic routes to the south and west leave from **Smíchovské nádraží** (*see p300*).

Hitchhiking

The usual rules of courtesy and common sense, especially for women, apply to hitchhiking within the Czech Republic. It's a time-honoured method of transport, particularly among students. As with hitching a ride in any country, travel with a friend and position yourself just outside the city limits with a sign bearing your destination of choice. You should offer to help with petrol money, though your money will most likely be waved away.

Karlovy Vary. See p281.

Excursions

Rocky outcrops and spa town decadence.

If you've only got time for a day-trip break from Prague, two choices loom largest of all. The first is to head to one of a variety of ancient castles within striking distance, all of which are accessed relatively easily from the city via public transport. However, if Prague Castle has sated your yearning for ageing fortifications, a number of towns are also worthy of a diversion – from handsome **Karlovy Vary**, home to a tremendous film festival, to **Terezín**, still dominated by the hideous legacy of World War II.

Castles

The long history of feudal plundering in the Czech lands means there are fortifications, keeps, battlements and baileys everywhere. Some of the finest are within reach of Prague, and a good few have been turned into restaurants and hostelries.

The wooded or mountainous setting of these monuments and palaces can be just as good as the treasures contained within. Find a rocky outcrop, preferably on the bend in a river, and someone, sometime will probably have built a redoubt on top. An hour's train journey or drive from Prague will land you at the foot of the palatial **Karlštejn** (*see below*), the impressive **Konopiště** (*see right*) or the Gothic grandeur of **Křivoklát** (*see right*).

KARLŠTEJN

Jutting up like the royal crown it is, Karlštejn Castle was once Charles IV's summer palace, perched over a lush bend of the Berounka river roughly 30 kilometres (19 miles) to the south-west of Prague. Castle aficionados maintain that Karlštejn looks better from without than from within. Dating from the 14th century, it was largely rebuilt in neo-Gothic style in the 19th century, but its interiors were sadly neglected.

The approach to the fort is an obstacle course of overpriced snack bars and hawkers of postcards, crystal and lace. But at least this stronghold, former home to the crown jewels, offers spectacular views to reward visitors for the short but strenuous hike up to the castle entrance from the train station.

One rewarding interior feature is the **Holy Rood Chapel**, its walls adorned with semi-precious stones and painted wooden panels by Master Theodoric, Charles IV's court portrait artist. There's also an altar with a diptych by Tomaso da Modena. Unfortunately, the other rooms can't match the chapel's splendour.

Owing to its proximity to Prague, Karlštejn is the Czech Republic's most visited castle, so a visit here inevitably comes with some jostling, courtesy of tour parties; the trip is probably best done early or late in the season. There are two tours of the castle in English, but they're both tedious in any language. The first runs for about an hour, while the second, which includes the Holy Rood Chapel, your main quarry, is otherwise an encyclopaedic chronicle of furnishings that runs for 100 minutes or longer.

Karlštejn Castle

Karlštejn (311 681 617/274 008 154/ www.hradkarlstejn.cz). **Open** *Nov-Jan, Mar* 9am-3pm Tue-Sun. *Apr, Oct* 9am-4pm Tue-Sun. *May, June, Sept* 9am-5pm Tue-Sun. *July, Aug* 9am-6pm Tue-Sun. Last tour 1hr before closing. **Admission** *Castle tour* 220 Kč; 120 Kč reductions. *Castle tour (incl chapel)* 300 Kč; 150 Kč reductions. **No credit cards.**

Where to eat

Pod Dračí Skálou

Karlštejn 130 (311 681 177). **Open** 11am-11pm Mon-Sat; 11am-10pm Sun. **Main courses** 65-155 Kč. **Credit** AmEx, MC, V.

This rustic place, just a short walk north of the castle, has a surprisingly diverse menu of Czech dishes, from boar to pheasant and venison, with tangy sauces and hearty mugs of beer on tap. It doubles as an atmospheric little pension.

U Janů

Karlštejn 90 (311 681 210). **Open** *Jan, Mar-May, Sept-Dec* 11am-5pm Tue-Sun. *June-Aug* 11am-10pm Tue-Sun. **Main courses** 160-180 Kč. **No credit cards**.

An old-fashioned place with antlers hanging from the ceiling, with a pleasant terrace garden too, this restaurant tends to be mobbed by tourists in high season, like everywhere else in this hamlet. However, the food is decent value, with dishes such as trout, duck and rabbit costing a fraction of Prague prices. There's also accommodation on the premises.

Getting there

By car

Karlštejn is 30km (19 miles) south-west of Prague. Take the E50-D5 or Route 5 towards Plzeň, then leave the motorway at exit 10 and follow the signs for Karlštejn.

By train

Trains leave Prague's Smíchovské nádraží or Hlavní nádraží stations for Karlštejn about every hour. The trip takes around 40mins. It's a 10min walk from the station up to the village, and a further 15mins from there up to the castle.

KONOPIŠTĚ

With more architectural appeal than Karlštejn and of equal historical significance, **Konopiště** is an exceptional castle in a land that's studded with hundreds. Built with seven French-style tower fortifications defending a rectangular bailey, Konopiště's contents are more stirring than most as well, particularly the fantastic collection of weapons and the gruesomely extensive display of hunting trophies.

The castle, which dates from the 14th century, was refurbished by the Habsburgs as a hunting lodge to satisfy the predatory passions of its most famous occupant, Archduke Franz Ferdinand. He lived here with his Czech wife, Sophie, who was shot along with him at Sarajevo in 1914. The assassination, aside from triggering World War I, spoiled Ferdinand's accession to the throne to which he was heir.

As you meander through his decadent digs, it will become apparent that he managed to do quite a bit of damage to the local fauna during his curtailed time on this earth. Ferdinand slaughtered nearly every kind of animal imaginable from the surrounding Sázava river woods and, incredibly, the countless trophies here represent only one per cent of the total collection. He supposedly felled an average of 20 animals a day, every day, for some 40 years.

The tour takes in sedate rooms featuring collections of wooden Italian cabinets and Meissen porcelain. A second tour of the castle, requiring a separate ticket, takes you through the archduke's private chambers, the chapel and a Habsburg version of a gentlemen's club. The castle has large grounds in which the peacocks and pheasants aren't affixed to a wall. Bears pace incessantly in the dry moat, oblivious to their unluckier brethren within.

Konopiště's popularity is second only to that of Karlštejn, so expect lots of coach parties.

Konopiště Castle

Konopiště (317 721 366/274 008 154/ www.zamek-konopiste.cz). **Open** *Apr, Oct* 9am-noon, 1-3pm Mon-Fri; 9am-noon, 1-4pm Sat, Sun. *May-Aug* 9am-noon, 1-5pm daily. *Sept* 9am-noon, 1-4pm daily. *Nov* 9am-noon, 1-3pm Mon-Fri, 9am-noon, 1-4pm Sat, Sun. **Admission** 190 Kč; 110 Kč reductions. 300 Kč English-speaking guide. **Credit** MC, V.

Getting there

By bus

Buses leave from Florenc station nearly every 45mins; the trip lasts a little over an hour. Note that it's a 2km walk from the station, but the path is marked with signs.

By car

Konopiště is 35km (22 miles) from Prague. Go south on the D1 and exit near Benešov, following the signs for Konopiště.

By train

Hourly trains to Benešov from Hlavní nádraží take about an hour. The castle is a 2km walk from the station but the way is well marked. Alternatively, you can catch one of the infrequent buses.

KŘIVOKLÁT

Křivoklát manages the unusual feat of being a living Gothic fortress. It does this, despite being founded 900 years ago, by functioning as a kind of living museum to medieval life and crafts, with resident artists and craftsmen operating a smithy and offering the resulting wares for sale. All the products are produced by ancient and authentic carpentry, ceramics and weaving techniques. It's also the perfect counterpoint to the tourist hordes that descend on overcrowded Karlštejn. Just inconvenient enough to remain peaceful, Křivoklát boasts one of the finest interiors in the country, featuring a magnificent knights' hall and royal hall plastered in late Gothic paintings and sculptures.

Křivoklát Castle.

ESCAPES & EXCURSIONS

Křivoklát was originally a Přemyslid hunting lodge, and was converted into a castle at the beginning of the 12th century by King Vladislav I. Fires followed, along with a spate of rebuilding by the Polish king Vladislav II Jagellon, whose trademark 'W' can be seen throughout the castle.

A fine altarpiece in the chapel portrays Christ surrounded by sweet-looking angels holding medieval instruments of torture. A more varied selection of these awaits in the dungeon, where you'll find a rack, a thumbscrew and the Rosary of Shame (a necklace made of lead weights), along with the Iron Maiden.

The castle's enormous Round Tower dates from 1280. English alchemist Edward Kelley was confined here for three years after Rudolf II tired of waiting for him to succeed in turning base metals into gold. Kelley managed to wangle his release, but failed to produce the gold, and was imprisoned in a different castle where he later died, supposedly from injuries suffered while trying to escape.

Two English-language castle tours set off every half-hour up to one hour before closing time. However, for the tours to run, there has to be a minimum of five English speakers willing to take part – or a smaller number willing to pay for the cost of five tickets.

The drive to Křivoklát is one of the attractions of a visit. The route follows the course of the Berounka river past fields, meadows and a forested hill before the castle dramatically appears, standing atop a lofty promontory.

★ Křivoklát Castle

Křivoklát (313 559 165/www.krivoklat.cz). **Open** *May, June* 9am-5pm Tue-Sun. *July, Aug* 9am-5.30pm Tue-Sun. *Apr, Sept* 9am-4pm Tue-Sun. *Oct* 10am-4pm Tue-Sun. *Nov-mid-Dec* 10am-3pm Sat, Sun. **Admission** *Long tour* 100 Kč; 70 Kč reductions (30 Kč for translator). *Short tour* (tower only) 70 Kč; 50 Kč reductions. **No credit cards.**

Where to eat

Hotel u Dvořáků

Roztoky 225 (313 558 355). **Open** 10am-11pm daily. **Main courses** 150 Kč. **No credit cards.** This is the only real place to eat near the castle. It serves a decent menu of the usual Czech fare at the usual better-than-Prague prices, and with friendlier service to boot.

Getting there

By bus

Direct buses leave from opposite the Hradčanská metro stop twice a day. The journey takes about 1hr 20mins.

By car

Křivoklát is 45km (28 miles) from Prague. Take the E50-D5 in the direction of Beroun. Turn off at junction 14 and follow the Berounka valley west, as if going to Rakovník.

By train

Direct trains to Křivoklát are infrequent, so take one to Beroun, which leaves from Smíchovské nádraží or Hlavní nádraží about every half-hour (journey time around 45mins), and change at Beroun for Křivoklát (a further 40mins).

Towns

There's more to life outside Prague than castles. From the spa town of **Karlovy Vary** (*see below*) to the fascinating silver mines of **Kutná Hora** (*see p282*), the postcard-perfect **Mělník** (*see p283*) to the dark wartime history of **Terezín** (*see p284*), Bohemia's towns make for ideal trips out of the capital.

KARLOVY VARY

Elegant if sleepy, at least when it's not high tourist season, **Karlovy Vary** tempts visitors with stately charms from another era. The promenades and colonnades of this West Bohemian spa town are looking finer than ever, following the infusion of much capital from Russian residents who have all but adopted the city. They're following in a grand tradition: Peter the Great was among the aristocrats and artists from the east, along with others from Western Europe, who once trekked here in search of luxurious cures in the hot springs.

Local lore has it that Karlovy Vary – or Karlsbad, as it was known until the last century – began its ascent to steamy fame and fortune in 1358, when one of Charles IV's hunting hounds leapt off a steep crag in hot pursuit of a more nimble stag. The unfortunate dog fell to the ground and injured its paw, then made a recovery as it limped through a pool of hot, bubbling water. Experts were summoned to test the restorative waters and declared them to be beneficial for all kinds of ills.

The Ohře river runs through the centre of town and disappears beneath the hulking **Hotel Thermal** (IP Pavlova 11, 359 001 111, www.thermal.cz, 1,230-2,500 Kč double), which

stands as a fascinating symbol of the communist notion of luxury, especially when contrasted with the gracious elegance of the **Grand Hotel Pupp** (*see below*). As for the town itself, the garish boutiques and inescapable wafer shops may not be everyone's idea of relaxation – but you can always retreat to the parks, which are adorned with busts of some of the spa's more famous guests, or self-medicate with a few Becherovkas, the famous local herbal liqueur that's made with the region's pure spring water.

The picture-postcard pretty streets grow very busy in late June and early July for the renowned **Karlovy Vary International Film Festival** (*see p226*), when the assortment of boulevards and thermal fountains becomes the Hollywood Boulevard of Central Europe. While it may be best known as a cineaste's festival, with endless screenings of new and avant-garde films, that's not to say that there aren't opportunities to indulge in some celebrity-spotting. For all other non-Film Festival cultural events, contact Čedok for tickets on 353 222 994 or 353 223 335.

Vojenské State Baths

Lázně 3, Mlýnské nábřeží 5 (353 119 111). **Open** 7am-3pm Mon-Sat. **Admission** 400 Kč. **Credit** AmEx, MC, V.
Not as plush as the Pupp baths, naturally, but you'll get a thorough and renewing treatment here, administered by no-nonsense pros.

Where to stay & eat

Grand Hotel Pupp

Mírové náměstí 2 (353 109 111/www.pupp.cz). **Open** *Roman baths* 8am-3pm Mon-Sat. *Castle baths* 7.30am-7.30pm daily. *Grand restaurant* noon-3pm, 6-10pm daily. **Rates** 4,500-5,500 Kč single; 4,520-7,040 Kč double; 7,500-10,000 Kč suite. **Main courses** 350-600 Kč. **Credit** AmEx, MC, V.
If you splurge on this lavish hotel, said to be the finest in the country, ask for a room that hasn't yet been refurbished; several have been rather unsympathetically 'modernised'. If you're feeling flush, the elegant restaurant is worth a visit, as is the hotel spa.

Promenáda

Tržiště 31 (353 225 648/www.hotel-promenada. cz). **Rates** 990-2,790 Kč single; 1,340-1,890 Kč double; 4,930-7,860 Kč apartments. **Main courses** 200-350 Kč. **Credit** AmEx, MC, V.
Known mainly these days for its award-winning gourmet restaurant, still something of a rarity in Karlovy Vary, this hotel is a cut above the usual. Service is excellent, and the muted decor shows off the current state of Czech high living. The bar offers high-quality wines from vineyards in Moravia.

ESCAPES & EXCURSIONS

Resources

Tourist information

Lázeňská 1 (353 224 097). **Open** *Apr-mid Nov*
9am-7pm Mon-Fri; 10am-6pm Sat, Sun. *Mid Nov-
Mar* 9am-5pm Mon-Fri; 10am-5pm Sat, Sun.
No credit cards.
The staff here are helpful, multilingual and have
information and tickets for all local events – except,
of course, the film festival.

Getting there

By bus

Buses run at least hourly from Prague's Florenc
station from 8am, with a journey time of about
2hrs 30mins. The private bus service Asiana (841
111 117, www.asiana.cz) also runs a bus hourly
from Florenc metro and bus station, the Dejvická
metro and Ruzyně Airport.

By car

Karlovy Vary is 130km (81 miles) west of Prague
on the E48.

By train

Trains leave Prague's Hlavní nádraží three times
a day. The journey time is about 4hrs.

KUTNÁ HORA

The soaring peaks of the cathedral in **Kutná
Hora** are visible for miles around, testifying to
the town's former role as a key source of wealth
in Bohemia. Kutná Hora's fame and status were
secured in the 13th century with the discovery
of silver. A Gothic boom town was born; for 250
years, Kutná Hora was second in importance
only to Prague in this part of the nation.

However, this fabled history might not be
apparent when you get off the train. Don't
worry, and don't be put off by the concrete
tower blocks that cluster around Sedlec station
like bad teeth – the UNESCO-designated World
Heritage Site old centre is a couple of kilometres
to the south-west. But before heading there, you
might want to stop at Sedlec's incredible bone
chapel, the **Ossuary**, where 40,000 skeletons
were arranged over the ages into fantastical
shapes by monks. The Cistercian abbey, which
was founded in 1142 and now houses a tobacco
factory, established the ossuary a few hundred
metres north of the church on Zámecká so the
monks might have a suitable memento mori.

To get from Sedlec to Kutna Horá's old
centre, either walk or catch the bus marked
'Centrum'. You'll soon find yourself at the
town's glory, the **Kostel sv. Barbory**
(**Cathedral of St Barbara**). Designed in Peter
Parler's workshop, it's a magnificent 1388
Gothic building with an exterior that outclasses

even St Vitus's Cathedral in Prague. St Barbara
was the patron saint of silver miners; their guild
emblems decorate the ceiling of the building.

For an idea of what life was like in a
medieval mine, head to the Hrádek or Little
Castle. Here, the **České museum stříba**
(**Czech Silver Museum**) kits you out in
protective suits and hard hats for a trip down
into the tunnels. If you want to see the silver
mine, a guided tour is compulsory. Booking
is advisable.

České museum stříbra
Czech Silver Museum & Medieval Mine

Barborská 28 (327 512 159/www.cms-kh.cz).
Open *Apr, Oct* 9am-5pm Tue-Sun. *May, June,
Sept* 9am-6pm Tue-Sun. *July, Aug* 10am-6pm
Tue-Sun. *Nov* 10am-4pm Tue-Sun. Last entry
90mins before closing time. **Admission** 60-130
Kč; 30-80 Kč reductions; 400 Kč tours in English.
No credit cards.

Kostel sv. Barbory
Cathedral of St Barbara

Barborská (327 512 115). **Open** *Nov-Mar*
10am-noon, 1-4pm Tue-Sun. *Apr, Oct* 9am-noon,
1-4.30pm Tue-Sun. *May-Sept* 9am-6pm Tue-
Sun. **Admission** 30 Kč; 15 Kč reductions.
No credit cards.

Sedlec Ossuary

Kostnice Zámecká (327 561 143). **Open**
Nov-Mar 9am-noon, 1-4pm daily. *Apr-Sept*
8am-6pm daily. *Oct* 9am-noon, 1-5pm daily.
Admission 35 Kč; 20 Kč reductions.
No credit cards.

Where to eat

Harmonia

Husova 105 (327 512 275). **Open** 10am-11pm
daily. **Main courses** 70-180 Kč. **No credit cards**.
Harmonia serves up good, traditional Czech food on
a beautiful terrace.

Resources

Tourist information

*Sankturinovský dům, Palackého náměstí 377
(327 515 556/327 512 378)*. **Open** *Apr-Sept*
9am-6pm daily. *Oct-Mar* 9am-5pm Mon-Fri;
10am-4pm Sat, Sun. **No credit cards**.
The helpful staff here can arrange for stays in private houses as well as providing the usual range of
tourist-related information.

Getting there

By bus

Buses leave 11 times a day from Florenc station.
The journey time is about 75mins.

By car

Kutná Hora is 70km (44 miles) from Prague. Head out through Žižkov and follow signs to Kolín to Route 12; then change to road 38 to Kutná Hora. A scenic alternative is Route 333 via Říčany, further south.

By train

Trains run from Hlavní nádraží or Masarykovo nádraží daily and take 50mins. The main Kutná Hora station is actually located in Sedlec. Local trains meet express trains coming from Prague and take visitors into Kutná Hora proper.

MĚLNÍK

An important town in the transplanting of viniculture from France to the Czech lands, **Mělník** is a quiet little hamlet within easy reach of Prague, offering pastoral views from its impressively restored castle. Just 33 kilometres (20 miles) north of Prague, the town also features yet another bizarre ossuary to go with its bucolic appeal. And, opera buffs note, the castle vineyards produce Ludmila wine, the tipple that Mozart supposedly drank while he composed *Don Giovanni*.

The main sights are near the lovely **castle**, now more château than stronghold. It occupies a prime position on a steep escarpment overlooking the confluence of the Vltava and Labe rivers, which was the inspiration for Smetana's anthem to Bohemia, *Ma Vlast* ('My Country'). The castle was rebuilt during the 16th and 17th centuries, when it lost much of its medieval character as a fort and was transformed into something more like a palace. Recent restitution laws have returned it to the ownership of the Lobkowicz family – once among the most powerful in Bohemia before being driven into exile – from whom the property was expropriated by the communists.

You can tour the castle's interior and, even better, take a separate tour round the splendidly gloomy wine cellars, wherein viniculture is followed, appropriately enough, by tastings and a chance to walk over an arrangement of thousands of upturned bottles. Although a settlement has existed here since the tenth century, it was Charles IV who introduced vines to the region from his lands in Burgundy. He also established a palace for the Bohemian queens, who would come here to escape Prague until the end of the 15th century.

Opposite the castle is the late Gothic **Kostel sv. Petr a Pavel (Church of Ss Peter and Paul)**. The ossuary in the crypt consists of skulls and bones piled to the ceiling. Two speakers precariously balanced on top of a stack of femurs broadcast a breathless English commentary delivered in Hammer horror style.

The site was established as a burial place for plague victims in the 16th century and sealed off. However, in 1914, a professor from Charles University cracked open the vault and brought his students to arrange the 15,000 skeletons he found within – revealing that ossuaries were not solely a medieval Czech fixation. The end result includes the Latin for 'Behold death!' spelled out in skulls.

Náměstí Míru, the main square below the castle, is lined with typically Bohemian Baroque and Renaissance buildings. The fountain dates from considerably later.

Kostnice
Ossuary

Church of Ss Peter & Paul (315 622 337). **Open** 9.30am-12.30pm, 1.15-4pm Tue-Fri; 10am-12.30pm, 1.15-4pm Sat, Sun. **Admission** 25 Kč; 15 Kč reductions. **No credit cards.**

Mělník Castle

Svatováclavská 19 (315 622 121/www.lobkowicz-melnik.cz). **Open** 10am-5pm daily. **Admission** *Castle tour* 80 Kč; 50 Kč reductions. *Wine-tasting tour* 70-220 Kč. **No credit cards.**

Where to eat

Castle vinárna

Svatováclavská 19 (315 622 121). **Open** 11am-6pm Tue-Sun. **Main courses** 195-575 Kč. **Credit** AmEx, MC, V.

The Castle vinárna is the swankiest dining room in town. The crockery is embossed with the insignia of the Lobkowicz family, the vaulted walls are painted a delicate peach colour and it's one of the better restaurants in the whole region.

Restaurace Stará Škola

Na vyhlídce 159 (no phone). **Open** 11am-11pm daily. **Main courses** 190 Kč. **No credit cards.**

Restaurace Stará Škola is a basic restaurant, close to the Church of Ss Peter and Paul, which does a decent plate of steak and chips with a more than decent backdrop: the terrace has a beautiful view over the surrounding countryside and the confluence of the Vltava and Labe rivers.

Resources

Tourist information

Náměstí Míru 30 (315 627 503). **Open** *May-Sept* 9am-5pm daily. *Oct-Apr* 9am-5pm Mon-Fri.

Getting there

By bus

There are roughly 15 departures a day from Prague's Holešovice metro and train station. Journey time is 50mins.

By car

Mělník is 33km (20 miles) from Prague. Head north out of Prague on Route 608; follow signs to Zdiby, then Mělník on Route 9.

TEREZÍN

Originally known as Theresienstadt, when it was built as a fortress town in 1780 on the orders of Emperor Joseph II to protect his empire from Prussian invaders, **Terezín** was briefly given its old name back when the Nazis took it over in 1941. It was here that Red Cross inspectors, visiting as a result of Danish pressure to ascertain what had happened to Danish Jews, were duped into believing that it was a model resettlement site when in fact the entire town was functioning as a holding camp for Jews en route to death camps further east.

Of 140,000 men, women and children who passed through Terezín, 87,000 were sent east, most of them to Auschwitz. Only 3,000 of these were to return alive. Another 34,000 people died within the ghetto of Terezín itself. Now little more than a Czech army barracks town, Terezín's atmosphere is still distinctly eerie, with lifeless, grid-pattern streets. The Nazis expelled the native population, few of whom chose to return after the war.

The **Muzeum ghetta** (**Ghetto Museum**) screens documentary films of wartime life here in several languages. Possibly the most chilling contains clips from the Nazi propaganda film, commonly called *The Führer Gives a Town to the Jews* although its correct title is *Terezín: A Documentary Film of the Jewish Resettlement*, part of the sophisticated strategy to hoodwink the world. Red Cross officials visited the camp twice and saw a completely staged, self-governing Jewish community with a flourishing cultural life. A Jewish prisoner, Kurt Gerron, directed the film. After shooting the film, most of the cast, and the director himself, were deported to Auschwitz and killed.

The harrowing ground-floor exhibition of artwork produced by the children of Terezín has now been removed to Prague's Pinkas Synagogue. Upstairs is an exhibition on the Nazi occupation of Czechoslovakia. Decrees of discriminating measures against Jews are detailed – including, in a telling detail of the dehumanisation of the Jews by the Nazis, the certificate that a customer in a pet shop intending to buy a canary was required to sign, which promised that the pet would not be exposed to any Jewish people.

A 15-minute walk back down the Prague road brings you to the **Malá pevnost** (**Small Fortress**), which was built at the same time as the larger town fortress. The Gestapo established a prison here in 1940, through which 32,000 political prisoners passed. Some 2,500 died within its walls. The approach to the Small Fortress passes through a cemetery containing the graves of 10,000 Nazi victims with, in the middle, a giant wooden cross.

The whole fortress is now a museum, and a free map (available from the ticket office) assists exploration of the Gestapo's execution ground and of courtyards and cells, some of which held more than 250 inmates at a time. The former SS commander's house is now a museum with displays detailing the appalling physical condition the inmates endured.

Malá pevnost
Small Fortress

Malá pevnost (416 782 225). **Open** *Nov-Mar* 8am-4.30pm daily. *Apr-Oct* 8am-6pm daily. **Admission** 180 Kč; 140 Kč reductions. **No credit cards.**
Guided tours run for groups of ten-plus. Book ahead.

★ Muzeum ghetta
Ghetto Museum

Komenského 411 (416 782 225/www. pamatnik-terezin.cz). **Open** *Nov-Mar* 9am-5.30pm daily. *Apr-Oct* 9am-6pm daily. **Admission** *Museum* 160 Kč; 130 Kč reductions. *Museum & Small Fortress* 200 Kč; 150 Kč reductions. **No credit cards.**

Where to eat

Light meals can be had in the former guards' canteen inside the entrance to the Small Fortress.

Hotel Salva Guarda

Mírové náměstí 12, Litoměřice (416 732 506/ www.salva-guarda.cz). **Open** 11am-11pm Mon-Thur, Sun; 11am-1am Fri, Sat. **Main courses** 150 Kč. **Credit** AmEx, DC, MC, V.
A traditional restaurant, serving decent and straightforward Czech cuisine.

Resources

Tourist information

Náměstí ČS armády 179 (416 782 616). **Open** 8am-5pm Mon-Thur; 8am-1.30pm Fri; 9am-3pm Sun.

Getting there

By bus

Buses leave Florenc station once every hour. Journey time is 60-75mins.

By car

Terezín is 50km (31 miles) north-west from Prague. Join Route 8 or the E55 at Holešovice, via Veltrusy, and follow it to Terezín.

Terezín.

ESCAPES & EXCURSIONS

Escapes

Head to the countryside, or discover the home of beer.

There's a variety of appealing day-long getaways within easy reach of Prague. But there are also a number of worthwhile options further afield, deeper into the heart of the Czech Republic.

Lovers of lager may care to make a pilgrimage to **Plzeň** (*see below*), birthplace of pilsner. Wine drinkers may prefer **Brno** (*see p288*), where you'll find plenty of fine Moravian vintages. However, there are also plenty of beautiful rural escapes that offer a chance to really get away from it all: in particular, the isolated town of **Kašperské Hory** (*see p296*) in the Šumava National Forest is a wonderful spot.

Towns & Villages

PLZEŇ

The West Bohemia city of **Plzeň**, or **Pilsen** to English-speakers, would be worth a visit even if it weren't synonymous with the greatest Czech invention and export, Pilsner Urquell lager. But, of course, after a century and a half of basking in the golden glow of its brewing expertise, it's impossible to separate the city from images of fine mugs of froth. Even non-drinkers will find it striking, memorable and wholly apart from Prague in look and feel. Praguers will secretly confess that folk from Pilsen are friendlier. And it's a handsome place: the town's old centre has been gussied up into an elegant 18th-century restoration, complete with promenades, a major zoo and some impressive museums.

The city's centre was officially founded by Wenceslas II in 1295 at the confluence of the Radbuza, Mže, Úhlava and Úslava rivers, though it was already a growing trade town at the crossroads linking the Czech lands with German cities Nuremburg and Regensburg. Italian architect Giovanni de Statia contributed much to the city's look after fires in the 16th century. A major university came later. And then Pilsen boomed during the industrial revolution, thanks to both Pilsner Urquell and the Škoda manufacturing plant (much prized by the Nazis as early spoils of World War II).

Venturing west across the Radbuza river from the train station, it's hard not to feel the frisson of history. Hulking pre-1989 concrete structures dominate the riverfront, but then you find yourself walking down Americká Street, a tribute to the Allied forces who liberated the city in 1945. Patton's Third Army was ordered to stay put and let the Red Army reach Prague first. It was a favour to Stalin, who repaid it by erasing every reference to the Americans from school books and history. Every 8 May, locals who hid US Army gear, including a Jeep or two, get it out and parade down the street.

For a longer-term sense of history, consider stopping in at the **Západočeské muzeum v Plzni** (**West Bohemian Museum**; Kopeckého sady 2, 377 329 380, www.zcm.cz), a multi-storey natural history collection in a stately building at the bottom of the green boulevard just north of Americká. The number of cafés and good restaurants in this area, which surrounds the city's main square, make it ideal for strolling.

If kids are in the equation, a trip to the **Zoo & Botanical Garden** (Pod Vinicemi 9, 378 038 301, www.zoopilzn.cz) is a good bet, particularly as it can be combined with a visit to the attached DinoPark, complete with roaring thunder lizards. Just bear in mind that it's on the north-west edge of town and best reached by car – or a lengthy ride on trams 1 and 4.

Every May, the Finale film fest (www.filmfestfinale.cz) celebrates the best in Czech film, most recently honouring, along with new indie achievements, street filmmaking during the Soviet-led invasion of 1968. There's also a lot of excitement at the celebration of pilsner's founding anniversary on 6 October, when the streets fill with musicians, fireworks and spilled lager.

Brewery Museum

Veleslavinova 6 (377 235 574). **Open** *Apr-Dec*
10am-6pm daily. *Jan-Mar* 10am-5pm daily.
Admission 100-120 Kč. **No credit cards**.
The thrilling history of the bottom-fermenting
process and its Czech origins, along with a self-
guided walk among improbably folksy mannequins.

Great Synagogue

*Sady Pětatřicátníko 11 (377 235 749/
www.zoplzen.cz).* **Open** 9am-1pm Mon-Fri.
Admission 120 Kč; 60 Kč reductions.
No credit cards.
The second-largest synagogue in Europe, founded
in 1894, stands as testament to the Jewish community that thrived here until World War II. Its pneu-
matic organ is a gem, still used for concerts, and
post-1989 restoration has done wonders.

Pilsner Urquell Brewery

U Prazdroje 7 (377 062 888/www.prazdroj.cz).
Open *Tours in English* 12.45pm, 2.15pm, 4.15pm
daily. **Admission** 150 Kč (250 Kč combined
brewery & museum ticket). **No credit cards**.
Ever-popular tours of the 166-year-old brewery
draw beer fans from around the world. The infectious smell of malting Czech hops precedes a tasting, naturally, of unpasteurised beer straight from
the barrel.

Where to eat & drink

Na Spilce

U Prazdroje 7 (377 062 755). **Open** 11am-10pm
Mon-Thur, Sat; 11am-11pm Fri; 11am-9pm Sun.
Main courses 150 Kč. **Credit** AmEx, DC, MC, V.

The grand beerhall within the Pilsner Urquell
brewery (for tours, *see above*) serves mountains of
authentic Czech cuisine, from garlic soup to strudel
for afters. So much the better for soaking up all
the booze.

U Salzmannů

Kopečná 50 (377 235 855/www.usalzmannu.cz).
Open 11am-11pm Mon-Thur, Sat; 11am-
midnight Fri; 11am-9pm Sun. **Main courses**
170 Kč. **No credit cards**.
Established in 1637, this elegant restaurant and pension just north-east of the main square, Náměstí
Republiky, specialises in game, great service and a
clientele of presidents.

Where to stay

Hotel Central

*Náměstí Republiky 33 (377 226 757/www.
central-hotel.cz).* **Rates** (incl breakfast) 2,200-
2,800 Kč double. **Credit** AmEx, MC, V.
Intentionally or not, this retro-cool operation right
on the main square is a classic of sorts, with moulded
glass and white stone in 1970s designs. (Note,
though, that the hotel guestrooms themselves have
mercifully been modernised.)

Hotel Continental

*Zbrojnická 8 (377 235 292/www.hotel
continental.cz).* **Rates** (incl breakfast)2,150-2,450
Kč double. **Credit** AmEx, MC, V.
Overlooking a riverside park in the old centre, this
grande dame (built in 1895) offers good value.
Facilities include a bar, a restaurant and, in the
cellar, a popular club.

Plzeň.

Resources

Tourist information

City Information Centre, Náměstí Republiky 41, Pilsen (378 035 330/www.plzen.eu). **Open** *Oct-Mar* 9am-6pm daily. *Apr-Sept* 9am-7pm daily. **No credit cards**.
Staff have all the latest on events, exhibitions and tours, with tickets to festivals as well.

Getting there

By bus

A dozen buses leave Prague daily for Pilsen, from Florenc station. The trip takes around 1hr.

By car

Pilsen is 80km (48 miles) south-west of Prague. Take the E50 motorway directly to Pilsen.

By train

A dozen trains leave from Hlavní nádraží daily; journey time is around 1hr 40mins.

BRNO

Compact, party-loving and spiked by tall medieval spires, the town of **Brno** is a cultural and visual oasis in the middle of the otherwise placid rolling hills and plains of Moravia, the Czech Republic's eastern half. Its population of 400,000, roughly half that of Prague, makes it the republic's second city, and it has a lot more going for it than just cathedrals, crypts and cobbled streets. A thriving cultural scene and nightlife nearly as varied as Prague's add up to an engaging but easygoing city without the capital's pretensions.

Having originated around 1100 as a ford across the Svratka river – the city's name is derived from the old Slavonic word for mud – Brno prospered from its location on important trade routes and swiftly became the capital of the Great Moravian Empire of old before it was annexed by the Czechs. The transfer thoroughly Catholicised the city, something still reflected in Brno's greatest treasures.

The vertiginous **Katedrála sv. Petr a Pavla (Petrov Cathedral)** rises above the old centre of town. Although the cathedral is a bit of a disappointment on the inside, it sits atop a suitably dramatic hill in defiance of heresy. Its 'noon' bells sound at 11am; the tradition originated during the Swedish siege of Brno, when the town was supposedly saved by an ingenious monk who knew that the attackers had decided to fight only until noon and then move on.

Český Krumlov. *See p290.*

The **Kapucínská krypta (Capuchin Crypt)**, just below Petrov Cathedral and adjoining the former coal market, offers a sobering confrontation with death. Through the action of constant draughts, several of the nobles and monks who were buried in the crypt have been mummified; they're now on display, many still in their original garb. If you haven't yet exceeded your squeamishness quota, further lugubrious sights await in the 13th-century fortress of **Špilberk**, on a hill even higher than Petrov's across Husova from the old centre. Here you can visit the labyrinth of dungeons, the casemates, where Emperor Joseph II had various prisoners suspended on the dank and dreary walls. Thankfully, they're no longer on show.

Back in the fresh air, Brno's streets revive you with their engaging possibilities for turning up the unexpected around every corner. Centuries-old pubs such as **Pegas** (*see below*), as well as the fruit and veg market on **Zelný trh** and half a dozen impressively ornate Baroque churches are within strolling distance of náměstí Svobody, the main square. Almost every tourist sees the **Dragon of Brno** – actually an overstuffed crocodile – hanging outside the tourist information bureau. It's said to be the gift of a Turkish sultan who rather exaggerated its status, hence the name.

The club scene in Brno is alive with its own particular vitality. The influence of local talents is typified by Iva Bittová, an avant-garde singer/violinist. You might even run into a local musician or performance artist at **Spolek**, the city's newest bookshop-café, which is also a good spot to try Moravia's greatest claim to fame: the delectable white wines.

For trips to the **Moravský kras**, or **Moravian Caves**, near Brno, *see p298*.

Kapucínská krypta
Capuchin Crypt
Kapucínské náměstí (542 213 232). **Open** *Mid Feb-Apr* 9am-noon, 2-4.30pm Tue-Sat; 11-11.45am, 2-4.30pm Sun. *May-Sept* 9am-noon, 2-4.30pm Mon-Sat; 11-11.45am, 2-4.30pm Sun. *Oct-mid Dec* 9am-noon, 2-4.30pm Tue-Sat; 11-11.45am, 2-4.30pm Sun. Closed mid Dec-mid Feb. **Admission** 50 Kč; 30 Kč reductions. **No credit cards**.

Katedrála sv. Petr a Pavla
Petrov Cathedral
Petrov 9 (543 235 031). **Open** *Crypt* 11am-5pm Mon-Sat; 11.45am-5pm Sun. **Admission** 35 Kč. **No credit cards**.

Špilberk Castle
Špilberk 1 (542 123 611/www.spilberk.cz). **Open** *Casemates* May-Sept 9am-6pm daily. Oct-Apr 9am-5pm Tue-Sun. *Observation tower* May-Sept 9am-6pm Tue-Sun. Oct-Apr 10am-5pm Sat, Sun. **Admission** 70-120 Kč; 35-60 Kč reductions. **No credit cards**.

Where to eat & drink

Charlie's Hat
Koblížná 12 (542 210 557). **Open** 11am-4am Mon-Thur; 11am-5am Fri; noon-5am Sat; 3pm-4am Sun. **No credit cards**.
A handy labyrinth of bars, Charlie's Hat holds a patio with DJs and local bands blaring forth on selected nights.

Restaurant Pegas
Jakubská 4 (542 210 104). **Open** 9am-midnight Mon-Sat; 10am-10pm Sun. **Main courses** 150 Kč. **Credit** AmEx, DC, MC, V.
Pegas is a classic, grand-scale beerhall with its own brew, served in wheat and cinnamon varieties. Foodwise, expect schnitzel and goulash galore, credibly done.

Šermířský klub L.A.G.
Kopečná 50 (543 237 068). **Open** 11am-midnight Mon-Fri; 5pm-midnight Sat, Sun. **Main courses** 170 Kč. **No credit cards**.
The waiters come clad in medieval tunics at this olde Moravian inn, serving up massive stuffed potato pancakes. It's also the headquarters of the local historic sword-fighting club.

Where to stay

Hotel Amphone
Třída kapitána Jaroše 29 (545 428 310/ www.amphone.cz). **Rates** (incl breakfast) 1,050-2,090 Kč double. **Credit** AmEx, MC, V.
Although it's not situated in a particularly enchanting building, Amphone is one of the most convenient and friendly hotels in Brno.

Hotel Royal Ricc
Starobrněnská 10 (542 219 262/www.romantic hotels.cz/royalricc). **Rates** (incl breakfast) 2,700-5,000 Kč double. **Credit** AmEx, MC, V.
The Hotel Royal Ricc is set in some particularly luxurious Renaissance-era quarters, with timbered ceilings, stained-glass windows and staff who try hard to make their guests' stays as enjoyable as possible. Modern amenities balance the historic trappings.

Resources

Tourist information
Radnická 8 (542 211 090). **Open** *Oct-Mar* 9am-6pm Mon-Fri; 9am-5pm Sat; 9am-3pm Sun. *Apr-Sept* 8.30am-6pm Mon-Fri; 9am-6.30pm Sat, Sun. **No credit cards**.
Staff at this tourist information spot can book rooms at hotels and pensions.

Getting there

By bus

Buses leave Prague for Brno every half-hour, from Florenc station. The trip takes around 2hrs 30mins.

By car

Brno is 110km (77 miles) east of Prague. Take the E50/E65 motorway directly to Brno.

By train

Trains leave from Hlavní nádraží 15 times a day and take about 3hrs 30mins.

ČESKÝ KRUMLOV

Český Krumlov's rocky setting in the foothills of the Šumava mountains makes it ideal for sport activities and hiking, all of which can be co-ordinated through the tourist information centre (*see p292*). However, the town itself has both a fine castle to explore and a lively, lovely centre, with a delectable beer of its own. In 1992, the tiny town so impressed UNESCO with its beauty that it was declared second in importance only to Venice on the World Heritage list.

The town is dominated by an enormous and well-maintained **castle complex**. It seems to grow straight out of a rocky escarpment, overlooking beautiful countryside, gabled inns and pubs overflowing with fine dark Eggenberg and Budvar. Krumlov's fantastic pink Renaissance tower rises high above the town, beautifully positioned on a double loop of the Vltava river on the eastern edge of the forested region. The streets below are a labyrinth of cobbled alleyways filled with medieval architecture, craft shops and homely eateries.

The castle is one of the most extensive complexes in Central Europe, with 40 buildings in five courtyards. Founded before 1250, the fortress was adopted by the Rožmberk clan in 1302. As the family's wealth and influence increased, it was transformed into a palace. Cross the dry moat to enter, noting the bored bears that roam below. Highlights of the castle tour include a gilded carriage built in 1638 to convey presents to the pope, and the Mirror and Masquerade Halls, both of which are triumphs of the arts of stucco and trompe l'oeil.

The tower was redone as a whimsical pink-and-yellow Renaissance affair in 1591, topped with marble busts and gold trimmings. Linking sections of the palace perched on two steep escarpments, the five-tiered **Plášťový Bridge** is equally spectacular. For the best view descend to the **Jelení zahrada** (**Stag Gardens**) and look upwards. In summer, the extensive formal garden is one of the venues for the **Český Krumlov International Music Festival** (www.festivalkrumlov.cz), which features everything from classical ensembles to costumed period performances to Roma music.

On the opposite side of the Vltava from the Castle district, **Latrán**, is **Nové Město** (**New Town**), laid out a mere seven centuries ago. On Horní is the impressive **Kostel sv. Víta** (**Church of St Vitus**), dating from 1439. The church's tower is visible from all parts of town.

Despite its attractions, though, Český Krumlov is not just a tourist town. Residents work in graphite mining, at the Eggenberg Brewery or at the nearby paper mills. Before World War II, the town was part of the predominantly German-speaking Sudetenland and so was annexed by Hitler in 1938. The majority of the region's German-speaking inhabitants were expelled in 1945 and the town's centuries-old bicultural life came to an end.

Český Krumlov Castle

Zámek 59 (380 704 711/www.castle.ckrumlov.cz). **Open** *Castle (with guided tour)* Sept-Apr 9am-5pm Tue-Sun. May-Aug 9am-6pm Tue-Sun. *Tower* Apr-Oct 9am-4.30pm Tue-Sun. June-Aug 9am-5.30pm Tue-Sun. **Admission** *Castle* 180-230 Kč; 100-130 Kč reductions. *Tower* 45 Kč; 35 Kč reductions. **Credit** MC, V.

Access to the castle tower, a manageable adventure that sets you back a very reasonable 45 Kč, is hard to pass up and offers stunning views over the town. Otherwise, there are two tours available, the first including Baroque and Renaissance interiors, the golden carriage and masquerade theatre. The second is a much drier chronicle of the Schwarzenberg family. Note that castle entry is only possible with the hour-long tour. The last tour is an hour before closing time.

Where to eat, drink & stay

Hospoda Na louži

Kajovská 66 (380 711 280). **Open** 10am-11pm daily. **Rates** 1,350-2,300 Kč. **Main courses** 150 Kč. **No credit cards**.

A good place to sample South Bohemian cuisine, Na louži is an old-fashioned and central pub with traditional food and walls covered in tin signs. The rooms are a bit like your granny's spare room, with creaky floors but wall-to-wall charm.

Hotel Růže

Horní 154 (380 772 100/www.hotelruze.cz). **Open** *Restaurants* 7am-10pm daily. **Rates** 4,200-6,100 Kč double. **Main courses** 350-700 Kč. **Credit** AmEx, MC, V.

A restoration of this towering Renaissance pile, a former Jesuit college, has created one of the country's most luxurious hotels. The carved wood furnishings, ceiling beams, three restaurants, cellar bar and amazing views fit in with the town perfectly.

The Sporting Life

Do as the locals do and go jump off a bridge…

Czech travellers have moved far beyond the old traditions of cheap Croatian beach holidays with bargain-price boxy hotels and, not infrequently, all-night bus rides there and back. These days, Praguers are living healthier lifestyles and want to carry on doing the same on holiday. Stables are offering riding lessons and treks are popping up everywhere. Passing cars carry mountain bikes well into the chilly months, and some have rafts on the roof during the summer. Go anywhere where there are mountains and you'll find climbers scaling the rocks; find a lake and you'll find a scuba class in progress.

Even if you're not a native, it's easy to join in all the fun. Most Prague travel agencies have English-speaking staff and several have become adept at arranging sport-related travel, with everything on offer from climbing to parachuting. The current trend in the latter, offered by **Paraškola Impact** and **Skyservice** (*see p266*), is to strap yourself to an instructor so you can experience freefall on your first jump, without having to advance through the usual static line-jump training. Staff will even video your terror for posterity.

KI Bungee Jump company (*see p264*) has been doing brisk business in pitching otherwise rational weekend travellers off bridges. The company also arranges less extreme activities such as kayaking, rafting and team-building activities for groups of up to 30 people, in addition to walking on

coals. This last activity may have been inspired by its work with Czech television stations on various reality shows in which fabulous-looking contestants must push themselves to the limit and overcome their primal fears. Staff can also arrange transport from Prague and help with finding accommodation.

Horse riding is another newly popular sport, with companies such as **Slupenec Horse Riding Club** (Slupenec 1, Český Krumlov province, 380 711 052, www.jk-slupenec.cz), a few minutes' drive outside Český Krumlov, offering riding lessons for beginners and day-long hacks for experienced riders.

More conventional sports weekends, such as ski trips, can be arranged at a host of Prague travel agents, such as **Čedok** (*see p311*) and **Adventura** (Voroněžská 20, Prague 10, 271 741 734, www.adventura.cz); **Happy Sport** (*see p266*) can offer affordable ski equipment and snowboard hire. Local tourist offices will also have listings for companies offering kayaking, rafting and similar activities.

Whether you choose a high-adrenalin activity like bungee jumping or parachuting, or a more conventional activity such as riding or kayaking, you will find one distinctly Czech aspect – participants invariably end up at the local pub, recounting tales of their daring over gallons of beer and platters of schnitzel.

ESCAPES & EXCURSIONS

The modern attractions almost feel out of place, but they're all here: a fitness centre and pool, business amenities, top-notch service and a disco.

Hotýlek a Hospoda u Malého Vítka
Radniční 27 (380 711 925/www.vitekhotel.cz). **Rates** (incl breakfast) 1,250-1,700 Kč double. **Credit** MC, V.
A restored Renaissance inn just off the main square of the city's Vnitřni Město district. Children and pets are welcome. A lobby pub sells light snacks.

Pension Ve věži
Pivovarská 28 (380 711 742/www.pension vevezi.cz/pensionvevezi). **Rates** (incl breakfast) 1,200-1,800 Kč double. **No credit cards.**
Phone well ahead to reserve one of the four rooms inside this fortress tower with metre-thick walls.

Resources

Tourist information
Náměsti Svornosti 2 (380 704 622/www. ckkrumlov.info). **Open** *June-Sept* 9am-7pm daily. *Apr, May, Oct* 9am-6pm daily. *Nov-Mar* 9am-5pm daily. **No credit cards.**
In addition to finding rooms, staff can book canoe and boat tours down the Vltava.

Vltava Travel Agency
Kájovská 62 (380 711 978/www.ckvltava.cz). **Open** *Jan-Mar* 9am-noon, 12.30-5pm Mon-Sat. *Apr-Dec* 9am-noon, 12.30-5pm daily. **Credit** MC, V.
Staff at the Vltava Travel Agency can book rooms, horse rides, canoe trips and numerous other activities in the area.

Tábor. *See p294*.

ESCAPES & EXCURSIONS

Getting there

By car

Český Krumlov is 136km (85 miles) from Prague. Either leave on the Brno motorway (D1-E50) and then take the E55 at Mirošovice past Tábor and České Budějovice, then the 159 road; or go via Pisek leaving Prague on Route 4, towards Strakonice.

By train

The trip from Hlavní nádraží takes 3hrs 30mins and includes a change at České Budějovice.

By bus

Buses leave Prague for Český Krumlov 6 times a day, from Florenc bus station. The trip takes 2hrs 50mins.

OLOMOUC

Located around 280 kilometres (170 miles) east of Prague in the heart of Moravia, **Olomouc** has a picturesque town centre, granted status as a UNESCO World Heritage Site. However, unlike other pretty and ancient Czech hamlets, it's also willing to stay up late, thanks to its population of university students. Strolling through the main squares of an evening (the town has three, cascading downhill from Václavské náměstí to Horní náměstí to Dolní náměstí), you'll see parties heading to the latest happening bar or club. All in all, the town is a friendly escape from Prague, while also making a good stopoff point on the way to Poland, the **Jeseníky mountains** or the impressive **Bouzov Castle** just nearby.

Dating back at least to 1017, Olomouc was a prize city in the Czech Přemyslid land-grab that ended the Great Moravian Empire. During the Hussite wars, the town, like much of Moravia, sided with the Catholics, saw Hussite rebels executed on its squares and was rewarded with a dozen handsome churches.

The **Old Town (Staré Město)** is defined by a bend of the Morava river and is criss-crossed by tiny lanes that twist up to **Kostel sv. Václava (St Wenceslas Cathedral)**. No doubt it was the last thing Václav III saw before he was murdered in the chapterhouse in 1306. It later inspired an 11-year-old Mozart to compose his *Sixth Symphony*.

The neighbouring **Přemyslid Palace**, with foundations dating back to 1204, is an evocative pile with Romanesque windows but no other pulse-quickening contents. Elsewhere, don't miss the socialist realist makeover of the **Town Hall Astronomical Clock Tower** on Horní náměstí, which includes a mosaic of a scientist discovering means of better living for all through chemistry.

Kostel sv. Václava
St Wenceslas Cathedral
Václavské náměstí (585 224 236). **Open** 9am-6pm daily. **Admission** free.
The towering spire of this neo-Gothic wonder more than merits the hike to the city's uppermost square.

Where to eat, drink & stay

Arigone
Univeritní 20 (585 232 351/www.arigone.cz). **Rates** (incl breakfast) 2,190 Kč double. **Open** *Restaurant* 6am-midnight daily. **Main courses** 100-300 Kč. **Credit** DC, MC, V.
Arigone, a restored townhouse hotel with raftered ceilings and warm service, also boasts a popular restaurant and bar.

Barumba
Mlýnská 4 (mobile 777 799 607). **Open** 7pm-3am Mon-Thur; 9pm-6am Fri, Sat. **Admission** free-120 Kč. **No credit cards**.
Barumba is a combination of internet café, split-level student bar and dance club, which often has DJs and live acts from Prague on its programme. It's home to a major scene at weekends.

Restaurace U Kapucínů
Dolní náměstí 23 (585 222 700). **Open** 10am-10pm Mon, Tue, Sun; 10am-11pm Fri, Sat. **Main courses** 200-350 Kč. **Credit** MC, V.
With good regional cuisine and frothy pints on tap, Restaurace U Kapucínů supplies just the basics on atmosphere, but still manages to be nice and cosy.

Resources

Tourist information
Town Hall, Horní náměstí (585 513 385/www. olomouc.eu). **Open** 9am-7pm daily.
The staff here can book rooms and arrange tours to Bouzov Castle just outside town. You can also pick up full listings of concerts, clubs, and food and drink in the area.

Getting there

By bus
Four buses depart Prague's Florenc station for Olomouc daily. The trip takes in the region of 3hrs 30mins.

By car
Olomouc is 280km (174 miles) east of Prague. Take the E50/E65 south-east towards Jihlava and Brno, merging on to the E462 south of Brno and on to Olomouc.

By train
Trains leave hourly from Hlavní nádraží and take about 3hrs to reach Olomouc.

TÁBOR

Though it's hard to imagine the friendly little town of **Tábor** as a key military stronghold against superior Habsburg forces, that's just what it was back in the 15th century. A band of religious radicals founded the town in 1420 following Jan Hus's execution. Led by the one-eyed general Jan Žižka, 15,000 Taborites battled the Catholic forces for nearly 15 years. However, their policies of equal rights for men and women and common ownership of property did not endear them to the ruling classes, and the Taborites were eventually crushed by more moderate Hussite forces under George of Poděbrady. A statue of Žižka sits astride a hill overlooking Prague; Tábor honours him with a more modest sculpture in its main square.

The **Hussite Museum** has more on this history, though it's almost entirely in Czech. One highlight is an unusual military innovation of Žižka's, a crude sort of tank consisting of cannons balanced on a wagon. The museum also runs tours of the underground passages (used as stores and refuges during the Hussite wars) in much of the centre. The main square, **Žižkovo náměstí**, is the spoke from which streets and alleys radiate. The confusing layout was a ploy to befuddle Tábor's enemies.

Hussite Museum

Náměstí Mikuláše z Husi 44 (381 252 242). **Open** *Apr-Oct* 8.30am-5pm daily. *Nov-Mar* 8.30am-5pm Mon-Fri. **Admission** *Museum* 60 Kč; 30 Kč reductions. *Tunnel tours* 40 Kč; 20 Kč reductions. **No credit cards**.

Where to eat, drink & stay

Beseda

Žižkovo náměstí (381 253 723). **Open** 10am-10pm daily. **Main courses** 150-300 Kč. **Credit** MC, V. Bohemian bureaucrats like their beer. But this beer-hall, within the town hall, also has a kitchen, serving meat platters, warming soups and dumplings.

Hotel Dvořák

Hradební 3037 (381 207 211/www.orea.cz). **Rates** 2,250-2,850 Kč double. **Credit** AmEx, MC, V. Tábor's newest and most stylish accommodation is set in the town's old heart. There's an impressive kitchen; other amenities include a sauna, a fitness centre and massage facilities.

Resources

Tourist information

Infocentrum, Žižkovo náměstí 2 (381 486 230/ www.tabor.cz). **Open** *May-Sept* 8.30am-7pm Mon-Fri; 10am-4pm Sat, Sun. *Oct-Apr* 9am-4pm Mon-Fri.

Getting there

By bus

About 6 buses depart Prague's Florenc station and Praha Roztyly for Tábor daily. Journey time is 2hrs.

By car

Tábor is 82km (51 miles) south of Prague. Take the D1 south-east towards Jihlava and Brno, exiting at junction 21 to motorway 3 south.

By train

Trains depart from Hlavní nádraží; journey time is 1hr 35mins. The train to Vienna from Prague also stops in Tábor.

TELČ

Lovely, quiet **Telč** may not be a prime destination in itself, but it's certainly worth the trip if you're passing through the region on the way to Krumlov or Tábor. With a main square chock-full of immaculately preserved Renaissance buildings, still partly enclosed by medieval fortifications and surrounded by lakes, Telč is yet another Czech town on UNESCO's World Heritage list.

The town's rhomboid central square dates back to the 14th century, with a delicate colonnade delineating three sides of the meeting place. This and the photogenic gabled houses were added in the 16th century by Zachariáš of Hradec. A trip to Genoa and a fortuitous marriage to Katerina of Wallenstein gave this Renaissance man the inspiration and means to rebuild the town following a devastating fire in 1530. Each of the pastel-hued buildings has a different façade adorned with frescoes, sgraffito or later Baroque and rococo sculptures.

On the narrow end of the square stands the onion-domed 17th-century Jesuit church on one side and the Renaissance castle on the other, their exteriors the work of Italian architect Baldassare Maggi, hired by Zachariáš in 1552 to spruce up his new home. The coffered ceilings of the Golden and the Blue Halls, and the monochrome trompe l'oeil decorations that cover the Treasury, are among the finest Renaissance interiors in Central Europe. The Marble Hall exhibits fantastic armour, while the African Hall contains a collection of hunting trophies.

The castle also houses a small municipal museum, which features an ingenious 19th-century mechanical nativity crib and a permanent exhibition of works by the Moravian surrealist Jan Zrzavý (1890-1977). The castle's peaceful gardens stretch down to the lake and make for a lovely afternoon walk.

Telč Castle
Státní zámek (567 243 943). **Open** *Apr, Oct*
9am-noon, 1-4pm Tue-Sun. *May-Aug* 9am-noon,
1-5pm Tue-Sun. **Admission** 70-80 Kč; 35 Kč
reductions. **No credit cards**.
Tours are conducted in Czech, but you can pick up
a detailed English text at the ticket counter.

Where to eat, drink & stay

Hotel Celerin
Náměstí Zachariáše z Hradce 43 (567 243 477/
www.hotelcelerin.cz). **Rates** 1,530-1,750 Kč
double. **Credit** AmEx, DC, MC, V.
A romantic and friendly restored hotel with 12
rooms on the town's main square.

Šenk pod věží
Palackého 116 (567 243 889). **Open** 11am-10pm
daily. **Main courses** 150 Kč. **No credit cards**.
Of the various restaurants in Telč, this is the most
charming place to eat. It serves good Czech fare, and
has friendly staff and a terrace.

Resources

Tourist information
Náměstí Zachariáše z Hradce 10 (567 112
411/www.telc-etc.cz). **Open** *May, Sept* 8am-5pm
Mon-Fri; 10am-5pm Sat, Sun. *June-Aug* 8am-6pm
Mon-Fri; 10am-6pm Sat, Sun. *Oct* 8am-5pm
Mon-Fri; 10am-4pm Sat, Sun. *Nov-Apr* 8am-5pm
Mon, Wed; 8am-4pm Tue, Thur; 8am-3pm Fri.
No credit cards.
The staff here can book accommodation, plus
fishing, horse riding and hunting expeditions for
around 300 Kč to 500 Kč for a day excursion.

Getting there

By bus
Buses leave several times daily from Florenc bus
station and twice from Roztyly. The journey
takes just under 4hrs.

By car
Telč is 150km (93 miles) south-east of Prague.
Head out of Prague in the direction of Brno on the
E50/D1 motorway. At Pávov, follow the signs to
Jihlava; at Třešť, follow signs to Telč.

Countryside

Spring and summer weather sends Praguers
dashing to every lake, meadow and wine cellar
outside the city. Berry-picking, snoozing in the
grass and jumping into rivers are all part of the
ritual, and all can be done easily in the densely
forested mountains of the **Šumava** region, near
Kašperské Hory and Český Krumlov.

Though the options are often basic, renting
a cottage is the best form of accommodation
to be had – camping is technically prohibited
in the Šumava region. However, you can pitch
tents at one of the campsites in **Český ráj**
(*see below*), a lush area of lakes, woods, rocks
and castles. The Czech-language *Šumava* by
Miloslav Martan is a handy and somewhat
decipherable guide that contains trail maps
along with pictures of regional flora and fauna.

Česká Pohoda
Pod sokolovnou 693, Prague 4 (241 402 222/
mobile 777 048 638/www.ceskapohoda.cz). *Metro
Pražského povstání, then bus 193*. **Open** 10am-
4pm Mon- Fri. **Rates** (per person) 1,000-3,000
Kč/wk. **No credit cards**.
This agency can organise stays in cabins in some
of the prettiest corners of Bohemia, at rates often
lower than those charged by small-town inns.
Though the website is in Czech only, staff speak
English; for online information in English, try
www.adventura.cz. The agency specialises in roughing it, but the lovely surroundings are worth the sac-
rifice and many cabins nowadays are fairly cosy and
some have internet or saunas.

ČESKÝ RÁJ

Although it's more crowded than Šumava,
in no small part because it's easier to reach,
Český ráj is still Czech paradise. In case you
think we're making extravagant eschatological
claims, that's simply the translation of its
name. As Central European wildernesses go,
this picturesque region – a protected national
park – is very nearly worthy of the name, even
if it's concentrated in a small area. Though
it's accessible by road, the best way to explore
it is on foot. Even reluctant amateurs can cross
the region in two days.

The neighbouring towns of **Jičín** and
Turnov provide a good base from which to
begin your exploration of the area's lake,
castles, woods and rock formations, as
signposted trails can be followed almost from
the town centre of each. One good way to see
Český ráj is to take the train to one town and
then hike over to the other for the return leg.

The greatest concentration of protruding
rocks is to be found around **Hrubá skála**:
follow any of the marked footpaths from
the village and you'll soon find yourself
surrounded by these pockmarked giants.
The most useful map is the *Český ráj
Poděbradsko*, which is available at any
decent Prague bookshop.

Supreme among ruined castles in the area
is **Trosky** (the name means 'ruins'). Its two
towers, built on dauntingly inaccessible basalt
outcrops, form the most prominent silhouette

in the whole region. The taller, thinner rock goes by the name of Panna (the Virgin), while the smaller one is Bába (Grandmother). The feminine appellations are somewhat misleading given Trosky's hulking muscular mass.

In the 14th century, Čeněk of Vartemberk undertook a monumental feat of medieval engineering by building a tower on top of each of the two promontories, with interconnecting ramparts between them. The towers remained virtually impregnable through the medieval, pre-gunpowder, period, as they could only be reached by an ingenious wooden structure that could be dismantled in times of siege, leaving invaders with the choice of scaling the impossibly steep rocks or, more likely, beating a hasty retreat. In the 19th century, the castle became a favourite haunt of Romantic poets, painters and patriots. Now you too can climb to the base of the tower for outstanding views of the countryside.

From 1 April until 31 October, climbers can scale the sandstone pinnacles in the region. Simply pay the 45 Kč entry fee at any park attendant's booth. However, you'll need to bring your own climbing gear, as there's nowhere to rent equipment.

Trosky Castle

Rovensko pod Troskami (481 313 925/ www.trosky.cz). **Open** *Apr, Oct* 8.30am-4pm Sat, Sun, public holidays. *May-Aug* 8.30am-6pm Tue-Sun. *Sept* 8.30am-4pm Tue-Sun. **Admission** 40 Kč; 25 Kč reductions. **No credit cards.**

Where to eat, drink & stay

There are plenty of places close to every main tourist sight that offer filling, if uninspiring, traditional Czech food.

We've listed convenient hotels below. If you want to sleep out, there are campsites, although most people just seem to pitch their tent on any appealing plot of land. Those who prefer the convenience of a campsite should try **Autocamp Sedmihorky** (*see below*) or **Podháj** (no phone). The latter is just north-west of Hrubá skála on the Libuška creek, and has the same rates and season as Sedmihorky.

Autocamp Sedmihorky

Turnov (481 389 160/162/www.campsedmi horky.cz). **Open** year-round. **Rates** *Tents* from 30 Kč/night. *Cars* from 30 Kč/night. *Trailers* from 50 Kč/night. *Additional charge* 25 Kč/adult; 20 Kč/child. **No credit cards.**
This campsite is convenient for exploring the sandstone rocks and as a starting point for hopping on the 268km-plus (167 miles) of cycling tracks. You can also rent bungalows for up to seven people from 210 Kč per night. High season runs Apr to Oct.

Hotel Štekl

Hrubá skála, Turnov (481 389 684). **Open** *Restaurant* 8am-10pm daily. **Rates** (incl breakfast) 890-1,300 Kč double. **Main courses** 150 Kč. **Credit** AmEx, MC, V.
A decent dining room with views over the surrounding valleys. The hotel is well worn and far from plush but perfectly serviceable.

Hotel Zámek

Castle Hrubá skála (481 659 111/www. hrubaskala.cz). **Open** *Restaurant* 10am-10pm daily. **Rates** 1,960 Kč double. **Main courses** 250 Kč. **Credit** AmEx, MC, V.
Fabulous location, good prices and fantastic views from the ivy-covered turret rooms. The food in the restaurant here is traditional Czech, with service that's a bit better than in Prague.

Getting there

By bus

Buses leave every 30mins from Černý Most metro station (Line C) to Jičín. If you opt not to walk from here (it's an ambitious hike), catch a bus on to Hrubá skála-Borek. Buses from Prague's Florenc station go daily to Turnov, where you change for a train to Doubravice. From there, it's a 20min walk to Hrubá skála.

By car

The Český ráj area is about 90km (56 miles) north-east of Prague. Follow signs to Mladá Boleslav and join the E65 or Route 10 to Turnov. Jičín is 23km (14 miles) south-west of Turnov. Hrubá skála and Trosky are both just off Route 35, which is the Turnov–Jičín road.

By train

Five trains a day leave Hlavní nádraží for Turnov. There are local connections from Turnov to Hrubá skála and Malá skála. A local train plies the line between Jičín and Turnov.

KAŠPERSKÉ HORY

Thoroughly isolated and ensconced in the **Šumava National Forest** yet only a two-hour drive from Prague, **Kašperské Hory** is an idyllic little town. Built on gold mining, it's guarded by the nearby fortress of **Kašperk**. The ruins make for a worthwhile five-kilometre hike from the town centre.

Once part of the Sudetenland, annexed by Hitler, the soothingly quiet country here is now on the edge of one of the largest forest reserves in Central Europe – a vast area of 685 square kilometres (264 square miles) is protected. The massif is one of the oldest in Europe and its large woods are home to deer, lynx, eagles and otters, as well as being the source of the Otava and Vltava rivers. For those wishing to explore, the forest – which is on the UNESCO Biosphere Reserve list – is crisscrossed by marked trails. The area gets a lot of rain, so be prepared.

Dining on river fish and Staropramen is your reward upon your return from the mountain trails. For a second day, particularly for those suffering from blistered feet and an excess of trees, another option is the **Muzeum Šumava (Šumava Museum)**, featuring stuffed versions of any wildlife species you may have missed in the woods, plus an assortment of dusty historic and glass-making exhibits.

In the surrounding countryside, horse riding is a local passion. The accommodating **Aparthotel Šumava 2000** can set you up for a day in the saddle.

Muzeum Šumava
Šumava Museum
Náměstí 140 (376 582 530/376 582 609). **Open** *May-Oct* 9am-5pm Tue-Sat; 9am-noon Sun. **Admission** 30 Kč. **No credit cards**. Excellent collection of Bronze Age and medieval relics, plus local flora and fauna.

Where to stay

Aparthotel Šumava 2000
Náměstí 8 (376 546 910/www.sumava2000.cz). **Rates** (per person) 950-1,650 Kč. **Credit** AmEx, DC, MC, V.
This modern hotel is equipped with a sauna. Staff are on hand to set you up with hiking maps, trekking gear or horse riding.

Pension Soňa
Karlova 145 (376 582 454/mobile 728 736 777). **Rates** (per person) 250-270 Kč. **No credit cards**.
A basic but friendly family-run guesthouse near the central square.

Resources

Tourist information
Městské informační centrum, Náměstí 1 (376 503 411/376 503 412/www.sumavanet.cz/khory). **Open** *Jan-Aug* 7.15am-noon, 12.30-5pm Mon, Wed; 7.15am-noon, 12.30-4pm Tue, Thur, Fri. *Oct-Dec* 7.15am-noon, 12.30-5pm Mon, Wed; 7.15am-noon, 12.30-4pm Tue, Thur; 7.15am-3pm Fri. **No credit cards**.

Šumava Museum.

Getting there

By bus

Nine buses per day from Na Knížecí (Metro Anděl, line B) leave for Vimperk or Sušice, where you need to change for Kašperské Hory.

By car

Kašperské Hory is 120km (75 miles) from Prague. Take motorway 4 south 90km (56 miles) to Strakonice. From here, take road 22, about 18km (11 miles) west to Horažďovice, then road 169, which is another 20km (12 miles) south-west to Sušice. From here, take road 145 and follow it 19km (12 miles) south to Kašperské Hory.

MORAVSKÝ KRAS

The stars of the Czech Republic's many cave systems (*jeskyně*) are those north of the Moravian capital of Brno (*see p288*). Busloads of children and even pensioners (the rarefied air is touted as a cure for allergies and asthma) go on the guided tours through the chilly limestone caves – a welcome respite in the hot months, but remember to bring a jumper. As this is a phenomenally popular summer attraction, long queues are inevitable.

The **Moravský kras** (**Moravian Caves**), comprising a series of 400 holes, is by far the most concentrated and accessible network of caves in the Czech Republic. Best visited as a day trip from Brno, these limestone caves were created over 350 million years by the erosive action of acidic rainwater and underground streams. The **Kateřinská**, **Sloupsko-Šošůvské** and **Balcarka** caves are all within striking distance of Brno.

If you're looking to do all your caving in one go, your best bet is the **Punkevní jeskyně**, the largest cave in the country. Some three kilometres of the cave's 12-kilometre length are open to the public. Passages of stalactites give way to the colossal **Macocha Abyss**: 140 metres (459 feet) deep, it was formed in part by the collapse of the ceiling of a cave further below. The tour then sends you down the narrow tunnels by boat. Visiting is a distinctly up-close experience: the passages are barely wide enough for the boats, and you'd be likely to be impaled by a stalactite if you stood up. Arrive early in peak season as tours can sell out by the middle of the morning. It's even better to reserve a place by phone, as queues can be long.

There are other attractions easily accessed by car. The most popular is the spectacular Gothic castle of **Pernštejn**. Elsewhere, you can visit the Napoleonic battlefield of **Austerlitz** (Slavkov) and the **Alfons Mucha**

Museum (515 322 789, closed Jan-May, Nov-Dec, Mon) housed in the Renaissance château of **Zamek Moravský Krumlov** (515 321 064, www.mkrumlov.cz).

Moravský kras
Moravian Caves

Skalní mlýn (516 413 575/www.cavemk.cz).
Open *Punkevní jeskyně* Jan-Mar 8.40am-2pm Tue-Sun. Apr-June 10am-3.50pm Mon; 8.20am-3.50pm Tue-Sun. July, Aug 10am-5pm daily. Sept 10am-3.50pm Mon; 8.20am-3.50pm Tue-Sun. Oct 8.20am-3.40pm Tue-Sun. Nov, Dec 8.40am-2pm Tue-Sun. *Other caves* Feb-Oct. **Admission** *Punkevní jeskyně* (incl chairlift to entrance & boat ride) 100 Kč adults; 80 Kč reductions. *Other caves* 50 Kč adults; 20 Kč reductions. **No credit cards**.

Where to eat, drink & stay

Hotel Skalní Mlýn

Skalní Mlýn (516 418 113). **Open** *Restaurant* 7am-11pm Mon-Fri; 8am-11pm Sat, Sun. **Main courses** 150 Kč. **Rates** (incl breakfast) 1,500 Kč double. **Credit** AmEx, MC, V.
This hotel is a popular place and the best base from which to explore the caves. There's also a reasonable restaurant.

Resources

Tourist information

Old Town Hall, Radnická 8 (542 211 089).
Open *Oct-Mar* 9am-6pm Mon-Fri; 9am-5pm Sat; 9am-3pm Sun. *Apr-Sept* 8.30am-6pm Mon-Fri; 9am-6.30pm Sat, Sun. **No credit cards**.
The staff here can book rooms in and around the town and can also supply you with maps, brochures and other information.

Getting there

By bus

Buses run roughly every hour between Brno and Prague (journey time 2hrs 30mins), from bus station Florenc.

By car

Brno is 202km (126 miles) south-east of Prague. The D1 motorway runs all the way to the city. The caves are 22km (14 miles) north-east of Brno.

By train

Trains to Brno from Prague run hourly and take 3-4hrs. About 12 trains a day leave Brno for the nearby town of Blansko. Local buses then take you onwards to the caves. A tourist train travels between the Punkevní caves and the centre of Skalní Mlýn, synchronised with the opening hours, from which the other three caves are accessible.

Directory

Getting Around

DIRECTORY

ARRIVING & DEPARTING

By air

Prague's only airport, the expanded and modernised **Ruzyně** (239 007 576), is 20 kilometres (12 miles) north-west of the city centre. It's not directly accessible by metro.

Airport buses ČEDAZ (221 111 111, www.cedaz.cz) runs express buses between the airport and Metro Dejvická and Náměstí Republiky for 90 Kč (6am-9pm daily). The white vans leave from outside the Arrivals terminal. The friendly, English-speaking **Prague Airport Shuttle** (602 395 421, www.prague-airport-shuttle.com) provides door-to-door transport. A ride to your hotel starts at 600 Kč for up to four people, rising to 1,800 for 13-16 passengers. Book online or send an SMS before you arrive.
Local buses Four local services run from the airport to metro stations about every 20mins (5am-midnight). Bus **119** departs from the airport to Metro Dejvická (green Line A), as does the slower **254**. Nos. **179** and **225** connect to Metro Nové Butovice (yellow Line B). You can also catch the **100** express service to the Zličín metro stop on the yellow Line B, which enters the city from the south. This is the cheapest, slowest and busiest route.

The buses depart from the stands in front of Arrivals, where you'll find orange ticket machines (you'll need 26 Kč in change). There are also ticket machines and an information office in the airport lobby. If you have lots of bags, you'll need to buy extra tickets for them. For ticket details, *see below*.
Taxis AAA, the taxi firm with the airport contract, is one of the city's reputable companies. The 20-25min ride should cost around 350 Kč (a 34 Kč boarding fee, 25 Kč/km and 5 Kč/min for waiting). Check at the airport information kiosk for the going rate to your destination.

By rail

International trains arrive at the **Main Station (Hlavní nádraží**, sometimes called Wilson Station or Wilsonovo nádraží), a beautiful if

crumbling art nouveau building with communist-period lower halls, and **Holešovice Station (Nádraží Holešovice)**. Both are on the red Line C of the metro. Caution: it's easy to get off at Holešovice thinking that it is the main railway terminus. If your train stops at both, wait for the last stop.

The Main Station has several food stalls and a PIS (Prague Information Service) office in the main hall. There are also public showers and a 24-hour left luggage area in the lower hall. Be warned, though, that at night, the station becomes a home for homeless people, drug addicts and hustlers. For 24-hour information on national and international rail travel, call 221 111 122 (English is spoken). For ticket prices, call 840 112 113.

**Hlavní nádraží
Main Station** *Wilsonova, Nové Město, Prague 2 (972 241 100/ www.idos.cz). Metro Hlavní nádraží/ tram 5, 9, 11, 26.* **Map** p329 P5.
**Nádraží Holešovice
Holešovice Station** *Vrbenského, Holešovice, Prague 7 (220 806 790/www.idos.cz). Metro Nádraží Holešovice/tram 12, 25.* **Map** p332 E1.
**Smíchovské nádraží
Smíchov Station** *Nádražní, Prague 5 (221 111 122/www.idos. cz). Metro Smíchovské nádraží/ tram 12.*

By coach

Florenc coach station may be the least pleasant place in Prague, but it's on two metro lines (yellow Line B and red Line C). Late arrivals can take the night tram or a taxi. The 24-hour helpline costs 14 Kč/min.

Florenc Station *Křižíkova 4, Prague 8 (information 900 144 444/www.csad.cz). Metro Florenc/tram 8, 24.*

PUBLIC TRANSPORT

Although walking is the best way to get around Prague's small centre, the city has an excellent, cheap and almost 24-hour integrated public transport system that will get you just about anywhere. There are bus and/or tram connections (and

usually taxi stands) at every metro station, and all of Prague's railway stations are connected to the metro.

Information

Day service with DP, the Prague Public Transit Company, runs from about 5am to about 12.10am daily, with peak times 5am-8pm Mon-Fri. Between midnight and 5am, night buses and trams take over. English-language content, maps and route changes are at www.dpp.cz. Metro, tram and bus lines are indicated on most city maps.

Timetables can be found at every tram and bus stop. The times apply to your stop, highlighted on the schedule. If your destination is listed below the highlighted stop, you're in the right place.

The DP maintains a number of information centres. Employees usually have at least a smattering of English, and can provide maps, booklets, schedules and tickets (cash only). See below for a full list.

Anděl metro station *Smíchov (222 646 055).* **Open** 7am-6pm Mon-Fri.
Můstek metro station *Nové Město (222 646 350).* **Open** 7am-6pm Mon-Fri. **Map** p328 M5.
Muzeum metro station *Nové Město (222 623 778).* **Open** 7am-9pm daily. **Map** p331 O7.
Nádraží Holešovice metro station *Holešovice (222 623 360).* **Open** 7am-6pm Mon-Fri.
Ruzyně Airport *220 111 111.* **Open** 7am-10pm daily.
Ruzyně Airport Tmnl 2 *296 669 652.* **Open** 7am-10pm daily.

Fares & tickets

Tickets (*jízdenky*) are valid for all modes of transport (metro, bus, tram, the funicular). Most locals have passes (*see right*); they're also the easiest option for visitors, as you can't buy a ticket on board trams or buses. It's worth stocking up on tickets in advance. You can buy them at most tobacconists, DP information offices (*see above*) and PIS offices (*see p311*), or anywhere displaying a red-and-yellow DP sticker. Most ticket outlets also sell transit passes, for unlimited travel on the metro, trams and buses.

Tickets Ticket machines dispense dozens of types of tickets, but only one needs concern you: a **26 Kč ticket**. It lasts for 75mins at peak times (5am-8pm Mon-Fri) and 90mins at off-peak periods (all other times) and allows unlimited travel in Prague, including transfers between metros, buses and trams. You can also buy a **24hr pass** from machines for 100 Kč.

The ticket machines themselves are marvels of Czechnology. Press the relevant button once for the ticket you want, twice if you want two tickets and so on; then press the 'enter' button. Insert the total amount in coins (change is given) and wait while the machine's screeching mechanism prints out each ticket individually.

Residents usually have **long-term passes**, available only at the DP windows and at the Karlovo náměstí metro station. You'll need a recent passport photo and ID. Passes cost 550 Kč for one month, 1,480 Kč for three months and 4,750 Kč for a year. There's a 'gliding' coupon valid for any 30- to 90-day period, so you needn't wait till the end of the month to start a pass.

Babies in buggies, children under six, handicapped people, small bags and skis ride for free. Children aged six to 15, large items of luggage and other sizeable items require a half-price ticket. Enormous bags and, quote, 'items that stink or look disgusting' are forbidden.

Using your ticket Stamp your ticket (face up in the direction of the arrow) in the machine as you board a bus or enter the 'paid area' of the metro. There are no guards or gates, but plain-clothes inspectors (*revizoři*) carry out random ticket checks, often on tourist-friendly routes. They can be merciless and may not speak English. The penalty for buying the wrong ticket, or failing to stamp the right one, is 700 Kč. It's always wise to demand a receipt if you are fined.

Disabled access

Public transport is still difficult to use. There are lifts at the following metro stations, although at some you'll need help to operate the lift: Dejvická, Muzeum, Strašnická and Skalka (green Line A); Zličín, Stodůlky, Luka, Lužiny, Hůrka, Vysočanská, Kolbenova, Hloubětín, Rajská zahrada, Nové Butovice, Smíchovské nádraží and Černý Most (yellow Line B); Nádraží Holešovice, Hlavní nádraží, Florenc, Muzeum, IP Pavlova, Vyšehrad,

Pankrác, Roztyly, Chodov, Opatov, Háje, Ládví, Kobylisy and Budějovická (red Line C).

Two bus routes are served only by kneeling buses. No.11 starts in Bryksova and runs via Černý Most, Florenc, Náměstí Republiky and IP Pavlova to Chodov. No.13 runs from Zličín via Hradčanská, Náměstí Republiky and Nádraží Holešovice to Sidliště Ďáblice. All of the newer, boxier trams also kneel. You can find out which lines use the newer cars at DP information offices (*see left*).

Metro

Prague's metro network is a scaled-down copy of the Moscow metro. The stations are well lit and clearly signposted; trains are clean and frequent. A digital clock on each platform informs you of the time elapsed since the last train.

The metro comprises three lines: the green Line A (Dejvická–Depot Hostivař); the yellow Line B (Černý Most–Zličín); and the red Line C (Ládví–Háje). Transfers (*přestup*) are possible at Muzeum (between Lines A and C), Můstek (Lines A and B) and Florenc (Lines B and C). Services run 5am-midnight daily; trains come every 2mins at peak times, and every 5-10mins off-peak. For a metro map, *see p336*.

Trams

The electric *tramvaje* service has been the preferred transport method for most Praguers for a century. Trams come every 6-8mins at peak times and every 10-15mins at other times. You may find you need to press the green button to open the doors.

The best lines for seeing the city are the 22, from the castle to Národní třída and beyond, and the Historic Tram (91), from the Výstaviště in Prague 7 through Malá Strana, across to the National Theatre, through Wenceslas Square, Náměstí Republiky and back to Prague 7. The 91 runs on weekends and holidays from Easter to mid Nov, leaving Výstaviště every hour from noon to 5.35pm. The ride takes 40mins; tickets cost 25 Kč for adults and 10 Kč for kids.

Buses

Autobusy in Prague provide links to the places where no other form of public transport is able to go. They run from about 5am-midnight, after which time ten night bus lines take

over (*see below*). Buses run every 5-18mins at peak times and every 15-30mins at other times. Call 900 144 444 for information. The line is open 24hrs, calls cost 14 Kč/min, and operators speak English.

Night trams & buses

Night buses and trams run about every 40mins (midnight to about 4.30am). All night trams have numbers in the 50s, and stop at Lazarská crossroads on Spálená. There's no central stop for night buses (nos.501-512), but many stop at the top of Wenceslas Square (near Metro Muzeum) and around the corner from Metro IP Pavlova. You can buy a guide to night transport at the DP information offices (*see left*) for about 10 Kč.

Funicular railway

The funicular (*lanovka*) runs for half a kilometre from the bottom of Petřín Hill at Újezd (around the corner from the tram stop of the same name), stops midway at Nebozízek (at the restaurant of the same name) and continues to the top of Petřín Hill. It runs every 10-15mins (9am-11.30pm daily), and costs 20 Kč for adults and 10 Kč for children. Transport passes are valid, but beware: scams by ticket sellers and inspectors have netted thousands of crowns. Don't get on board without buying a ticket and getting it stamped in the machine.

Rail services

Trains are generally useful only for travelling in the Czech Republic outside Prague. See *pp276-277*.

Water transport

The Prague Steamship Company had a monopoly on river traffic back in 1865, and still provides most boat services on the river. You'll find them, as well as other companies plus rowing boats for hire, on the Vltava's right bank.

Pražská paroplavební služba Prague Steamship Company *Rašínovo nábřeží, Nové Město, Prague 2 (224 931 013/224 930 017/www.paroplavba.cz). Metro Karlovo náměstí/tram 3, 16, 17.* **Map** p330 J10.

TAXIS

The appalling reputation of local taxi drivers has prompted City Hall

DIRECTORY

DIRECTORY

to introduce strict guidelines, but the odds are high that you'll get ripped off. The drivers waiting at ranks in obvious tourist locations are often crooks; it's a better bet to hail a moving cab or to call one of the services listed below.

Make sure that you use only authorised taxis, clearly marked with their registration numbers and with fares printed on the doors. If the driver doesn't turn on the meter, insist he does; if he still refuses, get out straight away or agree on a fee. If you don't, the driver will demand a ruinous fare at the end of your journey, and may even resort to violence in order to collect it.

Ideally, your taxi experience should go something like this: the driver does not turn on the meter (*taxametr*) until you enter the cab. When he does, 34 Kč appears as the initial amount (cash only is the norm). While you're driving within Prague, the rate is set at '1' and should never be more than 25 Kč per kilometre. At the end, the driver gives you a receipt (*účet* or *paragon*). (If he doesn't, you are theoretically not required to pay the fare.) Honest cabbies print one out on the machines; rip-off merchants will write you one out on a pad.

Cab companies
AAA *14014/www.aaataxi.cz.*
Halo Taxi *244 114 411/ www.halotaxi.cz.*
ProfiTaxi *844 700 800.*

Taxi complaints
Živnostenský odbor
Vodičkova 18, Prague 1 (221 097 111/222 231 640). **Open** 9am-5pm Mon-Fri.

DRIVING

Getting behind the wheel in Prague these days invariably means angst, delays and confusion, especially on Fridays and Sundays. Unless you have a residence permit, you'll need an international driver's licence.

There is zero tolerance for drinking and driving – drivers are not allowed to drink any alcohol at all; ditto for drugs. The use of seat belts is required in the front and – if the car is equipped – back seats. Children under 12 and anyone under 18 who is shorter than 150 centimetres (4ft 11in) cannot ride in the seat next to the driver unless they sit in approved safety seats and there's no airbag in the front seat. Small children must be in approved safety seats whether they're in the front or the back.

Trams, which follow different traffic lights to cars, always have the right of way. You must stop behind trams when passengers are getting on and off at a stop where there is no island, and you should avoid driving on tram tracks unless the road offers no alternative.

The speed limit for cars and buses is 90kph (56mph) on roads, 130kph (81mph) on motorways and 50kph (31mph) in towns/villages. Motorcyclists, along with their passengers, must wear protective helmets and eyegear, and the speed limit for motorcycles is 90kph (56mph) on roads and motorways and 50kph (31.25mph) in the villages and towns.

If you're driving your own car, you'll need to have international proof of insurance (known as a Green Card; contact your motoring organisation) and pay an annual toll for using the Czech roads. If you hire a car, insurance and toll should be taken care of for you. Otherwise, the toll sticker, which should be displayed on the windscreen, is 200 Kč for 15 days, 300 Kč for 2 months or 900 Kč for a year. It can be bought at post offices, most border-crossing points and petrol stations.

Car hire

Renting a car can be expensive. Shop around: some small local firms may charge far less than the big boys. The agency should provide you with a green insurance card, which you will be asked to show if you are stopped by police or drive across the border. Arrange your rental a few days in advance. **Student Agency** (*see p311*) also arranges car rental.

Alimex *Argentinská & Jatečni streets, Holešovice, Prague 7 (233 350 001/www.alimexcr.cz).* Metro Vltavská/tram 1, 3, 25. **Other locations** Ruzyně Airport, Prague 6 (220 114 860).
Budget *Hotel Inter-Continental, Náměstí Curieovych 5, Prague 1 (235 325 713/235 301 152/ www.budget.cz). Tram 22, 25.* **Other locations** Ruzyně Airport, Prague 6 (220 560 443).
Europe Car Rental *Pařížská 28, Staré Město, Prague 1 (224 811 290/www.europcar.cz). Metro Staroměstská/tram 17, 18.* **Other locations** throughout the Czech Republic.
Hertz *Karlovo náměstí 15, Prague 2 (225 345 031/www.hertz.cz). Metro Karlovo náměsti/tram 3, 4, 6, 14, 16, 18, 22, 24, 34.*

Fuel stations

Leaded fuel (octane 90) is called Special, leaded fuel (octane 96) is known as Super and unleaded fuel (95D) is called Natural. Super Plus 98 and diesel fuel are also widely available. A booklet listing all the petrol and service stations (and some car parks) in Prague is available from PIS offices (*see p311*). Many are open 24 hours.

Parking

Parking can be a nightmare. Watch for the zones reserved for area residents and businesses, and make sure you don't park in them. If you park illegally, your car may be clamped or towed (call 158 to get it back; it won't be cheap).

Coin-operated meters dispense tickets, which should be displayed on the dashboard. Streets in Prague 1 are divided into three zones: blue zones, for local residents and companies; orange zones, for stops of up to 2hrs (you'll pay a minimum of 10 Kč for 15mins and 40 Kč for 1hr); and green zones, for stays of up to 6hrs (15 Kč for 30mins, 30 Kč for 1hr, 120 Kč for 6hrs). Ignore the restrictions at your peril. You may be better off in a car park, ideally one with 24-hour security.

CYCLING

Pedalling in Prague is hazardous. However, Prague does have plenty of parkland inside and outside the city. Bikes are allowed in the last carriage of metro trains.

Bicycle hire

City Bike *Královdorská 5, Staré Město, Prague 1 (mobile 776 180 284/www.citybike-prague.com). Metro Náměstí Republiky/tram 5, 8, 14.* **Open** *Apr-Oct* 9am-7pm daily. **No credit cards. Map** p329 N3. Cycle tours of the city, three times a day: 10.30am, 1.30pm and 4.30pm. Rentals cost 650 Kč per day.

WALKING

The best way to get around the city centre is on foot. The excellent pocket-sized map *Praha do kapsy* is available at most newsstands. It's generally safe to walk anywhere at any time – using common sense and caution in the wee hours, of course. But beware of bad drivers, who've only just begun to stop for pedestrians at crossings because a recent law compels them to do so.

Resources A-Z

ADDRESSES

Czech buildings have two numbers posted on them: one in red, which is used in city records only, and one in blue, which denotes the address used for letters and callers (and is the one used throughout this guide). The street name comes first, followed by the street number; then, on a new line, a district code and district number, followed by the country:

> Jan Novak
> Kaprova 10
> 11 000 Praha 1
> Czech Republic

AGE RESTRICTIONS

The legal age for driving in the Czech Republic is 18, as it is for drinking and smoking, though it's virtually unheard of for clubs, bars and shops to ask for proof of age. The age of sexual consent for both straights and gays is 15.

ATTITUDE & ETIQUETTE

Praguers often seem stand-offish at first, especially in the service sector. But Czechs will quickly warm to you if you attempt to speak even a word or two of their language. When greeting, a polite *Těšim se* ('Pleased to meet you') with a handshake is safe; and the formal form of address, *vy*, is expected unless your host opens the door for the casual *ty* form.

Stand on the right side on metro escalators and let people out of a tram before boarding. Speaking in full voice may earn you stares, but not liberal drinking. People at a pub table tend to pay individually and don't assume drivers will always stop at zebra crossings on the way home.

BUSINESS

Couriers & shippers

DHL *800 103 000/220 300 111/www.dhl.cz.*
FedEx *800 133 339/www.fedex.com.*

Office services

Prague has dozens of good translation companies, with most offering services in all the major European languages along with many non-European languages. Translation rates are usually determined by the page.

For computer repairs/supplies, *see p197*.

Apple Center Anděl *Nádražní 23, Prague 5 (257 210 493/www.appleobchod.cz). Metro Anděl/tram 4, 7, 9, 10, 12, 14, 20.* **Open** 10am-6pm Mon-Sat.
If you're stuck for an iPod cable or MacBook RAM, this is the place.
APS *Rujanská 1223, Prague 4 (224 215 147/www.aps.cz; Czech only). Metro Opatov.* **Open** 9am-5pm Mon-Fri. **Credit** MC, V.
Flexible PC leasing options.
Artlingua *224 917 616/www.artlingua.cz.* Translations, specialising in legal and financial documents.
Copy General *Senovážné náměstí 26, Nové Město, Prague 1 (210 219 012/www.copygeneral.cz). Metro Náměstí Republiky/tram 3, 5, 9, 14, 24, 26.* **Open** 24hrs daily. **Credit** MC, V. **Map** p329 P4.
Copying, binding and finishing services, as well as pick-up and delivery. You can bring in a text file or PDF on a flash drive for printing or CD burning. There are a number of other locations throughout the city.
TaP Servis *224 226 629/www.tapservis.cz.* Translations.

Useful organisations

British Embassy Commercial Section *Na příkopě 21, Nové Město, Prague 1 (222 240 021-3/www.britain.cz). Metro Můstek/tram 3, 9, 14, 24.* **Open** 9am-noon, 2-5pm Mon-Fri. **Map** p329 N5.
Czechinvest *Štěpánská 15, Nové Město, Prague 2 (296 342 500/information 800 800 777/www.czechinvest.org). Metro Můstek/tram 3, 9, 14, 24.* **Open** 8am-4.30pm Mon-Fri. **Map** p331 N8.
This Czech government agency encourages foreign investment and assists in joint ventures.
Enterprise Ireland *Tržiště 13, Malá Strana, Prague 1 (257 531 585). Metro Malostranská/tram 12, 22.* **Open** 9am-1pm, 2-5pm Mon-Fri. **Map** p327 E4.
Hospodářská komora ČR Economic Chamber of the Czech Republic *Freyova 27, Prague 9 (296 721 300/www.komora.cz). Metro Hlavní nádraží, then tram 5, 9, 26.* **Open** 8am-4pm Mon-Fri.
Information on Czech industrial sectors, companies and finance.
Prague Stock Exchange (PX) *Rybná 14, Staré Město, Prague 1 (221 831 111/www.pse.cz). Metro Náměstí Republiky/tram 5, 8, 14.* **Open** 8am-4.30pm Mon-Fri. **Map** p329 N3.
PX trades about 50 companies in its top-tier listing. The big banks are among 40-odd brokerages that can place orders. Liquidity is good.

DIRECTORY

US Embassy Foreign Commercial Service *Tržiště 15, Malá Strana, Prague 1 (257 531 162/www.buyusa.gov). Metro Malostranská/tram 12, 22.* **Open** 9am-noon daily. **Map** p327 E4.

CONSUMER

There is a Czech Office of Consumer Protection. However, it doesn't have English-speaking services or a hotline and it's largely ineffective, so adopt a philosophy of 'buyer beware'. Shops may allow you to swap faulty goods but are generally unwilling to refund money.

CUSTOMS

There are no restrictions on the import and export of currency, but if you're carrying more than 350,000 Kč out of the country, you must declare it at customs. The allowances for importing goods are as follows:

● 200 cigarettes or 100 cigars at max 3g each, or 250g of tobacco;
● 1 litre of liquor or spirits and 2 litres of wine;
● Medicine in any amount for your own needs.

If you want to export an antique, you must have a certificate stating that it's not important to Czech cultural heritage. Ask about this when you purchase.

DISABLED ACCESS

According to the law, all new buildings must be wheelchair-friendly. Reconstructed buildings need not provide wheelchair access, though many do voluntarily.

But for all that, travelling around Prague in a wheelchair is no picnic. There are few ramps; most hotels provide no wheelchair access, and only five stations in the entire country are wheelchair-friendly. The guidebook *Přístupná Praha (Accessible Prague)*, available from the Prague Wheelchair Association, contains maps of hotels, toilets, restaurants, galleries and theatres that are wheelchair-friendly. For travel information, *see p301*.

Pražská organizace vozíčkářů
Prague Wheelchair Association
Centre for Independent Living (Centrum samostatného života), Benediktská 6, Staré Město, Prague 1 (224 827 210/www.pov.cz).

Metro Náměstí Republiky/tram 5, 8, 14. **Open** 9am-4pm Mon-Fri. **Map** p329 N3.
The PWA is run by the disabled for the disabled. In addition to its *Accessible Prague* book, it provides helpers and operates a taxi service and an airport pick-up service. Service is limited and should be ordered as far ahead as possible. It also has wheelchairs available for rent if you have any problems with your own.

DRUGS

Prague has historically been a crossroads between Europe and Asia and a major transit point for goods both legal and otherwise, and the people who traffic and buy them. Penalties for even minor drug possession are severe, so it's best not to take chances. Buying or selling street drugs is illegal, and a controversial Czech drug law outlaws the possession of even small quantities of drugs.

ELECTRICITY

Electricity is 220 volts with two-pin plugs almost everywhere. Bring continental adaptors or converters with you, as they're pricey here.

EMBASSIES & CONSULATES

All embassies and consulates are closed on Czech holidays (*see p312*) as well as their own national holidays. For other embassies, consult the *Zlaté stránky (Yellow Pages)* under 'Zastupitelské úřady'.

Australian Trade Commission & Consulate
Na Ořechovce 38, Prague 6 (224 310 743). Metro Dejvická, then tram 20, 26. **Open** 9am-1pm, 2-5pm Mon-Fri.
British Embassy *Thunovská 14, Malá Strana, Prague 1 (257 402 111). Metro Malostranská/tram 12, 22.* **Open** 8.30am-noon Mon-Fri; *telephone enquiries* 9am-9pm Mon-Fri. **Map** p327 E3.
Canadian Embassy *Muchova 6, Dejvice, Prague 6 (272 101 800/www.canada.cz). Metro Hradčanská/tram 18, 22.* **Open** 8.30am-12.30pm, 1.30-4.30pm Mon-Fri. **Map** p332 A3.
US Embassy *Tržiště 15, Malá Strana, Prague 1 (257 022 000/emergencies 257 532 716/www.usembassy.cz). Metro Malostranská/tram 12, 22.* **Open** 9am-noon Mon-Thur. **Map** p327 E4.

EMERGENCIES

All numbers are toll-free. *See also below* **Health**, *right* **Helplines** and *p308* **Police**.

Emergencies *112.*
Fire *150.*
First aid *155.*
Police *158.*

GAY & LESBIAN

Prague is a generally tolerant city and a popular destination for gay and lesbian travel. The proximity of Germany, a major market for sex tourism, has resulted in a boom in the commercial side of the scene. The **Gay Guide** (http://prague.gayguide.net) has the most complete and up-to-date information in English on the scene, legalities, accommodation and practicalities.

HEALTH

Prague isn't the healthiest place on earth. The Czech diet is fatty, pork-laden and low on fresh vegetables; the locals also top world beer-consumption charts and are unrepentant smokers. If that wasn't enough, the city also has serious smog problems these days.

The socialised healthcare system makes hospital visits cheap, but doctors spend little time with patients, preferring to dispense drugs rather than run tests. In general, if you pay cash (which is universally accepted), you'll get far better treatment than the locals, who must rely on their insurance.

Medical facilities are usually open from 7.15am to 6pm on weekdays only. It's usually best for expats to find a GP (*rodinný* or *practický lékař*), dentist (*zubní lékař*) and paediatrician (*dětský lékař*) close to their home or workplace. Many Czech doctors will speak English or German, especially at larger facilities, both hospitals (*nemocnice*) and medical centres (*poliklinika*).

Accident & emergency

Canadian Medical Care
Veleslavínská 30, Prague 6 (235 360 133/emergencies 724 300 301/www.cmcpraha.cz). Metro Dejvická/tram 20, 25, 26. **Open** 8am-6pm Mon, Wed, Fri; 8am-8pm Tue, Thur. **Credit** DC, MC, V.
This established general practice clinic has paediatricians, cardiologists, gynaecologists and other specialists, and on-site labs for many common tests.

Fakultní nemocnice v Motole Motol Hospital
V Úvalu 84, Smíchov, Prague 5 (224 431 111/emergencies 224 438 683 or 697/155 toll-free/ www.fnmotol.cz). Metro Hradčanská, then 108, 174 bus. **Open** 24hrs daily. **Credit** AmEx, MC, V.
Emergency treatment, plus a hospital department dedicated to the care of foreigners.

Medicover Clinic
Pankrác House, Lomnického 1705, Prague 4 (234 630 111/ emergencies 603 555 006/call centre 1221/www.medicover.cz). Metro Pražského povstání. **Open** 7am-7pm Mon-Fri; 9am-noon Sat. **Credit** AmEx, MC, V.
With a professional international staff, Medicover honours Central Health Insurance Office temporary insurance (*see p306*).

Nemocnice Na Homolce Na Homolce Hospital
Roentgenova 2, Smíchov, Prague 5 (257 271 111/emergencies 257 272 191/paediatrics 257 272 025/ emergencies 257 272 043/www. homolka.cz). Tram 4, 7, 9/bus 167. **Open** *Emergency* 24hrs daily. *Paediatric department* 8am-4pm daily. **Credit** AmEx, MC, V.
English-speaking doctors and a 24-hour emergency service. Care can be excellent but, given the state of the Czech public healthcare system, a private clinic is more advisable. Home visits are possible if needed.

Complementary medicine

Czechs have a long history of herbal cures, and many have embraced traditional Eastern medical practices with enthusiasm. The average pharmacy, or *lékárna*, will stock teas for everything from menstrual cramps to bronchitis, but you'll need to bring a Czech friend with you for help deciphering the labels. Check the *Zlaté stránky* (*Yellow Pages*; there's an English index at the back) for 'Health Care – Alternative Medicine'.

Contraception & abortion

Condoms are widely available in Prague and stocked at many grocers. Abortion is legal and can be arranged through most clinics.

Dentists

Many of the Western clinics have dentists on staff. However, the private practice listed below is also highly recommended.

Dental Emergencies
Palackého 5, Nové Město, Prague 1 (224 946 981). Metro Můstek/tram 3, 9, 14, 24. **Open** 7pm-6.30am Mon-Fri; 6.30am-6.30pm, 7pm-6.30am Sat, Sun, holidays. **No credit cards.** Map p330 M7.

Fakultní nemocnice v Motole Motol Hospital
V Úvalu 84, Smíchov, Prague 5 (224 433 681/224 431 111/ emergencies 224 436 107-8/155 toll-free/www.fnmotol.cz). Metro Hradčanská, then 108, 174 bus. **Open** 24hrs daily. **Credit** AmEx, MC, V.

Medicover Clinic *Pankrác House, Lomnického 1705, Prague 4 (234 630 111/emergencies 603 555 006/call centre 1221/www. medicover.cz). Metro Pražského povstání.* **Open** 7am-7pm Mon-Fri; 9am-noon Sat. **Credit** AmEx, MC, V.

Opticians

Most Western clinics have referral services with opticians, although shops such as **Eiffel Optic** (*see p205*) also have licensed opticians on staff.

Pharmacies

See p206.

STDs, HIV & AIDS

ČSAP (Česká společnost AIDS Pomoci) & Lighthouse (Dům Světla)
Malého 3, Prague 8 (224 814 284/AIDS helpline 800 800 980/ www.aids-pomoc.cz). Metro Florenc/ tram 8, 24. **Open** *Volunteers available* 9am-4pm Mon-Fri.
ČSAP is the Czech organisation for AIDS prevention and for the support of people with HIV or AIDS. In addition to a 24-hour hotline, it runs the Lighthouse, a hospice for HIV-infected individuals who would otherwise have nowhere to go. Donations are very welcome.

Women's health

Bulovka Hospital *Budínova 2, Libeň, Prague 8 (266 081 111). Metro Palmovka/tram 12, 14.* **Open** 24hrs daily.
Housed within a huge state hospital complex, the privately run MEDA Clinic is favoured by British and American women. Prices are reasonable, the gynaecologists speak English along with some other languages, and the facilities are clean and professional.

Dr Kateřina Bittmanová
Mánesova 64, Vinohrady, Prague 2 (office 222 724 592/ 603 551 393/home 272 936 895). Metro Jiřího z Poděbrad/tram 11. **Open** 7am-4pm Mon-Fri. **No credit cards.** Map p333 B3.
Dr Bittmanová speaks English, runs a friendly private practice and is on call 24 hours a day. Her fee for a general exam is 900 Kč.

RMA Centrum *Dukelských hrdinů 17, Holešovice, Prague 7 (233 382 809). Tram 4, 12, 14, 17, 26.* **Open** 7am-5pm Mon, Tue; 7am-7pm Wed; 7am-6pm Thur; 7am-1pm Fri. **No credit cards.** Map p332 E3.
An alternative medicine centre offering homeopathy, acupuncture and acupressure, traditional Chinese medicine and massage. There's also a beauty salon.

HELPLINES

Helplines generally run around the clock, though not all are staffed by English-speakers. You have a better chance of catching an English-speaker if you call during office hours. For AIDS helplines, *see left*.

Alcoholics Anonymous (AA)
Na Poříčí 16, Nové Město, Prague 1 (224 818 247). Metro Florenc or Náměstí Republiky/tram 5, 8, 14, 26. **Sessions** 5.30pm daily. Map p329 Q2.
English spoken.

Centrum krizové intervence – Psychiatrická léčebna Bohnice Crisis Intervention Centre
Ústavní 91, Prague 8 (284 016 666/www.plbohnice.cz). Metro Nádraží Holešovice, then bus 102, 177, 200. **Open** 24hrs daily.
The biggest and best-equipped mental health facility in Prague.

Drop In *Karolíny Světlé 18, Staré Město, Prague 1 (222 221 124/431 helpline/www.dropin.cz). Metro Staroměstská or Národní třída/ tram 6, 9, 17, 18, 22.* **Open** 9am-5.30pm Mon-Thur; 9am-4pm Fri. Map p328 J5/6.
An informal clinic devoted to problems related to drug addiction, with HIV testing and counselling.

ID

Spot checks of foreigners' documents are not unheard of, so it's best to carry ID. A photocopy of your passport is usually sufficient. Bars and clubs virtually never ask for ID but you may be asked to show a passport if changing money.

DIRECTORY

INSURANCE

Health insurance

Foreigners are technically required
to present documentary evidence
of health insurance in order to
enter the Czech Republic, though
it's rarely requested in practice.
Nationals of a country with which
the Czech Republic has a reciprocal
emergency healthcare agreement,
which includes the UK, Greece and
most of the republic's former allies
in the ex-Warsaw Pact countries,
are exempt. However, visitors
requiring a visa will have to
provide proof of insurance with
their application. The relevant
bodies will issue visas to foreigners
only for as long as they have valid
health insurance.

**Všeobecná zdravotní
pojišťovna (Central Health
Insurance, VZP**), the main health
insurance provider in the Czech
Republic, provides affordable
policies to foreigners for urgent
care coverage for up to a year.
Most state clinics and hospitals,
and a few private ones, accept VZP.
However, due to its massive debts
and delayed payments, it isn't
favoured by some doctors.

VZP *Orlická 4, Prague 3 (221
752 175/www.vzp.cz). Metro
Jiřího z Poděbrad/tram 11.*
Open 8am-4pm Mon-Thur;
8am-1pm Fri. **Map** p333 D2.
The main provider of health
insurance in the Czech Republic
offers reasonable rates for short-
term coverage, issued in terms of
30-day periods.
Other locations Na Perštýně 6,
Staré Město, Prague 1 (221 668 103);
Orlická 4, Žižkov, Prague 3 (221 753
114).

Travel & property insurance

Insuring personal belongings
is always wise and should be
arranged before leaving home.
Always ensure that your policy
covers Central and Eastern
European countries.

INTERNET

Many hotels in the city offer high-
speed internet access (*see pp124-
149*), and there are cafés with
Wi-Fi all over Prague. Try the
**Globe Bookstore &
Coffeehouse** if you have no
laptop of your own (*see p193*).
A list of Czech internet service
providers (O2 sells the most

competitive wireless access
packages) is available at the Czech-
language search engine **Seznam**
(www.seznam.cz).

LANGUAGE

The Czech language was exiled
from officialdom and literature
in favour of German for much of
the history of Bohemia, until the
National Revival in the 19th
century saw its triumphant
return as the national language.
Today, Czech is spoken
throughout Prague. However, most
places of business, at least in the
centre, should have some English-
speaking staff. German may help
you in speaking to some older
Czechs, while many middle-aged
people speak Russian, which was
taught compulsorily in schools
before the Velvet Revolution.
Czech is a difficult but rewarding
language to learn in that it helps
penetrate the wall put up by rather
shy Czechs. They invariably light
up upon hearing even the most
stumbling attempts at speaking
their mother tongue by a foreigner.
For essential vocabulary, *see p313.*

LEFT LUGGAGE

There are left luggage offices
and/or lockers at **Hlavní nádraží**
and **Nádraží Holešovice** stations,
and at **Florenc coach station**
(*for all, see p300*).

LIBRARIES

For a full list of Prague's libraries,
ask at the **National Library**
or look in the *Zlaté stránky*
(*Yellow Pages*) under 'knihovny'.
Admission rules vary – generally,
you don't need to register to use
reading rooms, but you will need
to sign up if you want to borrow
books. For this, you'll need your
passport and sometimes a
document stating that you're a
student, a teacher, a researcher
or a resident of Prague.
Most libraries have restricted
opening hours during July and
August, and some close entirely.

British Council *Politických vězňů
13, Nové Město, Prague 1 (221 991
160/www.britishcouncil.cz). Metro
Muzeum/tram 11.* **Open** 9am-5pm
Mon-Fri. **Map** p329 O6.
The interior of Bredovský Dvůr,
the British Council's new location,
was designed by Czech architect
Eva Jiřičná. The new classrooms
are designed in line with the latest

technology and come with all
manner of gadgets. The reading
room is stocked with all the major
British newspapers and magazines,
and there are free internet terminals
available. The library is packed
with materials and aids for TEFL
and TESL teachers, but most of
the literature in its collection now
resides at the Městská knihovna,
or City Library (*see below*).

**Městská knihovna v Praze
City Library** *Mariánské náměstí
1, Staré Město, Prague 1 (222
113 555/www.mlp.cz). Metro
Staroměstská/tram 17, 18.* **Open**
9am-8pm Tue-Fri; 10am-5pm Sat.
Map p328 K4.
The City Library is spacious, calm
and modern. You'll find an excellent
English-language literature section
bolstered by 8,000 books and
magazines from the British Council.
An impressive music and audio
collection also awaits, along with
plenty of comfortable spaces for
studying, scribbling and flipping
through tomes. Visitors wanting to
borrow books will need a passport
and 1,000 Kč for a cash deposit.

**Národní knihovna v Praze
National Library** *Klementinum,
Křížovnické náměstí 4, Staré
Město, Prague 1 (221 663 111/
www.nkp.cz). Metro Staroměstská/
tram 17, 18.* **Open** 9am-7pm Mon-
Sat. *Main reading room* 9am-10pm
Mon-Sat. **Map** p328 J4.
A comprehensive collection of just
about everything ever published
in Czech and a reasonable foreign
selection, housed in a confusing
warren of occasionally gorgeous
halls. This state-funded library
has an ancient system of ordering
books based on filling in little
leaflets and throwing them in a
box, which is emptied every two
hours. The orders are brought after
another hour (or a day, if it isn't
stored on site). Foreigners may
only take books as far as one of
the reading rooms.

LOST PROPERTY

Most railway stations have a lost
property office (*Ztráty a nálezy*).
If you lose your passport, contact
your embassy (*see p304*).

**Central Lost
Property Office**
*Karoliny Světlé 5, Staré Město,
Prague 1 (224 235 085). Metro
Národní třída/tram 6, 9, 17, 18,
22.* **Open** 8am-5.30pm Mon, Wed;
8am-4pm Tue, Thur; 8am-2pm Fri.
Map p328 J5.

MEDIA

English-language news & general-interest publications

Alongside the Czech publications listed below, foreign newspapers are available at various stalls on and around Wenceslas Square and at major hotels. The **International Guardian**, **International Herald Tribune** and the international **USA Today** are available on the day of publication. Most other papers arrive 24 hours later.

Czech Business Weekly

This Prague-based business magazine offers extensive coverage of the markets and financial trends in the Czech Republic.

New Presence

www.new-presence.cz

This is the English-language version of *Nová přítomnost*, a journal dating back to inter-war Bohemia that offers a liberal and stimulating selection of opinion writing (some translated from its original Czech) by both local and international writers. It's not easy to find, but still worth seeking out . Try the **Globe Bookstore & Coffeehouse** or **Big Ben Bookshop** (for both, *see p193*).

Newsline Radio Free Europe

www.rferl.org

A dry but highly informative daily overview of events in Eastern Europe and the countries that once formed the Soviet Union. It is produced in co-operation with Free Europe/Radio Liberty, the Prague-based radio station. Newsline's information is also available as an email service, and can be accessed from RFE's comprehensive website.

Prague Monitor

www.praguemonitor.com

A daily online digest of the Czech press translated into English, with good coverage of major political and financial events. It's also available as an email subscription.

Prague Post

www.praguepost.com

The principal English-language weekly in the Czech Republic has come a long way in recent years. The cultural coverage betters that of many papers in larger cities of the former Eastern bloc. There's also an events calendar, business and trends features, and a lively comment section.

Transitions Online *www.tol.cz*

Based in Prague, this fascinating internet-only, non-profit magazine covers current events in Central and Eastern Europe, the Balkans

and the former Soviet Union. A network of local correspondents provides unique, cross-regional analysis. Well worth a look.

Listings magazines

The *Prague Post* (*see above*) carries entertainment sections along with survival hints. Monthly entertainment listings can be found in **Kulturní přehled** (in Czech), **Kultura v Praze** and its shorter English equivalent **Culture in Prague**.

The **Prague Information Service** (PIS; *see p311*) publishes a free monthly entertainment listings programme in English.

Annonce

Bargain-hunting Czechs delve into this classified ad sheet in order to find good deals on second-hand washing machines, TVs, cars and the like. *Annonce* is also a good flat-hunting tool: place your ad for free, then simply wait by the phone.

Culture in Prague

An exhaustive monthly calendar of events held throughout Prague and the republic. Published mainly in Czech, it's also available in English at Wenceslas Square bookshops. It's considerably easier to decode than *Kulturní přehled* (*see above*), although be warned that the movie listings are notoriously unreliable.

Literary magazines

Though many have folded over the past few years, plenty of literary magazines are still published in Prague, in both Czech and English. You should be able to track down most of them at the well-stocked **Globe Bookstore & Coffeehouse** or **Big Ben Bookshop** (for both, *see p193*).

The Czech-language **Revolver Review**, supposedly published quarterly but distinctly irregular, is a hefty periodical with *samizdat* roots. It presents new works by well-known authors along with lesser-known pieces by pet favourites such as Kafka.

Labyrint Revue, a monthly, and **Literární noviny**, issued weekly, are the other two main Czech publications offering original writing and reviews of new work.

English publications tend to come and go. The best and most widely known is **Trafika**, a 'quarterly' – tending to lapse to an 'occasionally' – showcase for international writers.

The **Prague Review**, formerly the *Jáma Review*, is a slim quarterly of plays, prose and poetry from Czechs and Czech-based expats. Its editors – who have included such Czech literary heavyweights as Bohumil Hrabal, Ivan Klima and Miroslav Holub – subtitle the volume 'Bohemia's journal of international literature'.

Radio

BBC World Service (101.1 FM)

English-language news delivered on the hour plus regular BBC programming, with the occasional Czech and Slovak news broadcast. For 30 minutes a day, at around teatime, it transmits local Czech news in English, courtesy of Radio Prague.

Expres Radio (90.3 FM)

This newer station has been winning an increasing audience with fresh programming and alternative pop.

Radio Free Europe

Prague is now the world headquarters for RFE. It still beams the same old faintly propagandist stuff, mainly to the Middle East now, from its HQ at the former Czechoslovak Federal Assembly building, next to the National Museum.

Radio 1 (91.9 FM)

This excellent alternative music station plays everything from Jimi Hendrix through world music of various origins all the way to techno. It's unpredictable, however, with occasional evenings of call-in story-reading in Czech. The Friday-evening calendar show with Tim Otis has everything the hip party-goer needs to know.

Radio Prague (92.6 FM & 102.7 FM)

Daily news in English, plus interviews, weather and traffic. Nothing too inspired, but this is a well-established station with some history behind it.

Television

There are two national public channels. ČT1 tries to compete with TV Nova, but is out of its depth financially. Meanwhile, ČT2 serves up serious music (including lots of jazz greats), theatre and documentaries to the small percentage of the population that tunes in to it, and sometimes broadcasts English-language arthouse movies with Czech subtitles on Monday evenings.

DIRECTORY

MONEY

The currency of the Czech Republic is the *koruna*, or crown (Kč). One crown equals 100 hellers (*haléřů*) but don't let anyone dump these small, light coins in denominations of 50 on you – they're no longer legal currency. There are also 1, 2, 5, 10, 20 and 50 Kč coins in circulation. Notes are issued by the banks in denominations of 50, 100, 200, 500, 1,000, 2,000 and 5,000 Kč.

After the end of communist hegemony in Eastern Europe, the crown became the first fully convertible currency behind what had been the Iron Curtain. A bizarre indicator of its viability is the number of convincing counterfeit Czech banknotes in circulation. If someone stops you in the street asking if you want to change money, it's a fair bet he'll be trying to offload dodgy notes – and almost a certainty that he's scamming.

Banks & ATMs

The Czech Republic has long been a cash economy, and such conveniences as cash machines (ATMs), credit cards and cheques (travellers' cheques included) are not nearly as ubiquitous here as they are in EU countries or the US. However, the situation is changing; particularly in Prague, it's not difficult to find ATMs that will pay out cash on the major credit and charge card networks. Look for the symbol that matches the one on your card and use your usual PIN. Many smarter restaurants and shops, especially around Wenceslas Square and the Old Town, take credit cards and travellers' cheques.

American Express *Václavské náměstí 56, Nové Město, Prague 1 (222 800 237). Metro Můstek or Muzeum/tram 3, 9, 11, 14, 24.* **Open** 9am-7pm daily. **Map** p329 N6.
This office provides travel services but won't take client mail, and has generally slack-jawed service.
Československá obchodní banka (ČSOB) *Na příkopě 14, Nové Město, Prague 1 (261 351 111/www.csob.cz). Metro Můstek or Náměstí Republiky/tram 3, 5, 9, 14, 24.* **Open** 8am-5pm Tue-Thur; 8am-4pm Fri. **Map** p329 N5.
International currency transactions and transfers from abroad.
Komerční banka *Na příkopě 33, Nové Město, Prague 1 (222 432 408/information 800 111*

055/www.kb.cz). Metro Můstek or Náměstí Republiky/tram 3, 5, 9, 14, 24. **Open** 9am-6pm Mon, Wed; 8am-5pm Tue, Thur, Fri. **Map** p329 N5.
The country's largest full-service bank has branches throughout the Czech Republic. The ATM network accepts international credit cards and is a MasterCard (Eurocard) and Visa agent. Its card emergency number is 224 248 110.
Unicredit bank *Na příkopě 20, Nové Město, Prague 1 (224 121 111). Metro Můstek/tram 3, 5, 9, 14, 24.* **Open** 8.30am-5pm Mon-Fri. **Map** p329 N5.
This old trading bank, housed in one of Prague's most beautiful buildings, has long experience in working with foreign clients. Most staff speak reasonable English.

Bureaux de change

Exchange rates are usually the same all over the city, but banks take a lower commission (usually one to two per cent). Unfortunately, they are only open during business hours (usually 8am-5pm Mon-Fri), so try and ensure you have enough money before they close.

Bureaux de change usually charge a higher commission for changing cash or travellers' cheques, although some (such as those at the Charles Bridge end of Karlova street) may only take one per cent. Bear in mind that this means little if you're getting a poor exchange rate.

Lost or stolen credit cards

Komerční banka (*see above*) is a local agent for MasterCard and Visa; call the numbers given in case of loss or theft. For lost/stolen AmEx cards, the number is 222 412 241; for Diners Club, it's 267 314 485; and for missing travellers' cheques, it's 222 800 224 for AmEx and 221 105 371 for Travelex.

NATURAL HAZARDS

Deer ticks are known to transmit encephalitis in Central and Eastern Europe, for which a vaccine is available at many clinics. Ticks found should be smothered in soap or Vaseline, then removed by twisting in an anti-clockwise direction.

Lightning strikes are quite prevalent during Bohemia's muggy summer, but they pose little hazard unless you're on open ground at high elevations.

Air quality in Prague has improved, but pollution regulation is poorly enforced and the incidence of cancer is well above that in Western Europe.

OPENING HOURS

Standard opening hours for most shops and banks are from 8am or 9am to 5pm or 6pm from Monday to Friday. Many shops are open a bit longer, and from 9am to noon or 1pm on Saturday. Shops with extended hours are called *večerka* (open until 10pm or midnight) and 'non-stop' (open 24 hours daily). Outside the centre, most shops are closed on Sundays and holidays. Shops frequently close for a day or two for no apparent reason; some shops close for an hour or two at lunch; and some shops and many theatres close for a month's holiday in August.

Many businesses have shorter opening hours in winter (starting September or October) and extended hours in summer (starting April or May). Castles and some other attractions are open only in summer.

POLICE

Police in the Czech Republic are not regarded as serious crimefighters or protectors of the public, and are barely considered keepers of law and order. Their past as pawns for the regime, combined with a reputation for corruption, racism and incompetence, has prevented them from gaining much in the way of respect. If you're the victim of crime while in Prague, don't expect much help or even concern from the local constabulary.

For emergencies, call 158. The main police station, at Na Perštýně and Bartolomějská, is open 24 hours daily. In theory, an English-speaking person should be on call to assist crime victims with making a report. But in practice, any encounter with the Czech police is likely to be slow, unpleasant and ultimately ineffective.

You're expected to carry your passport or residence card at all times. If you have to deal with police, they're supposed to provide an interpreter for you. The legal drinking age is 18.

POSTAL SERVICES

Stamps are available from post offices, newsagents, tobacconists and most places where postcards are sold. Postcards as well as regular letters (up to 20 grams) cost 11 Kč within Europe and 20 Kč for airmail outside Europe. Packages should be wrapped in plain white or brown paper. Always use black or blue ink, or a snippy clerk will refuse to accept your mail. Even odd-shaped postcards are known to have been refused by the rule-obsessed Czech Post.

Post offices are scattered all over Prague. Though they are being modernised, many have different opening hours and offer varying degrees of service, and all are confusing. Indeed, the system designating what's on offer at which window is perplexing, even for some Czechs.

The **Main Post Office** on Jindřišská in Nové Město, Prague 1, offers the most services, some available 24 hours a day. Fax and international phone services are in the annexe around the corner at Politických vězňů 4. Some services, such as *poste restante* (general delivery) and EMS express mail, are theoretically available at all post offices, but are much easier to use at the main office on Jindřišská.

You can buy special edition stamps and send mail overnight within the Czech Republic and within a few days to Europe and the rest of the world via EMS, a cheaper but less reliable service than commercial couriers.

To send or collect restricted packages or items subject to tax or duty, you must go to the **Customs Post Office** (*see below*). Bring your passport, residence permit and any other ID. For incoming packages, you'll also need to pay duty and tax. The biggest queues here form between 11am and 1.30pm.

Hlavní pošta
Main Post Office
Jindřišská 14, Nové Město, Prague 1 (221 131 111/infoline 800 104 410). Metro Můstek/tram 3, 9, 14, 24. **Open** 2am-midnight daily. **No credit cards. Map** p329 N6.
Celní Pošta
Customs Post Office
Plzeňská 139, Smíchov, Prague 5 (257 019 108). Metro Anděl, then tram 4, 7, 9. **Open** 7am-3.30pm Mon, Tue, Thur, Fri; 7am-6pm Wed. **No credit cards.**

Useful vocabulary

letters *příjem – výdej listovin.*
packages *příjem – výdej balíčků* or *balíků.*
money transactions *platby.*
registered mail *doporučené.*

stamps *známky* – usually at the window marked *Kolky a ceniny.*
special issue stamps *filatelistický servis.*

RELIGION

There are plenty of churches in Prague, but services in English are held only at the churches below.

Anglican Church of Prague
Klimentská 5, Nové Město, Prague 1 (284 688 575). Metro Náměstí Republiky/tram 5, 8, 14. **Services** 11am Sun. **Map** p329 Q1.
Church of St Thomas *Josefská, Malá Strana, Prague 1 (257 532 675/www.augustiniani.cz). Metro Malostranská.* **Services** 6pm Sat, 11am Sun (in English). **Map** p327 F3. Catholic Mass.
International Baptist Church of Prague *Vinohradská 68, Žižkov, Prague 3 (mobile 731 778 735/www.ibcp.cz). Metro Jiřího z Poděbrad/tram 11.* **Service** 11am Sun. **Map** p333 C3.
International Church of Prague *Peroutkova 57, Smíchov, Prague 5 (296 392 228/www.internationalchurchofprague.cz). Metro Anděl, then bus 137, 508.* **Services** 10.30am Sun.
Prague Christian Fellowship *Eliášova 15, Prague 6 (222 532 675/www.praguefellowhip.cz). Metro Hradčanská.* **Services** 4.30pm Sun. **Map** p330 L9.

SAFETY & SECURITY

Street crime in the city consists mainly of pickpockets, not violent crime, though many practitioners are experts. Prague's pickpockets are concentrated in tourist areas such as Wenceslas Square, Old Town Square and Charles Bridge, and are particularly fond of the Slavia and tram No. 22 from Malostranské náměstí to Prague Castle. Keep an eye on your handbag or wallet, especially in crowds and on public transport. Seedier parts of Prague include some of Žižkov, parts of Smíchov, the park in front of Hlavní nádraží (the main train station), and the lower end of Wenceslas Square and upper end of Národní třída.

It's a good idea to use your room safe, if you have one. Thus, rather than carrying all your holiday money, only sufficient for the day is kept on your person and liable to loss. Keep a separate record of the numbers of any travellers' cheques and credit cards, along with contact information for reporting their loss.

SMOKING

Smoking isn't allowed on public transport in Prague, but that's about the only place in the city people don't light up. A new anti-smoking law is in effect but has had little practical impact. Restaurants must have non-smoking areas, but smoke still gets in your eyes.

STUDY

Charles University

Founded in 1348 by King Charles IV, Charles University (Univerzita Karlova) is the oldest university in Central Europe, and the hub of Prague's student activity. Its heart is the Carolinum, a Gothic building on Ovocný trh, which is home to the administration offices. Other university buildings are scattered all over the city.

Several cash-hungry faculties now run courses for foreigners. Contact the relevant dean or the International Relations Office during the university year (October to May) for information on courses and admissions procedures. It's best to enquire in person at the university, as staff can be difficult to reach by phone.

Below is a selection of popular offerings. For courses outside Prague, contact the British Council (*see p306*).

Charles University
International Relations Office, Univerzita Karlova, Rektorát, Ovocný trh 3-5, Staré Město, Prague 1 (224 491 302/ www.cuni.cz). Metro Staroměstská or Můstek/tram 3, 9, 14, 17, 18, 24. **Open** 9am-5pm Mon-Fri. **Map** p328 M4.
FAMU *Smetanovo nábřeží 2, Staré Město, Prague 1 (221 197 211/222). Metro Staroměstská or Národní třída/tram 6, 9, 17, 18, 22.* **Open** noon-4pm Mon, Wed; 10am-1pm Tue, Thur. **No credit cards. Map** p328 J5.
Famous for turning out such Oscar-winning directors as Miloš Forman, Prague's foremost school of film, TV and photography runs several English courses under its Film For Foreigners (3F) programme and Cinema Studies, including summer workshops (in co-operation with NY University, Washington, Miami and Boston), six-month and one-year courses in aspects of film and TV production and a BA in photography.

Institute of Language & Professional Training

Ústav jazykové a odborné přípravy. Univerzita Karlova, Vratislavova 10, Nové Město, Prague 2 (224 990 415/www.ujop.cuni.cz). Metro Karlovo náměstí/tram 3, 16, 17, 21. **Fees** 125,000 Kč/1yr course of training for future study; 95,000 Kč/1yr course of Czech; 20,000 Kč/ 6wk session; 46,000 Kč/intensive semester; 530 Kč/45mins individual lesson. **Open** *Oct-Dec* 10am-2pm Tue-Thur. *Feb-May* 10am-2pm Tue-Thur. **No credit cards**.

Aimed at preparing foreigners who want to embark on degree courses at Czech universities, this branch of Charles University offers Czech-language training in the form of a one-year course, intensive courses for a semester, or individual classes.

School of Czech Studies

Filozofická fakulta, Univerzita Karlova, Náměstí Jana Palacha 2, Staré Město, Prague 1 (221 619 381/www.ff.cuni.cz). Metro Staroměstská/tram 17, 18. **Open** 9-11am, 1-3pm Mon-Wed; 11am-3pm Thur; 9-11am, noon-2pm Fri. **Fees** 68,000 Kč/2-semester year for Czech Studies programme. **No credit cards**. **Map** p328 J3.

Year-long courses offer a mix of language instruction and lectures in Czech history and culture (Czech Studies programme). Language classes are available at beginner, intermediate and advanced level.

Other courses

Anglo-American College

Lázeňská 4, Malá Strana, Prague 1 (257 530 202/www.aac.edu/ www.aavs.cz). Metro Malostranská/ tram 12, 18, 22. **Open** 9am-5pm Mon-Fri. **Fees** 46,500 Kč/5-course semester; 11,800 Kč/1-course semester. **No credit cards**. **Map** p327 F4.

Western-style degree courses in business, law economics and humanities. The syllabus and classes are in English, but the student body is a mix of Czechs, Slovaks and foreign nationals.

Prague Center for Further Education

Karmelitská 18, Mala Strana, Prague 1 (257 534 013). Metro Malostranská/tram 20, 22. **Open** 9.30am-6pm Mon-Fri. **Fees** 2,600-5,600 Kč/course. **No credit cards**. **Map** p327 F4.

Provides Prague's international community access to English-language learning. Dynamic courses cover everything from Czech film history to wine tasting, plus sundry Prague-related subjects.

Language courses

Many schools offer Czech-language instruction. If you prefer a more informal approach, place a notice on one of the boards at the **Charles University Faculty**, the **Globe Bookstore** (*see p193*), **Radost FX** (*see p257*) or anywhere else where young Czechs and foreigners meet. Many students and young people happily offer Czech conversation in exchange for English conversation. But since Czech grammar is difficult, most serious learners need some professional instruction.

Akcent International House Prague

Bítovská 3, Kačerov, Prague 4 (261 261 638/www.akcent.cz). Metro Budějovická. **Fees** 9,300 Kč/3wk intensive; 8,190 Kč/standard 20wk course. **No credit cards**.

A co-op run and owned by the senior teachers, both Czech and foreign, this school has a good reputation for standards and quality. Choose a three-week intensive course or a more relaxed five-month course (two hours weekly). All classes have a maximum size of six. A bit out of the way, but worth the travel.

ARS Linguarum

Mánesova 27, Žižkov, Prague 2 (224 266 744/ www.arslinguarum.cz). Metro Muzeum/tram 11. **Open** 9am-4.30pm Mon-Fri. **Fees** 350-370 Kč/lesson. **No credit cards**. **Map** p333 A2.

Intensive courses include 20 lessons a week and are charged at 350 Kč per lesson. Standard courses of two 90-minute lessons a week cost up to 370 Kč per hour and run in classes of up to ten students. Instructors are both Czech and foreign.

LBS

Vinohradská 184, Prague 3 (267 132 127/www.lbspraha.cz). Metro Flora/tram 10, 16. **Open** 8am-5pm Mon-Fri. **Fees** 440 Kč/45 mins. **No credit cards**.

A medium-sized language school with reasonable prices and pleasant, professional staff. A programme including an intensive week-long course followed by a three-month standard course of two 90-minute lessons a week is the most popular.

Lingua Viva

Křemencova 10, Nové Město, Prague 1 (222 922 292/www.linguaviva.cz). Metro Národní třída/tram 6, 9, 18, 21, 22. **Open** 9am-7pm Mon-Thur; 9am-noon Fri. **Classes** of 5-9 students. **Fees** 5,990 Kč/72-hr course; 4,650 Kč/intensive 64-hr course; 405-630 Kč lesson. **No credit cards**. **Map** p330 K8.

Small, independent Lingua Viva is something of an upstart in comparison to the other language schools, with better rates and more informal instruction than most.

Státní jazyková Škola State Language School

Školská 15, Nové Město, Prague 1 (Slavonic languages & Czech for foreigners 222 230 016/ www.sjs.cz). Metro Můstek/ tram 3, 6, 9, 14, 17, 18, 22, 24. **Open** 12.30-3.30pm Tue; 12.30-6.30pm Wed; 12.30-3.30pm Thur, Fri. **Fees** 12,000 Kč/ intensive; 4,065 Kč/standard; 7,000 Kč/summer. **No credit cards**. **Map** p330 M7.

The largest and cheapest language school in Prague is state run and teaches just about every language. There are intensive Czech courses (16 hours weekly for five months) and standard courses (four hours weekly for five months) during the normal school year, as well as shorter intensive summer courses.

Ulrych Language Studio

Benešovská 21, Prague 10 (267 311 300/www.ulrych.cz). Metro Náměstí Míru/tram 10, 16. **Open** 8.30am-5pm Mon-Fri. **Fees** 670 Kč/60mins lesson; 1,000 Kč/90mins lesson. **No credit cards**.

Choose between intensive (20 hours' teaching each week) or standard courses running twice a week.

Student travel

GTS

Ve Smečkách 33, Nové Město, Prague 1 (222 119 700/ 296 211 717/call centre 844 140 140 or 257 187 100/www.gtsint.cz). Metro Muzeum/tram 3, 9, 14, 24. **Open** 9am-6pm Mon-Fri; 10am-3pm Sat. **Credit** AmEx, MC, V. **Map** p331 N8.

The best place for ISIC card-holders to find cheap fares. Especially good international flight bargains, as well as occasional deals on bus and train travel. GTS also offers travel insurance and issues ISIC cards – though only to applicants who have ID from local institutions.

Other locations Bechyňova 3, Dejvice, Prague 6 (224 325 235).

Student Agency

Ječná 37, Nové Město, Prague 2 (224 999 666/www.studentagency.cz). Metro IP Pavlova/ tram 4, 6, 11, 16, 22, 34. **Open** 9am-6pm Mon-Fri; 9am-1pm Sat. **Credit** MC, V. **Map** p330 L9.

Cheap flights, buses and trains outside the Czech Republic, especially for ISIC holders. Also offers Allianz travel insurance and issues ISIC cards, visas and working permits for programmes abroad. **Other locations** Ruzyně Airport, departure hall, plane tickets only (222 111 909/fax 222 111 902).

TELEPHONES

Since September 2002, all numbers in Prague have been on digital switchboards and should all have nine digits. Most operators speak some English. The *Zlaté stránky* (*Yellow Pages*) also has an English-language index at the back.

Dialling & codes

The Czech Republic's country code is 420. To call the numbers in this book from within Prague, simply dial the nine-digit number as listed in this guide. From abroad, dial your country's international access code (00 from the UK, 011 from the US) or the '+' symbol on your mobile phone, then 420 (the Czech country code), then the nine-digit local number as listed in this book. So, for instance, to reach the Savoy Hotel from the UK, dial 00 420 224 302 430.

To call abroad from Prague, dial the international access code of 00 (or the '+' symbol), then the relevant country code (see below), and then the number. When calling UK numbers, omit the first '0' of the area code. If you use the prefix 952 00, then the country code, then the number, you will be connected on a digital line at a significant discount.

Australia 61
Germany 49
Japan 81
New Zealand 64
UK 44
USA 1

Mobile phones

Mobile phone coverage in the Czech Republic is on the 900 and 1,800 MHz GSM frequency wavebands. Travellers from elsewhere in Europe should be able to connect to a local network with their existing handset, assuming their service provider has an arrangement with a Czech service provider. The same goes for most American phone users. Check before you leave if you're unsure, and be wary of high call charges.

Increased competition has led to better services and lower call charges among Czech networks. If you're here for a short time, it may be worth picking up a combination

SIM and pre-paid card for your phone. The main networks are **Vodafone** (800 777 777, www.vodafone.cz), **T-Mobile** (603 603 603, www.t-mobile.cz) and **O2** (800 123 456, www.cz.O2.com).

Phone cards

Pre-paid long distance phone cards – aka O2 Trick Cards – are on sale at newsagents' stands for 200 Kč up to 300 Kč. One unit is worth 10 Kč. The length of the unit differs with the time of the call and the destination to which the call is being made. Between 7am and 7pm during the week, one unit lasts 35 seconds; at weekends and public holidays it lasts 82 seconds. Callers can access the lines from any public or private phone via a code number.

Public phones

Virtually all of the public coin telephones that still take 2 Kč coins are perpetually broken. Other public phones run on telephone cards, which come in denominations of 50 to 150 units and can be bought at newsstands, post offices and anywhere you see the blue O2 sticker. Local calls cost 10 Kč; you'll get two minutes from 7am to 7pm during the week, and four and a half minutes at all other times.

TIME

The Czech Republic is on Central European Time (CET): one hour ahead of the UK, six hours ahead of New York and nine hours ahead of Los Angeles. The locals rely on the 24-hour clock.

TIPPING & VAT

Czechs tend to round up restaurant bills, often only by a few crowns, but foreigners are more usually expected to leave a ten per cent tip. If service is bad, however, don't feel obliged to leave anything. Service is often added on automatically for large groups. Taxi drivers expect you to round the fare up but, if you've just been ripped off, don't leave a heller.

A value-added tax of 19 per cent has been slapped on to retail purchases for years in the Czech Republic, but only in 2000 was a system set up to reimburse non-resident foreigners' VAT payments. You can claim a refund at the border or at Ruzyně Airport in the departure hall at the customs desk on the left. You'll need your

shop receipt, a passport and a VAT refund form, which staff can supply. Purchases of over 1,000 Kč are eligible if taken out of the country within 30 days of sale.

TOILETS

Usually called a 'WC' (pronounce it 'veh-tseh'), the word for toilet is *záchod*. There's sometimes a charge for using one of about 5 Kč. Calls of nature can be answered in all metro stations from at least 8am to 8pm, and at many fast-food joints and department stores. 'Ladies' is *Dámy* or *Ženy*, 'Gents' *Páni* or *Muži*. Czech public lavatories are often locked and are generally insalubrious, so you're better off finding one in a restaurant or hotel.

TOURIST INFORMATION

Bear in mind that the use of the international blue-and-white 'i' information sign is not regulated, so the places that are carrying it are not necessarily official.

The best map for public transport or driving is the widely available *Kartografie Praha Plán města* (a book with a yellow cover), costing about 100 Kč. However for central areas, the co-ordinates are sometimes far too vague. Instead, the free map from the PIS is useful.

Čedok *Na příkopě 18, Nové Město, Prague 1 (224 197 699/800 112 112/www.cedok.cz). Metro Můstek/tram 3, 5, 8, 9, 14, 24.* **Open** 9am-7pm Mon-Fri; 9.30am-1pm Sat. **Map** p329 N5.
The former state travel agency is still the biggest in the Czech Republic. It's a handy place to obtain train, bus and air tickets, and accommodation information.
Pražská informační služba Prague Information Service *Betlémské náměstí 2, Prague 1 (general info 12444/www.pis.cz). Metro Můstek/tram 3, 4, 8, 9,14, 24.* **Open** *Apr-Oct* 9am-7pm Mon-Fri; 9am-6pm Sat, Sun. *Nov-Mar* 9am-6pm Mon-Fri; 9am-5pm Sat, Sun. **Map** p328 K5.
PIS provides free information, friendly service and a handy map of central Prague.
Other locations Hlavní nádraží (Main Railway Station), Wilsonova, Nové Město, Prague 1 (no phone); Old Town Hall, Staroměstské náměstí, Staré Město, Prague 1 (no phone); Charles Bridge, in the Malá Strana-side Tower (summer only).

DIRECTORY

VISAS

Citizens of the US, UK and other EU members and most other European countries do not need a visa to enter the Czech Republic for stays of up to 90 days – just a valid passport with at least six months to run by the end of their visit. However, under a recent law aimed at preventing illegal residence by foreigners, border crossings can get complicated if you don't prepare. Foreigners who do need a visa to enter the Czech Republic, including Canadians, South Africans, New Zealanders and Australians can no longer get their visas at the border but must apply at a Czech embassy outside the Czech Republic. The process may take weeks, so planning is critical. Even visitors who don't require a visa may now be asked for proof they have sufficient finances, accommodation plans and health insurance.

Automated but confusing visa information is available in English at the **Foreigners' Police** (*see below*) or the **Ministry of Foreign Affairs** (224 181 111, www.mzv.cz). You're technically required to register at the local police station within 30 days of arriving (if you're staying at a hotel, this will be done for you). If you're from a country whose residents are allowed only 30 days in the Czech Republic, you must obtain an extended visa (confusingly called an exit visa, or *výjezdní vízum*) from the Foreigners' Police office, which allows you up to 90 days in total. The other option if you want to stay longer is a residence permit (*občanský průkaz*), which must be obtained from a Czech embassy abroad.

Beware staying here illegally, as police conduct periodic crackdowns on illegal aliens. They're usually aimed at Romanians, Ukrainians, Vietnamese and other nationals considered undesirable, but a few Brits and US citizens get caught.

Cizinecká policie
Foreigners' Police
Koněvova 32, Prague 3 (info 974 820 420). Metro Flora/tram 9. **Open** 7.30am-5pm Mon, Wed; 7am-2pm Tue, Thur. **Map** p333 D1. **Other locations** Olšanská 2, Žižkov, Prague 3.

WEIGHTS & MEASURES

Czechs use the metric system, even selling eggs in batches of five or ten. Things are usually measured out in decagrams or '*deka*' (10 grams) or decilitres or '*deci*' (10 centilitres). So a regular glass of wine is usually two *deci* (dcl for short), and ham enough for a few sandwiches is 20 *deka* (dkg).

WHEN TO GO

In **spring**, hotel prices rise, but Prague's most eagerly awaited season sees the city shaking off the long, cold winter. While snow can linger until early May, temperatures are often perfect for strolling.

In **summer**, locals usually leave for their country cottages (*chatas*) and abandon the city to the tourist hordes, leaving hotel bargains but many closed venues. Summers are warm but rarely hot, and are prone to thundery showers. The days are long – it stays light until 10pm.

Autumn brings crisp cool air and sharp blue skies, but it can also be wet. September is a good month to visit the city, with hotel prices falling but castles still open. But the days grow shorter very quickly: by the end of October, the sun sets at around 5.30pm.

In **winter**, street-side carp sellers and Christmas markets help break the monotony. Rooms are at their most affordable (except during the holidays) and the snow makes Prague so beautiful that you forget the wintery gloom. Sadly, the snow is rarely accompanied by clear blue skies; many Praguers still burn coal for heating, which doesn't help.

Public holidays

New Year's Day 1 Jan
Easter Monday
Labour Day 1 May
Liberation Day 8 May
Cyril & Methodius Day 5 July
Jan Hus Day 6 July

Statehood Day 28 Sept
Czech Founding Day 28 Oct
Struggle for Freedom Day 17 Nov
Christmas 24-26 Dec

WOMEN

Traditional gender roles are firmly entrenched in the Czech Republic and feminism is still not taken very seriously, but some women's organisations do exist. Most tend to emphasise women's rights as an integral part of human rights, rather than enter any debate about that tricky word 'feminism'. **Ženské Centrum** in Prague 2 (Gorazdova 20, 224 917 224) consists of two organisations: **proFem** focuses on protecting women against violence; while the **Centre for Gender Studies** deals with women's rights in general. The **Gender Studies Library** (224 915 666) has some material in English.

WORKING IN PRAGUE

To work legally here, you need a work permit and the necessary residency permit (termed a 'Temporary Visa for over 90 Days'). Unless you already have the residency permit (*see left*), there's little hope of finding legal work.

If you do have the residency permit, and are to be employed by a Czech company, the company needs to obtain a work permit for you. You'll need to give evidence of qualifications and sometimes relevant work experience, all with official notarised translations.

The *Prague Post*'s website (www.praguepost.com) has a mini-guide to living and working in the city, and its classifieds often feature advertisements from agencies that are willing to help for a fee.

THE LOCAL CLIMATE

Average temperatures and monthly rainfall in Prague.

	High (°C/°F)	Low (°C/°F)	Rainfall (mm/in)
Jan	0 / 32	-5 / 23	18 / 0.7
Feb	1 / 34	-4 / 25	18 / 0.7
Mar	7 / 45	-1 / 30	18 / 0.7
Apr	12 / 54	3 / 37	27 / 1.1
May	18 / 64	8 / 46	48 / 1.9
June	21 / 70	11 / 52	54 / 2.1
July	23 / 73	13 / 55	68 / 2.7
Aug	22 / 72	13 / 55	55 / 2.2
Sept	18 / 64	9 / 48	31 / 1.2
Oct	12 / 54	5 / 41	33 / 1.3
Nov	5 / 41	1 / 34	20 / 0.8
Dec	1 / 34	-3 / 27	21 / 0.8

Vocabulary

For food and drink vocabulary, *see* p152 **What's on the Menu?**

PRONUNCIATION

a	as in gap
á	as in father
e	as in let
é	as in air
i, y	as in lit
í, ý	as in seed
o	as in lot
ó	as in lore
u	as in book
ú, ů	as in loom
c	as in its
č	as in chin
ch	as in loch
ď	as in duty
ň	as in onion
ř	as a standard r, but flatten the tip of the tongue, making a short forceful buzz like ž
š	as in shin
ť	as in stew
ž	as in pleasure
dž	as in George

THE BASICS

Czech words are always stressed on the first syllable.

hello/good day	*dobrý den*
good evening	*dobrý večer*
good night	*dobrou noc*
goodbye	*nashledanou*
yes	*ano* (often *o* or just *jo*)
no	*ne*
please	*prosím*
thank you	*děkuji*
excuse me	*promiňte*
sorry	*pardon*
help!	*pomóc!*
attention!	*pozor!*
sir	*pán*
madam	*paní*
open	*otevřeno*
closed	*zavřeno*
where is...	*kde je...*
go left	*doleva*
go right	*doprava*
straight	*rovně*
far	*daleko*
near	*blízko*
good	*dobrý*
bad	*špatný*
big	*velký*
small	*malý*
no problem	*to je v pořádku*

I don't speak Czech	*nemluvím česky*
I don't understand	*nerozumím*
Do you speak English?	*Mluvíte anglicky?*
I would like...	*Chtěl bych...*
How much is it?	*Kolik to stojí?*
May I have a receipt, please?	*Účet, prosím?*
Can we pay, please?	*Zaplatíme, prosím?*
Do you have any light food?	*Máte nějaké lehké jídlo?*
Cool piercing!	*Dobrej piercing!*
It's a rip-off	*To je zlodě9jina*
I'm absolutely knackered	*Jsem úplně vyfluslý*
The lift is stuck	*Výtah zůstal viset*
Could I speak to Václav?	*Mohl bych mluvit s Václavem?*

STREET NAMES, ETC

In conversation most Prague streets are referred to by their name only, leaving off *ulice, třída* and so on.

avenue	*třída*
bridge	*most*
church	*kostel*
gardens	*sady* or *zahrada*
island	*ostrov*
lane	*ulička*
monastery, convent	*klášter*
park	*park*
square	*náměstí* or *nám*
station	*nádraží* or *nádr*
steps	*schody*
street	*ulice* or *ul*
tunnel	*tunel*

NUMBERS

0	*nula*
1	*jeden*
2	*dva*
3	*tři*
4	*čtyři*
5	*pět*
6	*šest*
7	*sedm*
8	*osm*
9	*devět*
10	*deset*
11	*jedenáct*
12	*dvanáct*
13	*třináct*
14	*čtrnáct*
15	*patnáct*
16	*šestnáct*
17	*sedmnáct*
18	*osmnáct*
19	*devatenáct*
20	*dvacet*
30	*třicet*
40	*čtyřicet*
50	*padesát*
60	*šedesát*
70	*sedmdesát*
80	*osmdesát*
90	*devadesát*
100	*sto*
1,000	*tisíc*

DAYS & MONTHS

Monday	*pondělí*
Tuesday	*úterý*
Wednesday	*středa*
Thursday	*čtvrtek*
Friday	*pátek*
Saturday	*sobota*
Sunday	*neděle*
January	*leden*
February	*únor*
March	*březen*
April	*duben*
May	*květen*
June	*červen*
July	*červenec*
August	*srpen*
September	*září*
October	*říjen*
November	*listopad*
December	*prosinec*
spring	*jaro*
summer	*léto*
autumn	*podzim*
winter	*zima*

PICK-UP LINES

What a babe!	*To je kost!*
What a stud!	*Dobrej frajer!*
Another drink?	*Ještě jedno?*
I love you	*Miluju tě*

PUT-DOWN LINES

What are you staring at?	*Na co čumíš?*
That pisses me off!	*To mě sere!*
You jerk!	*Ty vole!*
You bitch!	*Ty děvko!*

DIRECTORY

Further Reference

BOOKS

Literature & fiction

David Brierley
On Leaving a Prague Window
A readable but dated thriller set
in post-communist Prague.
Bruce Chatwin *Utz*
A luminous tale of a Josefov
porcelain collector.
Jaroslav Hašek
The Good Soldier Švejk
An ambling comic masterpiece set
in World War I, by Bohemia's most
bohemian writer.
Václav Havel *The Memorandum*;
Three Vaněk Plays; *Temptation*
The president's works for the stage.
Bohumil Hrabal *I Served The
King of England*; *Total Fears*
Hrabal's most Prague-ish novel,
I Served… tracks its antihero
through a decade of fascism, war
and communism. *Total Fears*
is a lush new translation by the
respected Twisted Spoon Press.
Milan Kundera *The Joke*; *The
Book of Laughter and Forgetting*;
The Unbearable Lightness of Being
Milan Kundera's tragicomic
romances are still the runaway
bestselling sketches of Prague.
Jonathan Ledgard *Giraffe*
A Cold War thriller about very
tall animals. Perfectly Czech.
Gustav Meyrink *The Golem*
The classic version of the tale of
Rabbi Loew's monster, set in
Prague's Jewish Quarter.
Jan Neruda *Prague Tales*
Wry and bittersweet stories of life
in 19th-century Malá Strana, from
Prague's answer to Dickens.
Josef Škvorecký
The Engineer of Human Souls
The magnum opus by the
chronicler of Czech jazz.
Jáchym Topol *Sister City Silver*
Three noir novellas by one of the
city's leading young writers.
Paul Wilson (ed) *Prague: A
Traveller's Literary Companion*
An excellent collection of stories
organised to evoke Prague's sense
of place.

Kafka

Franz Kafka *The Castle*;
*The Transformation & Other
Stories*; *The Trial*
Kafka classics.

Mark M Anderson
Kafka's Clothes
This erudite, unconventional book
encompasses Kafka, dandyism and
the Habsburg culture.
Max Brod
Franz Kafka: A Biography
The only biography by someone
who actually knew the man.
Ronald Hayman
K: A Biography of Kafka
Hayman's biography is widely
available and dependable.
Frederick Karl *Franz Kafka:
Representative Man*
A thorough account of the man
and his work.

History, memoir & travel

Peter Demetz
Prague in Black and Gold
A thoughtful exploration of
prehistoric to First Republic life.
Timothy Garton Ash
*The Magic Lantern: The Revolution
of 1989 Witnessed in Warsaw,
Budapest, Berlin and Prague*;
History of the Present
Oxford academic's on-the-spot 1989
history, and his look back a decade
later, painfully explore the morality
of the Velvet Revolution.
Dave Rimmer
Once Upon a Time in the East
Communism seen stoned and from
ground level.
Angelo Maria Ripellino
Magic Prague
A mad masterpiece of literary and
cultural history, which celebrates
the city's sorcerous soul.
Derek Sayer *Coasts of Bohemia*
A well-researched and witty
account of the millennium-long
Czech search for their national
identity, incorporating exhaustive
Prague references.
William Shawcross *Dubček*
Shawcross's biography of the
Prague Spring figurehead has been
updated to assess Dubček's role in
the 1989 Velvet Revolution.

Essays & argument

Karel Čapek
Towards the Radical Centre
Selected essays from the man
who coined the word 'robot'.
Václav Havel *Living in Truth*;
Letters to Olga; *Disturbing
the Peace*

Havel's most important political
writing, his prison letters to his
wife, and his reflections.

Miscellaneous

Miroslav Holub *Supposed to Fly*
This collecion of poetry by this
former dissident was inspired by
his youth in war-torn Plzeň.
Wilma Iggers *Women of Prague*
The fascinating lives of 12 women,
spanning 200 years.
Petr Sís *Three Golden Keys*
A children's tale set in Prague,
with wonderful drawings.
Various *Prague: 11 Centuries
of Architecture*
Solid and substantial.

FILM

Many of the following films can
be rented out from **Planet DVD**
(*see p208*).

Ecstasy (Extáze)
Gustav Machatý (1932)
Known for its groundbreaking
nude scene with the nubile actress
who would later be known as
Hedy Lamarr, this imagistic film
depicts a girl frustrated with her
relationship with an older man.
**The Long Journey (Daleká
cesta)** *Alfred Radok (1949)*
Banned by the communists
for 20 years, this film depicts
the deportation of Jews to the
concentration camps.
**The Great Solitude (Velká
samota)** *Ladislav Helge (1959)*
The Great Solitude is one of the few
movies made before the New Wave
that goes deeper than farm-tool
worship. It focuses on how tough
it is to be a rural party official.
**The Shop on Main Street
(Obchod na korze)** *Ján Kadár &
Elmar Klos (1964)*
Set during World War II in the Nazi
puppet state of Slovakia, *The Shop
on Main Street* concerns an honest
carpenter forced to 'Aryanise' a
button shop run by an old Jewish
woman. It was the winner of the
1966 Oscar for Best Foreign Film.
**Intimate Lighting (Intimní
osvětlení)** *Ivan Passer (1965)*
Possibly the most delightful film
of the Czech New Wave, *Intimate
Lighting* tells of the reunion of two
old friends after many years.

Larks on a String (Skřivánci na niti) *Jiří Menzel (1969)*
This tale of forced labour in the steel mills of industrial Kladno deals with politics a little, but love – and libido – somehow always triumph. Banned soon after its release, the film wasn't shown again until 1989, when it won the Berlin Film Festival's Golden Bear.

The Ear (Ucho)
Karel Kachyňa (1970)
The full force of surveillance terror and paranoia is exposed in this chilling film, the origins of which go further back than the communists to Kafka. The film was banned instantly.

Otesánek *Jan Švankmajer (2000)*
Švankmajer updates a classic Czech myth about a childless couple who adopt an insatiable baby made from tree roots.

Divided We Fall (Musíme si pomáhat) *Jan Hřebejk (2001)*
The Oscar-nominated tale of a small Czech village in wartime and its residents' moral dilemmas.

Želary *Ondřej Trojan (2004)*
This World War II melodrama, nominated for the Best Foreign Film Oscar, tells the story of a nurse hiding out in a village.

Citizen Havel *Pavel Koutecky & Miroslav Janek (2007)*
Behind-the-scenes access to the ex-dissident president's rise and fall makes for a heartfelt and funny documentary about politics versus humanity in the new Europe.

René *Helena Třeštíková (2008)*
A powerful, candid and disturbing documentary charting decades of soul-searching by a career criminal and writer.

MUSIC

Dan Bárta *Entropicture* (Sony)
Bárta, the soulful reigning prince of Czech pop rock, takes a thoughtful turn with some respected jazz men about town.

David Dorůžka *Silently Dawnging (Animal Music)*
Soulful and self-exploratory, the young jazz guitar prodigy here lays down contemplative and fascinating compositions that form a complex tapestry of emotion.

Ecstasy of St Theresa
In Dust 3 (EMI)
Jan P Muchow creates a textured digital background for the vocals of Kateřina Winterová.

Gipsy.cz *Reprezent* (Indies Scope)
The huge pop phenom has made waves at Glastonbury and on the Putumayo label, and here mixes up his best hip hop and MC work.

Moimir Papalescu & the Nihilists *Analogue Voodoo* (Panther)
All the rage on the club scene of late, this bizarre upbeat trio, of course, has nothing to do with the title.

Rene Trossman *Postmarked Illinois* (Faust Records)
The country's top electric blues guitar master, raised in Chicago but based in Prague since the 1990s, mixes luminous vintage pieces from old Windy City hands with a number of fresh originals.

Rok Ďábla (Sony Music/Bonton)
This soundtrack from the hit film of the same name presents the songs of beloved Czech folk balladeer Jarek Nohavica in a completely new light.

Homegrown classics

Czech Serenade (Supraphon)
The pantheon of great Czech composers – Antonín Dvořák, Josef Suk, Vitězslav Novák, Zdeněk Fibich, Leoš Janáček – in performances by a range of artists including the Czech Philharmonic and a gallery of top-class chamber players, mostly digitally recorded.

Czech Philharmonic Orchestra
Zdeněk Fibich: Symphony no.1 in F major; Symphony no.2 in E flat major; Symphony no.3 in E minor (Supraphon)
A set of symphonies by the little-known Romantic Czech composer now receiving a well-deserved revival. Performed by the Czech Philharmonic Orchestra under Karel Šejna, the disc also includes two excellent shorter works.

Orchestre National de France
Bohuslav Martinů: Double Concerto (Teldec/Erato)
This lyrical composition, performed with sensitivity by soloists Jean-François Heisser and Jean Camosi and conducted by James Conlon, provides a toothsome taste of the rarely heard modernist Czech composer at his best.

Prague Chamber Philharmonic
Jan Ladislav Dusík: Piano Concerto; Sonatas (Panton)
The Prague Chamber Philharmonic, conducted by Leoš Svárovský, delivers the energy that has set it apart from the city's larger orchestras in these excellent recordings of Dusík's Concert Concerto for Piano and Orchestra in E flat major (Op.70) and two of his more lyrical sonatas, the F sharp minor (Op.61) and the A flat major (Op.64).

Pavel Šporcl *Pavel Šporcl* (Supraphon)
This unorthodox Czech violin virtuoso has won over audiences with his deft treatment of Smetana, Dvořák, Janáček and Martinů. This is his star debut.

WEBSITES

Czech-English Dictionary
www.slovnik.cz
Millions of words translated from English, German, Italian, French and Spanish to Czech and back.

Czech Please
czechoutchannel.blogspot.com
International diner of mystery Brewsta never fails to find, chronicle and secretly photograph up close the latest and greatest cuisine discoveries in Prague.

Czech Techno
www.techno.cz
The party-list link contains the original, authoritative list of what's on in the dance clubs all over town.

www.dpp.cz/en
The website of Prague Public Transit has a section in English with the downloadable PDFs of the lastest tram, night tram and bus routes (handy, considering how often they change for street work projects).

www.expats.cz
An online bulletin board with handy classifieds: tips on residency, apartment hunting and jobs.

www.idos.cz
Searchable online train and bus timetables for every city and town in the Czech Republic.

Prague Information Service
www.pis.cz
A comprehensive source for city events with well-organised pages of general tourist information.

Prague Monitor
www.praguemonitor.cz
A witty daily round-up of all the latest links to English-language news and features related to the Golden City.

Prague Post
www.praguepost.com
Prague's main English-language weekly reports on the issues, trends and culture, with useful tourist information pages.

Prague TV
prague.tv
Tune in for outlandish columns, food and drink tips, links to maps and the beer counter.

Time Out Prague
www.timeout.com/prague
Shameless self-promotion it may be, but here's where you'll find the best of what's new in Prague.

DIRECTORY

Index

INDEX

INDEX

INDEX

INDEX

Index

Advertisers' Index

Please refer to the relevant pages for contact details.

Maps

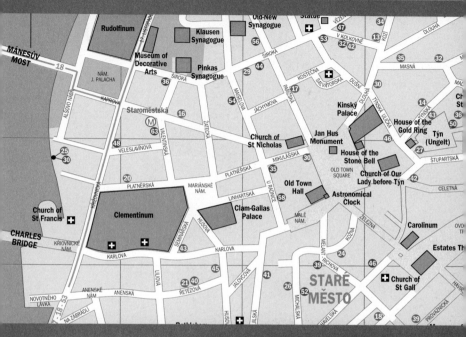

Major sight or landmark	■
Hospital or college	■
Railway station	■
Parks	■
River	■
Motorway	═══
Main road	──
Main road tunnel	─ ─
Pedestrian road	░░░
Airport	✈
Church	✚
Metro station	Ⓜ
Area name	JOSEFOV

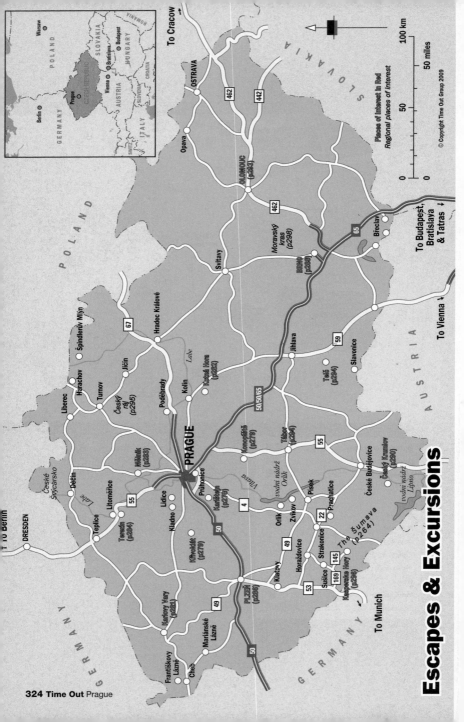

Escapes & Excursions

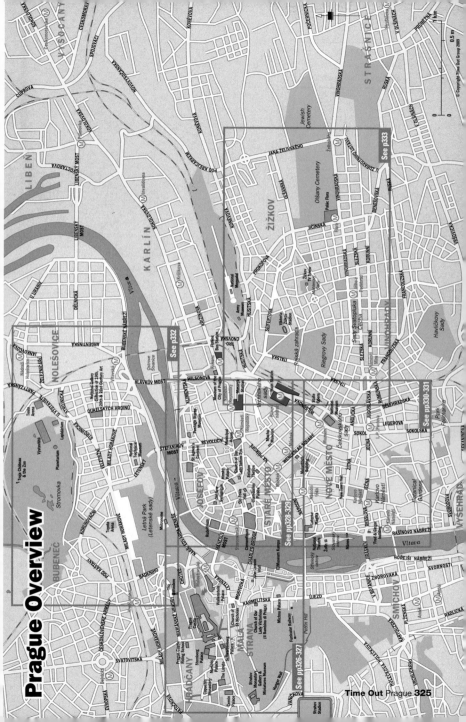

Prague Overview

See p332

See p333

See p330-331

See pp328-329

See pp326-327

Time Out Prague **325**

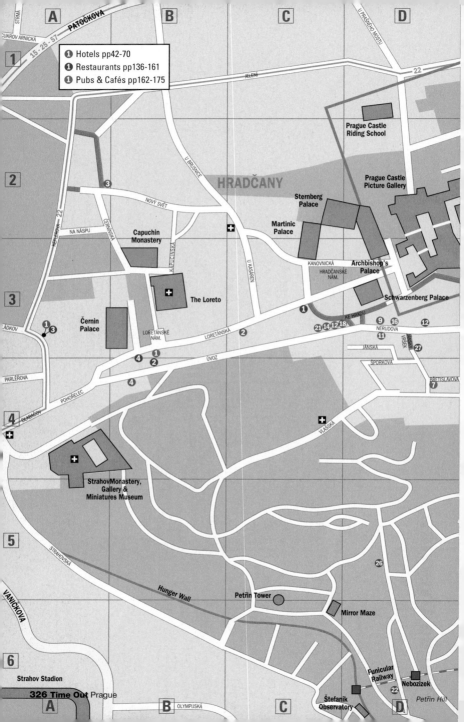

PATOČKOVA

STRMA

CUKROV ARNICKÁ

15 · 25 · 57

1 Hotels pp42-70
1 Restaurants pp136-161
1 Pubs & Cafés pp162-175

JELENÍ

U PRAŠNÉHO MOSTU

22

Prague Castle
Riding School

U BRUSNICE

HRADČANY

NOVÝ SVĚT

Prague Castle
Picture Gallery

Sternberg
Palace

Martinic
Palace

NA NÁSPU

KEPLEROVA 22

ČERNÍNSKÁ

KAPUCÍNSKÁ

Capuchin
Monastery

U KASÁREN

KANOVNICKÁ

HRADČANSKÉ
NÁM.

Archbishop's
Palace

The Loreto

Schwarzenberg Palace

JÁDKOV

Černín
Palace

LORETÁNSKÉ
NÁM.

LORETÁNSKÁ

1 **3**

KE HRADU

9 **16** **12**

NERUDOVA

21 **14** **12** **18**

11

JÁNSKÁ

JÁNSKÝ VRŠEK

27

ŠPORKOVA

PARLÉŘOVA

4 **1**
2

ÚVOZ

BRETISLAVOVA

7

POHOŘELEC

4

OLBRAMOV

VLAŠSKÁ

StrahovMonastery,
Gallery &
Miniatures Museum

STRAHOVSKÁ

VANICKOVA

Hunger Wall

Petřín Tower

Mirror Maze

26

Funicular
Railway

Nebozízek

22

Strahov Stadion

OLYMPIJSKÁ

Štefánik
Observatory

Petřín Hill

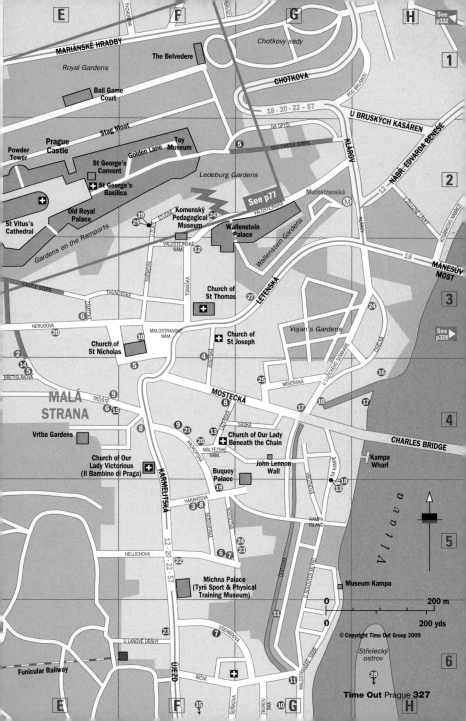

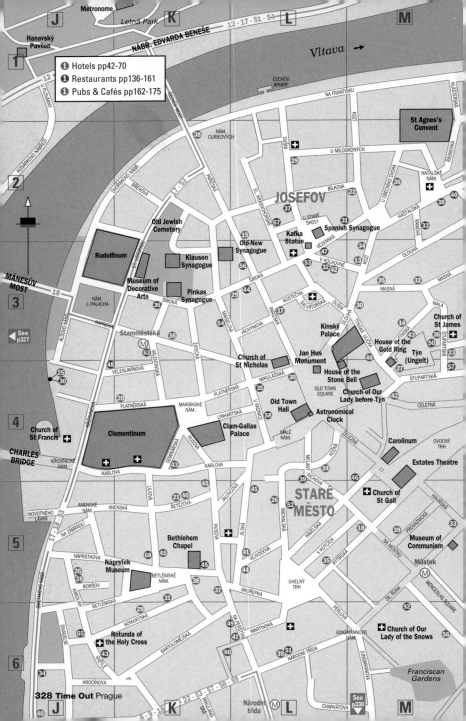

J **K** **L** **M**

Metronome

Letná Park

1

Hanavský
Pavilion

NÁBR. EDVARDA BENEŠE 12 - 17 - 51 - 54

Vltava →

1	Hotels pp42-70
1	Restaurants pp136-161
1	Pubs & Cafés pp162-175

ČECHŮV
WHARF

NA FRANTIŠKU

2

KOSARKOVO NÁBŘEŽÍ

NÁM.
CURIEOVÝCH

38

DVOŘÁKOVO NÁBŘ.

BŘEHOVÁ

PAŘÍŽSKÁ

U MILOSRDNÝCH

29

DUŠNÍ

St Agnes's
Convent

HAŠTALSKÉ
NÁM.

36

40

38

KLÁŠTERSKÁ

U OBECNÍHO DVORA

BÍLKOVA

JOSEFOV

22

HAŠTALSKÁ

RÁMOVÁ

33

DLOUHÁ

Old Jewish
Cemetery

37

67

U STARÉ
ŠKOLY

31

Spanish Synagogue

34

13

MASNÁ

**MÁNESŮV
MOST**

18

Rudolfinum

Klausen
Synagogue

Old-New
Synagogue

15

56

Kafka
Statue

47

53

V KOLKOVNĚ

32

42

35

32

MASNÁ

MALÁ

3

ALŠOVO NÁBŘ

NÁM.
J. PALACHA

Museum of
Decorative
Arts

36

ŠIROKÁ

Pinkas
Synagogue

29

44

ŠIROKÁ

KOSTEČNÁ

SALVÁTORSKÁ

DUŠNÍ

30

14

Church of
St James

36

23

STUPARTSKÁ

*See
p327*

KAPROVA

Staroměstská

54

MASELNÁ

JÁCHYMOVA

PAŘÍŽSKÁ

17

Kinsky
Palace

DLOUHÁ

TÝNSKÁ ULIČKA

House of
the Gold Ring

43

50

Týn
(Ungelt)

27

57

VELESLAVÍNOVA

VALENTINSKÁ

ŽATECKÁ

16

Church of
St Nicholas

Jan Hus
Monument

46

House of the
Stone Bell

STUPARTSKÁ

42

CELETNÁ

48

20

PLATNÉŘSKÁ

MARIÁNSKÉ
NÁM.

LINHARTSKÁ

MIKULÁŠSKÁ

35

OLD TOWN
SQUARE

Old Town
Hall

58

Church of Our
Lady before Týn

4

**CHARLES
BRIDGE**

Church of
St Francis

KŘIŽOVNICKÉ
NÁM.

Clementinum

KARLOVA

43

SEMINÁŘSKÁ

HUSOVA

Clam-Gallas
Palace

KARLOVA

MALÉ
NÁM.

Astronomical
Clock

ŽELEZNÁ

KOŽNÁ

24

46

MELANTRICHOVA

RYCHTOVA

Carolinum

OVOCNÝ
TRH

Estates Theatre

HAVÍŘSKÁ

45

JALOVCOVA

41

Church of
St Gall

NOVOTNÉHO
LÁVKA

21

40

ŘETĚZOVÁ

LILIOVÁ

ANENSKÉ
NÁM.

ANENSKÁ

26

**STARÉ
MĚSTO**

52

18

39

Museum of
Communism

33

Můstek

5

NA ZÁBRADLÍ

NÁPRSTKOVA

68

45

Bethlehem
Chapel

45

41

VENDOVA

44

HAVELSKÁ

V KOTCÍCH

RYTÍŘSKÁ

NA MŮSTKU

M

92

26

28

BORŠOV

Náprstek
Museum

BETLÉMSKÉ
NÁM.

38

37

ILSKÁ

SKOŘEPKA

UHELNÝ
TRH

PERLOVÁ

28. ŘÍJNA

WENCESLAS SQUARE

31

KONVIKTSKÁ

BETLÉMSKÁ

KAROLINY

DIVADELNÍ

65

Rotunda of
the Holy Cross

43

SVĚTLÉ

48

47

NA PERŠTÝNĚ

MARTINSKÁ

60

39

51

Church of Our
Lady of the Snows

JUNGMANNOVO
NÁM.

JUNGMANNOVA

6

34

KROČÍNOVA

328 Time Out Prague

40

J **K**

Národní
třída M

NÁRODNÍ TŘÍDA

L

CHARVÁTOVA

*Franciscan
Gardens*

*See
p330*

M

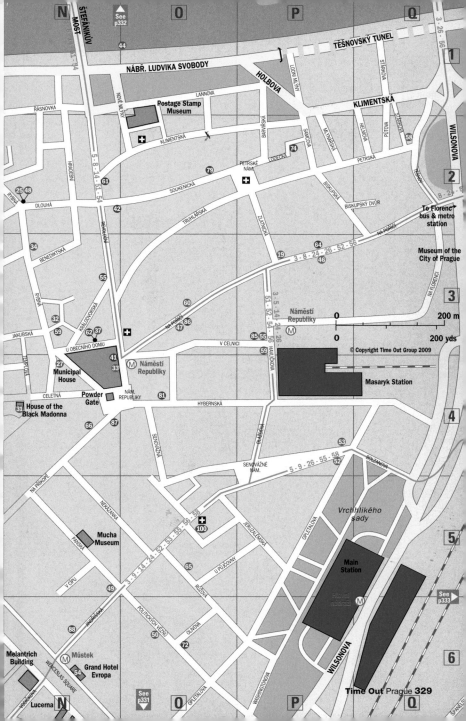

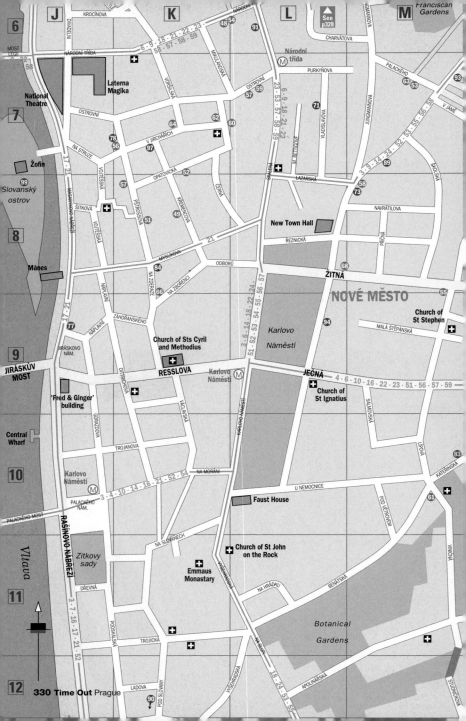

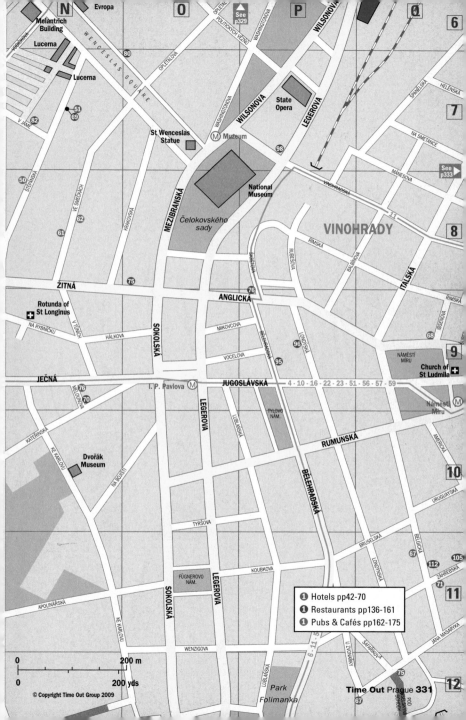

Evropa

Melantrich
Building

Lucerna

Lucerna

51
69

V JÁME

82

W E N C E S L A S   S Q U A R E

80

OPLETALOVA

POLITICKÝCH VĚZŇŮ

GPLEYALOVA

WASHINGTONOVA

See
p329

WILSONOVA

WILSONOVA

State
Opera

LEGEROVA

ŠPANĚLSKÁ

HELÉNSKÁ

St Wenceslas
Statue

Muzeum

98

NA SMETANCE

MÁNESOVA

See
p333

50

ŠTĚPÁNSKÁ

VE SMEČKÁCH

KRAKOVSKÁ

62

61

75

WASHINGTONOVA

MEZIBRANSKÁ

National
Museum

Čelokovského
sady

VINOHRADSKÁ

VINOHRADY

ŘÍMSKÁ

RUBEŠOVA

BALBÍNOVA

11

ITALSKÁ

ŘÍMSKÁ

ŽITNÁ

Rotunda of
St Longinus

NA RYBNÍČKU

V TŮNÍCH

HÁLKOVA

SOKOLSKÁ

ANGLICKÁ

76

MIKOVCOVA

VOCELOVA

BĚLEHRADSKÁ

96

95

LONDÝNSKÁ

ŠKRÉTOVA

NÁMĚSTÍ
MÍRU

Church of
St Ludmila

BLÁNICKÁ

68

JEČNÁ

MELOUNOVA

76

70

I. P. Pavlova

JUGOSLÁVSKÁ

4 · 10 · 16 · 22 · 23 · 51 · 56 · 57 · 59

Náměstí
Míru

KATEŘINSKÁ

KE KARLOVU

Dvořák
Museum

NA BOJIŠTI

LEGEROVA

LUBLAŇSKÁ

TYLOVO
NÁM.

RUMUNSKÁ

AMERICKÁ

URUGUAYSKÁ

TYRŠOVA

BĚLEHRADSKÁ

BRUSELSKÁ

LONDÝNSKÁ

BELGICKÁ

67

112

ZÁHŘEBSKÁ

105

71

APOLINÁŘSKÁ

FÜGNEROVO
NÁM.

KOUBKOVA

SOKOLSKÁ

LEGEROVA

KE KARLOVU

WENZIGOVA

6 · 11 · 5

U ZVONAŘKY

JANA MASARYKA

ŠAFAŘÍKOVA

0   200 m

0   200 yds

❶ Hotels pp42-70
❶ Restaurants pp136-161
❶ Pubs & Cafés pp162-175

© Copyright Time Out Group 2009

Park
Folimanka

LUBLAŇSKÁ

67

75

POD
SLAVÍNEM

Time Out Prague 331

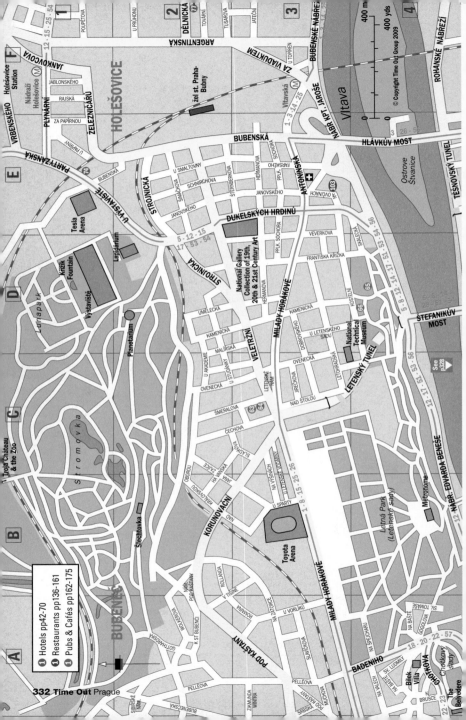

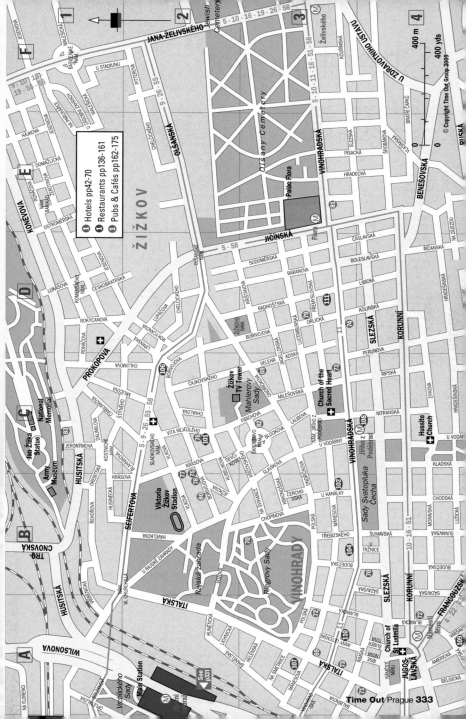

Street Index

STREET INDEX

Prague Metro

C Letňany
Prosek
Střížkov
Ládví
Kobylisy

B Černý Most
Rajská zahrada
Hloubětín
Kolbenova
Vysočanská
Palmovka
Invalidovna
Křižíkova
Florenc

Depo Hostivař
A Želivského
Skalka
Strašnická
Flora
Jiřího Z Poděbrad
Muzeum
Náměstí Míru

C Háje
Opatov
Chodov
Roztyly
Kačerov
Budějovická
Pankrác
Pražského Povstání
Vyšehrad
I.P. Pavlova
Karlovo náměstí
Národní třída

Nádraží Holešovice
Vltavská
Vltava
Náměstí Republiky
Florenc
Hlavní Nádraží
Českomoravská

Staroměstská
Můstek

Malostranská
Hradčanská
A Dejvická

Anděl
Smíchovské Nádraží
Jinonice
Nové Butovice
Radlická

Hůrka
Luka
Stodůlky
Lužiny
B Zličín

Vltava